Informatik aktuell

Herausgeber: W. Brauer
im Auftrag der Gesellschaft für Informatik (GI)

Springer
*Berlin
Heidelberg
New York
Barcelona
Budapest
Hongkong
London
Mailand
Paris
Santa Clara
Singapur
Tokio*

Günther Schmidt
Franz Freyberger (Hrsg.)

Autonome Mobile Systeme 1996

12. Fachgespräch
München, 14.–15. Oktober 1996

mit Sonderbeiträgen zu den
technischen Demonstrationen aus dem
Sonderforschungsbereich 331 „Informations-
verarbeitung in autonomen, mobilen
Handhabungssystemen" an der
Technischen Universität München

Herausgeber und wissenschaftliche Tagungsleitung

Günther Schmidt
Franz Freyberger
Technische Universität München
Lehrstuhl für Steuerungs- und Regelungstechnik
D-80290 München

Erweiterter Fachgesprächsbeirat

Prof. Dr.-Ing. habil. J. Detlefsen, Technische Universität München
Prof. Dr.-Ing. habil. R. Dillmann, Universität Karlsruhe
Prof. Dr.-Ing. G. Färber, Technische Universität München
Prof. Dr. V. Graefe, Universität der Bundeswehr München
Dr. G. Lawitzky, Siemens AG, München
Prof. Dr. rer.nat.habil. P. Levi, Universität Stuttgart
Prof. Dr. rer.nat. B. Radig, Technische Universität München
Prof. Dr.-Ing. G. Reinhart, Technische Universität München
Prof. Dr.-Ing. U. Rembold, Universität Karlsruhe
Prof. Dr.-Ing. G. Schmidt, Technische Universität München
Prof. Dr. G. Schweitzer, Eidgenössische Technische Hochschule Zürich

Die Deutsche Bibliothek - CIP-Einheitsaufnahme

Autonome mobile Systeme ... : ... Fachgespräch / Hrsg. und Tagungsleitung:
Universität München, Lehrstuhl für Steuerungs- und Regelungstechnik. - Berlin
; Heidelberg ; New York ; Barcelona ; Budapest ; Hongkong ; London ; Mailand ;
Paris ; Santa Clara ; Singapur ; Tokio : Springer.
  (Informatik aktuell)
12. 1996. München, 14. - 15 Oktober 1996. - 1996
  ISBN 3-540-61751-5

CR Subject Classification (1996): C.3, J.7, I.2.9

ISBN-13: 978-3-540-61751-8   e-ISBN-13: 978-3-642-80324-6
DOI: 10.1007/978-3-642-80324-6

Satz: Reproduktionsfertige Vorlage vom Autor/Herausgeber

SPIN: 10517407   33/3142-543210 – Gedruckt auf säurefreiem Papier

Vorwort

Das 12. Fachgespräch Autonome Mobile Systeme (AMS '96) findet am 14. und 15. Okt. 1996 an der Technischen Universität München statt. Die Organisation liegt in den Händen des Sonderforschungsbereiches „Informationsverarbeitung in autonomen, mobilen Handhabungssystemen" (SFB 331). Mit 26 Fachbeiträgen in zwei parallelen Sitzungsreihen, zwei Plenarvorträgen und einer offenen Podiumsdiskussion, die Trends in Anwendung und Forschung der AMS beleuchtet, bietet das 12. Fachgespräch während dreier Halbtage ein aktuelles Vortrags- und Diskussionsprogramm. Neben Fragen der Sensorik, Videosensorik, Lokalisation, Navigation, der Steuerung, Planung, Koordination und Kooperation werden auch neuartige Anwendungen und industrielle Komponenten vorgestellt und diskutiert. Eine breitere Beachtung im Vergleich zu vorausgegangenen Fachgesprächen finden Anwendungen autonomer Fahrzeuge im freien Gelände. So wird in diesem Jahre erstmals der Einsatz in der pflanzlichen Produktion und der Schiffsführung erörtert. Dies gilt in gleicher Weise für GPS (Global Positioning System)-Komponenten und deren Anwendung.

Dieses Fachgespräch versteht sich, wie auch seine Vorgänger, primär als eine Plattform des kritischen Wissens- und Informationsaustausches deutschsprachiger Forschergruppen im Bereich autonomer mobiler Roboter und Systeme. Dennoch oder gerade deshalb ist es befruchtend, auch internationale Gäste in das Fachgespräch eingebunden zu haben. Eine Bereicherung bilden auch verschiedene industrielle und institutionelle Ausstellungsobjekte, die im Foyer vor den Tagungsräumen einen angemessenen Platz finden und sicher ein lebhaftes Interesse auf sich ziehen werden.

Als eine Besonderheit dieses 12. Fachgesprächs finden am Nachmittag des zweiten Tages, im unmittelbaren Anschluß an das Vortragsprogramm, technische Demonstrationen des SFB 331 statt. Dabei geht es nicht um die Vorstellung einzelner Teilergebnisse, sondern um das integrierte Zusammenspiel erprobter Basisfunktionalitäten und Schlüsselkomponeten autonomer mobiler Roboter. Die Vorführungen, zu denen auch eine Videodokumentation bei den Herausgebern erhältlich ist, sind in zwei Szenarien eingebettet. Sie umfassen die Demonstratoren MACROBE, MOBROB und FLEXEL II im Szenario einer Produktionsumgebung sowie den mobilen Servicemanipulator ROMAN im Szenario einer belebten Laborumgebung. Ergebnisse und Perspektiven des SFB 331, der, wie auch der SFB 314 „Künstliche Intelligenz" (Universität Karlsruhe) dieses Fachgespräch seit seinen Anfängen begleitet, sind am Ende dieses Berichtsbandes in drei Sonderbeiträgen zusammengefaßt.

Bei der Auswahl der Beiträge zum Fachgespräch erhielt der Veranstalter wertvolle Unterstützung von seiten des erweiterten Fachgesprächsbeirates. Für die verantwortungsvolle Aufgabe, aus den 44 eingegangenen erweiterten Kurzfassungen die Auswahl der 26 Beiträge für das Vortragsprogramm zu treffen, sei allen Kollegen an dieser Stelle herzlich gedankt. Ebenso bedanken sich die Herausgeber bei den Autoren für ihre konstruktive und terminbewußte Mitarbeit und bei Herrn Prof. Dr. Brauer, dem Herausgeber von Informatik aktuell, sowie dem Springer-Verlag für die wohlwollende Förderung dieses Berichtsbandes.

Die Herausgeber:
Günther Schmidt und Franz Freyberger   München, im August 1996

Inhaltsverzeichnis

Kooperation, Koordination

Mensch/Roboter-Schnittstelle

Komponenten, Anwendungen

Sonderbeiträge zu den technischen Demonstrationen aus dem Sonderforschungsbereich 331 „Informationsverarbeitung in autonomen, mobilen Handhabungssystemen"

Übersichtsbeiträge

Autonomous Mobile Robots in France:
Some Projects and Scientific Approaches

Raja Chatila
LAAS-CNRS
7, Ave. du Colonel Roche 31077 Toulouse cedex - France
email: raja@laas.fr

Abstract

This paper overviews some of the main projects and activities on mobile robots in France.

1   Introduction

Research on autonomous mobile robots is active in France since the late seventies. The
HILARE project, started at LAAS-CNRS in 1977, was one of the first comprehensive
mobile robot projects in France and in Europe after the seminal SHAKEY project at SRI,
in the USA (1968-72). Today, many research and applicative projects exist, some of them
being a large scale collaboration of several institutions and industries at the national or
the european level.

The main institutions in mobile robotics in France are national research organizations.
Among them, CNRS (Centre National de la Recherche Scientifique) and INRIA (Institut
National de Recherche en Informatique et Automatique) in close relation with university
laboratories, pursue the broadest spectrum of studies in basic research such as : mobile
manipulation, navigation and motion planning, vision, perception and multi-sensor fusion, environment modelling,-time task planning and temporal reasoning, real-time control
architectures, etc.

Several domain-oriented organizations carry on important R&D efforts in this domain.
They are related, by alphabetical order : CEA (Commissariat à l'Energie Atomique:
Atomic energy commission), CEMAGREF (Centre National du Machinisme Agricole du
Génie Rural, des Eaux et des Forêts: agricultural machines), EDF (Electricité de France:
electricity natioanl company), CNES (Centre National d'Etudes Spatiales, the french space
agency), IFREMER (Institut Français de Recherche pour l'Exploration de la Mer, the
french agency for sea studies), ONERA (Office National d'Etude et Recherche Aérospa-
tiales: Aerospace studies).

Some industries have (or had) very active projects in mobile robotics in the past few years.
Alcatel Alsthom Recherche and Framatome developed two robots to investigate scientific
and technical issues in this domain. These companies, and others, such as Cybernetix and
ROL, ITMI, Matra Marconi Space, SAGEM, THOMSON participate also in National or
European projects with other european industries and research laboratories.

Finally, the french agency for military research and studies DRET has financed a program
called DARDS for the study and experimentation of an autonomous and semi-autonomous
land vehicle.

On the other hand, in October 1995, the french National Center of scientific Research (CNRS) has launched a "Strategic Action on Intelligent Machines" to foster research as well as applicative projects in the general domain of intelligent machines. We shall overview this action and some ongoing projects within it that pertain to mobile robotics.

2 Collaborative Projects

We overview in this section the main projects that are running or that terminated recently at the national or european level in which french partners play an important role [4, 5, 6]. References on these projects could be obtained directly from the participating institutions.

2.1 Esprit Project 2384 : PANORAMA - Perception and Navigation Systems Development for Outdoor Autonomous Mobile Robot

The participants are SAGEM (Prime), CEA (F), BAE, EASAMS, Univ.Southampton (UK), CRIF (B), SEPA (I), Universidad Politecnica de Madrid (SP), EID, LNETI (P), Rauma-Repola, Tamrock, VTT, and Helsinki University of Technology (Finland)

PANORAMA is a four years Esprit II project started on March 1989. It includes two users (TAMROCK and RAUMA-REPOLA), five information technology companies (SAGEM, FIAT, British Aerospace,...), four applied research institutes and three universities (Madrid, Helsinki, Southampton).

The objective of the Project is to develop a general purpose perception and navigation system for autonomous vehicles enabling path planning and motion in partially structured and partially known environments, especially outdoors. Typical applications cover open mine industry, construction, forest exploitation and agriculture. The PANORAMA system was adapted on an experimental TAMROCK (Finland) drilling tracked machine.

Besides the definition of the whole system and the approaches in its various aspects, the key results concern visual beacon and obstacle detection, basic piloting functions on three test-beds, path and perception actions planning, specification of a command language and prototyping of parts of the system controller.

The R&D developments have been developped and tested on several test-beds and most particularly on the vehicle REMI (a Mercedes 4 wheel drive) equipped by SAGEM.

2.2 ESPRIT BR 6946 - PROMOTION - Planning Robot Motion

This 3 years has ended August 1995. The participants were: Universitat Politecnica de Catalunya (Barcelona) (SP), Ecole Normale Suprieure (Paris) (F), Universita Degli Studi di Roma 'La Sapienza' (Roma) (I), INRIA (Sophia-Antipolis) (F), LAAS/CNRS (Toulouse) (F), and Utrecht University (Utrecht) (NL).

PROMotion is a research project dedicated to theoretical and practical issues in Robot Motion Planning [8]. The main goal is to create a synergy between four disciplines (Robotics, Algebraic Geometry, Computational Geometry and Control Theory) involved in Motion Planning, in order to provide theoretically well-founded methods that correspond to the motion planning issues in advanced robotics and its challenging real-world applications.

Motion planning relates to several disciplines, most notably robotics, computer science and mathematics, and has been developed along quite different directions with only little interaction. The coherence and the originality of PROMotion comes from its interdisciplinarity. PROMotion takes advantage of a common knowledge and understanding of the different theoretical issues in order to extend the state of the art in the domain. The theoretical work undertaken under this project is aimed at solving concrete problems.

The project has been successfully carried out and has been concluded by a final workshop in Roma on July 1995.

In addition to the continuation of the work, the third and last year has been dominated by four new experiments ; three of them put emphasis on the connection between planning and control for a mobile robot and the fourth integrates several issues in multiple mobile robot motion planning and control.

2.3   Esprit Project 6668 - MARTHA - Mobile Robots for Transportation and Handling Applications

This project started in june 1992 and ended in February 1996. The partners were FRAM-ATOME (F), SNCF (F), PROMIP (LAAS-MIDI ROBOTS) (F), MANNESMANN-DEMAG-GOTTWALD (D), FZI (D), and INDUMAT (D). The associated Partners were IKERLAN (SP), ROL (F), FAG (D), and ECT (NL).

The MARTHA project's ambition was to meet the pressing demands of European companies involved in fast intermodal transhipment.

Several key techniques and technologies are needed to make possible automated evolution of vehicle fleets under task-level programming or other high level operator control, hence being capable of some form of autonomy without the current limitation of expensive site preparation. Considered applications are generic and include rail, port and airport intermodal transhipment operations.

This R & D project comprises :

- research effort to supplement or to adapt the existing theoretical background ;
- important software development work to translate into operational codes working in real-time environments, new techniques as well as a significant portion of background know-how, yet never implemented as such at prototype stage ;
- sensor development, to satisfy a pressing need of the expected end-product application by an attractive and low-cost solution, based upon important background developments ;
- application, validation and demonstration on two test-beds, representing respectively a heavy-load sea-rail transhipment operation and a medium-load airport transportation and handling operation. Because the two applications are complementary and generic, they will be conducted in parallel. The considered test-beds are made available through other background projects of the contractors.

FRAMATOME, who is the prime of this project, is particularly involved in the CCS definition and implementation (they are assisted by Framentec for this particular task). Moreover, they are responsible for the study and the choice of the perception systems used on board the mobile robots (radars, sonars, infrared detector, laser scanner, etc).

One major milestone is the demonstration of several MARTHA scenarios on a set of laboratory robots provided by PROMIP at LAAS.

PROMIP has been involved in the design specifications of the Central Control Station. The main task of the CCS is to plan the missions for each mobile robot, and to control the proper execution of these missions. An approach proposed by Framatome make use of constraint-based programming techniques.

PROMIP main contribution to the MARTHA project concerns the design and the integration of the Robot Control System. This system includes all the functional modules of the mobile robot (perception modules, motion execution, motion planning, sensor based motion control, communication interface, etc) as well as the supervision system. The Supervision System controls the proper execution of the underlying modules and interprets the missions sent by the central station.

A special effort has been dedicated to the problem of multi-robot cooperation. For this purpose, LAAS has developed a new approach which is based on a paradigm where robots incrementally merge their plans into a set of already coordinated plans [1].

This is done through exchange of information about their current state and their future actions. This leads to a generic framework which can be applied to a variety of tasks and applications. The paradigm has been called Plan-Merging Paradigm.

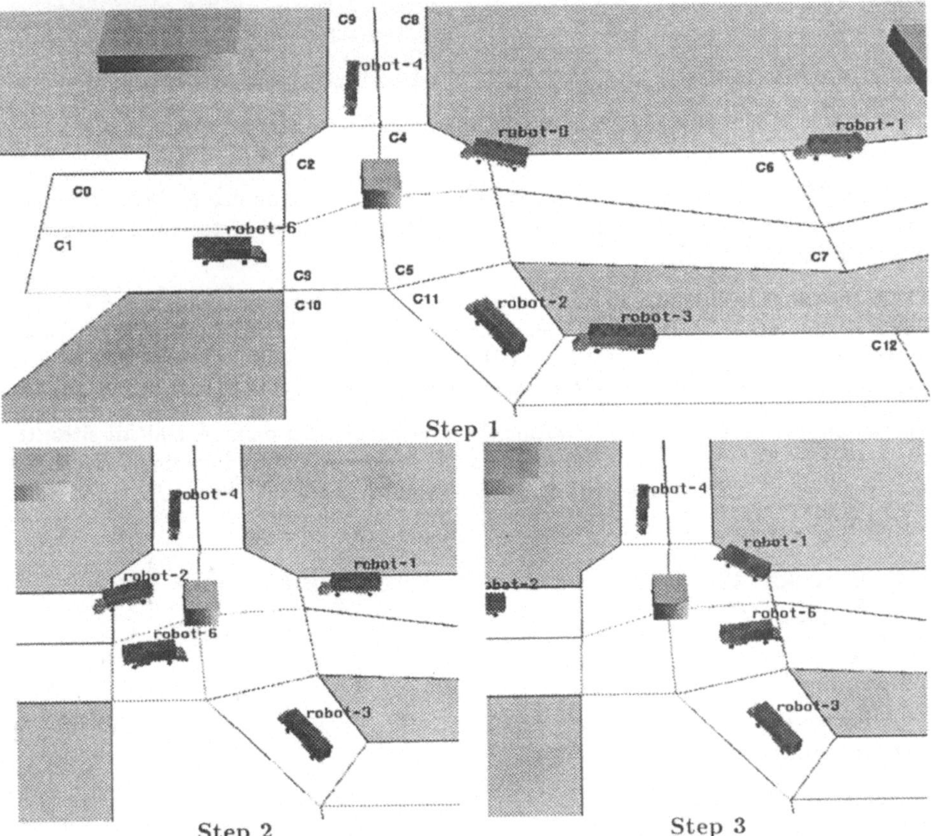

Figure 1: Coordination by plan merging for sharing space at an intersection (MARTHA).

Figure 2: The Three Hilare Robots in Action (MARTHA)

ROL and SNCF, who were heavily involved in the French Commutor project, are responsible for the heavy load demonstration (SNCF), and the design of the motion execution module of the RCS (ROL).

LAAS has implemented and demonstrated the plan-merging paradigm on a fleet of ten robots in simulation [2] (figure 1). The complete software has been also implemented and illustrated on three real robots from the HILARE family at LAAS (figure 2). The software is entirely installed on-board (a VME based multi-processor system under Vx Works).

The last phase consisted in demonstrating the same capabilities on more realistic sites: the SNCF experimental testbed at Trappes, and the Frankfort airport experimental testbed. The experiment at SNCF was carried out in very harsh condition (snow).

2.4 Eureka 474 FIRST: Friendly Interaction Robot for Service Tasks

This project had a duration of 4 years and ended in 1996.

The participants were : ITMI (Prime) (F), LIRMM (F), PIANELLI & TRAVERSA Industries (Turin) (I), and IRST (Trente) (I).

The objective of the project is to build industrial prototypes of mobile robot systems for transport of loads in hospitals.

The system developed by the French partners deals with transport and handling trolleys containing meal trays, linen, drugs, waste, etc... that weight up to 300 kg. The system comprises a fleet of mobile robots, a central control station and several decentralised control stations.

The central station is in charge of the technical management of the fleet of mobile robots. Its main functions are preparation of robot missions, scheduling of activities, on-line follow-up of missions, and replanning if a problem occurs. The ground station is continuously in communication with the robots via a radio link. It allows the users to have access to all the available functions of the system, to specify, modify and cancel missions, to display the current position of robots and the progress of missions, to stop one or several robots, etc...

The decentralised control stations are terminals of the central station located in different departments of the hospital (medical care departments, logistic units like kitchen, warehouse, etc...). They are linked to the central station by the hospital computer network. They allow users to have access to a subset of the system functionalities, for example requesting for an additional mission to be introduced into the planning, displaying the progress of a mission.

The robots navigate autonomously in a public indoor environment. They move close to patients and visitors and use public lifts. Autonomous navigation means automatic path and trajectory planning as well as reaction to unexpected events. Robots use different sensors to locate themselves, to perceive their surrounding environment in order to detect static and moving obstacles and avoid them when possible.

A prototype system is operational since June 1995. The electro-mechanical platform has been developed using standard AGV technology and its locomotion system has been designed to navigate in clustered environments. A learning and programming terminal is used off line to teach standard paths corresponding to the classical missions of the robot. The controller generate motions based upon the learnt geometric positions, the on-line information about unexpected obstacles and the position errors provided by an accurate localization system.

The complete system including the vehicle, the learning terminal and the control stations has been tested under real conditions in several departments of the Antoine Beclere Hospital (Clamart, France).

2.5 PROMETHEUS (Programme for European Traffic with Highest Efficiency and Unprecedented Safety)

This very well known program is now terminated (1988-1995). It involved all car-makers from France, Germany, Italy, Sweden, and the United Kingdom.

Its objectives were the study of highly computerized and sensor-equipped cars and the development of the corresponding equipment over (part of) the network of roads. This huge project is divided into eight sub-projects, each with the prefix PRO.

The sub-project PRO-ART is an R&D programme highly relevant to mobile robotics.

The PRO-ART French group was particularly interested by the development of an intelligent co-pilot in order to assist the driver. The development of such driver assistant is based on studies on car driving especially in cognitive psychology in order to take into account the characteristics of the different drivers. This kind of support systems is designed to help the driver in situations where he has some difficulties and is generally embedded in a larger architecture which includes real-time machine vision and sensor fusion capability.

The ProLab2 demonstrator has been realized by nine French laboratories (composing the French PRO-ART group), in collaboration with PSA and Renault corporations. It follows the demonstrator ProLab1 (embedded in a Renault 21) presented in 1991 in Compigne and in Torino. The demonstrator ProLab2 (embedded in a Peugeot 605) had been first presented in Paris in October 1994, and the Final presentation was in Toulouse, 9 June 1995.

ProLab2 is a system which provides information to help the driver to drive more safely. That means there is no automatic control of the vehicle. The system just observes and analyses the situation and informs the driver about perceived dangers and other safety information. The driver assistance system is decomposed into three different parts: a perception part, a decision part, and an information part.

For the perception part, the demonstrator is equipped with different sensors essentially cameras for front, lateral and rear vision, a laser telemeter and proprioceptive sensors for collecting information about the environment (static and dynamic) and the vehicle itself. The decision part integrates different processing modules like data fusion of several perceptive systems, situation analysis, planning and execution control of manoeuvres. The goal of this part is to generate adequate warnings and/or alarms according to the situation. The information part is a Human Computer Interface with three levels of interaction: an alarm mode in order to alert the driver to immediate danger; an advice mode in which the system informs the driver about the potential dangers and an assistance mode in which the system suggests some actions to the driver.

In a first stage, the different components were tested separately, and in a second stage, all the different parts were integrated on the vehicle. Real experiments of the demonstrator were realized and had allowed to optimize the global behavior of the copilot. The behavior of the driver assistance system tested in real contexts has been in adequation with the functional specifications and the results were very encouraging.

2.6 F12T - 0028 - IMPACT: A Light Mobile Tracked Machine with Advanced Sensing, World Modelling and Communication

This TELEMAN project (the programme of research for the European Atomic Energy Community in the field of remote handling in hazardous or disordered nuclear environments), started in March 1993 for a duration of 36 months.

Participants are EDF (F), INITEC (SP), KERNTECHNISCHE HILFSDIENST GmbH (G), TNO TPD (NL), Univ. College London (UK), KENTREE (IRL), LOUGHBOR-OUGH Univ. of Techn. (UK), FRAUNHOFER GESELLSCHAFT-IPA (G), Univ. Libre Brussels (B), CIEMAT (SP), CEA/LETI (F), and PIAP (P).

The overall objective of the IMPACT project is to develop a light mobile robot which can be quickly reconfigured, with different sensors and/or communications, for a variety of inspection tasks within nuclear plants. These interventions are to cover the range of normal, incident and accident situations and aim at surveillance (or data collecting) missions.

Among the sensors to be integrated within the project, let us quote the sensors used in 3D environmental reconstruction, using either the flight-time laser technique (the French Atomic Energy Commission Alis camera), or the stereovideogrammetry (the University College of London HAZMAP system). A radiation camera, giving a radiation "image" is also currently under study (the Spanish company CIEMAT). All these sensors have been implemented in 1994 in a Spanish plant, to reconstruct the plant's 3D environments on the one hand, and to establish a radiation cartography of certain areas on the other hand.

2.7 the DARDS Project

The DARDS project (Démonstrateur A Rapidité de Déplacement pour la Surveillance) of DRET (Bureau of Research of the French Ministry of Defence) aims to achieve an experimental autonomous surveillance rover. The first studies mainly carried out by industrial partners (Dassault Electronique, ITMI, Cybernetics), resulted in a vehicle that can autonomously perform basic motion tasks under global human supervision. CERT- ONERA joined the project to develop a decision layer in order to provide greater autonomy.

Autonomy can be defined as the ability to meet the mission goal(s) in spite of unexpected events. When such an event occurs, the decision layer has to detect it, then to update the current beliefs about the state of the worlds, and finally to modify the current plan of actions in accordance. The theoretical aspects of this problem were studied in the framework of the FIGARO project, and three sorts of methods were identified : reactive correction, pre-planned correction and plan revision. For an application to DARDS, the pre-planned correction method was selected ; it relies on the definition of behaviors that can be coded by Petri nets. Software was developed that allows execution monitoring to be performed by interpreting in real time the Petri nets code (Petri player).

The problem of mobile obstacle avoidance is also addressed in the CERT-DERA programme. The problem is not to deal with aggressive objects that try to obtain collision, but rather with quiet mobiles whose trajectory is badly known at the first detection. As new detection data are obtained, this trajectory is better estimated and the avoidance manoeuver is increasingly preferment. Game theory is used for the formalization of this problem and for the resolution procedure.

2.8 Planetary rovers

The following sections highlight the on-going programmes lead by the French Space Agency (CNES), and several laboratories and R&D organizations. At the core of these research projects, there are the robotics studies that are carried on by RISP, a consortium of Laboratories belonging to four research and R&D organizations (CEA, CNRS, INRIA, ONERA), in association with the French Space Agency (CNES) which started in 1989 a study project, VAP (Automated Planetary Vehicle) aiming to assess the state of the art and to develop the base-line system concepts for Planetary Rovers.

Various Lunar and Martian missions are currently considered with a main thrust on a technological mission on the Moon in 2002 (Lunar European Demonstration Approach: LEDA). The mission aims to demonstrate the feasibility and operational capacities of an autonomous rover covering hundreds kilometers in difficult terrains.

In this context, the group of RISP laboratories has pursued a broad spectrum of research activities scientifically related to CNES oriented projects, some of them just at the national level, some others expanding international collaboration.

2.8.1 The GEROMS testsite (Groupement pour les Essais en RObotique Mobile Spatiale)

GEROMS was created in August 1992 following a decision by the CNES/CST (Centre Spatial de Toulouse), the ONERA/CERT and the CNRS/LAAS to pool their individual competence and develop a common test facility for mobile robots in order to promote a centre of expertise unique in Europe for the testing of autonomous vehicles. GEROMS objectives are the experimentation, verification and validation of design concepts, the unit tests of subsystems fitted on a test vehicle, the development of complete systems with a view to integration and final acceptance, and finally, the experimentation and testing of mobile robot demonstrators in a representative context which considers mission peculiarities in terms of the environment.

In order to achieve these objectives, GEROMS has a main test site which consists of both an instrument-equipped automated test vehicle, and a calibrated test site including obstacles commonly met by robots during outdoor operation. This test site may be broken down into a "Moon" area, an "Earth" area and a "Mars" area.

The main test site is also equipped with the following:

- facilities for robot integration and maintenance,

- measurement facilities designed to firstly calibrate and characterize the site and then to assess the performance of both onboard subsystems and the robots themselves.

- software development equipment, which consists of workstations and analysis tools to debug and modify onboard software, whether on the main test site or during campaigns,

- computing facilities used to interface with and simulate the environment of systems or subsystems being tested,

- simple locomotion facilities (not autonomous, versatile, etc.) for subsystem testing,

- infrastructure providing the necessary support and resources (electrical power supply, air conditioning, etc.) during campaigns.

The test facilities and part of the infrastructure are "transportable" so that it is possible to move all such resources to an external test site considered more representative of the final operating environment (in situ tests).

2.8.2 Eureka Project 969 IARES

Following the research programme carried out by CNES in association with RISP, it was decided to build a demonstration rover to validate the robotics functionalities and to experimentally demonstrate the degree of operational and decisional autonomy offered by concepts developed since 1989. The Eureka pan-European structure appeared to offer a logical continuation to the French studies while also seeking to federate and transfer to the field of space the expertise and the achievements generated by other programmes in mobile robotics in which both industry and research participate. The reverse, i.e. the spin-off from space to industry is also a meaningful and important objective.

IARES associates 9 partners from 4 countries : France (ALCATEL ESPACE, CYBERNETIX, ITMI, MATRA MARCONI SPACE, SAGEM, and RISP); Spain (IKERLAN); Hungary (KFKI/RMKI) and Russia (VNIITRANSMASH). RISP, IKERLAN, KFKI and VNIITRANSMASH actually represent several organizations or sub-partners.

The objective of the IARES project [7] is to draw up a detailed definition of the sub-systems needed to produce a ground demonstrator that will be fully representative of robot functionalities and of the autonomy required for planetary exploration and therefore to develop the techniques that will allow the exploration and subsequent operation of planetary sites (Mars, the Moon). The following aspects relating to mobile robotics are developed :

- algorithms and systems for travel over natural and ill-known terrain,
- equipment required to autonomously determine the robot's position,
- equipment required for autonomous on-board environment perception,
- aspects related to on-board decision-making and the planning of operations associated with the operator station on Earth,
- handling and gripping tools.

The important perspectives that would open the ESA initiative of a Lunar scientific base to be situated in the South pole area as well as the difficulties in scheduling an ambitious exploration of Mars, have lead CNES to shift the current thrust of the work carried on within IARES to a lighter demonstrator, and to lead work and validation experiments aimed to anticipate and to support a first technical Lunar mission, LEDA.

The demonstrator IARES will be in particular tested on the GEROMS test site at CNES in Toulouse (France) from mid 1996 to end 1997.

2.8.3 CONCORDIA

An important international-wide science research oriented effort is conducted in Antarctica. France and Italy have programmed a major undertaking : the CONCORDIA project. From a robotics point of view, the work in this framework pertains to planetary rovers.

A scientific base, Dome C, is to be installed to carry on an ambitious scientific programme in the heart of Antarctica. Dome C is situated at a similar distance (approximately one thousand kilometers) of the Italian coastal base and the French one (Dumont d'Urville). Research groups in both countries have started studies related to robotics in two possible directions: logistics (coastal base - Dome C traverses) and scientific experiments (around Dome C, teleoperated experimentations, automatic monitoring,...).

For the French side, RISP, in charge of the studies, has focused its interest mainly in science-oriented robotic requirements. Work in progress includes a preliminary study with a science-oriented working group to be carried on in the Pyrénées mountains.

2.8.4 The Eden project

The objective of the EDEN project carried out at LAAS [3] is to achieve a canonical navigation task, i.e., the task: ``Go To [goal]'', where the argument goal is a distant target to reach autonomously. Any more complex robotic mission (exploration, sample collection...) will necessarily include one or more instances of this task. Given the variety of terrains the robot will have to traverse, this task involves in our approach several levels of reasoning, several environment representations, and three different motion modes. It raises a need for a specific decisional level (the *navigation* level), that is in charge of deciding which environment representation to update, which sub-goal to reach, and which motion mode to apply. This level, which is a key component of the system, controls the perception and motion activities of the robot for this task. Inded, in a natural environment, there may be regions that are rather flat, cluttered or not by obstacles, and regions of uneven terrain. To achieve an efficient behavior, the robot must adapt the manner in which it executes the navigation task to the nature of the terrain and the quality of its knowledge on it. Hence, three motion modes are considered:

- A **reflex** mode: on large flat and lightly cluttered zones, it is sufficient to determine robot locomotion commands on the basis of a goal (heading or position) and informations provided by "obstacle detector" sensors. The terrain representation required by this mode is just the description of the borders of the region within which it can be applied;

- A **2D planned** mode: when the terrain is mainly flat, but cluttered with obstacles, it becomes necessary for efficiency reasons to plan a trajectory. The trajectory planner reasons on a binary description of the environment, which is described in terms of empty/obstacle areas.

- A **3D planned** mode: when the terrain is highly constrained (uneven), collision and stability constraints have to be checked to determine the robot locomotion commands. This is done by a 3D trajectory planner, that reasons on a fine 3D description of the terrain (an elevation map or numerical terrain model);

The experimental robot, ADAM (figure 3), was provided by Matra Marconi Space and Framatome to LAAS, equipped with a 3D scanning laser range finder, two color cameras (for stereo, object recognition), and a 3-axis inertial platform. The motion controller also provides for odometry. On board computing equipement is composed of two VME racks, one for locomotion and attitude control, and the other for the perceptual and decisional functions.

Figure 3: *ADAM in the Geroms test site*

3 CNRS Strategic Action on Intelligent Machines

3.1 General overview

The assessment of the current development of advanced robotics, supported by information technology, microtechnologies and microsystems developments, has lead to consider for Robotics the new frontier of non-manufacturing applications.

Robust sensor-based systems with embedded intelligence are key issues in robotics research that will enable to make mobile robots come out the laboratories to a large variety of applicative domains such as service robots, in field-based applications such as mining, forestry, agriculture, underwater, space, and to public-oriented areas ranging from domestic and professional cleaning to assistance to the disabled and the aging.

This implies the actual development of machine-intelligence based robots, i.e. systems that would have to integrate perception to action throughout levels of sensing interpretation, task assessment, symbolic reasoning, sensor-based execution control, in a fully integrated system that could be controlled by a human throughout a sophisticated operator-machine interface.

Accordingly, CNRS has undertaken to organize a network of specific actions associating several other laboratories to a focal point laboratory and to open the cooperation with other domain-oriented institutions as well as to industrial partners. Among those specific actions, we shall mention Robotics in space, underwater, agriculture, construction, assistance to the disabled and the aging, assistance to the driver.

Actions that pertain to mobile robots and that started to be organized are the following:

1. Autonomous intervention robots for non-cooperative sites
2. Construction and civil work robots
3. Machine-Intelligence assisted driving
4. Personal robots to assist the impaired and the aging
5. Robotics in Agriculture and the food-industry
6. Subsea robotics
7. Intelligent household systems
8. Telerobotics for nuclear and related hostile environments
9. Entertainment robots
10. Domestic service robots

We develop some of these actions below.

3.2 Autonomous Intervention Robots for non-Cooperative Sites

objectives : the research programme is concerned with the design and the system development of autonomous mobile robots that can be remotely teleoperated in natural and non (or partly) cooperative environments.

The research themes include :

- Locomotion system design and control
- 3D perception and modelling
- Decisional real-time on-board autonomy
- Teleprogramming and telesupervision systems

The problem is supported by on-going projects such as IARES (see section 2.8.2) and CONCORDIA (section 2.8.3).

CNRS focal laboratory : LAAS
Other CNRS laboratories : LIFIA, LIRMM, LRP
Testbeds : LAAS facilities, GEROMS (section 2.8.1)
Main partners : CNES, RISP (consortium grouping CNRS, INRIA, ONERA) Industrial companies : Alcatel Espace, Cybernetix, ITMI, Matra Marconi Space, Sagem.

We shall develop in section 2.8.4 the technical work in this domain.

3.3   Construction and Civil Work Robots

objectives : the research programme comprises the system developments implied for a mobile machine to operate in construction works (road construction and maintenance, building construction,...).

It includes subjects such as : 6D dynamic localization, navigation and operator machine interfaces for soil automated handling, obstacle detection in complex dynamic work- environments.

CNRS focal laboratory : LAN
Testbed : LCPC site : Robot Melody, ...
Institutional partners : LCPC, CER (roadway experimentation center)
Industrial companies : Cochery Bourdin Chaussée, Scetauroute,...

3.4   Machine-Intelligence Assisted Driving

Project objectives : the research programme addresses the subjects related to the development of an intelligent co-pilot in order to assist a driver in continuity with a work carried on in the Pro-Art programme of PROMETHEUS.. The central aim remains improved and safer traffic conditions in roads and freeways.

The research programme includes

- algorithms improvement to suppress false alarms and to reduce system response-time
- data and multi-sensor signal fusion
- man-machine cooperation

CNRS focal laboratory : HEUDIASYC
Other CNRS laboratories : IEF, LAAS, LASMEA, LIFIA, LIAH
Institutional partner : INRETS
Industrial partners : PSA, RENAULT

3.5 Personal Robots to Assist the Impaired and the Aging

Objectives : the technical issues and scientific orientations of the research programme cover the following aspects :

- Perception and motion control problems as classically addressed in the scope of Robotics, but adapted to the actual application context,

- High-level of robustness and fault tolerance, including to user misuses.

- Person-machine interaction modes implementing the concept of co-autonomy, building on the interplay of the decisional levels of the machine and the user.

CNRS focal laboratory : LAAS
Other laboratories : IRIT, LAEI
Testbed : mobile robots, arm equipped wheelchairs (ENIT, LAAS)
Institutional partners : INSERM (CREA-Paris; U103, Montpellier), ENIT, CEA

3.6 Robotics in Agriculture & the Food-Industry

Objectives: the technical issues and the scientific orientations of the research programme cover the following aspects :

- 3D perception, natural and industrial environment modelling,

- techniques and models for computer-aided decision,

- development of automated machinery ; advanced control,

- methods, tools and interfaces for operator machine cooperation.

Important research objectives for the last theme are dynamic vision, virtual reality, sensor based adaptative control and AI based interfaces.

CNRS focal laboratory : LASMEA, Blaise Pascal University of Clermont-Ferrand
Other CNRS laboratories : IRISA, LIRMM, HEUDIASYC
Institutional partner : CEMAGREF.

3.7 Subsea Robotics

Objectives : the technical issues and scientific orientations of the research programme cover the field of underwater remote intervention. This can be envisioned in two modes: AUV (Autonomous Underwater Vehicles) or ROV (Remotely Operated Vehicles). The programme will mostly focus in medium term objectives in the last mode.

The research programme includes :

- development of operator machine interfaces (augmented reality,...)

- redundant on-board arm teleoperation including force feedback control

- sensor based control

- arm-vehicle coordination

CNRS focal laboratory : LIRMM
Test-bed: Toulon IFREMER site and LIRMM Montpellier
Other CNRS laboratories : LAN, I3S, LAG, LAAS Main partners : IFREMER, INRIA
and RSM (Mediterranean Subsea Robotics Group)

4 INRIA projects

INRIA is a french national institute for control and computer science. It carries out several
projects more or less pertaining to mobile robotics within the framework of its programme
Robotics, Image and Vision, mainly:

- ICARE, at Sophia-Antipolis. The project is involved in the investigation of problems
  associated with the control of mechanical systems, with Robotics as a privileged, but
  not exclusive, domain of application. The project focuses on control theory and application to Robotics, acquisition and processing of sensory data for control purposes,
  and real-time programming environments.

- MOVI at Grenoble. The project is focused on the perception of three dimensional
  shapes using cameras. Within this general frame, the study concerns more particularly
  the geometry of perception in order to be able to locate objects from a single or
  multiple views and to be able to recognize shapes or obstacles. 3D reconstruction
  using non calibrated or partially calibrated cameras is aimed towards improvement in
  speed, robustness and accuracy.

- PRISME at Sophia-Antipolis. The main interests of the project are computational
  geometry and geometric issues in robotics. The research is motivated by the many
  application domains, and most notably robotics, that require to solve geometric problems efficiently, and in particular motion planning for mobile robots.

- ROBOTVIS, at Sophia-Antipolis The scientific and technological objectives of the
  project are to develop theories of machine visual perception and in particular of
  three-dimensional vision and to demonstrate their validity.

- SHARP, at Grenoble. The Sharp project aims to develop techniques for task-level
  programming and autonomy to allow robots to be applied to novel, incompletely
  specified and non-repetitive tasks. The emphasis is on methods for planning and
  executing complex movements, dexterity, motion planning and control and reactivity.

INRIA participates through these projects to several french national and european projects.

5 Conclusion

During the last decade, dramatic developments in information technologies together with
an important progress in sensing devices, scientific results in autonmous robots have fos-
tered new perspectives in the domain of mobile robots.

The projects and developements overviewed in this paper tend towards achieving Autonomous Mobile Robots, i.e., machines endowed with the capacity to reason about a task
and about its execution, by intelligently relating perception to action.

Field robotics represents today a cutting-edge research stream in the domain of autonomous mobile robots, i.e. Intelligent Machines possessing decisional and operation al autonomy. There is a rich spectrum of application domains, most of them implying highly demanding technical advances in subjects such as automated locomotion, 3-D perception and modelling, on-board autonomy, and task-level teleprogramming. Multiple robot systems that imply several intelligent machines acting as semi-autonomous agents, are also a developing investigation domain.

The French National Centre for Scientific Research (CNRS) has undertaken to organize a network of specific actions on applicative issues of robotics, based on the association of several laboratories among which a focal centre, and with an open cooperation with other domain-oriented institutions as well as industries. Such actions arte intended to foster the real-world use of robots in the service and intervention domains, to then identify and study the new technological frontiers. What still is little more than "advanced prototype" should be actually used in real operations.

Acknowledgments: The author wishes to thank all the persons who provided data on their projects that are included in this paper.

References

[1] R.Alami, F.Robert, F.Ingrand, S.Suzuki. Multi-robot cooperation through incremental plan-merging. IEEE International Conference on Robotics and Automation (ICRA'95), Nagoya (Japon), 21-27 May 1995, pp.2573-2579

[2] Aguilar L., R. Alami, S. Fleury, M. Herrb, F. Ingrand, F. Robert. Ten autonomous mobile robots (and even more) in a route network like environment. IEEE International Workshop on Intelligent Robots and Systems (IROS'95), Pittsburgh (USA), 7-9 Aug. 1995, pp.260-267

[3] R. Chatila, S. Lacroix, T. Siméon, M. Herrb. Planetary exploration by a mobile robot: mission teleprogramming and autonomous navigation. Autonomous Robots Journal, Vol.2,4 , pp.333-344, 1995

[4] G. Giralt Programmes and perspectives for international research cooperation in Robotics and related areas. An assessment from France. Opening Workshop of SYROCO'94, Capri (Italy), 18 Septembre 1994, 16p.

[5] G. Giralt Mobile robots: decisional and operational autonomy Worshop on Intelligent Components for Autonomous and Semi-Autonomous Vehicles (ICASAV'95), Toulouse (France), 25-26 Octobre 1995, 8p.

[6] G. Giralt An overview of agricultural robotics in France Robotics and Automation in Food Processing, Melbourne (Australia), 15 May 1995, 8p.

[7] G. Giralt, L. Boissier, L. Marechal The IARES project: rovers for the human conquest of the moon and mars Workshop WT1 "Planetary Rover Technology and Systems", Minneapolis (USA), 23 April 1996, 20p.

[8] J.P. Laumond Motion planning for mobile robots: from academic to practical issues Robotics Research 6. Eds T.Kanade, R.Paul. International Foundation for Robotics Research. 1994. pp.21-27.

Leichtbau, Geschicklichkeit und multisensorielle Autonomie

- Schlüsseltechnologien für künftige Raumfahrt-Roboter wie für terrestrische Service-Roboter

Gerd Hirzinger

DLR

Deutsche Forschungsanstalt für Luft- und Raumfahrt e.V.
Institut für Robotik und Systemdynamik
Oberpfaffenhofen, 82234 Wessling

1 Einführung

Die Fortentwicklung der Industrie-Roboter in den letzten 10 Jahren weist ermutigende, aber auch viele frustrierende Aspekte auf. So wurden die Roboter durchaus schlanker, die Steuerungen schneller (kartesische Taktzeiten typischerweise von 30 auf 10 msec reduziert), vor allem der Preis fast auf die Hälfte reduziert; aber auf Sensorik basierende Intelligenz fehlt heutigen Industrie-Robotern eher noch mehr als vor 10 Jahren, als es viele Pilotprojekte gab (z.B. bildgestützte PKW-Rad-Montage, Griff auf das laufende Band etc.), die in der Folgezeit weitgehend eingestellt wurden. Sensorik wurde als zu teuer, zu unzuverlässig, zu kompliziert in der Programmierung dargestellt, und in den allermeisten Fällen führt man heute den Robotern die Teile wieder exakt und dementsprechend aufwendig zu. Dennoch weiß jeder Robotik-Fachmann, daß es nur eine Frage der Zeit (und insbesondere der Verfügbarkeit kostengünstiger Sensorik) ist, bis eine flexiblere, sich an Umweltveränderungen anpassende Robotergeneration, die dann auch komplexe Montagevorgänge beherrschen wird, auf den Markt kommt.
Der Raumfahrt-Robotik mit ihrem Ziel, Astronauten zumindest bei monotonen oder riskanten Arbeiten durch intelligente Automaten zu entlasten oder zu ersetzen, bzw. ganz allgemein der „Dienstleistungs-Robotik", kann dabei die Schrittmacher-Rolle für den Technologie-Durchbruch zufallen. Die dort insbesondere auf mobilen Plattformen benötigten Roboter sollten leicht (in der Raumfahrt sogar extrem leicht) und nicht von einer exakt strukturierten Umgebung abhängig sein, d.h. letztlich multisensorielle Autonomie aufweisen, leichte Programmierbarkeit und Lernfähigkeit sowie ggf. manipulative Geschicklichkeit durch feingliedrige Hände. Die Beiträge der DLR hierzu seien nachfolgend erläutert.

2 Vorarbeiten und Ziele

Ende April 93 führte erstmalig in der Geschichte der Raumfahrt bei der Spacelab-D2-Mission ein kleiner, mit lokaler, „multisensorieller" Intelligenz ausgestatteter Roboter an Bord eines

Raumfahrzeugs Aufgaben völlig flexibel in den unterschiedlichsten Betriebsarten durch; nämlich vorprogrammiert (und während der Mission vom Boden aus umprogrammiert), von Astronauten über die sog. DLR-Steuerkugel (Abb. 1) und einen TV-Stereo-Monitor ferngesteuert, aber auch vom Boden aus fernprogrammiert und ferngesteuert. Der Roboter mußte in diesen Betriebsarten Steckverbindungen in Form eines Bajonett-Verschlusses lösen bzw. wiederherstellen, mechanische Strukturen zusammen- bzw. auseinanderbauen und ein freifliegendes Objekt einfangen (Abb. 4).

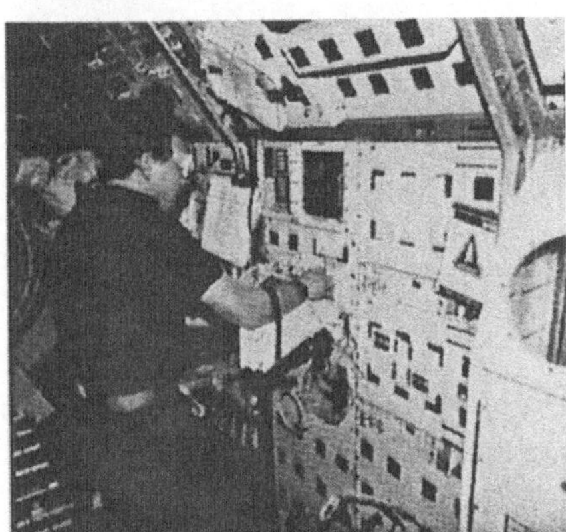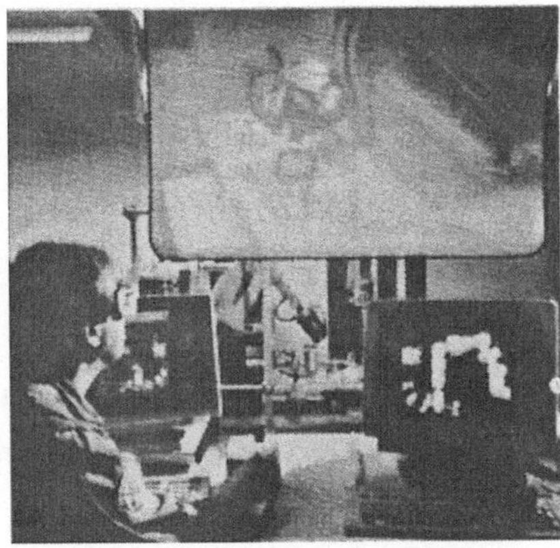

Abb. 1 Astronaut Hans Schlegel steuert den Roboter über sein Stereo-Display und die DLR Steuerkugel fern (links); ein Teil der Telerobotik-Bodenstation wurde auch für das Astronautentraining verwendet (rechts).

Schlüsseltechnologien für den Erfolg des von der DLR geführten Experiments waren u.a. [4]

- die multisensorielle „mechatronische" Greifertechnologie (Abb. 2); mit 16 Sensoren (redundante Kraft/Momentensensorik, 9 Laser-Entfernungsmesser, Stereo-Kameras, taktile Sensorik) und über 1000 Elektronik-Komponenten, integriert mit mehreren hundert Mechanik-Komponenten, war der ROTEX-2-Backen-Greifer der vermutlich komplexeste bisher gebaute Robotergreifer; er verlieh dem Roboter lokale Autonomie (shared autonomy).

Insofern war das Experiment auch gedacht als Demonstration des Potentials der intelligenten Sensorrückkopplung.

- die Methoden der prädiktiven, laufzeitkompensierenden 3D-Grafik-Simulation, die es erlaubten, das Roboterverhalten auch unter dem Einfluß der sensorischen Perzeption und der lokalen Signalrückkopplung vorauszurechnen und so die Gesamt-Signallaufzeiten von bis zu 7 Sekunden zu kompensieren (Abb. 3 und Abb. 10). Dadurch wurde neben der sensorgestützten Fernprogrammierung auch die sensorgestützte on-line Fernsteuerung durch den Operateur bzw. die rein maschinelle Intelligenz am Boden möglich.

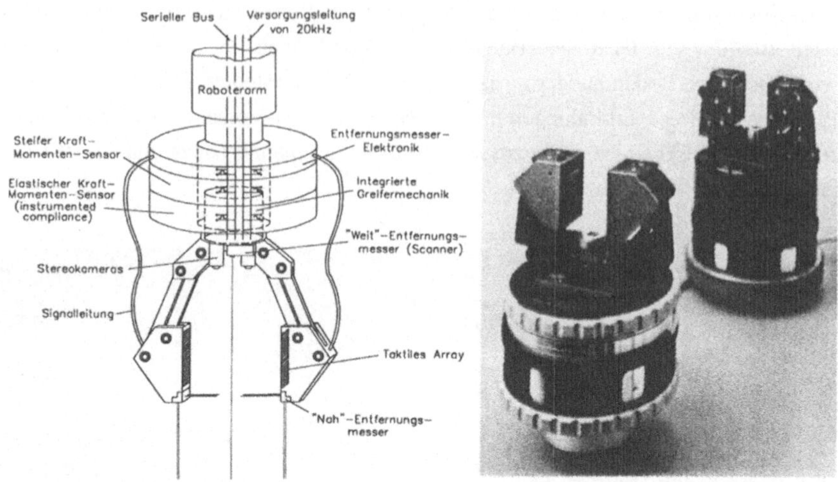

Abb. 2 Der ROTEX-Greifer (im Foto hinten) enthielt insgesamt 16 Sensorsysteme. Im Rahmen eines ESA-Auftrags wurde er inzwischen weiter optimiert (vorne).

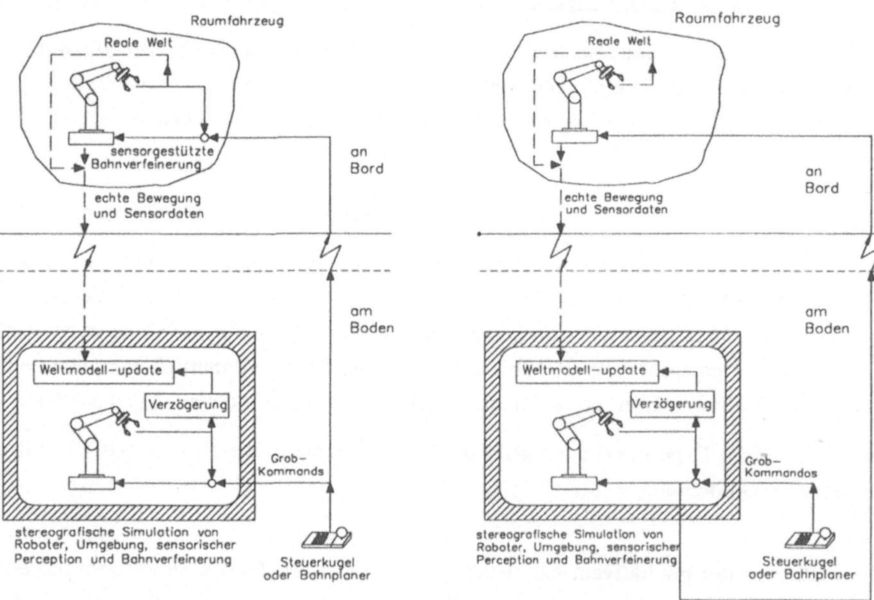

a) lokale Sensorrückkopplung an Bord (z.B. bei taktilem Kontakt)

b) Visuelle Sensorrückkopplung nur über die Bodenstation (Einfangen des Freifliegers).

Abb. 3 Prädiktive Simulation sensorischer Perzeption und Feinbahnplanung bei Bodenfernsteuerung durch Operateur oder maschinelle Intelligenz

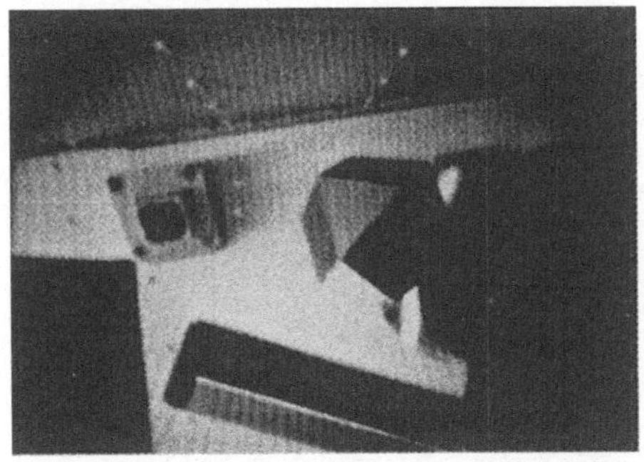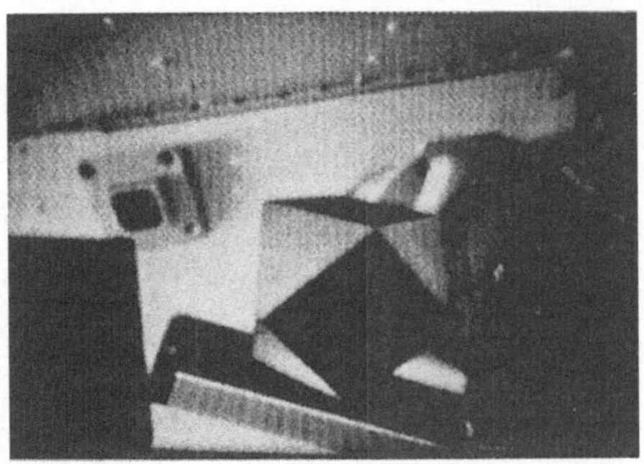

Abb. 4 Zwei aufeinanderfolgende Szenen aus einer der Greifer-Hand-Kameras kurz vor dem vollautomatisch vom Boden gesteuerten Greifen des „Freifliegers" bei ca. 6 sec. Gesamttotzeit. Die dunklen Flächen rechts und links stellen die Greiferbacken dar.

Inzwischen arbeitet die DLR intensiv an der Entwicklung einer neuen multisensoriellen, lernfähigen Leichtbau-Robotergeneration. Zwar sind diese Arbeiten zunächst durch Vorstellungen über künftige Weltraum-Roboter-Einsätze z.B. bei Inspektion, Wartung und Betrieb von Raumfahrt-Systemen motiviert, doch ist es gleichzeitig erklärtes Ziel, die für die Raumfahrt-Robotik entwickelten Technologien der terrestrischen Anwendung (u. a. im Bereich der medizinischen Service-Roboter) zugänglich zu machen. Die Arbeiten, eingebettet in eine strategische Leitkonzept-Kooperation mit dem DAIMLER-DASA-Konzern („Advanced Servicing Robot" ASR), zielen auf ein massives Vorantreiben der Basis-Technologien, um *operationelle* Robotik-Systeme für internes und externes „Servicing" in Raumlabors auf niedrigen Umlaufbahnen, aber auch *experimentelle* Systeme für externes Servicing (z.B. Wartung und Reparatur) von z.B. geostationären Nachrichten-Satelliten sowie für Planetenmissionen vorzubereiten.

Mobilität kommt dabei in unterschiedlicher Form zum Tragen:

- im Inneren von Raumstationen oder an deren Außenstruktur ist vornehmlich an mehrachsige, kartesische Transportschienen gedacht, die z.B. aus einem redundanten 7-Gelenk-Roboter ein 10 Freiheitsgrad-System machen. Allerdings werden auch Klettermechanismen (z.B. bei der DASA) vorbereitet.

- freifliegende Teleroboter-Systeme (Trägerfahrzeug mit Roboter), die zu den reparaturbedürftigen Systemen hinfliegen, sie inspizieren und ggf. dort manipulieren. Für ein solches Experimentalsystemen ESS (Experimental Servicing Satellite) werden bei der DLR derzeit die technologischen Voraussetzungen geschaffen. Es soll zu dem defekten TV-SAT1 (ein Solarpanel öffnete sich seinerzeit nicht) hinfliegen (Abb. 5), ihn mit dem Roboterarm am Apogäumsmotor ergreifen, heranziehen und in einer einfachen Halterung festklammern, um so den Roboter für das Aufschneiden der Klammern freizumachen, die das Solarpanel am Entfalten hindern.

Abb. 5 ESS - Inspektion und Reparatur durch einen freifliegenden Robotersatelliten

Neben dem dafür vorgesehenen video-gestützten Weltmodell-update ist für diese Art der Mobilität besonders die dynamische Wechselwirkung Roboter-Trägersatellit von Bedeutung, die im DLR-Labor mit 2 Robotern auch experimentell verifiziert wird und die insbesondere das visuelle „servoing" erschwert. Praktische Erfahrung wird die DLR hier auch durch die Kooperation mit der japanischen Raumfahrt Agentur NASDA sammeln, die 1997 erstmalig ein freifliegendes Teleroboter-Experimentalsystem ETS VII in den Weltraum schicken wird.

Zu den Basis-Technologien gehört in diesem Zusammenhang u.a. die Weiterentwicklung des multisensoriellen 2-Backen-Greifers (im ESA-Auftrag bereits zum europäischen Standard gereift, Abb. 2), aber auch die Realisierung der DLR-Leichtbauroboter-Konzepte, die längerfristig ein Verhältnis 1:1 zwischen Traglast und Eigengewicht anstreben. Höhere manuelle Geschicklichkeit soll durch die Entwicklung einer mehrfingrigen, feingliedrigen Roboterhand gewährleistet werden, mit einem „mechatronischen" Integrationsgrad, wie er bisher nirgendwo erreicht wurde. Im Bereich der Steuerungen ist insbesondere die im DARA-Auftrag vorangetriebene Entwicklung eines völlig modularen Steuerungskonzepts für künftige Raumfahrt-Automaten hervorzuheben, das eine sog. aufgabenorientierte, sensorbasierte Fernprogrammierung semi-autonomer Roboter einschließt. Mit ihr soll künftig auch der Nicht-Robotiker (also z.B. der wissenschaftliche Experimentator) in der Lage sein, Robotern im Weltraum die Abarbeitung komplexer Aufgaben im Sinne des verlängerten menschlichen Arms zu kommandieren. Selbstlernverfahren auf allen Ebenen wie auch der Geschicklichkeits-Transfer vom Menschen auf die Maschine (Lernen durch Vormachen) spielen darüberhinaus bei den DLR-Arbeiten eine wichtige Rolle.

Auf einige dieser von speziellen Raumfahrt-Szenarios unabhängigen Technologie-Entwicklungen sei im folgenden näher eingegangen.

3 Mechatronische Ansätze für eine neue Leichtbau-Roboter-Generation

Nach wie vor versuchen herkömmliche Industrie-Roboter, mit einer hohen Positioniergenauigkeit (in Wirklichkeit nur eine relative Wiederholgenauigkeit) zu brillieren, über schwere Massen und hohe mechanische Steifigkeiten, statt sich an der Leichtigkeit des menschlichen Arms zu orientieren, der über Multi-Sensorik (Auge, Gefühl) alle Positionier-Ungenauigkeiten sofort kompensiert.

Leichtbau ist für die Raumfahrt eine zentrale Forderung. Während herkömmliche Roboter nur etwa ein Zwanzigstel ihres Eigengewichts zuverlässig bewegen können, konnte dieses Verhältnis beim ersten DLR-Leichtbau-Roboter-Prototyp, der in einer Grundversion schon für das ROTEX-Astronauten-Training eingesetzt wurde, auf ein halb, d.h. um etwa eine Zehnerpotenz, verbessert werden. Der Entwurf dieses Roboters nach Konzepten der Mechatronik, insbesondere der Integration von Maschinenbau, Elektronik und Rechnerleistung auf kleinstmöglichem Raum erfolgte aus einem Guß, d.h. immer unter dem Aspekt der Optimierung des völlig modularen Gesamtsystems. Es hilft z.B. wenig, die Armstrukturen aus Faserverbundwerkstoff zu bauen, wenn man nicht gleichzeitig die Motor-Getriebe-Technik optimiert, inklusive der Krafteinleitung in die Faserstrukturen.

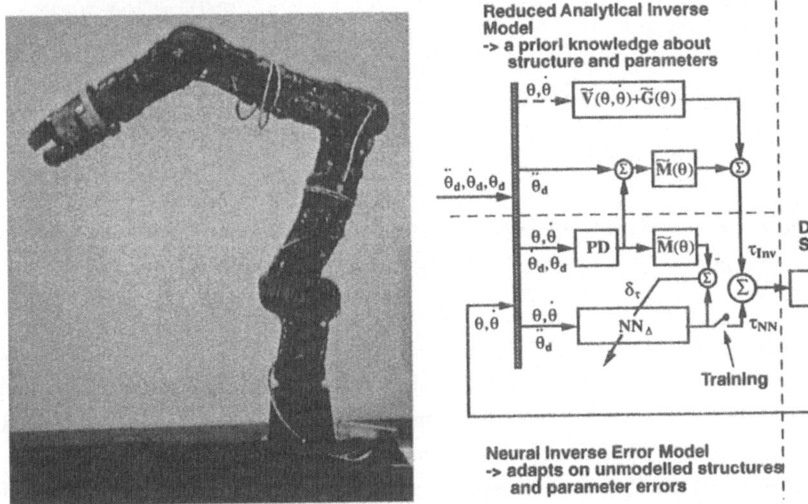

Abb. 6 Ein erster 7-Gelenk-Prototyp des DLR-Leichtbau-Roboters mit voll integrierter Elektronik und ca. 14 kg Gewicht bei ca. 1,5 m Reichweite; rechts die lernfähige „hybride" Invers-Dynamik-Steuerung (Kapitel 6).

Die komplette Steuer- und Leistungselektronik wurde u.a. aus Gründen der Kabelminimierung in den Arm integriert, d.h. der herkömmliche Steuerschrank verschwindet fast vollständig (Abb. 6). Damit sollen auch für die Industrie-Robotik, insbesondere aber die vielzitierte neue Generation von Service-Robotern für den häuslichen und medizinischen Bereich, Maßstäbe gesetzt werden. Auf die Analogie zum menschlichen Arm weist bei der neuesten Version auch die redundante 7-Freiheitsgrad-Kinematik hin, ebenfalls nicht üblich bei konventionellen Robotern. Der Arm ist aus CFK-Gitterstrukturen aufgebaut und enthält im Gegensatz zu herkömmlichen Robotern Drehmomentensensorik und -Regelung, so daß er nicht mehr wie heutige Roboter als reine Positioniermaschine arbeitet, sondern ähnlich wie der menschliche Arm durch Kräfte bzw. Momente in den Gelenken gesteuert wird. Hochdynamische bürstenlose Gleichstrommotoren (bis 18.000 U/min) in Verbindung mit extrem kompakten, hoch übersetzenden Doppelplaneten-Getrieben(1:500, Abb. 7) liefern ca. 120 Nm Drehmoment in den Gelenken bei nur 1 kg Gewicht.

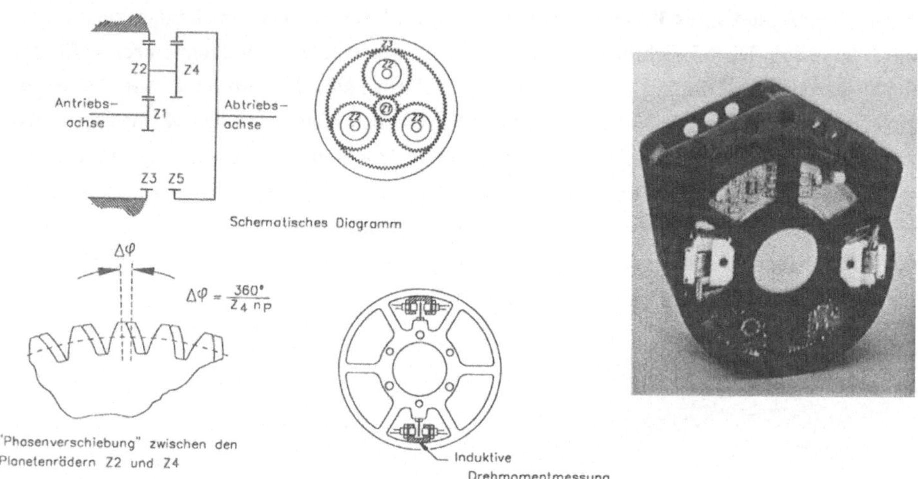

Abb. 7 Das extrem kompakte, hoch (1:500) übersetzende Doppelplaneten-Getriebe mit integriertem Drehmoment-Sensor (Foto rechts).

Der Drehmoment-Sensor ist integraler Teil des Getriebes und ähnelt einem Rad mit 6 Speichen, deren Verformung differentiell induktiv erfaßt werden. Die SMD-Auswerte-Elektronik ist in die Sensor-Mechanik integriert und liefert dem ebenfalls ins Gelenk integrierten Gelenk-Regelungsprozessor eine 12-Bit-Momenten-Information z.B. zur vollständigen Reibungs-Kompensation. Ein zweiter Prozessor in jedem Gelenk stellt die Kommunikation zum optischen Hochgeschwindigkeits-Bus vom Typ SERCOS her, der alle Gelenke mit 2-4 Mbaud mit der Zentralrechner-Karte, auf dem Echtzeit-Betriebs-System VxWorks basierend, verbindet. Kartesische Abtastzyklen von 1 msec auch bei Rückkopplung von Kraft-Sensor-Signalen sind das erklärte Entwicklungsziel. Mit heutigen Industrie-Robotern sind sensorgeregelte Montagevorgänge, ähnlich schnell wie von der menschlichen Hand durchgeführt, nach wie vor nicht möglich, da sich - bedingt vor allem durch die gängigen Steuerungsstrukturen - Reaktionszeiten von typischerweise 50-80 msec ergeben.

4 Die DLR-Mehrfinger-Hand auf Basis des künstlichen Muskels®

Die weltweit patentierte DLR-Planeten-Wälz-Gewindespindel (PWG) (Abb. 8 links), die im ROTEX-Greifer erstmalig eingesetzt wurde, setzt schnelle Drehbewegungen mit niedrigem Moment extrem reibungsarm in eine langsame Linearbewegung hoher Kraft um. Die mechanische Funktion der PWG kann als Kombination einer herkömmlichen Verschraubung mit einem Planetengetriebe und einem Wälzlager verstanden werden. Integriert man die Spindel ins Innere kleiner Spezialmotoren(Abb. 8 rechts), so entsteht ein hochkompaktes lineares Antriebselement, das vermutlich erstmalig eine echte Alternative zu pneumatischen und hydraulischen Stellgliedern darstellt. Mögliche Anwendungsgebiete reichen von der tonnenschweren Presse über den elektrischen Auto-Fenster-Heber, die voll-elektromechanische Bremse im Auto (break by wire), bis zur Flugzeugklappenverstellung und zur medizinischen Dosierpumpe. Inzwischen wird dieser „künstliche Muskel" in unterschiedlichen Versionen zu einer vollständig programmierbaren Feder mit „wählbarer Impedanz" (Dämpfung und Steifigkeit) weiterentwickelt. Entscheidend dafür sind die Entwicklung und Integration miniaturisierter Positions- und Kraft- bzw. Momenten-Sensoren sowie entsprechende Regelgesetze und deren Realisierung in Mikrocontrollern (Abb. 8 rechts). Diese neuen Linear-Antriebe sind die Basis einer neuen mehrfingrigen, mehrgliedrigen Roboterhand, bei der im Gegensatz zu allen bisher entwickelten Roboterhänden die gesamte Antriebstechnik in die Hand bzw. die Handwurzel integriert sein soll und dennoch maximale Greifkräfte um 1,5 kg garantieren soll (Abb. 9).

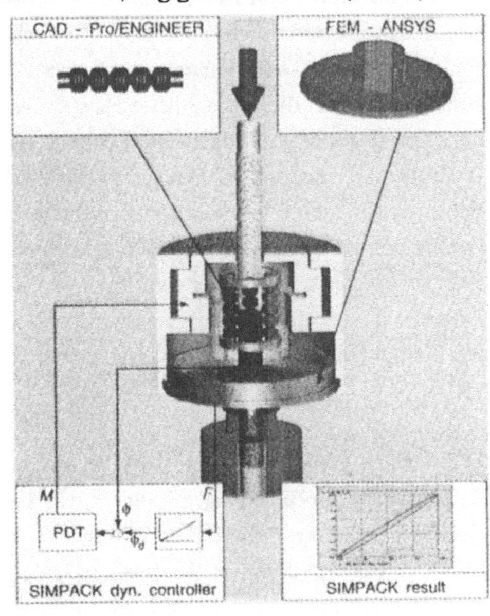

Abb. 8 Die DLR-Wälzgewindespindel (links). Integriert ins Innere kleiner Motoren (künstlicher Muskel) und ergänzt durch Positions- und Kraftsensorik kann sie durch regelungstechnische Maßnahmen zur Erzeugung einer programmierbaren Feder (aktiver Dämpfer) dienen.

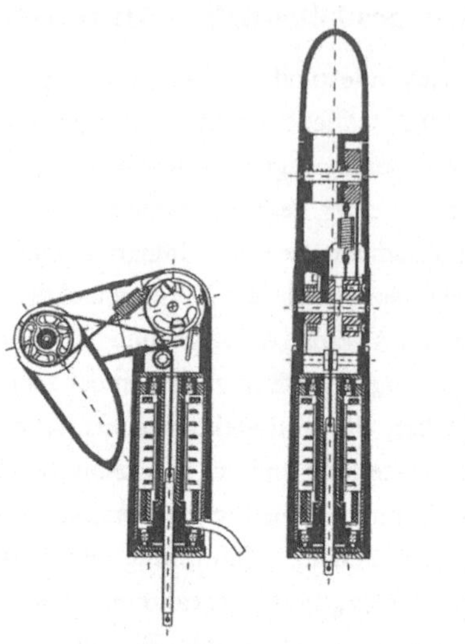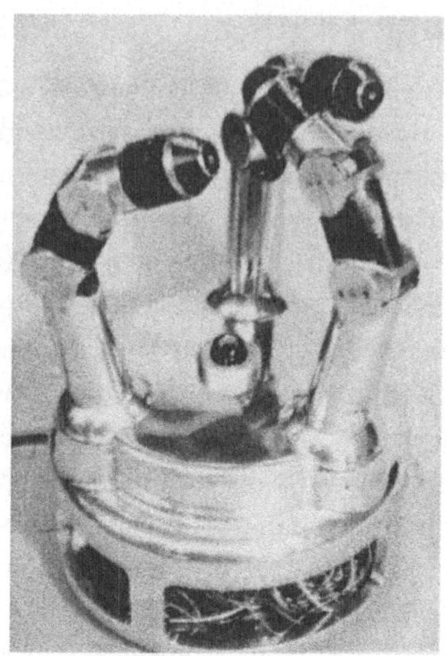

Abb. 9 Schematische Darstellung und erste Realisierung mehrgliedriger Finger mit integriertem „künstlichen Muskel"

Die o.a. Positions- und Kraft-Momenten-Sensorik für den künstlichen Muskel wird beim Einsatz in den Fingern durch miniaturisierte, optische Drehwinkelgeber und durch winzige, in die Finger integrierte Drehmoment-Sensoren realisiert und erlaubt so jede Form von „compliance control". Taktile, die menschliche Haut grob nachbildende Sensorik umhüllt alle Fingerglieder. Die 3-gliedrige Finger-Grundeinheit nach Abb. 9, links (ohne das 2 Freiheitsgrad-Basisgelenk) weist neben dem ins unterste Glied integrierten künstlichen Muskel bereits 14 Sensoren auf incl. einer kleinen Laserdiode in den Fingerkuppen, die einer Handkamera die Ortung von zu greifenden Objekten erleichtern soll. Die Anforderungen an „mechatronische" Echtwurfstechnik waren hier sehr hoch und nur durch modernste 3D-CAD-Technik erfüllbar. Angestrebt wird eine 4-fingrige anthropomorphe Hand mit 12 integrierten Antrieben, die auch die Manipulation von Objekten erlaubt und später zu einer Prothese weiterentwickelt werden soll.

Die meisten Handhabungsaufgaben in einem auf Roboter-Einsatz vorbereiteten Raumlabor ließen sich vermutlich zwar mit einem multisensoriellen 2-Backen-Greifer wie dem ROTEX-Greifer problemlos beherrschen. Trotzdem erscheint es sinnvoll, für komplexere Aufgaben (nicht vollständig planbare Reparaturen o.ä.) geschickte Roboterhände mit wenigstens 3 Fingern zu realisieren. Unabdingbar wird dies auch, wenn man an Haushaltsroboter (Hilfen für Alte und Behinderte) denkt. Bezüglich der Algorithmen für Mehr-Finger-Manipulation sei auf die Übersicht in [5] verwiesen.

5 Aufgabenorientiertes, sensorbasiertes Off-line-Programmieren (Tele-Sensor-Programmierung)

Roboter-Autonomie in einer nicht völlig exakt strukturierten Umgebung ist ohne (multi) sensorielle Informationsrückkopplung nicht denkbar; damit ist aber auch klar, daß die Sensorik (wenn auch ggf. simuliert) bereits in die Lern- oder Programmierphase einzubeziehen ist.

Die DLR-Arbeiten zur sensorgestützten „aufgabenorientierten Programmierung" zielen zwar vorrangig auf die Roboter-Fernprogrammierung durch den Raumlabor-Experten, sollen aber in gleicher Weise die einfache, sensorgestützte Roboterprogrammierung in den terrestrischen Fabriken vorantreiben. „Programmieren durch Vorzeigen in virtueller Umgebung" heißt hier das Schlüsselwort.

Das hierfür entwickelte Konzept der „Tele-Sensorprogrammierung" (bei ROTEX schon in den Grundzügen eingesetzt), erlaubt darüber hinaus sogar das schnelle Umschalten zwischen Fernprogrammierung und on-line-Fernsteuerung. Jede komplexe Aufgabe wird nach diesem Konzept in typischerweise sensorgeregelte Elementaroperationen zerlegt, die dem simulierten Roboter in der graphischen Umgebung gezeigt werden. Er registriert dabei automatisch die charakteristischen Sensormuster, die er später in der realen Welt zu erwarten hat.

Das derzeit realisierte Konzept basiert auf einer hierarchischen 2in2-Schichten-Struktur, bestehend aus einer expliziten, dem Experten vorbehaltenen Ebene, und einer impliziten, vom Anwender intuitiv verstehbaren Schicht.

Diese beiden werden aus Transparenzgründen in jeweils 2 weitere Ebenen unterteilt, so daß sich folgende Hierarchisierung ergibt:

Task — Operation — Elementaroperation — Sensorphase

- Die unterste Programmier- und Ausführungsebene repräsentiert die durch intelligente Sensordatenverarbeitung erreichte lokale Autonomie des Robotersystems. Als Bausteine dieser Ebene fungieren sogenannte *Sensorphasen*, die die enge Kopplung zwischen Sensoren und Manipulator beschreiben und dadurch eine sensorbasierte Regelung des Aktuators ermöglichen. Anstatt - wie bei herkömmlicher off-line-Programmierung oft gefordert -den Roboter inkl. seiner Arbeitsumgebung noch genauer zu kalibrieren (was wenig hilft, wenn sich die Umwelt verändert), werden in den Sensorphasen von der Simulation vorgegebene sensorische Referenzmuster abgelegt, die die Relativposition zwischen Greifer/Manipulator und Objekt charakterisieren. Der autonome Regelvorgang benötigt zur Transformation der sensorischen Abweichungen in Manipulatorbewegungen Prozeduren, die eben die Sensorfehler in entsprechende, zu korrigierende Positions- und Orientierungsfehler abbilden. Hier werden neben analytischen auch Neuronale-Netz-Konzepte verfolgt (Kapitel 6). Bei der Ausführung einer Sensorphase spielt es nun keine Rolle, wie sich die absolute Position von Roboter bzw. zu handhabendem Objekt darstellt.

- Können nicht alle kartesischen Freiheitsgrade durch die Sensorik ausgeregelt werden, so kommt das sog. „shared control"-Konzept zum Zuge, d.h. die freien Freiheitsgrade werden positionsgesteuert entweder vom Operateur bei der Telemanipulation oder durch einen übergeordneten Bahnplaner behandelt. Auf der Ebene der *Elementaroperationen* wird die durch die Sensorphasen erreichte Semi-Autonomie vervollständigt um Positionsvorgaben (relativ zu einer Objektklasse) sowie um Greiferoperationen. Lokal begrenzte, sensorgeregelte Manipulatorvorgänge müssen kartesisch geregelt werden. Großräumige Transferbewegungen, die als global im Arbeitsraum anzusehen sind, sollen aber kollisions- und singularitätsfrei sein, was sich nur im Gelenkwinkelraum des Manipulators bewerkstelligen läßt. Hierfür kommt ein schnelles globales Bahnplanungsverfahren zum Einsatz [10].

- Die *Operationsebene* stellt eine mächtige Mensch-Maschine-Schnittstelle auf implizitem Level zur Verfügung. Insbesondere bei internem Servicing muß die Kommandostruktur zur Steuerung einer Roboterarbeitszelle stark aufgaben- und objektbezogen sein, um den Experimentator von manipulatorspezifischen Details der Aufgabendurchführung zu entlasten. Mittels eines über die SPACE MOUSE gesteuerten „3D-cursors" – analog könnte auch ein Datenhandschuh verwendet werden – wählt der Experimentator, der jetzt kein Robotiker mehr sein muß, das zu handhabende Objekt aus und startet per Mausklick (oder Gestik) die Ausführung der zugeordneten Objekt- bzw. Ort-Operation. Der aktuelle Status des (simulierten bzw. realen) Systems wird dabei stets zurückgemeldet.

- Eine konsistente Folge von Operationen wird als komplette Aufgabe oder *Task* spezifiziert. Auf dieser Ebene erfolgt die Zuordnung einer Operation, die für eine Klasse von Objekten anwendbar ist, zu einer konkreten Objektinstanz, z.B. open door-2. Eine Task kann nun leicht off-line erstellt werden, indem die Objekt-Selektionen und Operations-Aktivierungen, die bei Anwendung der Operations-Ebene über den 3D-cursor geschehen, aufgezeichnet und als Task abgelegt werden.

Diese Strukturierung der Aufgabenorientierten Programmierung erlaubt dabei das schnelle Umschalten zwischen Fernprogrammierung und on-line Fernsteuerung, indem für letztere die Positionssteuerung des Manipulators über ein 3D-Eingabe-Gerät erfolgt, unterstützt durch den Aufruf von Elementaroperationen, und indem für eine intuitive Fernprogrammierung vorgefertigte Operations-Makros verwendet werden können. Somit ist dieses Konzept den Anforderungen der Raumfahrt-Robotik (internes und externes Servicing) wie auch denen des industriellen Einsatzes gewappnet. Von Brian Carlisle, Vorstands-Mitglied des führenden US-Roboter-Herstellers ADEPT, wurde oft als zentrale Aufgabe der Roboterforschung bezeichnet, einem Robotik-System innerhalb von 10 Minuten eine nicht triviale (z.B. Montage-Aufgabe) so beizubringen, daß es diese Aufgaben auch in einer zumindest leicht veränderlichen Umgebung zuverlässig wiederholen kann. Dieses Ziel rückt mit Hilfe der Aufgabenorientierten Programmierung in greifbare Nähe.

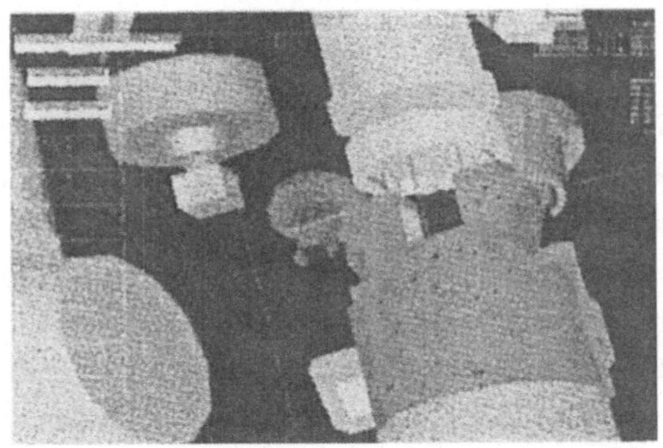

**Abb. 10 Bei der Tele-Sensor-Programmierung wird dem Roboter in der virtuellen Welt
die Aufgabe einschließlich der Sensormuster gezeigt
(hier: Laser-Abstandssensorik bei Annäherung an einen Bajonettverschluß).**

6 Neue Mensch-Maschine-Schnittstellen und Lernverfahren für die Robtik

Die im vorigen Abschnitt beschriebene Programmiertechnik kann als Lernen durch Vormachen charakterisiert werden und ist von daher auf optimierte Mensch-Maschine-Schnittstellen angewiesen. Ein dafür geeignetes 6-Freiheitsgrad-Interface, die bereits erwähnte SPACE MOUSE (als Nachfolger der bereits 1982 entwickelten DLR-Steuerkugel) wurde in den letzten Jahren zunehmend als 3D-Grafik-Interface vor allem in den CAD-Anwendungen der Automobilindustrie eingesetzt. Seit neuestem wird sie aber auch standardmäßig in den Programmiergeräten des führenden deutschen Roboterherstellers KUKA eingesetzt (Abb. 11) und kehrt so nach vielen Jahren in den Anwendungsbereich zurück, für den die Steuerkugel-Idee ursprünglich gedacht war; das natürliche, weil intuitive, Steuern eines Roboter-Greifers in gleichzeitig 6 Raumfreiheitsgraden.

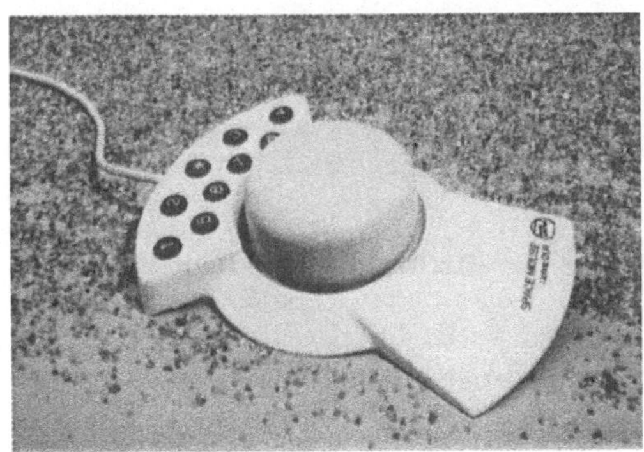
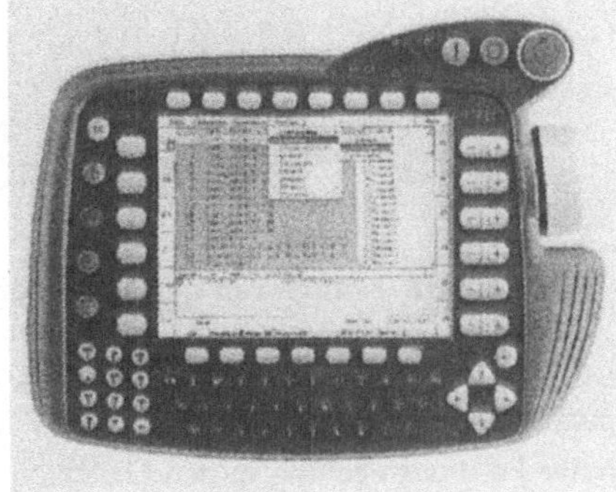

**Abb. 11 Die SPACE MOUSE als neue 3D-Mensch-Maschine-Schnittstelle mit dem
patentierten optoelektronischen Meßsystem und die Integration der Steuerkappe
in das KUKA Programmierpanel (rechts).**

Da sie sich zur Vorgabe von Kräften und Momenten eignet (ohne allerdings Kraftrückkopplung zu ermöglichen), wurden mit ihr die ersten Experimente zum „Skill-Transfer" in virtueller Umgebung durchgeführt. In der simulierten Welt wird dabei z.B. ein Roboter mit quaderförmigem Objekt im Greifer in eine Ecke gedrückt, unter visueller Kontrolle der dabei entstehenden, simulierten Kräfte (Abb. 12 links). Ein Neuro-Fuzzy-Netz erhält die Aufgabe, die zugrunde liegenden Gesetzmäßigkeiten zu beobachten und den Roboter nach der Lernphase (also mehreren Vormach-Versuchen) den Vorgang möglichst ohne Überschwingen von Kräften und Momenten ausführen zu lassen (auch wenn dies dem Lehrer nicht perfekt gelang). Schnellere Lernerfolge werden erzielt, wenn der menschliche Lehrer einen (allerdings wesentlich aufwendigeren) kraftreflektierenden Handcontroller, wie den am MIT entwickelten PHANTOM, zur Verfügung hat (Abb. 12 rechts). Aber auch andere Alternativen werden im DLR-Labor zum Vergleich herangezogen. So kann der Lehrer das Werkstück in der realen Welt über einen Kraft-Momenten-Sensor-Griff führen und damit z.B. eine Fügeaufgabe demonstrieren, wobei über einen berührungslosen Positions-Orientierungstracker (etwa dem POLHEMUS-Tracker) auch die Bewegungen der Hand erfaßt und gespeichert werden. Für ein abschließendes Urteil über die optimale Methodik des Skill-Transfers ist es noch zu früh, doch zeigen die Ergebnisse, daß die moderne Neuro-Informatik hier wesentliche Beiträge liefern kann [6].

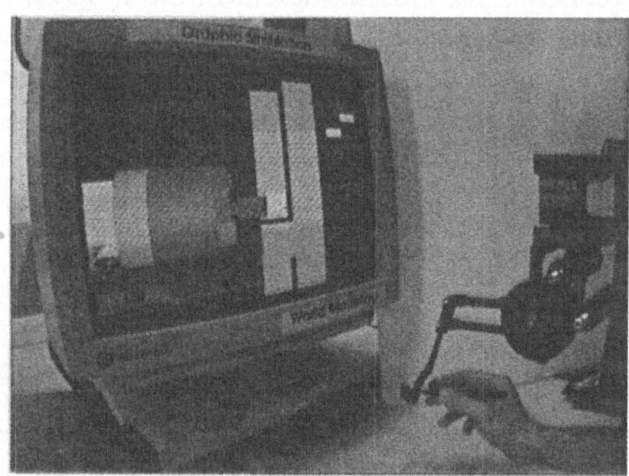

Abb. 12 Skill-Transfer in der virtuellen Welt mit kraftreflektierenden Handcontrollern

Lernen in Form der Selbstverbesserung ist vor allem im Bereich der Dynamik für schnelle, präzise Bewegungen gefragt, wie sie die Industrie fordert. Für Roboter mit klassischer dezentraler Positionsregelung in den Gelenken konnten über mehrstufige Lernverfahren schon bei der ersten Wiederholung einer hochdynamischen Bewegung die Bahnfehler um den Faktor 10-20 reduziert werden [7]. Inzwischen ist aber die Industrie-Robotik"reif" für die Integration „inverser" Dynamik -Modelle [8]. KUKA-Roboter, die solche Modelle aus dem DLR-Labor inklusive einer Reibungsmodellierung jetzt standardmäßig mitführen, konnten ihre Geschwindigkeiten um bis zu 30% steigern. Adaptive Regler, die erwartete und reale Motorströme vergleichen, werden in naher Zukunft auch in der Lage sein, die Anpassung an große Laständerungen automatisch vorzunehmen. Bei der in Kapitel 3 skizzierten Leichtbau-Roboter-

Entwicklung kommen „hybride" Verfahren für die Realisierung des sog. inversen dynamischen Modells zum Einsatz, die versuchen, a priori Wissen über Daten wie Trägheitsmomente, Motordynamik voll zu nutzen, aber die immer vorhandenen Modellierungsungenauigkeiten über neuronale Netze, insbesondere Multilayer-Perceptrons, zu lernen bzw. ständig im Betrieb zu kompensieren (Abb. 6 rechts).

Doch nicht nur im Bereich des Skill-Transfers und der Dynamik-Optimierung werden im DLR-Labor in großem Umfang mehrschichtige neuronale Netze eingesetzt, sondern auch für die Perzeption und Weltmodellierung. Unter Perzeption sei dabei die Fähigkeit verstanden, den Zustand der Umgebung und des Roboters zu erfassen und zu interpretieren. Mehrschichtige „Vorwärts"-Netze werden genutzt, um aus 2D-Intensitäts-Bildern und dem darin enthaltenen Schattenwurf die räumliche Gestalt eines Objekts zu ermitteln (Abb. 13), aber auch um z.B. aus multisensorieller Information nach einem Training die Relativlage des Greifers zu einem Objekt zu schätzen (s. Abschnitt 5).

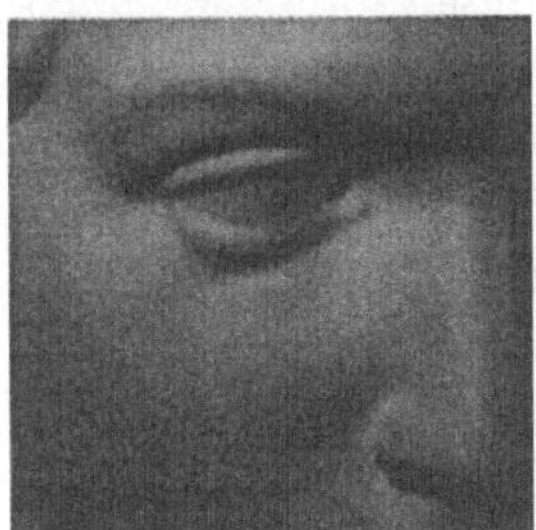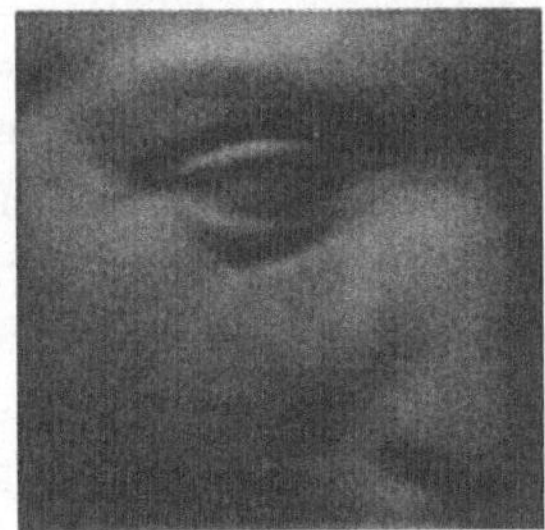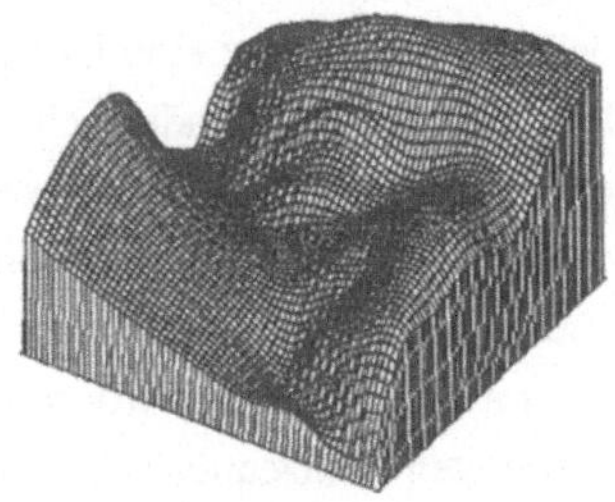

Abb. 13 Shape from Shading mit neuronalen Netzen [12]

Selbstorganisierende neuronale Netze, weiterentwickelt aus den sog. KOHONEN'schen Merkmalsarten, werden eingesetzt, um über spärlich verteilte räumliche Punkte (die etwa ein Lasersensor liefert) Kanten und Flächennormalen aus unterschiedlichsten Signalquellen im Sinne der sog. Sensorfusion räumliche Objektmodelle bis hin zum 3D-CAD-Format zu generieren [9]. Solche Netze werden aber auch eingesetzt, um im Bereich der kollisionsfreien Bahnplanung variable räumliche Auflösung zu erzeugen [10].

Auch beim Einsatz modellgestützter Bildverarbeitungssysteme für autonome Roboter werden bei der DLR zumindest fallweise neuronale Netzwerke herangezogen. Allerdings hängt dies von der Fragestellung ab:

a) Bei der Aktualisierung von Umweltmodellen (also Anpassung von 3D-CAD Modellen an Bildkonturen bei i.a. kleinen Abweichungen) werden vorzugsweise die sog. „Iterative Closest Point" (ICP)-Algorithmen [11] eingesetzt.

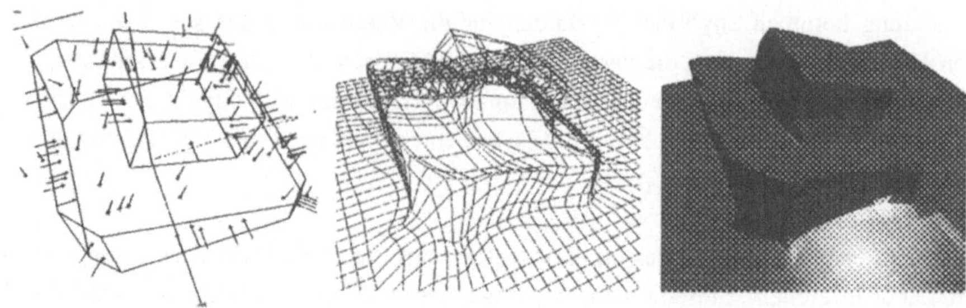

**Abb. 14 Selbstorganisierende Netze - abgeleitet aus den KOHONEN'schen Merkmals-
karten - erlauben den Aufbau von Weltmodellen aus multisensorieller Information
(in der Mitte ein Zwischenergebnis nach 2000 Iterationen,
rechts nach 3000 Iterationen das Endergebnis).**

b) Für die visuelle Lageregelung (visual servoing) in allen 6 Freiheitsgraden wurde ein modellbasierter Ansatz etnwickelt, mit dem die räumliche Lage eines bewegten Objekts in allen sechs Freiheitsgraden schnell und zuverlässig bestimmt und über die Zeit verfolgt werden kann. Der Algorithmus besteht aus zwei Schritten: Zunächst werden aus den Bilddaten
extrahierten Merkmale in räumliche Lageconstraints umgerechnet, mit denen unter Ausnutzung einer geometrischen Modellbeschreibung die dreidimensionale Objektlage bestimmt wird. Danach wird mit Hilfe eines geeigneten Kalman-Filters aus der bis dahin ausgewerteten Bildsequenz der Räumliche Objektzustand geschäftzt. Dieses Vorgehen bietet
eine Reieh von Vorteilen gegenüber der allgemein üblichen direkten Zustandsschätzung
aus Bildmerkmalen. Der Rechenaufwand steigt lediglich linear und nicht mit der dritten
Potenz der Zahl der berücksichtigten Bildmerkmale an, die gleichzeitige Auswertung der
Daten mehrerer Sensoren (Sensorfusion) wird vereinfacht und die zeitliche Auswertung
wird von der Wahl der Merkmale entkoppelt. Gerade der letzte Punkt ist entscheidend für
systematische Behandlung von Verdeckungen, die während des Trackingvorgangs auftreten können. Mit dem skizzierten Verfahren konnte ein Industrieroboter in einer über Bildverarbeitung geschlossenen Regelschleife in allen sechs Freiheitsgraden exakt an ruhenden
Objekten positioniert und bewegten Objekten zuverlässig nachgeführt werden. Der erzielte
Verarbeitungstakt lag trotz komplexen Bildmaterials bei 12,5 Hz.

c) Das Problem der modellbasierten 3D-Lageschätzung ohne jede Vorkenntnis über die mögliche räumliche Orientierung eines abgebildeten Objekts ist wegen der kombinatorischen
Explosion der Zahl möglicher 2D-Ansichten eine der schwierigsten Fragestellungen modellbasierter Bildverarbeitung. Unter der Randbedingung, daß dieses Problem nicht mit den
gleich hohen Genauigkeitsanforderungen gelöst werden muß wie die zuvor genannten,
wurde ein Ansatz auf Basis neuronaler Netze entwickelt. Verwendet werden dazu Ab-
wandlungen von Kohonens selbstorganisierenden Merkmalsarten mit einer auf die Pro-
blemstellung zugeschnittenen Topologie. Diese werden mit Objektansichten trainiert, die

man automatisch aus dem Modellwissen generiert. Dabei ist die Struktur so gewählt, daß das Netz auf ein Eingangsbild *in Echtzeit* mit einem oder mehreren Schätzwerten für die Objektorientierung antwortet. Es konnte gezeigt werden, daß die erzielbaren Ergebnisse geeignet sind, die für die oben genannten Verfahren benötigten Voraussetzungen zu liefern (Abb. 15).

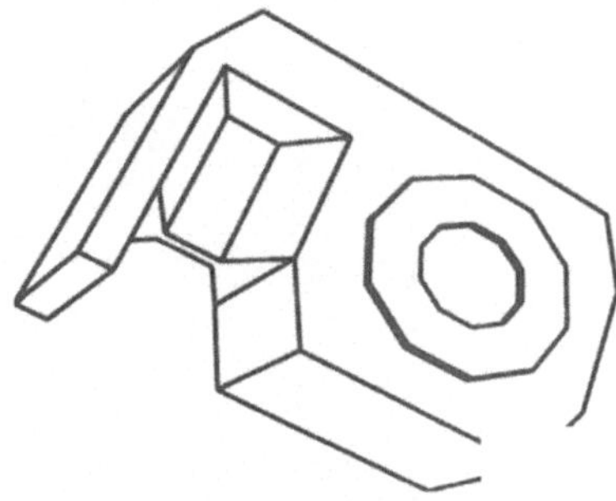

Abb. 15 3D-Lageerkennung mit starren Merkmalskarten: Aus automatisch vorsegmentierten Kamerabildern bestimmt das neuronale Netz einen Schätzwert für die Objektorientierung. Links ist das Eingangsbild, rechts das Objektmodell in der vom Netz gefundenen Orientierung dargestellt.

7 Ausblick

Die Entwicklung einsatzfähiger autonomer Roboter-Systeme geht wesentlich langsamer voran, als noch vor 10 oder 20 Jahren prognostiziert. Im Bereich der Raumfahrt-Robotik hat sich die Bundesrepublik mit dem Roboter-Technologie-Experiment ROTEX eine hervorragende Ausgangsposition verschafft. Wenn es jetzt gelingt, die Technologie-Entwicklung in einem Zeitrahmen von 5-10 Jahren konsequent voranzutreiben, dann sollte dem *operationellen* Einsatz von (ggf. freifliegenden) Raumfahrt-Robotern in Extrem-Leichtbau, die auf multisensorieller Teilautonomie basieren, nichts mehr im Wege stehen. Die Fernsteuerung bzw. Fernprogrammierung wird dann auf jeden Fall soweit sein, daß z.B. im normalen Raumlabor-Betrieb der Experimentator (d.h. nicht mehr notwendigerweise der Robotiker) am Boden die gewünschten Operationen auslöst und überwacht. Für Aktionen, die höhere Geschicklichkeit verlangen, sollten dann feingliedrige Mehr-Finger-Hände verfügbar sein.

Die für künftige Raumfahrteinsätze in den nächsten Jahren zu entwickelnde neue Robotergeneration sollte aber auch wesentlich dazu beitragen, die Entwicklung der Service-Roboter für den nichtindustriellen terrestrischen Bereich zu beschleunigen. Von kompetenten Institutionen wie dem Fraunhofer-Institut IPA werden diesem Technologiesektor nach dem Jahr 2000 Milliardenmärkte prognostiziert. Als Beispiel sei die Medizintechnik angeführt.

Insbesondere die minimal invasive Chirurgie hat u.a. wegen der Stereo-Bildübertragung vom nicht direkt zugänglichen Ort der Operation eine Reihe von Berührungspunkten zur Roboter-Fernsteuerung. Realisiert wurde von der DLR (auch schon im klinischen Versuch) eine vollautomatische Kameraführung, bei der statt des menschlichen Kamera-Assistenten ein kleiner Roboter das bildgebende Stereo-Endoskop durch ein Loch in der Bauchdecke des Patienten dem Werkzeug des Chirurgen nachführt (Abb. 16).

Abb. 16 Erstmalig fungierte im Dez. 95 am Klinikum rechts der Isar in München ein Roboter als selbständiger „Kamerassistent" bei einer minimal invasiven Operation. Die vollautomatische Nachführung des Endoskops nach den Instrumenten des Chirurgen wurde über Farb-Stereo-Segmentierung [2] realisiert und vermeidet Konzentrationsschwächen und Zitterbewegungen, die jeden menschlichen Assistenten charakterisieren.

Viel Interesse in der breiten Öffentlichkeit fanden aber auch die Arbeiten zur „Telekonsultation" durch ferngesteuerte Sonden (z.B. bei der Magenspiegelung) und Roboter. Im Grunde handelt es sich dabei (wegen nur geringer Signallaufzeiten) um eine einfache Form von „Telepräsenz", wie sie in der Roboter-Fernsteuerung üblich ist. Der (z.B. besonders erfahrene) Arzt sieht sich im Körper eines weit entfernt (z.B. in einer kleinen Klinik) liegenden Patienten um und erteilt Ratschläge, etwa zur Einschätzung von Gewebe auf Gut- oder Bösartigkeit. Er orientiert sich an den über ISDN-Kanäle übertragenen bewegten Bildern und steuert an Hand dieser Bilder mit einem 3D-Interface wie der SPACE MOUSE die Sonde oder den Endoskop-Roboter im/am Körper des ggf. weit entfernten Patienten. Die Ärzte geben i.a. dieser Ferndiagnose-Technik große Zukunftschancen. Die Übertragung bzw. Erweiterung solcher Ansätze auf die Diagnose, Wartung und ggf. Reparatur von Maschinen (Tele-Servicing) könnte vor allem für die exportabhängige mittelständische Industrie künftig zu einem bedeutenden Thema werden. Inwieweit auch die Telechirurgie in der Medizin (außer in militärischen Szenarien) Anwendung finden kann, wird in den nächsten Jahren sicher noch intensiv diskutiert. Technologisch ist dafür insbesondere eine feinfühlige Kraftrückkopplung erforderlich. An solchen Verfahren der Kraft-Rückkopplung arbeitet die DLR z.B. im Hinblick auf ein

„virtuelles" Chirurgentraining und im Zusammenhang mit der in Kap. 6 erwähnten Geschicklichkeitsübertragung Mensch-Roboter.

Man darf auf jeden Fall erwarten, daß die von den künftigen Dienstleistungsrobotern geforderte Flexibilität und sensorbasierte Intelligenz auch die weitere Entwicklung der Industrie-Roboter massiv beeinflussen wird.

8 LITERATUR:

[1]   G. Hirzinger, R. Koeppe, A. Baader, F. Lange, R. Staudte, G.Q. Wei, „Perception and Manipulation in Robotics: Neural Network Approaches", 7th. International Symposium on Robotics Research, ISRR'95, Herrsching, Oct. 20-24, 1995.

[2]   K. Arbter, G.Q. Wei, „Verfahren zum Nachführen eines Stereo-Laparoskops in der minimalinvasiven Chirurgie", Patent pending: 14.08.95.

[3]   G. Hirzinger, A. Baader, R. Koeppe, M. Schedl, „Towards a new generation of multisensory light-weight robots with learning capabilities", IFAC'93 World Congress, Sydney, Australia, July 18-23, 1993.

[4]   G. Hirzinger, B. Brunner, J. Dietrich, J. Heindl, „ROTEX - The First Remotely Controlled Robot in Space", IEEE Int. Conference on Robotics and Automation, San Diego, May 8-13, 1994.

[5]   K.B. Shimoga, "Robot Grasp Synthesis Algorithms: A Survey", Int. Journal of Robotics Research, Vol 15, Number 3, June 1996, ISSN 0278-3649, MIT Press.

[6]   R. Koeppe, G. Hirzinger, „Learning Compliant Motions by Task-Demonstration in Virtual Environments", Fourth International Symposium on Experimental Robotics, ISER'95, Stanford, California, 30.06. - 02.07.1996

[7]   F. Lange, G. Hirzinger, „Learning Force Control with Position Controlled Robots", IEEE Int. Conference on Robotics and Automation ICRA'96, Minneapolis, USA 22-28 April 1996.

[8]   L. Sciavicco, B. Siciliano, „Modeling and Control of Robot Manipulators", McGraw-Hill Companies, Inc. 1996 , ISBN 0-07-057217-8

[9]   A. Baader, G. Hirzinger, „A Self-Organizing Algorithm for Multisensory Surface Reconstruction, IROS'94, München, Sept. 12.-16. 1994.

[10]   E. Ralli, „A Global and Resolution Complete Path Planner for up to 6DOF Robot Manipulators", IEEE Int. Conference on Robotics and Automation ICRA'96, Minneapolis, USA 22-28 April 1996.

[11]   P.J. Besl, N.D. McKay, „A method for registration of 3-D shapes", IEEE Trans. Pattern Analysis and Machine Intelligence, 14(2):239-256, February 1992.

[12]   G.Q. Wei, G. Hirzinger, „Learning shape from shading by neural networks", Mustererkennung 1994, Erkennen und Lernen, DAGM, Wien, 1994.

[13]   E.D. Dickmanns, V. Graefe, „Dynamic monocular machine vision", Machine Vision and Applications, 1:223-240, 1988.

[14]   P.I. Corce, „Visual control of robot manipulators - A review", In K. Hashimoto, editor, Visual Sevoing, pages 1-31. World Scientific, 1993.

<hr>

Sensorik

Gitterkartenbasierte Fehlererkennung und Kalibrierung für Umgebungssensoren autonomer mobiler Systeme (AMS)

Martin Soika

Siemens AG, Zentralabteilung Technik
Otto-Hahn-Ring 6, 81730 München
email: Martin Soika@zfe.siemens.de

1. Einführung

Typische Einsatzumgebungen autonomer mobiler Systeme (AMS) [1] zeichnen sich dadurch aus, daß sie nur einen niedrigen Grad an Struktur aufweisen und zudem verschiedene dynamische Objekte (Menschen, andere Fahrzeuge) vorhanden sind. Um sich in seiner Umgebung zurechtzufinden, benötigt das AMS ein Modell, das durch Fusion der Sensormessungen erzeugt wird. Dabei müssen die jeweiligen Unzulänglichkeiten des Meßprinzips sowie der Sensorik selbst (systematische Meßfehler) berücksichtigt werden [2].

Fehlfunktionen oder gar Ausfälle einzelner Sensoren verfälschen das Umgebungsmodell. Aufbauende Funktionen wie Hindernisvermeidung, Navigation oder Lokalisierung werden durch solche Störungen wesentlich beeinträchtigt. Zum einen können nicht detektierte Hindernisse zu Kollisionen führen, zum anderen beschneiden "Geisterhindernisse" die Beweglichkeit des Roboters. Der Erfolg einer durchzuführenden Roboteroperation hängt demnach in starkem Maße vom Zustand der Sensoren ab. Fehler der Sensorik außerhalb der tolerierbaren Grenzen müssen deshalb sicher erkannt werden. An eine Fehlererkennung für Umgebungssensoren autonomer mobiler Systeme werden folgende Anforderungen gestellt:

- Unabhängigkeit von der Umgebung:
  Es sollen keine Referenz- oder Eichumgebungen notwendig sein, deren Einsatz im Hinblick auf kommende Produkte unpraktikabel und zu teuer ist.
- Unabhängigkeit von der Art des Fehlers:
  Wegen der Vielzahl der Fehlerarten, die im allgemeinen nicht alle a priori bekannt sind, soll der Ansatz möglichst alle Fehlerarten abdecken, die eine wesentliche Beeinträchtigung des Umgebungsmodells nach sich ziehen.
- Online-Fähigkeit:
  Aus Sicherheitsgründen soll eine ständige Überwachung der Sensoren möglich sein.
- Flexibilität:
  Bei Ausfall von Sensorik sollen die Verfahren, ggf. in Verbindung mit einer einfachen Adaption, weiterhin anwendbar sein.

Neben einem Hardwaredefekt eines Sensors kann es zudem passieren, daß durch mechanische Einwirkungen die Abbildungseigenschaften eines physikalisch an sich funktionierenden Sensors durch fehlerhafte Parameter erheblich beeinträchtigt sind. Mit der Durchführung eines Kalibrierexperiments kann diese Störung wieder aufgehoben werden. Das im folgenden vorgestellte Verfahren zur Fehlererkennung von Umgebungssensoren basiert auf einer Gitterkarte (Kapitel 2), deren Auswertung Rückschlüsse auf den Zustand der involvierten Sensorik zuläßt (Kapitel 3) und zudem die Kalibrierung in unpräparierten Umgebungen unterstützt (Kapitel 4). Experimentelle Ergebnisse (Kapitel 5) und eine kurze Zusammenfassung (Kapitel 6) runden den Artikel ab.

2. Aufbau der Gitterkarte

Das in dieser Arbeit vorgestellte Verfahren zur Fehlererkennung basiert auf einer, vom AMS mitgeführten Gitterkarte, wie sie in vielen anderen Arbeiten zur Hindernisvermeidung [3, 4] bzw. zur Lokalisierung verwendet wird. Sie wird hier in analoger Weise zu den Arbeiten von Elfes [5, 6] mit Hilfe eines vereinfachten probabilistischen Sensormodells [7] durch die eingehenden Messungen M aufgebaut. Durch die diskrete Zufallsvariable X mit den beiden Zuständen OCC und FREE wird für jede einzelne Gitterzelle C_i der Belegtzustand durch die Wahrscheinlichkeit

$$P(X(C_i) = OCC \mid \{M\}_t) = P(\ C_i \mid \{M\}_t)$$
$$P(X(C_i) = FREE \mid \{M\}_t) = P(\neg C_i \mid \{M\}_t) = 1 - P(C_i \mid \{M\}_t) \tag{1}$$

beschrieben. Abbildung 1 zeigt eine mit einem solchen Verfahren aufgebaute Gitterkarte.

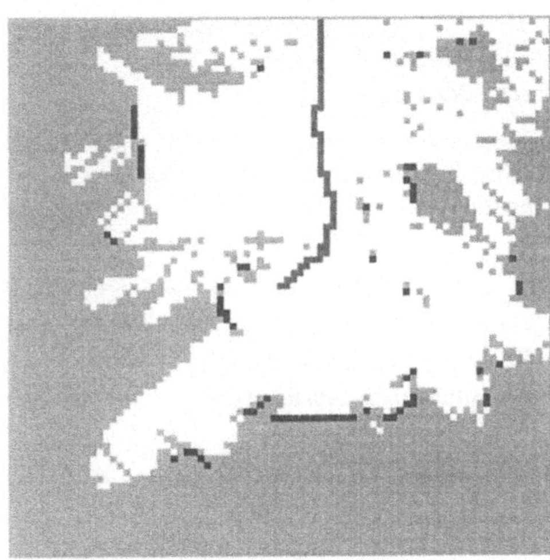

weiß:	$0.00 \leq P(\ C_i \mid \{M\}_t) \leq 0.25$
hellgrau:	$0.25 < P(\ C_i \mid \{M\}_t) < 0.75$
schwarz:	$0.75 \leq P(\ C_i \mid \{M\}_t) \leq 1.00$
dunkelgrau:	Spur des Fahrzeugs

Abb 1: Gitterkarte

Die Verwendung einer Gitterkarte ermöglicht den Vergleich von Sensormessungen, die, unterstützt durch die Bewegung des AMS,

- von unterschiedlichen Sensoren,
- zu verschiedenen Zeitpunkten sowie
- aus mehreren Blickwinkeln

aufgenommen wurden. Der Belegtzustand einer Gitterzelle ist die Aussage, über die von den Sensoren redundante Aussagen gemacht werden können. Als Maß für die Aussagekraft einer Gitterzelle über den Zustand von Sensoren dient die Redundanz R

$$R(C_i) = 1 - \frac{H(C_i)}{H_{max}(C_i)} \tag{2}$$

mit der Entropie H [8]

$$H(C_i) = -\left\{ P(C_i \mid \{M\}_t) \cdot \log_2(P(C_i \mid \{M\}_t)) + P(\neg C_i \mid \{M\}_t) \cdot \log_2(P(\neg C_i \mid \{M\}_t)) \right\} \tag{3}$$

Unter der Annahme, daß sich die fehlerfreien Sensoren in ihren Aussagen bestätigen, können fehlerhafte Sensoren anhand mehrfach auftretender Widersprüche bzgl. des Belegtzustandes von Gitterzellen erkannt werden. Bei einer Modifikation des Belegtzustandes infolge einer Messung werden zusätzlich die für diese Messung verantwortlichen Sensoren protokolliert. Demnach enthält jede in der Gitterkarte befindliche Zelle neben der Belegtwahrscheinlichkeit eine Liste von Sensoren, die dieses Pixel als belegt bzw. unbelegt "gesehen" haben.

3. Beurteilung der Sensoren

Für die Bewertung der Sensoren stehen in der im vorangegangenen Abschnitt beschriebenen Gitterkarte für jede Zelle C_i folgende Informationen zur Verfügung:

- l_{OCC} Liste der Sensoren, die dieses Pixel als belegt eingestuft haben.
- l_{FREE} Liste der Sensoren, die dieses Pixel als frei eingestuft haben.
- n_{OCC} Anzahl der Sensoren, die dieses Pixel als belegt eingestuft haben.
- n_{FREE} Anzahl der Sensoren, die dieses Pixel als frei eingestuft haben.
- $P(C_i \mid \{M\}_t)$ Belegtwahrscheinlichkeit nach Gleichung (1).

Aus jeder Zelle lassen sich somit Maße für den Zustand der beteiligten Sensoren ableiten. Um die Frage zu beantworten, welche Zellen zu welchen Zeitpunkten ausgewertet werden sollen, müssen zwei Anwendungsfälle unterschieden werden:

- **Selbsttest:**

  Für die Durchführung eines Selbsttests eignet sich als Fahrmanöver insbesondere das Drehen auf der Stelle. Dadurch wird eine hohe Überdeckung der Sensorwahrnehmungsbereiche und damit eine hohe Redundanz nach Gleichung (2) erreicht. Nach Abschluß der Drehbewegung sind dann alle Gitterzellen auszuwerten.

- **On-Line-Überwachung:**

  Die oft geradlinige Bewegung des Fahrzeugs führt dazu, daß sich die Wahrnehmungsbereiche nicht aller Sensoren überschneiden. Um eine hohe Redundanz zu erreichen, sollten die Gitterzellen erst dann ausgewertet werden, wenn sie sich außerhalb des Wahrnehmungsbereiches aller Sensoren befinden. Andererseits wird aus Speicherplatzgründen die verwendete Gitterkarte vom Fahrzeug fortlaufend mitgeführt. Die Bewegung des Fahrzeugs führt nun dazu, daß Zeilen und Spalten am Rand der Karte gelöscht werden. Dies ist notwendig, damit Speicherplatz für den Wahrnehmungsbereich geschaffen wird, in den das AMS vordringt. Genau diese Gitterzellen sind für eine On-Line-Fehlererkennung vor ihrer Vernichtung auszuwerten, da sie ein Maximum an Redundanz aufweisen.

Zur Beurteilung eines Sensors S_j zum Zeitpunkt t dient die Wahrscheinlichkeit

$$P(Y(S_j) = OK \mid \{K(C)\}_t) = P(\ S_j \mid \{K\}_t)$$
$$P(Y(S_j) = KO \mid \{K(C)\}_t) = P(\neg S_j \mid \{K\}_t) = 1 - P(\ S_j \mid \{K\}_t) \tag{4}$$

der Zufallsvariablen Y mit den Zuständen OK und KO. Diese ist abhängig von der Konsistenz K der bis zum Zeitpunkt t ausgewerteten Gitterzellen $\{C\}$. Die Konsistenz ist ein Maß dafür, inwieweit die Aussage eines Sensors S_j mit den Aussagen anderer Sensoren hinsichtlich der betrachteten Gitterzelle C_i übereinstimmt. Aus der Gitterkarte können für jede Zelle für jeden beteiligten Sensor S_j (d.h. dieser Sensor ist in mindestens einer der oben genannten Listen eingetragen) diese Konsistenzmaße abgeleitet werden.

$$P(K_i \mid S_j) = P(K(C_i) = CON \mid Y(S_j) = OK)$$
$$P(K_i \mid \neg S_j) = P(K(C_i) = CON \mid Y(S_j) = KO) \tag{5}$$

Die bedingte Wahrscheinlichkeit $P(K_i \mid S_j)$ beschreibt die Konsistenz für den Fall, daß die Aussage des Sensors richtig ist, $P(K_i \mid \neg S_j)$ unter der hypothetischen Annahme, daß sich der Sensor in seiner Aussage täuscht.

Mit Hilfe der Konsistenzmaße lassen sich unter Verwendung der Bayes'schen Regel die Wahrscheinlichkeiten für den Sensorzustand aus Gleichung (4) dann wie folgt aktualisieren.

$$P(S_j \mid \{K\}_i) = \frac{P(K_i \mid S_j) \cdot P(S_j \mid \{K\}_{i-1})}{P(K_i \mid S_j) \cdot P(S_j \mid \{K\}_{i-1}) + P(K_i \mid \neg S_j) \cdot P(\neg S_j \mid \{K\}_{i-1})} \tag{6}$$

Berechnung der Konsistenzmaße:

Die Konsistenz einer Gitterzelle C_i hinsichtlich einer Aussage von einem Sensor S_j wird in Gleichung (5) durch eine Wahrscheinlichkeit beschrieben. Diese wird abhängig davon, ob die Aussage des Sensors S_j für diese Gitterzelle richtig (OK) oder falsch (KO) war, wie folgt bestimmt. Zunächst werden dazu die Belegtwahrscheinlichkeiten der Gitterzelle für zwei Fälle berechnet. P_{ok} entspricht der hypothetischen Belegtwahrscheinlichkeit, falls der Sensor S_j eine wahre Aussage macht, P_{ko} ist die hypothetische Wahrscheinlichkeit, falls der Sensor S_j sich in seiner Aussage irrt.

Je nachdem, ob der betreffende Sensor die Gitterzelle belegt (OCC) oder frei (FREE) klassifiziert, berechnen sich diese Wahrscheinlichkeiten zu

OCC:
$$P_{ok}(S_j) = P(C_i \mid \{M_{k,k \neq j}\}_t, M_j = OCC) = P(C_i \mid \{M\}_t)$$
$$P_{ko}(S_j) = P(C_i \mid \{M_{k,k \neq j}\}_t, M_j = FREE) \tag{7}$$

FREE:
$$P_{ok}(S_j) = P(C_i \mid \{M_{k,k \neq j}\}_t, M_j = FREE) = P(C_i \mid \{M\}_t)$$
$$P_{ko}(S_j) = P(C_i \mid \{M_{k,k \neq j}\}_t, M_j = OCC) \tag{8}$$

Mit Hilfe von Gleichung (9) werden diese Größen auf die Konsistenzgrößen abgebildet.

$$P(K_i \mid S_j) = \alpha \cdot P_{ok}(S_j) + (1-\alpha) \cdot (1 - P_{ok}(S_j))$$
$$P(K_i \mid \neg S_j) = (1-\alpha) \cdot P_{ko}(S_j) + \alpha \cdot (1 - P_{ko}(S_j)) \tag{9}$$

Mit dem Parameter α kann eingestellt werden, wie stark sich die Auswertung einer Gitterzelle auf die Sensorbewertung auswirken soll. Für α sind je nach Klassifikation des betrachteten Sensors verschiedene Werte zu wählen:

OCC: $\qquad \alpha > 0.5$

FREE: $\qquad \alpha < 0.5$

Je weiter α von 0.5 entfernt ist, desto stärker schlägt sich die Auswertung der betrachteten Gitterzelle C_i auf die Bewertung des Sensors S_j nieder. Abbildung 2 und 3 zeigen die Konsistenzmaße $P(K_i \mid S_j)$ und $P(K_i \mid \neg S_j)$ in Abhängigkeit davon, wie viele Sensoren die betreffende Gitterzelle belegt (linke Achse n_{OCC}) bzw. frei (rechte Achse n_{FREE}) klassifiziert haben.

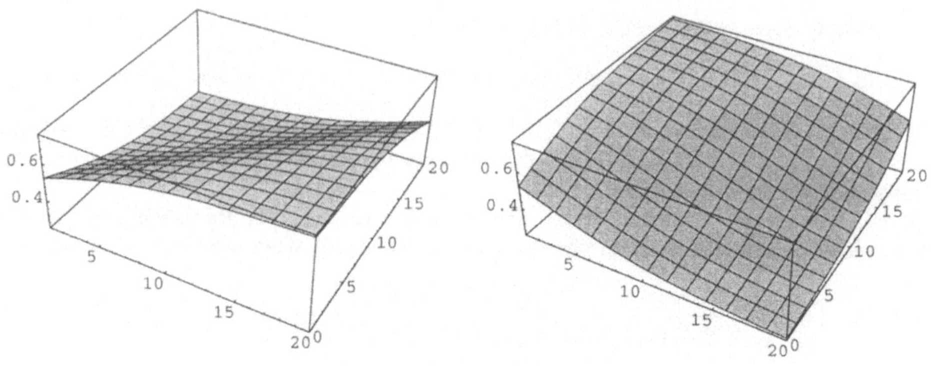

Abb. 2: $P(K_i \mid S_j)$ und $P(K_i \mid \neg S_j)$ für OCC-Klassifikation mit $\alpha = 0.75$

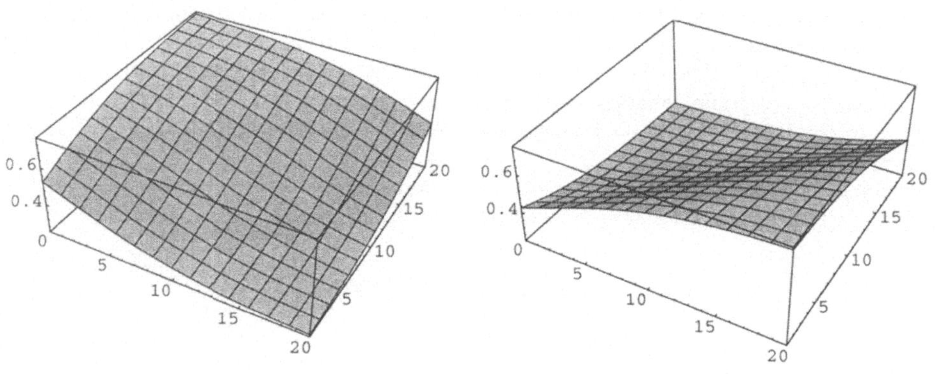

Abb. 3: $P(K_i \mid S_j)$ und $P(K_i \mid \neg S_j)$ für FREE-Klassifikation mit $\alpha = 0.25$

Anhand obiger Abbildungen wird folgendes deutlich:

- Für Gitterzellen mit $n_{FREE} = n_{OCC}$ beträgt die Belegtwahrscheinlichkeit 0.5. In der Information dieser Zelle ist praktisch keine Redundanz vorhanden. Deshalb läßt sich auch keine gesicherte Aussage über den Zustand der betreffenden Sensoren machen. Die Konsistenzmaße sind demnach nahezu 0.5 und haben damit in Verbindung mit Gleichung (6) kaum Einfluß auf die Sensorbewertung.

- Sehr stark unterschiedliche n_{FREE} und n_{OCC} führen zu von 0.5 verschiedenen Konsistenzmaßen, die in Verbindung mit Gleichung (6) Ausdruck von

Bestätigung	$P(K_i \mid S_j) > 0.5$	$P(K_i \mid \neg S_j) < 0.5$	bzw.
Widerspruch	$P(K_i \mid S_j) < 0.5$	$P(K_i \mid \neg S_j) > 0.5$	

sind.

Die Entscheidung, ob ein bestimmter Sensor als defekt oder funktionsfähig eingestuft wird, kann anhand von Schwellwerten für $P(S_j \mid \{K\}_i)$ durchgeführt werden.

4. Möglichkeiten einer Sensorkalibrierung

Neben der Erkennung von Sensordefekten in unbekannter Umgebung bietet die in dieser Arbeit verwendete Repräsentationsform der Umgebung zudem die Möglichkeit einer Sensorkalibrierung. Aufgabe einer Sensorkalibrierung ist es, die Parameter P eines funktionellen Zusammenhangs f

$$A = f(M; P) \tag{10}$$

zwischen Sensormeßwert M und einer weiterverarbeitbaren Aussage A zu bestimmen. Dazu wird zu jeder Messung M die zugehörige Aussage A benötigt. Verwandte Arbeiten stellen dies durch Verwendung von Eichkörpern bzw. -umgebungen sicher, die die in Kapitel 1 erwähnten Nachteile aufweisen. Der hier vorgestellte Ansatz basiert auf einer Erzeugung der Referenzaussagen durch die Messungen anderer funktionsfähiger und hinreichend gut kalibrierter Sensoren. Die Aussagen der eingehenden Sensormessungen beziehen sich auf den Belegtzustand der zugehörigen Gitterzelle. Die Frage nach der Gitterzelle, die einem Sensormeßwert entspricht, wird durch den Zusammenhang

$$C = f(M; P) \tag{11}$$

beantwortet. Zur Identifikation des Zusammenhangs, d.h. der Bestimmung der relevanten Parameter P muß zu einer Messung M eine gesicherte Hypothese für die zugehörige Gitterzelle C durch Auswertung der in der Gitterkarte gespeicherten Informaton bestimmt werden. Eine konkrete Realisierung für Ultraschall-Entfernungssensoren wird in Kapitel 5 beschrieben.

5. Realisierung und Ergebnisse

Obige Verfahren wurden für die bei der Siemens AG eingesetzte autonome mobile Plattform ROAMER 1 [1] implementiert und getestet.

An Sensorik wurden dabei 24 gleichartige, auf dem Umfang des Roboters angeordnete, in horizontaler Richtung messende Ultraschallsensoren mit einem Öffnungswinkel von ca. 20° verwendet. Zur Bestimmung der Robotereigenposition wurde auf Odometriedaten zurückgegriffen.

Die Experimente wurden mit einem 81x81 Pixel großen Gitter mit einer Zellengröße von 10x10 cm durchgeführt.

Durch die Erkennung mehrerer "eingebauter" fehlerhafter Sensoren wie

Abb. 4: ROAMER 1

- "schielende" Sensoren $\rightarrow$ Sensoren mit falsch parametrierter Hauptstrahlachsenrichtung
- "träumende" Sensoren $\rightarrow$ Sensoren, die nicht vorhandene Objekte sehen
- "blinde" Sensoren $\rightarrow$ Sensoren, die keine Objekte wahrnehmen

konnte die Eignung des Verfahrens sowohl für den Online-Einsatz sowie für einen Sensor-selbsttest nachgewiesen werden.

Die Abbildungen 5a und 5b zeigen als Ergebnis zweier Experimente zwei Bildschirmplots. Oben sind jeweils die aufgebauten Gitterkarten zu sehen (Farbgebung analog zu Abbildung 1), unten in Balkendarstellung von links nach rechts jeweils die Sensorbewertung für jeden der 24 Ultraschallsensoren. Der hellgraue Anteil des Balkens repäsentiert die Wahrscheinlichkeit $P(S_j \mid \{K\}_i)$ als Maß für die Fehlerfreiheit eines Sensors.

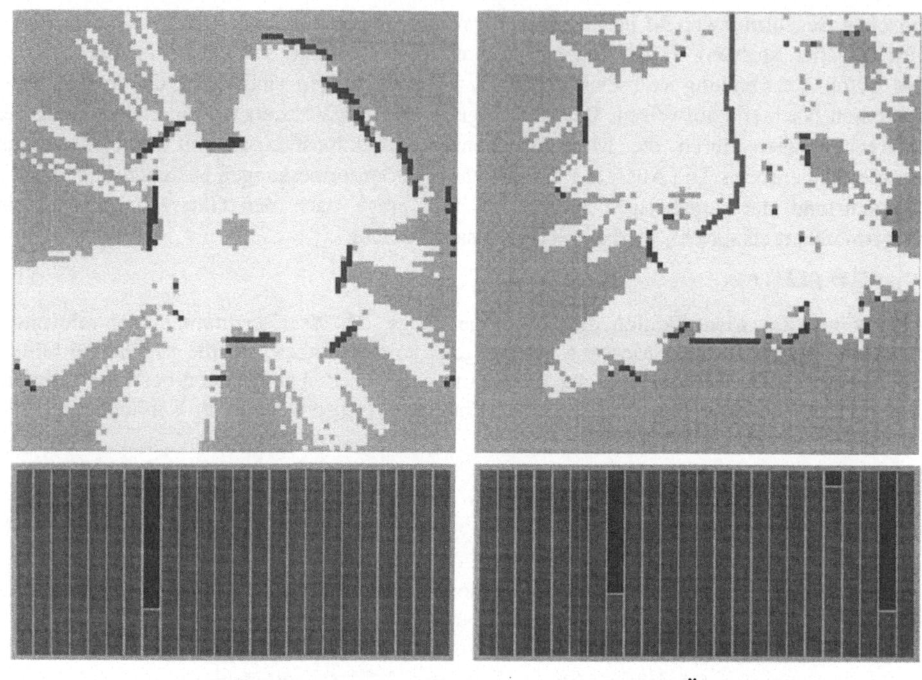

a. Selbsttest   b.: Online-Überwachung

Abb. 5: Gitterkarte und Sensorbewertung

Selbsttest:

Der Selbsttest wurde in der unpräparierten Büroumgebung unseres Labor durchgeführt. ROAMER 1 drehte sich dabei mit einer Winkelgeschwindigkeit von ca. 20°/s um 360°. Die Messungen wurden online in die Gitterkarte eingetragen. Nach Beenden der Drehung wurde die Gitterkarte ausgewertet. Abbildung 5a zeigt die Gitterkarte mit dem Ergebnis der Sensor-bewertung. Für die Klassifikation der Sensoren hat sich ein Schwellwert von 0.3 bewährt. Durch den Selbsttest konnte ein Defekt des Sensors S_8 detektiert werden.

Online-Fehlererkennung:

Die Online-Fehlererkennung wurde anhand von verschiedensten Fahrten durch unsere Büro-umgebung validiert. Abbildung 5b zeigt die Ergebnisse einer solchen Fahrt. Neben dem auch durch den Selbsttest als defekt klassifizierten Sensor S_8 konnte der in diesem Experiment zusätzlich manipulierte Sensor S_{23} (gegenüber dem Modell um 20° verstellte Hauptstrahl-achsenrichtung) als fehlerhaft erkannt werden.

Kalibrierung:

In Kapitel 4 wurden allgemein Möglichkeiten aufgezeigt, in welcher Weise die aufgebaute Gitterkarte für eine Kalibrierung der beteiligten Sensoren herangezogen werden kann. Ein konkrete Realisierung wurde mit der Bestimmung der tatsächlichen Hauptstrahlachsenrichtung β eines Ultraschallsensors gegenüber dem Roboterkoordinatensystem durchgeführt (siehe Abbildung 6).

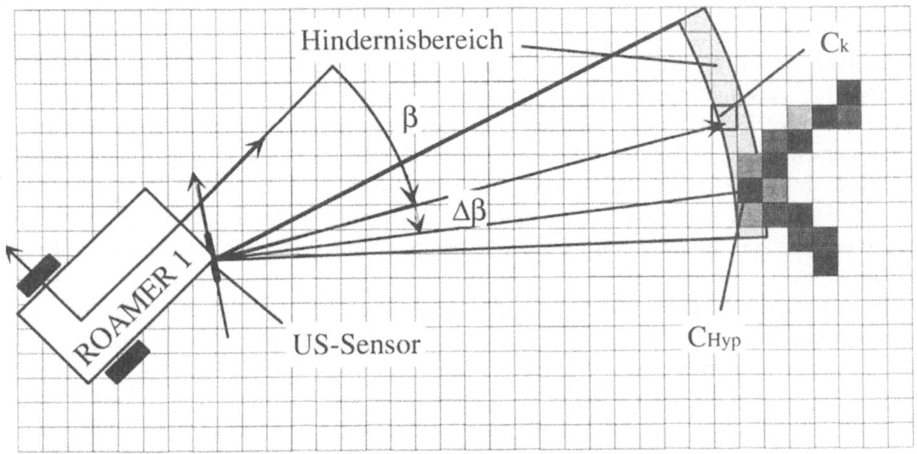

Abb. 6: Ermittlung von C_{Hyp}

Unter Verwendung von Gleichung (11) wird für jede Messung M_k eines zu kalibrierenden Sensors S_j mit den aktuellen Sensorparametern P_j die entsprechende Gitterzelle C_k der aus den Messungen der anderen Sensoren aufgebauten Gitterkarte bestimmt. Für die tatsächliche Position des detektierten Hindernisses ergibt sich wegen der niedrigen Winkelauflösung sowie der möglichen Verstellung des Sensors der in Abbildung 6 dargestellte Hindernisbereich. Innerhalb dieses Hindernisbereiches muß nun die wahrscheinlichste Hypothese C_{Hyp} für die zur Messung M_k gehörende Gitterzelle gefunden werden. Der Korrekturwert $\Delta\beta$ der Sensorhauptstrahlrichtung β ergibt sich mit

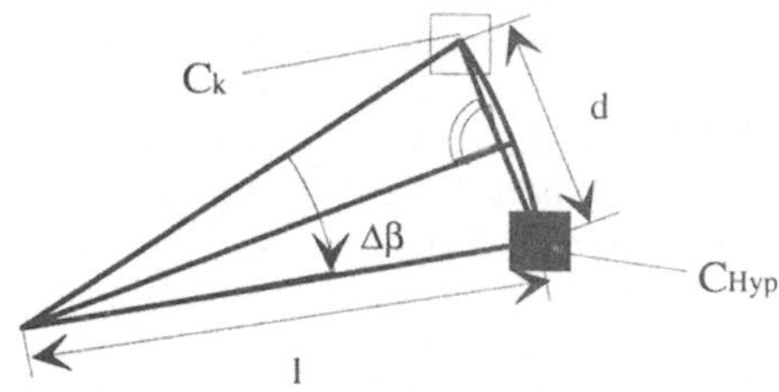

l	gemessene Entfernung
d	kartesischer Abstand zwischen den Gitterzellen C_k und C_{Hyp}

zu

$$\Delta\beta = 2 \cdot \arcsin(\frac{d}{2 \cdot l}) \qquad (12)$$

Abb. 7: $\Delta\beta$-Berechnung

und wird einem Optimierverfahren zugeführt. Als Algorithmus wurde ein Extended-Kalman-Filter implementiert. Eine Übertragung des Verfahrens auf einen Anwendungsfall, bei dem neben statischen Parametern auch dynamische Zustandsvariablen (z.B. Bestimmung von Odometrieparametern) geschätzt werden müssen, ist damit leicht realisierbar.

Durch das eben beschriebene Verfahren konnte die Hauptstrahlachsenrichtung bis auf ±3° genau korrigiert werden.

6. Zusammenfassung und Ausblick

Mit Hilfe des oben vorgestellen Verfahrens konnte die Aufgabe der Fehlererkennung für Umgebungssensoren autonomer mobiler Systeme gelöst werden. Besonders hervorzuheben ist dessen Anwendbarkeit in unpräparierten Alltagsumgebungen sowie die Flexibilität hinsichtlich der verwendbaren Sensorik. Eingehende Tests wurden anhand einer Implementierung für den mobilen Roboter ROAMER 1 durchgeführt. Die Ergebnisse haben gezeigt, daß mit dem entwickelten Ansatz Ausfälle der untersuchten Ultraschallsensoren sicher und schnell erkannt werden können.

Hinsichtlich den Möglichkeiten einer Sensorkalibrierung muß im Gegensatz zu anderen Arbeiten für dieses Verfahren eine ausreichende Anzahl funktionsfähiger und kalibrierter Sensorik zur Verfügung stehen. Für einen Einsatz bei der Inbetriebnahme eines autonomen Systems erscheint es, auch wegen der erreichbaren Genauigkeit, deshalb nur bedingt geeignet. Die Stärke des Ansatzes liegt in dessen Anwendbarkeit in einer Alltagsumgebung. Explizites Vorwissen in Form von Hindernispositionen und Freiräumen kann aber in die Gitterkarte abgebildet werden, wodurch das Verfahren auch in einer Referenzumgebung eingesetzt werden kann.

Demnächst soll ein IR-Laserscanner integriert werden, um die Anwendbarkeit des Verfahrens auch für verschiedene Sensormodalitäten nachgeweisen zu können. In diesem Zusammenhang soll untersucht werden, wie sich ein anderes Meßprinzip mit anderer Reichweite, Auflösung und Genauigkeit auf die Brauchbarkeit des Verfahrens auswirken.

Die weiteren Arbeiten konzentrieren sich auf die Fragestellung, auf welcher Basis andere Sensorik miteinander verknüpft werden muß, damit durch deren Messwerte redundante Aussagen gemacht werden, die wiederum eine Fehlererkennung für diese Sensoren ermöglichen.

Literatur

1   Rencken W.D, Leuthäusser I., Bauer R., Feiten W., Lawitzky G., Möller M., Low-Cost Mobile Robots for Complex Non-Production Environments, Proc. 1st IFAC Int. Workshop on Intelligent Autonomous Vehicles, April 1993.

2   Beckerman M., Oblow E. M.: Treatment of Systematic Errors in the Processing of Wide-Angle Sonar Sensor Data for Robotic Navigation, IEEE Transactions on Robotics and Automation, vol. 6, No. 2, April 1990.

3   Borenstein J., Koren Y.: The Vector Field Histogramm - Fast Obstacle Avoidance for Mobile Robots, IEEE Transactions on Robotics and Automation, Vol. 7, No. 3, 1991.

4   Borenstein J., Koren Y.: Real-Time Obstacle Avoidance for Fast Mobile Robots, IEEE Transactions on Robotics and Automation, Vol. 19, No. 5, 1989.

5   Matthies L., Elfes A.: Probablistic Estimation Mechanisms and Tesselated Representations for Sensor Fusion, Proceedings of the SPIE - The International Society for Optical Engeneering, Cambridge, MA, USA, 7-9 November 1988.

6   Elfes A.: Dynamic Control of Robot Perception Using Stochastic Spatial Models, Information Processing in Autonomous Mobile Robots, Proceedings of the International Workshop in Munich, Germany 6-8 March 1991, Springer-Verlag, Germany, 1991.

7   Elfes A.: Dynamic Control of Robot Perception Using Multi-Property Inference Grids, Proceedings of the 1992 IEEE International Conference on Robotics and Automation, Nice France, May 1992.

8   Shannon C.E., Weaver W.: The Mathematical Theory of Communication, University of Illinois Press, 1949.

Bewegungserfassung mit einem Millimeterwellen-Sensor

Thomas Troll, Jürgen Detlefsen

Technische Universität München
Lehrstuhl für Hochfrequenztechnik
D-80290 München, Germany
email: {troll,det}@hfs.e-technik.tu-muenchen.de

Kurzfassung. Der Einsatz autonomer, mobiler Systeme (AMS) in einer dynamischen Umgebung erfordert die sensorielle Erfassung und informationstechnische Bewertung von Umweltveränderungen. Dabei kann ein Bewegungsmonitor eine wesentliche Rolle bei der Definition von Aufmerksamkeitsbereichen spielen, da eine örtliche Veränderung von Objekten immer mit einer Bewegung verbunden ist. Der Beitrag befaßt sich mit der Erweiterung eines vorhandenen, entfernungsgebenden Millimeterwellen-Sensors um einen schnellen Bewegungsdetektor. Er ermöglicht einen direkten Zugriff auf die Geschwindigkeitsinformation über die Auswertung des Doppleranteils im Empfangssignal. Beschrieben wird die Systemerweiterung, die Verarbeitung der Bewegungsinformation und der experimentelle Einsatz des Systems zur Aufmerksamkeitssteuerung auf einer mobilen Plattform.

1 Einleitung

Halboffene oder geschlossene Türen, verstellte Durchfahrten, sich begegnende Fahrzeuge und nicht zuletzt Menschen im Umkreis eines autonomen, mobilen Systems, solchen Umgebungsbedingungen müssen sich mobile Roboter in der Zukunft verstärkt stellen. Während für die leitdrahtgebundenen und mit einfacher Schutzraumüberwachung ausgestatteten Systeme der Frühzeit noch starre Umgebungsbedingungen selbstverständlich waren, sind die Anforderungen an die Flexibilität heutiger Systeme deutlich gestiegen. Gerade im Servicebereich müssen sich autonome, mobile Systeme in einer belebten Umgebung bewegen können, die sich in gewissen Grenzen ständig ändert. In der jüngeren Forschung und in besonderem Maße innerhalb des Sonderforschungsbereichs 331 der TU München finden sich deshalb zahlreiche Ansätze zur Detektion, Erkennung und Bewältigung dynamischer Umgebungsbedingungen sowie zur Flexibilisierung und intelligenten Störungsbehandlung [1–4], [12].

Allen Ansätzen gemein ist eine geeignet geartete Repräsentation der Einsatzumgebung, sei sie a priori vorhanden oder exploriert. Dabei reicht die Bandbreite von einer sensornahen Darstellung bis zur verteilten Speicherung sehr abstrahierten Wissens. Sieht man von einer direkten Kommunikation zwischen den autonomen Systemen ab, kann die laufende Anpassung dieser Modellinformation an

Abb. 1. Ansicht des 3D-Millimeterwellen-Sensors nach der Neukonstruktion und
Verkleinerung

die sich ändernde Realität nur durch eine geeignete Verarbeitung und Bewertung sensorieller Information erreicht werden. Insofern kommt der Sensorik bei der Bewältigung dynamischer Szenarien eine entscheidende Rolle zu.

Um Umweltveränderungen mit Hilfe von Sensoren zu detektieren, gibt es mehrere Methoden. Die wohl gängigste ist der direkte Sensordaten-/Modellvergleich. Dabei ist es unerheblich, ob es sich um aktive, entfernungsgebende Sensoren wie z.B. Laserscanner oder um passive, bildgebende wie CCD-Kameras handelt. Voraussetzung für den Vergleich ist im allgemeinen sowohl eine Standorthypothese, um passende Modellinformation auswählen zu können, als auch ein entsprechendes Auflösungsvermögen des beteiligten Sensors, da sonst Veränderungen unentdeckt bleiben. Um alle Veränderungen in der Umgebung zu erfassen, muß der Sensordaten-/Modellvergleich grundsätzlich im ganzen Einzugsbereich des Systems ausgeführt werden, was mit der Verarbeitung einer erheblichen Informationsmenge verbunden ist.

In diesem Zusammenhang wäre eine Aufmerksamkeitssteuerung von Vorteil, die den Sensordaten-/Modellvergleich auf relevante Bereiche beschränken kann. Dazu genügt es, sich zunächst auf die Bewegungen im Raum zu konzentrieren, da diese Indikatoren für eigenbewegliche Objekte und potentielle Ursachen für statische Veränderungen sind.

Im Zuge einer Neukonstruktion und Verkleinerung wurde ein bereits vorhandener Millimeterwellen-Sensor um eine Einheit zur schnellen Bewegungserfassung erweitert (Abbildung 1). Der Sensor ist im Rahmen des Sonderforschungsbereichs 331 speziell für Perzeptionsaufgaben auf autonomen, mobilen Systemen entwickelt worden und wurde bisher in verschiedenen experimentellen Anwendungen u.a. zur initialen und schritthaltenden Standortbestimmung [11] sowie zur Schutzraumüberwachung [13] eingesetzt. Alle Anwendungen stützten sich dabei auf die Entfernungsinformation des Sensors.

Der Beitrag beschäftigt sich in Kapitel 2 zunächst kurz mit dem allgemeinen Problem der sensoriellen Erfassung von Bewegung, bevor in Kapitel 3 die konkrete Systemerweiterung des Millimeterwellen-Sensors beschrieben wird. Die Auswertung der Bewegungsinformation ist Gegenstand des vierten Kapitels, wobei auch die Validierung an zwei Beispielen demonstriert wird. Abschließend wird die Leistungsfähigkeit des Systems zur Aufmerksamkeitssteuerung auf einer mobilen Sensorikplattform in Kapitel 5 belegt.

2 Bewegungserfassung

Grundsätzlich gibt es zwei Methoden zur Bewegungsdetektion: direkt aufgrund des Dopplereffektes oder indirekt über die Ortsänderung der Objekte. Eine indirekte Bewegungsdetektion über die Verfolgung der Ortsänderung erfordert einen Sensor mit einem hohen Ortsauflösungsvermögen und eine störungsfreie Detektion der bewegten Objekte über einen längeren Zeitraum hinweg. Erfahrungen aus dem Automobilbereich mit Laser- und Millimeterwellensensoren haben gezeigt, daß diese Methode in vielen Fällen nicht robust genug ist.

Der direkte Zugriff auf die Geschwindigkeitsinformation via Dopplereffekt ist demgegenüber ein sehr effizientes Verfahren, das aber nur bei kohärenten Systemen zugänglich ist. Dazu zählen neben den Millimeterwellen-Sensoren auch Systeme mit optischen oder akustischen Trägersignalen. Im optischen Bereich, der z.B. durch Laserscanner stark in der Robotik vertreten ist, ergeben sich Dopplerfrequenzen im Bereich einiger Megahertz, die nur schwer schritthaltend zu verarbeiten sind. Akustische Systeme wie z.B. Ultraschallsensoren sind aufgrund geringer Reichweite, hoher Störempfindlichkeit und eines geringen Winkelauflösungsvermögen auf den extremen Nahbereich beschränkt.

Millimeterwellensysteme zeichnen sich in diesem Punkt durch eine genügend hohe Phasenempfindlichkeit des Trägersignals aus und durch Ausbreitungseigenschaften, die nahezu unabhängig von atmosphärischen Einflüssen sind. Die Dopplerfrequenzen liegen im Bereich einiger Kilohertz, sind also einer digitalen Datenverarbeitung leicht zugänglich. Neben einer quantitativen Auswertung des Signals hinsichtlich der Geschwindigkeit erlaubt eine spektrale Analyse grundsätzlich auch eine qualitative Bewertung der Bewegung.

3 Systembeschreibung

Wie schon angedeutet, baut der schnelle Bewegungsdetektor auf einem bereits vorhandenen Millimeterwellen-Sensor auf. Dieses Pulsradar, das bei einer Trägerfrequenz von 94 GHz arbeitet, ermöglicht die dreidimensionale Erfassung der Umgebung hinsichtlich der Entfernung und Geschwindigkeit von Objekten. Dazu verwendet es extrem kurze Pulse, aus deren Laufzeit auf die Entfernung des

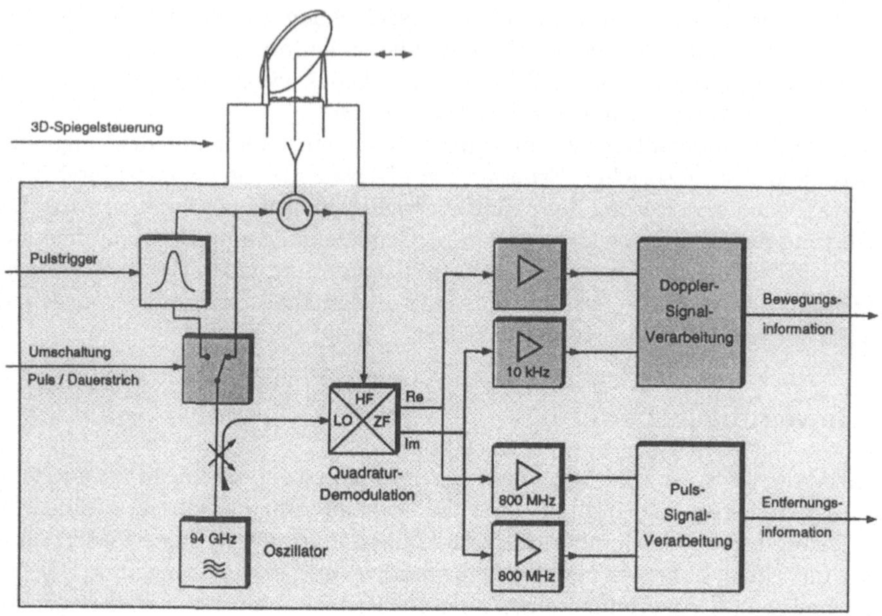

Abb. 2. Systemerweiterung des bestehenden Pulsradars um einen schnellen Bewegungsmonitor

Objektes geschlossen werden kann. Der Aufbau des Sensors und seine Systemparameter sind in [8] bereits ausführlich beschrieben, deshalb soll an dieser Stelle nur auf die Systemerweiterung näher eingegangen werden.

Die zur Bewegungserfassung notwendige Dopplerinformation war auch bisher schon in den Empfangssignalen des Pulssystems enthalten, jedoch immer auf das gerade vermessene Entfernungstor beschränkt. Eine reine Bewegungsüberwachung der Szene erfordert keine Entfernungsauflösung, es kann also für diesen Fall auf die gesamte Pulserzeugung und -verarbeitung verzichtet werden. Aus diesem Grund wurde der Sensor so erweitert, daß neben einem Pulsbetrieb auch ein sogenannter Dauerstrichbetrieb möglich ist, der einen schnellen Szenenüberblick erlaubt und mit einem deutlich geringeren Aufwand im Millimeterwellen- und Niederfrequenzbereich verbunden ist.

Abbildung 2 zeigt die Systemerweiterung. Der Bewegungsdetektor arbeitet wie das Pulssystem mit dem quadraturdemodulierten Empfangssignal, liefert also Amplitude und Phase des Bewegungssignals. Der Bandbreitebedarf ist mit $625\,\mathrm{Hz}/\frac{\mathrm{m}}{\mathrm{s}}$ für reale Geschwindigkeiten im Vergleich zur Trägerfrequenz von 94 GHz vernachlässigbar. Die Umschaltung zwischen Pulsbetrieb und Dauerstrichbetrieb erfolgt rechnergesteuert mit einem einfachen Digitalsignal. Erste Experimente haben gezeigt, daß auch ein gleichzeitiger Betrieb beider Modi möglich ist, da im Pulsbetrieb das Dauerstrichsignal nicht vollständig unterdrückt wird. Entsprechend der Leistungsminderung des Dauerstrichsignals ist diese Betriebsart aber weniger empfindlich.

4 Informationsverarbeitung der Bewegungsdaten

4.1 Signalbeschreibung

Ein Objekt im Erfassungsbereich eines kohärenten Systems mit Quadraturdemodulator, wie es in Abbildung 2 zu sehen ist, liefert im Dopplerfrequenzbereich das Ausgangssignal

$$u_a(t) = A\,e^{j2\pi f_d t}.$$

Die Signalamplitude A ist eine Funktion von Reflektivität und Abstand des beleuchteten Objekts, die Dopplerfrequenz f_d spiegelt das Bewegungsverhalten wieder. Der Zusammenhang zwischen der Dopplerfrequenz und der Radialkomponente der Objektgeschwindigkeit v_r ist mit

$$f_d = 2\frac{v_r}{\lambda_0}$$

entfernungsunabhängig und enthält im Vorzeichen die Bewegungsrichtung. Befinden sich mehrere Objekte im Sensorblickfeld, so überlagern sich ihre Dopplerfrequenzen linear und sind bei entsprechender Auflösung auch voneinander unterscheidbar. Für eine Trägerfrequenz von 94 GHz, das entspricht einer Freiraumwellenlänge λ_0 von 3,19 mm, ist mit einer Frequenz von 625 Hz bei einer Objektgeschwindigkeit von 1 m/s zu rechnen, d.h. nahezu alle Bewegungen einer Innenraumszene dürften in den Bereich bis 3 kHz abgebildet werden.

Grundsätzlich können mit dieser Anordnung beliebig tiefe Frequenzen ausgewertet werden, jedoch ist wegen des Auftretens großer Gleichspannungspegel im Empfänger durch unbewegte Objekte ($f_d = 0$) eine untere Grenzfrequenz von 2 Hz eingeführt worden. Das stellt im praktischen Betrieb keine Einschränkung dar, denn eine vernünftige Auflösung dieser Signale im Frequenzbereich würde eine Meßzeit im Sekundenbereich erfordern und einen schnellen Szenenüberblick verhindern.

4.2 Datenauswertung

Die Auswertung des Bewegungssignals erfolgt durch eine Analog-Digital-Wandlung mit anschließender Frequenzanalyse. Abtastrate und Meßzeit sind bei der Digitalisierung in weiten Grenzen frei wählbar, so daß sich bei den gegebenen Randbedingungen ein Geschwindigkeitsmeßbereich von $3\,\frac{\text{mm}}{\text{s}}$ bis $18\,\frac{\text{km}}{\text{h}}$ ergibt. Als guten Kompromiß zwischen Meßgenauigkeit und Verarbeitungsgeschwindigkeit hat sich eine Länge von 1024 Werten pro Datensatz herausgestellt. Die Frequenzanalyse erfolgt entweder durch eine schnelle Fouriertransformation (FFT) oder eine Phasenauswertung der Autokorrelation (PAKF). Letztere ist ein deutlich schnelleres Verfahren, das aber bei mehreren Objekten im Radarstrahl versagt. Die Reaktionszeit des Systems auf Bewegungen wird durch die Einschwingzeit der Filter bestimmt und liegt im Millisekundenbereich. Eine weiträumige Bewegungserfassung läßt sich mit den beschriebenen Verfahren bei zwei Spiegelumdrehungen pro Sekunde noch gut durchführen.

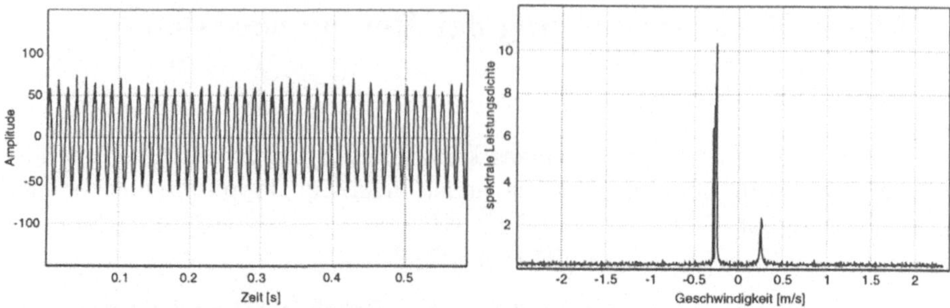

Abb. 3. Bewegungssignal und Spektrum eines mechanisch bewegten Reflektors

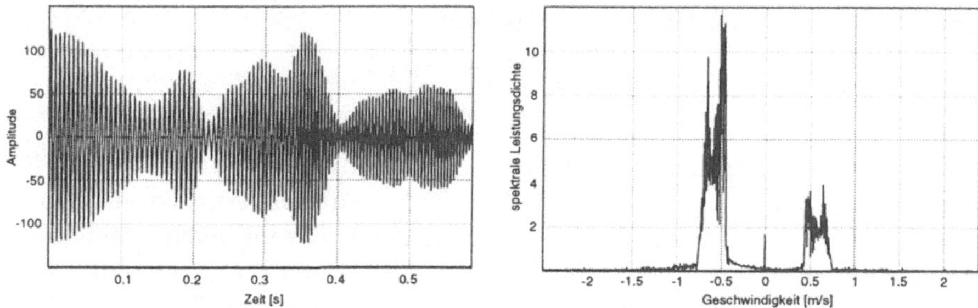

Abb. 4. Bewegungssignal und Spektrum einer Person

4.3 Validierung

Feste Blickrichtung Zur Validierung der Dauerstrich-Dopplereinheit wurde
eine reale Szene mit konstantem Blickwinkel durch den Sensor beleuchtet. Aus
den Meßergebnissen werden im folgenden zwei Situationen exemplarisch dargestellt. Abbildung 3 links zeigt das Zeitsignal eines Reflektors, der sich motorge-
trieben auf einem Verschiebetisch bewegt. Es ist durch hohe Konstanz in Amplitude und Frequenz gekennzeichnet. Sehr ungleichmäßig hingegen ist ein Signal
einer bewegten Person, wie es in Abbildung 4 links dargestellt ist. Im Zeitbereich
läßt sich die starke Schwankung der Amplitude, also der Reflektivität erkennen.

Beide Signale sind mit einer Fouriertransformation ausgewertet worden. Die
Spektren sind ebenfalls in den Abbildungen 3 und 4 neben den Zeitsignalen dargestellt. Die gleichförmige, maschinell erzeugte Bewegung des Radarreflektors ist
deutlich als schmale Frequenzlinie zu erkennen, die nur durch das Auflösungsvermögen des Systems begrenzt ist. Die sich bewegende Person erzeugt hingegen
ein sehr breites Spektrum um eine mittlere Geschwindigkeit von knapp 0.6 m/s.
Die Ergebnisse legen den Schluß nahe, daß neben einer Geschwindigkeitsmessung
auch eine qualitative Bewertung der Bewegung, also z.B. eine Unterscheidung in
Mensch und Maschine möglich sein müßte.

Rotierender Spiegel Etwas andere Signalformen ergeben sich, wenn der Spiegel des Systems mit konstanter Geschwindigkeit in einer Azimutalebene rotiert.
Der Radarstrahl überstreicht dann periodisch mit der Umlaufzeit das Szena-

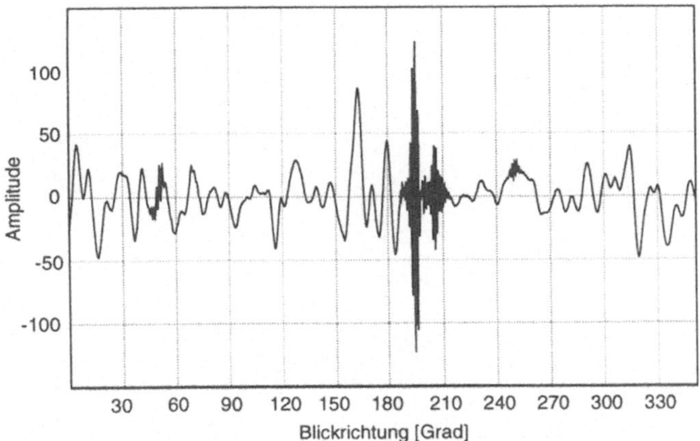

Abb. 5. Umgebungsabbildung über 360° bei einem mit 2 Hz rotierenden Spiegel. Die langsamen Schwankungen im Signal ergeben sich allein aus der unterschiedlichen Reflektivität der Objekte, die der Radarstrahl überstreicht. Unter 185° ein bewegtes Objekt.

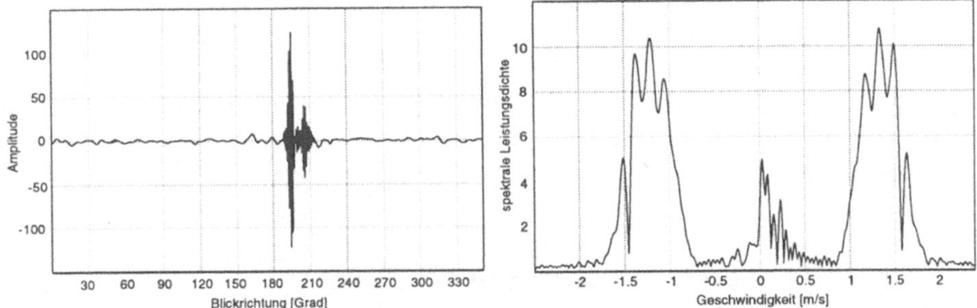

Abb. 6. Umgebungsabbildung nach Subtraktion des statischen Referenzsignals und spektrale Auswertung der verbleibenden Bewegung

rio. Je nach Entfernung und Reflektivität der Objekte, die der Radarstrahl in Folge trifft, ergeben sich so auch bei einer völlig statischen Szene Amplitudenschwankungen über dem Blickwinkel. Bei entsprechender Rotationsgeschwindigkeit überschreiten sie die untere Grenzfrquenz des Systems, sind wegen des Öffnungswinkels des Strahls aber auch nach oben hin begrenzt. Ihnen überlagert sich die Dopplerinformation von bewegten Objekten (Abbildung 5).

Durch seine Periodizität ist der statische Anteil des Signals einer Referenzierung gut zugänglich und kann sehr leicht auf Dynamik in der Szene hin untersucht werden (Abbildung 6). Die Refenzierung eröffnet auch die Möglichkeit, statische Veränderungen zu detektieren. Das völlige Fehlen oder Hinzufügen von Gegenständen äußert sich in starken Amplitudenschwankungen des Referenzsignals unter den entsprechenden Aspektwinkeln. Kleine Verschiebungen bis in den Submillimeterbereich hinein werden in der Phasenlage der komplexen Emp-

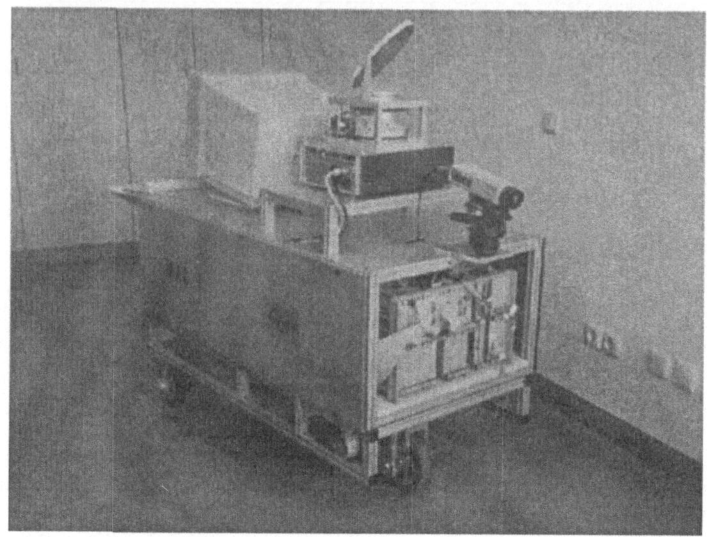

Abb. 7. Sensorikplattform MAC 1 mit Radar- und Videosensor

fangssignale sichtbar. Beide Arten von Veränderungen bleiben im Gegensatz zu den Dopplerfrequenzen nicht auf die Bewegung selbst beschränkt, sondern sind statischer Natur.

5 Experimenteller Einsatz des Systems

Eingesetzt wird der Sensor auf einer mobilen Plattform, die innerhalb des SFB 331 der Evaluierung der Sensorik [7], ihrer Informationsverarbeitung und naher Aspekte wie der Umgebungsmodellierung [6] dient. Dabei übernimmt der Radarsensor neben der initialen und schritthaltenden Lokalisation auch die Rolle eines Bewegungsmonitors. In einem Demonstrationsszenario [7], einer typischen Büroumgebung, überwacht der Millimeterwellensensor weiträumig einen Gangbereich im Hinblick auf bewegte Objekte und stellt Umgebungsänderungen fest. Quasistatische Änderungen, die vom Sensor detektiert werden, initiieren eine nähere Untersuchung durch videobasierte Objekterkennung (z.B. stehengelassener Papierkorb) [9] oder videobasierte Zustandsidentifikation (z.B. Türöffnungswinkel) [12]. Die Videosensorik wird dann durch die Vorgabe präziser Aufmerksamkeitsbereiche (Winkel- und Entfernungsbereich) in ihrer Schnelligkeit und Effizienz deutlich gesteigert.

Die Untersuchungen zum Bewegungsmonitor wurden zunächst auf einen ortsfesten Sensor beschränkt. Der Betrieb auf einer bewegten Plattform erscheint möglich, da grundsätzlich aus dem aspektwinkelabhängigen Bewegungsverhalten der statischen Umgebungselemente die Eigenbewegung nach Betrag und Richtung bestimmt und kompensiert werden kann.

6 Zusammenfassung und Ausblick

Der Beitrag zeigt, daß mit einfacher Radarsensorik weiträumig und schnell Bewegungen im Raum detektiert werden können, die vorübergehend oder dauerhaft auf missionsrelevante Veränderungen hinweisen. Da die beschriebene Dauerstrich-Dopplereinheit unabhängig von der entfernungsgebenden, aber aufwendigeren Puls-Dopplereinheit des Sensors arbeitet, ist heute schon eine Ausführung in integrierter Millimeterwellen-Schaltungstechnik vorstellbar. Die Dopplerfrequenzen liegen im Bereich bis maximal 10 kHz und sind damit einer kostengünstigen Auswertung zugänglich. Denkbare Anwendungen sind die eines autonomen, mobilen Nachtwächters, aber auch die Erweiterung eines Multisensorsystems um einen schnellen Bewegungsdetektor zur Aufmerksamkeitssteuerung.

Erste Ergebnisse der neuen Dauerstrich-Dopplereinheit lassen über die gezeigten Möglichkeiten hinaus eine Verwendung zur schnellen Lokalisation erwarten. Liegt die Geschwindigkeit des rotierenden Radarstrahls oberhalb einer gewissen Grenze, entsteht in einer statischen Umgebung auch bei ruhendem Sensor als Funktion des Aspektwinkels ein Signal, das von der unterschiedlichen Reflektivität aufeinanderfolgender Reflexionspunkte im Strahl herrührt (siehe Kapitel 4.3 und Abbildung 5). Dieses, mit einer Vollumdrehung des Ablenkspiegels periodische Signal zeigt besondere Ausprägung an stark reflektierenden Stellen des Raumes und eröffnet die Möglichkeit einer Lokalisation über Winkelmessung ähnlich [5] oder [10], jedoch an natürlichen Landmarken.

Danksagung

Die vorliegende Arbeit wurde im Rahmen des Sonderforschungsbereichs *Informationsverarbeitung in autonomen, mobilen Handhabungssystemen* (SFB 331), Teilprojekt L4, von der Deutschen Forschungsgemeinschaft gefördert. Die Autoren danken Herrn Georg Näger für die tatkräftige Unterstützung bei den Implementierungsarbeiten.

Literatur

1. D. Ansorge, G. Reinhart. Verhandlungsbasierte Koordinierung autonomer Einheiten in der Produktion. In G. Schmidt, F. Freyberger (Hrsg.), *Autonome Mobile Systeme*, Informatik aktuell. Springer-Verlag, 1996.
2. S. Blessing, D. Kugelmann, G. Reinhart. Sichere Handhabung mit 3D-Simulation und videobasierter Sensorik. In G. Schmidt, F. Freyberger (Hrsg.), *Autonome Mobile Systeme*, Informatik aktuell. Springer-Verlag, 1996.
3. W. Daxwanger, E. Ettelt, C. Fischer, U. Hanebeck, G. Schmidt. ROMAN: Ein mobiler Serviceroboter als persönlicher Assistent. In G. Schmidt, F. Freyberger (Hrsg.), *Autonome Mobile Systeme*, Informatik aktuell. Springer-Verlag, 1996.
4. C. Fischer, P. Havel, G. Schmidt, J. Müller, H. Stahl, M. Lang. Kommandierung eines Serviceroboters mit natürlicher, gesprochener Sprache. In G. Schmidt, F. Freyberger (Hrsg.), *Autonome Mobile Systeme*, Informatik aktuell. Springer-Verlag, 1996.

5. U. D. Hahnebeck and G. Schmidt. Absolute Localization of Fast Mobile Robots Based on an Angle Measurement Technique. In *IFAC Workshop on Intelligent Components for Autonomous and Semi-Autonomous Vehicles*, 1995.
6. A. Hauck, N. O. Stöffler. A Hierarchic World Model Supporting Video-based Localization, Exploration and Object Identification. In *2nd Asian Conference on Computer Vision*, volume 3, pages 176–180, 1995.
7. A. Koller, N. O. Stöffler. Basisfunktionen zur Steigerung der Autonomie mobiler Systeme. In G. Schmidt, F. Freyberger (Hrsg.), *Autonome Mobile Systeme*, Informatik aktuell. Springer-Verlag, 1996.
8. M. Lange, J. Detlefsen. 94 GHz Three-Dimensional Imaging Radar Sensor for Autonomous Vehicles. *IEEE Trans. on Microwave Theory Tech.*, 39(8):819–827, 1991.
9. S. Lanser, C. Zierl. MORAL: Ein System zur videobasierten Objekterkennung im Kontext autonomer, mobiler Systeme. In G. Schmidt, F. Freyberger (Hrsg.), *Autonome Mobile Systeme*, Informatik aktuell. Springer-Verlag, 1996.
10. T. Röfer. Navigation mit eindimensionalen 360°-Bildern. In R. Dillmann, U. Rembold, T. Lüth (Hrsg.), *Autonome Mobile Systeme*, Informatik aktuell. Springer-Verlag, 1996.
11. M. Rožmann, J. Detlefsen. Standortbestimmung in Innenräumen mit einem hochauflösenden 94-GHz-Radarsensor. In *8. Radarsymposium*, pages 43–50. Deutsche Gesellschaft für Ortung und Navigation, Verlag TÜV Rheinland, Köln, 1993.
12. N. O. Stöffler, A. Hauck, G. Färber. Ein geometrisch-symbolisches Umgebungsmodell zur Unterstützung verschiedener Perzeptionsaufgaben autonomer, mobiler Systeme. In G. Schmidt, F. Freyberger (Hrsg.), *Autonome Mobile Systeme*, Informatik aktuell. Springer-Verlag, 1996.
13. N. O. Stöffler, T. Troll. Model Update by Radar- and Video-based Perceptions of Environmental Variations. In *International Symposium on Robotics and Manufacturing*. ASME Press, New York, 1996. To appear.

Echtzeitfähige Merkmalsextraktion und Situationsinterpretation aus Laserscannerdaten

Kai O. Arras, Sjur J. Vestli, Nadine N. Tschichold-Gürman

Institut für Robotik
Eidgenössische Technische Hochschule Zürich
CH – 8092 Zürich
{arras, vestli, tschichold}@ifr.mavt.ethz.ch

Kurzzusammenfassung

Ein Verfahren für die Extraktion beliebiger, modellbasierter Merkmale aus Laserscannerdaten wird vorgestellt. Es arbeitet ohne Verwendung von Vorwissen über Ort und Anzahl der zu erkennenden Landmarken und besitzt dabei die Komplexität $O(n) + O(l^2)$ (n: Anzahl Messpunkte, l: Anzahl Umgebungsmerkmale). Seine Implementation zur Erkennung linienhafter Umgebungsstrukturen weist hohe Genauigkeit und Echtzeitfähigkeit auf. Eine Anwendung in der Positions- und Orientierungsbestimmung mobiler Roboter mittels eines Erweiterten Kalman Filters liegt vor.

Die darauf aufbauende Interpretationsmethode für strukturierte Indoor-Situationen liefert eine geometrische und symbolische Situationsbeschreibung. Diese ermöglicht eine im Sinne der Topologie richtige Situationsinterpretation, mit welcher konkave und konvexe Ecken, Öffnungen und potentielle Öffnungen erkannt werden können. Sie eignet sich zur Situationsklassifikation, zur situationsspezifischen Verhaltensauswahl oder zur Anweisung eines Explorationsalgorithmus, womit sowohl der metrische als auch der rein topologische Ansatz eines anschliessenden Map Buildings offensteht.

1. Einleitung

Die Frage nach der Umwelterkennung und Sensordateninterpretation ist wesentlicher Kern jeder Anwendung autonomer mobiler Roboter. Die Einsatzgebiete solcher Systeme weisen in der Regel einen gewissen Grad der Strukturiertheit auf, der sowohl von Gebäudemerkmalen als auch von Einrichtungsgegenständen herrührt. Für die Lösung des Problems von Navigation und Map Building ist die Extraktion geometrischer Primitive ein möglicher Weg, der hier durch die Detektion beliebiger, modellbasierter Umgebungsstrukturen beschritten werden soll.

Die Erkennung topologierelevanter Situationen und die Gewinnung metrischer Information sind zentrale Fragestellungen beim Kartographieren unbekannter Umgebungen. Verschiedene Methoden wurden für die Modellierung der Umwelt vorgeschlagen, welche sich in zwei sich gegenseitig nicht ausschliessende Klassen einteilen lassen. Es sind dies der metrische und der rein topologische Ansatz. Die Anwendung der hier vorgestellten Methode impliziert keine Festlegung auf eine dieser Ansätze. Das hier vorgestellte Verfahren der Situationsbeschreibung besteht aus der Ansammlung geometrischen Wissens über den betrachteten Umgebungsausschnitt und aus einer symbolischen String-Beschreibung, die auf hohem Abstraktionsniveau Aussagen über die Topologie der Situation zulässt.

2. Das Extraktionsverfahren

Im folgenden Abschnitt wird anfänglich die Extraktion von Geraden als eines der wichtigsten Landmarken beschrieben, das ausserdem von zentraler Bedeutung für die nachfolgende Situationsbeschreibung ist. Aus Gründen der Anschaulichkeit wird erst am Schluss die Verallgemeinerung für beliebige Umgebungsmerkmale vorgenommen.

Das Problem wird nach der Vorverarbeitung als erstes in ein Clusteringproblem umgewandelt. Der zentrale Teil ist ein wohlbekannter Clusteranalysealgorithmus, ein agglomeratives, hierarchisches Gruppierungsverfahren. Dieser Algorithmus mit der Komplexität $O(l^2)$ kann in einer Echtzeitanwendung nur durch erhebliche Reduktion der Eingangsinformation sinnvoll angewendet werden, was durch die vorhergehende Gewinnung der *beitragenden Segmente* erreicht wird. Schliesslich wird die Frage nach dem idealen Clustermittelpunkt optimal hinsichtlich einer präzisen Bestimmung der Geradenparameter beantwortet.

2.1 Vorverarbeitung

Die Vorverarbeitung der Rohdaten umfasst drei Schritte, welche gemeinsam das Ziel verfolgen, die Anzahl Messpunkte bei kleinstmöglichem Informationsverlust zu verringern: Der erste Durchgang verwirft Punkte, die ausserhalb eines festgelegten Abstandsintervalls liegen (zu weit weg oder zu nahe), der zweite entfernt alleinstehende Messungen und der dritte dünnt die Daten so aus, dass benachbarte Punkte in einer Mindestdistanz zueinander entfernt liegen [VESTLI95]. Eine vorverarbeitete Aufnahme eines Korridors mit Verzweigung ist in Figur 2–1 abgebildet.

Mit den vier, hier zu definierenden Parametern wird auf die Spezifikation des verwendeten Laserscanners eingegangen. Die Winkelauflösung, diejenige in radialer Richtung sowie der Charakter des Messrauschens sind die massgebenden Grössen des Sensors.

2.2 Gewinnung der Clusters im Parameterraum

Durch jeweils drei unmittelbar benachbarte Punkte $\{P_{i-1}, P_i, P_{i+1}\}$ wird eine Gerade im Sinne kleinster Fehlerquadrate eingelegt. Diese wird mittels den Parametern α und r in der Hesseschen Normalform der Geradengleichung beschrieben

$$x\cos(\alpha) + y\sin(\alpha) - r = 0, \qquad\qquad \text{(Gl. 2–1)}$$

wobei r die Länge des Lots von der Geraden zum Urprung angibt und α dessen Winkel mit der x-Achse des Sensorkoordinatensystems. Eine effiziente Berechnungsvorschrift für die Modellparameter α und r wird in [KANA89] vorgestellt.

Wenn nun mehrere Messpunkte in etwa auf einer Geraden liegen, so nehmen ihre assoziierten α/r-Parameter auch ähnliche Werte an, was sich in der Ausbildung homogener Bereiche in der Darstellung von α und r gegen den Messindex äussert (dünne Kurven in Figur 2–2). Wechselt man die Darstellungsart und trägt α gegen r ab, so erscheinen diese Bereiche jetzt als Clusters im Parameterraum, die jeweils zu einer der gesuchten linienhaften Strukturen korrespondieren (Punkte in Figur 2–3).

Damit konnte das Extraktionsproblem in ein Clusteringproblem umformuliert werden, wobei evident ist, dass weder Ort noch Anzahl der zu erwartenden Clusters bekannt sind. Einfache Hochrechnungen zeigen, dass der Einsatz herkömmlicher Methoden der Clusteranalyse an diesem Ort zu unpraktikabel hohen Rechenzeiten führen würde. Es muss daher eine Eigenschaft gefunden werden, mittels derer sich dieses Problem von einem allgemeinen Clusteringproblem unterscheidet.

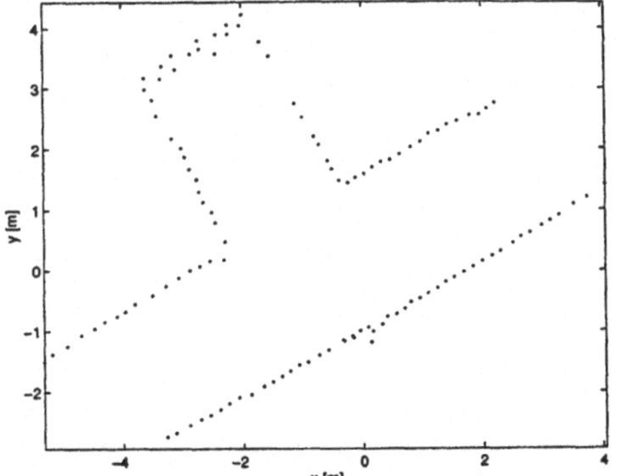
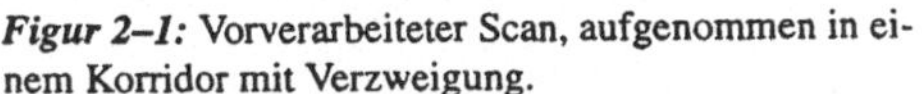

Figur 2–1: Vorverarbeiteter Scan, aufgenommen in einem Korridor mit Verzweigung.
Im ersten Schritt wird durch drei unmittelbar benachbarte Messpunkte des Scans eine Gerade im Sinne kleinster Fehlerquadrate eingelegt und mittels den Parametern α und r in der Hesseschen Normalform der Geradengleichung beschrieben.

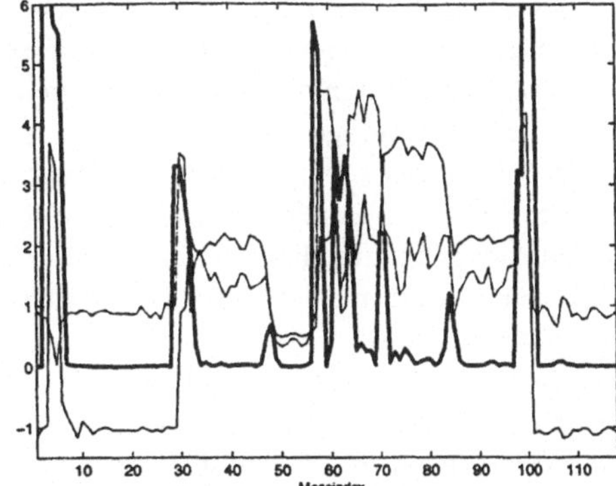

Figur 2–2: Assoziierte (α, r)-Wertepaare aufgetragen gegen den Messindex (dünne Kurven). Dort, wo Punkte auf einer Wand liegen, bilden sich sowohl in α als auch in r homogene Bereiche heraus.
Dick ausgezogen das Kompaktheitsmass e_i. In den Gebieten ähnlicher α/r-Werte ist e_i erwartungsgemäss nahe bei Null.

2.3 Bestimmung der beitragenden Segmente

Diese Eigenschaft gibt es und sie manifestiert sich als *Nachbarschaftsrelation* der Messpunkte: Der Aquisition der Messpunkte unterliegt eine Systematik durch die Tatsache, dass der Laserscanner die Umgebung in einer wohldefinierten Rotationsrichtung abtastet und nicht Messungen in beliebigen Winkeln und zufälliger Reihenfolge macht. Dieser Systematik ist es zu verdanken, dass sich die in Figur 2–2 beobachteten homogenen Bereiche herausbilden, die damit im Gegensatz zu einem gänzlich unstrukturierten Auftreten der (α, r)-Werte stehen.

Die Nachbarschaftsrelation lässt folglich die Aussage zu, dass Messpunkte auf Geraden nacheinander auftreten und somit nebeneinander im Verbund der Messungen abgelegt werden. Oben wurde zudem die Feststellung gemacht, dass auf Geraden liegende Messpunkte sich durch die Clusterbildung im Parameterraum auszeichnen. Diese zwei Aussagen ermöglichen nun den einfachen Schluss, dass die gesuchten, sich in Clustern befindlichen Punkte, *nebeneinander* anzutreffen sind.

Das eröffnet die im folgenden ausgenützte Möglichkeit, die Clusters aufzuspüren. Wir richten dafür unsere Aufmerksamkeit wiederum auf den α/r-Raum sowie auf ein zu definierendes Distanzmass, das die Nähe von darin befindlichen Punkten quantifiziert. Ein bekanntes Distanzmass für diesen Zweck ist die Abweichungsquadratsumme vom Mittelwertsvektor (Gl. 2–2), welches als ein Kompaktheitsmass eines Clusters C_j angesehen werden kann [SPÄTH83].

$$e(C_j) = \sum_{i \in C_j} \left\| x_i - \bar{x}_j \right\|^2, \qquad x_i \in \Re^s \qquad \text{(Gl. 2–2)}$$

Dieses tritt im Kontext des Varianzkriteriums auf, welches in der Clusteranalyse als mögliche Gütefunktion einer gegebenen Partition Verwendung findet, die es durch nachgeschaltete iterative Verfahren zu optimieren gilt. Hier interessiert uns nur die Kompaktheit dreier benachbarter Punkte $\{ x_{i-1}, x_i, x_{i+1} \}$, womit Gleichung 2–2 umgeschrieben werden kann zu

$$e_i = \sum_{j=i-1}^{i+1} \left\| x_j - \bar{x}_i \right\|^2, \qquad \bar{x}_i = \frac{1}{3} \sum_{j=i-1}^{i+1} x_i. \qquad \text{(Gl. 2–3)}$$

Hier gilt natürlich $x_i = (\alpha, r)_i$ und damit $s = 2$.

Dieser Wert ist offensichtlich dann nahe bei Null, wenn die drei Punkte dicht beieinander liegen. Trägt man ihn gegen den Messindex ab, so erscheint eine Kurve, die durch ihr Rausch- und Diskriminanzverhalten die homogenen Bereiche des α- und r-Graphen gut abtrennt (dick ausgezogene Kurve in Figur 2–2).

Ein *beitragendes Segment* ist nun definiert als Menge von Punkten, deren Indizes einen zusammenhängenden Bereich unterhalb des Schwellwertes ε bilden. Markiert man die so erhaltenen Punkte im ursprünglichen Scan, so wird ersichtlich, dass Punkte gefunden wurden, welche in Regionen liegen, die den Verlauf des gemessenen Linienstücks gut angeben (hervorgehobene Punkte in Figur 2–4).

Im allgemeinen kann jedoch dasselbe Umgebungsmerkmal durch mehrere beitragende Segmente repräsentiert sein. Die endgültige Lagebestimmung der Gerade sollte aber für bestmögliche Genauigkeit die Punkte aller Segmente in Betracht ziehen. Das Clusteringproblem ist demzufolge noch nicht gelöst und verlangt, diejenigen Segmente zu assoziieren, welche zu derselben linienhaften Umgebungsstruktur gehören.

2.4   Der Clustering-Algorithmus und die endgültige Lagebestimmung

Dafür wird für jedes beitragende Segment eine Annäherung der endgültigen Geradenparameter bestimmt. Diese Approximation erhält man durch ein erneutes Einpassen einer Gerade im Sinne kleinster Fehlerquadrate – jetzt jedoch durch jeweils alle Punkte des beitragenden Segments. So erhält man pro Segment einen Punkt im Parameterraum, die im Kollektiv an jenen Stellen clusterartige Strukturen ausbilden, wo schon die α/r-Wertepaare optisch zu erkennende Anhäufungen zeigten (Kreise in Figur 2–3). Was erreicht wurde, ist eine erhebliche Reduktion der Eingangsinformation, was erst jetzt die Anwendung bekannter Verfahren zur Clusteranalyse eröffnet, die den hohen Anforderungen des Problems hinsichtlich Echtzeitfähigkeit bei begrenzter Rechenleistung gerecht wird.

Die angewandte Gruppierungsmethode für die Assoziation der zum selben Linienstück gehörenden Segmente ist ein agglomeratives, hierarchisches Clusteringverfahren [HARTIG75], [SPÄTH83], was sich leicht und effizient implementieren lässt. Die Abstandsfunktion ist euklidisch, als Aktualisierungsmethode der Distanzmatrix wurde das konservative und monotone Average-Linkage gewählt.

Nach der Anwendung dieses Schritts, ist die Frage, *ob* ein Punkt zur Lagebestimmung der Gerade beiträgt, geklärt, d.h. die Korrespondenz von Messpunkt zu Merkmal ist hergestellt. Schliesslich verbleibt das Problem, *wie* ein Punkt zur Lagebestimmung beiträgt, was der Bestimmung des Clusterzentrums entspricht, das optimal hinsichtlich der ursprünglichen Fragestellung berechnet werden soll. Dazu wird wiederum eine Gerade im Sinne kleinster Fehlerquadrate eingepasst – diesmal jedoch durch *alle* Punkte, die einem beobachteten Linienstück zugeordnet sind.

In Figur 2–4 sind die endgültig extrahierten Geraden eingezeichnet. Die kurze Wand im oberen Teil der Figur wurde aufgrund dem starken Rauschen ihrer Messpunkte nicht extrahiert. Dies kann auch im Parameterraum eingesehen werden (Figur 2–3), wo dem im oberen Teil alleine liegende Cluster kein Zentrum (dicker Pfeil) zugeordnet ist.

2.5   Verallgemeinerung

Es ist offensichtlich erstrebenswert, verschiedene Merkmale extrahieren zu können, um einen höheren Grad der Allgemeinheit zu erlangen. Es lässt sich einsehen, dass das vorliegende

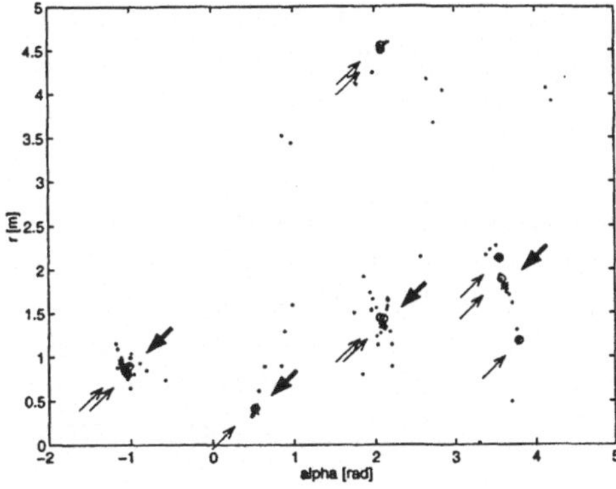

Figur 2–3: Clusters im Parameteraum, die zu den gesuchten Geraden korrespondieren.
Punkte: α/r-Clusters
Kreise: Segmentclusters (dünne Pfeile)
Sterne: Endgültige Clusterzentren (dicke Pfeile)

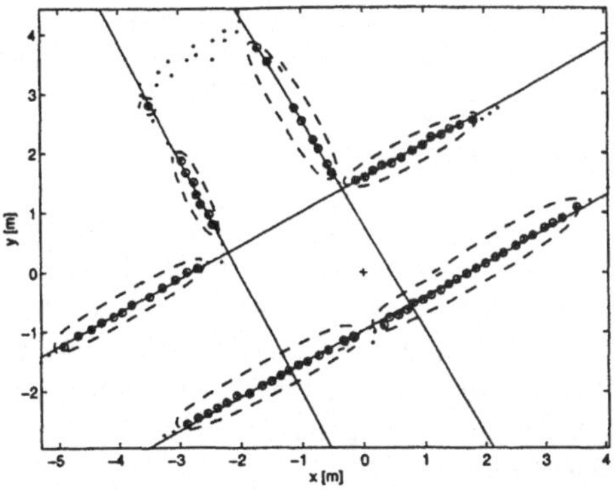

Figur 2–4: Beitragende Segmente, markiert in der Darstellung des ursprünglichen Plots. Die hervorgehobenen Punkte sind offenbar solche, die die Richtungen der Wände gut angeben. Ferner eingezeichnet sind die endgültigen Lagen der vier extrahierten Geraden.

Verfahren Allgemeingültigkeit besitzt und sich für die Extraktion beliebiger, modellbasierter geometrischer Primitive eignet. Verfolgen wir nun die eben kennengelernten Schritte für allgemeine Merkmale:

- **Schritt 1:** Lege das Merkmalsmodell im Sinne kleinster Fehlerquadrate in m benachbarte Messpunkte ein. Es bilden sich homogene Bereiche in den Kurven der Modellparameter aus, die mit den aufgenommenen Merkmalen korrespondieren. Trägt man die Parameter gegeneinander ab, entstehen Clusters im Parameterraum.

- **Schritt 2:** Wende ein Distanzmass auf benachbarte Punkte im Parameterraum an, um die Clusters aufzuspüren (Ausnützen der Nachbarschaftsrelation). Trägt man diese Distanz gegen den Messindex ab, zeichnen sich die Orte der Clusters durch zusammenhängende Gebiete sehr geringer Distanz aus. Die beitragenden Segmente erhält man schliesslich durch Anwenden eines Schwellwertes ε, der diese Gebiete isoliert.

- **Schritt 3:** Berechne eine Approximation der endgültigen Modellparameter für jedes beitragende Segment. Benutze diese dadurch entstehenden Punkte im Parameterraum als Eingang des agglomerativen, hierarchischen Gruppierungsverfahrens, welche die definitive Korrespondenz von Messpunkt zu Merkmal herstellt.

- **Schritt 4:** Bestimme die Clusterzentren durch erneutes Einpassen des Modells im Sinne kleinster Fehlerquadrate in die jetzt bekannten Menge von Messpunkten. Die endgültigen Parameter stehen somit fest.

Die Grösse m hängt von der Winkelauflösung des verwendeten Sensors ab. Bei hoher Winkelauflösung kann man sich den Detailverlust der stärker werdenden Glättung bei grossem m leisten. Bei niedriger Auflösung wird man von Vorteil ein detailerhaltendes, aber zugleich noch minimal glättendes m wählen.

Der Schwellwert ε steht in reiner Abhängigkeit des Sensorrauschens in radialer Richtung. Besitzt der eingesetzte Sensor geringe Genauigkeit, wird man ε vergrössern. Das führt jedoch zu einer Steigerung des Risikos von Fehlklassifikationen, da Umgebungsstrukturen mit ähnlicher Form fälschlicherweise als die gesuchten Merkmale interpretiert werden können. Bei Sensoren hoher Güte, kann ε vermindert werden, so dass nur Umgebungsstrukturen mit sehr grosser

Formtreue extrahiert werden. Hier muss ein Kompromiss zwischen geforderter Modelltreue der extrahierten Merkmale und dem Risiko von Fehlklassifikationen gefunden werden.

2.6 Ergebnisse

Es liegen Ergebnisse für Genauigkeit und Geschwindigkeit der Geradenextraktion vor. Diese beziehen sich auf die verwendete Hardware eines Motorola 68020 bei 20 MHz. Beim Laserscanner handelt es sich um einen Leuze Rotoscan RS 3 mit 2° Winkelauflösung und 4 mm radialer Auflösung. Die Standardabweichung in radialer Richtung beträgt ca. 7 mm. Der Roboter stand in einer Ecke mit zwei gut sichtbaren Wänden, wo 300 Messungen vorgenommen wurden. Es konnten folgende Werte für das Rauschen der Lageparameter der extrahierten Geraden identifiziert werden:

- Standardabweichung in α: $\sigma_\alpha = 0.2°$, Spannweite in α: $s_\alpha = 1.5°$
- Standardabweichung in r: $\sigma_r = 5\,\text{mm}$, Spannweite in r: $s_r = 2.5\,\text{cm}$
- Rechenzeit bei 90 prozessierten Messpunkten (inkl. Vorverarbeitung): < 240 ms.
- Rechenzeit für die Erhaltung der Situationsbeschreibung (siehe unten): < 10 ms

3. Geometrische und symbolische Situationsbeschreibung

Eine für das Map Building wesentliche Frage ist die Erkennung von Öffnungen oder allgemeiner, die der topologierelevanten Situationen. Es ist evident, dass ein Fehler in der Topologie eine schwerwiegende Unzulänglichkeit der Karte darstellt, was die Notwendigkeit einer im Sinne der Topologie korrekten Interpretation von Situationen verdeutlicht. Eine Situationsbeschreibung wird auch dann unumgänglich, wenn man auf den Einbezug metrischer Information in die Karte verzichten will und statt dessen ein rein topologiegeführtes Map Building- und Navigationskonzept verfolgt wie es z.B. in [KUIPERS88] vorgeschlagen wurde.

Hier sind wir in der Lage, eine geometrische und symbolische Beschreibungsart für strukturierte Indoor-Umgebungen zu entwickeln. Die gesamte Situationsbeschreibung basiert auf dem Schneiden benachbarter, linienhafter Umgebungsstrukturen und der Klassifikation des dabei entstehenden Schnittpunktes. Dazu wird auf die Ebene der beitragenden Segmente zurückgegriffen, da sie die Information über die Nachbarschaft aller extrahierten Merkmale enthält.

Ein für die erfolgreiche Unterscheidung erforderliches Klassifikationsmerkmal ist die Lage des gemeinsamen Schnittpunktes $C_{i,i+1}$, der entsteht, wenn die Geraden der benachbarten Segmente S_i und S_{i+1} geschnitten werden. In einer vorübergehenden Vereinfachung lässt sich sagen: wenn zwei Geraden parallel zueinander stehen und ihr Schnittpunkt im Unendlichen liegt, ergibt sich eine Öffnung, wenn er im Endlichen liegt eine konkave oder konvexe Ecke. Die hier zweckmässige Definition von "unendlich" und "endlich" lässt sich an Figur 3–1 verdeutlichen: Ein Schnittpunkt ist im "Unendlichen", wenn er ausserhalb des Kreises K_R liegt, andernfalls im "Endlichen". Der Kreisradius r_{max} ist ein in der Vorverarbeitung schon verwendeter Parameter, der den Rezeptionsradius des Roboters festlegt, indem alle Messpunkte mit grösserem Radialwert verworfen werden. Der Roboter "sieht" demnach nichts, was weiter weg ist als r_{max}.

In Figur 3–1 sind überdies alle möglichen Fälle abgebildet, die beim Schneiden benachbarter Segmentgeraden auftreten können. Abgebildet ist die schematische Darstellung einer Situation mit fünf extrahierten Segmenten S_1, S_2, ..., S_5; R bezeichnet die Roboterposition. Die Umgebungsgeraden sind dünn ausgezogen, die beitragenden Segmente durch dicke Linien hervorgehoben. Die drei ersten Schnittpunkte – eine konvexe Ecke ($C_{1,2}$), eine konkave Ecke ($C_{2,3}$) und eine Öffnung ($C_{3,4}$) – sind alle noch mit einfachen Mitteln unterscheidbar. Die zwei letzten Fäl-

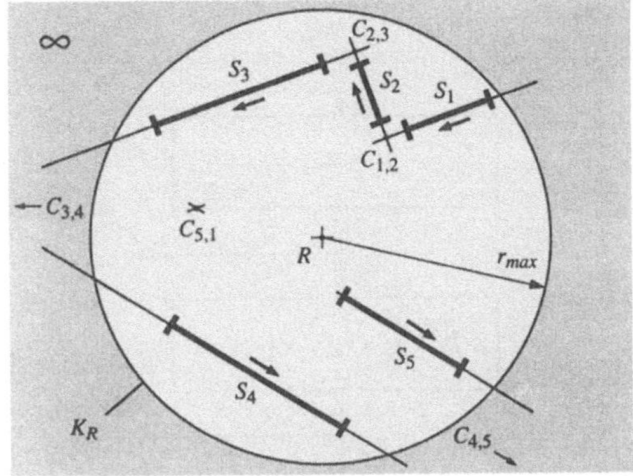
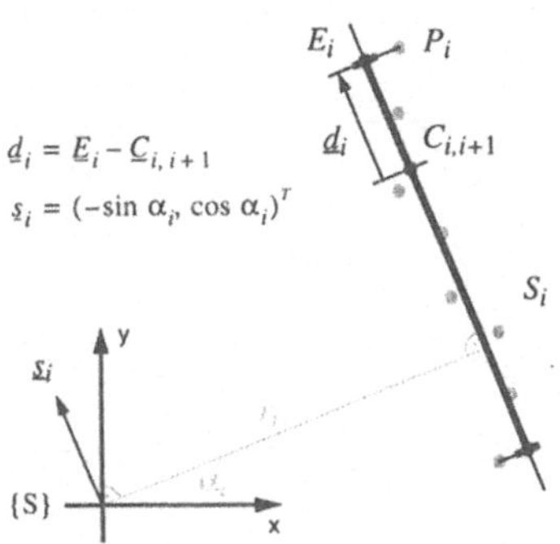

Figur 3–1: Alle möglichen Fälle beim Schneiden benachbarter Segmentgeraden. Mit einfachen Mitteln unterscheidbar sind die drei ersten Schnittpunkte: $C_{1,2}$ konvexe Ecke, $C_{2,3}$ konkave Ecke und $C_{3,4}$ Öffnung. Die zwei letzten Fälle benötigen die Direktionalität eines Segmentes λ als Klassifikationsmerkmal. Damit lassen sich $C_{4,5}$ als verdeckte Ecken und $C_{5,1}$ als Öffnung (obwohl $C_{5,1}$ im Endlichen liegt) identifizieren.

Figur 3–2: Bestimmung der Direktionalität eines Segmentes. Der Schnittpunkt $C_{i,i+1}$, der durch das Schneiden benachbarter Segmentgeraden entsteht, kann irgendwo auf der Segmentgerade liegen. Hier eingezeichnet ist der Fall, bei dem er sich innerhalb von S_i befindet. Die Direktionalität λ kann schliesslich als einfache Funktion von $\underline{s}_i$ und $\underline{d}_i$ angegeben werden (Gl. 3–1).

le jedoch, bei denen es sich um zwei Öffnungen handelt – halb verdeckt bei $C_{4,5}$ und obwohl der Schnittpunkt im Endlichen liegt auch bei $C_{5,1}$ –, können nicht ohne weiteres als solche erkannt werden. Sie erfordern das im folgenden beschriebene Klassifikationsmerkmal der *Direktionalität eines Segmentes*.

3.1 Die Direktionalität eines Segmentes

Die Direktionalität eines Segmentes λ ist definiert als die Scanrichtung bezüglich des gemeinsamen Schnittpunktes $C_{i,i+1}$. Es wird unterschieden zwischen *weg* vom Schnittpunkt (markiert durch einen Pfeil, der nach oben, vom Boden *weg* zeigt: ↑) und *hin* zum Schnittpunkt (angedeutet mit einem Pfeil, der nach unten, zum Boden *hin* zeigt: ↓). Die Scanrichtung eines Segmentes wird von derjenigen des Laserscanners bestimmt, die wohlbekannt entweder im Uhrzeigersinn oder im Gegenuhrzeigersinn definiert ist. Dadurch wird allen erkannten Umgebungsmerkmalen eine Richtung aufgeprägt und mittels der Erscheinungsreihenfolge können Aussagen über ihre Nachbarschaft gemacht werden.

Für die konkrete Bestimmung von λ betrachte man Figur 3–2. Gegeben sind die Lageparameter der Segmentgerade (α_i, r_i), die Koordinaten des Schnittpunktes $C_{i,i+1}$ mit der Geraden des folgenden, benachbarten Segmentes S_{i+1} und die Lage des letzten, dem Segment S_i zugehörigen Messpunkt P_i, welcher an demjenigen Ende von S_i liegt, das sich auf der Seite von S_{i+1} befindet. Den Segmentendpunkt E_i erhält man dann durch Projektion von P_i auf die Segmentgerade. Damit berechnet sich $\underline{d}_i$ als Differenz der Vektoren $\underline{E}_i$ und $\underline{C}_{i,i+1}$. Die Scanrichtung $\underline{s}_i$ kann für einen im Gegenuhrzeigersinn messenden Laserscanner durch Drehen des Lotes um $+\pi/2$ erhalten werden. Die Verwendung von P_i stellt den einzigen, bei der gesamten Situationsbeschreibung notwendigen Rohdatenzugriff dar.

Die Direktionalität λ_i von Segment S_i berechnet sich schliesslich aus der folgenden, einfachen Vorschrift:

$$\lambda_i = \frac{\underline{s}_i^T \underline{d}_i}{|\underline{d}_i|} = \begin{cases} 1, & weg\ (\uparrow) \\ -1, & hin\ (\downarrow) \end{cases} \qquad \text{(Gl. 3–1)}$$

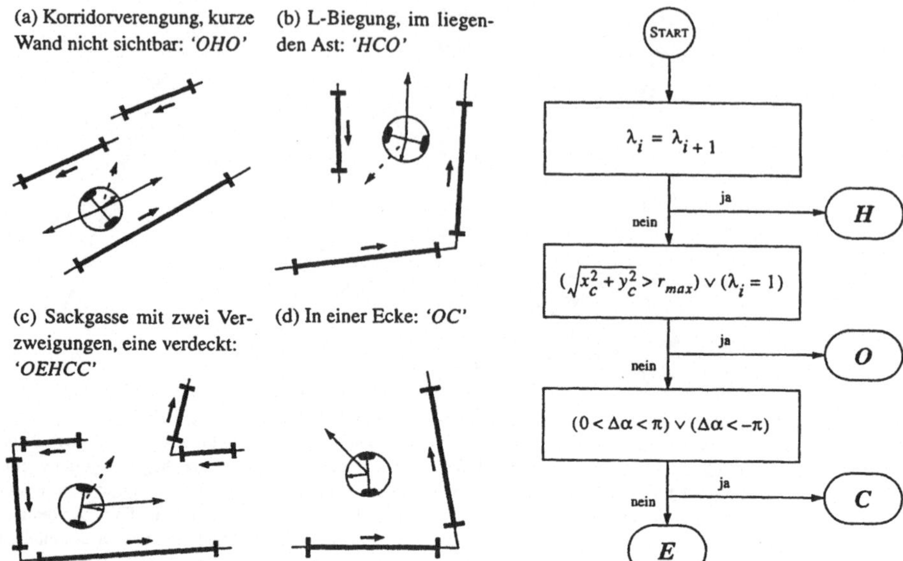

Figur 3–3: Schematische Darstellung einiger Situationen und ihre symbolische String-Beschreibung: Die Wände sind dünn ausgezogen, die beitragenden Segmente durch dicke Linien hervorgehoben.

Figur 3–4: Klassifikationsschema für die Unterscheidung der vier Schnittpunktstypen, welches für jedes benachbarte Segmentpaar S_i und S_{i+1} durchlaufen wird.

Die in Figur 3–1 eingezeichneten Pfeile geben die Scanrichtungen der Segmente für einen im Gegenuhrzeigersinn messenden Laserscanner an. Mit ihrer Hilfe lassen sich jetzt die Direktionalitäten der Segmente in der dargestellten Situation einfach ermitteln. Begonnen wird mit den Segmenten S_1 und S_2: Der Pfeil von Segment S_1 zeigt zum Schnittpunkt $C_{1,2}$ hin, also ist λ_1 als *hin* ($\downarrow$) definiert, λ_2 als *weg* ($\uparrow$). Analog die Fälle von $C_{2,3}$ und $C_{3,4}$. Beim Schneiden der Segmente S_4 und S_5 zeigt sich das erste Mal eine Anomalie in den Direktionalitäten. Sie ergeben sich beide als *hin* ($\downarrow$) zum Schnittpunkt $C_{4,5}$. Auch $C_{5,1}$ zeichnet sich wiederum durch abweichende λ-Werte aus, sie lassen sich als *weg* ($\uparrow$) bei λ_5 und *hin* ($\downarrow$) bei λ_1 identifizieren. Diese Wertekombinationen der Direktionalitäten sind für beide betrachteten Fälle charakteristisch. In [ARRAS96] wird hierzu eine detailliertere Diskussion geführt, wo durch die Definition einer geeigneten Notation die leichte Unterscheidung aller Fälle ermöglicht wird.

Die Direktionalität eines Segmentes ist somit ein Klassifikationsmerkmal, welches die Formulierung hinreichender Bedingungen für Fälle verdeckter Öffnungen und Öffnungen mit im Endlichen liegenden Schnittpunkten erlaubt. Die Bezeichnung "verdeckte Öffnung" ist im allgemeinen jedoch eine falsche Interpretation. Es sind Ecken, die verdeckt werden und zwar diejenigen, welche die fraglichen zwei Segmente verbinden. Betrachten wir dazu die Korridorverengung in Figur 3–3 (a). Es kann aus der Sicht des Roboters nicht entschieden werden, ob eine kurze Wand oder eine Öffnung verdeckt wird. In beiden Möglichkeiten werden jedoch Ecken verdeckt, eine konkave und eine konvexe im Falle der kurzen Wand und beliebig viele im Falle der Öffnung.

Die *symbolische Beschreibung* erhält man nun dadurch, dass jeder Ecke ihr entsprechendes Zeichen aus einem Alphabet von vier Buchstaben zugeordnet wird. Das Alphabet besteht aus den Zeichen *'E'* für konvexe Ecke (edge), *'C'* für konkave Ecke (corner), *'O'* für Öffnung (opening) und *'H'* für verdeckte Ecken (hidden corners). Somit ergibt sich ein String variierender

Länge, der die Situation auf einem sehr hohen Abstraktionsniveau beschreibt. Das endgültige Klassifikationsschema, welches für jedes benachbarte Segmentpaar S_i und S_{i+1} durchlaufen wird, ist in Figur 3–4 dargestellt. Die letzte Bedingung für die Unterscheidung konkaver und konvexer Ecken bedient sich der Differenz $\Delta\alpha$, welche durch $\Delta\alpha = \alpha_{i+1} - \alpha_i$ definiert ist. In Figur 3–3 sind weitere Situation mitsamt ihrer symbolischen String-Beschreibung dargestellt.

Die *geometrische Beschreibung* besteht in den Angaben jeweils adäquater geometrischer Grössen: Aus dem vorhergehenden Schritt sind die Lage aller linienhaften Umgebungsstrukturen mitsamt ihren Endpunkten bekannt. Im Falle von konkaven und konvexen Ecken werden Eckposition und Winkel berechnet, bei Öffnungen und verdeckten Ecken bestimmt man die Richtungen, in denen sie liegen.

Damit liegt schliesslich eine Fülle von Information über die momentane Situation des Roboters vor, welche vielfältige Anwendungen eröffnet. Die Anweisung eines Explorationsalgorithmus für unbekannte und komplexe aber bedingt strukturierte Umgebungen ist die hervorstechende Einsatzmöglichkeit der symbolischen String-Beschreibung. Die Implementation einer situationsspezifische Verhaltensauswahl, welche in Abhängigkeit des vorliegenden Umgebungsausschnitts ein angemessenes Fahrverhalten auswählt oder anwendungsspezifische Sonderverhalten aktiviert, ist ebenfalls denkbar.

4. Anwendung in der Positions- und Orientierungsbestimmung mobiler Roboter

Im hier angewandten, echtzeitfähigen Lokalisierungsverfahren kommt ein Erweitertes Kalman Filter zum Einsatz. Diese Möglichkeit wird schon vielerorts verfolgt, z.B. in [LEON92]. Dort werden aus Ultraschalldaten mehrere geometrischer Primitive – Linien, Ecken und Zylinder – extrahiert, allerdings ohne Echtzeitfähigkeit zu erlangen. Dennoch bestehen aufgrund gleicher Merkmalsmodelle für die Geraden Ähnlichkeiten, insbesondere in der Beobachtungsvorhersage (measurement prediction). Auch in [VESTLI95] werden obige Landmarken gefunden, jedoch unter Einsatz von Vorwissen über ihren Ort und ihre Anzahl. Mit der Implementation der Geradenextraktion wird Echtzeitfähigkeit erreicht.

Es konnte durch eine gute Harmonisierung mit dem hier eingesetzten, unterlagerten Positionsregler für nichtholonome mobile Roboter [KAISER95] ein ansprechendes Fahrverhalten realisiert werden. Wiederum liegen Resultate für Genauigkeit und Geschwindigkeit vor: Bei stehendem Roboter mit zwei gut sichbaren Wänden rauscht die Positions- und Orientierungsschätzung in x und y mit 6 mm Standardabweichung, in θ mit guten $0.05°$. Die Spannweiten betragen 2.5 cm in x und y, $1.5°$ in θ. Bei einer kleinen Tour durch den Laborraum, wo 160 Zyklen durchlaufen wurden, lag die durchschnittliche Zykluszeit bei 445 ms. Wiederum mit der schon erwähnten Hardware eines M68020 bei 20 MHz, auf der jedoch mittels eines Echtzeitbetriebssystems alle laufenden Prozesse quasi-parallel ausgeführt wurden.

5. Zusammenfassung und Ausblick

Es wurde ein neues Verfahren zur Extraktion beliebiger modellbasierter Merkmale aus Laserscannerdaten vorgestellt, das ohne Vorwissen über die Umwelt auskommt und bei der Geradenextraktion hohe Genauigkeit und Echtzeitfähigkeit aufzeigt. Das Verfahren besitzt die Komplexität $O(n) + O(l^2)$ (n: Anzahl Messpunkte, l: Anzahl Umgebungsmerkmale). Die so gewonnenen Lageparameter der linienhaften Umgebungsstrukturen wurden in einem Kalman Filter-basierten Verfahren zur Positions- und Orientierungsbestimmung erfolgreich eingesetzt.

Ausserdem wurde eine geometrische und symbolische Situationsbeschreibung vorgestellt, die mittels der eingeführten Direktionalität eines Segmentes elegant hergeleitet werden konnte. Diese ermöglicht eine im Sinne der Topologie richtige Situationsinterpretation, mit welcher konkave und konvexe Ecken, Öffnungen, potentielle Öffnungen und Öffnungen mit im Endlichen liegenden Schnittpunkten erkannt werden können.

Bis jetzt wurde die analytische Diskussion der Fehlerfortpflanzung im Extraktionsalgorithmus ausgelassen. Den Abstandswerten des Sensors wurde volles Vertrauen zugebilligt, was zu fehlerfreien und unkorrelierten Modellparametern führte. In Wahrheit besitzen die Abstandswerte Unsicherheiten, die sich fortpflanzen und auf die Parameter einwirken. Nur das konsequente Verfolgen dieser Unsicherheit wird es erlauben unter Berücksichtigung aller zur Modellierung notwendigen statistischen Momente das adäquate Distanzmass im Parameterraum zu definieren und den jetzt noch heuristisch gefundenen Schwellwert ε herzuleiten. Im Interesse grösstmöglicher Präzision kann ausserdem unter Einbezug der Intensität des reflektierten Lichtstrahls, welches ein Mass für die Sicherheit eines jeden Messpunktes ist, ein gewichtendes least-square-fit-Verfahren ins Auge gefasst werden. Unentbehrliche Grundlage hierfür ist ein statistisches Modell, welches das Sensorrauschen genügend gut charakterisiert.

In Vorbereitung befindet sich ein darauf aufbauendes Map Building. Die Exploration soll unter Ausnutzung der symbolischen Strings arbeiten. Die geometrische Beschreibung eröffnet zudem die Möglichkeit der autonomen Konstruktion eines Graphen.

Die Erkennung von Türen und Behandlung von "cluttered areas" ist Voraussetzung für ein allgemeines Map Building und muss angegangen werden. Dies wurde bis jetzt ausgeklammert, weil dabei zwangsläufig auf der Ebene der Rohdaten gearbeitet werden muss und robotergeometrieabhängige Gesichtspunkte ins Spiel kommen. In diesem Sinne bildet das hier vorgestellte Verfahren zur Situationsbeschreibung eine geschlossene Einheit.

Literaturverzeichnis

[ARRAS96]   Arras K.O., *"Map Building"*, Diplomarbeit am Institut für Robotik, ETH Zürich, 1996.

[HARTIG75]   Hartigan J.A., *"Clustering Algorithms"*, Wiley, New York, 1975.

[KAISER95]   Kaiser O., Pfiffner R., Vestli S.J., Astolfi A., *"Positionsregelung für nichtholonome mobile Roboter"*, 11. Fachgespräche Autonome Mobile Systeme, Karlsruhe, Deutschland, Nov. 1995.

[KANA89]   Kanayama Y., *"Spatial Learning by an Autonomous Mobile Robot with Ultrasonic Sensors"*, Technical Report of the University of California at Santa Barbara, Departement of Computer Science, TRCS89-06, February 1989.

[KUIPERS88]   Kuipers B.J., Byun Y.T., *"A Robust, Qualitative Approach to a Spatial Learning Mobile Robot"*, Proc. of the SPIE, Sensor Fusion: Spatial Reasoning and Scene Interpretation, Vol. 1003, 1988.

[LEON92]   Leonard J.J., Durrant-Whyte H.F., *"Directed Sonar Sensing for Mobile Robot Navigation"*, Kluwer Academic Publishers, 1992.

[SPÄTH83]   Späth H., *"Cluster-Formation und -Analyse"*, R. Oldenburg Verlag, 1983.

[VESTLI95]   Vestli S.J., *"Fast, accurate and robust estimation of mobile robot position and orientation"*, Doctoral Thesis Nr. 11360, ETH Zürich, 1995.

Die sehende Laufkatze als Autonomiebaustein moderner Containerkranbrücken

J. Hansemann, P. Kohlhepp, H. Haffner
Forschungszentrum Karlsruhe
Institut für Angewandte Informatik, Abteilung Industrielle Handhabungssysteme
D-76021 Karlsruhe
E-mail: kohlhepp@iai.fzk.de

Die Verladung von Containern mit großen Kranbrücken auf Containerschiffe oder landseitig auf Fahrzeuge wird zunehmend automatisiert. Eine dabei noch nicht gelöste Aufgabe ist die Feinpositionierung auf dem "letzten Meter". Dieser Beitrag beschreibt ein echtzeitfähiges Sensorsystem, das für diese Aufgabe entwickelt wird. Es basiert auf Laserabstandssensoren, die an der Laufkatze montiert werden und Sequenzen von 2D-Abstandsprofilen liefern. Mit Methoden der Entfernungsbildverarbeitung werden aus den Profilen charakteristische Hinweise auf Kantenpunkte der Objekte unterhalb der Laufkatze extrahiert, deren Akkumulation Container- und Greiferkanten ergibt. Die Verschmelzung der Informationen vieler Einzelprofile liefert schritthaltend die Position des Greifers, des Zielcontainers und das aktuelle Ladeprofil. In der gegenwärtigen Ausbaustufe des Systems ist damit unter anderem die visuelle Unterstützung des Kranführers möglich.

1 Einleitung

Aufgrund der stetig ansteigenden Umschlagszahlen in vielen großen Seehäfenterminals wird die Verladung von Containern mit Kranbrücken zunehmend automatisiert [1]. Bestimmte Arbeitsvorgänge, wie das Einfädeln eines Containers in die Ladebucht eines Schiffes oder das Absetzen auf einem Fahrzeug, bleiben davon ausgenommen. Gerade sie stellen besonders hohe Ansprüche an die Konzentrationsfähigkeit und Geschicklichkeit des Kranführers, der die Vorgänge aus 30-40m Höhe einsehen muß. Die Automatisierung dieses „letzten Meters", die auch der Vermeidung ermüdungsbedingter Unfälle dient, ist bisher durch große Unterschiede in den Fahrzeug- und Schiffskonstruktionen verhindert worden.

In diesem Beitrag wird ein Kransensorsystem vorgestellt, das die Objekte auf dem letzten Meter mit Hilfe von Lasersensoren und Entfernungsbildauswertung erkennen und lokalisieren soll. Es handelt sich um folgende Informationen:
- 3-D-Position und Schwingwinkel des Krangreifers ('Spreader')
- 3-D-Position des aktuellen Transportzieles (Zellgerüst und Einweiser einer Ladebucht auf dem Schiff, Zielcontainer, Fahrzeug(e) auf dem Kai)
- Datenbasis der 3-D Container-Eckpositionen innerhalb einer Ladebucht (Lade-Istprofil).

Im Betrieb kommen geschlossene sowie offene Container, verschiedene Greifer-, Schiffs- und Fahrzeugkonstruktionen (LKW-Chassis oder autonomes Fahrzeug), sowie unterschiedliche Licht- und Wetterverhältnisse (helles Sonnenlicht oder Nacht, Regen, Nebel) vor.

Dieses System, das am Institut für Angewandte Informatik des Forschungszentrums Karlsruhe im Rahmen eines Technologietransfer-Projektes gemeinsam mit dem Sensorhersteller IBEO, Hamburg, entwickelt wird, läßt sich zur visuellen Unterstützung des Kranführers auf dem letzten Meter einsetzen, aber auch in eine automatische Kransteuerung integrieren, um die Positionsregelung mit Zielkoordinaten oder die Anti-Schwingregelung mit Greiferpositionen und -winkeln zu versorgen. Die Logistik-Komponente wird durch den Vergleich zwischen Soll- und Ist-Profil unterstützt.

2 Merkmale des Lösungskonzeptes

Das System basiert auf mehreren Lasersensoren, die, an der Laufkatze des Containerkrans oberhalb des Greifers montiert, dessen Außenkanten sowie einen Teil seiner Umgebung ständig im Blick haben (Abb. 1). Der gewählte Ansatz unterscheidet sich von anderen darin, daß die Objekte unter der Laufkatze in ihrer 3-D Raumlage mit einer Genauigkeit erkannt werden, die ein automatisches Feinpositionieren ermöglicht und im Bereich der Auflösung bzw. Meßgenauigkeit der Sensoren liegt (ca. ±10mm). Dies gelingt ohne aufwendige Verarbeitung von 2.5-D oder 3-D-Entfernungsbildern, sondern durch schritthaltende Profilfolgenauswertung in Echtzeit, wobei die Redundanz der Informationen bei der Verschmelzung der einzelnen 1.5-D Höhenprofile ausgenutzt wird [2].

Bisherige Kransensorsysteme beschränken sich meist auf die Höhenmessung von Containerstapeln mit Hilfe von 1-D oder 2-D Entfernungssensoren, die an der Laufkatze oder am Spreader montiert sind [1][3]. Eine exakte Positionierung der Containerecken und -fußpunkte in den 3 Raumkoordinaten x, y, z ist damit ebensowenig möglich wie die Erkennung offener Container oder Einweiser. Videokameras zur Detektion der Containerfußpunkte, die -um freie Sicht zu haben- am Spreader selbst montiert sind, sind den mechanischen Erschütterungen und variablen Lichtverhältnissen ausgesetzt und daher nicht ausreichend robust für den industriellen Einsatz. Außerdem erweist sich das Fehlen eines festen Bezugspunktes am schwingenden Spreader als ungeeignet zur

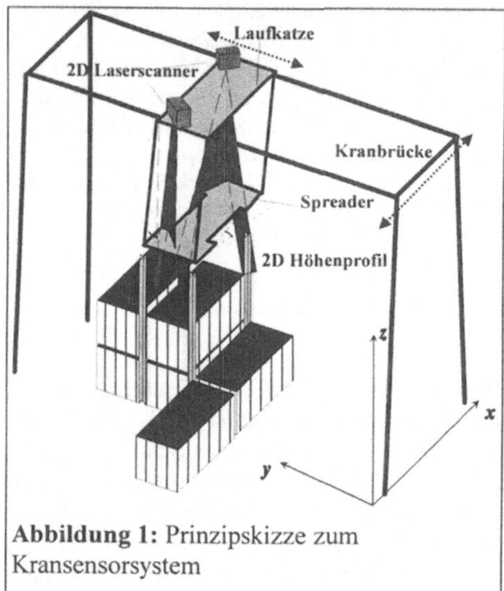

Abbildung 1: Prinzipskizze zum Kransensorsystem

Erstellung des Umgebungsmodells. Elektronische Pendeldämpfungsregelungen [4] verwenden zur Positions- und Winkelmessung des Spreaders die interne Sensorik (Winkel-Encoder, ggf. auch Beschleunigungssensoren) und können von einer genaueren, optischen Messung ebenfalls profitieren.

3 Systemaufbau und Sensorik

3.1 Laserabstandssensoren

Es handelt sich um hochauflösende, augensichere Laserradar-Sensoren (LADAR), die nach der „time of flight"-Methode arbeiten [5]. Dabei werden kurze (Infrarot-)Laserpulse abgesendet, welche diffus an den zu vermessenen Objekten reflektiert werden. Durch Ablenken der Laserpulse mit einem rotierenden Spiegel oder Prisma wird ein 2D-Höhenprofil der Umgebung in Polarkoordinaten abgetastet. Der Meßbereich der hier verwendeten Sensoren liegt zwischen ca. 3m und 40m, der Sektorwinkel reicht von -7.5° bis 7.5°, bezogen auf die optische Achse. Je nach verwendetem Sensortyp werden 8 oder 20 Profile pro Sekunde aufgenommen, wobei sich ein Profil aus bis zu ca. 240 Meßpunkten zusammensetzt. Das bedeutet eine Winkelauflösung von 0.06°. Die Vorteile der Meßmethode liegen in der Echtzeitfähigkeit und der weitgehenden Unabhängigkeit von der Beleuchtung. Einschränkungen ergeben sich durch das mögliche Auftreffen von Pulsen auf metallisch-spiegelnde oder auf stark absorbierende Oberflächen [6]. Im ersten Fall wird das Licht weggebrochen und die Reflektion von einem anderen Objektpunkt führt zu einem längeren optischen Weg des Pulses, im zweiten Fall reicht die Intensität des reflektierten Lichtes unter Umständen nicht für ein notwendiges Signal-Rauschverhältnis aus [6]. In der Praxis wirken sich diese Effekte kaum störend aus. Eine entsprechende Vorverarbeitung sorgt für das Eliminieren dieser Meßpunkte.

3.2 Kranteststand

Zum Entwickeln und Testen des Sensorsystems wurde ein Teststand aufgebaut, der die wichtigsten Komponenten eines realen Containerkrans im Größenverhältnis 1:10 abbildet. Der Arbeitsraum ist in Ladebuchten (Bays) eingeteilt, die durch Zellführungen mit Einweisern begrenzt sind (Abb. 2). Kern der Anlage ist ein Portalroboter, der die Kranbrücke nachbildet. Der am Portal entlangfahrende Wagen entspricht der Laufkatze. An 4 Seilen wurde eine schwingende Plattform zum Greifen der Container befestigt. Der Wagen mit den Sensoren und die Plattform sind synchron ausziehbar und damit an die Containerlänge anpaßbar. Ein Hubwerk sowie Haltemagnete erlauben das Verladen von (Styropor-)Containern, in die zusätzlich Eckbeschläge mit Container-Fußpunkten eingelassen sind. Die Sensoren sind an einer Längsseite der Laufkatze oberhalb des Greifers montiert; die Scanrichtungen bilden einen Winkel von 45° bzw. 135° zur Portalfahrtrichtung, um sowohl die Quer- als auch die Längskanten der Container vermessen zu können (Abb. 3). Die Abstände der Sensoren zu den Containern betragen 2-3m.

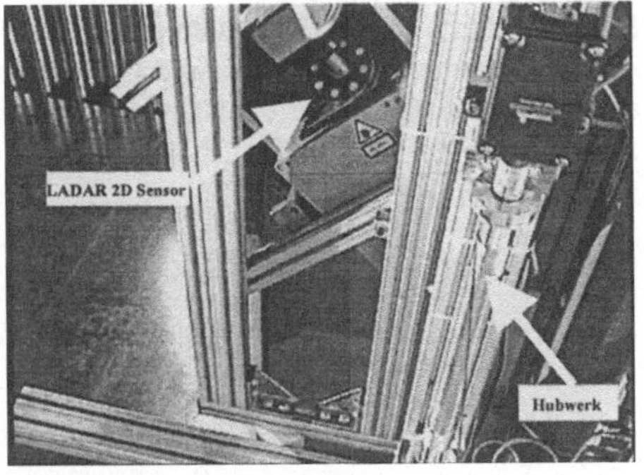

Abbildung 2: Testaufbau zur Containerverladung

Abbildung 3: Sensoranordnung am Kranteststand

3.3 Hardware
Die gesamte Steuerung und die Anwendungs-SW des Teststands sind auf einem Transputernetz (T805-TRAMs) realisiert, das über RS422-Schnittstellen mit den in den Sensoren integrierten Transputern kommuniziert. Es werden ausschließlich Standard-HW-Komponenten verwendet; die HW-Konfiguration ist modular und entsprechend der benötigten Rechnerleistung leicht skalierbar. Die Kommunikationstopologie wird per Software konfiguriert.

4 Sensordatenverarbeitung

Die Prozesse von der Vorverarbeitung bis zur graphischen Visualisierung werden jeweils auf einen Transputer abgebildet und bilden eine Pipeline, um die schritthaltende Verarbeitung der Sensorprofile zu erreichen (Abb. 4).

4.1 Einzelprofil-Verarbeitung

Der Prozeß zur Profilaufnahme übernimmt bereits die Umrechnung von Polarkoordinaten in sensorlokale kartesische Koordinaten. Die Vorverarbeitung beginnt mit der Medianfilterung (Fensterbreite 5 oder 7) der Meßpunkt-Koordinaten. Dadurch wird eine kantenerhaltende Glättung der verrauschten Profile erreicht und durch metallische Reflektionen verursachte Fehlmessungen werden „unschädlich" gemacht.

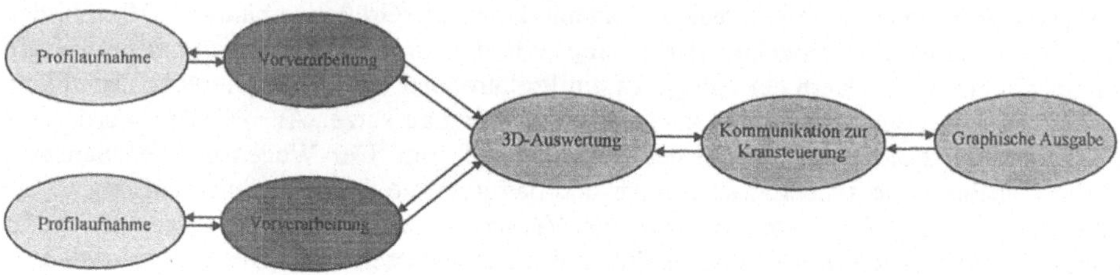

Abbildung 4: Pipeline der Prozesse zur Profilauswertung

Um stark verrauschte Profile zu verbessern, können aufeinanderfolgende Profile auch zeitlich gemittelt werden. Dies ist aber nur dann sinnvoll, wenn die Laufkatze und damit die Sensoren annähernd im Stillstand sind.

Die Profildaten (bis zu 500 Meßpunkte) werden nach Median-Filterung zu einem Polygonzug mit signifikanten Eckpunkten und Geradenstücken reduziert, wobei sowohl die Punktanzahl als auch die Approximationsgüte zur Laufzeit steuerbar sind (Abbildung. 5). Dazu wird ein „split-and-merge"-Algorithmus eingesetzt [7].

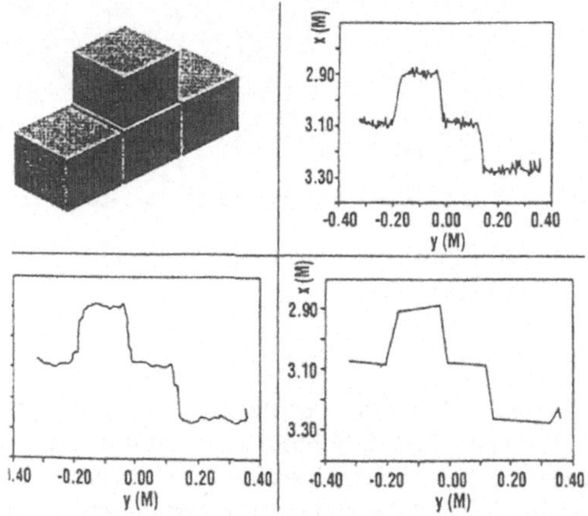

Abbildung 5: V.l.o.n.r.u graphisch dargestellte Testszene, Profil mit Originaldaten, gleiches Profil nach Medianfilterung und nach Polygonapproximation

Daran schließen sich eine Darstellung des Knickwinkels als Funktion der Bogenlänge (ψ(s)-Funktion [8]) und eine symbolische Beschreibung an. Diese charakterisiert für je zwei aufeinanderfolgende Stützpunkte des reduzierten Polygons die verbindende Kante qualitativ als

- *solide* ('**S**'), wenn zwischen beiden Stützpunkten im Rohdatenprofil ausreichend viele und ausreichend dicht liegende Meßpunkte vorhanden sind, andernfalls *transparent* ('**T**')
- annähernd *horizontal* ('_'), *vertikal* ('|'), *steigend* ('/') oder *fallend* ('\'), bezogen auf das Bodenniveau und unter Berücksichtigung der jeweiligen Scanrichtung

- zu einer Objektoberfläche gehörig (*Konturkante* '**C**'), oder *Sprungkante* ('**J**'), die zwei Objekte, von denen eines das andere verdeckt, durch einen Entfernungssprung verbindet (eine Sprungkante ist eine transparente Kante annähernd parallel zur Sensorblickrichtung)

Vor allem die Profilpunkte, die eine Sprungkante mit einer annähernd horizontalen Kante im Profil verbinden, liefern erste Hinweise auf Container- bzw. Spreaderkantenpunkte (*Kandidaten*). Solide, horizontale Konturkanten werden zusätzlich durch ihr *Niveau*, d.h. ihren Abstand vom Grund gekennzeichnet. Zwei Container auf beliebigen Niveaus, getrennt durch eine schmale Lücke, wären damit zum Beispiel durch folgende Kantenbeschreibungen erkennbar:**C_ J\ C| C_** oder **C_ C| J/ C_** oder **C_ J\ J/ C_**.

4.2 Greifererkennung

Da in jedem Zeitschritt (Profil) die aktuelle Greiferposition zu bestimmen ist, wird als erstes dessen Teilprofil von den übrigen Objekten separiert, wobei die Greifergeometrie a priori unbekannt ist. Um den Schwingwinkel berechnen zu können, muß zuerst eine *Referenzmessung* in schwingungsfreier Ruhelage erfolgen. Dabei kann o.B.d.A. angenommen werden, daß der Greifer das den Sensoren am nächsten liegende Objekt ist (dies gilt im Meßbetrieb i.a. nicht!), daß also die Trennung von Objekt und Hintergrund hier trivial wird.

Zur Laufzeit wird die in Ruhelage abgespeicherte $\psi(s)$-Funktion des Greifers in der $\psi(s)$-Funktion des aktuellen Profils wiedererkannt und lokalisiert. Die $\psi(s)$-matching-Methode eignet sich im Prinzip auch für komplexe Greifergeometrien, aber nur wenn es sich um 2-D-Konturen in einer Ebene handelt. Im allgemeinen überlagern sich Längs- und Querpendeln und Torsion, und der Sensor sieht je nach Schwingungslage des Greifers verschiedenartige Schnittprofile (z.B. Rollen, Aufbauten); es mangelt an invarianten Merkmalen. Zuverlässigere Ergebnisse erhalten wir, indem wir den Greifer innerhalb eines engen Suchbereiches verfolgen (region-of-interest), kombiniert mit einer Analyse der Niveaus der Objektkanten.

1. Wurde der Greifer im i-ten Profil erkannt - für i=0 (Referenzmessung) ist das sicher der Fall - so ergibt sich als Suchbereich für das i+1-te Profil die Bounding Box des i-ten Teilprofils, vergrößert um den maximalen Weg Δx, Δy, Δz, den der Greifer aufgrund der Hubgeschwindigkeit und der Pendelgesetze zwischen zwei Profilen zurücklegen kann. Die Auswertung erfolgt in einem mit der Laufkatze verknüpften Koordinatensystem, d.h. die Bewegung der Katze selbst und der Kranbrücke sind dafür unerheblich. Ist die Hubhöhe als Signal von der Kransteuerung verfügbar, so erhält man noch schärfere Grenzen.
2. Die Niveaus der annähernd horizontalen Konturkanten werden miteinander verglichen. Für jede solche Konturkante wird die Summe der Niveaudifferenzen modulo der Containerhöhe h zu allen anderen Horizontalniveaus bestimmt. Diese Summe wird in der Regel für den Greifer maximal, es sei denn, dessen Oberseite befindet sich exakt auf einem Containerniveau. Dazu sollten Containerniveaus aus früheren Profilen bereits bekannt sein, und die Container einer Ladebucht gleiche Höhe haben. Wegen dieser Einschränkungen kann das Niveaukriterium nur zusammen mit 1. angewandt werden.

Die Extraktion der Spreader-Teilprofile beider Sensoren liefert bei der gewählten Sensoranordnung i.d.R. zwei Kantenpunkte auf einer Längs-Außenseite des Spreaders und je einen Punkt auf beiden Querseiten. Durch Zuordnung zur bekannten Ruhelage ergeben sich
- die 3-D Raumkoordinaten der 4 Spreaderecken
- der Torsionswinkel in der x-/y-Ebene
- ggf. die Neigungswinkel der Plattform in der y-/z- und in der x-/z-Ebene.

Der Auslenkungswinkel der Seile in der y-/z-Ebene kann aus den Differenzen der Eckpositionen ebenfalls ermittelt werden, wenn der Drehpunkt bekannt ist, z.B. durch zwei definierte, verschiedene Auslenkungen aus der Ruhelage im Rahmen der Referenzmessung.

4.3 Containererkennung und -lokalisierung

Die nach Abzug der Greifer- und ggf. Zellgerüst-Anteile verbleibenden Teilprofile zeigen wegen des schmalen Sektorwinkels in der Regel nur partiell verdeckte Teilansichten der Zielobjekte (Container, Fahrzeug). Somit können anhand von Einzelprofilen keine Aussagen über die Abmessungen der Objektkanten getroffen werden. Verfahren zum Wiedererkennen von Objektkonturen wie das $\psi(s)$-Verfahren [8] versagen an dieser Stelle. Deshalb werden die Containerkantenpunkt-Kandidaten aus aufeinanderfolgenden Profilen gesammelt, um die Teilansichten zu verschmelzen. Abb. 6 zeigt einen solchen Kandidaten, der auf Niveau N1 (Containerniveau 1) liegt. Nach der Transformation der Kandidaten in das Kran- bzw. Weltkoordinatensystem werden diese klassifiziert. Für jeden Sensor gibt es 6 Möglichkeiten (p11...p16, p21...p26), einen einzelnen Container zu erfassen (Abb. 7), davon sind jeweils 4 relevant für die Detektion von Containerkantenpunkten. Abb. 6 zeigt als Beispiel das Profil p12 (Sensor1) in Seitenansicht. Unter Berücksichtigung der Scanrichtung liegt der Kandidat *nach* einer horizontalen Kante und *vor* einer verdeckenden Sprungkante. Damit gehört er zur Klasse CL5 und zur linken Längskante des Containers in Abb. 7.

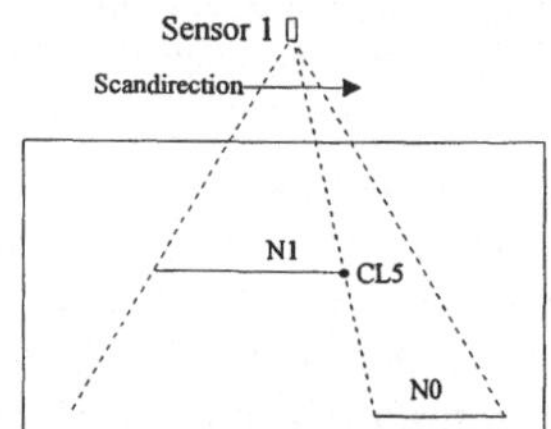

Abbildung 6: Einzelprofil mit Containerkantenpunkt-Kandidat

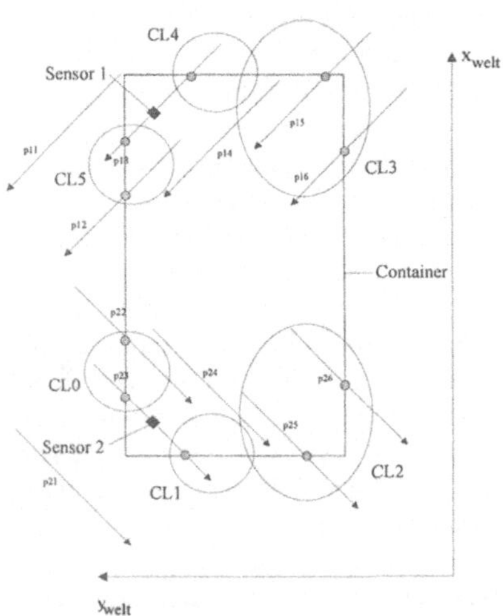

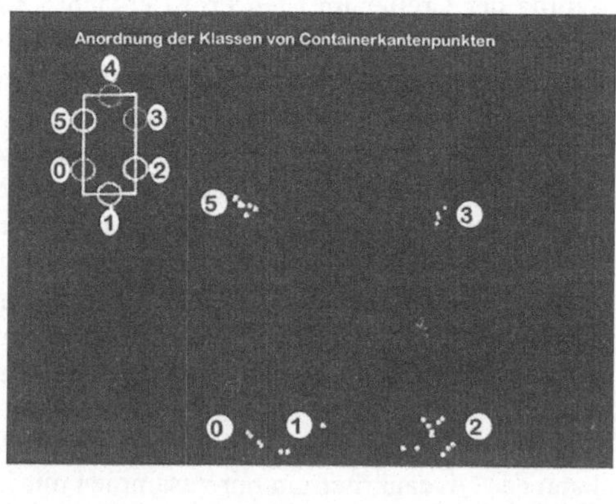

Abbildung 7: Profile mit Containerkantenpunkten und deren Klassen in Aufsicht

Abbildung 8: Containerkanten und zugeordnete Cluster mit gemessenen Kantenpunkten

Allgemein entspricht ein Containerkantenpunkt immer einem der beiden folgenden Ereignisse in der symbolischen Beschreibung:

C^a-Container"anfang"   **J/C_** $\vee$ **C|C_**   steigende Sprungkante oder vertikale Konturkante gefolgt von horizontaler Konturkante

C^e-Container"ende"   **C_J** $\vee$ **C_C|**   horizontale Konturkante gefolgt von fallender Sprungkante oder vertikaler Konturkante

wobei die an C^a, C^e beteiligten Konturkanten zu Containern, also weder zum Greifer noch zum Zellgerüst oder Fahrzeug gehören. Die Kantenpunkte müssen nun den *Containerpositionen*

$Bay_{i,j,s}$ *(i*:Ladebucht, *j*:Reihe,

$s \in \{o,u,l,r\}$ Seite, wobei *o[u]* die *obere[untere]* Querseite, *l[r]* die *linke[rechte]* Längsseite des Containers gemäß Abb. 7 bezeichnen)

korrekt zugeordnet werden. Bei unserer Sensoranordnung und der aufgrund des Sektorwinkels maximal möglichen Überdeckung sind die Zuordnungsmöglichkeiten stark eingeschränkt. Befindet sich der Greifer "logisch" bereits in der Ladebucht Nr. i (Reihe beliebig), und folgt im aktuellen Profil ein Container-Ende C^e direkt auf einen Anfang C^a (dies entspricht dem Profiltyp p13 für Sensor 1 und p23 für Sensor 2 in Abb. 7; zwischen C^a und C^e können sich aber Greiferkanten befinden), so handelt es sich um denselben Container, und dieser gehört entweder zur aktuellen Bay oder einer der Nachbar-Bays i+1 bzw. i-1. Handelt es sich hingegen um einzelne Ereignisse C^a oder C^e aktuellen Profil, so gibt es weitere Alternativen. Folgende Tabelle zeigt alle Zuordnungsmöglichkeiten für beide Sensoren.

Kantenpunkt	*Zuordnung für Sensor 1*	*Zuordnung für Sensor 2*
C^a, C^e kombiniert	$C^a \to Bay_{i,*,o} \wedge C^e \to Bay_{i,*,l} \vee$ $C^a \to Bay_{i+1,*,r} \wedge C^e \to Bay_{i+1,*,u}$	$C^a \to Bay_{i,*,l} \wedge C^e \to Bay_{i,*,u} \vee$ $C^a \to Bay_{i-1,*,o} \wedge C^e \to Bay_{i-1,*,r}$
C^a	$C^a \to Bay_{i,*,o} \vee Bay_{i,*,r} \vee Bay_{i+1,*,r}$	$C^a \to Bay_{i,*,l} \vee Bay_{i-1,*,l} \vee Bay_{i-1,*,o}$
C^e	$C^e \to Bay_{i,*,l} \vee Bay_{i+1,*,l} \vee Bay_{i+1,*,u}$	$C^e \to Bay_{i,*,u} \vee Bay_{i,*,r} \vee Bay_{i-1,*,r}$

Eine genaue Zuordnung, insbesondere die Bestimmung der durch (*) symbolisierten Reihennummer, erfordert die Koordinatenwerte und ihre geometrischen Beziehungen ((x,y,z) seien die Weltkoordinaten des Kantenpunktes, ($X_{i,j,s}$, $Y_{i,j,s}$, $Z_{i,j,s}$) die berechneten Container- bzw. Seitenposition zu $Bay_{i,j,s}$, und ε_x, ε_y, ε_z Toleranzwerte in der Größenordnung der Meßfehler bzw. der horizontalen Auflösung der Sensoren):

$$C \to Bay_{i,j,l} \Leftrightarrow \min_{k,m}\left|Y_{k,m,l} - y\right| = \left|Y_{i,j,l} - y\right| \le \varepsilon_y \wedge \left|Z_{i,j,l} - z\right| \le \varepsilon_z$$

$$C \to Bay_{i,j,r} \Leftrightarrow \min_{k,m}\left|Y_{k,m,r} - y\right| = \left|Y_{i,j,r} - y\right| \le \varepsilon_y \wedge \left|Z_{i,j,r} - z\right| \le \varepsilon_z$$

$$C \to Bay_{i,j,u} \Leftrightarrow \min_{k,m}\left|X_{k,m,u} - x\right| = \left|X_{i,j,u} - x\right| \le \varepsilon_x \wedge \left|Z_{i,j,u} - z\right| \le \varepsilon_z$$

$$C \to Bay_{i,j,o} \Leftrightarrow \min_{k,m}\left|X_{k,m,o} - x\right| = \left|X_{i,j,o} - x\right| \le \varepsilon_x \wedge \left|Z_{i,j,o} - z\right| \le \varepsilon_z$$

Für alle diese Positionen $Bay_{i,j,s}$ werden genügend viele Kandidaten akkumuliert (in Abb. 8 ist das Ergebnis für einen einzelnen Container dargestellt), und die Seiten werden durch iterative Ausgleichsrechnung immer genauer bestimmt. Die dabei aktualisierten Positionskoordinaten müssen stets folgende Konsistenzbedingungen einhalten (L Containerlänge, ΔL max. Bay-Abstand, B Containerbreite, ΔB max. Reihenabstand, $s \neq s'$ Seiten):

$$\left|X_{i,j,u} - X_{i,j,o} - L\right| \le \varepsilon_x \qquad X_{i,j,o} \le X_{i,j+1,u} \le X_{i,j,o} + \Delta L$$

$$\left|Y_{i,j,l} - Y_{i,j,r} - B\right| \le \varepsilon_y \qquad Y_{i,j,r} \le Y_{i,j-1,l} \le Y_{i,j,r} + \Delta B$$

$$\left|Z_{i,j,s} - Z_{i,j,s'}\right| \le \varepsilon_z .$$

Bei der Erkennung spielt die Sicherheit eine entscheidende Rolle: wird - aus welchen Gründen auch immer - ein Zielobjekt (Container, Einweiser) nicht zweifelsfrei erkannt, oder treten unerwartete bzw. nicht identifizierbare Objekte im Nahbereich des Greifers auf, wird ein Alarmsignal an die Kransteuerung ausgelöst und der manuelle Betrieb eingeleitet.

4.4 Lade-Ist-Profil

Das Lade-Istprofil eines Containerstapels auf einem Schiff oder -analog- auf dem Land umfaßt folgende Informationen:
- Anzahl der Ladebuchten (Bays)
- Für jede Ladebucht
    - Containerlänge (20'/40'/45'/48')
    - Nr. bzw. Position der ersten Containerreihe, Anzahl der beladenen Reihen
    - Für jede Reihe:
        - Nr. bzw. Position der untersten Lage, Anzahl der Lagen Container
        - Containerhöhe
        - die 4 Eckpositionen des obersten Containers (x,y,z)
        - Einweiserpositionen

Mit der Erst- oder Neuberechnung einer Containerposition geht die ständige Aktualisierung des Lade-Ist-Profils einher. Neben den Zu- und Abgängen von Containern werden auch Drift und Tidenhub des Schiffes berücksichtigt. Methodisch besteht eine starke Analogie zwischen dem Lade-Ist-Profil, das die Laufkatze durch schritthaltende Verschmelzung von Höhenprofilen aufbaut, und einer Landkarte, die ein mit Ultraschall- oder Lasersensorik ausgerüstetes autonomes Fahrzeug (AMS) aus Horizontalprofilen seiner Umgebung gewinnt [9]. In unserem Fall dient die „Landkarte" dazu, die Zielobjekte anzusteuern. Im Fall des AMS hat sie zum Ziel, mittels externer Sensorik die eigene Fahrzeugposition exakt zu bestimmen (Kompensation der durch die Odometrie verursachten Drift). Während ein AMS auch den Fahrkurs und die Geschwindigkeit der Explorationsfahrt im Sinne einer optimalen Datengewinnung „autonom" gestalten kann, sind diese Parameter im Umschlagsbetrieb vom Kranfahrer, bzw. von der Logistik durch die Reihenfolge der Be- und Entladevorgänge, im wesentlichen vorgegeben.

4.5 Kalibrierung und Referenzmessung

Wie bereits in Kap. 4.2 erwähnt, erfolgt vor dem eigentlichen Meßbetrieb eine Referenzmessung des Containergreifers in schwingungsfreier Ruhelage, wobei auch dessen Drehpunkt bestimmt wird. Diese Messung hat ferner den Zweck, die Sensoren zu kalibrieren, d.h. die Lage der beiden sensorlokalen 2-D-Koordinatensysteme in Bezug auf das KS der Laufkatze zu bestimmen. Die Konturen der Fahrzeuge zum Beladen (autonomes Fahrzeug, LKW-Chassis) werden ebenfalls durch eine Referenzmessung bekannt gemacht.
Vor dem ersten Beladen einer Bay eines Containerschiffes erfolgt eine Einmeßfahrt. Damit werden reihenweise die Positionen der Einweiser und der untersten Beladepositionen im Schiffsrumpf (Schachtboden) festgelegt.
Für den Spreader, die Einweiser und Container muß ferner eine eindeutige Korrespondenz der Weltkoordinaten, wie sie anhand eines charakteristischen Merkmals vom Sensor gesehen werden, zu den Koordinaten der Kransteuerung hergestellt werden, um das jeweilige Objekt anzufahren. Dazu genügt es z.B., einen beliebigen Container manuell zu greifen und nach Schließen der Twistlocks die Kran-, Katz- und Hubkoordinaten zusammen mit der sensoriell gemessenen Eckposition des Containers und des Spreaders zu notieren, um die Verschiebungsvektoren zu erhalten.

Hervorzuheben ist, daß die Kalibrierung keine externen Meßsysteme zur Vermessung von Krankomponenten oder gar CAD-Zeichnungen erfordert.

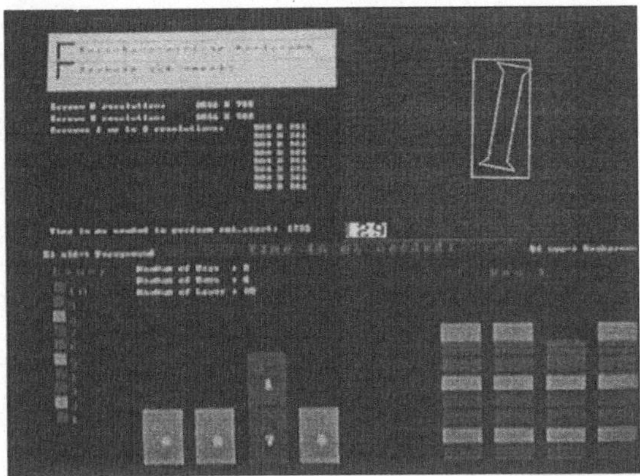

Abbildung 9: Visualisierung der Greiferlage relativ zum Ziel in der Aufsicht (oben rechts), Lade-Ist-Profil (unten)

5 Ergebnisse und Bewertung

Die Verfolgung des Greifers in Echtzeit und seine Visualisierung relativ zur gewünschten Zielposition zur Unterstützung des Kranfahrers wurde als erste Teilaufgabe realisiert. Dazu wurde ein spezielles Transputer-Grafik-Board eingesetzt. Die Zeitdifferenz zwischen der Aufnahme eines Profils und der resultierenden Aktualisierung der graphischen Darstellung liegt bei ca. 0.25 Sekunden und ist damit geeignet, den Kranführer visuell zu unterstützen. Abb. 9 zeigt den Greiferumriß in der x-/y-Ebene relativ zu einem rechteckig dargestellten Zielbereich. Drohende Kollisionsgefahr oder zu große Pendel-Amplitude signalisiert das System durch eine spezielle Warndarstellung.

Mit den oben beschriebenen Verfahren wurde die Position von Styropor-Containern mit den Abmessungen 1660*300*450 (L*B*H in [mm]) vermessen und die Meßgenauigkeit untersucht. Die exakte Position war durch eine vorausgegangene Referenzfahrt bekannt. Es wurden dabei Sensoren mit einer Winkelauflösung von 0.6° statt 0.06° verwendet. Die Winkelauflösung entscheidet, wie groß der Abstand zwischen dem „detektierten Randpunkt" auf der Containeroberfläche und dem tatsächlichen Kantenpunkt maximal sein kann. Da an einem realen Kran wegen der um Faktor 10 größeren Abstände zwei benachbarte Meßpunkte einen entsprechend größeren Abstand haben, werden durch die schlechtere Winkelauflösung die realen Verhältnisse gut simuliert (Abstand der Meßpunkte $\cong$2.5cm).

Es wurden in einer Meßreihe 15 Meßfahrten durchgeführt. Die Standardabweichung der Meßwerte für einzelne Containerkanten betrug dabei σ_n = 12.8 mm, der Mittelwert wich um 2.5 mm vom Sollwert ab.

Die Vermessung des Spreaders lieferte im Vergleich dazu schlechtere Ergebnisse. Das liegt daran, daß die Meßpunkte wegen der Spreaderbewegungen maximal über ca. 3 Profile gemittelt werden können und somit das Rauschen einen stärkeren Einfluß auf die Meßergebnisse hat. Der durchschnittliche Meßfehler für die Längenmessung des Spreaders betrug 5%. Bei einer Spreaderlänge von 1660 mm entspricht dies 83 mm.

Die zu vermessenden Objekte in realer Umgebung weisen größere Abmessungen auf als an unserem Teststand. Sie liegen auch in einem günstigeren Meßbereich, da die Entfernungen am Teststand mit knapp unter 3m den Grenzbereich für die verwendeten Sensoren markieren. Dadurch wird die Extraktion von Kantenpunkten in realer Umgebung begünstigt.

Ein offener Punkt beim Sensorentwurf ist die optimale Auslegung der Parameter: Scanrate R, Winkelbereich Θ, und Winkelauflösung $\Delta\theta$ im Hinblick auf die Meßaufgabe im Container-Terminal. Zwischen diesen Parametern besteht ein Zielkonflikt. Geht man von einer durch den Echtzeiteinsatz vorgegebenen Profilrate (z.B. 20 Hz) aus, so gilt: $R\sim\Theta/\Delta\theta$. Die Scanrate R zu vergrößern bedeutet, größere Abstandsfehler für den einzelnen Meßpunkt in Kauf zu nehmen. Die Filterung und Datenreduktion kann dann nicht mehr alle Störungen eliminieren, und es kommt zu falsch detektierten Kantenpunkten. Bei zu kleinem Blickfeld (Sektorwinkel Θ) ist keine ausreichende Überdeckung bzw. Redundanz der Teilprofile gewährleistet. Kleine Strukturen wie Einweiser sind dann nicht mehr sichtbar; die Container werden zu stark durch den Spreader verdeckt oder der Spreader liegt schon bei kleinen Schwingwinkeln außerhalb des Blickfeldes. Bei zu grober Auflösung $\Delta\theta$ schließlich werden die Lücken zwischen Containern bzw. zwischen Containern und Zellgerüst nicht detektiert. Andere Meßverfahren (Triangulation, Lichtschnittverfahren) bilden beim momentanen Stand der Technik auch keine Alternative; sie erreichen zwar weit höhere Scanraten, aber bei vertretbaren Kosten und Augensicherheit nicht annähernd die erforderliche Reichweite von 30-40m.

6 Ausblick

Um auch offene Container wie zum Beispiel Tankcontainer zu erkennen, ist es notwendig, die Containerfußpunkte an den Ecken der Container zu erkennen. Dies stellt besonders harte Anforderungen an die Winkelauflösung. Aber die Fußpunkte stellen nun einmal das *allen* Containerarten gemeinsame Merkmal dar.

Durch Verwendung von insgesamt 4 statt 2 Sensoren in anderer Anordnung soll zukünftig die Verdeckung der Container durch den Spreader verringert und die Meßgenauigkeit erhöht werden. Das Prinzip der 2D-Profilauswertung wird dabei in nächster Zukunft beibehalten werden. Die in der „dritten Dimension" (Bewegung der Laufkatze) erzielte Auflösung paßt sich automatisch den Anforderungen an: beim Überfahren einer Ladebucht mit hoher Geschwindigkeit ist die Auflösung ausreichend, um ein Lade-Ist-Profil zu erstellen, beim Einfädeln eines Containers ist die Geschwindigkeit der Laufkatze sehr niedrig und damit die Auflösung hoch genug, um Einweiser oder Fußpunkte zu erkennen.

7 Literatur

[1] A. Kleinschnittger: *Stufen der Automatisierung bei Brückenkranen*, Fördern und Heben 1(10), 1991, S. 824-825

[2] P.Kohlhepp, H.Haffner, J.Hansemann, J.Koprek: *Einsatz von Entfernungssensoren zur Vermessung und Erkennung dreidimensionaler Objekte*, KfK-Nachrichten 26(4), 1994, S.251-262

[3] J.Banks: *Hands off handling*, Cargo Systems, Juni 1991, S. 53-55

[4] C.D.R. Ill: *Comparison of container crane sway dampening systems*, 7th Terminal Operations Conference Exhibition, 16.-18.6.1992

[5] IBEO Lasertechnik: *LADAR2D, 2D LINEAR, 3D*, Interne Firmenschrift, Hamburg, 1990

[6] P. J. Besl: *Active Optical Range Imaging Sensors*, In: Advances in Machine Vision: Architecture and Application,. J: Sanz, Ed., Springer Verlag, New York, 1988

[7] H. Baessmann, P.W. Besslich: *Konturorientierte Verfahren in der digitalen Bildverarbeitung*, Springer Verlag, 1989

[8] R. Otterbach, R.Gerdes: *CORE - Ein Bildanalysesystem zur schnellen konturbasierten Objekterkennung und -lagebestimmung*, Vision&Voice Magazine 7(1), 1993

[9] K.-W. Jörg, E. von Puttkamer, H.-J. Richstein: *Integration und Fusion heterogener Multisensorinformation zur geometrischen Weltmodellierung für einen Autonomen Mobilen Roboter*, 9.Fachgespräch Autonome Mobile Systeme, TU Müchen, 28.-29.10.1993, S.287-298

Videosensorik

Real Time Pursuit and Vergence Control with an Active Binocular Head

K. Daniilidis, M. Hansen, G. Sommer

Institut für Informatik und Prakt. Mathematik
Christian-Albrechts Universität Kiel
Preusserstr. 1-9, 24105 Kiel, email:{kd,mha,gs}@informatik.uni-kiel.de

Abstract: This article is concerned with the design and implementation of a system for real time tracking of a moving object and binocular vergence control for depth estimation. Object detection relies only on the image motion without making any a priori assumptions about the object form. Using only the first spatiotemporal image derivatives subtraction of the normal optical flow induced by camera motion yields the object image motion. On the other hand, both the left and the right image are filtered hierarchically with Gabor functions. The phase difference of the responses yields a disparity map. The disparity in the center is the reference signal for vergence control of the binocular head. Both behaviors are implemented in parallel and the cycle rate achieved is 25 Hz.

1 Introduction

Traditional computer vision methodology regarded the visual system as a passive observer whose goal is the recovery of a complete description of the world. This approach led to systems unable to interact in a fast and stable way with a dynamically changing environment. The new paradigm of active behavioral vision showed that the ability to control the mechanical degrees of freedom during image acquisition as well as the behavior dependent selectivity in data processing facilitate more stable and real-time reactions in navigation and manipulation tasks.

The most evident reason for object pursuing is the limited field of view available by CCD cameras. The two degrees of freedom of panning and tilting enable keeping a moving object of interest in view for a longer time interval. Even if we had a sensor with 180 degrees field of view it would not be computationally possible to process every part of the field of view in the same detail. On the other hand, vergence control keeps the disparity magnitude bounded avoiding, thus, a computationally expensive search in large regions. Working with small disparities allows the use of filters with smaller support and reduces the computation time. Potential applications for the presented system are in the field of surveillance in indoor or outdoor scenes. The advantages are not only in the motion detection but mainly in the capability of keeping an intruder inside the field of view. Another application is in automatic video recording and video teleconferencing. The camera automatically tracks the acting or speaking person so that it always remains in the center of the field of view. In manufacturing or recycling environments, an active camera can track and estimate the depth to objects on the conveyor-belt so that they are recognized and grasped without stopping the belt. New directions are opened if such an active camera platform is mounted on an autonomous vehicle. As we will show in the results, vergence control supports scene exploration and the building of an environmental map.

The novelty of this approach is in the achievement of a video rate tracking and vergence control using sound image processing techniques. The performance of 25 Hz with a latency of about 100ms classifies our system together with the systems of Oxford and Stockholm among the fastest systems worldwide. Novel is also the design of the derivative and Gabor filters with respect to the limited support and accuracy in the given pipeline architecture. We demonstrate that real time implementation is not achieved by introducing heuristics but by systematic filter design.

As pursuing is one of the basic capabilities of an active vision system most of the research groups possessing a camera platform have reported results. The Oxford surveillance system [6] uses data from the motor encoders to compute and subtract the camera motion induced flow. It runs in 25 Hz with processing latency of about 110 ms. Camera behavior is modeled as either saccadic or pursuit motion and a finite state automaton controls the switching between the two reactions. The KTH-Stockholm system [10] computes the ego motion of the camera by fitting an affine flow model in the entire image. It is the only approach claiming pursuit in presence of arbitrary observer motion and not only pure rotation as assumed by the rest of the algorithms. However, this global affinity assumption is valid only if the object occupies a minor fraction of the field of view which is not a realistic assumption. Elimination of the flow due to known camera rotation is also applied by Murray and Basu [5]. The background motion is compensated by shifting the images. Then large image differences are combined with high image gradients to give a binary image. No real time implementation results are reported.

Regarding vergence control different approaches are developed. Olson and Coombs [7] used a cepstral filter for disparity estimation, and developed a real time vergence control with a servo rate of 10 Hz. Closer to our approach in disparity estimation was the work of Theimer & Mallot [9]. They also used a phase-based approach with Gabor filters on sub-sampled images with a rate of 1 Hz on common hardware. Westelius et al. [11] developed a vergence control based on phase differences. To get stable results they additionally computed the disparity from a pair of edge images. Uhlin et al. [10] also implemented a vergence control with phase-based disparity estimation and achieved the servo rate of 25 Hz.

2 Monocular pursuit of a moving object

A moving object in the image is defined as the locus of points with high image gradient whose image motion is substantially different from the camera induced image motion. We exploit the fact that the camera induced optical flow u_c is pure rotational

$$u_c = \begin{pmatrix} x_c y_c & -(1 + x_c^2) & y_c \\ (1 + y_c^2) & -x_c y_c & -x_c \end{pmatrix} \omega$$

where (x_c, y_c) are the camera coordinates and ω is the angular velocity computed from the angle readings of the axis encoders as follows.

The binocular camera mount[1] used in our system has four mechanical degrees of freedom: the pan angle χ of the neck, the tilt angle ϕ, and two vergence angle θ_l und θ_r for left and right, respectively (Fig. 1). The stereo basis is denoted by B.

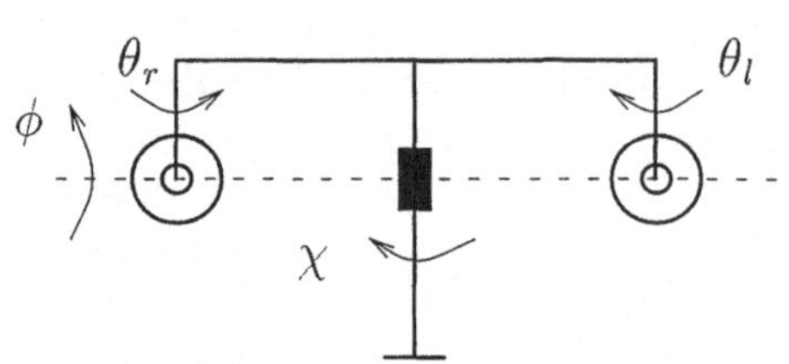

Abb. 1. The four degrees of freedom of the camera platform (left) and how it looks like (right).

Let $R(t) = R_{\phi(t)} R_{\theta(t)}$ be the time varying rotation of the camera coordinate system and Ω the skew-symmetric tensor of the angular velocity. Then we have $\dot{R}(t) = R(t)\Omega$ and the angular velocity with respect to the moving coordinate system reads $\omega = \left(\dot{\phi} \cos\theta \;\; \dot{\theta} \;\; \dot{\phi} \sin\theta \right)^T$. We assume the Brightness Change Constraint Equation $g_x u + g_y v + g_t = 0$ with g_x, g_y and g_t the spatiotemporal derivatives of the grayvalue function. From this equation we can compute only the normal flow - the projection of optical flow in the direction of the image gradient (g_x, g_y). The difference between the normal flow u_{c_n} induced by camera motion and the observed normal flow u_n

$$u_{c_n} - u_n = \frac{g_x u_c + g_y v_c}{\sqrt{g_x^2 + g_y^2}} + \frac{g_t}{\sqrt{g_x^2 + g_y^2}}$$

is the normal flow induced by the object motion. It turns out that we can test the existence of object image motion without the computation of optical flow. The sufficient conditions are that the object motion has a component parallel to the image gradient and the image gradient is sufficiently large. We can thus avoid the computation of full optical flow which would require the solution of at least a linear system for every pixel. Three thresholds are applied: the first for the difference between observed and camera normal flow, the second for the magnitude of the image gradient, and the third for the area of the points

---

[1] Consisting of the TRC BiSight Vergence Head and the TRC UniSight Pan/Tilt Base

satisfying the first two conditions. The object position is given as the centroid of the detected area.

2.1 Real time spatiotemporal filtering

Special effort was given to the choice of filters suitable for the used pipeline-processor [2] so that the frequency domain specifications are satisfied without violating the real time requirements. Whereas up to 8×8 FIR-kernels can be convolved with the image with processing rate of 20 MHz the temporal filtering must be carried out by delaying the images in the visual memory. We chose IIR filtering for the computation of the temporal derivatives since its computation requires less memory than temporal FIR filtering for the same effective time lag.

The temporal lowpass filter chosen is the discrete version of the exponential [3]

$$E(t) = \begin{cases} \tau e^{-t\tau} & t \geq 0 \\ 0 & t < 0. \end{cases}$$

If $E_n(t)$ is the n-th order exponential filter ($n \geq 2$) its derivative reads

$$\frac{dE_n(t)}{dt} = \tau(E_{n-1}(t) - E_n(t)).$$

The discrete recursive implementation for the second order derivative filter reads

$$h_1(k) + rh_1(k-1) = q(g(k) + g(k-1))$$
$$h_2(k) + rh_2(k-1) = q(h_1(k) + h_1(k-1)) \qquad g_t(k) = \tau(h_1(k) - h_2(k)),$$

where $g(k)$ is the input image, $h_1(k)$ and $h_2(k)$ are the lowpass responses of first and second order, respectively, and $g_t(k)$ is the derivative response. We note, that the lowpass response is used to smooth temporally the spatial derivatives. The spatial FIR-kernels are binomial approximations to the first derivatives of the Gaussian function.

2.2 Estimation and Control

The control goal of pursuing is to hold the gaze as close as possible to the projection of a moving object. Output measurements are the absolute position of the object denoted by o obtained from the centroid in the image and the angle readings. Let v and a be the velocity and acceleration of the object, c be the absolute position of the optical axis, and $\Delta u(k)$ the incremental correction in the camera position. The state is described by the vector $s = \begin{pmatrix} c^T & o^T & v^T & a^T \end{pmatrix}^T$. A motion model of constant acceleration and a linear control function $\Delta u(k) = -K\hat{s}(k)$ with $\hat{s}$ an estimate of the state enables the use of the separation principle stating that optimal control can be obtained by combining the optimum deterministic control with the optimal stochastic observer. The minimization of the difference $\|o - c\|$ between object and camera position in the reference coordinate system can be modeled as a Linear Quadratic Regulator problem with the minimizing cost function $\sum_{k=0}^{N} s^T(k)Qs(k)$ where Q is a symmetric matrix with $Q_{11} = 1$,

---

[2] Datacube MaxVideo 200 board

$Q_{12} = Q_{21} = -1, Q_{22} = 1$ and the rest of its elements zero. In steady state modus a constant control gain K is assumed resulting in an algebraic Ricatti equation with the simple solution that input camera position should be equal the predicted position of the object. One of the crucial problems in vision based closed loop control is how to tackle the delays introduced by a processing time longer than a cycle time. We emphasize here that the delay in our system is an estimator delay. The normal flow detected after frame k concerns the instantaneous velocity at frame $k-1$ due to the mode of the IIR temporal filter. At time $k-1$ the encoder is also asked to give the angle values of the motors. To the delay amount of one frame we must add the processing time so that we have the complete latency between motion event and onset of steered motion.

Concerning optimal estimation we also assume steady state modus obtaining a stationary Kalman Filter with constant gains. The special case of a second order plant yields the well known α-β-γ-Filter with update equation

$$\hat{s}^+(k+1) = \hat{s}^+(k) + (\ \alpha\ \beta/\Delta t\ \gamma/\Delta t^2\ )^T(m(k+1) - m^-(k+1)),$$

where s^+ is the state after updating and m^- is the predicted measurement. The gain coefficients α, β and γ are functions of the target maneuvering index λ. This maneuvering index is equal to the ratio of plant noise covariance and measurement noise covariance. The lower is the maneuvering index the higher is our confidence in the motion model resulting to a smoother trajectory. The higher is the maneuvering index the higher is the reliability of our measurement resulting to a close tracking of the measurements which may be very jaggy. This behaviour was thoroughly studied in [1].

We proceed with a real experiment. In Fig. 2 the system is tracking a Tetrapak moving from right to left. The images in Fig. 2 are chosen out of 20 frames saved "on the fly" during a time of 8s. The centroid of the detected motion area is marked with a cross. We show the tracking error by drawing the trajectory of the centroid in the image as well as the control values for the tilt and the vergence angle, ϕ and θ for the entire time interval of 8s. Although the target might move smoothly the orbit of the centroid depends on the distribution of the detected points in the motion area. Therefore, it is corrupted with an error of very high measurement variance. Allowing a high maneuvering index which enables close tracking would result in a extreme jaggy motion of the camera. The estimator would forget the motion model and yield an orbit as irregular as the centroid motion. Therefore, we decrease the maneuvering index to 0.01 and obtain as expected a much higher pixel error. Only a post processing of the binary images could improve the position of the detected centroid. The small size of the target enables a relatively small pixel error (the target is always observed left from the center). Because the centroid variation is only in the vertical direction - due to the rod holding the target - the tilt angle changes irregularly. The average angular velocity is 8.5 deg/s. The reader is referred to [1] for numerous real and synthetic experiments.

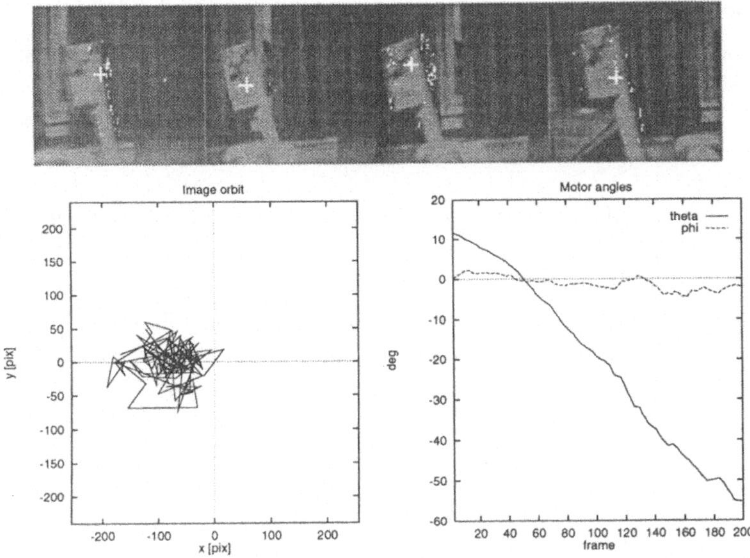

Abb. 2. Four frames recorded while the camera is pursuing a Tetrapak moving from right to left. The pixel error (bottom left) shows that the camera remains behind the target and the vergence change (bottom right) shows the turning of the camera from right to left with an average angular velocity of 8.5 deg/s.

3 Phase-based Disparity Estimation for Vergence Control

The idea of a phase-based approach is to implicitly solve the correspondence problem. Without explicit feature extraction these approaches can be described similarly by a local correlation of bandpass-filtered images. The local phase response contains the information of the spatial position of the matched structure. According to the Fourier shift-theorem

$$f(x) \circ\!\!-\!\!-\!\!-\!\!\bullet\ F(\omega) \quad f(x+D) \circ\!\!-\!\!-\!\!-\!\!\bullet\ F(\omega)e^{i\omega D},$$

a global spatial shift D of a signal $f(x)$ can be detected as a phase shift in the Fourier spectrum. Extracting the local phase in both images of a stereo pair with complex filters like Gabor filters leads to a direct computation of local disparity. Fleet [2] and Sanger [8] have employed phase-based approaches to recover disparity information with complex Gabor filters on different scales. The spatial shift $D(x) = \frac{\Delta\Phi(x)}{\omega}$ is computed in the *constant frequency model* from local phase difference [2]:

$$\Delta\Phi(x) = \phi_l(x) - \phi_r(x). \tag{1}$$

The phases are denoted $\phi_r(x)$ for the right and $\phi_l(x)$ for the left image.

Our Approach for a fast real-time algorithm [4] is influenced by the given hardware to obtain real time performance. Small filters and a simple algorithm can perform a high clock rate. We developed such a simple algorithm based on the theoretical principles of the phase-based approach.

3.1 Filter design

Our Gabor filters with an odd size of 7x7 regard the following four constraints, noticed in [11]:

a. *No DC component* to get an optimal phase behaviour.

b. *Suppression of wrap around* of the phase for maximizing the measurable disparity.

c. *Monotonous phase* to assure the one to one relation between phase difference and disparity.

d. *Small support* to get low computational costs.

To get no wrap around and to have a maximum measurable horizontal disparity related to the filter size a wavelength $\lambda = 2\pi/\omega_x = 6$ pixel is optimal.

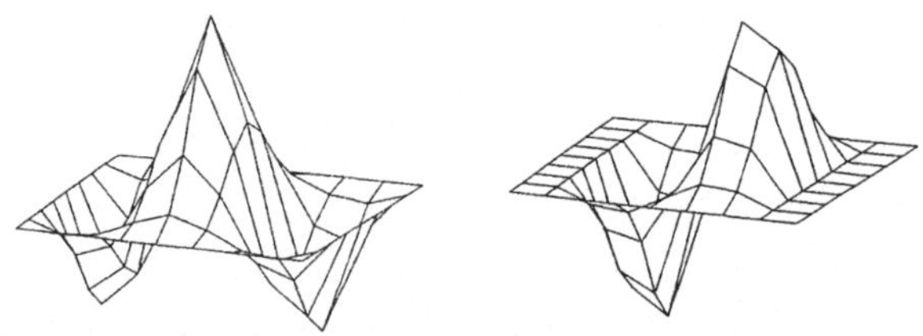

Abb. 3. Odd and Even Gabor filter 7x7.

Without a consistency check of the measured phases in the left and the right image, disparity estimation can produce arbitrary results. Our method to check the stability of phase information based on thresholding the magnitude of the filter responses. First, in each image the magnitudes are thresholded (by 20 % of the maximum magnitude) and second, the sum of magnitudes of both images are calculated and thresholded again (by 40 % of the sum maximum magnitude). The estimated phase difference at image pixel x is called stable if these two constraints are fulfilled. This map of stable phase differences is our *confidence map $c(x)$*.

The small filter size demands a strategy to deal with larger disparities in stereo images. Our approach is to compute a Gaussian pyramid $f_i(x)$ by approximating the Gaussian filter by a 7x7 binomial filter B. Sub-sampling S reduced the image resolution from 512x512 at the finest level to 16x16 at the coarsest level. This results in a maximal measurable disparity of ± 192 pixel at the coarsest level.

$$f_g(x)_i = G(x, \sigma, \omega) * f_i(x) \quad f_i(x) = S(B * f_{i-1}(x)).$$

4 Vergence Control and one Application

The camera mount (Fig. 1) has four mechanical degrees of freedom: pan angle, tilt angle ϕ, and two vergence angle θ_r and θ_l. The right camera has been declared as the dominating eye of our system. Pan, tilt and right vergence angle are controlled by a gaze-controller. Regarding vergence movement we only have to control the left vergence angle θ_l to reduce the horizontal stereo disparity D_c in the center of view. The disparity D_c is picked out from the center of the computed disparity map. The vergence control is designed as a feedback loop.

The estimated disparities D_c are compared with the reference signal $D_0 = 0$ in the case of convergence. The left vergence angle θ_l is controlled by the PD-controller because of its robust behaviour in real time applications. The offsets $\Delta\theta_l$ is defined by the PD-control law:

$$\Delta\theta_l = K_p D_c + K_d \dot{D}_c \tag{2}$$

The controller gains K_p and K_d are tuned by the Ziegler-Nichols method to have robust control and minimal settling time.

One application of combining vergence and gaze control is active depth estimation in an unknown area. The gaze controller has to move the gaze direction of the dominating right camera to interesting points in the world. These are edges and corners in the case of well structured areas. Then the left camera can fixate the same points by vergence control. After verging depth can be computed. We use the responses of our Gabor filters for controlling the right camera by choosing the local maxima of one confidence map (128x128) as gaze points. Normally a lab scene contains 10 - 25 selected local maxima in a view. After estimating the range of all points a new confidence map is computed. Then local maxima can be detected again at this new view until the chosen segment of the unknown area is explored.

4.1 Depth computation

In the case of convergence on a gaze point P we need the knowledge of the left and right vergence angles θ_l, θ_r to compute the depth of this point. Additionally the baseline of the stereo rig is known. We compute the depth in a cyclopean frame (see Fig. 4). The origin O is at half base line B. The cameras are verging on selected gaze point P. The gaze point is denoted by the angles (γ, ϕ), where ϕ is the tilt angle and $\gamma = \arctan(\sin(\theta_l - \theta_r)/(2\cos\theta_l \cos\theta_r))$.

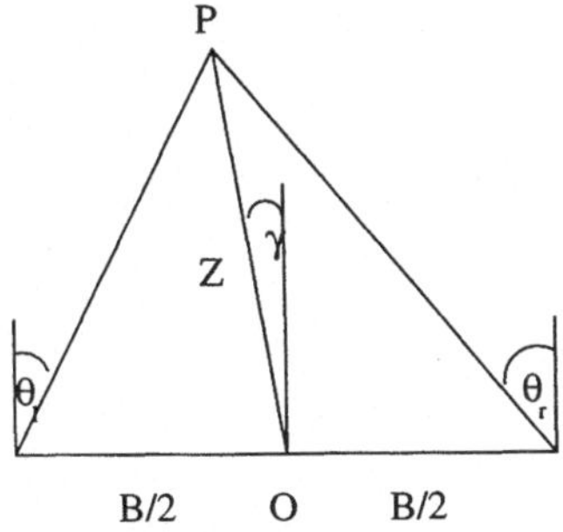

Abb. 4. Stereo geometry of our vision system at convergence at gaze point P.

We define the depth Z of the point P as the length of the line P to O. With trigonometric transforms the equation for $Z(\theta_l, \theta_r, B)$ follows:

$$Z^2 = B^2 \left(\frac{\sin^2(\theta_l - \theta_r)}{4\sin^2(\theta_l + \theta_r)} + \frac{\cos^2\theta_r \cos^2\theta_l}{\sin^2(\theta_l + \theta_r)} \right). \tag{3}$$

We represent the depth map $Z(\gamma, \phi)$ with a resolution of $2\pi/360$ for γ and ϕ. The vergence angles have an intrinsic resolution of $0.006°$. This results in a theoretical error in depth estimation $\frac{\Delta Z}{Z}$ from 0.09% at $Z = 1.0$ m up to 0.9% at $Z = 10.0$m in the case of symmetric vergence.

5 Experiments and results

The example shows a typical view of our lab. We explore this scene with our system to get depth information. Fig. 5 shows a fly of four images (u.) and their resulting confidence maps at a resolution 128x128 (l.). The confidence maps are

Abb. 5. The view of our lab which has to be explored. (l.) The confidence maps of the same images at resolution 128x128.

used for control the gaze direction (γ, ϕ). In this example the tilt angle $\phi = 0$ is hold constant. The range of the gaze angle γ is $-55°...50°$. The gaze controller selected 14 points from the four confidence maps. The white scan line (Fig 5.) is the area, where local maxima are detected. It represents the constraint $\phi = 0$ The gaze of the right camera is directed to each gaze point $(\gamma_i, 0)$. After verging the depth $Z(\gamma_i, 0)$ is computed. The tabular shows the estimated depth values (rounded in 0.05 m) and computed gaze directions (rounded in 1 degree).

γ_i	-53	-50	-42	-38	-32	-27	-21	-12	-5	5	7	15	21	43
Z	3.30	3.65	3.95	4.30	4.70	5.30	6.15	5.95	5.90	6.00	6.10	4.05	4.50	2.30

Figure 6 shows a result of depth exploration. The depth $Z(\gamma, 0)$ is the radius of the polar figure. Linear interpolation is applied between gaze points $(\gamma_i, 0)$. In Fig. 6 it can be recognized the approximate rectangular outline of our lab. At the right side the windows, at the front side the open cupboards and the door and clipboard at the left wall have good structure, so that vergence control with Gabor filters was possible.

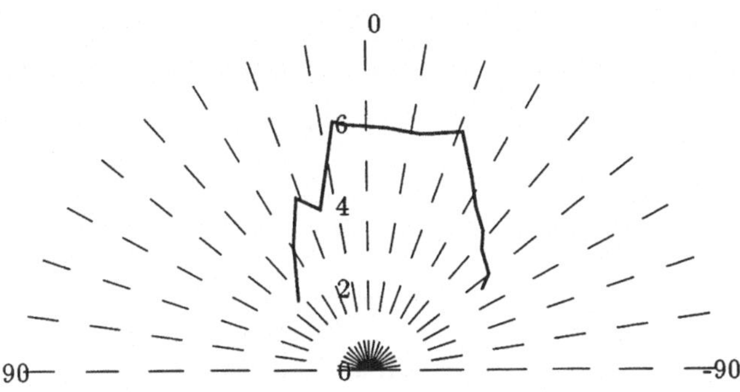

Abb. 6. Depth map $Z(\gamma_i, 0)$ of our lab. The gaze directions range from $-53... + 43°$.

References

1. K. Daniilidis, Ch. Krauss, M. Hansen, and G. Sommer. Real Time Tracking of Moving Objects with an Active Camera. Technical Report 9509, Inst. f. Inf. u. Prakt. Math., October 1995. submitted also to the *Real Time Imaging* Journal.
2. D. J. Fleet, A. D. Jepson, and M. R. M. Jenkin. Phase-Based Disparity Measurement. *CVGIP: Image Understanding*, 53(2), 3 1991.
3. D.J. Fleet and K. Langley. Recursive filters for optical flow. *IEEE Trans. Pattern Analysis and Machine Intelligence*, 17:61–67, 1995.
4. M.Hansen and G.Sommer. Real Time Vergence Control using Local Phase Differences. *Machine Graphics and Vision*, 5(1/2):51–63, 1996.
5. D. Murray and A. Basu. Motion tracking with an active camera. *IEEE Trans. Pattern Analysis and Machine Intelligence*, 16:449–459, 1994.
6. D.W. Murray, P.L. McLauchlan, I.D. Reid, and P.M. Sharkey. Reactions to peripheral image motion using a head/eye platform. In *Proc. Int. Conf. on Computer Vision*, pp. 403–411, Berlin, Germany, May 11-14, 1993.
7. T.J. Olsen and D.J. Coombs. Real-Time Vergence Control for Binocular Robots. *International Journal of Computer Vision*, 1:76–89, 1991.
8. T.D. Sanger. Stereo Disparity Computation Using Gabor Filters. *Biol.Cybernetics*, 59:405–418, 1988.
9. W.M. Theimer and H.A. Mallot. Phase-based binocular vergence control and depth reconstruction using active vision. *CVGIP: Image Understanding*, 60:343–358, 1994.
10. T. Uhlin, P. Nordlund, A. Maki, and J.A. Eklundh. Towards an Active Visual Observer. In *Proc. Int. Conf. on Computer Vision*, pp. 679–686. Boston, MA, June 20-23, 1995.
11. C.J. Westelius, H. Knutsson, J. Wiklund, and C.F. Westin. Phased-Based Disparity Estimation. In H.I.Christensen J.L. Crowley, editor, *Vision as Process*. Springer Verlag, Heidelberg, 1994.

MORAL: Ein System zur videobasierten Objekterkennung im Kontext autonomer, mobiler Systeme

Stefan Lanser, Christoph Zierl

Technische Universität München
Forschungsgruppe Bildverstehen (FG BV), Informatik IX
Orleansstr. 34, 81667 München
email: {lanser,zierl}@informatik.tu-muenchen.de

Kurzfassung. Zu den grundlegenden Anforderungen an ein autonomes, mobiles System (*AMS*) gehört die Fähigkeit, in einer à priori bekannten Umgebung zu navigieren und missionsrelevante Objekte zu identifizieren sowie ihre räumliche Lage relativ zum AMS zu bestimmen. Zur Bewältigung dieser Aufgaben muß die Umgebung des AMS mit geeigneter Sensorik erfaßt werden. Dieser Beitrag stellt das videobasierte Objekterkennungssytem MORAL [1] vor, das auf der modellbasierten Auswertung einzelner Bilder eines CCD-Sensors beruht. Durch geeignete Parametrisierung läßt sich das System dynamisch an unterschiedliche Aufgaben anpassen. Die Einbindung in konkrete AMS erfolgt transparent über *remote procedure calls*. Insgesamt ermöglicht diese Architektur ein hohes Maß an Flexibilität in bezug sowohl auf die verwendete Hardware (Rechner, Kamera) als auch auf die zu erkennenden Objekte.

1 Einleitung

Im Kontext autonomer, mobiler Systeme (*AMS*) können durch ein videobasiertes Objekterkennungssystem u.a. folgende Aufgaben übernommen werden:

- Erkennung missionsrelevanter Objekte
- Lokalisierung von Objekten (Unterstützung von Manipulationsaufgaben)
- Navigation in bekannter Umgebung

Diese Aufgaben lassen sich formal auf die Bestimmung einer Interpretation

$$\mathcal{I} = \langle\ obj, \{(I_{j_1}, M_{i_1}), \ldots, (I_{j_k}, M_{i_k})\}, (\mathcal{R}, \mathcal{T})\ \rangle \tag{1}$$

zurückführen. Dabei bezeichnet *obj* die Objekthypothese, (I_{j_l}, M_{i_l}) eine Korrespondenz zwischen Bildmerkmal I_{j_l} und Modellmerkmal M_{i_l} und $(\mathcal{R}, \mathcal{T})$ die berechnete 3D-Lage des Objekts.

Das in diesem Beitrag beschriebene videobasierte Objekterkennungssystem MORAL erfüllt diese Aufgaben durch den Vergleich von prädizierten Modell-

---

[1] **M**unich **O**bject **R**ecognition **A**nd **L**ocalization

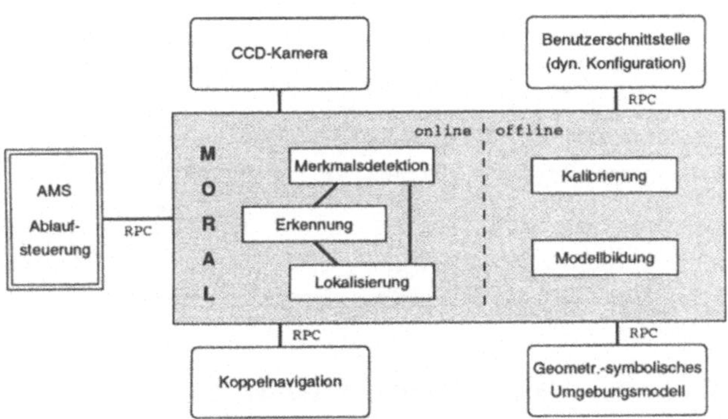

Abb. 1. Das videobasierte Objekterkennungssystem MORAL .

und im Videobild detektierten Bildmerkmalen, vgl. [14, 15]. Die dafür benötigten 3D-Modelle sind Polyederapproximationen der Umwelt, die aus bestehenden CAD-Darstellungen abgeleitet oder durch das in [9] vorgestellte geometrisch-symbolische Umgebungsmodell zur Verfügung gestellt werden.

Weitere videobasierte Ansätze zur modellbasierten Objekterkennung finden sich u.a. in [10, 8, 5]. Der Spezialfall der videobasierten Lokalisierung eines AMS wird z.B. in [7, 3, 11] behandelt.

2 Systemarchitektur

2.1 Übersicht

Das vorgestellte Objekterkennungssystem ist als RPC-Server (*remote procedure call*) realisiert, dessen Dienste von beliebigen Clientprozessen aufgerufen werden können, insbesondere von der Fahrzeugsteuerung eines AMS. Die Verwendung des standardisierten RPC-Mechanismus erlaubt die transparente Kommunikation mit anderen Komponenten. Damit ist das vorgestellte Objekterkennungssystem weitgehend unabhängig von der konkreten Hardwarestruktur des AMS. Mit Hilfe desselben Mechanismus nimmt das System auch Dienste weiterer Komponenten wie z.B. des *Geometrisch-symbolischen Umgebungsmodells* in Anspruch, vgl. Abb. 1. Spezielle RPC's dienen zur dynamischen Umkonfigurierung des Systems, das sich so flexibel an geänderte Aufgabenstellungen anpassen läßt.

Die interne Struktur von MORAL besteht im wesentlichen aus folgenden fünf Modulen (vgl. Abb. 1), die in ANSI-C bzw. C++ implementiert sind:

- Die *Kalibrierung* bestimmt die inneren Parameter der verwendeten CCD-Kamera sowie die relative Lage der Kamera bzgl. des AMS (*hand-eye-calibration*).
- Die *Modellgenerierung* überführt offline die vorliegende geometrische Objektbeschreibung in ein für die Erkennung geeignetes Objektmodell. Bei der Navigation wird darüberhinaus online auch direkt auf die Geometriedaten zugegriffen.

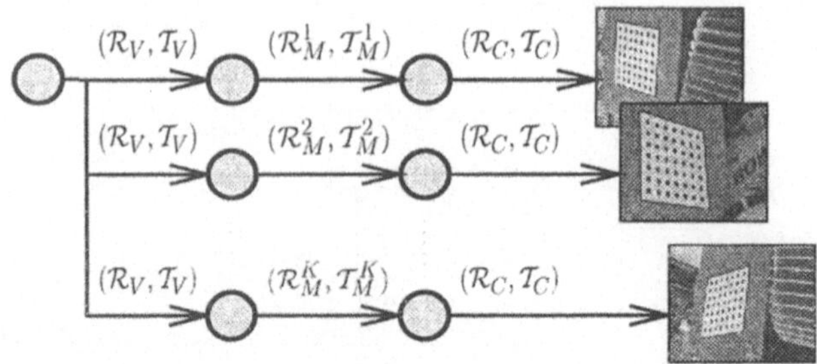

Abb. 2. Bestimmung der relativen Lage der Kamera basierend auf bekannten Bewegungen des Endeffektors des Manipulators eines AMS.

- Die *Merkmalsdetektion* extrahiert online die benötigten Merkmale aus dem Videobild.
- Die *Erkennung* generiert online Hypothesen über Objekte im Sichtbereich der Kamera und deren ungefähre räumliche Lage.
- Die *Lokalisierung* bestimmt ausgehend von einer Starthypothese die räumliche Lage von Objekten relativ zum AMS bzw. die räumliche Lage des AMS in seiner Umgebung.

2.2 Kalibrierung

Für die Bestimmung der 3D-Lage von Objekten aus Videobildern müssen sowohl die inneren Kameraparameter (Abbildung der 3D-Umgebung in Pixel) als auch die Lage der CCD-Kamera relativ zum Manipulator bzw. Fahrzeug ausreichend genau bestimmt werden. Ein Kameramodell nähert die Abbildung eines 3D-Punktes in der Umgebung auf ein 2D-(Sub-)Pixel im Videobild einer CCD-Kamera an. Im vorgestellten System wird das Modell einer Lochkamera mit radialer Verzerrung verwendet [18]. Es beinhaltet im wesentlichen die folgenden inneren Kameraparameter: Kammerkonstante b, Verzerrungskoeffizient κ, Skalierungsfaktoren S_x und S_y sowie den Hauptpunkt $[C_x, C_y]$.

Bestimmung der inneren Kameraparameter. Im ersten Teil des Kalibrierungsprozesses werden die inneren Kameraparameter ermittelt. Dazu werden Videobilder eines 2D-Eichkörpers mit N kreisförmigen Marken P_i von K unterschiedlichen Standpunkten aufgenommen (*Multibildkalibrierung* [18]). Durch ein Bündelausgleichsverfahren wird simultan in allen Bildern der Abstand zwischen den projizierten 3D-Mittelpunkten der Marken und den korrespondierenden 2D-Bildpunkten minimiert. Da lediglich die Geometrie des Eichkörpers à priori bekannt sein muß, ist das Verfahren am Einsatzort des AMS einfach anwendbar.

Hand-Auge-Kalibrierung. Im zweiten Teil des Kalibrierungsprozesses wird ggf. die Lage der Kamera relativ zum Werkzeugkoordinatensystem des Manipulators ermittelt (*hand-eye calibration* [17]). Bezüglich ihrer Umgebung setzt

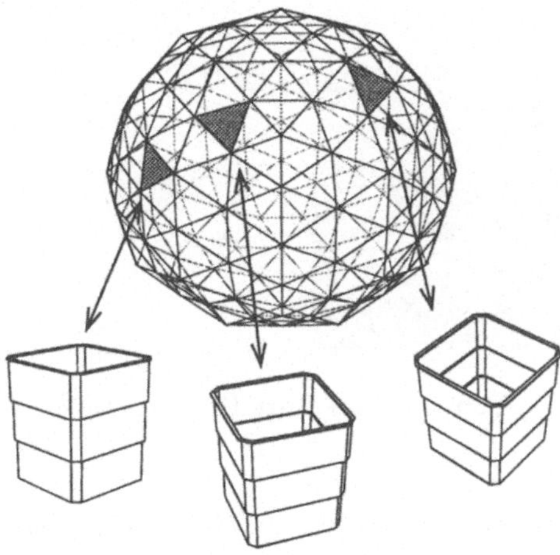

Abb. 3. Jedes Dreieck der triangulierten Gaußschen Sphäre definiert eine 2D-Ansicht des betrachteten Objekts.

sich die absolute 3D-Lage einer CCD-Kamera im Manipulator eines AMS aus der Lage $(\mathcal{R}_V, \mathcal{T}_V)$ des AMS, der relativen Lage $(\mathcal{R}_M, \mathcal{T}_M)$ des Endeffektors und der relativen Lage $(\mathcal{R}_C, \mathcal{T}_C)$ der Kamera zusammen, vgl. Fig. 2. Mit Hilfe kontrollierter Bewegungen $(\mathcal{R}_M^k, \mathcal{T}_M^k)$ des Endeffektors läßt sich die gesuchte Lage $(\mathcal{R}_C, \mathcal{T}_C)$ durch einen weiteren Bündelausgleich bestimmen [17].

Ist der 2D-Eichkörper im Sichtbereich der Handkamera auf dem AMS montiert (Abb. 6 rechts), können die unterschiedlichen Aufnahmepunkte automatisch angefahren werden. Die gesamte Kalibrierung kann so in wenigen Minuten durchgeführt werden.

2.3 Modellgenerierung

Unter Verwendung einer triangulierten Gaußschen Sphäre wird jedes zu erkennende Objekt durch maximal 320 normalisierte 2D-Ansichten repräsentiert (*multiview representation*), vgl. Abb. 3. Diese normalisierten Ansichten beinhalten die Modellmerkmale, die zur Korrespondenzbildung verwendet werden, vgl. Glg. (1). Die Eingabe für dieses Modul ist die *boundary representation* des durch Polyeder approximierten 3D-Objekts, die von einem CAD-System übernommen oder vom Umgebungsmodell bereitgestellt wird.

Um die Vergleichbarkeit zwischen dem i.a. zu detaillierten CAD-Modell und den extrahierten Bildmerkmalen zu gewährleisten, werden die Ausgangsmodelle durch Simulation von Bildvorverarbeitungsoperatoren entfeinert. Somit besteht jede normalisierte 2D-Ansicht eines Objekts aus denjenigen Modellmerkmalen, die im Videobild detektierbar sind.

Desweiteren werden abhängig von der verwendeten Erkennungsstrategie spezifische Eigenschaften der Modellmerkmale berechnet. Mögliche Eigenschaften

Abb. 4. Detektierte Bildmerkmale.

sind beispielsweise Formmerkmale für die Generierung von *Aspektbäumen* [20] oder auch topologische Beziehungen zwischen Modellmerkmalen [16].

Im Fall der videobasierte Navigation bezeichnet *obj* in Glg. (1) die Umgebung des AMS. Anstelle von offline berechneten 2D-Ansichten werden dann zur Interpretation des Videobildes die vom Umgebungsmodell online in Abhängigkeit von der aktuellen Lage des AMS prädizierten Modellmerkmale verwendet [9].

2.4 Merkmalsdetektion

Die Detektion der Bildmerkmale (Abb. 4) stützt sich im wesentlichen auf das Bildanalysesystem HORUS [6] ab. HORUS stellt dazu eine umfangreiche Bibliothek von Bildverarbeitungsoperatoren zur Verfügung. Objekt- und kontextspezifisches Wissen kann während des Segmentationsprozesses berücksichtigt werden. Dieses Wissen betrifft beispielsweise den Merkmalstyp (Linie/Fläche/Kontur) oder die Farbe des Objekts bzw. des Bildhintergrundes.

Die Parametrisierung dieses Moduls erfolgt entweder systemintern (vom Erkennungs- bzw. Lokalisierungsmodul) oder durch externe Module wie die AMS-Steuerung oder eine externe Fehlerbehandlung [2].

2.5 Objekterkennung

Das Objekterkennungsmodul identifiziert Objekte im Sichtbereich der Kamera und bestimmt ihre ungefähre 3D-Lage. Dazu werden Korrespondenzen zwischen den Merkmalen der gespeicherten 2D-Modellansichten und den detektierten Bildmerkmalen aufgestellt. Das Ergebnis dieses Prozesses ist eine sortierte Liste von Objekthypothesen inkl. den zugehörigen Lagehypothesen gemäß Glg. (1), die anschließend vom Lokalisierungsmodul verfeinert werden. Stellt ein externes Modul (z.B. die Fahrzeugkoppelnavigation) bereits eine grobe 3D-Lagehypothese zur Verfügung, wird nur das Lokalisierungsmodul aufgerufen.

Generierung von Assoziationen Der erste Schritt während des Erkennungsprozesses ist die Generierung einer Menge von *Assoziationen*. Eine Assoziation

Abb. 5. Die zwei am höchsten bewerteten Objekthypothesen des Erkennungsmoduls.

ist definiert als Quadrupel (I_j, M_i, v, c_a), wobei I_j ein Bildmerkmal, M_i ein Modellmerkmal, v eine der 2D-Modellansichten eines Objekts und c_a die Konfidenz der Korrespondenz $\langle I_j, M_i \rangle$ bezeichnen. Die Berechnung dieses Konfidenzwertes erfolgt entweder durch die Traversierung der Aspektbäume [21, 20] oder durch geometrischen Vergleich der Merkmale unter Berücksichtigung topologischer Nebenbedingungen [16].

Generierung von Hypothesen Die Assoziationen zu jeder 2D-Modellansicht werden zu *Hypothesen* $\{(obj, \mathcal{A}_i, v_i, c_i)\}$ zusammengefaßt. Dabei wird zu jeder 2D-Ansicht v_i aus der Menge der zugehörigen Assoziationen mit ausreichender Konfidenz eine Teilmenge $\mathcal{A}_i$ ausgewählt. Diese Teilmenge muß sowohl geometrisch als auch topologisch konsistent sein: Geometrische Konsistenz bedeutet hier, daß die 2D-Transformation zwischen Modell und Bild für alle Merkmale einheitlich ist, die Einzeltransformationen also einen Cluster im Transformationsraum bilden. Topologische Konsistenz bedeutet, daß die Bildmerkmale dieselben topologischen Nebenbedingungen wie die korrespondierenden Modellmerkmale erfüllen [16]. Der Konfidenzwert c_i der Hypothese hängt von den Konfidenzwerten der enthaltenen Assoziationen und dem Prozentsatz der zugeordneten Modellmerkmale ab.

Die sortierte Liste der aufgestellten Hypothesen wird im Anschluß durch das Lokalisierungsmodul verifiziert und ggf. verfeinert. Während der Hypothesengenerierung wird ein Verschiebungsvektor und ein Skalierungsfaktor in der Bildebene berechnet. Aus dieser *schwachen Perspektive* läßt sich eine ungefähre 3D-Lagehypothese mit allen 6 Freiheitsgraden bestimmen.

2.6 Lokalisierung

Das Lokalisierungsmodul von MORAL bestimmt die Lage der Kamera entweder relativ zu einem Objekt[2] oder absolut in der Umgebung des AMS. Ausgangspunkt dafür ist eine grobe Lagehypothese, die entweder vom Erkennungsmodul, von der Fahrzeugsteuerung oder einem *Tracking*-Prozeß bereitgestellt wird.

---

[2] damit ist natürlich auch umgekehrt die Lage des Objekts relativ zur Kamera bzw. relativ zum Manipulator/Fahrzeug bekannt.

Die benötigte Modellinformation (3D-Linien im Sichtbereich der Kamera) wird entweder vom Erkennungsmodul übergeben oder vom Umgebungsmodell gemäß der Lagehypothese prädiziert. Für die einzelnen Modellmerkmale werden dann in einem ersten Schritt Korrespondenzkandidaten unter den extrahierten Bildmerkmalen ermittelt. Ist die Unsicherheit der Lagehypothese, beschrieben durch eine entsprechende Kovarianzmatrix, bekannt, wird die Kandidatenauswahl eingegrenzt, indem spezifische Suchräume für die Modellmerkmale berechnet werden [13].

Die endgültigen Korrespondenzen werden durch Traversierung eines Interpretationsbaumes ermittelt [8]. Die Suche wird dabei durch topologische Nebenbedingungen gesteuert. Bereits aufgestellte Korrespondenzen beeinflussen wiederum durch topologische Nebenbedingungen das Aussehen der tieferen Ebenen des Interpretationsbaumes. Während dieses Prozesses werden durch eine gewichtete Ausgleichsrechnung Bild- und Modellinien zur Deckung gebracht und somit die aktuelle 3D-Lagehypothese schrittweise verfeinert [19, 12]. Gleichzeitig werden durch Berücksichtigung der *Consistent-Viewpoint*-Nebenbedingung Sackgassen im Interpretationsbaum frühzeitig erkannt.

Stehen nur koplanare Modellmerkmale zur Verfügung, die aus relativ großer Distanz betrachtet werden, wird die Schätzung aller 6 Freiheitsgrade aufgrund der starken Korrelation der Lageparameter instabil. In diesem Fall können zwei rotatorische Freiheitsgrade gebunden werden, wenn z.B. die Orientierung der „Grundebene" des Objekts relativ zur Kamera bekannt ist. Eine flexiblere Lösung besteht in der Verwendung zweier Videobilder mit bekannter Kamerabewegung zwischen den Aufnahmestandpunkten (*Bewegungsstereo*): Die gleichzeitige Modellanpassung an beide Videobilder beseitigt obige Instabilität. Bei Modellen mit nicht ausschließlich koplanaren Merkmalen liefert bereits die 3D-Lageschätzung aus nur einem Videobild gute Ergebnisse.

3   Anwendungen

Im folgenden werden einige Anwendungen von MORAL im Kontext autonomer, mobiler Systeme beschrieben, die im Rahmen des Sonderforschungsbereiches 331 an der TU München Verwendung finden. Die verwendeten AMS sind jeweils mit einer CCD-Kamera ausgestattet (Abb. 6). Durch die Flexibilität von MORAL gestaltet sich die Integration auf diesen Plattformen mit unterschiedlicher Hardware und verschiedenen Aufgaben einfach. Eine typische Sequenz von RPC's an MORAL ist in Abb. 7 zu finden.

Ein Beispiel für die videobasierte Navigation eines AMS in einer bekannten Umgebung mit MORAL ist in Abb. 8 zu sehen. An geeigneten Stellen wird dabei das Lokalisierungsmodul von MORAL beauftragt, die odometriegestützte aktuelle Lagehypothese des AMS zu korrigieren. Dazu wird diese Lagehypothese via RPC abgerufen, das Umgebungsmodell via RPC mit der Prädiktion der sichtbaren Modellmerkmale beauftragt und ein Videobild eingezogen. Aus diesen Eingaben wird die tatsächliche 3D-Lage des AMS in seiner Umgebung berechnet, vgl. Abb. 8. Auf einer SPARC-10 Workstation benötigt ein kompletter Naviga-

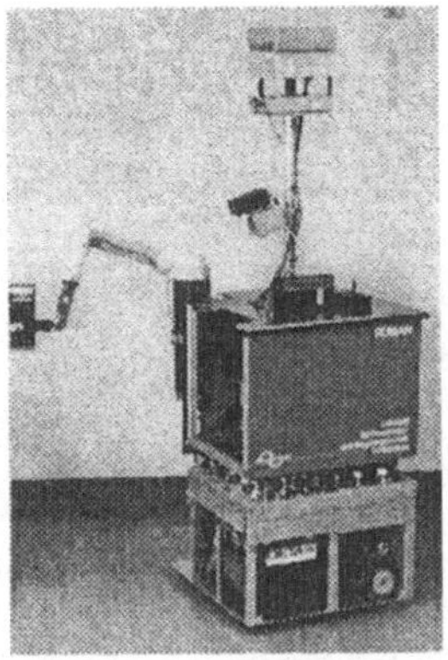

Abb. 6. Die autonomen, mobilen Systeme MAC 1, ROMAN und MOBROB.

```
ok = video_init(&ID)
ok = video_load_param(ID,Configuration)
ok = video_load_param(ID,CameraParameter)
ok = video_load_object(ID,Object)
    ⋮
ok = video_rec_object(ID,&Object,&Pose)
    ⋮
ok = video_finish(ID)
```

Abb. 7. Beispiel für eine Aufrufsequenz an MORAL .

tionsaufruf etwa 2 Sekunden. Die erzielbare Genauigkeit liegt bei 5 – 10 cm in der Position[3] und bei etwa 0.4° im Azimutwinkel. Als Referenz liegt dabei die Lasernavigation des Serviceroboters ROMAN zugrunde [4].

Das linke Bild in Abb. 9 zeigt das Ergebnis einer videobasierten Zustandsidentifikation: Nach der Lokalisierung des Türrahmens durch MORAL wird der Öffnungswinkel des Türflügels in einem zweiten Schritt durch ein externes Modul bestimmt [9]. Ein AMS ist somit in der Lage zu entscheiden, ob eine Tür passierbar ist oder ob sie ggf. geöffnet werden muß [4]. Letzteres kann durch die videobasierte Lokalisierung der Türklinke unterstützt werden (Abb. 9 rechts).

In Abb. 10 ist die videobasierte Objekterkennung eines Werkzeugwagens bzw. eines Rollcontainers zu sehen. Der Rechenzeitbedarf liegt dabei abhängig von der Anzahl der Bild- bzw. Modellmerkmale zwischen 3 und 10 Sekunden auf einer SPARC-10 Workstation. Die erzielbare Genauigkeit bei der Lokalisierung liegt bei 1 – 2 % des Objektabstandes.

Eine weitere Anwendung von MORAL – die Unterstützung des Greifvorgangs eines Werkstückes durch den mobilen Roboter MOBROB – ist in Abb. 11 dargestellt. Da die exakte Lage des Objekts nicht à priori bekannt ist, beauftragt der Führungsrechner des Roboters MORAL mit der Identifikation und der Bestimmung der 3D-Lage des Werkstückes mit Hilfe einer Kamera im Handflansch

---

[3] Dabei ist die Genauigkeit in Blickrichtung deutlich geringer als senkrecht darauf.

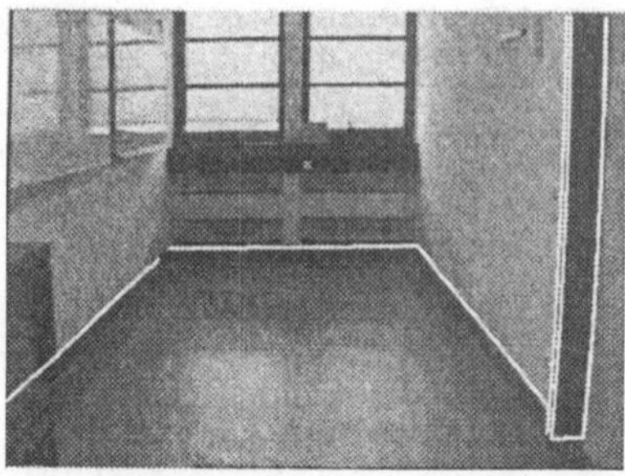

Abb. 8. Beispiele für die videobasierte Navigation mit natürlichen Landmarken.

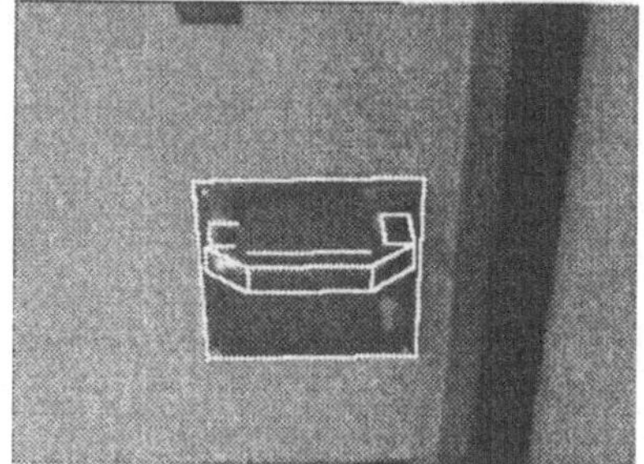

Abb. 9. Bestimmung des Türöffnungswinkels [9] und Lokalisierung der Klinke.

des Manipulators [2, 1]. In diesem Beispiel wird der Bewegungsstereoansatz verwendet, vgl. Abschnitt 2.6. Die Genauigkeit der Lokalisierung liegt hier bei etwa 1 mm bei einem Aufnahmeabstand von etwa 90 cm. Die Objekterkennung ist dabei auch unter schwierigen Aufnahmeverhältnissen möglich (Abb. 12). Die Gesamtlaufzeit beträgt in diesen Fällen zwischen 2 und 5 Sekunden.

4 Zusammenfassung

In diesem Beitrag wurde das videobasierte 3D-Objekterkennungssystem MORAL vorgestellt. Im Kontext autonomer, mobiler Systeme können damit modellbasiert Aufgaben wie das Erkennen und Lokalisieren missionsrelevanter Objekte erfüllt werden. Die Flexibilität des Systems wurde anhand von verschiedenen Experimenten auf unterschiedlichen Plattformen demonstriert.

Künftige Arbeiten werden sich u.a. mit der Handhabung einer größeren Modelldatenbasis, mit der videobasierten Modellgenerierung und der Integration des Merkmalstyps *gekrümmte Linie* beschäftigen.

Danksagung

Die vorliegende Arbeit wurde im Rahmen des Sonderforschungsbereichs *Informationsverarbeitung in autonomen, mobilen Handhabungssystemen* (SFB 331), Teilprojekt L9, von der Deutschen Forschungsgemeinschaft (DFG) gefördert.

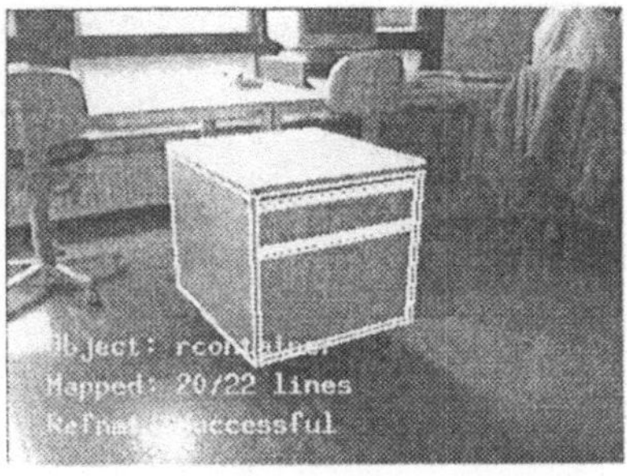

Abb. 10. Videobasierte 3D-Objekterkennung mit MORAL .

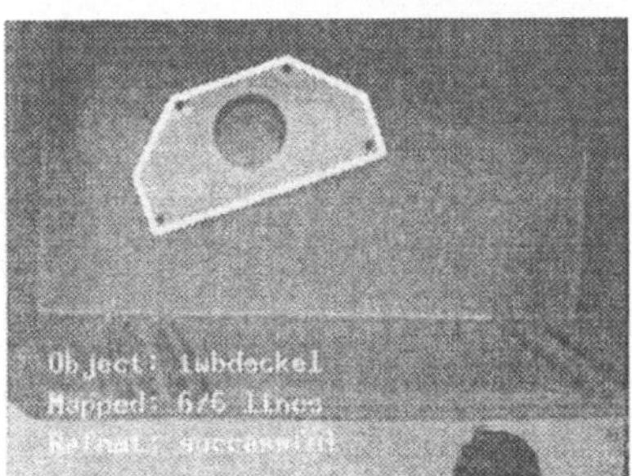

Abb. 11. Lokalisierung eines Werkstückes zur Unterstützung des Greifvorganges.

Literatur

1. S. Blessing, D. Kugelmann und G. Reinhart. Sichere Handhabung mit 3D-Simulation und videobasierter Sensorik. In G. Schmidt und F. Freyberger (Hrsg.), *Autonome Mobile Systeme*, Informatik aktuell. Springer-Verlag, 1996.

2. S. Blessing, S. Lanser, and C. Zierl. Vision-based Handling with a Mobile Robot. In *6th International Symposium on Robotics and Manufacturing*. TSI Press, 1996.

3. H. Christensen and N. Kirkeby. Model-driven vision for in-door navigation. *Robotics and Autonomous Systems*, 12:199–207, 1994.

4. W. Daxwanger, E. Ettelt, C. Fischer, F. Freyberger, U. Hanebeck und G. Schmidt. ROMAN: Ein mobiler Serviceroboter als persönlicher Assistent in belebten Innenräumen. In G. Schmidt und F. Freyberger (Hrsg.), *Autonome Mobile Systeme*, Informatik aktuell. Springer-Verlag, 1996.

5. S. Dickinson, A. Pentland, and A. Rosenfeld. From Volumes to Views: An Approach to 3-D Object Recognition. *CVGIP: Image Understanding*, 55(2):130–154, March 1992.

6. W. Eckstein and C. Steger. Interactive Data Inspection and Program Development for Computer Vision. In *Visual Data Exploration and Analysis III*, volume 2656 of SPIE Proceedings. SPIE - The Intern. Soc. for Optical Engineering, 1996.

7. C. Fennema, A. Hanson, E. Riseman, J. R. Beveridge, and R. Kumar. Model-Directed Mobile Robot Navigation. *IEEE Trans. on Systems, Man, and Cybernetics*, 20(6):1352–1369, November 1990.

8. W. Eric L. Grimson. *Machine Vision for Three Dimensional Scenes*, chapter Object Recognition by Constrained Search, pages 73–108. Academic Press, Inc., 1990.

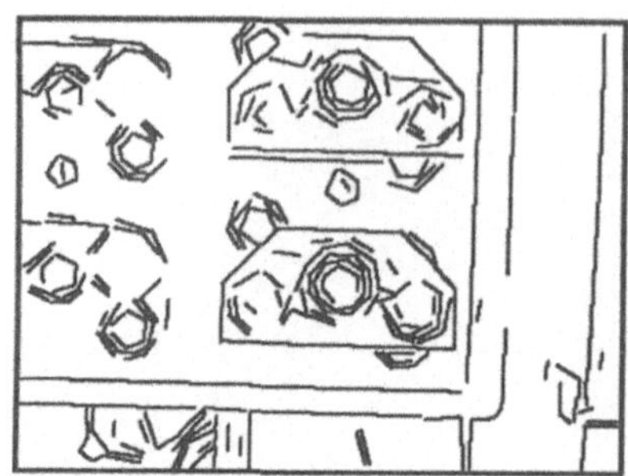

Abb. 12. Lokalisierung von Werkstücken bei schwierigen Beleuchtungsverhältnissen und strukturiertem Hintergrund.

9. N. O. Stöffler, A. Hauck und G. Färber. Ein geometrisch-symbolisches Umgebungsmodell zur Unterstützung verschiedener Perzeptionsaufgaben autonomer, mobiler Systeme. In G. Schmidt und F. Freyberger (Hrsg.), *Autonome Mobile Systeme*, Informatik aktuell. Springer-Verlag, 1996.

10. K. Ikeuchi and T. Kanade. Automatic Generation of Object Recognition Programs. *IEEE Trans. on Computers*, 76(8):1016–1035, August 1988.

11. A. Kosaka and J. Pan. Purdue Experiments in Model-Based Vision for Hallway Navigation. In *Workshop on Vision for Robots in IROS'95*, pages 87–96, 1995.

12. R. Kumar and A. R. Hanson. Robust Methods for Pose Determination. In *NSF/ARPA Workshop on Performance versus Methodology in Computer Vision*, pages 41–57. University of Washington, Seattle, 1994.

13. S. Lanser and T. Lengauer. On the Selection of Candidates for Point and Line Correspondences. In *International Symposium on Computer Vision*, pages 157–162. IEEE Computer Society Press, 1995.

14. S. Lanser, O. Munkelt und C. Zierl. Robuste videobasierte Identifizierung von Hindernissen und Werkstücken sowie die Bestimmung ihrer räumlichen Lage. In P. Levi (Hrsg.), *Autonome Mobile Systeme*, Informatik aktuell, pages 95–106. Springer-Verlag, 1994.

15. S. Lanser, O. Munkelt, and C. Zierl. Robust Video-based Object Recognition using CAD Models. In U. Rembold, R. Dillmann, L.O. Hertzberger, and T. Kanade, editors, *Intelligent Autonomous Systems IAS-4*, pages 529–536. IOS Press, 1995.

16. S. Lanser and C. Zierl. On the Use of Topological Constraints within Object Recognition Tasks. In *13th ICPR*, volume 1. IEEE Computer Society Press, 1996.

17. S. Lanser und Ch. Zierl. Robuste Kalibrierung von CCD-Sensoren für autonome, mobile Systeme. In R. Dillmann, U. Rembold und T. Lüth (Hrsg.), *Autonome Mobile Systeme*, Informatik aktuell, pages 172–181. Springer-Verlag, 1995.

18. S. Lanser, Ch. Zierl und R. Beutlhauser. Multibildkalibrierung einer CCD-Kamera. In G. Sagerer, S. Posch und F. Kummert (Hrsg.), *Mustererkennung*, Informatik-Fachberichte, pages 481–491. Deutsche Arbeitsgemeinschaft für Mustererkennung, Springer-Verlag, 1995.

19. D. G. Lowe. Fitting Parameterized Three-Dimensional Models to Images. *IEEE Trans. on Pattern Analysis and Machine Intelligence*, 13(5):441–450, 1991.

20. O. Munkelt. Aspect-Trees: Generation and Interpretation. *CVGIP: Image Understanding*, 61(3):365–386, May 1995.

21. O. Munkelt and C. Zierl. Fast 3-D Object Recognition using Feature Based Aspect-Trees. In *12th ICPR*, pages 854–857. IEEE Computer Society Press, 1994.

Absolute Lokalisation mobiler Roboter
durch farbige Codierung der Einsatzumgebung

Thomas Cord
Forschungszentrum Informatik (FZI)
Abteilung Technische Expertensysteme und Robotik
Haid-und-Neu-Straße 10-14, 76131 Karlsruhe

Dejan E. Lazic
Universität Karlsruhe
Institut für Algorithmen und Kognitive Systeme
Am Fasanengarten 5, 76128 Karlsruhe

Kurzfassung

Autonome mobile Systeme benötigen zur Navigation leistungsfähige Verfahren zur Bestimmung ihrer Position und Orientierung in der Einsatzumgebung. Dieser Beitrag beschreibt ein zuverlässiges Konzept für ein Lokalisationssystem, das auf einer vollständigen Codierung der Einsatzumgebung beruht. Der Boden der Einsatzumgebung wird dabei lückenlos mit farbigen Kacheln versehen. Zur Positions- und Orientierungsbestimmung wird ein zweidimensionales farbiges Muster auf den Kacheln benutzt, das jeden Punkt in der Arbeitsumgebung eindeutig festlegt. Dies ist auf zwei verschiedene Arten möglich: Entweder werden die Koordinaten des Mittelpunktes jeder Kachel bezüglich des Hauptkoordinatensystems der Einsatzumgebung mittels farbiger Codezeichen zusätzlich auf die Kacheln des Fußbodens aufgetragen oder es werden handelsübliche Fußbodenplatten mit einem zufälligen bunten Muster verwendet, das als farbiger Zufalls-Code interpretiert wird. In beiden Fällen nimmt der Roboter ein Bild einer ganzen Kachel und Teile angrenzender Kacheln mit einer CCD-Kamera auf und identifiziert mit Hilfe von Methoden der Kanalcodierung und der Farbbildverarbeitung die Information auf der Kachel.

1.   Einführung

Die Arbeiten auf dem Forschungsgebiet der Bewegungssteuerung von autonomen mobilen Robotern haben die Steigerung der Flexibilität und Betriebssicherheit bei Transportaufgaben durch Erhöhung ihrer Autonomie, d.h. eine Verbesserung der Fähigkeit, unvorhergesehene Ereignisse und Veränderungen der Umwelt zu beherrschen, zum Ziel [1]. Durch den Einsatz leistungsfähiger Sensoren und Navigationssysteme kann auf aktive und passive Leitspuren verzichtet werden. Hierdurch wird eine flexiblere Nutzung von Fahrtrassen und Rangierflächen möglich. Den Fahrzeugen wird so eine größtmögliche Unabhängigkeit und Flexibilität gegeben.

Die in der Literatur beschriebenen Navigationssysteme basieren auf einer internen Repräsentation der Einsatzumgebung, die meist in kartenartiger Form in absoluten kartesischen Koordinaten dargestellt wird. Zur Planung von Bewegungsbahnen und zur Planausführung mittels dieser Karte ist die genaue Kenntnis der absoluten Position des Fahrzeugs erforderlich. Die existierenden Navigationssysteme verwenden indirekte Meßmethoden, um einen Schätzwert für die Lokalisierung zu gewinnen. In [2, 3 und 4] wird beispielsweise ein hochauflösendes Laser-Scanner-System zur Positionsbestimmung verwendet, während in [5] einfachere Ultraschallsensoren eingesetzt werden. Zur Positionsschätzung zwischen zwei Messungen werden interne Sensoren, die keine Referenzen außerhalb des mobilen Roboters benötigen, verwendet.

Der Einsatz des Satelliten-Navigationssystems GPS zur Lokalisation mobiler Roboter wäre vielversprechend, allerdings schließt die Genauigkeit der für nicht-militärische Anwendungen verfügbaren Systeme einen Einsatz in der Robotik aus. Damit die hohe Präzision militärischen Anwendungen vorbehalten bleibt, werden die Signale für die zivile Nutzung künstlich modifiziert. Durch die Verwendung eines differentiellen GPS läßt sich diese Genauigkeitsverschlechterung zwar wieder aufheben, aber die Positionswerte eines solchen Systems schwanken dennoch um einige Meter. Außerdem ist der Einsatz von GPS prinzipbedingt auf Outdoor-Anwendungen beschränkt.

Zur Verbesserung der absoluten Lokalisation mobiler Roboter wird in diesem Beitrag ein zuverlässiges Verfahren vorgestellt, das auf einer vollständigen Codierung der Einsatzumgebung beruht. Der Boden der Einsatzumgebung wird dabei komplett mit farbigen Kachelmustern versehen. Solche farbig codierten Fußböden sind heute in optisch und ästhetisch ansprechenden Formen als Standardprodukt erhältlich. Zur Positions- und Orientierungsbestimmung wird ein zweidimensionales farbiges Muster benutzt, das durch eine Kachelcodierung jeden Punkt in der Arbeitsumgebung eindeutig festlegt. Durch den Einsatz fehlerkorrigierender Codes wird eine effiziente und sichere Lokalisation mobiler Roboter ermöglicht. Außerdem erlaubt dieser Navigationscode eine wesentliche Verbesserung der Navigation und Umweltmodellierung.

Die Idee der vollständigen Markierung der Einsatzumgebung wurde bereits mit großem Erfolg im FROG-System (*Free Ranging On Grid Navigation System*) umgesetzt [6, 7]. Die flexible und spurfreie Bewegung der Transportfahrzeuge findet bereits weltweit praktische Anwendung in Großregallagern und Fertigungsumgebungen. Allerdings wird bei diesem System die Einsatzumgebung relativ markiert, so daß die absolute Position nur inkrementell bestimmt werden kann. Das in dieser Arbeit beschriebene absolute Verfahren ermöglicht eine zuverlässigere und effizientere Lokalisierung mobiler Roboter.

2. Entwicklung des Navigationscodes

Bei diesem System wird der Boden der Einsatzumgebung vollständig mit quadratischen Kacheln $T = \{T_{ij} \mid i = 1, ..., I; j = 1, ..., J\}$ versehen. Die Koordinaten des Mittelpunktes P jeder Kachel T_{ij} bezüglich des Hauptkoordinatensystems der Einsatzumgebung werden mit farbigen Codezeichen auf die Kacheln des Fußbodens geschrieben, so daß ein entsprechendes Kachelmuster bzw. Codewort entsteht. Die Menge der Kacheln mit verschiedenen Mustern stellt den Navigationscode dar. Mit einer CCD-Kamera nimmt der Roboter ein Bild Im einer ganzen Kachel T^{*}_{ij} und Teile der angrenzenden Kacheln auf (Abb. 1). Durch Methoden der Bildverarbeitung kann das Bild in Normalposition, d.h. kollinear zur Roboterachse X_R gebracht und somit die Orientierung des Roboters Θ_R bestimmt werden. Der Roboter decodiert die Information, die in der nächstliegenden Kachel eingeschrieben ist (Koordinaten X^{*}_{i} und Y^{*}_{j} des Mittelpunktes P^{*} in T^{*}_{ij}) und erhält so einen Schätzwert seiner eigenen Position. Mit Verfahren der Bildverarbeitung ist es möglich, die Roboterposition noch präziser zu bestimmen, da diese von den Kameraeigenschaften und der Dichte der codierten Information abhängig ist.

Bei der Decodierung der codierten Positionsdaten sind folgende Fehlerquellen zu berücksichtigen:

* Staub oder Schmutz bedeckt die Kacheln teilweise
* Kratzer oder Beschädigungen der Kacheln
* Verfälschung des Kachelmusters durch einfallendes Licht oder Schatten
* Störungen die durch das Bildaufnahmesystem verursacht werden.

Durch die Verwendung eines fehlerkorrigierenden Codes ist es möglich, die Auswirkungen dieser Fehlerquellen zu vermindern und so eine zuverlässige und sichere Navigation des Fahrzeugs zu erreichen.

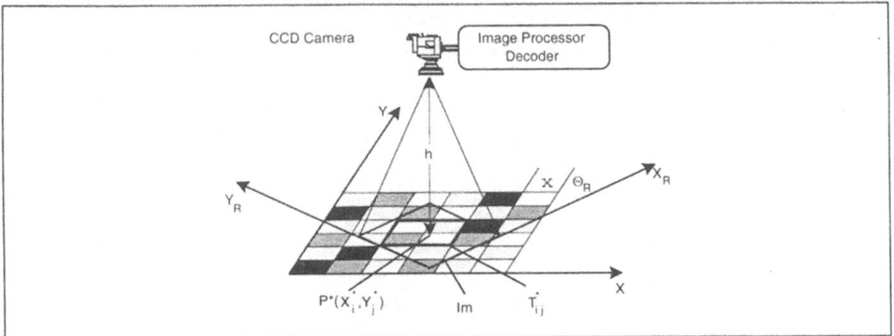

Abb. 1:   Lokalisation eines mobilen Roboters mit farbig codierten Kacheln

Zur Darstellung der Codewörter auf den Kacheln kann je nach Anwendung zwischen zwei verschiedene Verfahren gewählt werden:

1) Die Codezeichen, welche die Koordinaten des Mittelpunktes jeder Kachel bezüglich des Hauptkoordinatensystems der Einsatzumgebung repräsentieren, werden mit Hilfe eines speziell entwickelten Designs direkt auf den Fußboden geschrieben. Beim Entwurf des Kachelmusters können ästetische Aspekte berücksichtigt werden, so daß ein optisch ansprechender Bodenbelag entsteht (Abb. 2a).

2) Es werden Fußbodenplatten aus Kautschuck oder PVC mit einem zufälligen bunten Muster verwendet, das als farbiger Zufalls-Code interpretiert wird. Solche Fußböden werden in unterschiedlichsten Formen und Farben als Standardprodukt hergestellt und eignen sich besonders für Serviceroboteranwendungen (Abb. 2b).

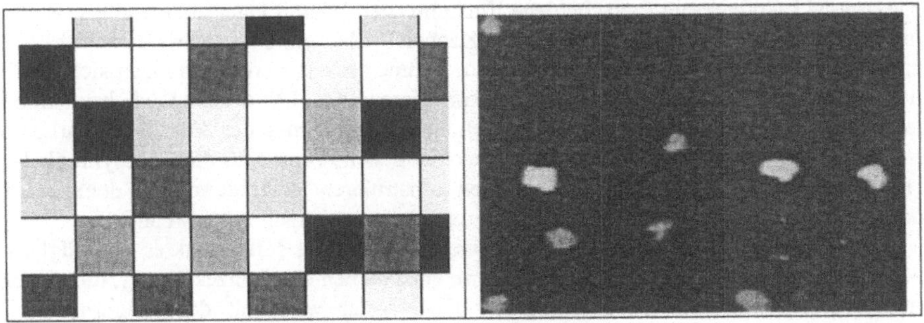

Abb. 2:   Darstellung der Codewörter auf den Kacheln
            a) speziell entwickeltes Design (links)
            b) Fußboden mit buntem zufälligen Muster (rechts)

2.1 Entwicklung eines codierten Kacheldesigns

Ausgehend von den Grundflächenmaßen der Einsatzumgebung und der erforderlichen Positioniergenauigkeit des Roboters muß ein Code ausgewählt werden, der die gewünschten Fehlerkorrekturmöglichkeiten besitzt und gleichzeitig genügend Codewörter zur Verfügung stellt, um die Einsatzumgebung mit einer ausreichenden Anzahl von Kacheln bedecken zu können. Die Verwendung eines Reed-Solomon Codes für die Muster, die auf den Kacheln anzuordnen sind, ist am geeignetsten, weil diese Codes aus mehrwertigen Symbolen bestehen, die durch verschiedene Farben dargestellt werden. Außerdem eignen sich Reed-Solomon Codes für Übertragungskanäle mit bündelartiger Fehlerstruktur [8]. Reed-Solomon Codes haben die allgemeine Form:

$$\{x_i = (x_{i1}, ..., x_{iN}) \,|\, x_{in} \in GF(2^m), i = 1, ..., M\}$$

$$GF(2^m) = \{\Psi_1, ..., \Psi_q\}$$

und folgende Eigenschaften:
- Anzahl der verschiedenen Symbole: $q = 2^m$
- Länge des Codewortes: $N = 2^m - 1$
- Länge des Informationswortes: $K = 2^m - 2t - 1$
- Minimale Hamming-Distanz: $d_{min} = 2t + 1$
- Anzahl korrigierbarer Fehler: t
- Anzahl möglicher Codewörter: $M = 2^{mK}$.

Die verschiedenen Codewörter werden von einem Generatorpolynom erzeugt,

$$g(z) = (z - \alpha)(z - \alpha^2) ... (z - \alpha^{2t})$$

wobei α ein primitives Element von $GF(2^m)$ ist.

Die Symbole des Reed-Solomon Codes werden in dieser Arbeit durch acht verschiedene Farben dargestellt, d.h. es wurde ein Reed-Solomon Code mit Codesymbolen aus dem Galois-Feld $GF(2^3)$ gewählt, der Codewörter der Länge $N=7$ mit 8 verschiedenen Symbolen (Farben) produziert. Die Anzahl der möglichen Codewörter ist abhängig von den gewünschten Fehlerkorrekturmöglichkeiten. Ein guter Kompromiß ist die Wahl von $t=2$ möglichen Symbolfehlerkorrekturen. Dieser Code beinhaltet $K=3$ Informationssymbole pro Codewort und erzeugt insgesamt 512 Codewörter (verschiedene Kachelmuster). Damit kann man eine Einsatzumgebung von ca. $46\ m^2$ mit $30 \times 30\ cm^2$ großen Kacheln bedecken. Diese Variante ist für kleinere Einsatzumgebungen geeignet. Müssen größere Räume codiert werden, so bietet sich die Wahl eines Codes an, der nur einen Symbolfehler korrigieren kann. Mit diesem Code kann eine Fläche von ca. $3000\ m^2$ gekachelt werden. Durch eine Vergrößerung der Anzahl der Farben oder durch eine zusätzliche Verwendung von unterschiedlichen Formen für die Codesymbole lassen sich weitere Codes für grössere Umgebungen konstruieren. Außerdem ist es denkbar, einen Code in verschiedenen Bereichen der Einsatzumgebung mehrfach zu verwenden.

Für jede Kachel T_{ij} werden die Koordinaten (X_i, Y_j) des Mittelpunktes P bezüglich der Kachelgröße normiert. Diese normierten Werte entsprechen den Indizes i und j, die ein Informationswort bilden. Die Decodierung der Codewörter wird mit dem Algorithmus von Berlekamp-Massey durchgeführt [9, 10].

Eine weitere wichtige Aufgabe ist die Auswahl der Farben und der Größe der Symbole, so daß das gesamte Kachelmuster leicht und möglichst fehlerfrei decodiert werden kann. Es wurden acht Farben mit einem optimalen Farbabstand ausgewählt. Die Codewörter der Länge $N=7$ werden in Form einer $3x3$-Matrix auf den Kacheln angeordnet. Die beiden ungenutzten Felder werden zur Beschreibung der Kachelorientierung und zur eindeutigen Festlegung des Beginns jedes Codewortes verwendet. Hierzu dient das spezielle Synchronisationssymbol S, das sich bei jeder Kachel in der unteren rechten und der unteren linken Ecke befindet. Durch das Synchronisationssymbol ist es möglich, die gesamte Bodenfläche mit Codewörtern auszufüllen und auf Begrenzungsflächen zwischen den Kacheln zu verzichten (Abb. 3).

Abb. 3:   Anordnung der Codesymbole und der Synchronisationsymbole auf einer Kachel

Zur Analyse der möglichen Fehlerquellen bei der Detektion der codierten Informationen wurde ein Datenkanalmodell eines uniformen symmetrischen Kanals entwickelt (Abb. 4). Dieses Modell beschreibt die Symbolfehlerwahrscheinlichkeit $p(x)$ in Abhängigkeit von der Kantenlänge x der farbigen Codezeichen. Mit q wird die Anzahl der Symbole (Farben) bezeichnet. Es ist zu erkennen, daß die Fehlerwahrscheinlichkeiten $p(x)$ und $\varepsilon(x)$ sinken, wenn die Symbolgröße x vergrößert wird. Durch Untersuchung verschiedener Störungsursachen hat sich gezeigt, daß die Fehlerwahrscheinlichkeit $p(x)$ durch folgende Formel dargestellt werden kann:

$$p(x) = \frac{1}{2}e^{-x^4/2}.$$

Mit Methoden der Informations- und Codierungstheorie kann die Kanalkapazität, die Informationsdichte und andere Parameter des entworfenen Systems berechnet werden [11].

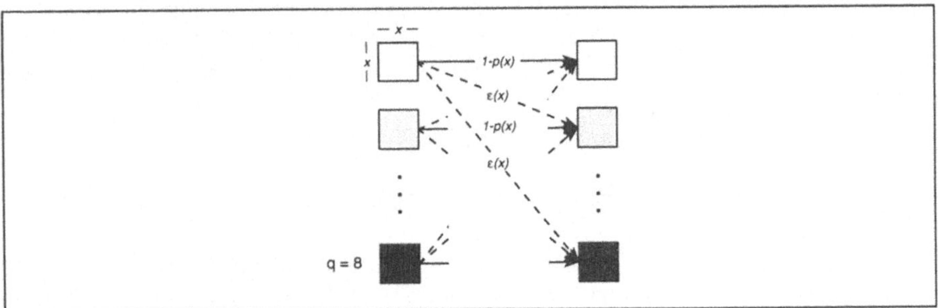

Abb. 4:   Uniformer symmetrischer Übertragungskanal mit 8 Symbolen (Farben)

2.2 Verwendung von Kacheln mit zufälligem Muster

Bei der Verwendung von Fußböden mit einem zufälligen Muster werden die einzelnen Bodenplatten vor dem Verlegen in der Einsatzumgebung des Roboters analysiert. Jede Kachel wird dabei in N Teilflächen zerlegt. Durch Auswertung der Farbinformationen jeder Teilfläche wird ein binäres Codewort $v=(v_1, v_2, ..., v_N)$ erzeugt. Die Codewörter einer Menge von Fußbodenplatten bilden einen nichtlinearen fehlerkorrigierenden Code. Durch Auswahl von Kacheln mit Codewörtern mit einer größtmöglichen Hamming-Dinstanz läßt sich ein nichtlinearer Code mit fast optimalen Fehlerkorrektureigenschaften finden.

Praktische Versuche mit dem Kautschukbelag *noraplan viva* der Fa. Freudenberg haben gezeigt, daß eine Unterteilung einer Kachel der Größe *305 x 305 mm* in *36* Teilflächen einen nahezu optimalen Code liefert. Bei der Herstellung dieses Bodenbelags werden durch einen

Zufallsprozeß Flecken in zwei verschiedenen Farben erzeugt. Überschreitet die Anzahl der Farbflecken in einer Teilfläche einen vorgegebenen Schwellwert, so steht an der entsprechenden Stelle des binären Codewortes eine „1", sonst „0" (Abb. 5).

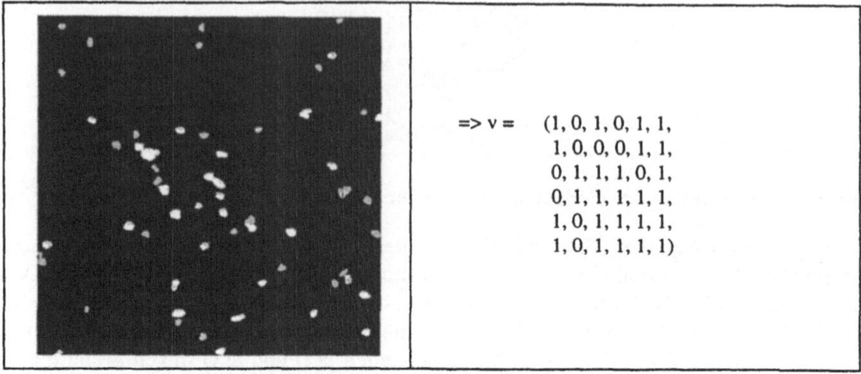

Abb. 5:   Beispiel für die Detektion eines Codewortes

Durch eine statistische Analyse einer großen Anzahl von Bodenkacheln wurde gezeigt, daß die Hamming-Distanzen der Codewörter binomialverteilt sind. Der Code ist daher fast optimal [12]. Es ist möglich, während des Lernvorganges für eine Einsatzumgebung nur Codewörter auszuwählen, die eine größtmögliche Hamming-Distanz haben. Bei der Decodierung des Codes ist eine maximale Anzahl von Symbolfehlern korrigierbar. Zur Decodierung der Codewörter wurde ein Maximum-Likelihood Verfahren realisiert. Mit Hilfe einer Lookup-Tabelle, die die Koordinaten (X_i, Y_j) jeder Kachel T_{ij} speichert und beim Verlegen des Fußbodens erstellt wurde, kann für jedes detektierte Codewort die entsprechende Positionsinformation bestimmt werden.

3.   Detektion und Decodierung der Codewörter

Die Detektion der farbigen Informationen, die auf die Kacheln geschrieben sind, wird mit Methoden der Farbbildverarbeitung durchgeführt. Da die Farbeigenschaften des Fußbodens durch unterschiedliche Beleuchtungsverhältnisse sehr stark variieren, müssen sehr robuste Auswerteverfahren verwendet werden. Die Erkennung der Codezeichen in einem Farbbild, das der Roboter mit einer CCD-Kamera vom Boden der Einsatzumgebung aufgenommen hat, beruht auf einer echtzeitfähigen Farbanalyse. Hierzu wird vorab in einem Lernvorgang die Farbverteilung der verschiedenen Codesymbole erfaßt. Nach Auswertung dieser Verteilung wird ein Farbklassifikator mit einer Funktionstabelle geladen, um für jedes Pixel im Videotakt zu entscheiden, um welches Codezeichen es sich handelt. Während des Meßvorgangs liefert der Farbklassifikator ein Klassifikationsbild, das nachbearbeitet werden muß, um kleine Störungen zu unterdrücken und die zumeist zerstückelten Detektionsgebiete zu verschmelzen. Anschließend kann die Position der einzelnen Codezeichen bestimmt werden.

4.   Zusammenfassung

Es wurde ein zuverlässiges Verfahren zur absoluten Lokalisation mobiler Roboter vorgestellt, das auf einer vollständigen Codierung der Einsatzumgebung beruht. Der Boden der Einsatzumgebung wird dabei lückenlos mit farbigen Mustern versehen. Solche farbig codierten Fußböden werden in optisch ansprechenden Formen als Standardprodukt hergestellt. Die verwendete Codierung erlaubt die Korrektur möglicher Fehler, die beispielsweise bei Verschmutzungen von Kacheln oder Schatten auftreten, wenn die Kacheloberfläche bis zu einem Drittel bedeckt ist. Das realisierte System erlaubt eine Positionsbestimmung in Echtzeit, wenn sich der mobile Roboter mit moderater Geschwindigkeit fortbewegt. Mobile Roboter können durch dieses Verfahren neuartige Anwendungsfelder bei Dienstleistungs- und Serviceaufgaben im industriellen sowie nichtindustriellen Bereich, etwa zur Übernahme von Überwachungs-, Reinigungs- oder Transportaufgaben, erschließen.

Schlußbemerkung

Die Autoren danken Prof. Dr.-Ing. U. Rembold sowie Prof. Dr. T. Beth von der Universität Karlsruhe für ihre Ratschläge und die Unterstützung. Die Arbeiten wurden am Forschungszentrum Informatik (FZI), Abteilung Technische Expertensysteme und Robotik und am Europäischen Institut für Systemsicherheit (E.I.S.S.) durchgeführt.

Literaturverzeichnis

[1] P. Hoppen, *Autonome mobile Roboter: Echtzeitnavigation in bekannter und unbekannter Umgebung*, Dissertation an der Universität Kaiserslautern, BI-Wiss.-Verlag, 1992

[2] F. Dierks, *Freie Navigation autonomer Fahrzeuge*, 10. Fachgespräch „Autonome Mobile Systeme 1994", P. Levi et. al. (Hrsg.), Stuttgart, 1994

[3] G, Weiß, C. Wetzler, E. von Puttkamer, *Positions- und Orientierungsbestimmung von bewegten Systemen in Gebäuden durch Korrelation von Laserradardaten*, 10. Fachgespräch „Autonome Mobile Systeme 1994", P. Levi et. al. (Hrsg.), Stuttgart, 1994

[4] U.D. Hanebeck, G. Schmidt, *Absolute Localization of Fast Mobile Robots Based on an Angle Measurement Technique*, IFAC Workshop on Intelligent Components for Autonomous and Semi-Autonomous Vehicles, Toulouse, France, 1995

[5] F. Wallner, R. Dillmann, *Situationsabhängige Einsatzplanung kooperierender aktiver Sensoren auf einem mobilen Robotersystem*, 10. Fachgespräch „Autonome Mobile Systeme 1994", P. Levi et. al. (Hrsg.), Stuttgart, 1994

[6] D. Taylor, *New Developments in Automatic Guided Vehicles*, The fabricator, January/February 1991

[7] J. Manji, *Manufacturing the Mac with Automated Material Handling*, Automation, February 1991

[8] D.E. Lazic, F.J. Hampson, *Error Control in Position Determination of Autonomous Mobile Robots*, Proc. of the International Symposium on Communication Theory & Applications, Lake District, UK, 1993

[9] E. Berlekamp, *Algebraic Coding Theory*, Mc Graw-Hill, New York, 1968

[10] J. Massey, *Shift-Register Synthesis and BCH Decoding*, IEEE Transaction on Information Theory, Vol. IT-15, 1969

[11] D.E. Lazic, T. Cord, *A Highly Reliable Navigation System for Autonomous Mobile Robots in a Structured Environment*, Proc. of the Second ECPD International Conference on Advanced Robotics, Intelligent Automation and Active Systems, Vienna, Austria, 1996

[12] D.E. Lazic, V. Senk, *A Direct Geometrical Method for Bounding the Error Exponent of any Specific Family of Channel Codes - Part I: Cutoff Rate Lower Bound for Block Codes*, IEEE Transactions on Information Theory, IT-38(5), 1548-1559, September 1992

Umweltmodelle, Lokalisation

Ein geometrisch–symbolisches Umgebungsmodell zur Unterstützung verschiedener Perzeptionsaufgaben autonomer, mobiler Systeme

Norbert O. Stöffler, Alexa Hauck, Georg Färber

Lehrstuhl für Prozeßrechner
Technische Universität München
email: {stoffler,hauck,faerber}@lpr.e-technik.tu-muenchen.de

Kurzfassung. Wesentlich für die Autonomie eines mobilen Systems ist die Interaktion mit einer dynamischen Umgebung. Hierzu benötigt es Sensorik, um sein Modell der Umgebung stets aktuell zu halten. Das Modell wird schritthaltend korrigiert, so daß es sich mit den Sensordaten zur Deckung bringen läßt.
Dieser Beitrag beschreibt ein Umgebungsmodell das auf autonomen, mobilen Systemen mit unterschiedlichen Sensoren eingesetzt wird. Die Modellierung erfolgt geometrisch, sensorspezifische Transformationen finden während des Zugriffs statt. Durch seine hierarchische, symbolische Struktur kann auf das Modell während unterschiedlicher Perzeptionsaufgaben (absolute und relative Lokalisation, Objekterkennung, Zustandsbestimmung) einheitlich zugegriffen werden.

1 Einleitung

Ein wichtiger Beitrag zur Autonomie eines mobilen Systems ist die Fähigkeit, seine Umgebung sensoriell zu erfassen (*Perzeption*) und diese Information adäquat zu interpretieren. Abhängig von der Intention der Interpretation lassen sich mehrere Perzeptionsaufgaben unterscheiden. Zentrales Problem eines mobilen Systems ist die eigene Lokalisation in der Umgebung. Eine weitere wichtige Aufgabe ist die Erkennung von relevanten Objekten und die Lokalisation relativ zu diesen Objekten, respektive die Bestimmung der absoluten Objektlage.

Unterschiedlichste Sensorsysteme werden hierfür zur Zeit eingesetzt, entwickelt und weiterentwickelt [5]. Sensorrohdatensätze werden im allgemeinen vorverarbeitet, um sie auf Wesentliches zu reduzieren, i.e. sogenannte (sensorspezifische) Merkmale zu extrahieren. Als Beispiele hierfür seien Kanten (Diskontinuitäten des Grauwerts) in Videobildern oder Flächen in Entfernungsbildern genannt.

Eine große Klasse in der Literatur beschriebener Verfahren bedient sich zur Interpretation dieser Merkmale modellbasierter Ansätze, d.h. ein geometrisches Modell wird mit den Sensordaten zur Deckung gebracht. Vereinfacht dargestellt heißt das, daß Modellhypothesen solange algorithmisch variiert werden, bis sich damit ein Merkmalssatz prädizieren läßt, der dem extrahierten Satz entspricht.

Meist werden je nach Sensortyp und Perzeptionsaufgabe unterschiedliche Modelle verwendet. Während sich für Videosensoren und kantenbasierte Algorithmen dreidimensionale "Drahtmodell"-Repräsentationen eignen, lassen sich Rundum-Scans - wie sie beispielsweise von Radarsensoren geliefert werden - gut mit zweidimensionalen Raumschnitten vergleichen [12]. Abhängig von der Perzeptionsaufgabe unterscheidet man auch Umgebungsmodelle und Objektmodelle.

1.1 Ansatz

Bei der Realisierung eines autonomen mobilen Systems ist es wünschenswert, nur ein Modell der Umgebung zu halten, mit dem sich alle anfallenden Perzeptionsaufgaben für alle installierten Sensortypen behandeln lassen. Andernfalls ergeben sich Konsistenz-, und bei komplexen Modellen auch Speicherplatzprobleme. Im Rahmen des Teilprojektes Q5 des Sonderforschungsbereiches 331 (SFB 331) wurde eine Modellstruktur entwickelt, die den gestellten Anforderungen genügt und auf den Demonstratoren des SFB bei unterschiedlichen Aufgaben zum Einsatz kommt [6, 2, 13].

Modellzugriffe können hierarchisch auf Welt-, Objekt- und Klassenebene erfolgen. Sensorspezifische Merkmalssätze werden, entsprechend gewähltem Modellausschnitt und zu testenden Parametern, zur Laufzeit prädiziert. Das entwickelte Zugriffskonzept erlaubt den parallelen Zugriff mehrerer Modell-Clients und das gleichzeitige Testen eventuell konkurrierender Hypothesen. Über einen sensorunabhängigen, symbolischen Kommunikationsmechanismus [5] sind die lokalen Modelle kooperierender AMS gekoppelt, um für globale Konsistenz zu sorgen.

Da die Untersuchung von Videosensorik immer noch ein sehr aktuelles Forschungsgebiet mit hoher Dynamik in Methoden und Repräsentationen ist, wurde hier eine generische Merkmalsbeschreibung geschaffen, mit der sich ein breites Spektrum von unterschiedlichen Auswertungs- und Interpretationsalgorithmen bedienen und untersuchen läßt, ohne auf den Vorteil eines einheitlichen Modells verzichten zu müssen.

2 Modellstruktur

Um eine möglichst einheitliche Umgebungsbeschreibung für unterschiedliche Sensoren mit unterschiedlichen Sensormerkmalen zu erreichen, erfolgt die Modellierung primär geometrisch. Körper werden durch ihre Oberflächen (*Boundary Representation*, kurz *B-Rep*) dargestellt. Jede Oberfläche besteht aus einer Menge von Eckpunkten und den durch diese aufgespannten Polygonen.

Für entfernungsgebende Sensoren können Sensormerkmale wie Flächen oder Schnittlinien direkt aus der *B-Rep* abgeleitet werden. Im Falle von Videosensoren müßten Oberflächeneigenschaften und Beleuchtung sehr genau modelliert werden, um ein realistisches Sensorbild berechnen zu können. Auch der rechnerische Aufwand hierfür wäre enorm. Deshalb werden die vom Sensor gut detektierbaren Kanten als separate Referenzen auf die Eckpunkte der *B-Rep* dargestellt. Dies reduziert die Berechnung eines Sensorbildes zum reinen Sichtbarkeitstest der 3D-Kanten gegen die *B-Reps*. Weitere Sonderbehandlungen der Videomerkmale werden in Kapitel 2.2 erläutert.

Rotatorische oder translatorische Freiheitsgrade werden ähnlich den Konventionen der Manipulator-Kinematik beschrieben. Achsen und Koordinatensysteme sind in Anlehnung an den Denavit-Hartenberg-Formalismus [3] gewählt (siehe Abb. 1): Die Z-Achse fällt mit der Rotations- bzw. Translationsachse zusammen. Ihre Richtung wird so gewählt, daß sich ein positiver Drehsinn ergibt. Da Objekte mit mehreren parallelen Gelenken nicht mehr einer kinematischen Kette, sondern einer baumartigen Struktur entsprechen, konnten die Konventionen für die X-Achse nicht befolgt werden. Um eine einheitliche Struktur von Perzeptionsalgorithmen zu erleichtern, werden die Gelenkzustände auf das Intervall [0, 1] normiert. Darüberhinaus existiert noch ein Wert "unbekannt". Zu jedem Gelenk wird außerdem der vom Unterobjekt überstrichene Raumbereich (im folgenden als "Maske" bezeichnet) gespeichert, um bei unbekannten Zuständen für die Verdeckungsrechnung eine schnelle Worst-Case-Abschätzung zu erhalten.

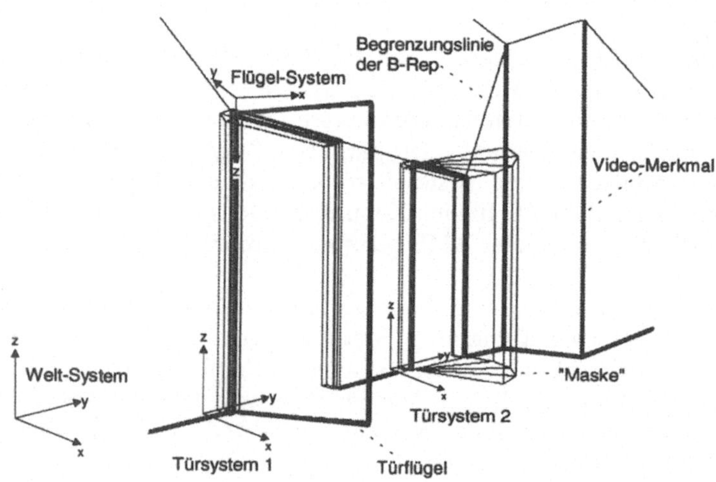

Abb. 1. Geometrische und kinematische Struktur der Modellierung

Jeder Knoten des Objektbaumes trägt die *B-Rep* und die Merkmalsbeschreibung des Teilobjektes. Da die geometrische Beschreibung gleicher Objekte identisch ist, werden Objekte zu Klassen zusammengefaßt. Instanzen unterscheiden sich nur in ihrer Weltposition und ihrem Zustand, also der Menge aller Gelenkzustände. Da es realistischerweise weder möglich noch nötig ist, die gesamte Umgebung eines AMS in einzelne Objekte aufzuteilen, wurde zusätzlich ein Pseudoobjekt, die sogenannte *Kulisse*, eingeführt. Sie enthält alle Umgebungselemente unbekannter oder irrelevanter Objektzugehörigkeit in Form einer einzigen, umfassenden *B-Rep*. Um schnell auf alle Umgebungselemente im Sensorsichtbereich zugreifen zu können, werden zwei Ortsindizes verwendet. Objekte sind über ein äquidistantes Gitter referenziert, die Kulisse aufgrund des ungleich höheren Speicherbedarfs über einen s2d-Baum [8].

Als weitere Indizes fungieren Gelenk-, Objekt- und Klassennamen. Auf symbolischer Ebene ergibt sich damit eine Modellstruktur wie in Abb. 2.

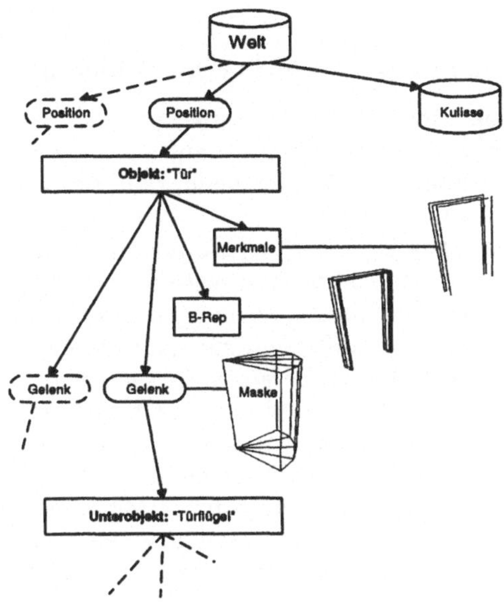

Abb. 2. Symbolische Struktur der Modellierung

2.1 Merkmalsprädiktion

Merkmale entfernungsgebender Sensoren gehen durch einfache geometrische Transformationen aus der Oberflächenbeschreibung hervor [10].

Für die Sichtbarkeitsberechnung der Videomerkmale wurde der aus der Computergraphik bekannte z-Buffer Algorithmus angepaßt. Die im Sichtkegel des Sensors erfaßten Polygone der Oberflächenbeschreibung werden in die Bildebene projiziert und gerastert. Dabei wird für jedes Pixel nur die geringste Tiefe gespeichert (beim üblichen Koordinatensystem mit x und y in der Bildebene ist die z-Koordinate eben gerade die Tiefe). Das Ergebnis dieses Vorgangs ist eine zweidimensionale, gerasterte Tiefenkarte. In einem zweiten Schritt werden die im Sichtkegel enthaltenen, linienförmigen Videomerkmale gegen diese Karte getestet. Dazu werden sie ebenfalls projiziert und gerastert. Hat ein Pixel eines Merkmals eine geringere Tiefe als das Pixel der Tiefenkarte, ist das zugehörige Liniensegment sichtbar.

Im Gegensatz zu Computergraphik-Anwendungen wird der selbe Rasterisierungsalgorithmus für Polygone und Linien verwendet. Da die Linien auch auf den selben 3D-Eckpunkten basieren wie die Polygonränder, werden somit Quantisierungsartefakte vermieden.

Neben den günstigen Realzeiteigenschaften des z-Buffer-Algorithmus durch Hardwareunterstützung [11] und regelbare Auflösung der Tiefenkarte lassen sich auch einfache Gütekriterien für die Sichtbarkeit eines Merkmales, wie z.B. Länge in Pixel, ableiten.

2.2 Erweiterungen in der Definition von Videomerkmalen

Die Interpretation von Videobildern ist immer noch eine der anspruchsvollsten Aufgaben bei der Sensordatenverarbeitung auf autonomen, mobilen Systemen. Hier kann eine Unterstützung durch die Modellprädiktion auf verschiedenen Ebenen zum Tragen kommen.

Die *Segmentierung* (*figure–ground–separation*) wird durch die von den Modellmerkmalen aufgespannten Aufmerksamkeitsbereiche (*regions of interest*) unterstützt, Lage- und Nachbarschaftsbeziehungen können zur *Gruppierung* von Sensormerkmalen genutzt und außerdem zur quantitativen Bewertung potentieller Bild-Modell-Korrespondenzen herangezogen werden.

Um je nach Perzeptionsaufgabe und verwendetem Algorithmus die relevante Information bereitstellen zu können, wurde eine generische Struktur entwickelt: Aufbauend auf dem beschriebenen Basismerkmal "Linie" können durch Attribuierung und Aggregation sogenannte *aggregierte Merkmalsklassen* definiert werden; ein typisches Beispiel wäre eine Merkmalsklasse "Video–Kontur", welche eine Liste von Liniensegmenten und ein Attribut enthält, das angibt, ob die Kontur geschlossen ist.

Aggregierte Merkmalsklassen fallen in zwei Hauptgruppen: *aufgabenspezifische* und *topologische* Merkmale. Erstere sind auf eine bestimmte Perzeptionsaufgabe spezialisiert; sie enthalten genau die Modellinformation, die für die jeweilige Aufgabe relevant ist. Beispiele finden sich in Kap. 4, in dem die experimentelle Realisierung einer Perzeptionsaufgabe beschrieben wird. *Topologische* Merkmalsklassen modellieren geometrische Relationen, wie sie bei der Gruppierung von Merkmalen entstehen und speziell bei der videobasierten Objekterkennung Anwendung finden. Die "Sichtbarkeit" eines aggregierten Merkmals wird durch Auswertung einer merkmalsspezifischen Regel bewertet. Diese Regel verknüpft eine Reihe von Maßzahlen wie Linienlängen und Orientierungen, die wiederum bei der Sichtbarkeitsprüfung der Linien bestimmt werden.

Eine Korrespondenzfindung auf der Ebene topologischer Merkmale ist sowohl schneller als auch robuster als auf der Ebene der Einzelmerkmale, da die Zahl der zu testenden Zuordnungen erheblich geringer ist und die Wahrscheinlichkeit der Verwechslung sinkt. Ersteres gilt umso mehr, wenn Merkmalsextraktionsmethoden eingesetzt werden, die schon auf der Sensorseite topologische Eigenschaften extrahieren, wie z.B. in [9, 7].

3 Anwendungsarchitektur

Abb. 3 zeigt eine typische Anwendungsarchitektur, bestehend aus dem Umgebungsmodell-Server und einigen als Clients realisierten Perzeptionsprozessen. Eine experimentelle Version dieser Systemarchitektur wurde im Rahmen des SFB 331 implementiert.

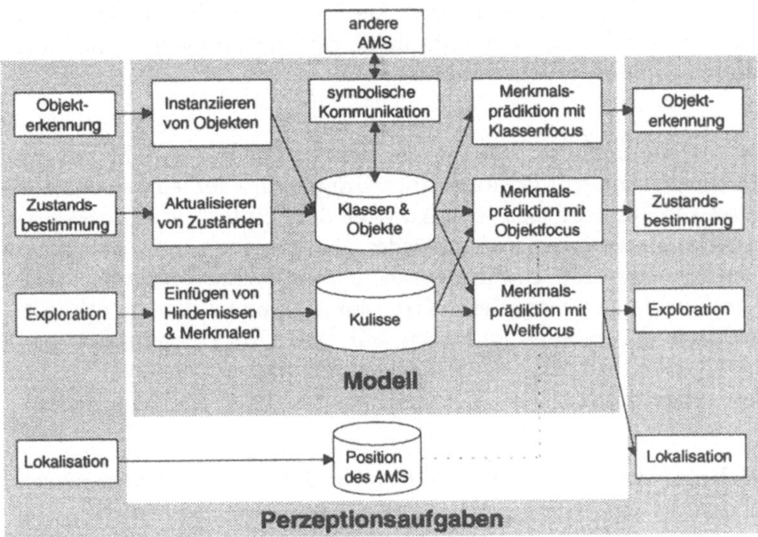

Abb. 3. Anwendungsarchitektur

Mittels der Perzeptionsprozesse wird das Umgebungsmodell kontinuierlich aktualisiert. Jeder Prozeß extrahiert die für seine Aufgabe relevante Information aus den Sensordaten und vergleicht sie mit der Modellinformation. Die Differenzen werden entsprechend der Aufgabe interpretiert und die entsprechenden Parameter angepaßt.

Jeder Client besitzt einen privaten Kommunikationskanal zum Modell, einen sogenannten *Accessor*, der sich wie eine lokale Modellkopie verhält. Die Prozesse können somit parallel ablaufen, ohne sich beim Testen diversitärer Hypothesen zu beeinflussen. Desweiteren enthält der Accessor Zugriffsparameter wie z.B. das Sensormodell, die Sensorposition und Objektzustände. Zugriffe können somit inkrementell erfolgen, was die Datenhaltung im Accessor optimiert. Zwei virtuelle Zeiger, als *Focus* und *Zoom* bezeichnet, referenzieren den relevanten Ausschnitt aus dem in Abb. 2 dargestellten Objektbaum. Der *Focus* wird entsprechend der durchzuführenden Perzeption gesetzt, er zeigt für Lokalisationsaufgaben auf die Welt, für Objekterkennungen auf eine zu erkennende Klasse und für die Bestimmung von Objektzuständen auf Objekte oder Teilobjekte. Nur die Zustände des gerade fokussierten Objektes sind parametrierbar. Änderungen der Zustände eines Objektes werden solange auf einer privaten Kopie ausgeführt, bis sie explizit vom Client ins Modell zurückgeschrieben werden. Der *Zoom* beeinflußt die Auswahl der prädizierten Merkmale. Er wird algorithmusspezifisch gesetzt.

Lokalisation. Ein Parameter, auf dem die meisten Perzeptionsaufgaben aufbauen, ist die Position des AMS. Diese wird von einem oder mehreren Lokalisationsprozessen aktualisiert [12]. Da die Genauigkeit der Lokalisation stark von der Qualität der gefundenen Korrespondenzen abhängt, werden nur Merkmale mit sehr guter Sichtbarkeit prädiziert. Teilobjekte mit unbekanntem Gelenkzustand werden durch ihre Maske ersetzt. Die Projektion der Maske in den z-Buffer "maskiert", im wörtlichen Sinne, all diejenigen Merkmale aus, die vom beweglichen Teilobjekt verdeckt sein könnten.

Exploration. Signifikante Differenzen zwischen Bild- und Modellinformation lassen auf eine veränderte Position eines Umgebungselementes oder auf ein noch unbekanntes Objekt schließen. Die Aufgabe der Explorationsprozesse ist es, diese Differenzen auszuwerten und entweder Modellelemente zu aktualisieren oder neue einzutragen [1, 13]. Dafür werden neu entdeckte Merkmale verfolgt, stabilisiert und nach geometrischen Kriterien gruppiert. Daran schließt sich die Rekonstruktion der B-Reps und eventuell eine Objekterkennung an. Falls die gefundene Struktur keiner bekannten Objektklasse zuzuordnen ist, wird sie in der Kulisse eingetragen.

Zustandsbestimmung. Eine Perzeptionsaufgabe, die die hierarchische Struktur des Modells besonders gut nutzt, ist die rekursive Bestimmung von Gelenkzuständen. Sie wird anhand eines experimentellen Beispiels in Kap. 4 dargestellt.

Objekterkennung. Innerhalb der experimentellen Systemarchitektur wurden mehrere Algorithmen zur *Objektidentifikation* untersucht [4, 6]. Der Accessor wird jeweils auf Objektklassen fokussiert, die Sensorposition wird zunächst im Koordinatensystem der zu erkennenden Klasse angegeben. Falls ein Objekt erkannt werden kann, wird eine neue Instanz angelegt und im Modell an der entsprechenden Position eingetragen.

Kommunikation. Zusätzlich zu den sensorspezifischen Zugriffen kann auch auf symbolischer Ebene Modellinformation abgefragt und manipuliert werden. Unabhängig voneinander operierende AMS können miteinander kommunizieren, indem sie Objektnamen und -attribute (i.e. Zustände und Positionen) mittels eines symbolischen Kommunikationsmediums [5] austauschen.

4 Anwendungsbeispiel

Die Anwendung des Modells soll nun am Beispiel der videobasierten *Zustandsbestimmung* veranschaulicht werden. Im Gegensatz zur 3D-Objektlokalisation wird diese Aufgabe nur selten in der Literatur beschrieben, nicht zuletzt weil Objekte mit internen Freiheitsgraden viele sehr unterschiedliche Ansichten aufweisen, was bei konventionellen Lokalisationsalgorithmen schnell zu einer kombinatorischen Explosion der Zahl der möglichen Korrespondenzen führt.

Die vorgestellte hierarchische Objektstruktur erlaubt hingegen ein rekursives Vorgehen. Zuerst wird der statische Teil, also die "Wurzel" eines Objekts und damit gleichzeitig die Achsen der Teilobjekte lokalisiert. Hierauf wird der Gelenkzustand des ersten Teilobjektes bestimmt, gefolgt von denen seiner Teilobjekte und so fort, bis alle Freiheitsgrade gefesselt sind. Auf mobilen Systemen ist die Zustandsbestimmung ein Autonomiebaustein, der beispielsweise beim Öffnen und Durchfahren von Türen zum Einsatz kommt. Ausgehend vom bestimmten Öffnungswinkel kann die Bewegungsplanung entsprechend angepaßt und die Türklinke videogestützt gegriffen werden.

Für die Bestimmung von Gelenkzuständen haben sich drei aufgabenspezifische, aggregierte Merkmalsklassen als geeignet erwiesen: *radialvariante Kanten*, das sind Kanten, deren Startpunkt auf der Achse liegt, *parallelvariante Kanten* (achsenparallele Kanten) und *variante Ecken*, eine Kombination der beiden genannten Kantentypen. Abb. 4 (a) zeigt die aufgabenspezifischen Merkmale eines Türflügels.

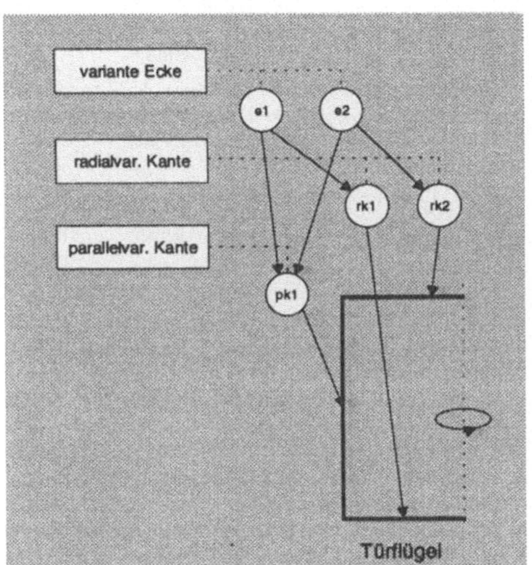

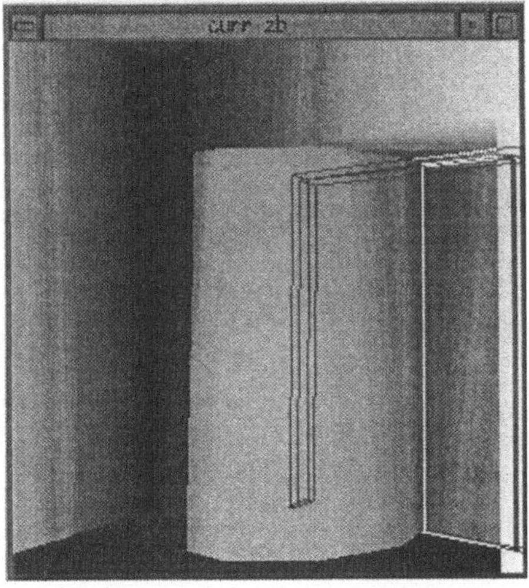

Abb. 4. (a) Merkmale des Türflügels, (b) z-Buffer bei noch unbekanntem Zustand

Um einen Gelenkwinkel zu bestimmen, genügt es, eine variante Ecke im Bild zu lokalisieren; aus dem Schnitt des Sehstrahls durch die Ecke und ihrer Bahn (ein Kreis im Falle eines rotatorischen Freiheitsgrades) ergibt sich der Winkel.

Erster Schritt der Zustandsbestimmung ist also die Lokalisation des statischen Teils, im Falle der Tür des Türrahmens. Dazu wird der Modell-Accessor auf die Tür fokussiert und eine Merkmalsprädiktion angefordert. Da der Gelenkwinkel des Türflügels noch unbekannt ist, werden nur die Merkmale des Rahmens zurückgeliefert (siehe Abb. 5, die linke Hälfte des Rahmens wird noch durch die "Maske" verdeckt, siehe Abb. 4 (b)). Die eigentliche Lagebestimmung des Rahmens erfolgt mit dem System MORAL [6].

Im nächsten Schritt werden der Zoom auf die "varianten Ecken" gesetzt und Modellansichten für verschiedene Gelenkwinkelwerte abgefragt (Abb. 6). Für jede Ansicht werden Korrespondenzen zwischen Bild- und Modell–Merkmalen gesucht; die Ecke im Bild, die mit einer der Ansichten am besten korrespondiert, wird für die Winkelberechnung herangezogen. Der Winkel wird anschließend im

Modell eingetragen und über die symbolische Schnittstelle an die anderen AMS weitergemeldet.

Der Algorithmus wurde auf der Experimentierplattform MARVIN und auf dem Serviceroboter ROMAN [2] implementiert und getestet.

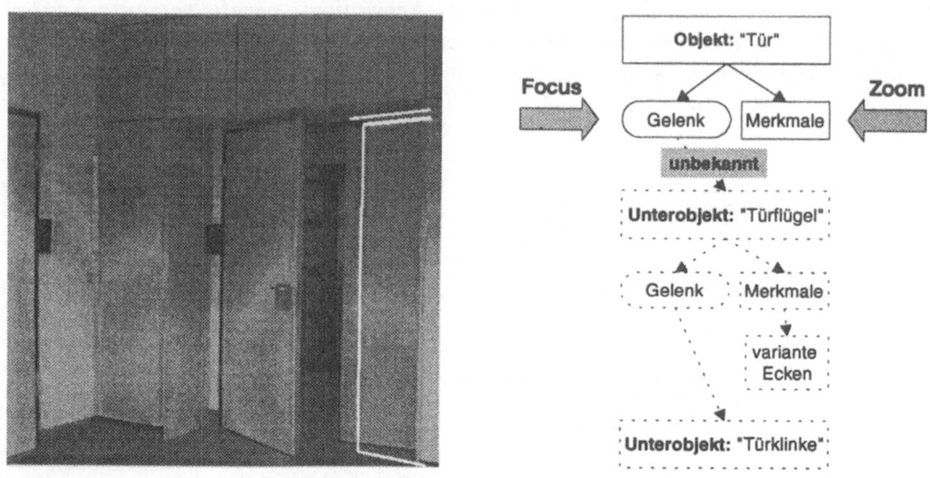

Abb. 5. Lokalisation des statischen Teils

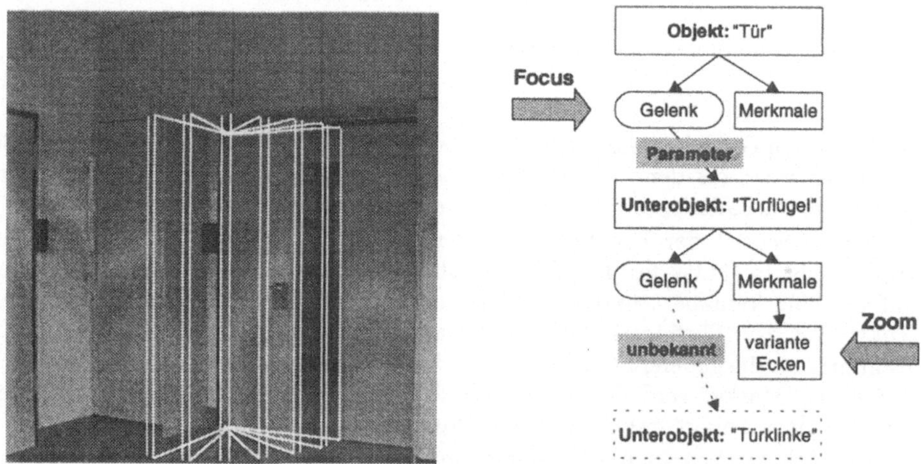

Abb. 6. Bestimmung des Öffnungswinkels

Danksagung

Diese Arbeit wurde von der *Deutschen Forschungsgemeinschaft* im Rahmen des *Sonderforschungsbereichs 331, "Informationsverarbeitung in autonomen, mobilen Handhabungssystemen", Teilprojekt Q5*, unterstützt.

Literatur

1. D. Burschka and C. Eberst. Exploration of Unknown or Partially Known Environments. In *Proceedings of the 2nd ACCV*, volume 2, pages 727–731, 1995.

2. W. Daxwanger, E. Ettelt, C. Fischer, F. Freyberger, U. Hanebeck und G. Schmidt. ROMAN: Ein mobiler Serviceroboter als persönlicher Assistent in belebten Innenräumen. In G. Schmidt und F. Freyberger (Hrsg.), *Autonome Mobile Systeme*, Informatik aktuell. Springer-Verlag, 1996.

3. J. Denavit and R.S. Hartenberg. A Kinematic Notation for Lower-Pair Mechanisms Based on Matrices. *Journal of Applied Mechanics*, pages 215–221, June 1955.

4. C. Eberst and J. Sicheneder. Generation of Hypothetical Landmarks Supporting Fast Object Recognition with Autonomous Mobile Robots. In *Proc. of IEEE/RSJ Int. Conf. on Intelligent Robots and Systems (IROS'96)*, Osaka, Japan, November 1996.

5. A. Koller und N. O. Stöffler. Basisfunktionen zur Steigerung der Autonomie mobiler Systeme. In G. Schmidt und F. Freyberger (Hrsg.), *Autonome Mobile Systeme*, Informatik aktuell. Springer-Verlag, 1996.

6. S. Lanser und C. Zierl. MORAL: Ein System zur videobasierten Objekterkennung im Kontext autonomer, mobiler Systeme. In G. Schmidt und F. Freyberger (Hrsg.), *Autonome Mobile Systeme*, Informatik aktuell. Springer-Verlag, 1996.

7. G. Magin and C. Robl. A Single Processor Realtime Edge-Line Extraction System for Feature Tracking. In *IAPR Workshop on Machine Vision Applications (IAPR MVA '96)*, 1996.

8. G. Magin, A. Ruß, D. Burschka, and G. Färber. A Dynamic 3D Environmental Model with Real-Time Access Functions for Use in Autonomous Mobile Robots. *Robotics and Autonomous Systems*, 14:119–131, 1995.

9. C. Rothwell, J. Mundy, and B. Hoffman. Representing Objects using Topology. In *Proceedings of the International Workshop Object Representation for Computer Vision*, 1996.

10. A. Ruß. *Sensornahe Umgebungsmodellierung mit echtzeitfähigen Zugriffsfunktionen*. Dissertationsschrift, TU München, 1994.

11. A. Ruß and G. Färber. Real-Time Prediction of Sensor Images using Computer Graphics Hardware for Autonomous Mobile Robots in Complex Structured Environments. In *Third International Conference on Computational Graphics and Visualisation Techniques COMPUGRAPHICS'93*, pages 68–73, 1993.

12. A. Ruß, S. Lanser, O. Munkelt und M. Rožmann. Kontinuierliche Lokalisation mit Video- und Radarsensorik unter Nutzung eines geometrisch-topologischen Umgebungsmodells. In G. Schmidt (Hrsg.), *Autonome Mobile Systeme*, Seiten 313–327. TU München, 1993.

13. N. O. Stöffler and T. Troll. Model Update by Radar- and Video-based Perceptions of Environmental Variations. In *International Symposium on Robotics and Manufacturing*. ASME Press, New York, 1996. To appear.

Mobile Robot Navigation under Sensor and Localization Uncertainties

Hiroshi Noborio
Dept. Engineering Informatics
Osaka Electro-Commun. Univ.

Günther Schmidt
Lehrstuhl f. Steuerungs- u. Regelungstechnik
Technische Universität München

Abstract

In a real environment, a mobile robot always operates under several kinds of uncertainties, e.g. sensor and localization ones. However in previous reported sensor-based navigation, most algorithms have unfortunately neglected the uncertainties and consequently they cannot be straightforwardly applied to a mobile robot. Based on this observation, we discuss how to make some of the previous sensor-based navigation algorithms robust with respect to uncertainties. Then, we ascertain feasibility of extended robust algorithms by using a mobile robot Nomad equipped with a ring of ultrasonic sensors, wheel encoders, and a gyrocompass, and its robot simulator with sensory physical characteristics.

1. Introduction

Sensor-based navigation for a mobile robot is concerned with selecting a sequence of sensor-based operators between the present and the goal positions. If a mobile robot does not know its 2-D environment completely or partially, it regards sensor information reflected from closer obstacles in order only to avoid them in a real-time manner. In an on-line framework, we focus on how a mobile robot reaches its goal in an uncertain 2-D world.

Based on this observation, we have analyzed in several surveys [8, 9, 13] all sensor-based navigation algorithms for a mobile robot while turning our attention to the convergence of the robot to the goal. As mentioned in the surveys, all previous algorithms can be completely classified into three types, i.e., the metric, geometric, and topologic ones (Fig.1). Each of them has its own robustness of the convergence with respect to a robot uncertainty.

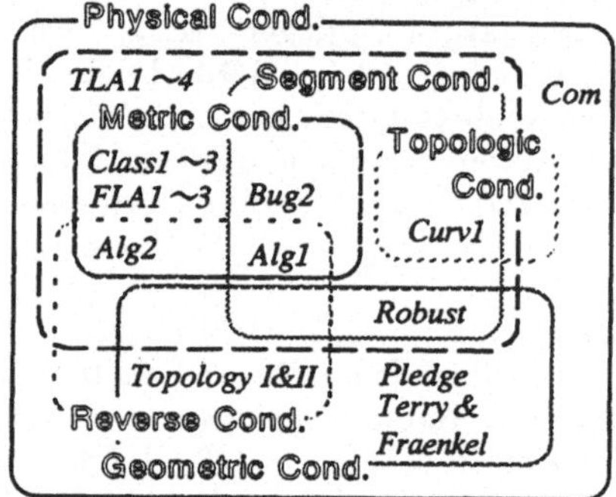

Fig.1 A classification of all previous sensor-based navigation algorithms [13].

In a real environment, a mobile robot and its sensors have to cope with several uncertainties. However, all the sensor-based navigation algorithms except one did not consider such uncertainties. In the exceptional one [15, 16], the authors pioneered a practical sensor-based navigation scheme by using a mobile robot with precise GPS (Global Positioning System) and a ring of ultrasonic sensors. However they did not discuss how each or both of such uncertainties affects the convergence of a mobile robot to or near its goal in an arbitrary unknown environment. Thus in this paper, we analyze how each or both of sensor and localization uncertainties disturbs the convergence in each kind of sensor-based navigation algorithm. In other words, we make a good match between each sensor-based algorithm and each uncertainty. As a result, we find how each algorithm is improved in order for a mobile robot to arrive at or near its goal in overcoming such uncertainties.

Firstly, many researchers have developed and analyzed appropriate sensors and their capabilities in obstacle detection and avoidance [1, 3, 5, 14, 18]. By using these non-contact sensors, a mobile robot can detect and avoid an unknown obstacle. However, each sensing scheme unfortunately includes some distance and orientation error with respect to closer obstacles. On this observation, we extended previous metric and topologic algorithms to robust sensor-based navigation algorithms [12]. In the extended algorithms, we still assume that a mobile robot can identify its position exactly by using precise GPS information, e.g. [4, 17].

However we easily find many uncertain environments when no GPS is available, e.g. in a real indoor human world. When a mobile robot operates in such an environment by use of the sensor-based navigation, the robot should be always prepared for some localization error. In this framework, a mobile robot needs to calculate its position by the usual dead-reckoning data. Firstly, we theoretically described what kind of position and orientation errors can maintain the convergence of a mobile robot near its goal in all the previous sensor-based navigation algorithms. The answer is as follows: The convergence is perfectly kept if and only if an estimated position corresponds to its real position by the homeomorphism [11, 19]. In other words, if we assume all the other errors, e.g. a kind of random error, all the algorithms lose their convergence. However many researchers have unfortunately pointed out an existence of the random error [7]. Therefore we must design a new robust sensor-based navigation algorithm for managing some localization error.

As a first step, we tried to design a family of robust algorithms from the previous metric algorithms [2, 20]. Roughly speaking, if there are obstacles sparsely distributed in an uncertain world, the extended algorithms can maintain their convergence, otherwise, a mobile robot sometimes enters into a deadlock situation and consequently cannot even arrive near its goal. The reason is that the metric property is strongly damaged by the position error. And truth to tell, the topologic property is also affected by the position error. Thus we tried to design another robust algorithm from the previous geometric algorithm [10, 21]. In this framework, if a mobile robot has a good on board gyrocompass, i.e., an accurate orientation information [6], and also has a good sensing scheme, i.e., an accurate recognition of an unknown obstacle boundary, the robot can arrive near the goal with the help of geometric characteristic. Therefore, we firstly measure errors of sensing and orientation in order to determine their upper bounds. Then according to geometric characteristic using such bounds, a robust geometric algorithm guides a mobile robot near to its goal in a practical environment.

This paper is organized as follows: Section 2 explains how a sensor uncertainty is modeled in our sensor-based navigation. Also we describe major problems in the previous sensor-based navigation assuming that there is uncertainty. Then we explain robust metric algorithms *NC-Class* for a mobile robot with some sensing error. Finally we ascertain feasibility of these extended algorithms by a dynamic simulator of an ultrasonic ring on the *Nomad*. In section 3, we explain how to model a localization uncertainty in our sensor-based navigation. Then by using a well-known evaluation of the uncertainty, we design a robust geometric algorithm *NC-Robust** for a mobile robot with sensing and localization errors. Finally we ascertain feasibility of the extended algorithm by using the *Nomad* with an ultrasonic ring, wheel encoders, and gyrocompass. Section 4 contains a few concluding remarks and future research problems.

2. A Metric Algorithm *NC-Class* under Some Sensory Uncertainty

In this section, we design a robust metric algorithm *NC-Class* for a mobile robot with sensor and orientation uncertainties. Then we ascertain feasibility of the new algorithm by using a dynamic simulation of an ultrasonic ring on the Nomad.

2.1 A Mobile Robot and its Uncertain Environment

A mobile robot expressed by a point detects its absolute position R exactly by precise GPS (General Positioning System) information, and also detects its orientation by a good gyrocompass with a bounded error α, which is small enough. The error α means the orientation difference between absolute and robot (sensor) coordinates (Fig.2). On the other hand, there are many uncertain obstacles in a finite or infinite 2-D environment, whose shape and location are to be free. Needless to say, the number of obstacles and the perimeter of each obstacle are assumed finite. Moreover, a mobile robot is equipped with some of outer sensors (vision, a ring of ultrasonic sensors, and a ring of infrared sensors) so as to detect closer obstacles omnidirectionally [3, 5, 14, 18]. In the sensor-based navigation, a mobile robot goes straight to its goal G if its direction is not closed by any obstacle within a given distance threshold T, otherwise, a mobile robot starts to follow the detected obstacle with the help of its normal vector VN' and its clockwise or counter-clockwise tangential vector VT' in the robot (sensor) coordinate system. Note that the vectors VN' and VT' correspond to the vectors VN and VT in the absolute coordinate system and the maximum difference between VN and VN' or VT and VT' is bounded by α. In the sensor-based navigation, a mobile robot should avoid each obstacle continuously unless it sometimes loses its goal G as described in Fig.2. The continuity of obstacle avoidance is to be very important [1]. In general, if we consider a narrow environment, a robot should follow its detected obstacle faithfully as close as possible, otherwise, the robot does not always follow the obstacle faithfully under the influence of kinematics and dynamic restrictions.

Now we define some sensor uncertainty as follows: A robot sensor usually misunderstands a true point P' on an unknown obstacle as a virtual one P''. In this research, the sensing error is formulated by the maximum difference between the points P' and P'', and it is directly proportional to the distance d' by a coefficient β, i.e., $ES(d')=\beta*d'$ $(VN'=RP', d'=|VN'|, 0<\beta<<1)$. In addition to this, we denote an error circle $CS(d')$ whose center is to be at the point P' and its radius is given by the $ES(d')$. Note that the circle $CS(d')$ is a kind of Gaussian error distribution around the true point P'.

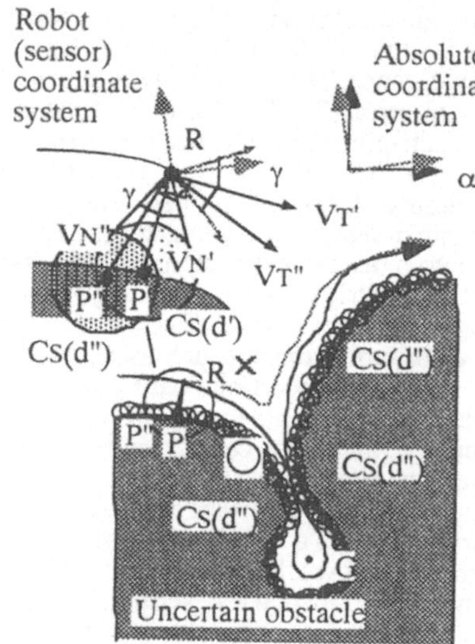

Fig.2 In a continuous obstacle tracing based on a sensor-feedback control, a robot R firstly measures only a point P'' and secondly calcurates the vectors $-VN''$, VT'', and the error circle $CS(d'')$.

In the formulation, we denote normal vectors VN' and VN'' or (clockwise) tangential vectors VT' and VT'' for the points P' and P'', respectively, as shown in Fig.2. In general, the sensor-based navigation forbids a mobile robot not to overlook its detected obstacle, and therefore the distance d' should be bounded as a smaller value. Consequently, the maximum angle between VN' and VN'' or VT' and VT'' is bounded by a small angle γ in the robot (sensor) coordinate system. In consequence, the maximum angle between the VN and VN'' or VT and VT'' is completely bounded by the angle $\alpha+\gamma$ in the absolute coordinate system (Fig.2).

Finally, we clearly obtain two relative sets of inequalities $d'-\beta*d'<d''<d'+\beta*d'$ and $d''-\beta*d''/(1-\beta)<d''-\beta*d''/(1+\beta)< d'<d''+\beta*d''/(1-\beta)$ $(VN''=RP'',d''=|VN''|)$, and then we denote another error circle $CS(d'')$ whose center is at the point P'' and its radius is by the $ES(d'')= \beta*d''/(1-\beta)$.

2.2 The Detail of an Extended Algorithm

The metric algorithms *Class1~3* commonly consist of two conditions, i.e., physical and metric ones. Thus in the paragraph, we improve these conditions for dealing with some sensing error, and then explain the algorithm details.

Physical condition: In the contact tracing, a mobile robot can go straight to its goal if the goal direction VG is to be open, otherwise, the robot follows the detected obstacle in one of the clockwise and counter-clockwise orders. However in a non-contact tracing, the goal direction VG is always open and therefore the alternative behaviors are not switched at all. In addition, we unfortunately have no solution by thresholding the Euclidean distance against the detected obstacle (Fig.3(a)). To overcome this problem, we adopt the inner product $VG\cdot(-VN)$ or the outer product $VG\times VT$ as a tool for switching two behaviors. That is, a mobile robot goes straight to its goal G if the inner product $VG \cdot (-VN)$ or the outer product $VG \times VT$ is negative, otherwise, the robot follows the detected obstacle as shown in Fig.3(b).

In this section, the vector VG is not affected by any error because it can be calculated by precise present and goal positions. However the vector $-VN$ or VT is unfortunately affected by the orientation error α and sensing error γ. However as mentioned in the previous paragraph, the error, that is, the difference between $-VN$ and $-VN''$ or between VT and VT'' is completely bounded by the angle $\alpha+\gamma$. Then, the switching the inner or outer product is to be fortunately stable as long as the angle $\alpha+\gamma$ is fully smaller than 90 degrees. As a result, the new physical condition is still robust against sensing and orientation errors.

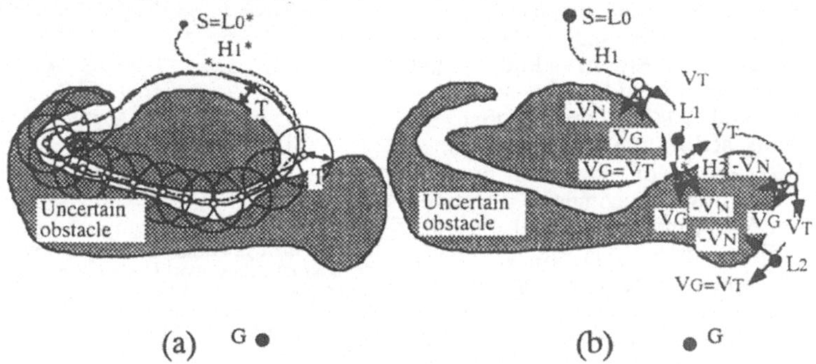

Fig.3 The old physical condition (a), and a new physical condition in a non-contact tracing (b).

Arrival of the goal between a mobile robot and its tracing obstacle: In the contact tracing, a mobile robot needs not consider any goal between the robot and its following obstacle. However in a non-contact tracing, a mobile robot should consider such a goal. In a clockwise or counter-clockwise tracing, if the sign of the outer product $SG \times VG$ is changed and also if the distance $dg(=|RG|)$ is smaller than or equals to the distance $d''+\beta*d''/(1-\beta)$ $(d''=|RP''|)$, a mobile robot should go straight to the goal G in order to check its goal arrival (Fig.4(a)). Moreover, if and only if the distance dg is larger than $d''+\beta*d''/(1-\beta)$ in the checking, the robot starts to trace the detected obstacle again because there is no goal between them (Fig.4(b)). Based on the procedure, a mobile robot arrives at the goal G surely between the robot and its tracing obstacle.

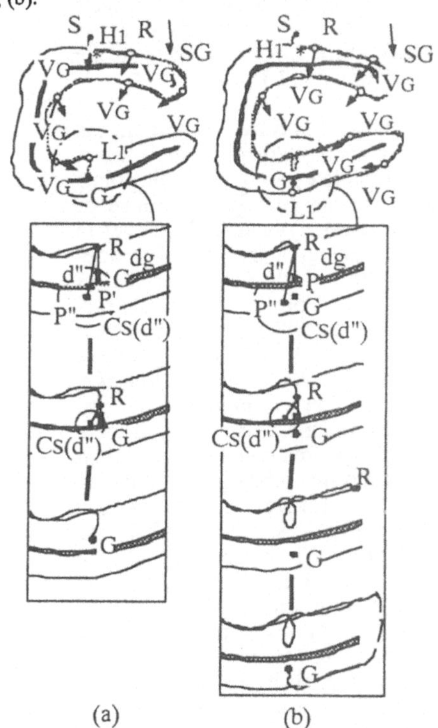

Fig.4 If and only if the goal distance dg is smaller than or equals to the distance $d''+\beta*d''/(1-\beta)$, a mobile robot goes straight to the goal G for checking its arrival (a), otherwise, it traces the detected obstacle again (b).

{132}

Metric condition: By using the above procedure, if a mobile robot has its goal between the robot and its tracing obstacle, it arrives at the goal G. Otherwise, the robot finds a leave point $Li(=RN)$ at worst when it senses the nearest point N on the detected obstacle against the goal G. Firstly at the point RN, a mobile robot can keep the physical condition. The reason is as follows: At RN, the angle between VG and $-VN$ is 180 degrees or the angle between VG and VT is 90 degrees. In addition, the maximum error $\alpha+\gamma$ between the $-VN$ and $-VN''$ or VT and VT'' is smaller than 90 degrees. Thus at RN, the sign of the inner product $VG\cdot(-VN'')$ or the outer product $VG\times VT''$ always becomes negative. Secondly at RN, a mobile robot keeps the metric condition since it is always closer than the previous hit point Hi against the goal G (Fig.5). Thus a mobile robot always leaves its detected obstacle at RN as Li at worst as long as there is a deadlock-free path in an unknown world.

Now as long as a mobile robot selects such a leave point Li, the robot arrives at the goal G finally since Li comes close to the goal G monotonously [13].

No return for a visited point: In the contact tracing, a mobile robot can always return several visited points, e.g. hit points Hi and leave points Li, again because of topology of a detected obstacle. However in a non-contact tracing, a mobile robot does not always return such visited points as shown in Fig.6(a). For this reason, sensor-based navigation algorithms controlled by a set of memorized points, e.g. the algorithms *Alg1&2*, *Topology I&II*, *Telly*, *Fraenkel* are not useful at all in a non-contact tracing. As an exception of this, if and only if there is not any deadlock-free path in an uncertain 2-D world, a mobile robot goes round an uncertain obstacle forever. In this case, a mobile robot memorizes a path P from the previous hit point Hi around its detected obstacle, and then it can find a perpetual cycle around it as a deadlock situation by checking if the vector VG increases by more than 2π in the tracing order and simultaneously the path P crosses itself before leaving the obstacle as illustrated in Fig.6(b). Therefore in a non-contact tracing, all the algorithms with this procedure are to be robust for finding no deadlock-free path.

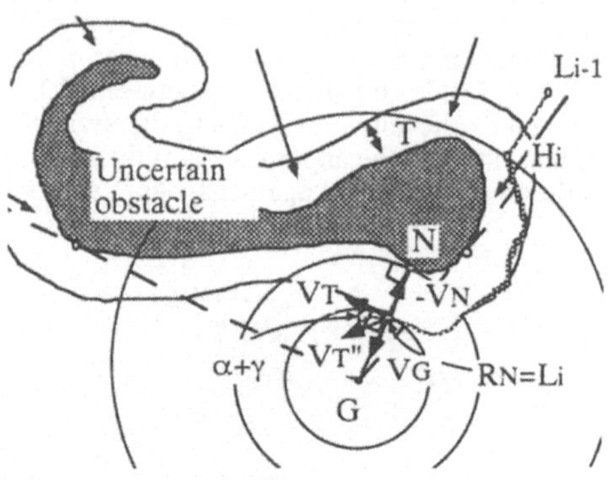

Fig.5 If there is a deadlock-free path toward the goal G in an uncertain world, a mobile robot finds the point RN as a leave point Li at least, which is located on the segment NG (N: the nearest point around a detected obstacle from the goal G). Because the robot always keeps physical and metric conditions at the RN.

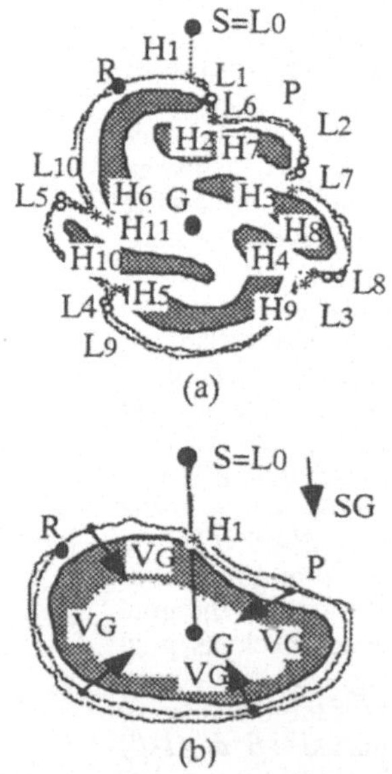

Fig.6 In a non-contact tracing, a mobile robot R does not always identify a perpetual cycle with leave points since it cannot return any visited point around a detected obstacle (a). On the other hand, the robot can recognize a perpetual cycle without any leave point stably if it joins the cycle around it (b).

To maintain the convergence of a mobile robot to its goal, we design a non-contact metric algorithm *NC-Class* with all the previous conditions/functions.

0. A mobile robot R initializes its position by the start position $S(=L0)$, and sets $i=1$, and then we move to Step 1.

1. The robot R moves along the goal vector $VG=SG$ until one of the following occurs:
  a. If the robot R arrives at the goal position G, the algorithm stops with success.
  b. If the Euclidean distance for the goal vector VG against an uncertain obstacle is smaller than a threshold T, the robot R registers its position as a hit point Hi and then we go to Step 2.

2. The robot R traces the detected obstacle by using the vectors VN'' and VT'' while memorizing its path P from the Hi until one of the following occurs:
  a. If the robot R arrives at the goal position G, the algorithm stops with success.
  b. If the outer product $VG{\times}VT''$ or the inner product $VG{\bullet}(-VN'')$ becomes negative and also if the Euclidean distance RG is smaller than the distance HiG, the robot R registers its position as a leave point Li, set $i=i+1$, and we return to Step 1.
  c. If the sign of the outer product $SG{\times}VG$ is changed and also if the distance $dg(=|RG|)$ is smaller than or equals to the distance $d''+\beta*d''/(1-\beta)$, the robot R goes straight to the goal G (Fig.4(a)). Then if the robot R arrives at the goal G, the algorithm stops with success. On the other hand, if the distance dg is larger than the distance $d''+\beta*d''/(1-\beta)$, the robot R traces the detected obstacle again (Fig.4(b)).
  d. If the path P crosses itself after the vector VG increased by more than 2π in the tracing order, the algorithm stops with failure (Fig.6(b)).

Finally we should note that a mobile robot influenced by kinematics and dynamic restrictions does not always trace a detected obstacle faithfully. In the sensor-based navigation, it is no problem as long as a mobile robot continues to trace the detected obstacle without colliding with or losing track of it [1]. Moreover in the improved algorithm, a mobile robot always finds a leave point around a detected obstacle by the procedure **2b**. As a result, the leave point comes close to the goal and finally the robot arrives near it after avoiding many unknown obstacles. The detail proof was described in [12].

2.3 A Simulation Result

In this paragraph, we ascertain feasibility of the algorithm *NC-Class* by using a dynamic simulator of an ultrasonic ring of the *Nomad* (Nomadic Tech. Inc.). A set of closer unknown obstacles is omnidirectionally recognized by a ring of ultrasonic sensors, whose physical characteristics are completely installed in the dynamics simulator. Figure 7 indicates the convergence of a mobile robot to its goal G in the extended algorithm *NC-Class*.

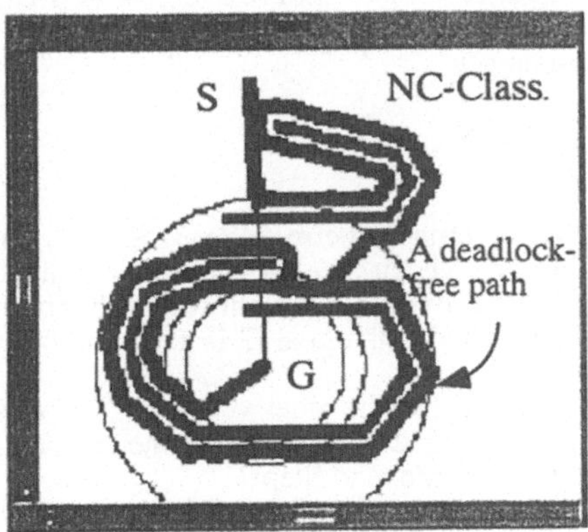

Fig.7 A deadlock-free path is made by the *NC-Class* in the *Nomad* dynamic simulator.

3. A Geometric Algorithm *NC-Robust** under Both Uncertainties

In this section, we consider that a mobile robot does not have any GPS, and consequently we are obliged to assume some position error. In this case, metric and topologic conditions are completely damaged by the position uncertainty [10]. Therefore we must rely on a geometric algorithm *Robust* so as to design a robust sensor-based navigation algorithm for a mobile robot with sensor, orientation, and position uncertainties [10]. Firstly we propose a robust sensor-based navigation algorithm *NC-Robust** for a mobile robot with these uncertainties. Then we ascertain feasibility of the algorithm by using the *Nomad* with wheel encoders, a gyrocompass, and a ring of ultrasonic sensors.

3.1 The Difference against the Previous Section's Definition

If we assume a position error, a true goal vector VG is always misunderstood as a virtual one VG". In the physical condition, the problem is how much is the angle δ between VG and VG". As described in [7], the position error is boundlessly accumulated. However, we assume that the sum of angles α, γ, δ is smaller than 90 degrees in order to keep the physical condition. Furthermore in the geometric condition based on the segment SG, the problem is how much is the error ellipse EE. Here we also assume that the maximum ellipse is smaller than a free space CG around the goal G as illustrated in Fig.8.

3.2 The Detail of an Extended Algorithm NC-Robust*

To maintain the convergence of a mobile robot to its goal G, we design a non-contact geometric algorithm *NC-Robust** with all the previous conditions/functions (Fig.8).

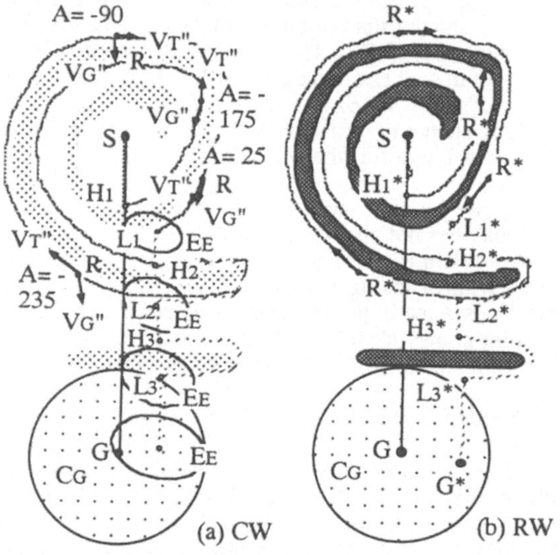

Fig.8   A robot head R always monitors the angle A between VG" and VT" and also checks the intersection between EE and SG in CW (a) while its robot body $R*$ always follows a detected obstacle by a non-contact sensor-feedback control in RW (b).

0. A robot head R initializes a permanent error ellipse EE by S. Then we go to Step 1.

1. A head R moves while the vector VG" is consistent with the vector SG in CW, and simultaneously its body $R*$ moves in RW until one of the following occurs:
   a. If the error ellipse EE includes the goal G in CW, the body $R*$ stops with success in RW.
   b. If the Euclidean distance for the goal vector VG" against an uncertain obstacle is smaller than a threshold T in CW, the head R memorizes its present position as a hit point H in CW and then we move to Step 2.

2. The head R initializes a temporary error ellipse E by H, and defines a line I on H, which is parallel with SG. Then the body $R*$ continues to trace the detected obstacle in the clockwise or counter-clockwise order in RW, and simultaneously the head R memorizes a path P from H and also monitors the angle A between VG" and VT" in CW until one of the following occurs:
   a. If the error ellipse EE includes the goal G in CW, the body $R*$ stops with success in RW.
   b. If the angle A is to be within the interval $[0-\rho, 180+\rho]$ ($\rho=\alpha+\gamma+\delta$) and also if the error ellipse E intersects the line I in CW, we return to Step 1.

c. If the path P crosses itself after the vector VG'' increased by more than $2*(\pi+\delta)$ in the tracing order in CW, the body R^* stops with failure in RW (Fig.6(b)).

Finally in the robust algorithm, a mobile robot always finds a leave point around a detected obstacle by the procedure **2b**. As a result, the robot arrives near the goal G surely along the segment SG after avoiding many unknown obstacles. The detail proof was described in [21].

3.3 An Experimental Result

In this paragraph, we ascertain feasibility of the algorithm *NC-Robust** by using a mobile robot *Nomad 200* (Nomadic Tech. Inc.) with a ring of ultrasonic sensors, gyrocompass, and wheel encoders (Fig.9). The *Nomad* can recognize surrounding unknown obstacles omnidirectionally and trace one of them by a sensor-feedback control.

Fig.9 A photograph of the *Nomad* in our experiment.

The *Nomad* also has a good gyrocompass to measure its orientation. Furthermore the *Nomad* calculates its position and error ellipse (67%) by the usual dead-reckoning. Needless to say, since our sensor-based navigation algorithm and sensor-feedback control scheme are compact, they can be completely installed into an on-board computer on the *Nomad*.

Now *Nomad* supervised by *NC-Robust** generates a deadlock-free path toward its goal surely in a complicated unknown world (Fig.10). In the result, the *Nomad* always arrives near the goal G although it is strongly affected by sensing, position, and orientation errors. Therefore we can see that the proposed algorithm *NC-Robust** keeps the convergence of a mobile robot near its goal in an uncertain world under these uncertainties.

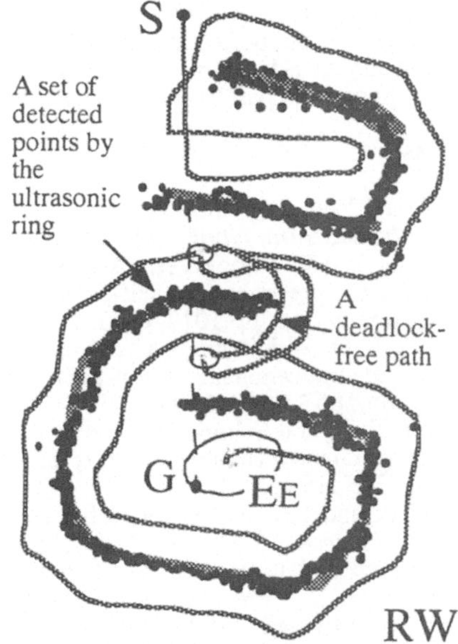

Fig.10 The *Nomad* arrives near the goal G via a deadlock-free path in a complicated unknown environment by using the *NC-Robust**.

4. Conclusions and Future Research Problems

All the previous sensor-based navigation algorithms have been built as the following two assumptions: (1) A mobile robot identifies its position and orientation exactly in an uncertain 2-D world; and (2) A mobile robot faithfully follows an unknown boundary of its encountered obstacle by a sensor-feedback control. Under these assumptions, all the algorithms maintain their convergence of a mobile robot to its goal in a 2-D unknown world. However in general, each or both of these assumptions is broken for a real robot running in a practical environment because of sensor and localization uncertainties. Consequently the convergence is strongly damaged.

To overcome the status quo, we discussed how three types of sensor-based navigation algorithms (metric, geometric, and topologic algorithms) are fit for two kinds of robot uncertainties (sensor and localization uncertainties). As a result, the metric and topologic algorithms can be easily improved to robust ones for a sensor uncertainty because the metric and topologic conditions are completely kept by no localization uncertainty. On the other hand, the geometric algorithm is modified to a robust one for sensor and localization uncertainties since the obstacle geometry can be available if and only if some sensor uncertainty is not accumulated and small enough.

Secondly as one of future research problems, we must pay attention to the non-holonomic property of a mobile robot. In section 2, we described "a mobile robot influenced by kinematics and dynamic restrictions does not worry about how to trace an uncertain obstacle as long as it does not collide with or lose track of the obstacle. It is right, but it is difficult for a non-holonomic mobile robot to achieve the obstacle following in a narrow environment. As a result, I believe that this is a future research problem in the sensor-based navigation.

Finally due to limitations of space, some important information have to be eliminated in this paper as follows: (1) In the same framework of section 2, we can design another metric algorithm *NC-Bug2*, and a topologic algorithm *NC-Curv1* as robust algorithms. They were completely described in [12]; and (2) The convergence of a mobile robot to its goal in the algorithms *NC-Class*, *NC-Bug2*, and *NC-Curv1* are theoretically ensured in [12], and also that in the algorithm *NC-Robust** is theoretically ensured in [21].

Acknowledgments
This research was supported in part by 1994 and 1995 Grants-in-aid for Scientific Research from the Ministry of Education, Science and Culture, Japan (No.06750266 and 07750299), and is also supported in part by the Alexander von Humboldt-Stiftung, Germany (No.15599).

References

[1] Ando Y. and Yuta S., Following a wall by an autonomous mobile robot with a sonar-ring, *Proc. of the IEEE Int. Conf. on Robotics and Automation*, pp.2599-2605, 1995.

[2] Hamaguchi T. and Noborio H., A sensor-based bridge between gross and fine motion-planning in the presence of a self-positioning error, *Proc. of the Japan-USA Symp. on Flexible Automation*, pp.1017-1020, 1994.

[3] Hanebeck U.D. and Schmidt G., A new high performance multisoner system for fast mobile robot applications, *Proc. of the IEEE/RSJ/GI Int. Conf. on Intelligent Robots and Systems*, pp.1853-1860, 1994.

[4] Hanebeck U.D. and Schmidt G., Set theoretic localization of fast mobile robots using an angle measurement technique, *Proc. of the IEEE Int. Conf. on Robotics and Automation*, pp.1387-1395, 1996.

[5] Kleeman L. and Kuc R., Mobile robot sonar for target localization and classification, *J. Robotics Research*, Vol.14, No.4, pp.295-318, 1995.

[6] Komoriya K. and Oyama E., Position estimation of a mobile robot using optical fiber gyroscope (OFG), *Proc. of the IEEE/RSJ/GI Int. Conf. on Intelligent Robots and Systems*, pp.143-149, 1994.

[7] Leonard J. and Durrant-Whyte H., Mobile robot localization by tracking geometric beacons, *IEEE Trans. on Robotics and Automation*, pp.376-382, 1991.

[8] Noborio H., On a sensor-based motion planning for a mechanical mobile robot, *Technical Report: ISC94-09*, Inform. Sci. Center., Osaka Electro-Commun. Univ., pp.95-118, March 1995.

[9] Noborio H., Sensor-based motion planning for mobile robots, A tutorial material TM-4 "Sensor-based robot motion planning" in the *1995 IEEE Int. Conf. on Robotics and Automation*, pp.1-17.

[10] Noborio H., et al., On a deadlock-free characteristic of sensor-based path-planning algorithms under a self-positioning error, *Proc. of the 7th Int. Conf. on Advanced Robotics*, pp.839-846, 1995.

[11] Noborio H., et al., On-line deadlock-free path-planning algorithms in the presence of a dead reckoning error, *Proc. of the IEEE Int. Conf. on Systems, Man and Cybernetics*, pp.483-488, 1995.

[12] Noborio H., et al., On-line deadlock-free path-planning algorithms by means of a sensor-feedback tracing, *Proc. of the IEEE Int. Conf. on Systems, Man and Cybernetics*, pp.1291-1296, October, 1995.

[13] Noborio H., On a sensor-based navigation for a mobile robot, *Journal of Robotics Mechatronics*, Vol.8, No.1, pp.2-14, Feb. 1996.

[14] Ohya A., et al., High speed measurement of normal direction of walls by ultrasonic sensor, *J. Robotics Society of Japan*, Vol.13, No.5, pp.700-703, 1995 (in Japanese).

[15] Skewis T. and Lumelsky V.J., Experiments with a mobile robot operating in a cluttered unknown environment, *Proc. the IEEE Int. Conf. Robotics and Automation*, pp.1482-1487, 1992.

[16] Skewis T. and Lumelsky V.J., Experiments with a mobile robot operating in a cluttered unknown environment, *J. Robotic Systems*, Vol.11, No.4, pp.281-300, 1994.

[17] Tsumura T., et al., A 3-d position and attitude measurement system using laser scanners and corner cubes," *Proc. of the IEEE/RSJ Int. Conf. on Intelligent Robots and Systems*, pp.604-611, 1993.

[18] Yagi Y., Kawato S., Tsuji S., Collision avoidance using omnidirectional image sensor (COPIS), *Proc. of the IEEE Conf. Robotics and Automation*, pp.910-915, 1991.

[19] Yoshioka T. and Noborio H., On deadlock-free characteristics in previous sensor-based path-planning algorithms by a dead reckoning error, *Proc. of the Japan-USA Symp. on Flexible Automation*, Vo.2, pp.645-648, July 1994.

[20] Yoshioka, T., et al., On the sensor-based navigation for a real mobile robot in its practical environment, *Proc. of the USA-Japan Symposium on Flexible Automation*, 1996 (to appear).

[21] Yoshioka, T., et al., A gross sensor-based navigation algorithm for a mobile robot with self-positioning, sensing, control errors, *Proc. of the IECON*, 1996 (to appear).

Zum Lokalisationsproblem für Roboter*

Oliver Karch   Hartmut Noltemeier

Lehrstuhl für Informatik I
Universität Würzburg
Am Hubland, 97074 Würzburg
EMail: {karch,noltemei}@informatik.uni-wuerzburg.de

Zusammenfassung. Wir untersuchen die erste Phase des *Lokalisationsproblems für Roboter*: Für ein gegebenes Kartenpolygon $\mathcal{P}$ und ein sternförmiges Polygon $\mathcal{V}$ sind alle Punkte aus $\mathcal{P}$ zu bestimmen, deren Sichtbarkeitspolygon gleich $\mathcal{V}$ ist. In [6] beschreiben Guibas, Motwani und Raghavan (für Kartenpolygone *ohne Löcher*) ein Verfahren mit Preprocessing–Aufwand $\mathcal{O}(n^4 r)$, so daß eine solche Lokalisationsanfrage mit bestmöglichem Zeitbedarf von $\mathcal{O}(m + \log n + A)$ beantwortet werden kann. Hierbei bezeichnen m und n die Eckenzahlen von $\mathcal{V}$ und $\mathcal{P}$, r ist die Anzahl der Reflex–Ecken des Kartenpolygons $\mathcal{P}$ und A ist die Größe der Ausgabe, d.h. die Zahl der gefundenen Punkte.

Wir zeigen, daß die Komplexitätsschranke für das Preprocessing zu $\mathcal{O}\big(n^2 r \cdot (n + r^2)\big)$ verschärft werden kann. Dies ist besser als die ursprüngliche Abschätzung, falls die Zahl r der Reflex–Ecken klein gegenüber der Zahl n der Gesamtecken des Kartenpolygons ist.

Außerdem beschreiben wir einen Ansatz, das Verfahren von Guibas et al. so zu modifizieren, daß es auch in der Praxis (z.B. bei ungenauer Sensorik, etc.) sinnvoll eingesetzt werden kann.

1 Das Lokalisationsproblem

Wir betrachten das *Lokalisationsproblem für Roboter* (siehe z.B. [4, 13]): Ein Roboter befindet sich an einer unbekannten Position innerhalb seiner Einsatzumgebung und seine Aufgabe besteht darin, seine Konfiguration (d.h. Position und Orientierung) innerhalb der Einsatzumgebung zu bestimmen. Dies ist beispielsweise nötig, wenn der Roboter nach einer Störung (z.B. Stromausfall) wieder selbständig starten soll und *kein Vorwissen* über seine Konfiguration vor der Störung besitzt.

Als Hilfsmittel verfügt der Roboter über eine *Umgebungskarte* und einen sog. *range finding*-Sensor (z.B. Laser-Radar), der dem Roboter das zum aktuellen Standort gehörende *Sichtbarkeitspolygon* liefert. Die besondere Herausforderung hierbei ist, das Lokalisationsproblem nur mit dieser Minimalausstattung an Sensoren zu lösen; insbesondere dürfen also

---

*Diese Arbeit wird von der Deutschen Forschungsgemeinschaft (DFG) gefördert, Proj.nr. No 88/14-1.

keine Ortsmarken (z.B. Markierungen an den Wänden oder auf dem Boden) verwendet werden.

Das Problem wird in der Regel in zwei Phasen bearbeitet:

1. Zunächst generiert der *stillstehende* Roboter eine Menge von *hypothetischen Positionen*, die konsistent mit seinen Sensordaten sind. Beispielsweise kann es in einer Lagerhalle mit mehreren gleichartigen Regalreihen, zwischen denen sich der Roboter aufhält, mehrere Positionen geben, die dasselbe Sichtbarkeitspolygon liefern und die der stillstehende Roboter nicht zu unterscheiden vermag.

   Unter der zusätzlichen Voraussetzung, daß die Orientierung des Roboters schon bekannt ist (d.h. der Roboter besitzt einen "Kompaß"), haben Guibas et al. [6] hierfür eine Basislösung angegeben (siehe Abschnitt 2).

2. Falls die erste Phase keine eindeutige Position geliefert hat, *bewegt* sich in der zweiten Phase der Roboter solange innerhalb der Umgebung, bis er genügend Information besitzt, um alle "falschen" Hypothesen über seinen ursprünglichen Standort eliminieren zu können. Dieses *online-Problem*[1] wird in [5, 10, 12] behandelt.

Der vorliegende Artikel konzentriert sich auf die erste Phase der Lokalisation, d.h. auf das Generieren der möglichen Standorte des Roboters. Im folgenden Abschnitt skizzieren wir zunächst das in [6] beschriebene Verfahren und geben dann in Abschnitt 3 für einige der dabei auftretenden Größen genauere Aufwandsabschätzungen an.

Da die Methode von Guibas et al. die *genaue Kenntnis der Orientierung* des Roboters sowie eine *präzise Sensorik* voraussetzt, ist es nicht direkt in die Praxis umsetzbar. In Abschnitt 4 gehen wir auf diese Probleme ein und zeigen eine Möglichkeit auf, sie zu umgehen.

2 Das Verfahren von Guibas et al.

Im folgenden gehen wir davon aus, daß die Umgebung des Roboters mittels einer 2-dimensionalen Darstellung beschrieben werden kann, der Roboter sich also auf einer ebenen Fläche mit vorwiegend senkrecht stehenden Wänden und Hindernissen bewegt. Der range finding-Sensor des Roboters liefert somit ein sternförmiges Sichtbarkeitspolygon $\mathcal{V}$ und unter der zusätzlichen Annahme, daß der Roboter einen Kompaß besitzt, besteht das Lokalisationsproblem darin, alle Positionen innerhalb des Kartenpolygons $\mathcal{P}$ zu ermitteln, deren Sichtbarkeitspolygon gleich $\mathcal{V}$ ist.

Zerlegung in Sichtbarkeitszellen

Bei der von Guibas et al. beschriebenen Methode wird in einem Preprocessing-Schritt das Kartenpolygon $\mathcal{P}$ (bestehend aus n Ecken, davon r Reflex-Ecken[2]) in *Sichtbarkeitszellen* zerlegt. Eine Sichtbarkeitszelle $\mathcal{C}$ ist dadurch bestimmt, daß jeder Punkt $p \in \mathcal{C}$ innerhalb der Zelle *annähernd dasselbe* Sichtbarkeitspolygon $\mathcal{V}(p)$ induziert. Genauer: Jeder Punkt $p \in \mathcal{C}$ besitzt dasselbe *Sichtbarkeitsskelett* $V^*(p) = V_{\mathcal{C}}^*$.

---

[1] Der Roboter muß die eintreffenden Informationen online verarbeiten, um so einen möglichst effizienten Weg zu finden, auf dem die falschen Hypothesen eliminiert werden.

[2] Eine Reflex-Ecke besitzt einen Innenwinkel $> 180°$. Solche Ecken sind die Ursache für Verdeckungen: Wenn das Sichtbarkeitspolygon nicht das gesamte Kartenpolygon umfaßt, werden die nicht sichtbaren Teile durch eine oder mehrere Reflex-Ecken (und die daran angrenzende Streckenzüge) verdeckt.

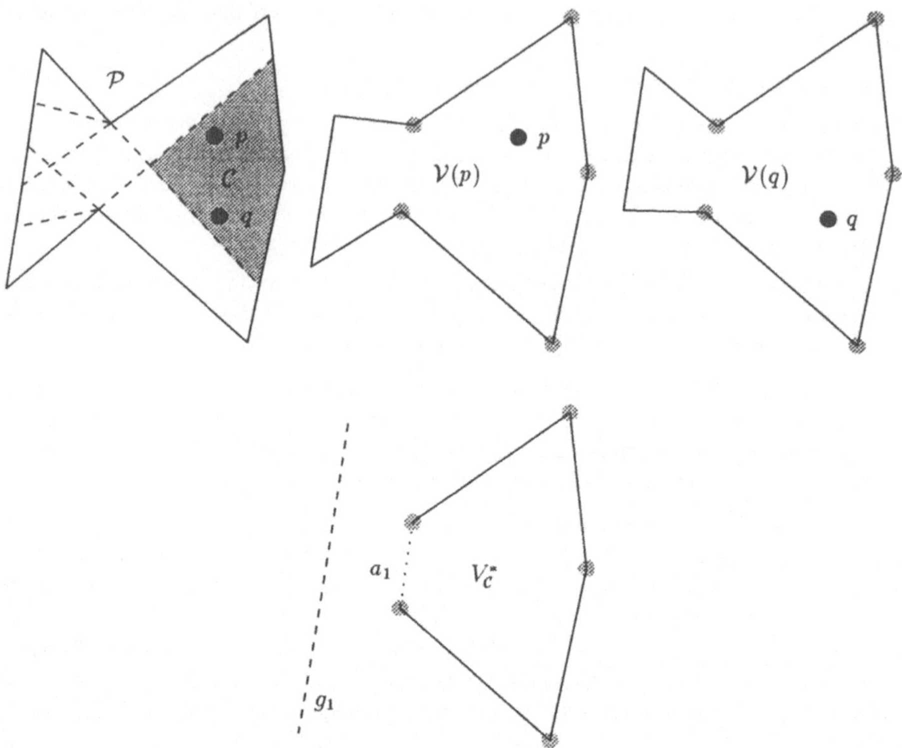

Abbildung 1: Die Zerlegung eines Kartenpolygons $\mathcal{P}$ in Sichtbarkeitszellen sowie die Sichtbarkeitspolygone zweier Punkte p und q aus *derselben* Zelle $\mathcal{C}$. Darunter das *gemeinsame* Sichtbarkeitsskelett $V_{\mathcal{C}}^* = V^*(p) = V^*(q)$ mit der künstlichen Kante a_1 und der zugehörigen Geraden g_1.

Das Sichtbarkeitsskelett

Anschaulich besteht das zu einem Sichtbarkeitspolygon $\mathcal{V}(p)$ gehörende Skelett $V^*(p)$ aus denjenigen Ecken und Kanten von $\mathcal{V}(p)$, die *zweifelsfrei* zur Karte $\mathcal{P}$ gehören müssen und nicht durch Verdeckungen induziert worden sein können. Die restlichen Kanten des Sichtbarkeitspolygons $\mathcal{V}(p)$ sind dann entweder *Scheinkanten*, die kollinear zum Betrachterpunkt p liegen oder Kanten von $\mathcal{P}$, die nur *teilweise* sichtbar sind. Für jede Kante des zweiten Typs wird zu $V^*(p)$ eine *künstliche Kante* a_i hinzugefügt, zusammen mit der zugehörigen Geraden g_i, auf der die ursprüngliche Kante von $\mathcal{V}(p)$ lag (Für eine exakte Definition des Skelettbegriffs und der noch folgenden Begriffe siehe [6]).

Abbildung 1 zeigt eine Zerlegung eines Kartenpolygons $\mathcal{P}$ in Sichtbarkeitszellen (links) sowie die Sichtbarkeitspolygone zweier Punkte p und q aus *derselben* Zelle $\mathcal{C}$ (rechts daneben). Beide Sichtbarkeitspolygone besitzen jeweils zwei zu p bzw. q kollineare Scheinkanten, verursacht durch die beiden Reflex-Ecken des Kartenpolygons. Die Menge der sichtbaren Ecken des Kartenpolygons (grau hinterlegt) ist in $\mathcal{V}(p)$ und $\mathcal{V}(q)$ jeweils dieselbe. Das zur Zelle $\mathcal{C}$ gehörende Skelett $V_{\mathcal{C}}^*$ (unten) besitzt eine künstliche Kante a_1 mit

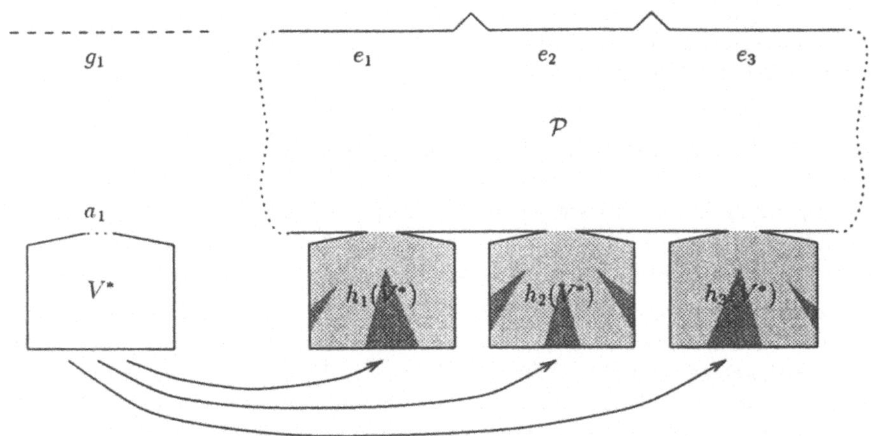

Abbildung 2: Die drei Einbettungen $h_1, \ldots, h_3$ des Skeletts V^* in das Kartenpolygon $\mathcal{P}$.

zugehöriger Geraden g_1, auf der die entsprechenden Kanten der Sichtbarkeitspolygone liegen.

Einbettungen eines Skeletts

Genauso wie ein sternförmiges Polygon $\mathcal{V}$ an mehreren Stellen in die Karte $\mathcal{P}$ "passen" kann, gilt dies auch für das oben definierte Skelett V^*. Eine solche Abbildung $h(V^*)$ eines Skeletts in die Karte $\mathcal{P}$ wird *Einbettung* des Skeletts genannt. Man kann zeigen, daß es für jedes Skelett nur $\mathcal{O}(r)$ verschiedene Einbettungen in die Karte gibt. Demzufolge kann es auch nur $\mathcal{O}(r)$ verschiedene hypothetische Roboterstandorte bei einer Lokalisationsanfrage geben.

Der Begriff der Einbettung ist in Abbildung 2 veranschaulicht: Das Skelett V^* mit einer künstlichen Kante a_1 besitzt die drei Einbettungen $h_1, \ldots, h_3$ in die Karte $\mathcal{P}$. Diejenigen Sichtbarkeitszellen, deren Skelett gleich V^* ist, sind dunkelgrau dargestellt. Man beachte, daß von jeder dieser Sichtbarkeitszellen aus *genau eine* der drei *Kandidatkanten* $e_1, \ldots, e_3$ für die (eingebettete) künstliche Kante $h_i(a_1)$ sichtbar ist. Diese drei Kanten sind kollinear und liegen auf der (eingebetteten) Geraden $h_i(g_1)$.

Der Zusammenhang zwischen dem Sichtbarkeitspolygon und der Einbettung seines Skeletts wird in folgendem Satz deutlich:

Satz 1 (Guibas et al. [6]) *Sei $\mathcal{V}(p)$ ein Sichtbarkeitspolygon, $V^*(p)$ das zugehörige Skelett, $h(V^*(p))$ eine Einbettung dieses Skeletts in die Karte $\mathcal{P}$ und $h(p)$ der dem Beobachterpunkt p entsprechende Punkt in der Einbettung. Dann ist $\mathcal{V}(h(p)) = \mathcal{V}(p)$ genau dann erfüllt, wenn $V^*(h(p)) = V^*(p)$ gilt.*

Obiger Satz besagt also, daß es für ein gegebenes Polygon $\mathcal{V}(p)$ genügt, alle Einbettungen des zugehörigen Skeletts $V^*(p)$ zu betrachten, um diejenigen Punkte in der Karte mit Sichtbarkeitspolygon $\mathcal{V}(p)$ zu finden, und danach zu prüfen, ob die zugehörigen eingebetteten Beobachterpunkte $h_i(p)$ dasselbe Skelett $V^*(p)$ induzieren.

Das *kontinuierliche*[3] Problem, ein Sichtbarkeitspolygon in eine Karte einzupassen, wurde also durch die Reduktion der Sichtbarkeitspolygone auf ihr Skelett und die Zerlegung der Karte in Sichtbarkeitszellen auf natürliche Weise *diskretisiert.*

Das Verfahren und sein Preprocessing–Aufwand

Die Zerlegung in Sichtbarkeitszellen erhält man durch Einfügen von $\mathcal{O}(nr)$ Halbstrahlen in die Karte $\mathcal{P}$. Die Zahl der so entstehenden Zellen ist bei einem Kartenpolygon *ohne Löcher* (d.h. keine frei stehenden Hindernisse) aus $\mathcal{O}(n^2r)$, sonst aus $\mathcal{O}(n^2r^2)$.

Die einzelnen Zellen werden bezüglich ihrer Skelette in *Äquivalenzklassen* eingeteilt. Für die daraus resultierende Menge an Äquivalenzklassen wird eine Suchstruktur (z.B. ein mehrdimensionaler Suchbaum) aufgebaut, die es erlaubt, die zu einem Skelett gehörende Klasse, effizient (d.h. mit logarithmischer Zeit in der Zahl der Klassen) zu bestimmen. Für jede Äquivalenzklasse werden außerdem die darin enthaltenen Sichtbarkeitszellen in einer Point Location–Suchstruktur verwaltet, so daß für einen Anfragepunkt p diejenigen Zellen der Äquivalenzklasse bestimmt werden können, die den Punkt $h(p)$ enthalten (vgl. Satz 1).

Bei der eigentlichen Lokalisationsanfrage wird dann das zum Sichtbarkeitspolygon $V(p)$ des Roboters gehörende Skelett $V^*(p)$ berechnet, die zugehörige Äquivalenzklasse bestimmt und in dieser Äquivalenzklasse diejenigen Zellen gesucht, die den Punkt $h(p)$ enthalten. Auf diese Weise erhält man eine optimale Anfragezeit von $\mathcal{O}(m + \log n + A)$, wobei m die Eckenzahl von $V(p)$ und A die Größe der Ausgabe (d.h. die Zahl der möglichen Roboterstandorte) bezeichnet.

Der Gesamtaufwand an Zeit und Speicher für das Preprocessing beträgt (für ein Kartenpolygon *ohne Löcher*) $\mathcal{O}(n^2r \cdot |\mathcal{EC}|)$, wobei $|\mathcal{EC}|$ die Beschreibungskomplexität einer Äquivalenzklasse im worst case bezeichnet.

Die Beschreibungskomplexität einer Äquivalenzklasse

Für ein gegebenes Skelett V^* sei $|\mathcal{EC}(V^*)|$ die (Beschreibungs-)Komplexität der zugehörigen Äquivalenzklasse, d.h. die Anzahl aller Ecken und Kanten *aller* Sichtbarkeitszellen, die das Skelett V^* besitzen.

Ein naiver Ansatz liefert eine grobe Abschätzung von $\mathcal{O}(n + r^4)$ für diese Komplexität: Jede zu V^* äquivalente Sichtbarkeitszelle liegt in einer der $\mathcal{O}(r)$ Einbettungen von V^*. Man kann sich leicht überlegen, daß es in jeder Einbettung maximal $\mathcal{O}(r^2)$ zu V^* äquivalente Zellen (d.h. Zellen C mit Skelett $V_C^* = V^*$) geben kann. Außerdem besitzt jede Zelle zusätzlich zu den Kanten, die sie mit dem Kartenpolygon gemeinsam hat, höchstens $\mathcal{O}(r)$ weitere Kanten. Insgesamt ist also die Gesamtkomplexität von $\mathcal{EC}(V^*)$ aus $\mathcal{O}(n + r^4)$. Im worst case (d.h. $r \in \Omega(n)$) gilt also $|\mathcal{EC}(V^*)| \in \mathcal{O}(n^4)$.

In [6] wurde allerdings schon gezeigt, daß die Komplexität einer Äquivalenzklasse nur aus $\mathcal{O}(n^2)$ ist.

---

[3]Kontinuierlich in dem Sinne, daß sich kein $\varepsilon > 0$ finden läßt, so daß sich das Sichtbarkeitspolygon $V(p)$ eines sich um maximal ε bewegenden Punktes p nicht ändert.

3 Eine schärfere Abschätzung für die Beschreibungskomplexität einer Äquivalenzklasse

In diesem Abschnitt wollen wir eine genauere obere Schranke von $\mathcal{O}(n + r^2)$ für die Komplexität einer Äquivalenzklasse angeben und zeigen, daß diese Schranke worst case-optimal ist. Aus Platzgründen soll der Beweis nur grob skizziert werden; der vollständige Beweis findet sich in [9].

Ein worst case–Beispiel

Betrachten wir das in Abbildung 2 dargestellte Kartenpolygon. Durch Hinzufügen weiterer kollinearer Kandidatkanten e_j und weiterer Einbuchtungen $h_i(V^*)$ erhalten wir eine Karte mit $\Omega(r)$ Einbettungen von V^* und jeweils $\Omega(r)$ Kandidatkanten für die künstliche Kante $h_i(a_1)$. Durch geeignetes Skalieren der Szene ist es möglich, daß *jede* Kante e_j in *jeder* Einbettung $h_i(V^*)$ eine Sichtbarkeitszelle mit Skelett V^* induziert. Die Gesamtkantenzahl aller zu V^* äquivalenten Sichtbarkeitszellen ist also aus $\Omega(r^2)$ plus die Zahl der Kanten, die die Zellen mit der Karte $\mathcal{P}$ gemeinsam haben. Durch geeignetes Einfügen weiterer Punkte zu V^* kann man erreichen, daß diese zweite Kantenzahl aus $\Omega(n)$ ist.

Insgesamt erhält man somit eine Komplexität von $\Omega(n + r^2)$ für die Äquivalenzklasse des Skeletts V^*.

Beweisskizze für die $\mathcal{O}(n + r^2)$–Schranke

Sei V^* ein Sichtbarkeitsskelett und $h(V^*)$ eine seiner Einbettungen. Die Kanten der zu V^* äquivalenten Sichtbarkeitszellen in $h(V^*)$ werden begrenzt durch

- Kanten des Kerns $\mathrm{Ker}(h(V^*))$,

- Kanten von *Sichtbarkeitskeilen*, die durch die zu den künstlichen Kanten gehörenden Kandidatkanten induziert werden. Für eine künstliche Kante $h(a)$ in einer Einbettung $h(V^*)$ und einer Kandidatkante e ist der dazugehörende Sichtbarkeitskeil die Menge aller Punkte, für die beim Blick durch die künstliche Kante $h(a)$ *ausschließlich Punkte der Kandidatkante e* sichtbar sind.

Abbildung 3 veranschaulicht diesen Sachverhalt: Jede der drei Kandidatkanten $e_1, \ldots, e_3$ induziert in Einbettung $h(V^*)$ einen Sichtbarkeitskeil. Die Vereinigung der drei Keile für die künstliche Kante $h(a_1)$, geschnitten mit $\mathrm{Ker}(h(V^*))$, ergibt die Menge der zu V^* äquivalenten Sichtbarkeitszellen.[4]

Die Kanten des zweiten Typs sind der dominierende Teil an der Komplexität von $\mathcal{EC}(V^*)$. Deren Zahl wird bestimmt durch die Zahl der Sichtbarkeitskeile, und somit durch die Zahl der Kandidatkanten für die künstlichen Kanten. Sei deshalb $\overline{E}$ die Menge *aller* Kandidatkanten für *alle* künstlichen Kanten in *allen* Einbettungen von V^*. Für die Kardinalität von $\overline{E}$ kann man dann folgendes zeigen:

---

[4]Falls das Skelett V^* mehr als eine künstliche Kante besitzt, so ist in entsprechender Weise zunächst für jede künstliche Kante die Vereinigung der zugehörigen Sichtbarkeitskeile zu bilden. Die Sichtbarkeitszellen ergeben sich dann durch Schnitt des Kerns mit dem Schnitt aller Vereinigungsmengen.

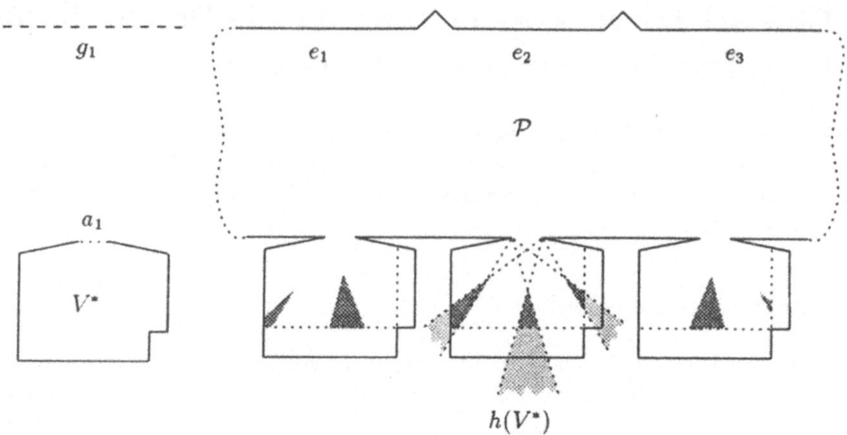

Abbildung 3: Die drei zu V^* äquivalenten Sichtbarkeitszellen (dunkelgrau) in Einbettung $h(V^*)$ sind die Schnittmenge der drei Sichtbarkeitskeile (hellgrau) mit dem Kern $\mathrm{Ker}(h(V^*))$.

Lemma 2 *In Kartenpolygonen ohne Löcher bzw. mit ausschließlich konvexen Löchern ist die Kardinalität von $\overline{E}$ aus $\mathcal{O}(r)$.*

Könnte nun jede Kandidatkante aus $\overline{E}$ eindeutig einem Sichtbarkeitskeil zugeordnet werden, so wäre die Komplexität des Arrangements aller Keile, $\mathcal{O}(|\overline{E}|^2) = \mathcal{O}(r^2)$, eine obere Schranke für die Zahl der Kanten des zweiten Typs. Dies ist jedoch *nicht* möglich, wie Abbildung 3 zeigt: Die Kante e_2 induziert in *allen drei* Einbettungen von V^* einen Sichtbarkeitskeil. Dieser naive Ansatz führt somit nicht zum Erfolg.

Allerdings zeigt ein topologisches Argument, daß jedes *Paar von Kandidatkanten* maximal einem *Paar von Sichtbarkeitskeilen* zugeordnet werden kann. Hiermit kann dann der folgende Satz gezeigt werden:

Satz 3 *Die Gesamtkomplexität einer beliebigen Äquivalenzklasse (in einem Kartenpolygon ohne Löcher) ist aus $\mathcal{O}(n + r^2)$.*

Für den Extremfall vieler Reflex–Ecken, d.h. $r \in \Omega(n)$, erhält man damit wieder die in [6] gezeigte Schranke. Ist jedoch die Zahl der Reflex–Ecken deutlich geringer als die Gesamtzahl aller Ecken, erhält man eine bessere Abschätzung für die Komplexität der Äquivalenzklasse. Falls beispielsweise die Zahl r der Reflex–Ecken nur aus $\mathcal{O}(\sqrt{n})$ ist, hängt die Komplexität einer Äquivalenzklasse nur noch linear von der Gesamtzahl n der Ecken ab, und nicht mehr quadratisch.

Auswirkung auf den Preprocessing–Aufwand

Unter Verwendung von Satz 3 kann somit die Abschätzung des Zeit- und Speicherbedarfs beim Preprocessing (siehe Abschnitt 2) von $\mathcal{O}(n^4 r)$, wie in [6] gezeigt, auf $\mathcal{O}\big(n^2 r \cdot (n + r^2)\big)$ verschärft werden.

Kartenpolygone mit Löchern

Die obigen Komplexitätsbetrachtungen gelten nur für Kartenpolygone *ohne Löcher*, d.h. in der Einsatzumgebung des Roboters befinden sich keine *frei stehenden Hindernisse*. Für Kartenpolygone mit Löchern verschlechtern sich die Abschätzungen (siehe hierzu [6, 9]). Für den Spezialfall eines Kartenpolygons mit l konvexen Löchern konnten wir zeigen, daß die worst case–Komplexität einer Äquivalenzklasse aus $\mathcal{O}(n + (l+1)r^2)$ ist, d.h. linear in der Anzahl der Löcher.

4 Anwendbarkeit des Verfahrens in der Praxis

Das in Abschnitt 2 beschriebene Lokalisationsverfahren von Guibas et al. ist aus mehreren Gründen nicht direkt für den Praxiseinsatz geeignet:

1. Bei der Lokalisation wird schon die *genaue Kenntnis der Orientierung* des Roboters vorausgesetzt. Diese ist jedoch häufig nicht bekannt bzw. mit Ungenauigkeiten behaftet. Ein praktikables Verfahren sollte also entweder ohne diese Information auskommen (d.h. beim Einpassen des Sichtbarkeitspolygons in die Karte sind außer Translationen auch Rotationen zugelassen), oder aber zumindest kleine Abweichungen tolerieren.

2. Der range finding–Sensor des Roboters besitzt in der Realität ebenfalls nur eine beschränkte Genauigkeit und liefert zudem nicht direkt das Sichtbarkeits*polygon* des Roboters, sondern in der Regel nur eine Folge von *Abtastwerten* (bei einem Rundum–Scan mit einer Winkelauflösung von 0.5° ergibt dies z.B. eine Folge von 720 Entfernungswerten). An solche *Sensorungenauigkeiten* muß das Verfahren in geeigneter Weise angepaßt werden.

Distanzfunktionen zwischen Scans und Skeletten

Eine Möglichkeit, die oben beschriebenen Probleme zu umgehen bzw. abzuschwächen, ist die Einführung einer geeigneten *Distanzfunktion* $d(S, V^*)$, die die *Ähnlichkeit* eines Scans S (den der range finding–Sensor liefert) zu einem Sichtbarkeitsskelett V^* modelliert. Diese Distanz sollte die folgenden Eigenschaften besitzen:

1. Sie sollte *unabhängig vom Referenzpunkt* des Scans bzw. des Skeletts sein, d.h. eine Translation des Scans oder des Skeletts im jeweiligen lokalen Koordinatensystem sollte keine Veränderung der Distanz bewirken.

2. Falls der Roboter keinen Kompaß besitzt, sollte die Distanz auch *unabhängig von der Orientierung* des Scans bzw. des Skeletts sein.

3. Die Distanz sollte *stetig* sein in dem Sinne, daß eine kleine Veränderung der Abtastwerte (verursacht z.B. durch ungenaue Sensordaten) auch nur eine kleine Distanzänderung bewirkt. Diese Forderung wird unter anderem auch dadurch motiviert, daß bei der Methode von Guibas et al. gerade die Einteilung der Kanten des Sichtbarkeitspolygons in verschiedene Typen (Scheinkanten, Teilkanten, usw.) das Verfahren anfällig für Störungen macht: Schon eine geringe Verschiebung eines

Eckpunkts kann den Typ einer Kante ändern, was zur Folge hat, daß das aus dem Sichtbarkeitspolygon resultierende Skelett i.d.R. keiner Äquivalenzklasse zugeordnet werden kann.

In Frage kommen hier beispielsweise Modifikationen der *Arkin-Metrik* [2] oder der *Minimalen Hausdorff-Distanz* [1, 8]. Eine Lokalisationsanfrage entspricht dann einer *Nearest Neighbor-Query* in der Menge der Skelette bezüglich der gewählten Distanzfunktion $d(S, V^*)$. Damit diese Anfrage effizient ausgeführt werden kann, sollten die Skelette in einer geeigneten Datenstruktur gespeichert werden.

Verwalten der Skelette

Hierfür bietet sich beispielsweise der *Monotone Bisektor-Baum* [11] an, ein *räumlicher Index*, der es erlaubt, die Menge der Skelette bezüglich einer weiteren Distanzfunktion $D(V_1^*, V_2^*)$, die die Ähnlichkeit zweier Skelette V_1^* und V_2^* beschreibt, *hierarchisch* zu partitionieren. Die Menge der Skelette wird hierbei rekursiv in *Cluster* mit monoton fallenden *Clusterradien* unterteilt. Diese Aufteilung spiegelt dann die Ähnlichkeiten der Skelette untereinander wider.

Damit bei einer Nearest Neighbor-Anfrage nicht immer alle Cluster durchsucht werden müssen, sollte die Distanz $D(V_1^*, V_2^*)$ so gewählt werden, daß sie "kompatibel" zur Distanz $d(S, V^*)$ ist, d.h. es sollte die *Dreiecksungleichung*

$$d(S, V_2^*) \leq d(S, V_1^*) + D(V_1^*, V_2^*)$$

erfüllt sein. Auch für diese Distanzfunktion scheinen die Arkin-Metrik und die Minimale Hausdorff-Distanz (in einer modifizierten Form) geeignete Kandidaten zu sein.

5 Zukünftige Arbeiten

Der oben beschriebene Ansatz wird zur Zeit von uns implementiert und getestet. Entscheidend für die Effizienz und Güte des Verfahrens ist offensichtlich die Wahl der beiden Distanzfunktionen $d(S, V^*)$ und $D(V_1^*, V_2^*)$. Ziel ist es deshalb, weitere Distanzfunktionen mit den oben beschriebenen Eigenschaften zu finden und in Beispielszenarien zu testen.

Literatur

[1]   Helmut Alt, Oswin Aichholzer, Günther Rote. Matching Shapes with a Reference Point. In *Proceedings of the 10th Annual ACM Symposium on Computational Geometry*, 1994, S. 85–92.

[2]   Esther M. Arkin, L. Paul Chew, Daniel P. Huttenlocher, Klara Kedem, Joseph S. B. Mitchell. An Efficiently Computable Metric for Comparing Polygonal Shapes. *IEEE Transactions on Pattern Analysis and Machine Intelligence*, 13 (1991), S. 209–216.

[3]   Udo Braun. Lernen von Ähnlichkeitsmaßen und Nearest-Neighbour-Klassifikation in einem ausgewählten Szenario. Diplomarbeit, Lehrstuhl für Informatik I, Universität Würzburg, April 1996.

[4] Ingemar J. Cox. Blanche — An Experiment in Guidance and Navigation of an Autonomous Robot Vehicle. *IEEE Transactions on Robotics and Automation*, 7 (1991), S. 193–204.

[5] Gregory Dudek, Kathleen Romanik, Sue Whitesides. Localizing a Robot with Minimum Travel. In *Proceedings of the 6th Annual ACM–SIAM Symposium on Discrete Algorithms*, 1995, S. 437–446.

[6] Leonidas J. Guibas, Rajeev Motwani, Prabhakar Raghavan. The Robot Localization Problem. In Ken Goldberg, Dan Halperin, Jean-Claude Latombe, Randall Wilson (Hrsg.), *Algorithmic Foundations of Robotics*, 1995, S. 269–282. A K Peters.

[7] Leonidas J. Guibas, Rajeev Motwani, Prabhakar Raghavan. The Robot Localization Problem, Juli 1995, `http://theory.stanford.edu/people/motwani/postscripts/localiz.ps.Z`.

[8] Daniel P. Huttenlocher, Klara Kedem. Computing the Minimum Hausdorff Distance for Point Sets Under Translation. In *Proceedings of the 6th Annual ACM Symposium on Computational Geometry*, 1990, S. 340–349.

[9] Oliver Karch. A Sharper Complexity Bound for the Robot Localization Problem. Technischer Bericht Nr. 139, Lehrstuhl für Informatik I, Universität Würzburg, Juni 1996.

[10] Jon Kleinberg. The Localization Problem for Mobile Robots. In *Proceedings of the 35th Annual IEEE Symposium Foundation Computer Sciences*, 1994.

[11] Hartmut Noltemeier, Knut Verbarg, Christian Zirkelbach. A Data Structure for Representing and Efficient Querying Large Scenes of Geometric Objects: MB*-Trees. In G. Farin, H. Hagen, H. Noltemeier (Hrsg.), *Geometric Modelling*, Band 8 von *Computing Supplement*, 1993, S. 211–226. Springer.

[12] Kathleen Romanik, Sven Schuierer. Optimal Robot Localization in Trees. In *Proceedings of the 12th Annual ACM Symposium on Computational Geometry*, 1996.

[13] C. Ming Wang. Location estimation and uncertainty analysis for mobile robots. In I. J. Cox, G. T. Wilfong (Hrsg.), *Autonomous Robot Vehicles*, 1990 Springer, Berlin.

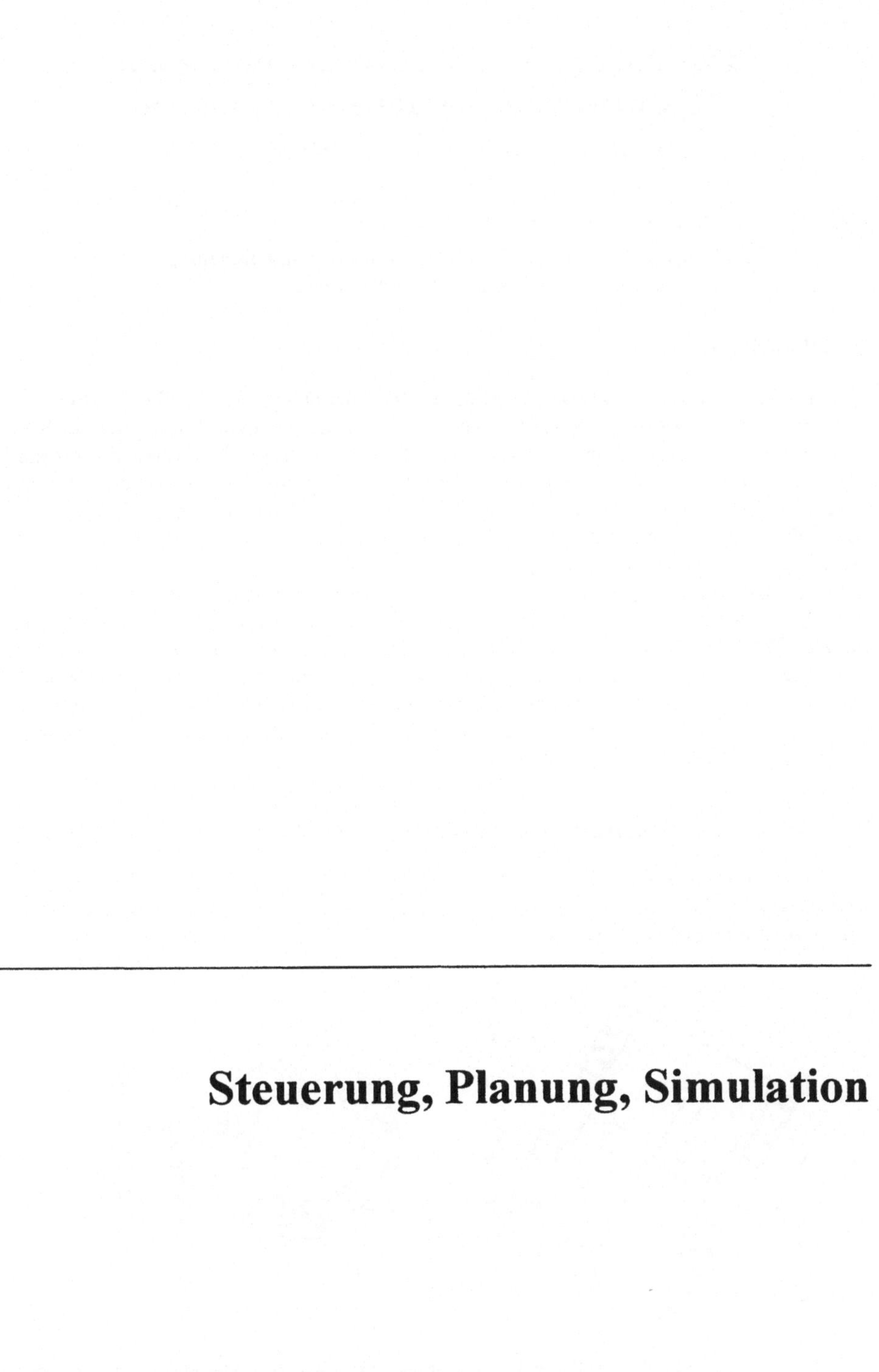

Steuerung, Planung, Simulation

Die Ausgangsgrößenverkopplung zur Reduzierung des Radschlupfes bei omnidirektionalen Fahrzeugen

Andreas Jochheim
FernUniversität Hagen
Fachbereich Elektrotechnik, Prozeßsteuerung und Regelungstechnik
Postfach 940, 58084 Hagen

1. Einleitung

Ist bei radangetriebenen Fahrzeugen die Zahl der Antriebe größer als die Anzahl der Freiheitsgrade der Bewegung, so müssen diese synchronisiert werden, damit erhöhter Schlupf durch Gegeneinanderarbeiten vermieden und die gewünschte Bahntrajektorie eingehalten wird. Drehzahlsynchronität läßt sich mechanisch durch Getriebe realisieren. Allerdings steigt der Aufwand immer dann beträchtlich, wenn die Ausgangsgrößen "Drehzahl" bei einem Fahrzeug oder einer Anlage örtlich weit verteilt sind. Im Einzelfall ist eine Getrieberealisierung auch gar nicht möglich.

In diesem Beitrag wird die Anwendung der in [1] entwickelten Ausgangsgrößenverkopplung beim Entwurf einer Geschwindigkeitsregelung zur Schlupfreduzierung für ein omnidirektionales Fahrzeug, das mit vier Mecanum-Antriebseinheiten ausgestattet ist, beschrieben. Die Ausgangsgrößenverkopplung stellt ein Reglerentwurfsverfahren dar, welches es erlaubt, vorgegebene, durch lineare Gleichungen beschreibbare Ausgangsgrößenverkopplungen direkt im Entwurf zu berücksichtigen. Sie gestattet es somit, ein allgemeines "elektronisches Getriebe" zu realisieren.

2. Die kinematischen Gleichungen des Mecanum-Fahrzeuges

Eine Mecanum-Antriebseinheit besteht aus einem motorangetriebenen Rad, auf dessen Radumfang sich diagonal angeordnetete, ballig geformte, antriebslose Rollen befinden. Bild 1 zeigt ein solches Rad.

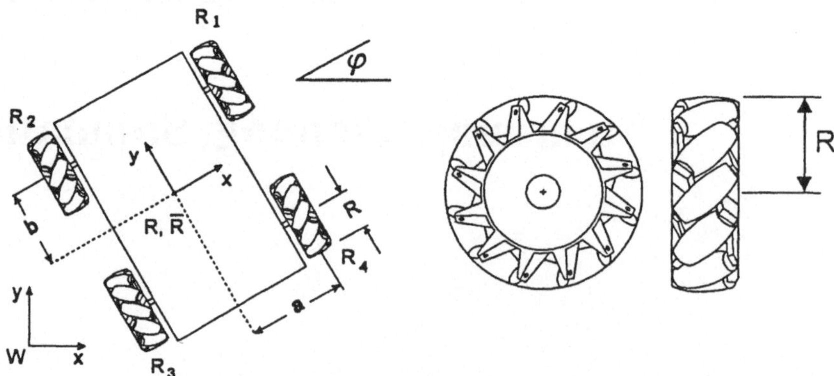

Bild 1: Schematische Darstellung eines vierradangetriebenen Mecanum-Fahrzeuges und seiner Räder

Die Ausstattung eines Fahrzeuges mit mindestens drei einzeln angesteuerten Antrieben erlaubt es, dieses Fahrzeug ohne zusätzliche Lenkeinrichtungen auf jeder beliebigen Trajektorie in der Ebene zu bewegen. Es besitzt alle drei Freiheitsgrade (x, y, φ) und somit die Mobilität eines Luftkissenfahrzeuges. Üblicherweise werden Fahrzeuge, wie in Bild 1 schematisch in der Draufsicht dargestellt, mit vier Antrieben ausgestattet. Unter der Annahme einer schlupffreien Bewegung lauten die Beziehungen zwischen den Radgeschwindigkeiten und den Geschwindigkeitskomponenten $v_x^F(t)$, $v_y^F(t)$ und $v_\varphi^F(t)$ des Fahrzeuges im Weltkoordinatensystem [2]:

Vorwärtstransformation:

$$\begin{pmatrix} v_x^F \\ v_y^F \\ v_\varphi^F \end{pmatrix} = \frac{R}{4} \begin{pmatrix} \cos\varphi & -\sin\varphi & 0 \\ \sin\varphi & \cos\varphi & 0 \\ 0 & 0 & 1 \end{pmatrix} \begin{pmatrix} -1 & 1 & -1 & 1 \\ 1 & 1 & 1 & 1 \\ \frac{1}{a+b} & \frac{-1}{a+b} & \frac{-1}{a+b} & \frac{1}{a+b} \end{pmatrix} \begin{pmatrix} \omega_{R1} \\ \omega_{R2} \\ \omega_{R3} \\ \omega_{R4} \end{pmatrix} \tag{1}$$

Rückwärtstransformation:

$$\begin{pmatrix} \omega_{R1} \\ \omega_{R2} \\ \omega_{R3} \\ \omega_{R4} \end{pmatrix} = \frac{1}{R} \begin{pmatrix} -1 & 1 & (a+b) \\ 1 & 1 & -(a+b) \\ -1 & 1 & -(a+b) \\ 1 & 1 & (a+b) \end{pmatrix} \begin{pmatrix} \cos\varphi & \sin\varphi & 0 \\ -\sin\varphi & \cos\varphi & 0 \\ 0 & 0 & 1 \end{pmatrix} \begin{pmatrix} v_x^F \\ v_y^F \\ v_\varphi^F \end{pmatrix} \tag{2}$$

Der Zusammenhang zwischen den Geschwindigkeiten bezüglich des stationären, augenblicklich mit dem Roboterkoordinatensystem R deckungsgleichen Koordinatensystems $\bar{R}$ und denen in W läßt sich über die Gleichung

$$\begin{pmatrix} v_x^F \\ v_y^F \\ v_\varphi^F \end{pmatrix} = \begin{pmatrix} \cos\varphi & -\sin\varphi & 0 \\ \sin\varphi & \cos\varphi & 0 \\ 0 & 0 & 1 \end{pmatrix} \begin{pmatrix} v_x \\ v_y \\ v_\varphi \end{pmatrix} \tag{3}$$

beschreiben. $v_x(t)$ ist somit für die Seitwärtsbewegung, $v_y(t)$ für die Vorwärts-Rückwärtsbewegung und $v_\varphi(t)$ für die Drehbewegung des Fahrzeuges verantwortlich. Der Winkel zwischen $\bar{R}$ und dem Weltkoordinatensystem W ist $\varphi(t)$.
Wie an der Rückwärtstransformation (2) zu erkennen, ist die Geschwindigkeit eines Rades eine Linearkombination der anderen drei Räder. Es besteht somit die Notwendigkeit, bei einem derartigen Fahrzeug die Räder so anzusteuern, daß stets die Rollbedingung

$$\omega_{R1}(t) + \omega_{R2}(t) - \omega_{R3}(t) - \omega_{R4}(t) = 0 \tag{4}$$

erfüllt ist, um Schlupf durch Gegeneinanderarbeiten der Räder zu vermeiden.
Zur Beschreibung der Verkopplungsbedingung werden die Verkopplungsmatrix T und die Synchronitätsmatrix S eingeführt:

$$T = \begin{pmatrix} 1 & 1 & -1 & -1 \end{pmatrix} \qquad S = \begin{pmatrix} 1 & 0 & 0 \\ 0 & 1 & 0 \\ 0 & 0 & 1 \\ 1 & 1 & -1 \end{pmatrix} \tag{5}$$

Die Multiplikation der Verkopplungsmatrix mit dem Vektor der vier Radgeschwindigkeiten ergibt genau die linke Seite der Rollbedingung (4), während die Multiplikation der Synchronitätsmatrix mit dem Vektor der ersten drei Radgeschwindigkeiten genau zusätzlich die vierte Radgeschwindigkeit so erzeugt, daß (4) erfüllt ist. Es gilt weiterhin $TS = 0$.

3. Die dynamischen Gleichungen des Mecanum-Fahrzeuges

Zur Bestimmung des dynamischen Modells des Mecanum-Fahrzeuges wird ein in [3] vorgestellter erweiterter Lagrange-Ansatz genutzt, der die nichtholonomen Nebenbedingungen bei rollenden Rädern miteinschließt. Um die Überschaubarkeit des Modells für den Reglerentwurf zu gewährleisten, werden Reibungsphänomene im Modell selbst nicht berücksichtigt, sondern als Störungen interpretiert. Man erhält das in der Tabelle 1 angegebene Gleichungssystem, welches zum Reglerentwurf herangezogen wird [1]. Das Modell impliziert, daß die Rollbedingung erfüllt ist. Jedoch kann angenommen werden, daß auftretende Verkopplungsfehler so gering sind, daß das gesamtdynamische Verhalten des Fahrzeuges gleich bleibt.

Tabelle 1: Gleichungssystem Mecanum-Fz zum Reglerentwurf

Zustandsgleichung: Ausgangsgleichung:

$$\dot{x}(t) = a(x) + \underbrace{B_V V J_V}_{B(x)}\, u(t) \qquad\qquad y(t) = \underbrace{J_R V^{-1} v}_{c(x)}$$

Zustands-, Eingangs- und Ausgangsvektor:

$$x(t) = \begin{pmatrix} v_x^F(t) \\ v_y^F(t) \\ v_\varphi^F(t) \\ v_f(t) \\ \varphi(t) \end{pmatrix} \qquad u(t) = \begin{pmatrix} M_1(t) \\ M_2(t) \\ M_3(t) \\ M_4(t) \end{pmatrix} \qquad y(t) = \begin{pmatrix} \omega_{R1}(t) \\ \omega_{R2}(t) \\ \omega_{R3}(t) \\ \omega_{R4}(t) \end{pmatrix}$$

Systemvektoren und Matrizen:

$$a(x) = \begin{pmatrix} -Ax_2x_3 \\ Ax_1x_3 \\ 0 \\ 0 \\ x_3 \end{pmatrix} \quad B_V = \begin{pmatrix} B & 0 & 0 & 0 \\ 0 & B & 0 & 0 \\ 0 & 0 & C & 0 \\ 0 & 0 & 0 & D \\ 0 & 0 & 0 & 0 \end{pmatrix} \quad V = \begin{pmatrix} \cos x_5 & -\sin x_5 & 0 & 0 \\ \sin x_5 & \cos x_5 & 0 & 0 \\ 0 & 0 & 1 & 0 \\ 0 & 0 & 0 & 1 \end{pmatrix}$$

$$J_V = \begin{pmatrix} -1 & 1 & -1 & 1 \\ 1 & 1 & 1 & 1 \\ 1 & -1 & -1 & 1 \\ 1 & 1 & -1 & -1 \end{pmatrix} \quad J_R = \frac{1}{R}\begin{pmatrix} -1 & 1 & k & v_1 \\ 1 & 1 & -k & v_1 \\ -1 & 1 & -k & -v_1 \\ 1 & 1 & k & -v_1 \end{pmatrix} \quad v = \begin{pmatrix} x_1 \\ x_2 \\ x_3 \\ x_4 \end{pmatrix}$$

Abkürzungen und Bedeutungen:

$$A = \frac{4\Theta_R}{4\Theta_R + mR^2}; \qquad B = \frac{R}{4\Theta_R + mR^2}; \qquad C = \frac{Rk}{4\Theta_R k^2 + \Theta_W R^2}; \qquad D = \frac{1}{\Theta_R}$$

$v_f(t) = \omega_{R1}(t) + \omega_{R2}(t) - \omega_{R3}(t) - \omega_{R4}(t)$

$k = a + b$ (siehe Bild 1), $v_1 \approx 0$

m Masse des Fahrzeuges einschl. Räder und Rollen

Θ_W Trägheitsmoment des Fahrzeuges um die z-Achse einschl. Räder und Rollen

Θ_R Trägheitsmoment der Räder einschl. der Rollen um die Drehachse der Räder

R Radius des MECANUM-Rades

M_i an den Rädern durch die Antriebe angreifende Drehmomente

4. Der Reglerentwurf

Differenziert man jede Komponente des Ausgangsvektors $y(t)$ der Ausgangsgleichung in Tabelle 1 nach der Zeit und setzt anschließend die Zustandsgleichung ein, gelangt man zur "Direkten Systembescheibung":

$$y^*(t) = c^*(x) + D^*(x)u(t) \tag{6}$$

mit $y_i^*(t) = \dot{y}_i(t)$, $c_i^*(x) = \left[\frac{\partial}{\partial x}c_i(x)\right]^T a(x)$ und $D_i^*(x) = \left[\frac{\partial}{\partial x}c_i(x)\right]^T B(x)$. Für eine ausführliche Betrachtungsweise der Direkten Systembeschreibung für lineare Systeme sei an dieser Stelle auf [4] und für eine Klasse von nichtlinearen, zeitvarianten Systemen auf [5] verwiesen.

Wählt man nun als Regelungsgesetz

$$u(t) = -\underbrace{D^{*-1}(x)c^*(x)}_{k_1(x)} - \underbrace{m_0 D^{*-1}(x)M_0 c(x)}_{k_2(x)} + \underbrace{m_0 D^{*-1}(x)w(t)}_{V(x,t)} \tag{7}$$

mit $w(t)$ als Führungsvektor mit den Sollgeschwindigkeiten $\omega_{Ri,soll}(t)$ der Räder, so wird das Führungsgrößenverhalten des Gesamtsystems durch das Differentialgleichungssystem

$$y^*(t) + m_0 M_0 y(t) = m_0 w(t) \tag{8}$$

oder im Frequenzbereich durch

$$Y(s) = \underbrace{m_0(sI + m_0 M_0)^{-1}}_{G_W(s)} W(s) \tag{9}$$

beschrieben. Über die skalare Größe m_0 und die Gewichtungsmatrix M_0 können nun die Dynamik und die Verkopplung des Gleichungssystems vorgegeben werden.
Setzt man die Gewichtsmatrix mit einem noch freien Parameter g zu

$$M_0 = \begin{pmatrix} 1+g & g & -g & -g \\ g & 1+g & -g & -g \\ -g & -g & 1+g & g \\ -g & -g & g & 1+g \end{pmatrix} \tag{10}$$

an (es ist dann $M_0 S = S$), so gilt für die Übertragungsmatrix

$$G_W(s) = \frac{m_0}{N(s)} \begin{pmatrix} s+m_0\tilde{g} & -m_0 g & m_0 g & m_0 g \\ -m_0 g & s+m_0\tilde{g} & m_0 g & m_0 g \\ m_0 g & m_0 g & s+m_0\tilde{g} & -m_0 g \\ m_0 g & m_0 g & -m_0 g & s+m_0\tilde{g} \end{pmatrix} \tag{11}$$

mit $N(s) = (s + m_0)(s + m_0(1 + 4g))$ und $\tilde{g} = 1 + 3g$. Damit die Führungsgrößen die Rollbedingung erfüllen, werden nur die ersten drei Radgeschwindigkeiten durch $\hat{w}(t)$ vorgegeben und dann $w(t)$ über $w(t) = S\hat{w}(t)$ ermittelt, so daß $W(s) = S\hat{W}(s)$ gilt. Damit wird Gleichung (9) mit (11) zu

$$Y(s) = \frac{m_0}{s + m_0} S\,\hat{W}(s) \tag{12}$$

Wie sofort einsichtig, erfüllt $Y(s)$ die Rollbedingung, da jetzt $TY(s) = 0$ wegen $TS = 0$ ist. Über den Gewichtungsfaktor m_0 wird somit unabhängig der Wahl von g in der

Gewichtungsmatrix M_0 genau der Eigenwert vorgegeben, welcher bei Erfüllung der Synchronität das Systemverhalten beschreibt. Bei Nichterfüllung der Synchronität durch den Einfluß äußerer Störungen muß die Gleichung (9) mit (11) betrachtet werden. Es wird zusätzlich eine Eigenbewegung, beschrieben durch $s+m_0(1+4g)$ im Polynom $N(s)$ in dem Sinne angeregt, daß sie dem Verkopplungsfehler entgegenwirkt. Über den Koeffizienten m_0 kann somit die Dynamik des ungestörten Systems festgelegt werden, während über g dann anschließend die Dynamik der Ausregelung des Verkopplungsfehlers eingestellt wird.

5. Realisierung des Reglers

Berechnet man die einzelnen Anteile des Regelungsgesetzes (7) über (6) bei Wahl der Gewichtungsmatrix nach (10), so erhält man nach einigen Umformungen und Umsortierungen unter Nutzung der Transformationen (1) bis (3):

Entkopplungszweig:

$$k_1(x) = \frac{1}{8}mR^2 \begin{pmatrix} -(\omega_{R2,ist} + \omega_{R4,ist}) \\ (\omega_{R1,ist} + \omega_{R3,ist}) \\ -(\omega_{R2,ist} + \omega_{R4,ist}) \\ (\omega_{R1,ist} + \omega_{R3,ist}) \end{pmatrix} \tag{13}$$

Vorwärtszweig:

$$\begin{aligned}
V(x,t) \;=\;\; & m_0\Theta_R \begin{pmatrix} \omega_{R1,soll} \\ \omega_{R2,soll} \\ \omega_{R3,soll} \\ \omega_{R4,soll} \end{pmatrix} \quad \longrightarrow \text{ Anteil Radgeschw.} \\[2mm]
+\; & \frac{m_0}{4}mR\,u_x\,v_{x,soll} \qquad \longrightarrow \text{ Anteil x-Komponente in } \bar{R} \\[2mm]
+\; & \frac{m_0}{4}mR\,u_y\,v_{y,soll} \qquad \longrightarrow \text{ Anteil y-Komponente in } \bar{R} \\[2mm]
+\; & \frac{m_0}{4}\frac{R}{k}\Theta_W\,u_\varphi\,v_{\varphi,soll} \quad \longrightarrow \text{ Anteil } \varphi\text{-Komponente in } \bar{R}
\end{aligned} \tag{14}$$

Rückkopplungszweig:

$$\begin{aligned}
k_2(x) \;=\;\; & m_0\Theta_R \begin{pmatrix} \omega_{R1,ist} \\ \omega_{R2,ist} \\ \omega_{R3,ist} \\ \omega_{R4,ist} \end{pmatrix} \quad \longrightarrow \text{ Anteil Radgeschw.} \\[2mm]
+\; & \frac{m_0}{4}mR\,u_x\,v_{x,ist} \qquad \longrightarrow \text{ Anteil x-Komponente in } \bar{R} \\[2mm]
+\; & \frac{m_0}{4}mR\,u_y\,v_{y,ist} \qquad \longrightarrow \text{ Anteil y-Komponente in } \bar{R} \\[2mm]
+\; & \frac{m_0}{4}\frac{R}{k}\Theta_W\,u_\varphi\,v_{\varphi,ist} \quad \longrightarrow \text{ Anteil } \varphi\text{-Komponente in } \bar{R} \\[2mm]
+\; & m_0\hat{g}\Theta_R\,u_f\,v_f \qquad \longrightarrow \text{ Anteil Verkopplung}\,(\hat{g} = 1 + 4g)
\end{aligned} \tag{15}$$

Hierbei gilt für die Vektoren u_x, u_y, u_φ und u_f in Gleichung (14) und (15) der Zusammenhang

$$\begin{pmatrix} u_x & u_y & u_\varphi & u_f \end{pmatrix} = J_V^T \qquad (16)$$

mit der Matrix J_V der Tabelle 1.

Die Gleichungen (13) bis (16) ermöglichen eine sehr anschauliche Betrachtung des über den Entwurf gewonnenen Reglers:

Neben dem Entkopplungsanteil $k_1(x)$ teilt sich der Regler auf in die Regelung der einzelnen Radgeschwindigkeiten und die Regelung der einzelnen Geschwindigkeitskomponenten in $\bar{R}$. Zusätzlich wirkt ein Verkopplungsterm bei Verletzung der Verkopplungsbedingung im qualitativ richtigen Sinne.

Bild 2 zeigt schematisch die zum Aufbau der Regelung genutzten Stell- und Meßgrößen der Steuerung des am Lehrgebiet entwickelten mobilen Roboters. Als Antriebseinheiten dienen Synchron-Servomotoren mit Getriebe und Resolverrückführung, welche über Servoregler angesteuert werden. Über einen $\pm 10V$ Analogeingang wird diesen das Motorsollmoment als Stellgröße vorgegeben.

Als Meßgrößen werden die Radgeschwindigkeiten aus den Resolversignalen gewonnen. Zur genauen Orientierungsbestimmung des Fahrzeuges wird weiterhin ein Lasergyroskop eingesetzt, so daß als weitere Meßgrößen $\varphi(t)$ und $v_\varphi^F(t)$ vorliegen.

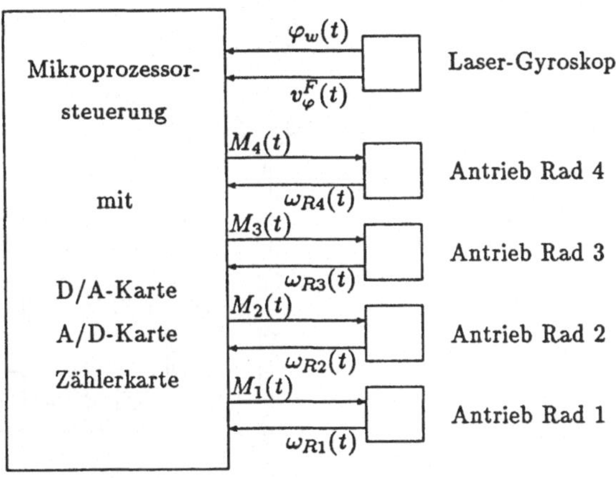

Bild 2: Stell- und Meßgrößen zur Reglerrealisierung

Die in die Steuerung implementierte Gesamtregelstruktur zeigt Bild 3. Die Geschwindigkeitssollwerte werden von einer übergeordneten Bahnregelung im Weltkoordinatensystem geliefert. Die Bahnregelung besteht aus drei Proportionalreglern, die den einzelnen Positionskomponenten zugeordnet werden. Die Reglermatrix K_L hat somit Diagonalgestalt. Die zum Aufbau der Regelung benötigten translatorischen Geschwindigkeitswerte in $\bar{R}$ werden über die Transformationen (1) bis (3), ausgedrückt durch die Matrix J in Bild 3, bestimmt. Die Matrizen J^* und V lassen sich ebenfalls daraus entnehmen.

Die Korrekturmatrix S_K dient zur Kompensation der Berechnungsfehler bei der x- und y-Position durch die systematischen Bahnabweichungen aufgrund von Spurfehlern, des durch Roll- und Wälzreibung entstehenden Schlupfes, der wandernden Bodenkontaktfläche der Rolle usw. Auf die Bestimmung dieser Matrix soll an dieser Stelle nicht weiter eingegangen werden, da sie für den Reglerentwurf keine Bedeutung hat, sondern lediglich die Genauigkeit in der Berechnung der absoluten Position erhöht.

Der Regelungsalgorithmus arbeitet mit einer Abtastzeit von $T_A = 5\,ms$. Da der übergeordnete Interpolator aus den vorgegebenen Kursdaten die Sollwerte ebenfalls im $5\,ms$ Zyklus errechnet, liegt zu jedem Regeltakt ein aktueller neuer Sollwertvektor vor. Der im Gesamtregelungskonzept vorhandene, übergeordnete Bahnregler im Weltkoordinatensystem kann über einen Software-Schalter überbrückt werden, so daß zu Untersuchungszwecken der hergeleitete Regler allein genutzt werden kann.

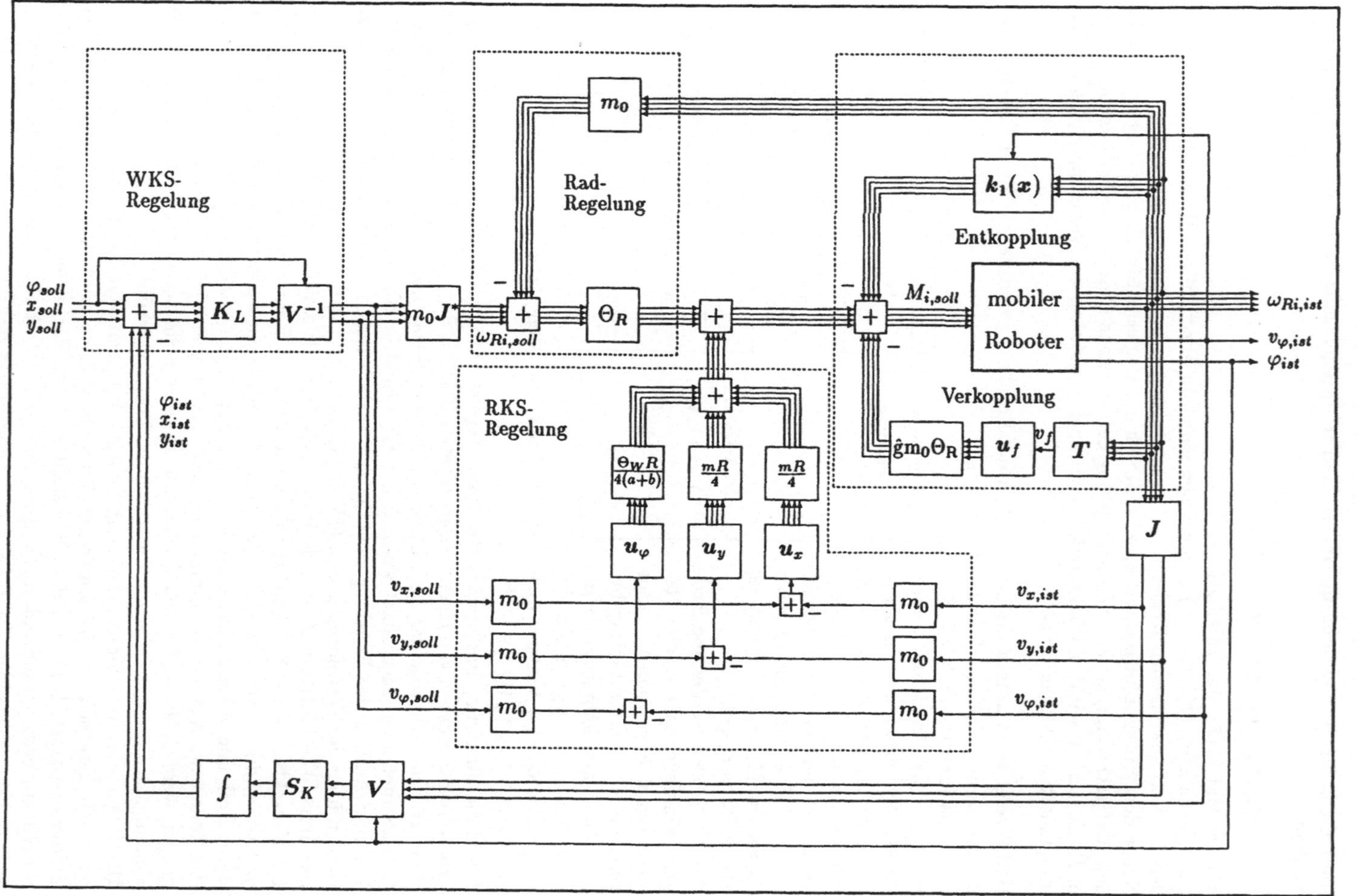

Bild 3: Gesamtregelstruktur

6. Ergebnisse

Zunächst wird das Verhalten des Fahrzeuges bei Bewegung in seinen drei Hauptrichtungen Vorwärtsfahrt, Seitwärtsfahrt und Drehfahrt anhand der Sprungantworten untersucht. Hierzu wird der Bahnregler überbrückt und in $\bar{R}$ jeweils eine Geschwindigkeitskomponente vorgegeben. Die Geschwindigkeit in allen drei Richtungen ist so gewählt worden, daß sich stets gleiche Radsollgeschwindigkeiten von $5\,rad/s$ ergeben.

Bild 4 zeigt den Verlauf der Verkopplungsfehler beim Vergleich der Regelung einmal mit und einmal ohne Verkopplungsanteil. Zum quantitativen Vergleich ist zusätzlich mit d_I das Integral über $(v_f(t))^2$ angegeben.

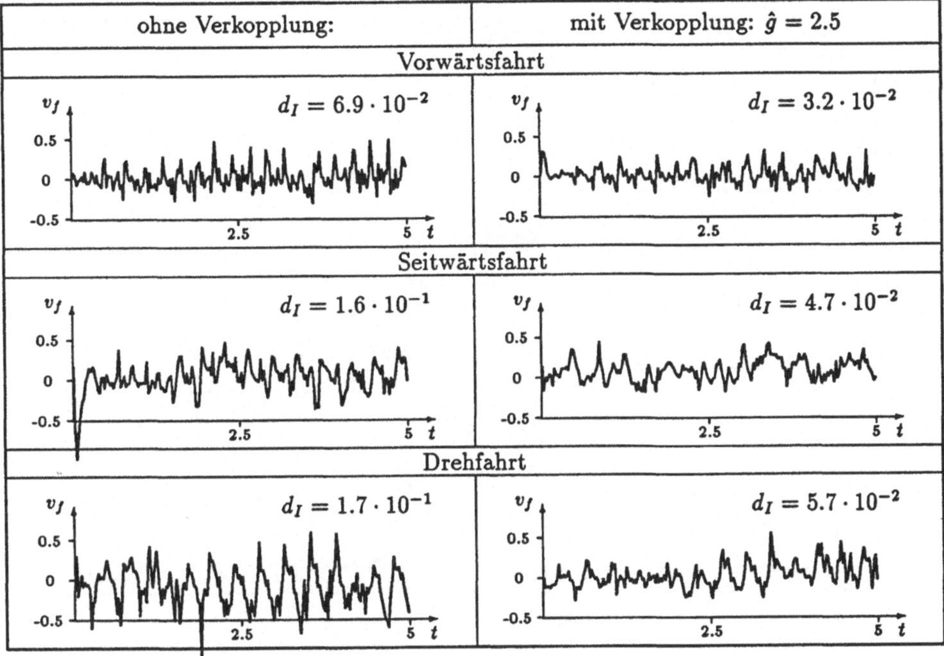

Bild 4: Verkopplungsfehler bei der Fahrt in die drei Grundrichtungen

Die Ausschläge im Fehler $v_f(t)$ haben sich nach der Verkopplung für alle drei Bewegungsrichtungen verringert, und das Fehlermaß hat sich stets um den Faktor 2 – 3 reduziert. Der prinzipiell größere Verkopplungsfehler und sein unruhigerer Verlauf bei der Seitwärts- und Drehfahrt werden dadurch verursacht, daß hier die Rollen des Rades an der Bewegung beteiligt sind, während sie bei der Vorwärtsfahrt stillstehen.

Bild 5 zeigt die Stellgrößenverläufe, repräsentiert durch den Motorstrom in A, beispielhaft für Rad 1 bei allen drei Hauptbewegungen des Fahrzeuges. Gut erkennbar ist hier die Wirkung der Verkopplungsregelung, da der Stellgrößenverlauf jeweils erheblich mehr Aktivität zeigt. Dieses ist unmittelbar einsichtig, da jetzt jedes Rad auch auf alle Störungen an den anderen Rädern reagiert.

Betrachtet man die Maximalströme von unter $5\,A$ bei den Stellwertverläufen und vergleicht diese mit dem maximal erzielbaren und zulässigen Spitzenstrom von $22\,A$ pro Antrieb, so ist klar, daß noch eine erheblich bessere Dynamik durch Verändern der Reglerparameter m_0 und g erzielt werden kann. Die erzielbare Dynamik der Drehzahlregelung ist in den vorangegangenen Untersuchungen bewußt nicht ausgenutzt worden, weil u.a. die Mechanik des Fahrzeuges (Getriebe und Lager) bei den Sprungantwortuntersuchungen erheblich in Anspruch genommen wird und die Gefahr des Durchrutschens einzelner Räder in der Beschleunigungsphase bei der Seitwärts- und Drehbewegung ohne Verkopplungsregelung erheblich zunimmt. Die Verkopplungsregelung verhindert dieses, da der Verkopplungsfehler im Falle des Durchrutschens einzelner Räder sehr groß wird, so daß sie hier den zusätzlichen positiven Nebeneffekt besitzt, als Antischlupfregelung der Einzelräder zu wirken (falls nicht an allen Räder gleichzeitig die Rollreibung zu klein wird).

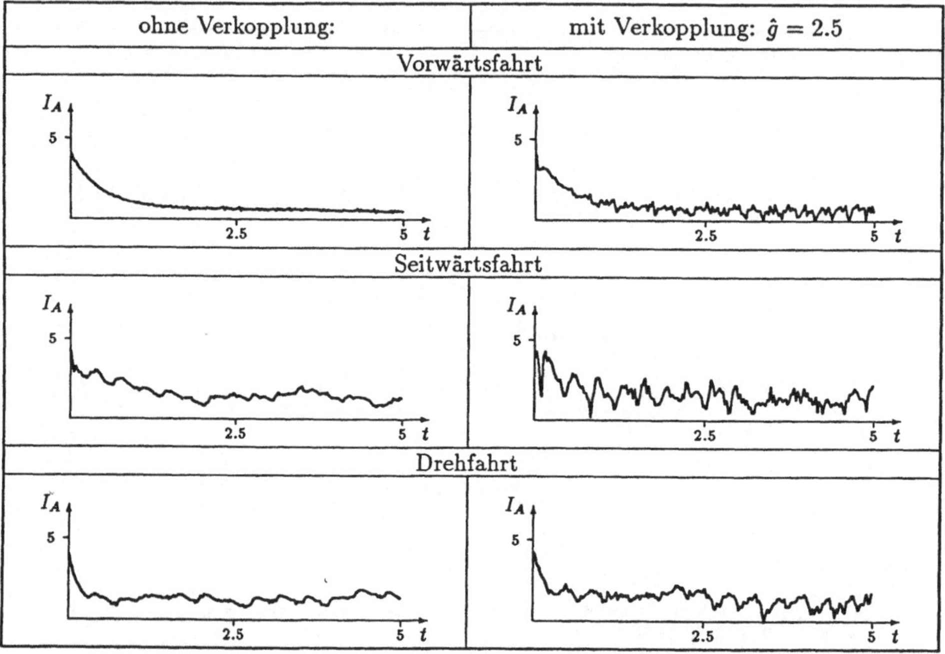

Bild 5: Stellgrößenverläufe beim Rad 1 bei der Fahrt in die drei Grundrichtungen

In dem nachfolgenden Versuch wird die Wirkung der Verkopplungsregelung anhand einer Testfahrt, bei welcher alle Bewegungskomponenten beteiligt sind, im Zusammenspiel mit dem übergeordneten Bahnregler untersucht. Da der Bahnregler zu Geschwindigkeitssollwertverläufen führt, die geglättet sind, und der die Bahnsollwerte berechnende Interpolator den translatorischen Bewegungskomponeten zur weiteren Schonung der Antriebe ein Sinusquadratprofil aufprägt, werden jetzt die Tests mit optimierten Parametern für m_0 und g durchgeführt.

Bild 6 zeigt den Testkurs und die dabei entstehenden Verkopplungsfehler, wenn dieser mit einer Bahngeschwindigkeit von $400\,mm/s$ durchfahren wird. Wie aus den Sprungantwortuntersuchungen schon zu erwarten, wirkt sich die Verkopplungsregelung wiederum positiv auf die Reduzierung des Verkopplungsfehlers aus. Weiterhin ist aus den Untersuchungsreihen festzustellen, daß nicht nur der Fehler selbst, sondern auch die Streuung des Fehlers bei der Verkopplungsregelung erheblich kleiner wird. Die Reproduzierbarkeit sich wiederholender Bewegungsvorgänge wird dadurch größer und sicherer.

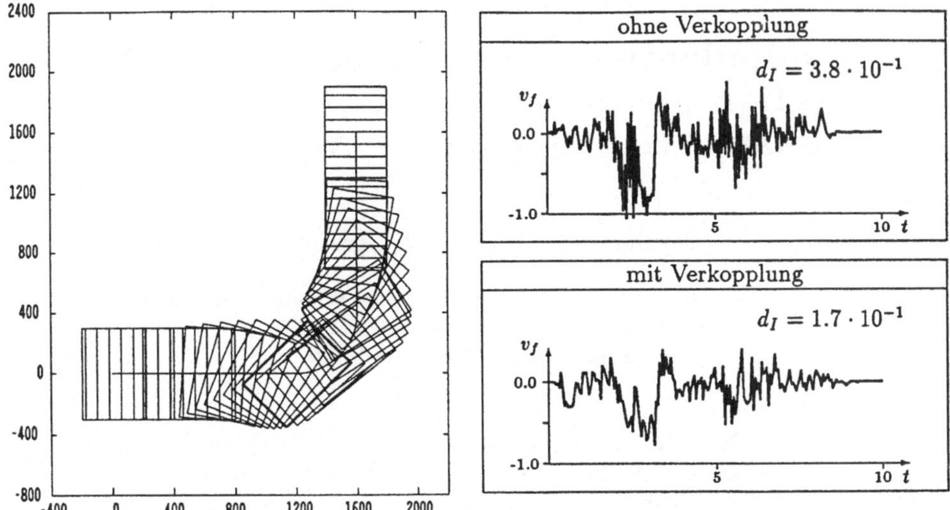

Bild 6: Fahrbewegung beim Testkurs (die Größendarstellung der Fahrzeugumrandung ist nicht maßstabsgerecht) und Verlauf des Verkopplungsfehlers

7. Zusammenfassung

Mit der Ausgangsgrößenverkopplung verfügt man über ein Entwurfsverfahren, welches einzuhaltende Verkopplungsanforderungen direkt mit in den Entwurf einbezieht. Insbesondere zur Synchronisation von Antrieben eignet sich dieses Verfahren, wenn auf mechanische Getriebekonstruktionen verzichtet werden soll. Anhand des Beispiels eines Mecanum-Fahrzeuges — hier ist die Verkopplungsanforderung durch eine Rollbedingung gegeben — wird die Leistungsfähigkeit des Verfahrens demonstriert. Bei Verletzung der Rollbedingung entsteht zusätzlicher Schlupf, der zu erhöhter und bei odometrischer Positionsbestimmung nicht bestimmbarer Positionsabweichung führt.
Die Anwendung der Verkopplungsregelung zeigt deutliche Vorteile: neben einem stets geringeren Fehler in der Einhaltung der Rollbedingung wird die Reproduzierbarkeit sich wiederholender Bewegungsvorgänge höher und sicherer. Weiterhin wirkt die Regelung wie eine Antischlupfregelung der Einzelräder. Die Verkopplungsregelung ist somit einer Einzelradregelung vorzuziehen.

8. Literatur

[1] *Jochheim, A.:* Reglerentwurf für Mehrgrößensysteme unter der Nebenbedingung vorgegebener Ausgangsgrößenverkopplungen. Düsseldorf: VDI-Verlag, 1995

[2] *Muir, P.F.:* Modeling and control of wheeled mobile robots. Dissertation, Carnegie-Mellon University, 1988

[3] *Lehmann, T.:* Elemente der Mechanik III: Kinetik. Braunschweig: Vieweg & Sohn Verlag, 1977.

[4] *Falb, P.L.; Wolovich, W.A.:* Decoupling in the Design and Synthesis of Multivariable Control Systems. IEEE Transactions on Automatic Control AC-12 (1967), S. 651-659.

[5] *Freund, E.; Hoyer, H.:* Das Prinzip nichtlinearer Systementkopplung mit der Anwendung auf Industrieroboter. Regelungstechnik 28 (1980), S. 80-87 und 116-126.

AMOS: Schnelle Manipulator-Bewegungsplanung durch Integration potentialfeldbasierter lokaler und probabilistischer globaler Algorithmen

Bernhard Braun und Ralf Corsépius

Forschungsinstitut für anwendungsorientierte Wissensverarbeitung
FAW Ulm, Postfach 2060, D-89010 Ulm
{braun,corsepiu}@faw.uni-ulm.de

Zusammenfassung Es wird ein praktikables Verfahren zur Generierung kollisionsfreier Manipulator-Bahnen für den echtzeitnahen Einsatz unter Berücksichtigung aller Freiheitsgrade und beliebiger Nutzlasten in realistisch komplexen Umweltszenarien beschrieben. Dabei wächst die mittlere Laufzeit des Verfahrens zum einen nur sublinear (logarithmisch) mit der Komplexität des Umweltmodells und hängt zum anderen nicht kritisch (insbesondere nicht exponentiell) von der Anzahl der Freiheitsgrade ab. Das Verfahren stützt sich im wesentlichen auf die Kombination der Effizienz eines lokalen, potentialfeldbasierten Planers mit der Vollständigkeit eines globalen, probabilistischen Roadmap-Verfahrens sowie auf eine hierarchische geometrische Umweltrepräsentation zur schnellen Berechnung euklidischer Distanzvektoren in realistisch komplexen, nicht-konvexen Arbeitsräumen. Wie Simulationsexperimente bestätigen, werden kollisionsfreie Bahnen für sechsachsige Manipulatoren in komplexen Umweltmodellen auf Standardworkstations innerhalb weniger Sekunden generiert.

1 Einführung

Im Projekt AMOS (Autonome Mobile Systeme[1]) werden grundsätzliche Fragestellungen zur durchgängigen Integration symbolischer und subsymbolischer Formen der Informationsverarbeitung am Beispiel eines mobilen Robotersystems untersucht. Um die hierbei gewählten Ansätze [Kni94] in einer weiteren Aktionsdomäne zu validieren, wurde die mobile Plattform um einen Manipulator ergänzt. Durch die besonderen Anforderungen an einen mobilen Manipulator, wird ein schneller Wegeplaner erforderlich um den Manipulator in die Lage zu versetzen, auch in komplexen, teilweise unstrukturierten oder über Sensoren erfaßte Umgebungsmodellen unter On-line-Bedingungen zu operieren.

Ein wichtiger Bestandteil der auszuführenden Greif- und Transportoperationen ist die Planung von Bewegungsabläufen, bei denen zu einer vorgegebenen

---

[1] Als Verbundprojekt mit industriellen Partnern durch das BMBF gefördert, Förderungsnummer 01 IW 302A|1.

kartesischen Zielposition und -orientierung des Endeffektors und einer gegebenen geometrischen Beschreibung von Einsatzumgebung, Roboter und Nutzlast, eine Sequenz von Steueranweisungen der einzelnen Armgelenke so zu generieren ist, daß die Zielkonfiguration unter Vermeidung von Kollisionen erreicht wird.

Folgende Annahmen liegen dem hier betrachteten Lösungsansatz des Wegeplanungsproblems zugrunde:

— Geometrie und Position des Roboters und der Arbeitsraumhindernisse sowie direkte und inverse Kinematik sind zum Planungszeitpunkt bekannt.
— Mit Ausnahme der Nutzlast sowie der bewegten Armsegmente (Selbstkollisionen) werden alle Hindernisse als während der Bewegungsplanung und -ausführung *statisch*, d.h. als unbeweglich angesehen.
— Dynamische Aspekte (Gravitation, Trägheit) werden vernachlässigt.

Demgegenüber stehen die folgenden Anforderungen:

— Berücksichtigung von mindestens $m = 6$ Freiheitsgraden.
— Betrachtung von Umgebungsmodellen realistischer Komplexität (Büroumgebungen, Innenräume).
— *Keine* vereinfachenden Annahmen bezgl. der mathematischen Eigenschaften der Arbeitsraumhindernisse, wie z.B. Konvexität.
— Echtzeitnahe *On-line*-Planung, d.h. die Planungs-Rechenzeit sollte in der selben Größenordnung wie die Plan-Ausführungszeit auf dem realen Roboter, also im Bereich von Sekunden bis zu wenigen Minuten, liegen.
— Berücksichtigung von Selbstkollisionen und beliebigen Nutzlasten.

2 Frühere Forschungsarbeiten

Umfassende Darstellungen der wichtigsten Roboter-Bewegungsplanungsalgorithmen (*path planning, motion planing, mover's problem*) sind z.B. in [Lat91] und [Can88] zu finden.

Zahlreiche deterministische, globale Verfahren (s. z.B. [Lat91]) wurden vorgeschlagen, von denen hier nur eine kleine Auswahl genannt werden soll: Konfigurationsraum-Diskretisierung, Zellzerlegung, Sichtbarkeitsgraph-Methode (*visibility graph method*) für translatorische Roboterbewegungen und $m \leq 3$ Freiheitsgraden, verallgemeinerte Voronoi-Diagramme (Sceletonization) für zwei- oder dreidimensionale Konfigurationsräume, Freeway-Methode, Canny-Roadmap [Can88] (oder Silouette-Algorithmus), quadratische Programmierung [Che93] und viele andere mehr.

Die praktische Anwendbarkeit der meisten der beschriebenen Verfahren bleibt allerdings wegen der bei wachsender Zahl der Freiheitsgrade auftretenden „kombinatorischen Explosion" des Suchraumes auf die niedrigdimensionale ($m \leq 4$ Freiheitsgrade) Bahnplanung beschränkt. Dies ist eine unmittelbare Konsequenz der komplexitätstheoretischen Resultate von Reif [Rei79], wonach „die Planung eines Pfades für einen aus einer Menge von über Gelenke verbundenen Polyedern bestehenden Roboter im dreidimensionalen Raum mit polyederförmigen Hindernissen *PSPACE*-hart", also mindestens NP-schwierig ist.

Daher existiert wahrscheinlich kein deterministisches und vollständiges Wegeplanungsverfahren, dessen Worst-Case-Laufzeit nicht mindestens exponentiell in der Anzahl der Freiheitsgrade wächst.

Die vorliegende Arbeit kombiniert und erweitert im wesentlichen die folgenden Ansätze:

- Schnelle, aber unvollständige, lokale Planung im Konfigurationsraum, basierend auf Potentialfeldmethoden, vgl. [Kha86, Vol90].
- Einsatz des Verfahrens zur Bestimmung von euklidischen Distanzvektoren nach Quinlan [Qui94].
- Globale Planung mit probabilistischen Roadmap-Methoden, vgl. [Gla91, Kav94].

3 Lokale Planung und künstliche Potentialfelder

Bei lokalen Planungsverfahren werden anstatt einer erschöpfenden Suche auf dem gesamten Konfigurationsraum nur niedrigdimensionale, beschränkte Untermannigfaltigkeiten des hochdimensionalen Suchraumes exploriert.

3.1 Potentialfelder

Ein verbreiteter Ansatz zur Realisierung lokaler Wegeplanungsverfahren sind künstliche Potentialfelder [Kha86, Vol90, Lat91]. Dabei werden die Hindernisse mit einem „abstoßenden Kraftfeld" U_{rep} umgeben. Gleichzeitig ist der Roboter einem „anziehenden Kraftfeld" U_{att} ausgesetzt, dessen Zentrum sich an der Zielposition befindet. Beide Komponenten überlagern sich additiv zu einem kombinierten Potential $U = U_{att} + U_{rep}$.

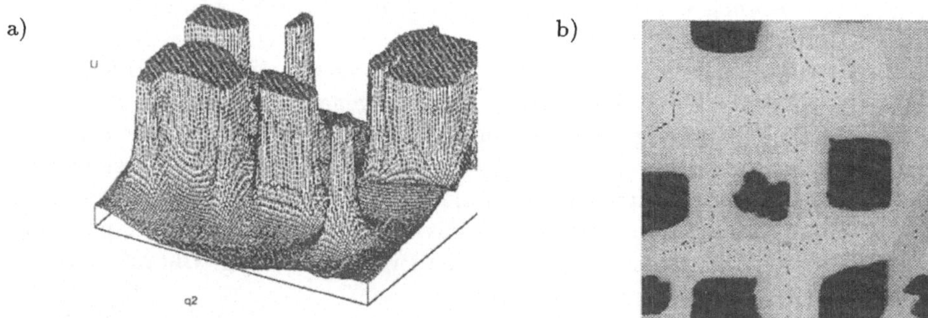

Abbildung 1. Konfigurationsraum-Potentialfelder (2D-Schnitte für Gelenkwinkel q_1, q_2 des 6D-Konfigurationsraumes): a) 3D-Darstellung; b) 2D-Darstellung (Hindernisse schwarz), Verteilung der optimierten Zwischenziele (gepunktet);

Während die hindernisunabhängige Potentialfeldkomponente U_{attr} ohne weiteres etwa mit den in [Vol90] aufgeführten Standardfunktionen (parabolisches oder konisches Potential) realisiert werden kann, ist die Konstruktion eines geeigneten *hindernisabhängigen*, „abstoßenden" Feldes U_{rep} problematisch. U_{rep} sollte die geometrische Struktur der Umgebung in jedem Punkt des Konfigurationsraumes möglichst gut widerspiegeln, um einem Planungsverfahren so viel *lokale* „Ausweich-Information" wie möglich zu liefern.

Wir verwenden die in Gl. 1 beschriebene Potentialfunktion [Bra95], bei der die Stärke der Abstoßung proportional zur Summe der Kehrwerte aller kollisionsrelevanten Abstände $d_{i,j}$ zunimmt (Segment 0 = Basis und Umwelt, Segment m = Endeffektor+Last).

$$U_{rep}(\mathbf{q}) = \eta \sum_{i,j \in I} \frac{1}{d_{i,j}^{\nu}(\mathbf{q})} \tag{1}$$

$$d_{i,j} := \text{Euklidische Distanz zw. Segment } i \text{ und } j$$

3.2 Gradientenauswertung

Wir nutzen für die lokale Planung die Möglichkeit, daß zusätzlich zum Funktionswert $U_{rep}(\mathbf{q})$ auch der *Gradient* $\nabla U_{rep}(\mathbf{q})$ des Potentialfeldes an jeder Stelle $\mathbf{q}$ analytisch und effizient berechnet werden kann:

$$\nabla U_{rep}(\mathbf{q}) = -\eta\nu \sum_{i,j \in I} \frac{1}{d_{i,j}^{\nu+1}(\mathbf{q})} \mathbf{J}_{i,j}(\mathbf{q})^T \cdot \mathbf{d}_{i,j}(\mathbf{q}) \tag{2}$$

Die Berechnung des Gradienten wird also auf je eine Matrixmultiplikation von Jacobimatrix $\mathbf{J}_{i,j}$ und Distanzvektor $\mathbf{d}_{i,j}$ für jedes kollisionsrelevante Armsegment-Paar $d_{i,j}$ zurückgeführt.

Dabei bereitet zunächst die Berechnung der euklidischen Arbeitsraum-Distanzen $d_{i,j}$ und Distanzvektoren $\mathbf{d}_{i,j}$ Schwierigkeiten, denn die meisten Standardalgorithmen zur Distanz(vektor)bestimmung [Lat91, Gil90] basieren auf der Zerlegung der Objekte in konvexe Primitive mit anschließender (konvexer) Abstandsbestimmung zwischen allen *Paaren* konvexer Teilobjekte. Zudem ergibt sich für die Konvex-Zerlegung beliebiger nicht-konvexer Objekte i.a. eine große Zahl von Primitiven, welche letztlich nur durch die Anzahl der (dreiecksförmigen) Oberflächenfacetten selbst beschränkt ist, weshalb die Laufzeit dieser Distanzberechnungsverfahren mindestens quadratisch mit der Komplexität des Umweltmodells wächst.

Daher verwenden wir eine Variante eines von Quinlan [Qui94] vorgeschlagenen Verfahrens. Dieser Algorithmus basiert auf einer hierarchischen Hüllkörper-Repräsentation (BS-Baum) des Arbeitsraumes und erlaubt im Gegensatz zu vielen Hüllkörper-Verfahren nicht nur eine effiziente Kollisionserkennung, sondern darüberhinaus auch die Berechnung von Distanzen und Distanzvektoren mit einem mittlerem Aufwand von $O(\log n)$ [Qui94, Bra95]. Hinzu kommt eine einmalige $O(n \log n)$-Vorverarbeitungsphase, bei der die Hüllen beliebiger Körper vorab berechnet werden.

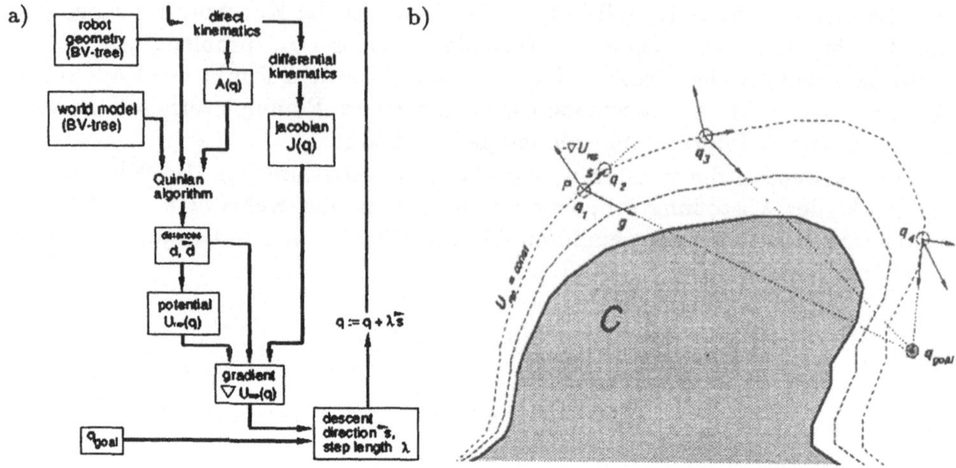

Abbildung 2. Lokale Planung: a) Blockdiagramm; b) Gradient-Sliding-Algorithmus;

3.3 Gradient-Sliding-Algorithmus

Bei dem folgenden, von uns [Bra95] vorgeschlagenen *Gradient-Sliding-Verfahren*, wird mit Hilfe der analytischen Gradientenauswertung eine verallgemeinerte Form der „Hindernisvermeidung durch Vorbeigleiten" realisiert:

Algorithmus 3.1 Gradient-Slide(q_{start}, q_{goal})

Eingabe: Start- und Zielkonfigurationen $q_{start}, q_{goal} \in \mathcal{C}_{free}$
Ausgabe: Kollissionsfreier Pfad $\tau : \mathbf{N} \to \mathcal{C}$ oder $\tau = \emptyset$, wenn keine Lösung
Ablauf :

$q \leftarrow q_{start}$
for $i \leftarrow 1$ **to** $n_{maxstep}$ **do**
    if $U_{rep}(q) = \infty$ **then return** $\emptyset$
    $\tau(i) \leftarrow q$
    $g \leftarrow (q_{goal} - q)_{\mathrm{mod}_{2\pi}}$
    if $\|g\| < \lambda$ **then return** τ
    $s \leftarrow \lambda(\frac{g}{\|g\|} + \alpha_{grad}(-\frac{\nabla U_{rep}(q)}{\|\nabla U_{rep}(q)\|}))$
    $q \leftarrow (q + s)_{\mathrm{mod}_{2\pi}}$
return $\emptyset$

Dieser Algorithmus kann als Simulation eines den Roboter repräsentierenden Partikels (Punktroboter) veranschaulicht werden, das sich unter Einfluß virtueller Kraftfelder durch den Konfigurationsraum bewegt. Abb. 2b zeigt ein solches Partikel P, das sich zum Zeitpunkt i an der Position $q = q_1$ in einem zweidimensionalen Konfigurationsraum in der Nähe eines Hindernisses C befindet. C ist von einem Potentialfeld U_{rep} umgeben, welches in P einen vom Hindernis weggerichteten Kraftvektor $-\nabla U_{rep}(q)$ induziert. ∇U_{rep} ist orthogonal zu der durch P verlaufenden $(m-1)$-dimensionalen Äquipotentialhyperfläche

$U_{rep} = const$ (gestrichelte Linie), welche die Oberfläche des Konfigurationsraumhindernisses lokal in P approximiert. Gleichzeitig ist P einer auf Ziel gerichteten Kraft **g** ausgesetzt, die von einem hindernisunabhängigen Potentialfeld U_{att} induziert wird. Die Bewegung des Partikels wird somit von der resultierenden Kraft **s**, als Vektorsumme der Komponenten **g** und $-\nabla U_{rep}$ bestimmt. Die resultierende Flugbahn entspricht also einem stetigen, zum Ziel hin gerichteten, tangentialen „Gleiten" entlang der durch den Gradienten lokal repräsentierten Aquipotentialhyperflächen des Konfigurationsraum-Potentialfeldes, wodurch die Namensgebung des Verfahrens motiviert ist.

a)   b)

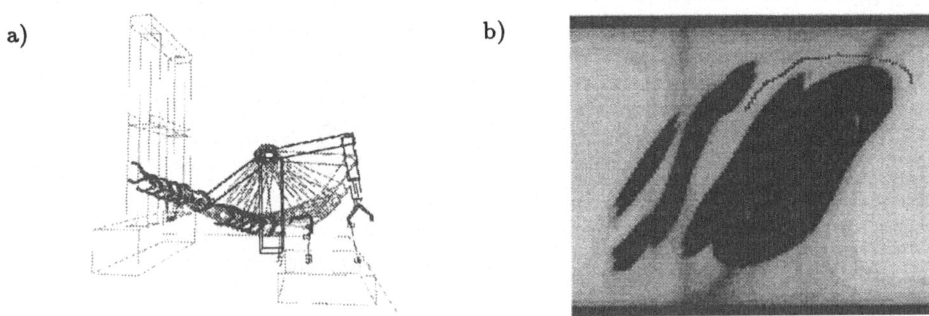

Abbildung 3. Lokale Planung mit dem Gradient-Sliding-Algorithmus: a) Ergebnispfad im Arbeitsraum (mit Distanzvektoren), b) Querschnitt durch den Konfigurationsraum (Ergebnispfad gepunktet)

3.4 Merkmale des lokalen Planers

In jeder Iteration des Verfahrens ist genau eine Potentialfunktions- und Gradientenauswertung erforderlich, d.h. die je Schritt benötigte Anzahl von Funktionsauswertungen ist konstant, also insbesondere *unabhängig* von der Dimension des Konfigurationsraumes, während bei nicht-gradientenbasierten Methoden eine lineare bis exponentielle Abhängigkeit von m besteht.

Dies und der Einsatz des Quinlan-Verfahrens bewirkt eine bemerkenswert hohe Ausführungsgeschwindigkeit des lokalen Planers.

Der Preis für die hohe Ausführungsgeschwindigkeit des lokalen Planers $\mathcal{LP}$ ist der Verzicht auf die Verfahrens-Vollständigkeit, d.h. er wird nicht immer in der Lage sein, *beliebige* Paare von Start- und Zielkonfigurationen zu verbinden.

4 Globale Planung

Im allgemeinen sind lokale Planer, so auch der in Abs. 3 vorgestellte, schnell aber unvollständig, globale Verfahren hingegen vollständig aber sehr langsam.

Wir umgehen die Unvollständigkeit von $\mathcal{LP}$ durch die Hinzunahme einer *globalen Planungskomponente* $\mathcal{GP}$, welche beim Scheitern von $\mathcal{LP}$ in der Lage ist, geeignete, eventuell leichter erreichbare *Zwischenziele* zu generieren. Dieser Ansatz wird in erster Linie durch zwei entscheidende Beobachtungen motiviert:

1. „Natürliche" Roboter-Einsatzumgebungen zeichnen sich durch ein vergleichsweise hohes Maß an räumlicher und zeitlicher Kohärenz und Stetigkeit aus: Die *Worst-Case*-Situation „labyrinthartiger", extrem „zerklüfteter" Strukturen tritt im globalen Maßstab so gut wie überhaupt nicht auf. Meist existieren viele Lösungen, von denen aber nur eine einzige benötigt wird.
2. Mit dem beschriebenen potentialfeldgradienten-basierten lokalen Planungsalgorithmus können „gutartige" (z.B. lokal konvexe) Bereiche des Suchraumes weiträumig und mit annähernd von der Suchraumdimension unabhängiger Geschwindigkeit kollisionsfrei überbrückt werden.

Ein vielversprechender Ansatz, wie er in ähnlicher Form auch in den Arbeiten von Glavina [Gla91] und Kavraki [Kav94] verfolgt wird, besteht nun in der Entwicklung von Methoden, die die Vorteile der lokalen und globalen Planung kombinieren, ohne gleichzeitig die jeweiligen Nachteile zu übernehmen.

Die globale Planungskomponente $\mathcal{GP}$ wird von der aufwendigen „raumfüllenden" Exploration ganzer m-dimensionaler Konfigurationsraumbereiche entbunden, und beschränkt sich auf die Erzeugung *punktförmiger Zwischenziele*, deren effiziente Verbindung von $\mathcal{LP}$ übernommen wird.

Dabei entwickelt sich im Laufe der Suche ein *dynamischer Graph* $G = (V, E)$ (Roadmap), dessen Knotenmenge V aus Start- und Zielkonfigurationen sowie allen bisher von $\mathcal{GP}$ generierten Zwischenzielen besteht. Zwischen zwei Knoten wird eine Kante in die Menge der Kanten E aufgenommen, wenn durch einen Aufruf von $\mathcal{LP}$ eine kollisionsfreie Verbindung der beiden Zwischenziele hergestellt werden kann. Auf dem so konstruierten gerichteten Graphen G kann nun mit Standard-Graphsuche eine globale Lösung extrahiert werden, sobald Start und Ziel in derselben Zusammenhangskomponente liegen.

Die Erzeugung der Zwischenziele erfolgt probabilistisch, wobei zunächst eine Gleichverteilung auf dem freien Konfigurationsraum zugrundeliegt.

Anders als in [Gla91, Kav94] wird jedoch jedes neue Zwischenziel s einer Optimierung unterzogen, indem, ausgehend von s, eine feste Zahl von Gradientenabstiegs-Schritten auf dem Konfigurationsraum-Potential U_{rep} durchgeführt wird. Damit erhalten wir als neues Zwischenziel s^* eine Näherung an das nächstliegende *lokale Minimum* des Potentialfeldes. Durch dieses Vorgehen konzentrieren wir die Wahrscheinlichkeitsverteilung der Zwischenziele auf mit dem lokalen Planer i.a. leichter erreichbare Konfigurationsraum-Regionen in den Potential„mulden" und -„tälern" (vgl. Abb. 1b).

5 Simulationsergebnisse

Der in diesem Text beschriebene Planer wurde in umfangreichen Simulationen von Manipulatoren in unterschiedlichen Arbeitsräumen erprobt [Bra95], von denen hier nur ein Beispiel gezeigt werden kann.

Um das Laufzeitverhalten der Wegeplanung aufzuzeigen, simuliert das in Abb.4 gezeigte Szenario einen MANUS-Manipulator (sechsachsig, PUMA-artige Kinematik) in einer komplexen, wenig strukturierten und lokal zerklüfteten Umgebung. Dabei werden Arbeitsraumhindernisse mit fraktalen Oberflächen und eine sperrige Nutzlast, insgesamt ca. $2 \cdot 10^4$ Oberflächenfacetten, generiert. In dieser Umgebung ist der Bewegungsspielraum des Manipulators derart eingeschränkt, daß der Anteil des freien Konfigurationsraumes nur 4.5% beträgt. Es waren $n = 1000$ unabhängige Wegeplanungsaufgaben, bestehend aus je einer zufälligen, über $\mathcal{C}_{free}$ gleichverteilten Start- und Zielkonfiguration, zu lösen.

Die Simulationsresultate auf einer Standard-Workstation (SPARC 2) können Abb. 4b entnommen werden. Die mittlere Planungsdauer beträgt ca. sechs Sekunden. In 99.5% der Fälle werden weniger als 30 Sekunden benötigt.

a)

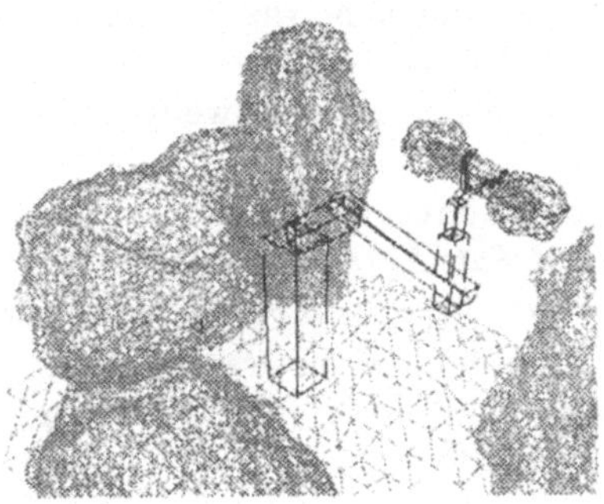

b)

	Potential-auswertungen	CPU-Zeit (Sek.)
Mittelwert	299.3	6.4
Minimum	4	0.2
Maximum	1299335	644.8
Varianz	4319.2	53.5

Abbildung 4. Simulationsszenario: komplexe Umwelt, sperrige Nutzlast (Freiraumanteil 4.5%)

6 Bewertung und Ausblick

Wie die durchgeführten Simulationsexperimente zeigen, konnte ein praktikabler Planer für den echtzeitnahen Einsatz von Manipulatoren unter Berücksichtigung aller Freiheitsgrade und beliebiger Nutzlasten in realistisch komplexen Umweltszenarien realisiert werden.

Der Schlüssel für die Effizienz des Verfahrens liegt dabei in der Kombination der Schnelligkeit der potentialfeldbasierten lokalen Planers mit der (probabilistischen) Vollständigkeit des globalen Planers.

Mit Hilfe der analytischen Gradientenauswertung konnte ein *lokales Planungsverfahren* (Gradient-Sliding-Algorithmus) realisiert werden, dessen Laufzeit nahezu unabhängig von der Anzahl der Freiheitsgrade ist, was insbesondere für den geplanten Einsatzbereich gegenüber den verbreiteten *Hill-Climbing*-Techniken eine entscheidende Leistungssteigerung bedeutet. In Kombination mit der probabilistischen *globalen Planungskomponente* wird in den meisten Fällen schnell *eine gültige Lösung* des Wegeplanungsproblems gefunden, indem die „gutartige" Struktur von Nicht-Worst-Case-Szenarien ausgenutzt wird.

Einschränkend ist zu erwähnen, daß das Verfahren nur im probabilistischen Sinne vollständig ist, d.h. trotz der im *mittleren* Fall sehr schnelleren Laufzeit gibt es keine obere Schranke für die Worst-Case-Laufzeit, d.h. sehr schwierige Probleme nehmen unter Umständen wesentlich mehr Zeit in Anspruch als z.B. die erschöpfende Breitensuche.

Der vorgestellte potentialfeldbasierte lokale Planer basiert auf der Auswertung des Gradientenvektors eines Konfigurationsraumpotentialfeldes, also auf der Ableitung erster Ordnung und ist somit im Kern ein Steepest-Descent-Optimierungsverfahren mit der aus der mathematischen Optimierungstheorie bekannten Problematik der nicht optimalen Konvergenzgeschwindigkeit. Wenn es daher gelänge, Ableitungsinformation zweiter Ordnung (Hessematrix) für die lokale Planung in ähnlicher Weise nutzbar zu machen, wie dies in der nichtlinearen Optimierungstheorie mit Hilfe der bekannten (Quasi-)Newtonverfahren (BFGS-Verfahren) geschieht, würde dies vermutlich zu einer weiteren Leistungssteigerung führen.

Bei der globalen Zwischenzielgenerierung könnten als optimierte Zwischenziele nicht nur lokale Minima, sondern auch *Sattelpunkte* der Potentialfunktion verwendet werden. Dies erscheint vor allem deshalb vorteilhaft, da sich Sattelpunkte in der Regel an „kritischen" Engstellen des Freiraumes befinden, wo zusätzliche Zwischenziele besonders hilfreich sind, um die lokale Planung erfolgreich „hindurchzuleiten".

7 Zukünftige Arbeiten in AMOS

Der in dieser Arbeit beschriebene Algorithmus wurde als Teil einer Studie über Manipulator-Wegeplanung im Rahmen des AMOS-Projektes am FAW Ulm entwickelt und in umfassenden Simulationen unseres Manipulatorsystems eingesetzt.

Zusätzliche Arbeiten wurden auf den Gebieten Weltmodellierung, Task-Planung, strategische Bewegungsplanung, Integration von Sensordaten sowie der Simulation und Integration symbolischer Informationsverarbeitung durchgeführt.

Um die prinzipiellen Beschränkungen „klassischer" Bewegungsplaner zu umgehen, untersuchen wir alternative Ansätze zur Bewegungsplanung auf der Basis genetischer Algorithmen. Diese ermöglichen uns die flexible Realisierung verschiedener Planungsstrategien (z.B. Einbeziehung von strategischen Nebenbedingungen) für eine Vielzahl von Kinematiken innerhalb desselben Planers ohne explizite Verwendung der inversen Kinematik.

Literatur

[Bar91] Barraquand J., Latombe, J.-C.: Robot Motion Planning: A Distributed Representation Approach. Int. J. Robot. Res. (1991) 10(6) 628–649

[Ber94] Berchtold, S.: Kosten-Nutzen-optimale Verbesserung kollisionsfreier Roboterbewegungen mittels Polygon-Manipulation. Autonome Mobile Systeme, 10. Fachgespräch (1994) 167–178

[Bra95] Braun, B.: Vergleich von Algorithmen zur Bahnplanung eines Manipulators. Diplomarbeit an der Univ. Ulm (durchgef. am FAW) Fak. f. Informatik (1995)

[Can88] Canny, J.F.: The Complexity of Robot Motion Planning. MIT Press (1987)

[Che92] Chen, P.C., Hwan, Y.K.: SANDROS: A Motion Planner with Performance Proportional to Task Difficulty. Proc. IEEE Int. Conf. on Robotics and Automation (1992) 2346–2353

[Che93] Cheng, F.-T., Chen, T.-H., Wang, Y.-S., Sun, Y.-Y.: Obstacle Avoidance for Redundant Manipulators Using the Compact QP Method. Proc. IEEE Int. Conf. on Robotics and Automation (1993) 262–269

[Gla91] Glavina, B.: A Fast Motion Planner for 6-DOF Manipulators in 3D-Environments. Proc. Fifth Int. Conf. on Advanced Robotics Pisa/It. (1991) 1176–1181

[Gil90] Gilbert, E.G., Foo, C.-P.: Computing the Distance Between General Convex Objects in Three-Dimensional Space. IEEE Transactions on Robotics and Automation 6(1) (1995) 53–61

[Kha86] Khatib, O.: Real-Time Obstacle Avoidance for Manipulators and Mobile Robots. Int. J. Robot. Res. 5(1) (1986) 90–98

[Kav94] Kavraki, L., Latombe, J.-C.: Randomized Preprocessing of Configuration Space for Fast Path Planning. Proc. IEEE Int. Conf. on Robotics and Automation (1994) 2138–2145

[Kni94] Knick, M., Schlegel, C.: AMOS: Active Perception of an Autonomous System. IROS Intelligent Robots and Systems (1994) 281–289

[Kon91] Kondo K.: Motion Planning with Six Degrees of Freedom by Multistrategic Bidirectional Heuristic Free-Space Enumeration. IEEE Trans. on Robotics and Automation 7(3) (1991) 267–271

[Lat91] Latombe, J.C.: Robot Motion Planning. Kluwer Academic Publishers (1991)

[Qui94] Quinlan, S.: Efficient Distance Computation between Non-Convex Objects. Proc. IEEE Int. Conf. on Robotics and Automation (1994) 3324–3329

[Qui93] Quinlan, S., Khatib, O.: Elastic Bands: Connecting Path Planning and Control. Proc. IEEE Int. Conf. on Robotics and Automation (1993)

[Ral93] Ralli, E., Hirzinger, G.: Fast Path Planning for Robot Manipulators Using Numerical Potential Fields in the Configuration Space. IROS Intelligent Robots and Systems (1994) 1922–1929

[Rei79] Reif, J.: Complexity of the mover's problem and generalizations. Proc. of the 20th Annual Symposium on the Foundations of Computer Science (1979) 421–427

[Vol90] Volpe, R., Khosla, P.: Manipulator Control with Superquadric Artificial Potential Functions: Theory and Experiments. IEEE Transactions on Systems, Man and Cybernetics 20(6) (1990) 1423–1436

Bahnplanung in dynamischen Umgebungen: Berechnung und Minimierung von Kollisionswahrscheinlichkeiten auf Basis statistischer Daten

E. Kruse, R. Gutsche und F. M. Wahl

Institut für Robotik und Prozeßinformatik
Technische Universität Braunschweig
Hamburger Str. 267, D-38114 Braunschweig

Zusammenfassung. In dynamischen Umgebungen muß eine effiziente Bahnplanung für mobile Roboter in der Lage sein, unbekannte, sich bewegende Hindernisse angemessen zu berücksichtigen. Wir haben daher in früheren Artikeln die Verwendung statistischer Daten zur Beschreibung typischer, häufiger Hindernisbewegungen vorgeschlagen. In diesem Artikel konzentrieren wir uns auf die Herleitung mathematischer Formeln zur Berechnung von Kollisionswahrscheinlichkeiten. Durch Verallgemeinerung der Ergebnisse lassen sich statistische Daten als Berechnungsgrundlage verwenden. Darauf aufbauend präsentieren wir einen Bahnplanungsalgorithmus, welcher sich an gängige Potentialfeldverfahren anlehnt, darüberhinaus jedoch unter Berücksichtigung der statistischen Daten Bahnen mit näherungsweise minimaler Kollisionswahrscheinlichkeit berechnet.

1 Einführung

Um Bahnplanungsverfahren für mobile Roboter sinnvoll in der Praxis einsetzen zu können, müssen in den meisten Fällen sich bewegende Hindernisse berücksichtigt werden. Gegenwärtig lassen sich für solche dynamischen Umgebungen im wesentlichen zwei Ansätze unterscheiden:

1. Es wird vorausgesetzt, daß die Bewegungen sämtlicher Hindernisse genau bekannt sind. Die Bahn des Roboters kann dann zum Beispiel im Konfigurations-Zeit-Raum geplant werden [6, 3].
2. (Bewegliche) Hindernisse werden ignoriert, bis sie sich in der unmittelbaren Nähe des Roboters befinden. Der Roboter macht dann eine Ausweichbewegung, z.B. [9, 10].

Beide Ansätze werden praktischen Problemen nur eingeschränkt gerecht, da in realen Umgebungen meist die *genauen* Bewegungen einzelner Hindernisse nicht vorhergesagt werden können, jedoch Wissen über das *durchschnittliche* Verhalten der Hindernisse leicht verfügbar ist. Der erste Ansatz ist somit primär von theoretischer Bedeutung, während der zweite recht ineffizient sein kann, da nur lokales Wissen berücksichtigt wird.

Aufgrund dieser Überlegungen haben wir in einem früheren Artikel die Einbeziehung statistischer Daten vorgeschlagen [5]. Es werden hierbei Bahnen geplant, welche dem Aufkommen und den erwarteten Bewegungen der Hindernisse angepaßt sind. Die Kollisionswahrscheinlichkeit, d.h. die Wahrscheinlichkeit, daß ein Roboter auf ein Hindernis trifft, wird deutlich verringert, beim Abfahren der Bahn wird somit eine aufwendige Neuplanung bzw. ein reaktives Verhalten entsprechend seltener notwendig.

Ein offensichtliches Ziel im Rahmen der *statistischen Bahnplanung* ist die Erzeugung von Pfaden mit *minimaler Kollisionswahrscheinlichkeit*. Eine typische Aufgabenstellung ist in Abbildung 1 dargestellt: Um die Zielposition zu erreichen, muß der mobile Roboter einen der beiden Korridore durchqueren. Der untere sei häufig von Hindernissen belegt, welche sich in Roboterrichtung bewegen, der obere sei sehr selten von entgegenkommenden Hindernissen belegt. Welcher Pfad minimiert die Kollisionswahrscheinlichkeit? Da Belegungswahrscheinlichkeiten und Hindernisgeschwindigkeiten eine entscheidende Rolle spielen, ist eine direkte, intuitive Antwort nicht möglich. Wir geben in diesem Artikel eine *mathematisch fundierte* Antwort: Wir stellen eine Methode zur Berechnung von Kollisionswahrscheinlichkeiten vor. Dazu betrachten wir im nächsten Abschnitt Kollisionen zunächst anhand elementarer, charakteristischer Situationen, für die sich Kollisionswahrscheinlichkeiten formal berechnen lassen. In den darauf folgenden Abschnitten werden die Ergebnisse durch Einführung statistischer Größen verallgemeinert und führen zu einem Bahnplanungsverfahren, welches Bahnen mit (näherungsweise) minimaler Kollisionswahrscheinlichkeit plant.

2 Kollisionszeit

Wir betrachten zunächst mögliche Kollisionen des Roboters mit einem einzelnen Hindernis. Zur Vereinfachung nehmen wir dabei den Roboter als punktförmig an.[1] Die Geschwindigkeiten des Roboters R und des Hindernisses O seien v_R bzw. v_O. Das Hindernis ist rechteckig mit den Maßen $l_O \times w_O$. Es bewegt sich parallel zu den Kanten der Länge l_O. Die Pfade des Roboters und des Hindernisses sind parallel oder schneiden sich mit dem Winkel α. Betrachtet wird ein lineares Segment des Schnittbereiches mit der Länge d (Abb. 2).

Von besonderem Interesse ist das *Kollisionszeitintervall* t_{coll}: Beginnt der Roboter in diesem Zeitintervall seine Bewegung entlang des Pfadsegmentes d, so kollidiert er mit dem Hindernis. Abbildung 3 illustriert das Problem mit Hilfe eines Raum-Zeit-Diagrammes. Die Robotertrajektorie ist eine Gerade, die vom Hindernis belegten Pfadelemente bilden ein Parallelogramm. Schneiden sich beide, so bedeutet dies eine Kollision, während sich der Roboter entlang d bewegt. Das Intervall t_{coll} setzt sich aus mehreren Anteilen zusammen: Die Belegungsdauer t_{occ} ist die Länge des Zeitabschnittes, während dessen ein einzelner Punkt des Roboterpfades durch ein Hindernis belegt ist. Sie ist unabhängig von

---

[1] Diese Einschränkung wird später aufgehoben; in guter Näherung wenden wir unser Verfahren auch auf reale (rechteckige) Roboter an.

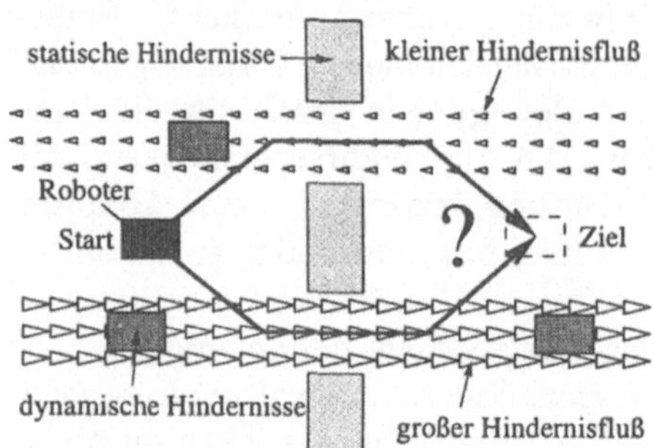

Abb. 1. Welche Bahn ist besser?

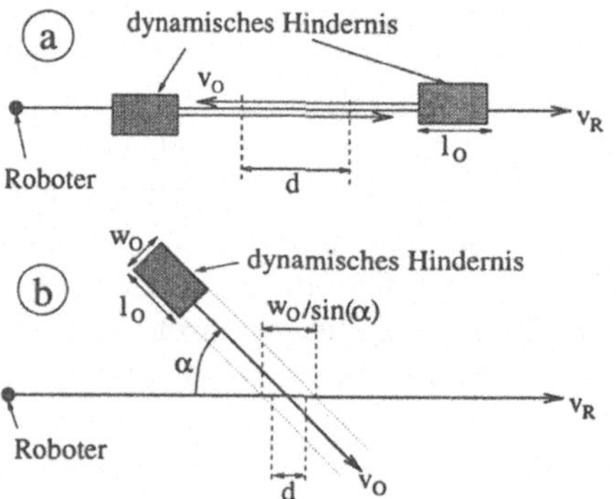

Abb. 2. Kollision Hindernis↔Roboter

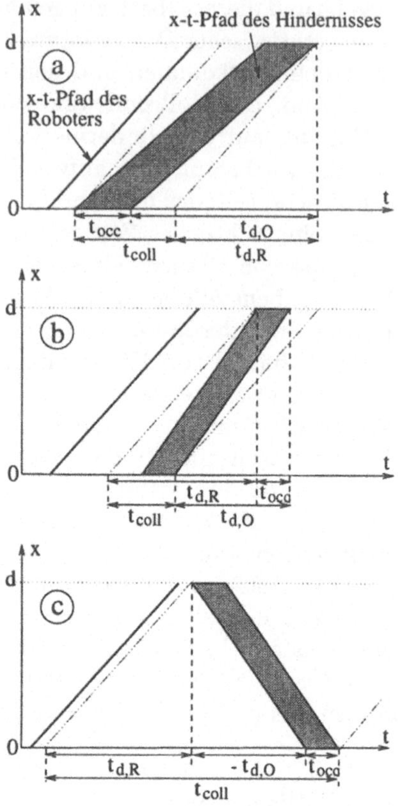

Abb. 3. x-t-Diagramm

der betrachteten Position auf dem Segment d:

$$t_{occ} = \frac{l_O}{v_O} \tag{1}$$

Die Zeit für den Roboter, um sich entlang d zu bewegen, beträgt:

$$t_{d,R} = \frac{d}{v_R} \tag{2}$$

Ein analoges Zeitintervall für das Hindernis ergibt sich aus seiner Geschwindigkeitskomponente entlang der Roboterbewegungsrichtung (das Vorzeichen von $t_{d,O}$ gibt die Bewegungsrichtung an):

$$t_{d,O} = \frac{d \cos \alpha}{v_O} \tag{3}$$

Betrachten wir zunächst den Fall, daß sich Roboter und Hindernis in parallele Richtungen bewegen ($\alpha = k\pi$, Abb. 2a). Zur Berechnung von t_{coll} werden drei Fälle unterschieden (Abb. 3): Das Hindernis bewegt sich in die gleiche Richtung wie der Roboter und ist langsamer (a), schneller (b), oder es bewegt sich in entgegengesetzter Richtung (c). Wie in Abbildung 3 ersichtlich, ist die folgende einfache Beziehung für alle drei Fälle gültig:

$$t_{coll} = |t_{d,R} - t_{d,O}| + t_{occ} \tag{4}$$

Durch Einsetzen der vorigen Gleichungen (1), (2) und (3) ergibt sich:

$$t_{coll} = \left(\frac{d}{l_O} \left| \frac{v_O}{v_R} - \cos\alpha \right| + 1 \right) t_{occ} \tag{5}$$

Nun sei angenommen, daß sich der Roboter und das Hindernis nicht in parallele Richtungen bewegen ($\alpha \neq k\pi$, Abb. 2b). Während im vorigen Fall die Länge des betrachteten Pfadelementes d beliebig gewählt werden konnte, beschränken wir es nun auf den (endlichen) Schnitt beider Pfade:

$$d \leq \frac{w_O}{\sin\alpha} \tag{6}$$

Es läßt sich zeigen, daß Abbildung 3 auch für diesen Fall gültig ist; die Beziehungen zwischen den verschiedenen Zeitintervallen ändern sich nicht. Wenn d gemäß (6) beschränkt ist, ist Gleichung (5) somit für beliebige Winkel α gültig.

3 Kollisionswahrscheinlichkeit

Die Kollisionswahrscheinlichkeit p_{coll} hängt davon ab, wie häufig Hindernisse erscheinen. Als Maß hierfür verwenden wir das Zeitintervall T_O; es bezeichnet die Dauer, während welcher im Durchschnitt genau *ein* Hindernis im betrachteten Pfadelement erscheint.[2] Damit kann p_{coll} einfach angegeben werden:

$$p_{coll} = \frac{t_{coll}}{T_O} \tag{7}$$

Diese Gleichung ist auch für mehrere, nacheinander erscheinende Hindernisse gültig – vorausgesetzt, daß ihre jeweiligen Kollisionszeitintervalle nicht überlappen. Andernfalls ist die tatsächliche Kollisionswahrscheinlichkeit etwas kleiner. Unter der Annahme $t_{coll} \ll T_O$ wird der aus dieser Näherung resultierende Fehler vernachlässigbar. Dies verdeutlicht die folgende Gleichung; sie berücksichtigt den Term zweiter Ordnung, welcher sich durch überlappende Kollisionzeiten zweier Hindernisse ergibt.

$$p_{coll} = \frac{t_{coll}}{T_O} - \frac{t_{coll}(t_{coll} - t_{occ})}{4T_O^2} \tag{8}$$

(Es wird vorausgesetzt, daß ein Punkt nicht von zwei Hindernissen gleichzeitig belegt sein kann, d. h. t_{occ} Intervalle können sich nicht überlappen. Es erscheint daher im zweiten Term der Faktor $t_{coll} - t_{occ}$.)

---

[2] Eine alternative Notation wäre die Hindernis-Frequenz, d. h. die durchschnittliche Anzahl von Hindernissen innerhalb eines festen Zeitintervalls: $f_O = T_O^{-1}$.

Im Rahmen der statistischen Daten ist die *Belegungswahrscheinlichkeit* p_{occ} von großer Bedeutung. Für einen Punkt oder Bereich des Arbeitsraumes ist dies die Wahrscheinlichkeit, zu einem zufällig gewählten Zeitpunkt belegt zu sein. Unter der Annahme, daß sich Hindernisse nicht überlappen, kann diese Wahrscheinlichkeit direkt zu t_{occ} in Beziehung gesetzt werden:

$$p_{occ} = \frac{t_{occ}}{T_O} \tag{9}$$

Die Kollisionswahrscheinlichkeit kann nun analog zu Gleichung (5) in Abhängigkeit von der Belegungswahrscheinlichkeit ausgedrückt werden:

$$p_{coll} = \left(\frac{d}{l_O}\left|\frac{v_O}{v_R} - \cos\alpha\right| + 1\right) p_{occ} \tag{10}$$

Gleichung (10) beschreibt die Kollisionswahrscheinlichkeit unter der Voraussetzung, daß die Größe, Bewegungsrichtung und Geschwindigkeit eines potentiellen Hindernisses von vornherein bekannt sind. Lediglich der Zeitpunkt seines Erscheinens ist unbekannt und wird durch die Belegungswahrscheinlichkeit ersetzt. Unser Ziel ist jedoch die ausschließliche Verwendung allgemeiner, leicht zu gewinnender statistischer Daten. Im folgenden werden daher weitere Verallgemeinerungen notwendig, um auf individuelle Hindernisparameter verzichten zu können.

Die Hindernisgeschwindigkeit v_O wird durch eine Wahrscheinlichkeitsverteilung ersetzt. Mit Hilfe der Dichtefunktion $p(v)$ (mit $\int_{-\infty}^{\infty} p(v)\,dv = 1$), läßt sich die Kollisionswahrscheinlichkeit $\bar{p}_{coll}$ berechnen:

$$\bar{p}_{coll} = \int_{-\infty}^{\infty} p_{coll}(v)\,p(v)\,dv$$

$$= p_{occ} \int_{-\infty}^{\infty} \left(\frac{d}{l_O}\left|\frac{v}{v_R} - \cos\alpha\right| + 1\right) p(v)\,dv = \left(\frac{d}{l_O}k_\alpha + 1\right) p_{occ} \tag{11}$$

Die Konstante k_α hängt von α, $p(v)$ und v_R ab:

$$k_\alpha = \int_{-\infty}^{\infty} \left|\frac{v}{v_R} - \cos\alpha\right| p(v)\,dv \tag{12}$$

Zur Vereinfachung nehmen wir an, daß die Hindernisgeschwindigkeiten im Intervall $[v_{min}, v_{max}]$ gleichverteilt sind; k_α kann dann analytisch berechnet werden:

$$k_\alpha = \frac{s_1(v_R\cos\alpha - v_{max})^2 + s_2(v_R\cos\alpha - v_{min})^2}{2v_R(v_{max} - v_{min})} \tag{13}$$

$$s_1 = sign(v_{max} - v_R\cos\alpha)$$
$$s_2 = sign(v_R\cos\alpha - v_{min})$$

Analog zur Hindernisgeschwindigkeit kann auch die Hindernisgröße durch statistische Daten dargestellt werden. Ist die Wahrscheinlichkeitsverteilung bekannt, so kann das zugehörige Integral (numerisch) berechnet werden. In der gegenwärtigen Implementierung wird die Hindernisgröße allerdings durch Konstanten dargestellt, d. h. es wird angenommen, daß die tatsächlichen Größen nur innerhalb enger Grenzen schwanken. Der Näherungsfehler ist dann vernachlässigbar gegenüber anderen, unvermeidlichen Näherungen bei der Verallgemeinerung vom punktförmigen zum rechteckigen Roboter.

Der Winkel α läßt sich nicht ohne weiteres mit obigem Verfahren durch eine Wahrscheinlichkeitsverteilung darstellen: Er hängt von der Bewegungsrichtung des Roboters ab und variiert über den gesamten Bereich $[0, 2\pi)$. Sein Einfluß auf die Kollisionswahrscheinlichkeit ist entscheidend, er muß daher genau repräsentiert werden. Um sich auf sinnvolle statistische Daten beziehen zu können, wird das Intervall $[0, 2\pi)$ in acht gleichgroße Teilintervalle aufgeteilt (entlang der Koordinatenachsen und Winkelhalbierenden). Bei der Bahnplanung werden diese statistisch erfaßten Bewegungsrichtungen in das Roboterkoordinatensystem transformiert.

4 Statistische Daten

In den vorherigen Abschnitten haben wir Formeln zur Schätzung von Kollisionswahrscheinlichkeiten vorgestellt, welche auf einer Reihe von einfach zu gewinnenden statistischen Daten aufbauen. Diese Daten lassen sich danach unterscheiden, ob sie vom Ort abhängen (ortsvariant) oder für den gesamten Arbeitsraum als konstant angesehen werden können (ortsinvariant).

Ortsvariante Daten werden in einem zweidimensionalen Raster verwaltet. Jede Zelle $\mathbf{c} \in \{0, 1, \ldots, res_x - 1\} \times \{0, 1, \ldots, res_y - 1\}$ dieses *statistischen Rasters* enthält die folgenden Informationen:

- Belegungswahrscheinlichkeit $p_{occ}(\mathbf{c})$.
  Belegungswahrscheinlichkeiten sind ein verbreitetes Konzept zur Modellierung statischer Umwelten basierend auf unsicheren bzw. verrauschten Sensordaten [2]. Unser Modell unterscheidet sich davon: Eine Zelle hat einen eindeutigen Zustand (frei oder belegt), welcher sich jedoch im Laufe der Zeit ändern kann.
- Hindernisfluß $p_\alpha(\mathbf{c})$.
  Dies ist die Wahrscheinlichkeit, daß eine Zelle mit einem Hindernis belegt ist, welches sich in Richtung α (bzgl. des Weltkoordinatensystems) bewegt. Zur Repräsentation von p_α wird der Bereich $[0, 2\pi)$ in acht gleichgroße Teilintervalle aufgeteilt $(p_0, p_{\frac{1}{4}\pi}, p_{\frac{1}{2}\pi}, \ldots, p_{\frac{7}{4}\pi})$.
- Teilweise dynamische Belegungswahrscheinlichkeit $p_{partly}(\mathbf{c})$.
  Teilweise dynamische Hindernisse bewegen sich nicht, sondern sie erscheinen und verschwinden wieder von Zeit zu Zeit (z.B. Objekte, welche im Arbeitsraum für einige Zeit abgestellt und später wieder aufgenommen werden). Die entsprechenden Zeitintervalle ihrer Existenz sind groß im Verhältnis zur

Zeit, um die Roboterbahn abzufahren. Es wird somit angenommen, daß sich der Zustand dieser Hindernisse während der Bewegung des Roboters nicht ändert.[3] Der Wert $p_{partly}(\mathbf{c})$ wird nicht explizit im statischen Raster abgelegt, da er aus den anderen statistischen Daten berechnet werden kann:

$$p_{partly}(\mathbf{c}) = p_{occ}(\mathbf{c}) - \sum_{\alpha} p_{\alpha}(\mathbf{c}) \tag{14}$$

Ortsinvariante statistische Daten werden als (näherungsweise) konstant für den gesamten Arbeitsraum angenommen:

- Hindernisgeschwindigkeit v_O.
  Die Hindernisgeschwindigkeit sei gleichverteilt im Intervall $[v_{min}, v_{max}]$.
- Hindernisgröße $l_O \times w_O$.
  Kleine Abweichungen der tatsächlichen Hindernisgröße von diesem Wert haben keinen signifikanten Einfluß auf die Ergebnisse der Bahnplanung.

Die Annahme, daß diese Daten ortsinvariant sind, kann unter Umständen eine zu grobe Näherung darstellen. Für eine genauere Erfassung lassen sich die Daten dann ebenfalls ortsvariant im statistischen Raster repräsentieren.

In unserem praktischen Versuchsaufbau werden die statistischen Daten mit Hilfe von Kameras, welche an der Hallendecke montiert sind, gewonnen [4]. Hindernisse werden erkannt und ihre Bewegungen erfaßt. Abbildung 7 zeigt ein typisches Kamerabild und einige von der Bildverarbeitung erfaßte Pfade. Aus diesen Daten werden die Einträge für das statistische Raster gewonnen, sowie durchschnittliche Hindernisgrößen und -geschwindigkeiten ermittelt. Prinzipiell sind auch einfachere Erfassungsmethoden ohne Objektsegmentierung denkbar (z.B. basierend auf dem optischen Fluß), für die Zukunft planen wir jedoch Experimente, welche die Objektbewegungen auf einer höheren Ebene (*statistische Beispielpfade*) berücksichtigen.

5 Bahnplanung mit dem cp-Feld

Unser in [5] vorgestelltes statistisches Bahnplanungsverfahren wurde mit Hilfe der Formeln zur Berechnung von Kollisionswahrscheinlichkeiten weiterentwickelt. Das Verfahren ist an übliche Potentialfeldmethoden [1] angelehnt, seine Grundlage bilden nun jedoch sogenannte *cp-Felder* (cp = collision probability). Ein cp-Feld wird für eine vorgegebene Zielposition des Roboters berechnet. Es beschreibt Kollisionswahrscheinlichkeiten für Pfade von beliebigen Punkten des Arbeitsraumes zur Zielposition. Für einen punktförmigen Roboter kann ein Pfad mit (näherungsweise) minimaler Kollisionswahrscheinlichkeit direkt abgeleitet werden.

---

[3] Dementsprechend fallen auch Hindernisse, die sich mit deutlich geringerer Geschwindigkeit als der Roboter bewegen, näherungsweise in diese Kategorie.

Ausgangspunkt der cp-Feld-Berechnung ist die (von der Roboterbewegungsrichtung abhängige) Kollisionswahrscheinlichkeit für die Durchquerung einer Zelle $\mathbf{c}$ (für eine ausführlichere Darstellung der folgenden Betrachungen siehe [8]):

$$p_{coll}(\mathbf{c}) = p_{occ}(\mathbf{c}) + \frac{d_{cell}}{l_O} \sum_\alpha k_\alpha p_{\alpha-\alpha_R}(\mathbf{c}) \tag{15}$$

(d_{cell}: Größe der Zelle, α_R: Roboterbewegungsrichtung, k_α: siehe Gleichung (13), $p_{\alpha-\alpha_R}$: In das Robotersystem transformierter Hindernisfluß)

Im Verlaufe eines Pfades müssen eine Reihe jeweils benachbarter Zellen durchquert werden. Bei der Verknüpfung der zugehörigen Kollisionswahrscheinlichkeiten ist zu berücksichtigen, daß diese zu einem gewissen Grad korrelieren. Als Kompromiß zwischen den Grenzfällen keine bzw. vollständige Korrelation verwenden wir die folgende allgemeine Formel mit einem variablen Korrekturterm $p_{cor}(\mathbf{c}_1, \mathbf{c}_2)$:

$$p_{coll} = p_{coll}(\mathbf{c}_1) + p_{coll}(\mathbf{c}_2) - p_{cor}(\mathbf{c}_1, \mathbf{c}_2) \tag{16}$$

Eingehendere Untersuchungen (unterstützt durch Ergebnisse aus Experimenten) führten zu folgendem Korrekturterm:

$$p_{cor}(\mathbf{c}_1, \mathbf{c}_2) = \max \left\{ p_{coll}(\mathbf{c}_1) * p_{coll}(\mathbf{c}_2) ,\ \min\{p_{occ}(\mathbf{c}_1), p_{occ}(\mathbf{c}_2)\} \right\} \tag{17}$$

Die Verknüpfung mehrerer Zellen erfolgt iterativ in analoger Weise:

$$p_{coll,i+1} = p_{coll,i} + p_{coll}(\mathbf{c}_{i+1}) - p_{cor,i}(\mathbf{c}_i, \mathbf{c}_{i+1}) \tag{18}$$

$$p_{cor,i}(\mathbf{c}_i, \mathbf{c}_{i+1}) = \max\{p_{coll,i} * p_{coll}(\mathbf{c}_{i+1}) ,\ \min\{p_{occ}(\mathbf{c}_i), p_{occ}(\mathbf{c}_{i+1})\}\}$$

Um das cp-Feld zu berechnen, verwenden wir einen Algorithmus ähnlich dem, wie er in [5] vorgestellt wurde. Die Berechnung beginnt dabei am Zielpunkt und breitet sich im freien Arbeitsraum aus, indem eine Art A^*-Suche durchgeführt wird. Freie Zellen des Rasters entsprechen Knoten, benachbarte Zellen (8-er Nachbarschaft) sind durch Kanten verbunden. Die Bewegung entlang einer Kante vergrößert die Kollisionswahrscheinlichkeit des Pfades zum Ziel gemäß der Gleichung (18).

Für einen punktförmigen Roboter kann ein Pfad mit (näherungsweise) minimaler Kollisionswahrscheinlichkeit direkt aus dem cp-Feld abgeleitet werden. Abbildung 4 stellt das cp-Feld für das einführende Beispiel (Abb. 1) dar. Für verschiedene Startpositionen sind die Lösungspfade mit ihren Kollisionswahrscheinlichkeiten (gemäß dem cp-Feld) angegeben.

Zur Bewertung der berechneten Pfade lassen sich drei Maße gegenüberstellen: 1. Die formal berechenbare Kollisionswahrscheinlichkeit. 2. Der Wert der Roboterstartposition im cp-Feld. 3. Das Simulationsergebnis. Abbildung 6 zeigt eine gute Übereinstimmung für das Beispiel, insbesondere die *Verhältnisse* zwischen den Kollisionswahrscheinlichkeiten verschiedener Pfade sind für das cp-Feld und die realen bzw. theoretischen Werte ähnlich. Dies deutet darauf hin, daß das Verfahren tatsächlich meistens in der Lage ist, den optimalen Pfad zu finden.

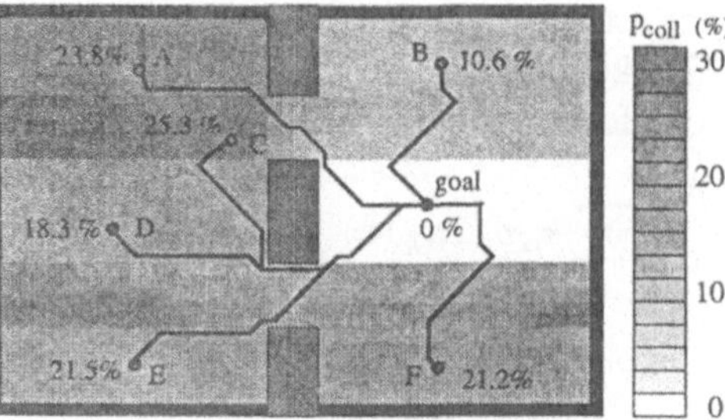

Abb. 4. Das *cp*-Feld

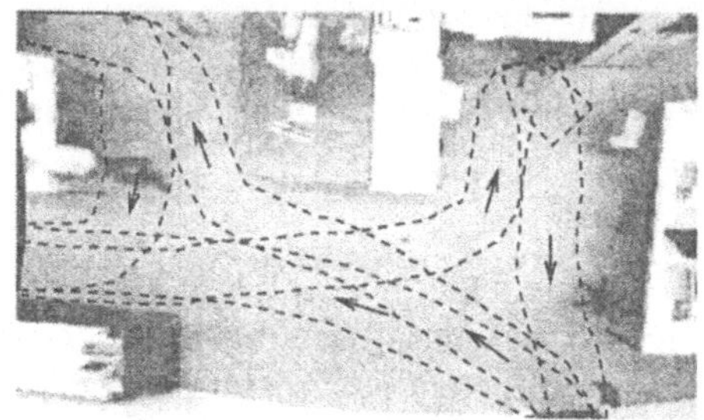

Abb. 5. Rechteckiger Roboter

Kollisionswahrscheinl. (%)		
Pfad	theor.	*cp*-Feld	Sim.
A	23.9	23.8	19.9
B	10.5	10.6	9.0
C	26.8	25.3	20.6
D	17.2	18.3	15.0
E	21.3	21.5	17.9
F	21.0	21.2	17.6

Abb. 6. Experimentelle Ergebnisse

Abb. 7. Blick auf reale Arbeitszelle

Der vorgestellte Ansatz läßt sich von punktförmigen Robotern auf reale (rechteckige) Roboter verallgemeinern. Dazu werden während der Berechnung des *cp*-Feldes benachbarte Zellen nur dann miteinander verbunden, wenn das senkrecht zur Verbindungskante nächstgelegene Hindernis einen größeren Abstand als die halbe Roboterbreite hat. Die Bahnplanung erfolgt dann gemäß [1] mit Hilfe eines über Kontrollpunkte definierten Konfigurationsraumpotentials und mit Zufallsbewegungen, um aus lokalen Minima zu entkommen. Im Gegensatz zu üblichen Näherungen mit einem umschriebenen Kreis (durch entsprechende Vergrößerung der Hindernisse, bzw. Transformation vom Arbeits- in den Konfigurationsraum) bietet dieses Verfahren einige Vorzüge: Das *cp*-Feld bleibt für den gesamten Arbeitsraum definiert, und der Roboter kann auch durch schmale Korridore eine Bahn finden, die bei kreisförmiger Approximation blockiert wären. Abbildung 5 zeigt das veränderte *cp*-Feld und Beispielpfade für einen rechteckigen Roboter.

6 Ausblick

In diesem Artikel haben wir Grundlagen zur Schätzung von Kollisionswahrscheinlichkeiten für mobile Roboter in dynamischen Umgebungen vorgestellt. Es wurde hierbei insbesondere auf eine konsequente mathematische Herleitung geachtet, um sich nicht auf heuristische oder inituitive Abschätzungen gründen zu müssen. Die entwickelten Formeln flossen unmittelbar in ein statistisches

Bahnplanungsverfahren ein, welches Pfade mit näherungsweise minimaler Kollisionswahrscheinlichkeit liefert.

Die Repräsentation komplexer Bewegungsmuster durch eine überschaubare Menge statistischer Daten verdient in der Zukunft einer genaueren Untersuchung. Wir planen unter anderem, die Informationen nicht auf Flußfelder zu beschränken, sondern z.B. durch aussagekräftigere *statistische Beispielpfade* darzustellen. Dabei bietet sich die Anpassung des *probabilistic roadmap*-Bahnplanungsverfahrens [7] mit gewichteten Kanten an. Andere entscheidende Kriterien, wie z.B. die Länge des Pfades, sollten zusätzlich berücksichtigt werden. Eine weitere Richtung für interessante Untersuchungen besteht darin, die Robotergeschwindigkeit nicht als konstant, sondern nur als nach oben begrenzt zu betrachten. Dies ist insbesondere bei Berücksichtigung der möglichen reaktiven Verhaltensweisen bei Erscheinen eines Hindernisses bedeutend: Potentielle Kollisionen, die sich bei Beibehaltung des geplanten Pfades durch Abbremsen des Roboters vermeiden lassen, sind weniger kritisch als Situationen, in denen der Roboter ausweichen oder gar umkehren muß. Auch diese Aspekte wollen wir in der Zukunft eingehend und systematisch untersuchen.

Literatur

1. J. Barraquand, B. Langlois, and J.-C. Latombe. Numerical potential field techniques for robot path planning. *IEEE Transactions on Systems, Man, and Cybernetics*, 22(2), Mar. 1992.
2. A. Elfes. Occupancy grids: A stochastic spatial representation for active robot perception. *Proceedings of the Sixth Conference on Uncertainty in AI*, July 1990.
3. K. Fujimura. *Motion Planning in Dynamic Environments*. Springer Verlag, 1991.
4. R. Gutsche, C. Laloni, and F. M. Wahl. Factory floor monitoring system with intelligent control for mobile robot guidance. *International Conference on Advanced Mechatronics (ICAM '93)*, pages 185–190, 1993.
5. R. Gutsche, C. Laloni, and F. M. Wahl. Path planning for mobile vehicles within dynamic worlds using statistical data. In *IEEE/RSJ International Conference on Intelligent Robots and Systems*, 1994.
6. K. Kant and S. W. Zucker. Toward efficient trajectory planning: The path-velocity decomposition. *The International Journal of Robotics Research*, 5(3):72–89, 1986.
7. L. Kavraki and J.-C. Latombe. Randomized preprocessing of configuration space for fast path planning. In *IEEE International Conference on Robotics and Automation*, 1994.
8. E. Kruse, R. Gutsche, and F. M. Wahl. Estimation of collision probabilities in dynamic environments for path planning with minimum collision probability. In *IEEE/RSJ International Conference on Intelligent Robots and Systems*, Nov. 1996.
9. D. W. Payton, J. K. Rosenblatt, and D. M. Keirsey. Plan guided reaction. *IEEE Transactions on Systems, Man, and Cybernetics*, 20(6):1370–1382, Nov. 1990.
10. S. Ratering and M. Gini. Robot navigation in a known environment with unknown moving obstacles. In *IEEE International Conference on Robotics and Automation*, pages 25–30, 1993.

Situationserkennung als Grundlage der Verhaltenssteuerung eines mobilen Roboters

Klaus Peter Wershofen und Volker Graefe
Institut für Meßtechnik
Universität der Bundeswehr München
85577 Neubiberg

Kurzfassung

Ein neuartiges Systemkonzept für verhaltensbasierte mobile Roboter, die objektorientierte verhaltensbasierte Navigation, wird vorgestellt. Kernpunkt dabei ist, daß die Verhaltensauswahl situationsgesteuert erfolgt. Der hierfür maßgebliche Situationsbegriff wird erläutert; er ergibt sich im wesentlichen aus den Zuständen der in der Umgebung des Roboters befindlichen körperlichen Objekte und des Roboters selbst. Voraussetzungen für eine Realisierung des Konzepts sind eine leistungsfähige Sensorik und eine angepaßte Wissensrepräsentation. Ein globales Koordinatensystem und eine genaue Kenntnis der geometrischen Gegebenheiten des Einsatzgebiets des Roboters sind dagegen nicht erforderlich.

Das Konzept wurde in Form eines mobilen Roboters, der sichtgesteuert in Wegenetzen von Gebäuden navigieren kann, realisiert. Dabei zeigte sich, daß sich auf der Grundlage des vorgestellten Systemkonzepts sowohl eine Lernfähigkeit des Roboters als auch ein hohes Maß an Benutzerfreundlichkeit bei der Kommunikation mit dem Roboter erreichen läßt.

Einführung

Verhaltensbasierte Ansätze finden bei der Planung und Koordinierung der Handlungen von autonomen Robotern seit etwa zehn Jahren besonderes Interesse. Während bei klassischer Vorgehensweise ein Roboter vor dem Ausführen einer Bewegung erst einmal eine „optimale" Bahn errechnet und sich dann entsprechend dieser Bahn bewegt, wählt ein verhaltensbasierter Roboter aus einem Repertoire verfügbarer, sozusagen eingebauter, Verhaltensmuster (Anhalten, Abbiegen, Geradeausfahren o.ä.) ein in diesem Moment angemessenes oder erfolgversprechendes aus und führt es sofort aus. Komplexe Missionen, etwa die Fahrt durch ein Wegenetz, werden ausgeführt, indem nacheinander verschiedene Verhaltensmuster aktiviert werden.

Gegenüber dem klassischen Ansatz mit der dort üblichen Bahnplanung und -optimierung werden durch einen verhaltensbasierten Ansatz wesentliche Nachteile vermieden, u.a. der hohe typischerweise benötigte Zeitbedarf vor dem Beginn der Bewegung, die Notwendigkeit, zahlreiche kinematische, dynamische und sensorische Systemparameter des Roboters genauestens zu kennen, und die Schwierigkeit, das benötigte interne „Weltmodell" (auch wenn es in Wahrheit nur ein Modell eines kleinen Umgebungsbereichs ist) aus real verfügbaren Sensordaten mit der erforderlichen Vollständigkeit und Genauigkeit aufzubauen. Der verhaltensbasierte Ansatz ersetzt die aufwendige quantitative Optimierungsrechnung und Bahnplanung durch eine qualitative Abwägung zwischen den aktuell ausführbaren Verhaltensmustern, was sehr schnell und in vielen Fällen schon auf der Grundlage ungefährer, qualitativer Sensordaten und ohne Verwendung eines quantitativ genauen Weltmodells geschehen kann.

Ein zentrales Problem bei jedem verhaltensbasierten Ansatz ist, wie und auf welcher Grundlage die fortlaufende Auswahl des jeweils zu aktivierenden Verhaltens geschehen soll. Im folgenden wird hierzu ein Lösungsansatz vorgestellt, der auf der Fähigkeit eines Roboters beruht, Situationen in Echtzeit zu erkennen und die Verhaltensauswahl auf dieser Grundlage situationsabhängig vorzunehmen.

Da es die in der Umgebung des Roboters sichtbaren Objekte sind, welche die Situation, und damit die Verhaltensauswahl, wesentlich mitbestimmen, bezeichnen wir unseren Ansatz, zur Abgrenzung von anderen verhaltensbasierten Ansätzen, auch als objektorientiert.

Die Begriffe „Objekt" und „Situation"

Bei der objektorientierten verhaltensbasierten Navigation spielen die Begriffe „Objekt" und „Situation" im Zusammenhang mit der Umwelterfassung sowie der Auswahl und der Ausführung von Verhaltensmustern eine wichtige Rolle. Da diese Begriffe häufig mit unterschiedlichen Inhalten verwendet werden, soll hier ihre Bedeutung im Zusammenhang mit der objektorientierten verhaltensbasierten Navigation klargestellt werden.

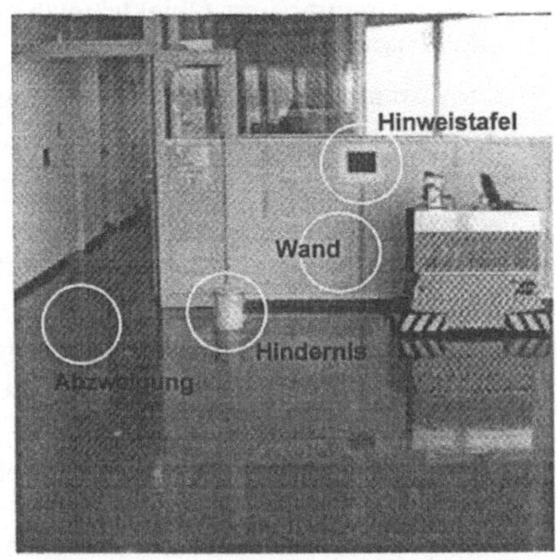

Abb. 1
Teile der Versuchsumgebung mit Beispielen für „Objekte", die im Zusammenhang mit der Navigation in Wegenetzen relevant sind (mit weißem Kreis markiert). Rechts im Bild ist der nach dem hier beschriebenen Konzept aufgebaute mobile Roboter *ATHENE II* zu sehen.

Objekt

Ein mobiler Roboter operiert in einer Umgebung, die sich aus körperlichen Gegenständen zusammensetzt. Alle körperlichen Gegenstände (oder Teile davon), die für den Roboter bei der Verhaltenskoordination oder der Ausführung von Verhaltensmustern von Bedeutung sind, werden hier als „Objekte" bezeichnet. Welche körperlichen Gegenstände das im Einzelfall sind, ist abhängig vom Verhaltensrepertoire des Roboters und seinen Möglichkeiten, Verhaltensmuster auszuwählen bzw. zu koordinieren. Somit hängt es von den Fähigkeiten des Roboters ab, welche Teile der Umwelt als „Objekte" angesehen werden.

In Abb. 1 sind Beispiele für Objekte, die für einen mobilen Roboter im Zusammenhang mit der Navigation in Wegenetzen von Gebäuden relevant sind, mit einem weißen Kreis markiert. Die dort zu sehenden „Objekte" „Hindernis", „Abzweigung" und „Wand" sind sowohl zur Verhaltensauswahl als auch zur Verhaltensausführung geeignet, während das Objekt „Hinweistafel" nur für Zwecke der Verhaltenskoordination herangezogen wird.

Situation

Große Lexika, z.B. [Brockhaus 1989] oder [Meyer 1977] definieren den Begriff „Situation" als „augenblickliche Lage", eine „Sachlage", eine „Stellung" oder einen „Zustand". Eine weitergehende Erklärung, die auch im Hinblick auf die Eingrenzung des Begriffs „Situation" im Zusammenhang mit der objektorientierten verhaltensbasierten Navigation wertvoll ist, erlauben die von beiden Lexika angeführten philosophischen Erläuterungen:

> „Situation ist im Sinne der Existenzphilosophie der einmalige, unwiederholbare Augenblick, in dem sich für den Einzelnen in der Wechselbeziehung zwischen innerer Bestimmtheit und äußerer Lage die unmittelbare konkrete Wirklichkeit darstellt. Der in ihm gegebene Entscheidungszwang habe die nun sichtbare Unangemessenheit aller allgemeinen Normativität zu überbrücken. Die Situation sei somit als 'hermeneutische Situation' (M. Heidegger) zugleich Chance und Schranke des Menschen" [Brockhaus 1989].

„In der philosophischen Pragmatik ist Situation ein Konstrukt, das den Komplex von Bedingungen, Möglichkeiten und Determinanten von Handlungen zusammenfassen soll" [Meyer 1977].

Ähnlich wie bei den vorstehenden Definitionen ist auch bei der objektorientierten verhaltensbasierten Navigation der Begriff „Situation" als die Gesamtheit der Umstände, die vom Roboter bei der Auswahl eines in dem jeweiligen Moment geeigneten Verhaltensmusters zu berücksichtigen sind, zu verstehen. Dazu gehören

- die wahrnehmbaren Objekte in der Umgebung des Roboters und deren vermutete oder erkennbare Zustände;

- der Zustand des Roboters (Bewegungszustand, gerade ausgeführtes Verhaltensmuster etc.);

- die Gegebenheiten der Umgebung, welche dem Roboter bekannt sind (z.B. Lageplan), auch wenn diese momentan mit seinen Sensoren nicht erfaßbar sind;

- die Ziele des Roboters, und zwar sowohl permanente Ziele (z.B. Überleben, Unfallfreiheit), als auch transiente, die sich aus der aktuellen Mission ergeben (z.B. Fahrtziel, zu befahrende Wege);

- das Repertoire an verfügbaren Verhaltensmustern sowie die gegebenen Möglichkeiten, Verhaltensmuster zu koordinieren und zu verketten und so bestimmte Änderungen der Situation herbeizuführen.

Die Situation ergibt sich somit nicht direkt aus objektiv vorhandenen externen Gegebenheiten, sondern aus den unvollkommenen internen „Bildern" der externen Gegebenheiten, wie sie im Roboter aus der Sensordatenverarbeitung in Verbindung mit gespeichertem Wissen entstehen, zusammen mit den ebenfalls internen Zielen und Zuständen des Roboters.

Der Benutzer spielt insofern indirekt eine Rolle, als er über die Benutzerschnittstelle Ziele vorgeben oder unmittelbar in die Verhaltensauswahl eingreifen kann.

Systemarchitektur

Überblick

Abbildung 2 gibt einen Überblick über die realisierte Systemarchitektur. Eine ausführliche Beschreibung der Systemarchitektur und ihrer Komponenten findet sich in [Wershofen 1996].

Zentrale Instanz ist das Situationsmodul. Die Situationserkennung spielt bei unserem Ansatz eine zentrale Rolle, weil fast alle Entscheidungen im System auf der Grundlage der vom Roboter erkannten Situation getroffen werden. Die Situationserkennung geschieht durch eine Verknüpfung von Sensordaten mit gespeichertem Wissen über die Umwelt und über die Mission.

Eine wesentliche Grundlage der objektorientierten verhaltensbasierten Navigation bilden außerdem elementare sensorische und motorische Fähigkeiten, aus denen, wenn sie in koordinierter Form ausgeführt werden, Verhaltensmuster resultieren. Bei der hier im Vordergrund stehenden Navigation in Wegenetzen zählen zu den sensorischen Fähigkeiten die Erkennung von Wänden, Abbiegemöglichkeiten, Zielobjekten (auf die ggf. zugefahren werden soll) und Landmarken. Aus dem Bereich der motorischen Fähigkeiten ist z.B. das Geradeausfahren oder das Kurvefahren zu nennen.

Die Verhaltensmuster sind wiederum die Basis für komplexes Verhalten, welches durch eine situationsabhängige Verkettung der (elementaren) Verhaltensmuster entsteht. Auch das Abarbeiten vorgegebener Fahraufträge wird durch die situationsabhängige Verkettung von Verhaltensmustern realisiert. Dazu wird der erteilte Auftrag in eine Datenstruktur (Missionsbeschreibung) umgesetzt, auf die ein Management-Prozeß zugreift, welcher das Gesamtverhalten – einschließlich der Kommunikation mit dem Benutzer – koordiniert.

Drei weitere Module sind somit, neben dem Situationsmodul, wichtige Bestandteile des Systems: eine sehr leistungsfähige Sensorik zur Erfassung der Gegebenheiten der Umwelt als Grundlage der fortlaufenden Situationserkennung, eine Aktorik zur Realisierung der vom Situationsmodul jeweils ausgewählten Verhaltensmuster und eine an die Erfordernisse der Systemarchitektur angepaßte Wissensrepräsentation.

Situationserkennung und Verhaltensauswahl

Ein Beispiel soll die Funktionsweise dieses Moduls verdeutlichen. Ein Roboter habe die Aufgabe, sich in einem Netz von Korridoren in einem Gebäude zu bewegen. Eine typische Situation ist gegeben, wenn der Roboter sich mitten in einem Korridor befindet. Ein angemessenes Verhaltensmuster wäre in dieser Situation, dem Korridor entlangzufahren; Alternativen wären anzuhalten oder vielleicht auch umzukehren. Das Situationsmodul wird aufgrund der Sensordaten das Bestehen der genannten Situation erkennen und z.B. veranlassen, daß die Aktorik das Verhalten „Korridor Folgen" realisiert. Die Aktorik wird dabei mit den erforderlichen Sensordaten, z.B. Abstand zur Wand, versorgt.

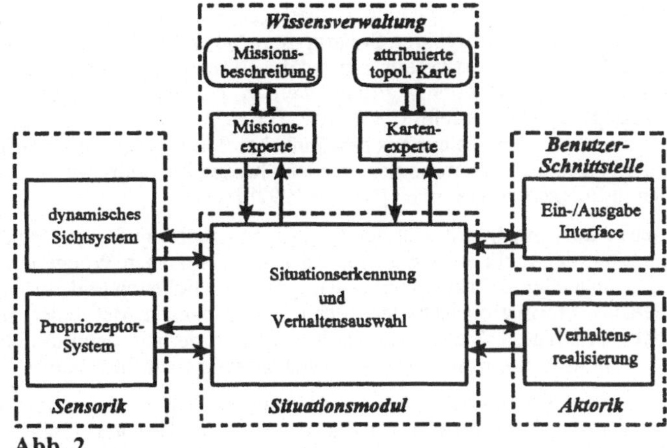

Abb. 2
Überblick über die Systemarchitektur der objektorientierten verhaltensbasierten Navigation.

Eine neue Situation tritt ein, wenn der Roboter aufgrund einer groben Positionsschätzung erkennt, daß er in die Nähe einer Kreuzung gekommen ist, an der er (zur Erfüllung seiner aktuellen Mission) abbiegen sollte. Da weder eine genaue Grundrißkarte noch ein genau arbeitendes Navigationssystem vorausgesetzt werden soll, muß rechtzeitig vor dem Erreichen der Kreuzung ein Suchverhalten der Sensorik aktiviert werden, mit das Eintreten der wiederum neuen Situation „Kreuzung erreicht" erkannt wird, sobald sie eingetreten ist. Anschließend kann die Kreuzung relativ zum Roboter vermessen werden und das Verhaltensmuster „Abbiegen" aktiviert werden.

Durch eine geeignete Verkettung von Verhaltensmustern kann der Roboter so jeden Punkt im Wegenetz erreichen; wichtig ist dabei, daß eine geometrisch ungenaue Karte des Wegenetzes genügt, wenn diese nur die Topologie des Netzes richtig repräsentiert. Weder für die Situationserkennung noch für die Ausführung von Verhaltensmustern muß der Roboter seine Position relativ zu irgendeinem globalen Koordinatensystem kennen, auch nicht zum Passieren von Engstellen. Es genügt, wenn er weiß, in welchem Korridor er sich befindet, in welcher der beiden möglichen Richtungen er sich bewegt, und wann er sich einer in der Karte nur ungenau eingetragenen Kreuzung soweit angenähert hat, daß es sich lohnt, das betreffende Suchverhalten zu aktivieren. Eine hochgenaue Navigation relativ zu in der Nähe befindlichen Objekten, z.B. Wänden, ist dennoch möglich, nämlich durch Auswertung der aktuellen Sensordaten.

Diese Vorgehensweise ist der eines Autofahrers vergleichbar, der mit einer ungenauen Anfahrtsskizze ein Ziel erreicht und dort seinen Wagen in einer engen Parklücke parkt, ohne sich dabei für genaue geographische Koordinaten zu interessieren.

Sensorik und Aktorik

Wichtige Voraussetzung für eine Situationserkennung ist reichhaltige sensorische Information über die in der Umgebung des Roboters befindlichen Objekte. Grundsätzlich kommen für die Gewinnung derartiger Information die verschiedensten Sensoren in Betracht. Einige Tiere, wie beispielsweise Fledermäuse und Delphine, stellen unter Beweis, daß reine Sonarsysteme sehr leistungsfähig sein können. Andererseits zeigt die Natur, daß das Sehen den akustischen Verfahren in nahezu allen Umgebungen überlegen ist [Graefe 1992a]. Hinzu kommt, daß die momentan für Roboter verfügbaren Sonarsysteme nur schlecht geeignet sind, Objekte zu erkennen und die Informationen zu liefern, die für die Erkennung von nicht-trivialen Situationen notwendig sind. Andererseits konnte gezeigt werden, daß ein Sichtsystem, dessen Architektur auf dem Konzept des in [Graefe 1989] bzw. [Graefe 1991] beschriebenen objektorientierten Sehens basiert, selbst wenn es nur aus gewöhnlichen Mikroprozessoren aufgebaut ist, die Informationen liefern kann, die ein autonomes Straßenfahrzeug benötigt, um Verkehrssituationen auf Autobahnen in Echtzeit zu erkennen [Graefe 1992b].

Neben dem Sichtsystem ist noch ein Propriozeptorsystem vorhanden, das im wesentlichen aus zwei mit den nicht angetriebenen Rädern verbundenen Weggebern besteht. Es dient vor allem dazu, ungefähre Information über Fahrgeschwindigkeiten und zurückgelegte Wege zu gewinnen. Genaue Information ist wegen der unvermeidlichen Meßfehler mit einer solchen Anordnung nicht zu erhalten. Sie ist aber auch nicht erforderlich, denn die Navigation beruht – wie auch beim Menschen – primär auf der visuell gewonnenen Information.

Die Aktorik verfügt über ein Repertoire an sozusagen eingebauten motorischen Fähigkeiten, die jeweils als eigene Regler für die Motoren des Roboters realisiert sind. Durch koordinierte Aktivierung solcher motorischer Fähigkeiten in Verbindung mit sensorischen Fähigkeiten ergeben sich die elementaren Verhaltensmuster.

Wissensrepräsentation

Das für die Situationserkennung und die Steuerung des Roboters erforderliche Wissen ist nicht zentral in einer einzigen Wissensbasis gespeichert, sondern – in Anlehnung an das von [Graefe 1989] vorgeschlagene Konzept der objektorientierten Sichtsysteme – im gesamten System verteilt. Dabei wird das jeweilige Wissen so repräsentiert, wie es zur Lösung der jeweiligen Teilaufgabe optimal ist. Ganz bewußt wird dabei in Kauf genommen, daß dadurch unter Umständen gleiches Wissen zum Teil mehrfach an verschiedenen Stellen im System gespeichert wird.

Ein Teil des Wissens, z.B. für die Erkennung von Objekten und Situationen oder für die Regelung des Roboters, ist in Form von prozeduralem Wissen unmittelbar innerhalb der für diese Fähigkeiten zuständigen Module gespeichert. Der andere Teil des Wissens wird in Form von deklarativem Wissen in Datenbasen gespeichert.

An deklarativem Wissen benötigt der Roboter bei der objektorientierten verhaltensbasierten Navigation Wissen über die statischen Eigenschaften der Umgebung und Wissen über die auszuführende Aufgabe.

Er verfügt deshalb über zwei unterschiedliche Wissensbasen:

- eine attribuierte topologische Karte, die das Wissen über das Operationsgebiet sowie über dort vorhandene Objekte beinhaltet;

- eine Missionsbeschreibung, welche die aktuelle Aufgabe des Roboters spezifiziert.

Zu jeder der beiden Wissensbasen gehören neben einer Datenstruktur zur Speicherung quasi statischen Wissens die für den Zugriff auf das gespeicherte Wissen und die Verwaltung der Datenbestände zuständigen Prozeduren. Diese sind hier als „Missionsexperte" und als „Kartenexperte" bezeichnet.

Die beiden Wissensbasen sollen nachfolgend kurz vorgestellt werden.

Attribuierte topologische Karte

Eine topologische Karte, die durch geeignete Attribute erweitert ist, hat sich als adäquat erwiesen, um bei der objektorientierten verhaltensbasierten Navigation das zum Agieren in einem Wegenetz benötigte Wissen über die Umwelt zu repräsentieren. Sie wird, wie in [Graefe, Wershofen 1991] vorgeschlagen, „attribuierte topologische Karte" genannt.

Die grundsätzliche Struktur der attribuierten topologischen Karte ist aus Abb. 3 ersichtlich. Die Abbildung zeigt einen kleinen Ausschnitt aus einer solchen Karte für ein Wegenetz. Die wichtigsten Eigenschaften der attribuierten topologischen Karte sind:

- im Wegenetz vorhandene Kreuzungen und Abzweigungen (z.B. A, B und C) sowie aufgabenrelevante Orte wie etwa Beladestationen (z.B. G) werden als Punkte modelliert;

- die Verbindungswege zwischen den Orten werden als Paare von entgegengesetzt gerichteten Pfaden modelliert;

- sowohl Punkte als auch Pfade tragen als Attribute Listen, die wichtige Hinweise beinhalten.

Ein Vorzug der attribuierten topologischen Karte ist, daß in ihr neben Informationen über die Topologie der Einsatzumgebung auch explizite Hinweise enthalten sein können, die das Bewältigen von Aufgaben erheblich erleichtern. Schon in [Kuhnert 1990], [Kuhnert, Wershofen 1990] und [Thorpe, Gowdy 1990] wird darauf hingewiesen, daß es für einen Roboter von Vorteil ist, nicht nur Informationen bezüglich der Geometrie bzw. Topologie der Einsatzumgebung zu speichern, sondern diese mit Hinweisen zu ergänzen, wie z.B. aufgabenrelevante Orte erkannt werden können oder welche Handlungen an einer bestimmten Stelle ausgeführt werden müssen.

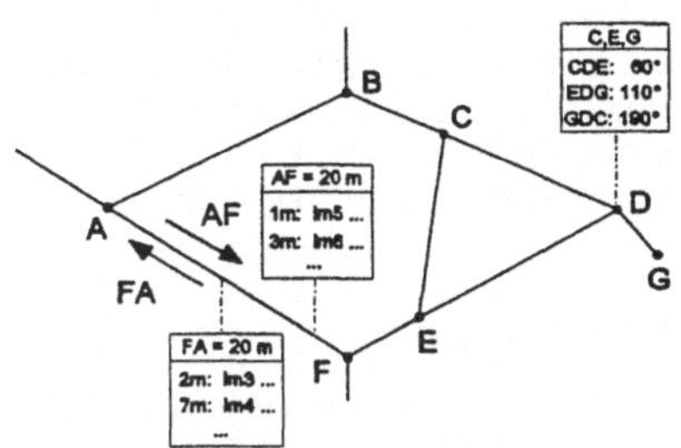

Abb. 3
Ausschnitt einer attribuierten topologischen Karte. Attribut-Listen (hier in gekürzter Form angedeutet) sind jedem Knoten und jedem gerichteten Pfad zugeordnet.

Missionsbeschreibung

Abhängig von den Fähigkeiten des Roboters kann eine Missionsbeschreibung sehr kompakt oder sehr ausführlich sein. Im günstigsten Fall ist es schon ausreichend, wenn die Missionsbeschreibung den Namen des zu erreichenden Zielortes und optional eine Liste mit den Namen von Zwischenpunkten, an denen vorbeigefahren werden soll, beinhaltet. Im Gegensatz dazu besteht eine detaillierte Missionsbeschreibung aus einer Sequenz von Aktionen, die ausgeführt werden müssen, um die gewünschte Mission auszuführen.

Die bei der objektorientierten verhaltensbasierten Navigation möglichen Missionsbeschreibungen können mit Hinweisen verglichen werden, die einem Menschen gegeben werden, wenn ihm erklärt wird, wie er zu einem bestimmten Ort gelangen kann. Dies bedeutet, daß der Bediener mit dem objektorientierten verhaltensbasierten Roboter auf eine für ihn naheliegende Weise kommunizieren kann.

Benutzerschnittstelle

Daß die Kommunikation zwischen Bediener und Roboter schon auf einer relativ hochsprachlichen Ebene erfolgen kann, ist ein großer Vorzug der objektorientierten verhaltensbasierten Navigation. Ursächlich dafür ist, daß der Systemarchitektur Konzepte wie „Situation" und „Verhalten" zugrundeliegen und daß dadurch der Roboter ein Kommunikationsverhalten zeigen kann, das in gewissen Grenzen dem eines intelligenten Lebewesens ähnelt. Insbesondere kann die Kommunikation situationsabhängig und unter Bezugnahme auf Sachverhalte und Objekte der Umgebung erfolgen, wie sie für den Benutzer erkennbar sind, und ohne Bezugnahme auf Roboter-interne Gegebenheiten wie etwa Speicheradressen, Variablennamen, Prozeßbezeichnungen o.ä..

Voraussetzung für diese Art der Kommunikation ist, daß das Situationsmodul als zentrale Schaltstelle im System auch an der Steuerung der Kommunikation mit dem Benutzer beteiligt ist.

Aufgrund der Tatsache, daß die Handlungen des Roboters auf Verhaltensmustern basieren, können die Anweisungen des Bedieners an den Roboter in sehr kompakter Form erfolgen.

Beispiele hierfür sind: „Fahre der Wand entlang" oder „Biege an der nächsten Kreuzung ab". Die Umweltrepräsentation in Form einer attribuierten topologischen Karte ermöglicht es darüber hinaus, in Fahraufträgen gewohnte Ortsbezeichnungen in Form von Ortsnamen zu verwenden. So ist dem Roboter nicht mitzuteilen, daß er zu irgendeiner Koordinate (x, y) zu fahren hat, sondern der Fahrauftrag lautet z.B.: „Fahre zum Manipulatorlabor".

Realisierung

Am Beispiel der auftragsbezogenen Navigation in hindernisfreien Wegenetzen von Gebäuden erfolgte die Validierung des vorgestellten Ansatzes. Als Experimentiergerät wurde der mobile Roboter *ATHENE II* (vgl. Abb. 1 bzw. [Wershofen 1996]) eingesetzt. Die Informationsverarbeitung erfolgte mit einem an Bord des Roboters befindlichen PC, der für die Bildverarbeitung mit einer Transputer-Framegrabber-Karte versehen war.

Erkennungsprozesse

Bei der genannten Anwendung des vorgestellte Konzepts wurden Erkennungsprozesse für Wände, Abbiegemöglichkeiten, Zielobjekte und Landmarken benötigt.

Bei der Erkennung von Abbiegemöglichkeiten wird vorausgesetzt, daß der Roboter weiß, daß er sich in der Nähe einer Abzweigung befindet, und in welche Richtung abgebogen werden soll. Diese Information wird aus der Karte bzw. dem Fahrauftrag entnommen. Befindet sich der Roboter in der Nähe einer Abbiegemöglichkeit, schwenkt er seine Kamera quer zur Fahrtrichtung in die erwartete Richtung des abzweigenden Weges und sucht nach dem typischen Erscheinungsbild eines in Längsrichtung gesehenen Korridors.

„Zielobjekte" sind z.B. Objekte auf oder am Rand von frei befahrbaren Flächen. Ein Roboter kann solche Objekte für die Navigation auf freien Flächen benutzen. „Landmarken" hingegen dienen nur der Orientierung. Im Rahmen der Implementation des vorgestellten Konzept wurden Erkennungsprozesse für Zielobjekte und Landmarken mit rechteckförmiger Kontur entwickelt.

Verhaltensmuster

Verhaltensmuster entstehen, wenn sensorische und motorische Fähigkeiten koordiniert ausgeführt werden. Für *ATHENE II* wurden „Wand Folgen", „Abbiegen" und „Anhalten" als einfache Verhaltensmuster implementiert. Beim sichtbasierten Verhaltensmuster „Wand Folgen" wird *ATHENE II* so gesteuert, daß die Ablage zur Wand einem vorgegeben Wert entspricht. Das realisierte Verhaltensmuster „Abbiegen" gliedert sich in drei Phasen, in denen die Führung des Roboters ohne Sichtrückkopplung erfolgt. Zunächst wird mit geschwenkter Kamera nach der Abbiegemöglichkeit gesucht. Nach erfolgreicher Erkennung wird ihre Position relativ zum Roboter gemessen. Erreicht dieser einen Wert, der unter den gegebenen Umständen ein kollisionsfreies Abbiegen erlaubt, wird durch eine mittels der Propriozeptoren gesteuerte Kurvenfahrt die gewünschte Orientierungsänderung durchgeführt.

Die Mitte eines Zielobjektes wird beim Verhaltensmuster „Auf ein Objekt Zufahren" bei nach vorn gerichteter Kamera mit der Bildmitte zur Deckung gebracht. So wird erreicht, daß *ATHENE II* in Richtung eines Objektes fährt.

Situationserkennung und Verhaltensauswahl

Grundlage für die Koordination des Gesamtverhaltens ist eine fortlaufende Situationserkennung mit dem Ziel, in jedem Moment das jeweils angemessene Verhaltensmuster auszuwählen. Bei der Navigation in hindernisfreien Wegenetzen von Gebäuden sind die möglichen Situationen weitgehend durch den Fahrauftrag und den jeweils erreichten Ort bedingt.

Realisiert ist die Situationserkennung und Verhaltensauswahl in Form eines endlichen Automaten.

Ergebnisse

Zur Bestimmung der Leistungsfähigkeit des vorgestellten Ansatzes wurden zahlreiche Experimente und Testfahrten mit dem mobilen Roboter *ATHENE II* durchgeführt. Die Versuchsfahrten fanden in verschiedenen, willkürlich ausgewählten Teilbereichen des weitläufigen Laborgebäudes der Universität statt, wobei der Roboter sich jeweils in einem mehrfach zusammenhängenden Netz von Korridoren und frei befahrbaren Flächen, die in keiner Weise hierfür besonders hergerichtet worden waren, zu bewegen hatte (Abb. 1). Aufgrund der Abmessungen des Roboters und der Korridore stellten Abbiegemöglichkeiten in der Regel Engstellen dar, die jedoch mit angemessen reduzierter Geschwindigkeit ohne Probleme durchfahren wurden.

Ausführung von Fahraufträgen

Fahraufträge können dem Roboter wahlweise als Aktionslisten (Abfolgen von Verhaltensmustern) oder in benutzerfreundlicher Weise als Namenslisten übergeben werden. Abb. 4 zeigt den Verlauf einer typischen Versuchsfahrt, (Abb. 5) die dazu gehörende Missionsbeschreibung, die in diesem Fall dem Roboter als Namensliste vorgegeben wurde.

Ortsbestimmung

In den Experimenten wurde auch gezeigt, daß selbst wenn Engstellen zu passieren sind, Fahrtziele auch dann problemlos erreicht werden, wenn die Startposition und die metrischen Angaben in der Karte um mehrere Meter falsch sind. Hier zeigt sich ein hohes Maß an Robustheit, und zugleich resultiert im Vergleich zu bisher bekannten Ansätzen eine hohe Aufwandsreduzierung bei der Erstellung der Missionsbeschreibung und der Karte. Weiter konnte gezeigt werden, daß der Roboter *ATHENE II* in der Lage ist, seinen Standort innerhalb des kartierten Einsatzbereiches, z.B. zu Beginn einer Mission, durch den Vergleich der visuellen Erscheinungsbilder von erkannten Landmarken mit den entsprechenden Einträgen in der Karte selbständig zu bestimmen.

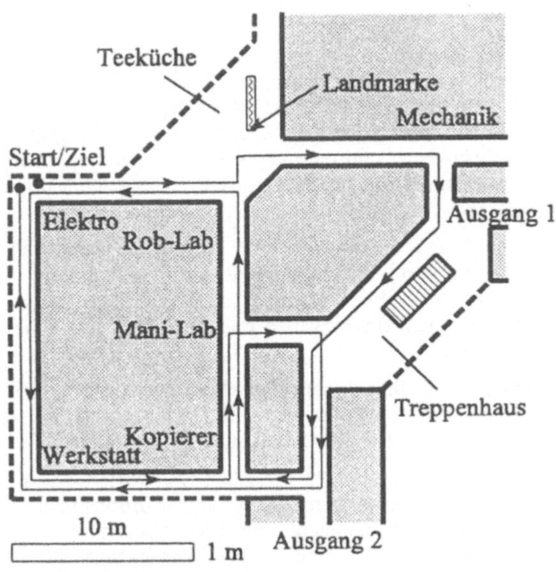

Abb. 4
Vom Roboter zurückgelegter Weg bei der Ausführung des nebenstehenden Fahrauftrags

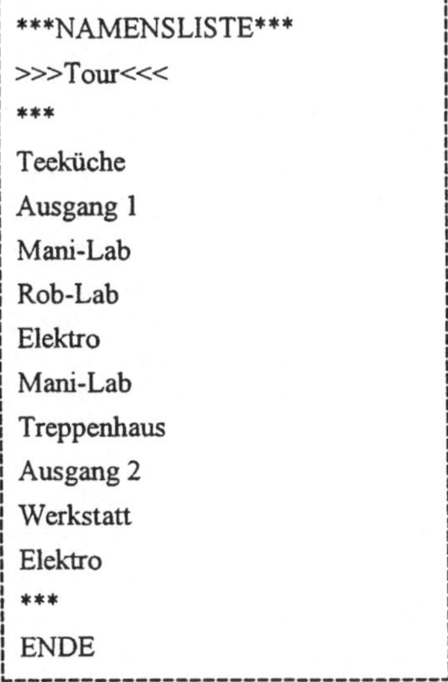

Abb. 5
Namensliste als Missionsbeschreibung für die in Abb. 4 dargestellte Fahrt

Wissenserwerb durch Lernen

Die objektorientierte verhaltensbasierte Navigation bildet eine sehr gute Basis zur Realisierung eines lernfähigen Roboters [Wershofen, Graefe 1993]. Der Nachweis hierfür wurde zunächst für das überwachte Erlernen von Kartenwissen erbracht. In Experimenten wurde erstmals demonstriert, daß ein sehender mobiler Roboter die zur selbständigen Navigation benötigte Karte im Rahmen von geführten Erkundungsfahrten erlernen kann.

Darüber hinaus wurde in einem ersten Experiment gezeigt, daß auch eine selbständige, von keinem Bediener unterstützte Erkundungsfahrt möglich ist. Um hierbei ähnliche Leistungen wie bei der geführten Erkundungsfahrt zu erreichen, sind allerdings die sensorischen Fähigkeiten von *ATHENE II* noch zu erweitern.

Hinderniserkennung

Die Erkennung von Hindernissen und die Vermeidung von Kollisionen wurden zunächst zurückgestellt. Um einen Roboter im Alltagsbetrieb einsetzen zu können, sind diese Fähigkeiten jedoch notwendig. Erste Versuche zur Hindernisvermeidung [Efenberger 1996] bestätigen, daß hierfür der von [Graefe et al. 1988] und von [Graefe 1990] vorgestellte Ansatz für die Hinderniserkennung auf Straßen ebenfalls eingesetzt werden kann. Dieser Ansatz ist durch einen ständig aktiven Entdeckerprozeß und nachgeschaltete Klassifizierer charakterisiert.

Fahrversuche mit einem Entdeckerprozeß, der einerseits schlagartige zeitliche Veränderungen im Blickfeld der Kamera und andererseits Bildbereiche mit starker Textur registriert, ergaben, daß damit bei günstigen Bedingungen schnell und zuverlässig auf Hindernisse, z.B. mit einem Nothalt, reagiert werden kann [Efenberger 1996].

Als äußerst schwer beherrschbar erwiesen sich jedoch die sehr stark ausgeprägten Spiegelungen, z.B. von Lampen und Fenstern, im Fußboden und in einem Teil der Wände sowie die örtlich und zeitlich sehr stark variablen Beleuchtungsverhältnisse (Sonnenschein bzw. künstliche Beleuchtung, teilweise in Abb. 1 erkennbar). Diese Probleme müssen noch gelöst werden.

Zusammenfassung und Ausblick

Es wurde ein Ansatz zur Steuerung sehender Roboter, die objektorientierte verhaltensbasierte Navigation, vorgestellt. Hauptmerkmal dieses verhaltensbasierten Ansatzes ist, daß die Verhaltensauswahl aufgrund einer Erkennung und Beurteilung der Situation, in der sich der Roboter befindet, erfolgt. Voraussetzungen für eine Realisierung des Konzepts sind eine leistungsfähige Sensorik, typischerweise in Form eines Sichtsystems, und eine angepaßte Wissensrepräsentation. Eine 3D- oder 4D-Weltbeschreibung ist weder für die Situationserkennung noch für die Ausführung von Verhaltensmustern erforderlich.

Vorteile eines solchen Ansatzes sind die sehr klare, modulare Struktur, die sich bei der Realisierung eines Roboters nach diesem Konzept ergibt, und die Möglichkeit, mit dem Roboter, z.B. bei der Auftragserteilung, auf einer ähnlichen Abstraktionsebene zu kommunizieren wie mit einem Menschen, was für praktische Anwendungen im Interesse der Benutzerfreundlichkeit dringend erwünscht ist.

Als angepaßte Umweltrepräsentation wurde eine attribuierte topologische Karte entwickelt. Die Erstellung dieser Karte wird in hohem Maße dadurch erleichtert, daß in ihr primär nur die Topologie des Wegenetzes gespeichert ist, während metrische Angaben allenfalls in Form überschlägiger Hinweise enthalten sind.

Die Leistungsfähigkeit der objektorientierten verhaltensbasierten Navigation wurde am Beispiel der auftragsbezogenen Navigation in hindernisfreien Wegenetzen eines nicht besonders präparierten Gebäudes nachgewiesen. Hierfür wurde die objektorientierte verhaltensbasierte Navigation auf dem mobilen Roboter *ATHENE II* implementiert. Dabei konnte *ATHENE II* nicht nur solche Aufträge, die in allen Einzelheiten als Abfolgen von Verhaltensmustern spezifiziert waren, abarbeiten, sondern auch selbständig (d.h., ohne zusätzliche Information vom Benutzer) namentlich vorgegebene Zielorte anfahren.

Der objektorientierte verhaltensbasierte Ansatz läßt sich übrigens nicht nur für die Navigation eines Fahrzeugs, sondern auch für die Steuerung eines Manipulatorarms einsetzen. Wie in [Graefe, Ta 1995] gezeigt, gelingt dabei aufgrund einer Lernfähigkeit des Systems das sichtgesteuerte Greifen auch ohne Kalibrierung der Gesamtanordnung. Es ist beabsichtigt, hierauf aufbauend und auf der Grundlage des hier vorgestellten Konzepts einen intelligenten mobilen Roboter in Form eines fahrenden Manipulators zu realisieren. Dieser soll einerseits (nahezu) keine Eichung seiner optischen und mechanischen Teilsysteme benötigen und andererseits Wissen über die Gegebenheiten der Einsatzumgebung und über die Erscheinungsbilder von zu manipulierenden Objekten durch Lernen erwerben können.

Literatur

Brockhaus 1989: Der Große Brockhaus, Bd. 10, Wiesbaden.

Efenberger, W. (1996): Zur Objekterkennung für Fahrzeuge durch Echtzeit-Rechnersehen. Dissertation, Fakultät für Luft- und Raumfahrttechnik der Universität der Bundeswehr München.

Graefe, V. (1989): Dynamic Vision Systems for Autonomous Mobile Robots. Proc. IEEE/RSJ International. Workshop on Intelligent Robots and Systems IROS '89. pp 12-23.

Graefe, V. (1990): An Approach to Obstacle Recognition for Autonomous Mobile Robots. IEEE/RSJ International. Workshop on Intelligent Robots and Systems IROS '90. Tsuchiura, pp 151-158.

Graefe, V. (1991): Robot Vision Based on Coarsely-grained Multi-processor Systems. In Vichnevetzky; Miller (eds.): Proc. IMACS World Congress. Dublin, pp 755-756.

Graefe, V. (1992a): Vision for Autonomous Mobile Robots. Proc. IEEE Workshop on Advanced Motion Control. Nagoya, pp 57-64.

Graefe, V. (1992b): Visual Recognition of Traffic Situations by a Robot Car Driver. Proc. 25th ISATA; Conference. on Mechatronics. Florence, pp 439-446.

Graefe, V.; Regensburger, U.; Solder, U. (1988): Visuelle Entdeckung und Vermessung von Objekten in der Bahn eines autonom mobilen Systems. In H. Bunke et al. (Eds.): Mustererkennung 1988. Informatik-Fachberichte 180, Springer, pp 312-318.

Graefe, V.; Wershofen, K. P. (1991): Robot Navigation and Environmental Modelling. International. Advanced Robotics Programme – Proc. of the Second Workshop on Multi-Sensor Fusion and Environmental Modelling, Oxford.

Graefe, V.; Ta, Q. (1995): An Approach to Self-learning Manipulator Control Based on Vision. IMEKO International Symposium on Measurement and Control in Robotics, ISMCR '95. Smolenice, pp 409-414.

Kuhnert, K.-D. (1990): Fusing Dynamic Vision and Landmark Navigation for Autonomous Driving. Proc. of IEEE Workshop on Intelligent Robots and Systems IROS '90. pp 113-119.

Kuhnert, K.-D.; Wershofen K.P. (1990): Echtzeit-Rechnersehen auf der Experimental-Plattform ATHENE. Fachgespräch Autonome Mobile Systeme. Karlsruhe, pp 59-68.

Meyer (1977): Meyers Enzyklopädisches Lexikon, Bd. 21, Mannheim.

Thorpe, C.; Gowdy, J. (1990): Annotated Maps for Autonomous Land Vehicles. In Masaki, I. (ed.): Proc. of IEEE Round table Discussion on Vision-based Vehicle Guidance, pp 4.1-4.7.

Wershofen, K. P. (1996): Zur Navigation sehender mobiler Roboter in Wegenetzen von Gebäuden – Ein objektorientierter verhaltensbasierter Ansatz. Dissertation, Fakultät für Luft- und Raumfahrttechnik der Universität der Bundeswehr München.

Wershofen, K. P.; Graefe, V. (1993): Ein sehender mobiler Roboter als Experimentierplattform zur Erforschung des maschinellen Lernens. In Schmidt, G. (ed.): Autonome Mobile Systeme – Methoden, Technologien, Anwendungen – 9. Fachgespräch. München, pp 115-126.

Exploration und Navigation mit hierarchischen Neuronalen Netzen

Michael Pauly

Lehrstuhl für Technische Informatik, RWTH Aachen
Ahornstr. 55, D-52074 Aachen
email: pauly@techinfo.rwth-aachen.de

Zusammenfassung Serviceroboter halten immer mehr Einzug in Bereiche des Dienstleistungssektors. Dabei werden diese Roboter oft mit neuen, sich ändernden Einsatzumgebungen konfrontiert. In diesem Beitrag wird ein Verfahren zur Exploration und Navigation eines teil- oder vollautonomen Roboters in bekannten und unbekannten Umgebungen vorgestellt, welches auf in zwei Schichten hierarchisch angeordneten Neuronalen Netzen basiert. In der oberen Schicht befindet sich ein Neuronales Netz zur Situationsanalyse. Die in der unteren Schicht verwendeten Neuronalen Netze sind auf einzelne Teilaufgaben spezialisiert. Dadurch können diese Teilbereiche getrennt voneinander entwickelt, getestet und modifiziert werden.

1 Einleitung

Neben klassischen Verfahren werden heute auch Methoden der Fuzzy-Logic, z.B. [8], und Neuronalen Netze [9], [10], [11] erfolgreich bei der Navigation und Exploration von Umgebungen eingesetzt.

Ein Nachteil all dieser Methoden ist, daß bei der Neuerstellung oder einer Änderung immer die Wechselwirkungen im gesamten System betrachtet werden müssen. Von Vorteil wäre ein modularer Aufbau, der die Möglichkeit bietet, die für die einzelnen Aufgaben notwendigen Module getrennt voneinander erstellen und testen zu können.

Hierarchische Neuronale Netze bieten diese Möglichkeit. Jedes der einzelnen Teilnetze kann unabhängig von den anderen erstellt, trainiert, modifiziert und getestet werden. Ferner besteht bei dem hier verwendeten verhaltensorientierten Ansatz [2] die Möglichkeit, für jedes Grundverhalten eine unterschiedliche auf das spezielle Problem abgestimmte Netzarchitektur zu wählen. Dadurch kann das gesamte System leicht modifiziert oder für neue Aufgaben erweitert werden.

Am Lehrstuhl für Technische Informatik der RWTH Aachen wurde die Navigation des Serviceroboter systems TAURO (<u>T</u>eil<u>AU</u>tonomes <u>RO</u>botersystem) [6] mit Hilfe von hierarchischen Neuronalen Netzen, basierend auf diesem Ansatz, realisiert. Dabei setzt sich die komplexe Navigationsaufgabe aus mehreren einfachen Verhaltensmustern (Basisverhalten) zusammen.

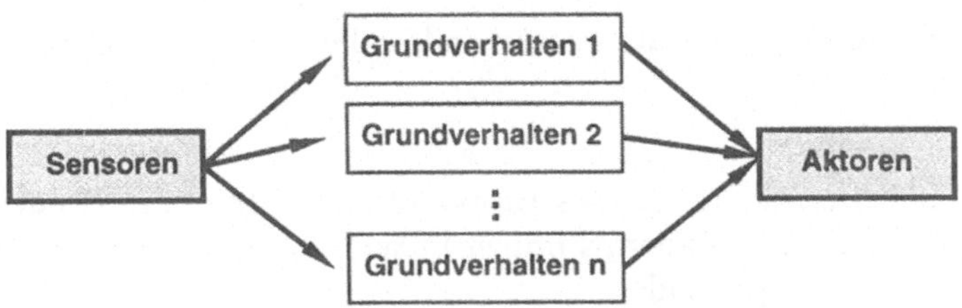

Abbildung 1: Verhaltensorientierte Kontrollstruktur mit n parallel agierenden Basisverhalten

1.1 TAURO

TAURO wurde als kooperatives System entwickelt mit der Aufgabe, Gebäudeinnenräume, wie z.B. Museen oder Lagerhallen zu überwachen [7]. Dazu erfolgte die Aufteilung in einen Leitstand, in dem alle rechen- und speicherplatzintensiven Operationen durchgeführt werden, sowie eine oder mehrere mobile Plattformen, die die zur Navigation und Erfüllung der Überwachungsaufgabe notwendige Software 'onboard' besitzen. Eine sechsrädrige 30 x 40 cm große mobile Plattform dient als Testbed für die bei TAURO entwickelten Algorithmen.

Als Sensoren stehen für die Navigation Ultraschall- sowie Infrarotsensoren zur Verfügung. Erfaßt wird die weitere Umgebung des Fahrzeugs mit Ultraschall mit zwei unterschiedlichen Meßmethoden. Einerseits steht eine Entfernungsmessung für die direkte Fahrzeugumgebung (bis 50 cm) zur exakten Navigation um Hindernisse oder durch enge Passagen, mit einer Genauigkeit von 2 mm, zur Verfügung. Andererseits wird für größere Entfernungen bis 10 m eine Entfernungsmessung, mit einer Genauigkeit von 15 mm benutzt. Im Nahbereich bis 20 mm werden Infrarotsensoren verwendet, die ggf. eine Notabschaltung vornehmen können.

1.2 Verhaltensorientierte Navigation

Die bei der Navigation zu erfüllende Aufgabe setzt sich aus mehreren Grundverhalten (Basisverhalten), wie z.B. Kollisionsvermeidung, Wandfolgen oder Freiraumsuche, zusammen (Abb. 1), die jeweils die aktuell anliegenden Sensordaten direkt verarbeiten und in Steuerbefehle für die Motoren (Aktoren) umsetzen.

Die einzelnen Basisverhalten verfolgen zum Teil entgegengesetzte Ziele. So wird in dem Verhalten 'Wandfolgen' versucht, kollisionsfrei entlang einer Objektkontur zu navigieren. Im Gegensatz dazu versucht das Verhalten 'Freiraumsuche', freie Gebiete aufzuklären. Erst das Zusammenspiel aller Basisverhalten ergibt die für die Navigation notwendige komplexe Verhaltensstruktur. Folgende fünf Basisverhalten erwiesen sich als ausreichend [5]:

Kollisionsvermeidung Bei der Kollisionsvermeidung wird versucht, im Sensorbereich auftretende Hindernisse berührungsfrei zu umfahren. Dabei ist es egal, ob es sich bei den Objekten um feststehende oder bewegliche Hindernisse handelt.

Wandfolgen links/rechts Dieses Basisverhalten folgt einer Hinderniskontur (Wand) so, daß sich das Hindernis immer links bzw. rechts in einem konstanten Abstand vom Fahrzeug befindet.

Freiraumsuche Bei der Freiraumsuche wird ein möglichst großer Abstand zu allen im Sensorbereich befindlichen Hindernissen gehalten. Dieses Verhalten wird benötigt, um bei der Exploration einzeln im Raum stehende Objekte zu finden.

Zielsuche Hierbei fährt das Fahrzeug direkt auf einen vorgegebenen Zielpunkt zu und versucht, diesen auf geradem Wege zu erreichen. Gleichzeitig werden, wie bei der Kollisionsvermeidung, vor dem Fahrzeug auftretende Hindernisse umfahren.

Sackgassenbefreiung Befindet sich der Roboter in einer Ecke oder einer Sackgasse, so dreht sich der Roboter mit Hilfe dieses Basisverhaltens um die Hochachse, wenn dies möglich ist, bis die Fahrt weiter durchgeführt werden kann.

2 Hierarchische Neuronale Netze

Der Aufbau des verwendeten hierarchischen Neuronalen Netzes gliedert sich in zwei Ebenen. In der oberen Ebene analysiert ein Kontrollnetzwerk die jeweils vorliegende Situation und steuert die Teilnetze in der darunterliegenden Ebene entsprechend an (Abb. 2).

Bei dieser Art der hierarchischen Trennung benötigt das Kontrollnetzwerk keine Information darüber, wie die einzelnen Basisverhalten funktionieren und wie diese realisiert sind.

2.1 Kontrollnetzwerk

Im Kontrollnetzwerk sind zwei grundlegende Strategien realisiert: die direkte Navigation zu einem Zielpunkt und die Exploration der Umgebung. In Standardsituationen versucht der Roboter, den vorgegebenen Zielpunkt auf direktem Weg zu erreichen. Treten dabei Hindernisse auf, so werden diese umfahren. Eine Exploration der Umgebung wird dann gestartet, wenn TAURO auf unerwartet viele unbekannte Objekte stößt oder in einer unbekannten Umgebung neu startet.

Das Kontrollnetzwerk ordnet die Eingangsdaten fünf unterschiedlichen Situationsklassen zu. Nach dieser Situationsanalyse werden die jeweiligen Grundverhalten ausgewählt.

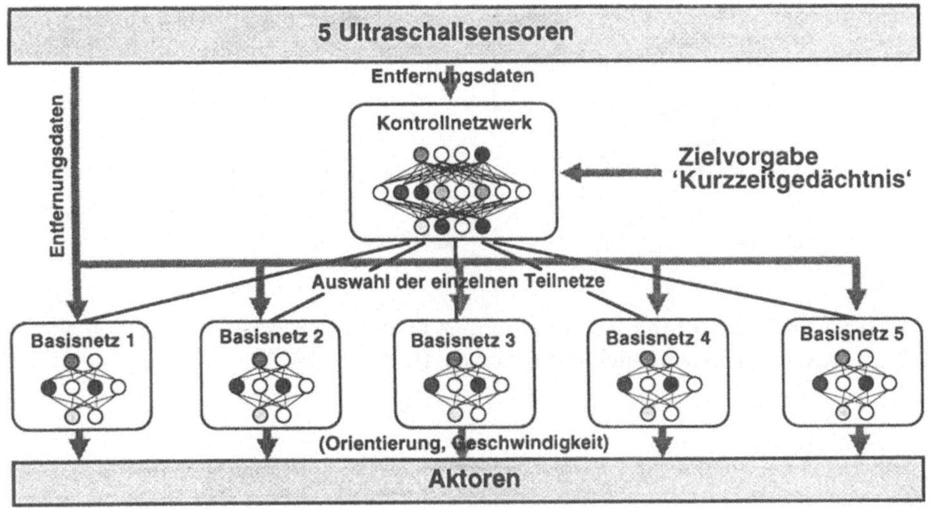

Abbildung 2: Aufbau eines hierarchischen Neuronalen Netzes bestehend aus einem Kontrollnetzwerk und 5 Basisnetzen

Als Kontrollnetzwerk wird ein Backpropagation Netzwerk mit folgenden Eingangsdaten verwendet: den Entfernungsdaten der Sensoren, dem Fahrzeugstatus und einem 'Kurzzeitgedächtnis'. Dieses 'Kurzzeitgedächtnis' beinhaltet Informationen über die aktuell ausgewählten Grundverhalten sowie Informationen über die Positionen, in denen sich das Fahrzeug bei einem Wechsel der Basisverhalten befand. Die Ausgangsdaten sind die Aktivierungen für die fünf Basisnetzwerke.

2.2 Basisnetzwerke

Die einzelnen Grundverhalten sind jeweils in getrennten Backpropagation-Netzwerken realisiert. Diese wurden separat entwickelt, trainiert (überwachtes Lernen) und in unterschiedlichen Umgebungen getestet. Die Daten für das Training der Netze wurden aus mehreren manuell gesteuerten Testfahrten generiert.

Nachdem das Kontrollnetzwerk ein Grundverhalten ausgewählt hat, werden in einem ersten Schritt die von den Ultraschallsensoren ermittelten Entfernungsdaten normiert und als Eingangsdaten auf die Teilnetze gegeben. Nach der Berechnung liefert das Neuronale Netz die notwendige Richtungs- und Geschwindigkeitsänderung.

3 Exploration

Die Exploration startet, wenn sich das System in einer vollständig oder teilweise unbekannten Umgebung befindet, oder wenn größere Veränderungen aufgetreten

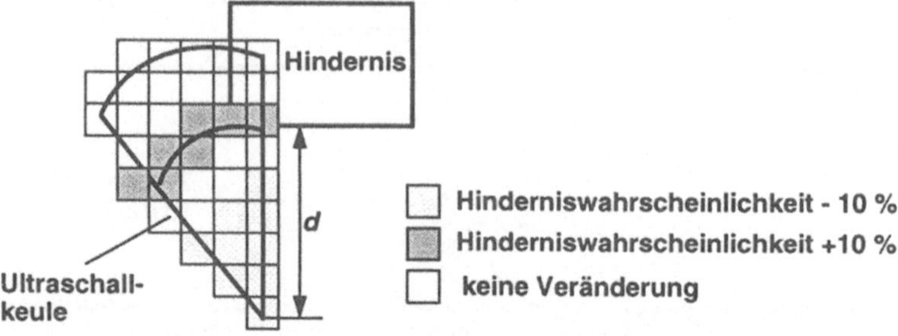

Abbildung 3: Änderung der Eintragung in der Wahrscheinlichkeitskarte aufgrund eines im Sensorbereich detektierten Hindernisses.

sind. Um die Einsatzumgebung zu speichern wird eine rasterorientierte Karte verwendet, in der die einzelnen Wahrscheinlichkeiten eingetragen werden, mit denen sich ein Hindernis an der jeweiligen Stelle befindet [3]. Bei der Neuerkundung einer vollständig unbekannten Umgebung legt TAURO eine neue Karte an, wogegen sonst die bereits vorhandenen Karten erweitert bzw. korrigiert werden.

Abbildung 3 zeigt die Auswertung des Sensorsignals. Wird in der Entfernung d ein Hindernis detektiert, so werden die entsprechenden Koordinaten als belegt gekennzeichnet. Da nicht genau ermittelt werden kann, an welchem Punkt der Ultraschallkeule sich das Hindernis befindet, wird der gesamte Kreisbogen bei dieser Entfernung als Hindernis gekennzeichnet. Die Hindernis-Wahrscheinlichkeit wird dort um den Wert 10 % erhöht. Über den Bereich hinter dem Hindernis kann keine Aussage gemacht werden; dieser Bereich bleibt deshalb unverändert. Da der Sektor vor dem Hindernis frei sein muß, wird seine Wahrscheinlichkeit um den Wert 10 % verringert. Die Felder des Bogens unmittelbar vor dem Hindernis bleiben unverändert [5].

Die Exploration einer unbekannten Umgebung startet damit, daß der Roboter solange fährt bis der erste Sensorkontakt mit einem Objekt auftritt. Daraufhin folgt der Roboter der Objektkontur, um die Ausdehnung des Hindernisses zu erfassen. Ist ein Objekt vollständig erfaßt, so wechselt das Kontrollnetzwerk zu dem Basisverhalten 'Freiraumsuche' und sucht neue unbekannte Objekte (siehe Abb. 4).

Abgebrochen wird die Exploration dann, wenn entweder die Umgebung hinreichend genau erfaßt wurde oder, wenn vom Kontrollnetz Aufgaben mit einer höheren Priorität zugewiesen wurden. Die so gewonnene Repräsentation der Umgebung (Abb. 5) kann im folgenden für die durchzuführende Navigation und Wegplanung verwendet werden. Bereiche, die z.B. aus Zeitgründen, nicht erkundet werden konnten, werden als frei von Hindernissen gekennzeichnet, damit diese für eine spätere Wegplanung zur Verfügung stehen.

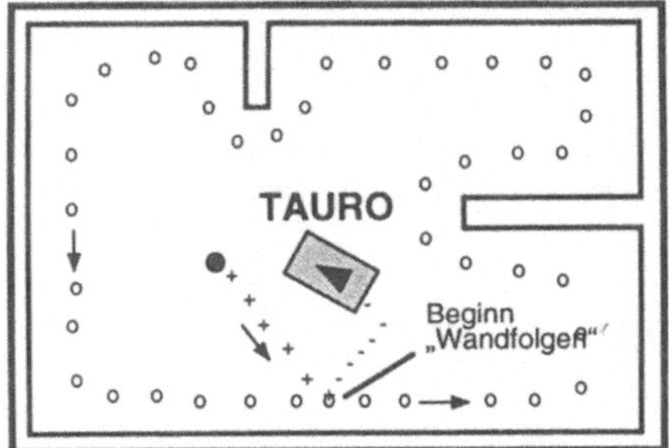

Abbildung 4: Beispiel für die Exploration einer unbekannten Umgebung. Zuerst fährt der Roboter geradeaus (+). Nachdem er ein Objekt erreicht hat, schaltet das Kontrollnetzwerk auf 'Wandfolgen' (o). Nach einem Umlauf, d.h. nach Erreichen des Startpunktes von 'Wandfolgen' beginnt das System mit der Freiraumsuche (-).

4 Navigation

Dem Erreichen eines vorgegebenen Zielpunktes dient eine Punkt-zu-Punkt Navigation. Dabei wird die zu fahrende Trajektorie entweder von einem übergeordneten Wegplanungsmodul ermittelt oder mit Hilfe der bei der Exploration erstellten Karte berechnet. Auf der Zieltrajektorie werden in einem vorgegebenen Abstand Wegpunkte ermittelt, die der Roboter dann der Reihe nach gesteuert von dem hierarchischen Neuronalen Netz anfährt.

Die interne Repräsentation der Umgebung bildet die während der Exploration ermittelte Wahrscheinlichkeitskarte. Diese wird zur Berechnung des Zielpfades in eine Neuronale Karte, basierend auf einem topologisch angelegten zweidimensionalen Hopfield-Netzwerk mit zeitkontinuierlichen Neuronen [4], umgerechnet.

Das Netzwerk besteht aus N identischen Neuronen, die in einem zweidimensionalen Gitter angeordnet gedacht sind. Jedes Neuron ist mit seinen nächsten 8 Nachbarn symmetrisch durch verstärkende Gewichte T_{ij} verbunden und besitzt den Aktivierungszustand σ_i, mit $i = 1..N$ und $\sigma_i \in [0,1]$. Die Zustandsvariablen σ_i ändern sich durch Eingangswerte von verbundenen Neuronen. Der gesamte Eingangswert u_i des Neurons i besteht aus der gewichteten Summe der Aktivitäten seiner benachbarten Neuronen und eines externen Eingangs I:

$$u_i = \sum_{j}^{N} T_{ij}\sigma_j(t) + I_i \tag{1}$$

Für die Gewichte T_{ij} gilt:

$$T_{ij} = \begin{cases} 1 & \text{für} \quad \rho(i,j) < r \\ 0 & \text{sonst} \end{cases} \tag{2}$$

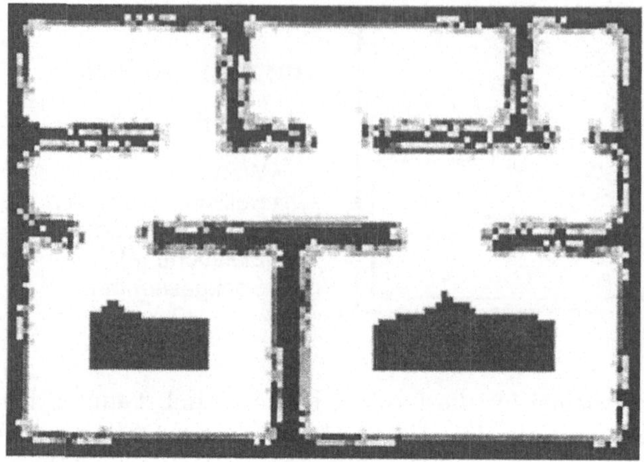

Abbildung 5: Nach einer Erkundungsfahrt ermittelte Verteilung der Hinderniswahrscheinlichkeiten (weiß: kein Hindernis, schwarz: Hindernis)

Hierbei ist r eine positive Zahl und $\rho(i, j)$ der euklidische Abstand zwischen den Neuronen i und j. Im zeitdiskreten Fall berechnet sich die Aktivierung der Neuronen durch

$$\sigma_i(t+1) = g\left(\sum_j^N T_{ij}\sigma_j(t) + I_i\right) \tag{3}$$

wobei $g(x)$ eine Sigmoidfunktion ist.

Die Neuronale Karte ist so dimensioniert, daß deren Größe mit der der Wahrscheinlichkeitskarte übereinstimmt, ein Neuron also einem Rasterfeld in der Wahrscheinlichkeitskarte entspricht [5]. Zum Zeitpunkt $t = 0$ werden alle Aktivierungen auf Null gesetzt. Neuronen, die in der korrespondierenden Karte Hindernissen entsprechen, werden auf den Wert Null fixiert, das Neuron, welches den Zielpunkt repräsentiert, auf den Wert Eins.

Die Aktivierung breitet sich vom Zielpunkt ausgehend über alle Neuronen der Karte aus, die kein Hindernis darstellen. Diese Berechnung der Neuronenzustände wird solange fortgeführt, bis die Aktivierungsfront den Startpunkt des Roboters erreicht hat, oder bis keine Änderungen mehr auftreten (Equilibrium). Die Berechnung kann im ersteren Falle bereits abgebrochen werden, weil sich der Verlauf der Aktivierungsausbreitung nicht mehr ändert, sondern nur deren Niveau.

Die Berechnung des Zielpfades geschieht, indem ausgehend vom Startpunkt des Roboters immer auf das benachbarte Feld mit der höchsten Aktivierung übergegangen wird, solange bis der Zielpunkt erreicht ist (Abb. 6).

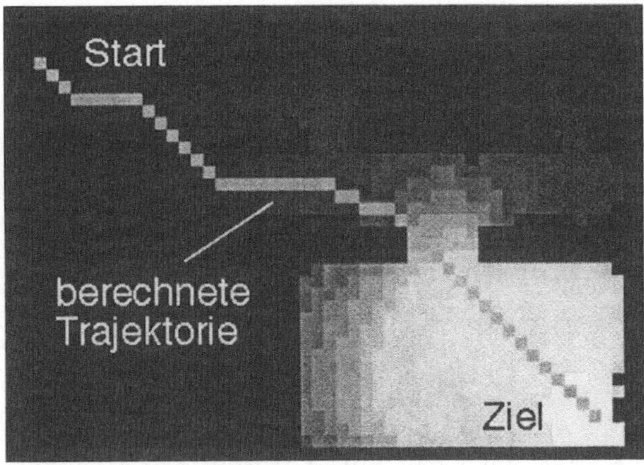

Abbildung 6: Verlauf der Aktivierung in der Neuronalen Karte mit eingezeichnetem Zielpfad

5 Ergebnisse

Jedes der einzelnen Basisverhalten zeigte nach einem angemessenen Training ein gutes und robustes Verhalten. Neben den verwendeten Backpropagation-Netzwerken wurden auch Elman-, Jordan- und Time-Delay Netzwerke getestet. Diese erwiesen sich jedoch als weniger geeignet für die hier durchzuführenden Navigationsaufgaben [5].

Die einzelnen Module der Basisverhalten ließen sich leicht modifizieren und erweitern. Desweiteren war eine gleichzeitige Entwicklung mehrerer Basisverhalten möglich.

Getestet wurde die Exploration mit 25 unterschiedlichen simulierten Testumgebungen in denen sich geometrisch einfache Objekte befinden. Die Umgebungen sind dabei in zwei Kategorien aufgeteilt. Zum einen in Umgebungen, die lediglich aus einem einzigen Raum bestehen, in dem sich eine unterschiedliche Anzahl von Objekten befindet (10 Räume). Zum anderen standen Umgebungen mit einer unterschiedlichen Raumanordnung und Raumstruktur zur Verfügung (5 Umgebungen mit Labyrinthstruktur, 10 Umgebungen mit unterschiedlicher Anordnung von Räumen). Dabei wurde die durchzuführende Erkundungsfahrt nach einer vorher festgelegten Zeit abgebrochen. Die Ergebnisse der Testläufe zeigen, daß fast alle Objekte während der vorgegebenen Zeit gefunden und kartographiert wurden (90 - 95 %).

In einem zweiten Versuch wurden unterschiedliche Raumstrukturen (Labyrinth, diverse Büroumgebungen) erkundet. Steht ausreichend Zeit für die Erkundung zur Verfügung, so werden auch diese Umgebungen nahezu vollständig erfaßt.

Auf Basis der ermittelten Wahrscheinlichkeitskarten wurden jeweils mehre-

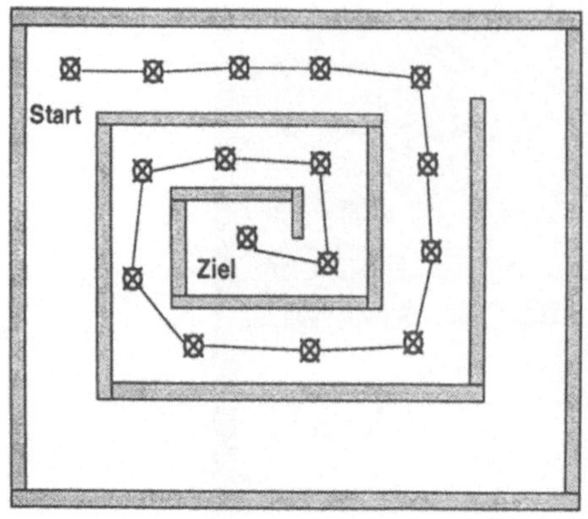 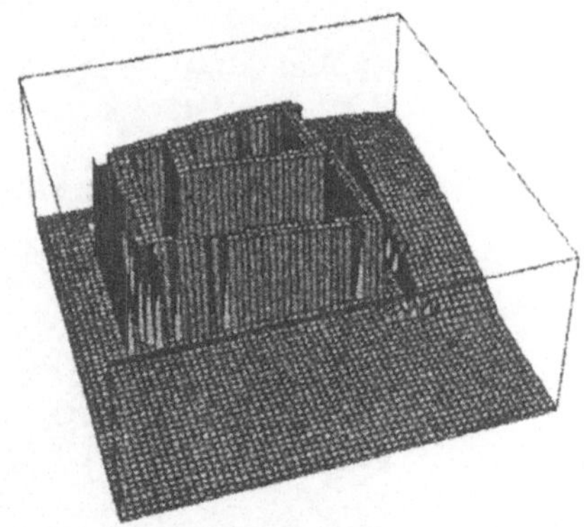

Abbildung 7: Beispiel für einen mit Hilfe der Neuronalen Karte berechneten Zielpfad, bestehend aus Zielpunkten.

Abbildung 8: Dreidimensionale logarithmische Darstellung der Neuronalen Karte von Abb. 7.

re Routenplanungen durchgeführt. Dabei wird die Berechnung der Neuronalen Karte abgebrochen, sobald die Aktivierungsfront den Roboter erreicht hat, d.h. sobald die Aktivierung des Feldes der Neuronalen Karte, auf dem sich der Roboter befindet, größer als Null wird. Ist das Ziel nicht erreichbar, so kann die Aktivierung den Roboter auch nicht erreichen. In diesem Fall wird die Berechnung nach Erreichen des Equilibriums abgebrochen. Aufgrund der Liapunov-Funktion kann nachgewiesen werden, daß ein solches existiert [4].

Existieren mehrere Zielpfade, so wird aufgrund der schnelleren Ausbreitung der Aktivierung immer der kürzere gewählt, selbst wenn dieser bedeutend schmaler ist [5]. Das unterscheidet diese Methode u.a. von der Potentialfeldmethode [1], bei der der Zwischenraum zwischen nahestehenden Hindernissen ein höheres abstoßendes Potential aufweist als der zwischen weit auseinanderliegenden, was darin resultiert, daß in obigem Beispiel der längere Weg bevorzugt würde.

Wird die Berechnung des Zielpfades nicht bei Erreichen der ersten Aktivierung abgebrochen, so kann sich bei mehreren möglichen Zielpfaden die Aktivierung durch gegenseitige Verstärkung der Neuronen so erhöhen, daß nicht der kürzeste Weg gewählt wird, sondern ein anderer, breiterer.

6 Zusammenfassung und Ausblick

In diesem Bericht wurde ein Navigations- und Explorationsverfahren vorgestellt, welches auf hierarchisch angeordenten Neuronalen Netzen basiert. Dazu wurden zwei Hierarchiestufen verwendet. In der oberen Schicht analysiert ein Kontrollnetzwerk die aktuelle Situation und wählt eines der sich in der unteren Schicht befindenen Netze aus. Diese sind vorab auf ein vorgegebenes Verhaltensmuster (Basisverhalten) trainiert.

Die vorgestellte Exploration kartographiert selbständig unbekannte Umgebungen. Die dabei ermittelten Informationen über die Umgebung werden in einer gerasterten Wahrscheinlichkeitskarte abgelegt, die als Grundlage für die bei der Navigation benötigten Routenplanung dient. Berechnet wird die benötigte Trajektorie zum gewünschten Zielpunkt mit Hilfe eines zweidimensionalen Hopfield-Netzwerkes.

References

[1] Borenstein J., Koren Y.: Real-time Obstacle Avoidance for Fast Mobile Robots. IEEE Transactions on Systems, Man, and Cybernetics, Vol. 19, No. 5, pp. 1179-1187 (1989)

[2] Brooks R.A.: A Robust Layered Control System for a Mobile Robot. IEEE Journal of Robotics and Automation, Vol. 2, No. 1, pp. 14-23 (1986)

[3] Elfes A.: Sonar-Based Real-World Mapping and Navigation. IEEE Transactions on Robotics and Automation, Vol. 3, No. 3, pp. 249-265 (1987)

[4] Glasius R., Komoda A., Gielen S.: Neural networks dynamics for path planning and obstacle avoidance. Neural Networks, Vol. 8, No. 1, pp. 125-133 (1995)

[5] Hansen O.: Echtzeitnavigation eines Roboterfahrzeuges mit dynamischen Neuronalen Netzen. Diplomarbeit, Lehrstuhl für Technische Informatik, RWTH Aachen (1995)

[6] Pauly M.: TAURO - Teilautonomer Serviceroboter für Überwachungsaufgaben. In: Dillmann R., Rembold U., Lüth T. (Hrsg.): 11. Fachgespräch Autonome Mobile Systeme 1995, Springer Verlag, Berlin, Heidelberg, pp. 30-39 (1995)

[7] Pauly M., Kraiss K.-F.: A Concept for Symbolic Interaction with Semi-Autonomous Mobile Systems. 6th IFAC/IFIP/IFORS/IEA Symposium on Analysis, Design and Evaluation of Man-Machine Systems, Boston, USA (1995)

[8] Saffiotti A., Ruspini E.H., Konolige K.: A Fuzzy Controller for Flakey, an Autonomous Mobile Robot. Technical Report, SRI Artificial Intelligence Center, Menlo Park, California (1993)

[9] Thrun S.B., Möller K.: Active Exploration in Dynamic Environments. In: Moody J.E., Hanson S.J., Lippmann R.P. (Hrsg.): Advances in Neural Information Processing Systems 4, Morgan Kaufmann, California (1992)

[10] Vestli S.J., Tschichold-Gürman N., Andersson H.: Learning control and localisation of mobile robots. In: Levi P., Bräunl Th. (Hrsg.): 10. Fachgespräch Autonome Mobile Systeme 1994, Springer Verlag, Berlin, Heidelberg, pp. 201-213 (1994)

[11] Yamauchi B.: Dynamical neural networks for mobile robot control. NRL Memorandum Report AIC-033-93, Naval Research Laboratory, Washington, DC (1993)

LAURON II – Simulation und Realisierung einer sechsbeinigen Laufmaschine

Stefan Cordes[1] und Peter Bührle[2]

[1] Interaktive Planungstechnik, Forschungszentrum Informatik,
Haid–und–Neu–Straße 10–14, 76131 Karlsruhe, email: cordes@fzi.de
[2] Institut für Technische Mechanik, Universität Karlsruhe,
Kaiserstraße 12, 76128 Karlsruhe, email: buehrle@itm.uni-karlsruhe.de

Zusammenfassung Im folgenden Artikel wird die Realisierung einer sechsbeinigen Laufmaschine präsentiert. Die Entwicklung wurde unter Zuhilfenahme einer Dynamiksimulation durchgeführt. Um die Funktionsfähigkeit eines solch komplexen Systems zu garantieren, muß die Eignung der Einzelkomponenten (Abmessungen, Antriebe, Getriebe, Steuerungsalgorithmus) noch vor der Gesamtkonstruktion geprüft werden. Aus diesem Grund wurde die Laufmaschine als Vielkörpersystem modelliert und simuliert, wodurch insbesondere die Dynamik der Antriebseinheiten berücksichtigt werden konnte. Durch die optimierte Auslegung der Mechanik und Antriebe sowie der verbesserten Steuerungshardware konnte die Leistungsfähigkeit des Roboters im Vergleich zum Vorgänger erheblich gesteigert werden.

1 Einführung

Im Gegensatz zu radgetriebenen, mobilen Systemen begann die ernsthafte Entwicklung von Laufmaschinen erst vor ungefähr 30 Jahren, obwohl Laufmaschinen im Vergleich zu radgetriebenen Systemen auf unebenem und unstrukturiertem Gelände erheblich mobiler sind. Sie können in Gebieten operieren, in denen ein äußerstes Maß an Beweglichkeit gefordert wird. Darüberhinaus besteht ein wichtiger ökologischer Vorteil, der nur durch Fortbewegung auf Beinen ermöglicht wird: Laufmaschinen hinterlassen keine kontinuierliche Zerstörungsspur auf dem Untergrund, sondern nur einzelne Fußabdrücke. Aus diesen Eigenschaften ergeben sich die speziellen Anwendungsbereiche von Laufmaschinen, zum Beispiel als Telemanipulator oder mobile Trägerplattform für Analysesysteme.

Laufmaschinen sind ein Paradebeispiel für komplexe Syteme. Neben den anwendungsorientierten Aspekten stellt ihre Steuerung eine besondere Herausforderung dar. Ein System mit veränderlicher Topologie und einer großen Anzahl von Freiheitsgraden muß in teilweise unbekannter Umgebung unter Echtzeit-Bedingungen gesteuert werden.

Abhängig von der gewählten Gangart können Laufmaschinen mit vielen Beinen entweder gute statische Stabilität oder hohe Geschwindigkeiten erreichen. Allerdings erhöht jeder zusätzliche Freiheitsgrad die Anforderungen an die Steuerung der Maschine. Unter den Laufmaschinen mit einer unterschiedlichen Anzahl von Beinen haben sich sechsbeinige Laufmaschinen als guter Kompromiß herausgestellt, daneben besitzen sie natürliche Vorbilder (Brooks, 1989, Hartikainen et al., 1992, Krotkov et al., 1991, Pfeiffer et al., 1993, Raibert et al., 1989).

Abbildung 1. Der Vorgänger: Die Laufmaschine LAURON I

Die sechsbeinige Laufmaschine LAURON I (**Laufender Ro**boter **N**euronal gesteuert) wurde 1993 am Forschungszentrum Informatik (FZI) der Universität Karlsruhe entwickelt (Cordes, 1995). LAURON I (Abb. 1) wird nun im Deutschen Museum für Wissenschaftsgeschichte in Bonn ausgestellt. Die Entwicklung des Nachfolgers LAURON II begann Ende 1994 in einer interdisziplinären Zusammenarbeit zwischen dem Forschungszentrum Informatik und dem Institut für Technische Mechanik der Universität Karlsruhe. Konzeption und Design von LAURON II berücksichtigen sowohl die Schwachstellen von LAURON I als auch die Ergebnisse der Dynamiksimulation.

2   Dynamische Beschreibung des Systems

Die Bewegungsgleichungen eines Vielkörpersystems bestehend aus starren Körpern und idealen Gelenken können nach (Wittenburg, 1977) computergestützt generiert werden. Für den Fall eines baumstrukturierten Systems mit f Freiheitsgraden liefert das Prinzip der virtuellen Leistung die Bewegungsgleichungen

$$\underline{A}(\underline{q},t)\underline{\ddot{q}} = \underline{B}(\underline{q},\underline{\dot{q}},\underline{k}_A,t) \tag{1}$$

mit der $(f,1)$ Matrix $\underline{q}$ der verallgemeinerten Koordinaten, die symmetrische (f,f) Massen-Matrix $\underline{A}$ und der $(f,1)$ Matrix $\underline{B}$, die alle übrigen Kräfte und Momente, insbesondere die Kräfte und Momente $\underline{k}_A$ der p Aktuatoren, beinhaltet. Die Stellwirkungen der Aktuatoren werden durch innere, masselose Kraft-

und Momentelemente übertragen, die jeweils zwischen zwei Körpern wirken. Dadurch kann auch die Dynamik des Antriebssystems berücksichtigt werden. Eine Transformation von (1) in den Zustandsraum mit der Einführung von $2f$ Zustandsvariablen $\underline{y}_{MKS}$ ergibt

$$\underline{\dot{y}}_{MKS} = \underline{F}(\underline{y}_{MKS}, \underline{k}_A, t). \tag{2}$$

Sei $f_{A,i}$ die Anzahl der Zustandsvariablen eines Aktuators i $(1 \leq i \leq p)$, dann stellt

$$f_A = \sum_{i=1}^{p} f_{A,i}$$

die Gesamtanzahl aller Zustandsvariablen der Aktuatoren dar. Die Wirkungen der Aktuatoren $\underline{k}_A$ können in Abhängigkeit von f_A Zustandsvariablen des Antriebssystems $\underline{y}_{AS}$ und der kinematischen Kopplungsterme $\underline{g}$ geschrieben werden

$$\underline{k}_A = \underline{k}_A(\underline{y}_{AS}, \underline{g}, t), \tag{3}$$

in denen $\underline{g}$ als eine Funktion der Zustandsvariablen $\underline{y}_{MKS}$ des Vielkörpersystems ausgedrückt werden kann:

$$\underline{g} = \underline{g}(\underline{y}_{MKS}). \tag{4}$$

Die Gleichungen, die die Dynamik des Antriebssystems beschreiben, können in folgender Weise geschrieben werden:

$$\underline{\dot{y}}_{AS} = \underline{G}(\underline{y}_{AS}, \underline{g}, \underline{u}, t) \tag{5}$$

wobei $\underline{u}$ die $(p, 1)$ Matrix der Stelleingriffsgrößen darstellt, zum Beispiel die Spannung an einem Gleichstrommotor. Werden die Gleichungen (3) und (4) in die Gleichungen (2) und (5) eingesetzt, dann erhält man das gekoppelte System von Differentialgleichungen (Bührle, 1994)

$$\underline{\dot{y}}_{ALL} = \begin{pmatrix} \underline{\dot{y}}_{MKS} \\ \underline{\dot{y}}_{AS} \end{pmatrix} = \begin{pmatrix} \underline{F}(\underline{y}_{MKS}, \underline{y}_{AS}, t) \\ \underline{G}(\underline{y}_{MKS}, \underline{y}_{AS}, \underline{u}, t) \end{pmatrix} \tag{6}$$

für die $(2f + f_A)$ unabhängigen Zustandsvariablen $\underline{y}_{ALL}$.

3 Modellierung

Um das dynamische Verhalten der sechsbeinigen Laufmaschine LAURON II zu simulieren und und die korrekte Auslegung der verwendeten Antriebe zu überprüfen, muß sowohl das mechanische System, als auch das Antriebssystem modelliert werden. Die Modelle hierfür werden in den beiden nächsten Abschnitten vorgestellt.

3.1 Mechanisches System

Die Laufmaschine besteht aus $n = 19$ Starrkörpern und $m = 19$ idealisierten Gelenken. Ihre Struktur und Geometrie ist in Abb. 2 dargestellt. Jedes Bein i ist am Hauptkörper mit einem Drehgelenk (α_i) unter einem Winkel von $\psi = 30°$ gegenüber der xy-Ebene des Körperkoordinatensystems verbunden. Die vorderen und hinteren Beine sind zusätzlich noch um $\varphi = 30°$ nach vorne bzw. hinten gedreht. Die Position und die Orientierung des Hauptkörpers kann durch drei translatorische (x, y, z) und drei rotatorische Freiheitsgrade (Bryant-Winkel ϕ_1, ϕ_2, ϕ_3) beschrieben werden. Ein Bein besteht aus drei Segmenten, die durch zwei achsenparallele Drehgelenke (β_i und γ_i) verbunden sind. Insgesamt besitzt die Laufmaschine $f = 24$ mechanische Freiheitsgrade, die in der Matrix $\underline{q}$ der verallgemeinerten Koordinaten zusammengefaßt werden:

$$\underline{q}^T = (\phi_1, \phi_2, \phi_3, \alpha_1, \ldots, \alpha_6, \beta_1, \ldots, \beta_6, \gamma_1, \ldots, \gamma_6, x, y, z). \tag{7}$$

In diesem Ansatz wird der Bodenkontakt nicht als kinematische Bedingung betrachtet. Bei einem Bodenkontakt von Bein i wirken horizontal und vertikal ausgerichtete Federn und Dämpfer auf die Fußspitze.

Die Elemente der $(6, 6)$ Feder- und Dämpfermatrizen $\underline{C}$ und $\underline{K}$ können nichtlinear sein und führen zu folgender Gleichung.

$$\underline{F}_G = \underline{C}(\underline{r}_F) \cdot (\underline{r}_F - \underline{r}_G) + \underline{K}(\underline{r}_F) \cdot \dot{\underline{r}}_F \tag{8}$$

$\underline{r}_F$ beschreibt die Position der Fußspitze und $\underline{r}_G$ die Position des Bodenkontakts. Diese Methode hat den Vorteil, daß nur ein Satz von Gleichungen für alle Phasen der Laufbewegung notwendig ist. Es befinden sich keine geschlossenen kinematischen Schleifen im System, wodurch die Anzahl der Freiheitsgrade konstant bleibt.

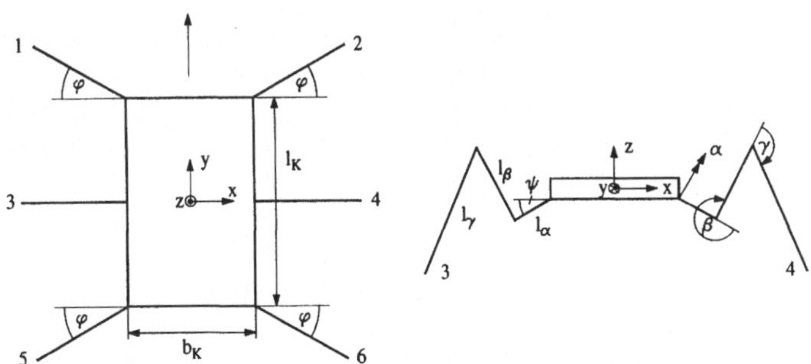

Abbildung 2. Struktur und Geometrie der Laufmaschine

Die Modellierung des Bodenkontakts als kinematische Randbedingung hat mehrere Nachteile. Mit jedem Wechsel eines Bodenkontakts ändert sich die Anzahl der Freiheitsgrade. Bei einer sechsbeinigen Laufmaschine existieren insgesamt $2^6 = 64$ Möglichkeiten für die Beine, einen Bodenkontakt zu besitzen oder nicht. Es müßten also für alle 64 Möglichkeiten unterschiedliche Differentialgleichungssysteme aufgestellt werden. Darüberhinaus besteht keine Möglichkeit, das Rutschen eines Fußes zu simulieren.

Mit der gewählten Methode kann jedes Kraftgesetz untersucht werden, insbesondere auch Rutschen oder ein Reibungsmodell. Eine kleine Einschränkung wird allerdings an die Steifigkeit der Federn gestellt: sie dürfen nicht unendlich steif sein, da dies zu numerischen Instabilitäten während der Integration führt. Ein fester Boden kann also nicht simuliert werden. Dies ist jedoch für die Dynamiksimulation ohne Bedeutung, denn auch in der realen Welt existiert kein unendlich fester Untergrund. Eine Restelastizität bleibt immer vorhanden.

Als externe Kräfte wirken die 19 Gewichtskräfte $\boldsymbol{F}_{Wi}$ und die Reaktionskräfte $\boldsymbol{F}_{Gj}$ des Bodens, wenn Bein j Bodenkontakt hat. Das Antriebssystem wird durch 18 innere Momentelemente berücksichtigt.

Die Bewegungsgleichungen für das mechanische System (1) werden durch das Programm für Vielkörpersysteme (Wittenburg und Wolz, 1985) bereitgestellt.

3.2 Antriebssystem

Die Laufmaschine besitzt $p = 18$ Antriebe, die mit permanenterregten Gleichstrommotoren realisiert wurden. Werden die Kirchhoff'schen Maschengesetze und das Induktionsgesetz (Fischer, 1988) angewendet, dann ergeben sich Differentialgleichungen der $(18,1)$ Matrix $\underline{I}_R$ der Motorströme zu:

$$\frac{d\underline{I}_R}{dt} = \text{diag}(\underline{L}_R)^{-1}\left[\underline{U}_R - \text{diag}(\underline{R}_R)\underline{I}_R - \text{diag}(\underline{k}_M)\text{diag}(\underline{i}_G)\underline{\dot{q}}_D\right] \qquad (9)$$

Mit den folgenden $(18,1)$ Matrizen: Induktivität $\underline{L}_R$, Motor-Spannung $\underline{U}_R$, Spulenwiderstand $\underline{R}_R$, Motorkonstante $\underline{k}_M$ und Getriebeuntersetzung $\underline{i}_G$. Die $(18,1)$ Winkelgeschwindigkeiten $\underline{\dot{q}}_D$ korrespondieren mit den verallgemeinerten Koordinaten der angetriebenen Gelenke. Für den Fall $\underline{y}_{DS} = \underline{I}_R$ entspricht die Gleichung (9) der Gleichung (6b). Mit der $(18,1)$ Matrix $\underline{M}_M$ der Motor-Drehmomente ergibt sich zu

$$\underline{M}_M = \text{diag}(\underline{k}_M)\underline{I}_R - \underline{M}_R(\underline{\dot{q}}_D) \qquad (10)$$

mit der $(18,1)$ Matrix der Reibdrehmomente $\underline{M}_R$, wobei sowohl die Coulombsche als auch viskose Reibung berücksichtigt wird. Die $(18,1)$ Matrix $\underline{M}_D$ der Drehmomente der Getriebeausgänge, kann mit der $(18,1)$ Matrix $\underline{\eta}_G$ der Getriebewirkungsgrade zu

$$\underline{M}_D = \text{diag}(\underline{i}_G)\text{diag}(\underline{\eta}_G)\underline{M}_M. \qquad (11)$$

angegeben werden. Die verwendeten Getriebe werden im nächsten Abschnitt beschrieben. Insgesamt wird die Dynamik des Gesamtsystems durch 66 gekoppelte Differentialgleichungen erster Ordnung beschrieben.

4 Gang-Generierung

Um die gewünschte Bewegung der Laufmaschine zu erreichen, müssen die Sollwerte für die Gelenke bestimmt werden. Diese Winkel sind die Eingaben für die PID-Regler der Gelenke. Es wurde ein Computerprogramm entwickelt, um diese Werte für einige periodische Gangarten berechnen zu können, wie z.B. der *pentapod wave gait* oder der *tripod equal phase gait* (Song und Waldron, 1989).

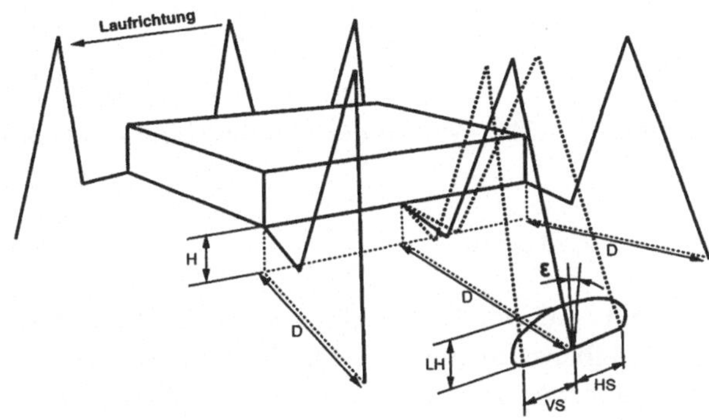

Abbildung 3. Trajektorie eines Fußpunktes

Für eine bestimmte Bewegungsart (Geradeauslaufen, Drehen auf der Stelle, Seitwärtslaufen) ist die Trajektorie $r_{Fi}(t)$ jedes einzelnen Fußpunktes entsprechend geometrischer Werte vorgegeben (siehe Abb. 3). Hat der Fußpunkt keinen Bodenkontakt (Schwingphase), so wird angenommen, daß die Trajektorie eine Zykloide ist, deren Fläche in einem Winkel ε gegen die Vertikale geneigt ist.

Diese Art der Trajektorie hat gute kinematische Eigenschaften für die Beinbewegung. Insbesondere die zum Boden relative Fußpunktgeschwindigkeit kurz vor dem Aufsetzen kann so minimiert werden. Alternativ kann der Fußpunktvektor auch in verallgemeinerten Koordinaten angegeben werden. Über die inverse Kinematik können dann die gesuchten Gelenkwinkel bestimmt werden.

5 Realisierung von LAURON II

Ausgehend von den Erfahrungen, die mit der Laufmaschine LAURON I gemacht wurden, konnte die neue Laufmaschine LAURON II (Abb. 4 und 5) weiterentwickelt werden. Mechanik, Antriebssystem, Sensorik und Steuerung sind optimiert worden. Im Gegensatz zur alten Laufmaschine kann jetzt eine onboard-Energieversorgung mitgeführt werden, um ein autonomes Arbeiten des Roboters zu ermöglichen. Die konkrete Umsetzung wird im folgenen Abschnitt beschrieben.

Abbildung 4. CAD–Modell der Laufmaschine LAURON II

5.1 Mechanik und Antriebe

Einer der Hauptaspekte bei der Entwicklung einer Laufmaschine ist die Anforderung nach einem möglichst geringen Eigengewicht. Aus diesem Grund und der leichten Bearbeitbarkeit wegen wurde fast ausschließlich Aluminium als Werkstoff verwendet.

Hauptkörper LAURON II besteht aus einem Hauptkörper und sechs Beinen, die bis auf Symmetrien identisch sind. Der Hauptkörper dient als Träger für die mitgeführte Rechnerhardware. Der Hauptkörper dient auch als Träger für die Erweiterungen der Laufmaschine um eine Stereokamera, Sprach-Ein/Ausgabe, ein drahtloses Kommunikationssystem sowie eine integrierte Energieversorgung.

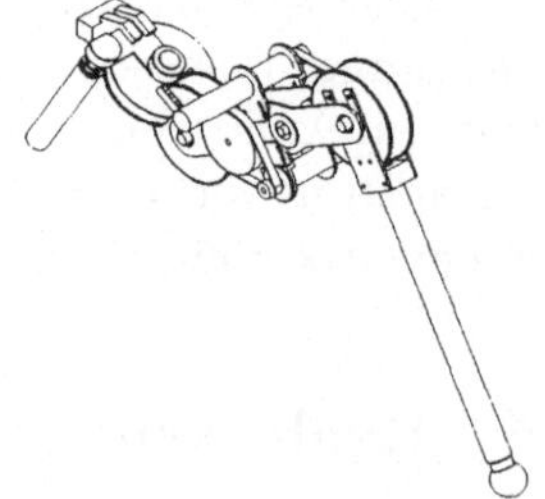

	Abmessungen	Arbeitsbereich	Masse
Körper	$\ell_K = 440$ $b_K = 240$		$m_M = 4500$
Bein	$\ell_\alpha = 66$ $\ell_\beta = 200$ $\ell_\gamma = 300$	$-40° \leq \alpha \leq 40°$ $-97° \leq \beta \leq 108°$ $-143° \leq \gamma \leq 143°$	$m_L = 1900$
Gesamt			$m_T = 15900$

Tabelle 1. Konstruktionsdaten von LAURON II und CAD-Modell eines Einzelbeins

Beine Jedes Einzelbein besteht aus drei Segmenten, die durch zwei Drehgelenke (β– und γ–Gelenk) verbunden sind. Die Beine wiederum sind durch ein weiteres Drehgelenk (α–Gelenk) am Hauptkörper befestigt. Die hohe Mobilität der Beine erlaubt das Laufen sogar in Rückenlage.

Jedes der 18 Gelenke wird von einem 12V Gleichstrommotor (Faulhaber 2342–012CR, $R_R = 2.1\,\Omega, \mathrm{L}_R = 2.5 \cdot 10^{-5}\,\mathrm{H}$, $k_M = 13.95 \cdot 10^{-3}\,\mathrm{Nm/A}$) mit unterschiedlichen Untersetzungsgetrieben in Serie angetrieben. Für die Beine und die Befestigung wurde eine Modulstruktur geschaffen, damit der Zusammenbau und das Zerlegen leicht durchführbar sind.

α–**Gelenk** Die Drehmomentübertragung wird durch zwei aufeinanderfolgende Getriebe vorgenommen. Beim ersten handelt es sich um ein Planetengetriebe (Untersetzungsverhältnis $i = 66 : 1$), das an den Motor angeflanscht ist. Das zweite ist ein Seilzug mit einer Untersetzung von $i = 100 : 8$. Der Motor sowie die Getriebe sind am Hauptkörper montiert.

β–**Gelenk** Die Kraftübertragung wird durch drei Getriebe unterschiedlichen Typs vorgenommen. Auch hier ist das erste wieder ein Planetengetriebe ($i = 43 : 1$). Beim zweiten handelt es sich um ein Zahnriemengetriebe ($i = 72 : 14$). Das letzte ist wiederum ein Seilzug mit $i = 100 : 8$ wie im α–Gelenk. Alle Getriebe und der Motor sind auf dem β-Segment installiert, da dies aufgrund der Gewichtsverteilung zu einer geringeren Belastung der Motoren führt.

γ–**Gelenk** Bis auf einen Unterschied gleicht der γ–Antrieb dem β– Antrieb, und zwar ist das Übertragungsverhältnis des Planentengetriebes $i = 14 : 1$.

Massen und Abmessungen In Tabelle 1 sind die Abmessungen (in mm), Arbeitsbereiche und Massen (in g) der einzelnen Komponenten von LAURON II zusammengefaßt.

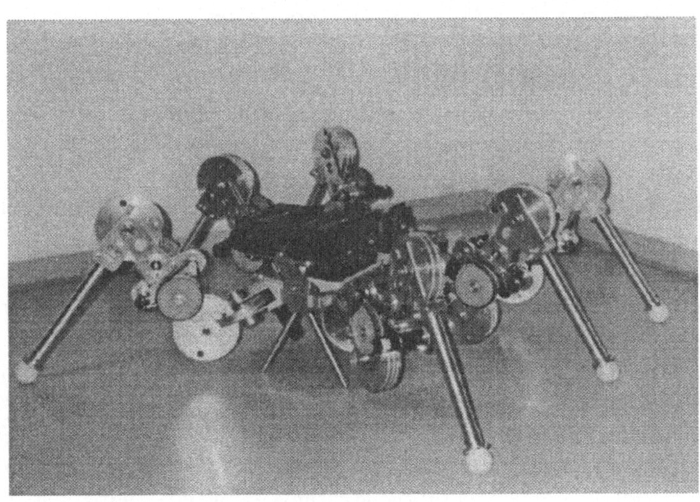

Abbildung 5. LAURON II

6 Die Hardwarearchitektur

Die Hardwarearchitektur für LAURON II ist hierarchisch aufgebaut und beschreibt die Laufmaschine auf verschiedenen Abstraktionsebenen. Die höchste Abstraktionsebene beschreibt den mobilen Roboter als ein System, das in der Lage ist, komplexe Aufgabenstellungen in unbekannter Umgebung zu lösen. Die nächste Stufe stellt den Roboter als ein System dar, daß aus höheren Kontrollsystemen und dem Antriebssystem besteht. Die unterste Abstraktionsebene im Bereich Antriebssysteme beschreibt intelligente Antriebe. In Abb. 6 ist die Hardwarearchitektur der Laufmaschine dargestellt.

Der hierarchische und modulare Aufbau stellt die Mittel bereit, die für die Handhabung eines komplexen Systems wie LAURON II notwendig sind. Einzelne Komponenten können Schritt für Schritt implementiert und in Betrieb genommen werden, Wartung und Fehlersuche vereinfachen sich. Einzelne funktionale Einheiten können unabhängig voneinander realisiert und parallel in Hardware implementiert werden. Der modulare Ansatz erlaubt den einfachen Austausch von Steuerungskomponenten, etwa um eine leistungsfähigere Hardware zu benutzen. Neue Komponenten können über die Kommunikationsverbindungen hinzugefügt werden, ohne daß die Hardwarestruktur des Systems geändert werden muß.

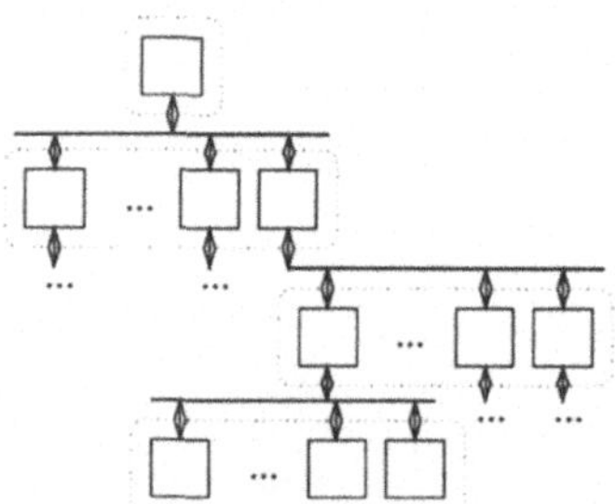

Abbildung 6. Hierarchisch organisierte Module bilden die Hardwarearchitektur

Durch die Verwendung von frei programmierbaren Controller-Boards bei der Implementierung der Hardwarearchitektur können leicht verschiedene Kontrollstrategien verwendet werden. Es ist möglich eine voll zentralisierte Kontrollarchitektur zu schaffen, wenn alle Module zu reinen Datentransmittern gemacht werden. In diesem Fall werden alle Berechnungen auf der höchsten Ebene ausgeführt. Auf der anderen Seite kann ein gegensätzlicher Ansatz gewählt werden, indem eine dezentralisierte Steuerungsstrategie verwendet wird. Die Module der unterschiedlichen Ebenen in der Hierarchie müssen miteinander kooperieren, um ein Problem zu lösen. Eine dritte Möglichkeit der Implementierung einer Steuerung liegt in der dynamischen Kombination der beiden genannten Varianten, was zu adaptiven Steuerungsmechanismen führt.

6.1   Gelenk-Ebene

Die kleinste funktionale Einheit stellt ein Gelenk dar. Die Aufgabe ist es, den aktuellen Drehwinkel des Gelenkes zu bestimmen und den Motor für dieses Gelenk zu regeln. Aufgrund der speziellen Sensorauswertung besitzten die Drehwinkelgeber ein zyklisch absolutes Verhalten bei einer Auflösung von ca. 14 Bit. Die Motortreiber sind um SMD-MOSFETS aufgebaut. Sie eignen sich bei 20KHz Schaltfrequenz und 10Bit Auflösung sehr gut für die Motoransteuerung. Es kann sowohl eine Spannungsregelung und eine Stromregelung des Motors durchgeführt werden.

Ebenfalls in die Gelenk-Ebene ist der Fußsensor integriert. Mit ihm werden die auftretenden Bodenkontaktkräfte (Richtung und Quantität) bestimmt. Wie der Drehwinkelgeber ist auch der Fußsensor über an den CAN-Bus eines Beines angeschlossen.

6.2   Bein-Ebene

Die nächste funktionale Einheit ist ein Bein, es umfaßt drei Gelenke pro Bein und den Fuß (Abb. 7). Die Hardware der Beinsteuerung ist um ein scheckkartengroßes (85mmx55mm) Mikrocontrollermodul der Firma Phytec (Phytec, 1995) aufgebaut. Der eingesetzte C-167 Mikrocontroller bietet eine große Anzahl von Schnittstellen und eine Rechenleistung von etwa 10 MIPS. Die Beinsteuerung beinhaltet die gesamte Hardware für Sensorinterfaces und Kommunikationsverbindungen. Sie ist im Hauptkörper der Laufmaschine montiert.

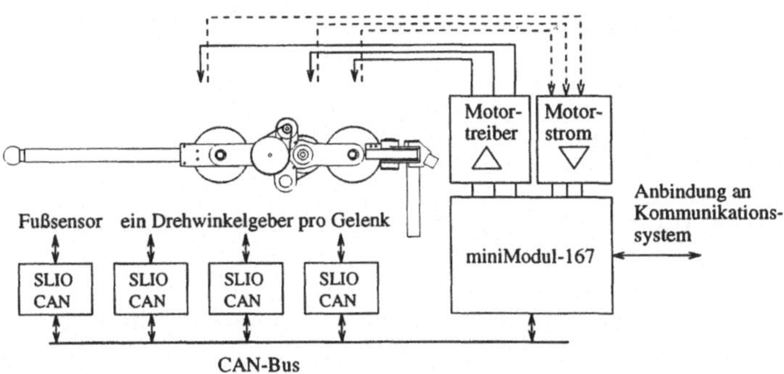

Abbildung 7. Ein Bein-Subsystem von LAURON II beinhaltet eine Verarbeitungseinheit und ein lokales Kommunikationssystem, den Bein-Bus

Die Aufgaben des Mikrocontrollers teilen sich in zwei Bereiche auf: zum einen ist es die Informationsverarbeitung für ein Bein, wozu die Kommunikation über den CAN-Bus gehört, an den die Drehwinkelgeber angeschlossen sind,

die Spannungs- oder Stromregelung der Motoren und die Auswertung der Fuß-
sensordaten. Zum anderen werden Dienste für die übergeordneten Ebenen bereitgestellt, die es erlauben, ein Bein als unabhängige Einheit zu betrachten.
Diese beinhalten die Verwaltung der Kommunikation mit dem übergeordneten
Körperrechner.

6.3 Körper-Ebene

Die zur Zeit höchste Ebene ist mit auf Körperrechner realisiert. Er ist für die
Körperbewegung verantwortlich und führt die Körpersteuerung aus. Die Steuerung beinhaltet die Beinkoordination für verschiedene Gangarten, Lageregelung
des Körpers und Überwachung der Beine.

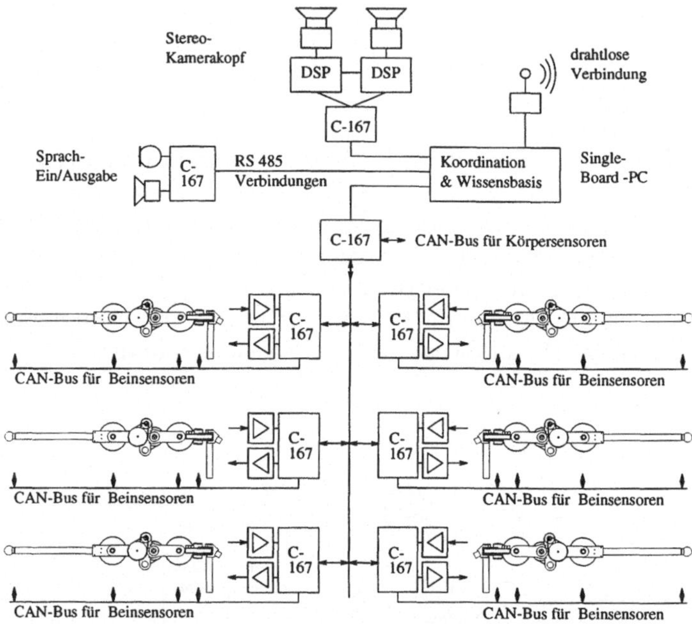

Abbildung 8. Die vollständige Architektur von LAURON II

Die Informationen, die für die Regelung von Körperlage und -geschwindigkeit
benötigt werden, werden aus den aktuellen Gelenkwinkeln oder den Werten der
Körpersensoren bestimmt. Die Körpersensoren bestehen aus zwei Neigungssen-
soren und zwei Gyroskopen.

6.4 Komplexe Teilsysteme

Auf der Ebene der komplexen Teilsysteme ist ein einfaches Sprach-Ein/Ausgabe-
system und ein Stereo-Sichtsystem geplant. Um den Datenstrom zu reduzieren,
werden lokale Rechner eingesetzt.

6.5 Mobiler Roboter

Auf der obersten Ebene wird das Gesamtsystem gesteuert. Diese Ebene soll mit einem Single-Board-PC realisiert werden und koordiniert die untergeordneten Ebenen. Eine drahtlose Kommunikationsverbindung wird verwendet, um Kommandos an die Laufmaschine oder Statusinformationen von der Laufmaschine zu übertragen. Innerhalb dieser obersten Ebene werden Weltmodelle verwaltet, mit der die Steuerung der Laufmaschine an die aktuelle Situation angepaßt wird. Abb. 8 zeigt den detaillierten Gesamtaufbau des Systems.

7 Simulationsergebnisse

Im folgenden werden nun einige Ergebnisse der Dynamiksimulation für die Laufmaschine LAURON II dargestellt. Bis jetzt sind noch keine Vergleiche mit Messungen an der realen Maschine möglich.

Für den Tripod-Wellengang (jeweils 3 Beine wechseln sich am Boden oder in der Schwingphase ab) ist folgender Bewegungsablauf vorgegeben: zwei Schritte geradeaus, zwei Schritte zum Drehen des Hauptkörpers um die Vertikalachse und zwei Seitwärtsschritte.

Die Abb. 9(a)–10(a) zeigen die aktuellen Werte der α–, β– und γ–Koordinaten für Bein 2 und Bein 4. Diese beiden Beine gehören unterschiedlichen Gruppen an, sodaß ihre Bewegungsphasen zeitlich versetzt sind. Die Koordinatenwerte entsprechen den Sollwerten aus der inversen Kinematik.

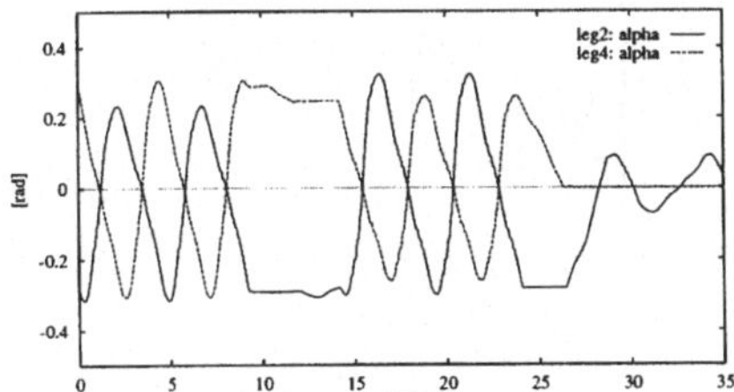
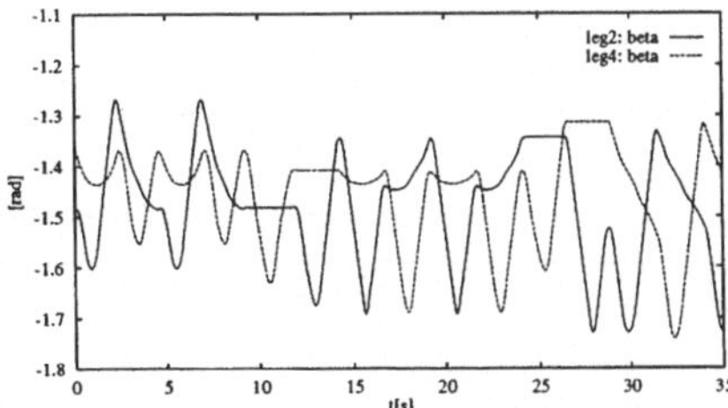

Abbildung 9. Simulationsergebnisse für den Tripod-Gang (Beine 2 und 4). Links: (a) α–Gelenk. Rechts: (b) β–Gelenk.

In Abb. 10(b) sind die Motorströme I_R des Gleichstrommotors im β–Gelenk der Beine 2 und 4 dargestellt. Dies ist das am stärksten belastete Gelenk. Die Werte für Bein 4 liegen hier höher als die für Bein 2, da Bein 4 sich in der Schwingphase alleine halten muß, während Bein 2 und Bein 6 sich diese Phase auf der rechten Seite teilen. Der thermisch zulässige Dauerstrom des verwendeten Motors liegt bei $I_{RM} = 1.4\,$A. In der Simulation wird dieser Wert nicht erreicht,

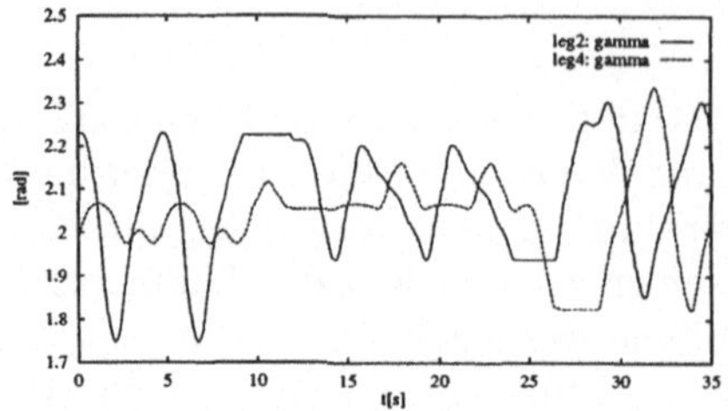 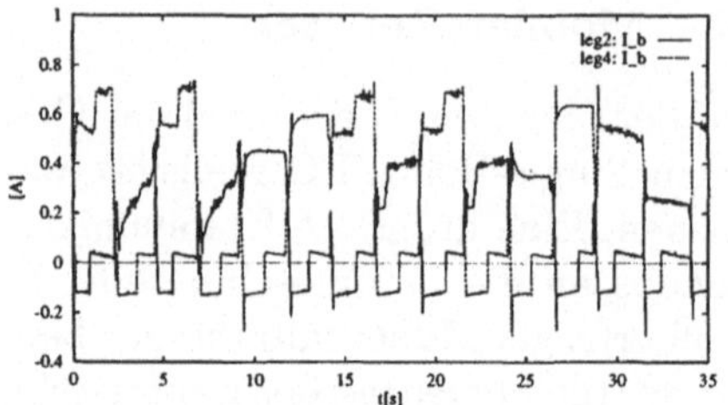

Abbildung 10. Simulationsergebnisse für den Tripod-Gang (Beine 2 und 4). Links: (a) γ–Gelenk. Rechts: (b) Motorstrom I_R im β–Gelenk.

es stehen also noch genügend Reserven zur Verfügung. Die Ergebnisse der α–, β– und γ–Koordinaten des Beines 4 für einen Tetrapod-Wellengang sind in Abb. 11(a) dargestellt. Hier erkennt man den periodischen Verlauf für das reine Geradeauslaufen. Zu jedem Zeitpunkt befinden sich zwei Beine auf jeder Seite des Roboters in der Schwingphase. Deshalb ist die Belastung des β–Gelenkes bei allen Beinen etwa gleich groß. Dies wird durch Abb. 11(b) bestätigt. Hier sind die Simulationsergebnisse für die Drehmomente M_D an den Getriebeabgangswellen des β–Gelenkes (Beine 2 und 4) dargestellt.

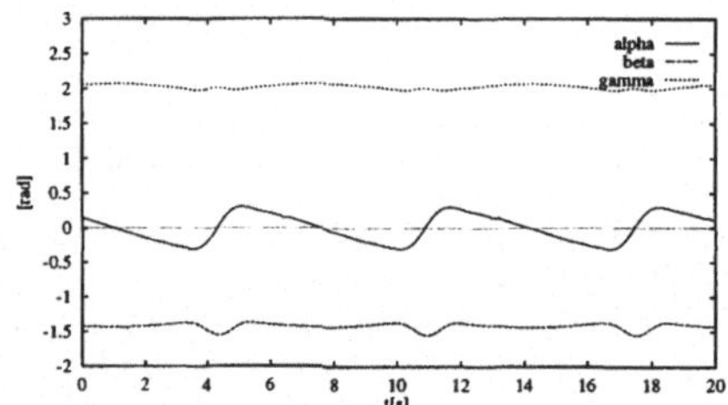 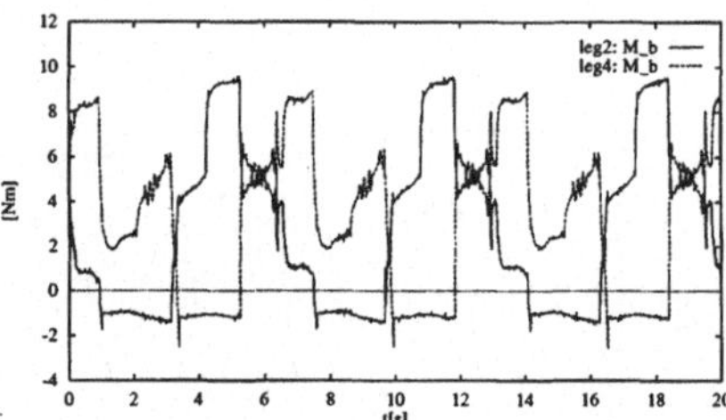

Abbildung 11. Simulationsergebnisse für den Tetrapod-Wellengang. Links: (a) α–, β– und γ–Winkel. Rechts: (b) Drehmoment M_D im β–Gelenk (Beine 2 und 4)

8 Zusammenfassung

In dieser Arbeit wurde die Dynamiksimulation und die Realisierung einer sechsbeinigen Laufmaschine vorgestellt. Dazu wurde der Roboter zunächst als Mehrkörpersystem modelliert. Es wurden Simulationen für den Roboter durchgeführt, wobei die dynamischen Eigenschaften der Antriebe berücksichtigt wurden. Die Simulationen führten zu Ergebnissen, nach denen die mechanische Struktur und die Antriebe für den realen Roboter ausgewählt wurden.

Der Aufbau der realisierten Laufmaschine wurde vorgestellt, einschließlich der verwendeten Antriebselemente, Getriebe, Sensoren und der Steuerungsarchitektur. In Zukunft sollen Messungen an LAURON II durchgeführt werden und mit den Ergebnissen der Simulation verglichen werden, um die Durchführbarkeit der beschriebenen Methode zu bestätigen. Erste experimentelle Untersuchungen am Einzelbein haben gezeigt, daß die Leistungsfähigkeit gegenüber LAURON I erheblich gesteigert werden konnte.

Literaturverzeichnis

[Brooks, R. A., 1989], "A Robot that Walks; Emergent Behaviors from a Carefully Evolved Network", *Neural Computation*, 1:2, pp. 365–382.

[Bührle, P., 1994], "Simulation geregelter Mehrkörpersysteme unter Berücksichtigung der Eigendynamik der Antriebselemente", *Zeitschrift für angewandte Mathematik und Mechanik*, Vol. 74(4), pp. T104–T106.

[Cordes, S., 1995], "A Flexible Hardware Architecture for the Adaptive Control of Mobile Robots", *Proceedings of the 3rd International Symposium on Intelligent Robotic Systems*, Pisa, Italy, pp. 75–82.

[Fischer, R., 1992], "*Elektrische Maschinen*", Hanser–Verlag, München–Wien.

[Hartikainen K. et al., 1992], "Control and Software Structures of a Hydraulic Six-Legged Machine Designed for Locomotion in Natural Environment", *Proceedings of the 1992 IEEE/RSJ International Conference on Intelligent Robots and Systems*, Raleigh, pp. 590–596.

[Krotkov E. et al., 1991], "Ambler: A Six–Legged Planetary Rover", *ICAR 91*, pp. 717–722.

[Pfeiffer, F., Eltze, J., Weidemann, H.–J., 1993], "The TUM–Walking Machine", *Intelligent Automation and Softcomputing, Trends in Research, Development and Applications*, TSI Press, Albuquerque, New Mexico, USA.

[Phytec, 1995], "*miniMODUL-167 Data Sheet*", Phytec GmbH, Mainz, Germany.

[Raibert, M. et al., 1989], "Dynamically stable Legged Locomotion", *MIT Artificial Intelligence Laboratory, Technical Report 1179, LL-6*.

[Song, S.–M., Waldron, K. J., 1989], "*Machines that Walk: The Adaptive Suspension Vehicle*", MIT Press, Cambridge–London.

[Wittenburg, J., 1977], "*Dynamics of Systems of Rigid Bodies*", B.G. Teubner, Stuttgart.

[Wittenburg, J., Wolz, U., 1985], "MESA VERDE — Ein Computerprogramm zur Simulation der nichtlinearen Dynamik von Vielkörpersystemen", *Robotersysteme 1*, Springer–Verlag, Berlin, pp. 7–18.

Sichere Handhabung mit 3D-Simulation und videobasierter Sensorik

Stefan Blessing, Doris Kugelmann, Gunther Reinhart

Technische Universität München
Institut für Werkzeugmaschinen und Betriebswissenschaften
Prof. Dr.-Ing. G. Reinhart, Prof. Dr.-Ing. J. Milberg
Karl-Hammerschmidt-Straße 39, D-85609 Aschheim
e-mail: {bl,kl}@iwb.mw.tu-muenchen.de

Kurzfassung. Am Institut für Werkzeugmaschinen und Betriebswissenschaften (iwb) der Technischen Universität München wurde ein autonomer mobiler Roboter aufgebaut, der selbständig Handhabungsaufgaben ausführt. Durch den zusätzlichen Einsatz eines Bildverarbeitungs- und eines 3D-Bewegungssimulationssystems kann er auch zur Handhabung ungeordneter Teile oder zum Entfernen falsch plazierter Objekte eingesetzt werden. Zur Bestimmung der Position der zu greifenden Objekte wird mit der CCD-Kamera im Handflansch des Roboters ein Bild aufgenommen, anhand dessen ein 3D-Objekterkennungssystem die exakte Position des Objekts bestimmt. In einer Produktionsumgebung wird der videobasierte Erkennungsprozeß jedoch häufig durch verschiedene Umgebungseinflüsse, z. B. ungünstige Lichtverhältnisse, gestört. Um dennoch eine hohe Sicherheit bei der Objekterkennung und damit die Verfügbarkeit des Handhabungssystems insgesamt zu gewährleisten, wurde eine Störungsbehandlungseinheit in das Objekterkennungssystem integriert. Die Detektion und Identifikation der Störungen ermöglicht ein situationsangepaßtes Handeln zur Behebung der Störung. Mit den von der störungstoleranten Objekterkennung bestimmten Objektkoordinaten wird das Umgebungsmodell des am iwb entwickelten 3D-Bewegungssimulationssystems USIS (Universal Simulation System) aktualisiert, das dann als Grundlage für die automatische Generierung eines Handhabungsprogramms für den Roboter genutzt wird. Komplexe Handhabungsaufgaben, z. B. bei übereinander liegenden Objekten, erfordern eine intelligente Planung des Handhabungsprozesses unter optimaler Nutzung der zur Verfügung stehenden Ressourcen, die vom Simulationssystem USIS durchgeführt wird.

1 Einleitung

Die Komponenten einer automatisierten Produktion, d. h. Maschinen, Fahrzeuge und Handhabungseinheiten, müssen eine hohe Zuverlässigkeit und Verfügbarkeit aufweisen, um einen wirtschaftlichen Betrieb der gesamten Produktion zu ermöglichen. Können auftretende Störungen im Ablauf, z. B. durch falsch plazierte oder fehlende Rohteile, von den Komponenten nicht selbständig behoben werden, kann die Hilfe eines autonomen mobilen Systems in Anspruch genommen werden [1].

Zur Handhabung von Objekten, wie Roh- oder Fertigteilen und kleineren Betriebsmitteln, wird im allgemeinen ein Steuerungsprogramm benötigt. Für bereits im Vorfeld geplante Handhabungsaufgaben sind derartige Programme vorhanden. Tritt jedoch eine Störung auf, die u.a. durch falsch plazierte Teile verursacht werden kann, so ist in der Regel kein geeignetes Roboterprogramm vorhanden. D. h. mit den vorhandenen Programmen ist aufgrund der veränderten Objektpositionen nicht gewährleistet, daß das zu handhabende Objekt korrekt gegriffen wird und Kollisionen mit anderen Objekten vermieden werden.

Der autonome mobile Roboter des iwb verfügt deshalb über eine Sensoreinheit zur Bestimmung der Position der zu handhabenden Objekte sowie ein 3D-Bewegungssimulationssystem [9] zur Generierung eines kollisionsfreien Handhabungsprogramms (s. Abb. 1). Diese Komponenten werden von dem Führungsrechner [7], einer intelligenten Steuerung, koordiniert. In den folgenden Abschnitten werden Sensoreinheit und 3D-Bewegungssimulation näher erläutert.

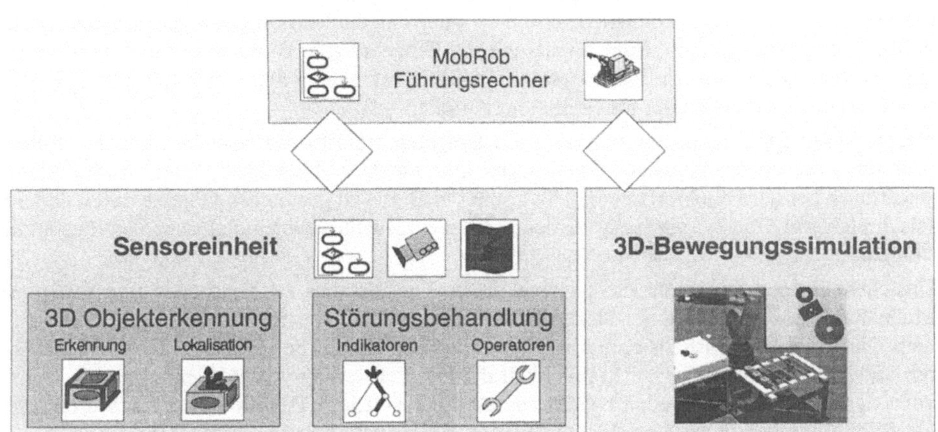

Abb. 1. Komponenten des autonomen mobilen Roboters des iwb

2 Störungstolerante Objekterkennung

Aufgabe der Sensoreinheit ist die Bestimmung der Position eines zu handhabenden Objekts in Bezug auf den Greifer des mobilen Roboters. Die hierzu eingesetzte videobasierte Objekterkennung bietet mit vergleichsweise geringem technischen Aufwand eine robuste Möglichkeit zur Bestimmung der Position des zu greifenden Objekts.

2.1 Aufbau der Sensoreinheit

Die Sensoreinheit erhält vom Führungsrechner des mobilen Roboters den Auftrag, Objekte an einer vermuteten Position zu lokalisieren. Der Erkennungsauftrag wird von der Ablaufsteuerung der Sensoreinheit entgegengenommen und durchgesetzt. Die Ablaufsteuerung koordiniert dabei die Erfassung des aktuellen Kamerabildes, die eigentliche videobasierte Objekterkennung und eine eventuell erforderliche Störungsbehandlung.

Zur Bilderfassung wurde der mobile Roboter des iwb mit einer Miniatur-CCD-Kamera im Handflansch des Roboterarmes ausgestattet [11]. Die Kamera schränkt damit, im Gegensatz zu außen am Roboter angebrachten Systemen, weder den Arbeitsraum des Roboters noch die Auswahl an passenden Greifern ein.

Basierend auf dem aufgenommenen Videobild findet eine Identifikation und Lokalisation des gesuchten Objekts mit Hilfe des im Teilprojekt L9 des SFB 331 entwickelten 3D-Objekterkennungssystems MORAL [6] statt, das es ermöglicht, Objekte in nahezu beliebigen Raumlagen zu erkennen.

Da die Lage der Kamera relativ zum Werkzeugkoordinatensystem vorher durch eine Hand-Auge-Kalibrierung bestimmt wurde [2], kann das Ergebnis der Objekterkennung direkt in Werkzeugkoordinaten des Roboters angegeben werden.

2.2 Häufige Störungsursachen und Reaktionsmöglichkeiten

Die Randbedingungen der videobasierten Objekterkennung in einer Produktionsumgebung, z. B. die für die Bildverarbeitung relevanten Lichtverhältnisse, unterliegen sehr starken Schwankungen. Bei stationären Systemen kann diese Klasse von Störungen durch Anpassung und Optimierung der Umgebungsbedingungen nahezu ausgeschlossen werden. Mobile Systeme müssen jedoch an verschiedenen Orten unter unterschiedlichen Umgebungsbedingungen zuverlässig operieren können. Eine Anpassung der Umgebung, z. B. durch am mobilen System angebrachte zusätzliche Beleuchtungseinrichtungen, ist häufig nicht mit vertretbarem Aufwand und ohne Einbußen der Flexibilität herzustellen.

Neben diesen Störungen, die aufgrund von Umgebungseinflüssen entstehen können, führen auch unvorhersehbare Konstellationen in der im Videobild abgebildeten Szene zu Fehlinterpretationen bei der Objekterkennung. So können z. B. die zu greifenden Objekte durch andere, falsch plazierte Objekte verdeckt werden, oder die gesuchten Objekte sind nur unvollständig sichtbar.

Unsichere Erkennungsergebnisse zu detektieren, ihre Ursache zu bestimmen und geeignete Maßnahmen zur Behebung der Störung einzuleiten ist Aufgabe der Störungsbehandlungseinheit. Die Vorteile der Realisierung in einem separaten Modul liegen neben der überschaubaren, modularen Struktur in der Möglichkeit der Parallelisierung von Rechenprozessen. Damit kann es weitgehend vermieden werden, durch die zusätzliche Funktionalität der Störungsbehandlung Einbußen in der Verarbeitungsgeschwindigkeit hinnehmen zu müssen.

Eine qualitative Analyse der häufigsten Ursachen für eine ungenaue oder gescheiterte Erkennung [3] ergab, daß diese meist auf eine Reihe von Basisfehlern, die einzeln oder in überlagerter Form auftreten, zurückgeführt werden können. Demnach stellen z. B. Reflektionen, die bei der Erkennung metallischer Werkstücke durch die Oberflächenbeschaffenheit des Objekts auftreten, eine Ausprägung des Basisfehlers „ungünstiger Lichteinfall" dar. Eine weitere Ausprägung dieses Basisfehlers kann durch teilweise übereinander liegende Objekte entstehen, wenn vermehrt Schatten auftreten, die ebenfalls zu Fehlinterpretationen führen können. Der Basisfehler „falsches Objekt" liegt vor, wenn ein fehlendes oder zum Teil verdecktes Objekt ein zuverlässiges und sicheres Erkennungsergebnis verhindert.

Die zur Auswahl stehenden Reaktionsmöglichkeiten unterteilen sich in interne und externe. Interne Reaktionen finden innerhalb des Sensorsystems statt, der aufrufende Führungsrechner wird über die Störungsbehandlung nicht informiert. Derzeit sind die folgenden internen Reaktionen implementiert:

- Abrufen weiterer Lagehypothesen:
  Wird die erste, formal beste Lagehypothese der Objekterkennung aus einem bestimmten Grund als nicht plausibel erachtet, so werden weitere Lagehypothesen abgerufen. Häufig kann dadurch ein Ergebnis gefunden werden, das den Plausibilitätskriterien genügt.

- Anpassung der Parameter der Bildvorverarbeitung:
  Ist z. B. die Farbe des Hintergrunds bekannt kann mit dieser Information die Anzahl der extrahierten Bildlinien reduziert werden. Dadurch kann die Zahl der Fehlinterpretationen reduziert werden.

- Anpassung der Parameter der Bildinterpretation:
  Liegt Vorwissen über die vermutliche Lage des Objekts vor, z. B. wenn bekannt ist, daß das gesuchte Objekt flach auf dem Boden einer Kiste liegt, kann diese Information genutzt

werden, den Suchraum der Objekterkennung einzuschränken und die Erkennungssicherheit zu steigern.

Weitere interne Reaktionsmöglichkeiten können neben der Anpassung weiterer Parameter der Objekterkennung auch aus dem Bereich der Bildmanipulation stammen. Hierbei ist allerdings sehr viel Vorwissen über die Art der Störung (Unschärfe, mangelnder Kontrast, o.ä.) erforderlich. Im Regelfall lassen sich diese Störungen auch durch o.g. Parameteranpassungen oder durch die folgenden externen Reaktionen beheben.

Externe Reaktionen beziehen die Fähigkeiten des mobilen Roboters mit ein. Dies ist in erster Linie die Möglichkeit, die Kamera in eine andere Aufnahmeposition zu bringen. Hauptsächlich bei verdeckten oder unvollständig sichtbaren Objekten ermöglicht diese Reaktion eine einfache aber wirkungsvolle Störungsbehebung. Ebenfalls denkbar ist es, störende Objekte zu identifizieren und zu entfernen, bevor das eigentlich gesuchte Objekt lokalisiert und gegriffen werden kann.

2.3 Aufbau der Störungsbehandlungseinheit

Wie bereits angesprochen, stellt die Grundlage der Störungsbehandlung die Identifikation der aufgetretenen Störung dar. Dazu wurden Störungsindikatoren entwickelt, die jeweils auf die Detektion eines Basisfehlers spezialisiert sind. Diese Indikatoren analysieren die abgebildete Szene und die Ergebnisse der Objekterkennung und liefern jeweils ein Maß für das Vorhandensein des jeweiligen Basisfehlers. Auf Basis dieser Fehlermaße wird die Zuverlässigkeit der Erkennung beurteilt und, wenn erforderlich, die Störungsursache identifiziert.

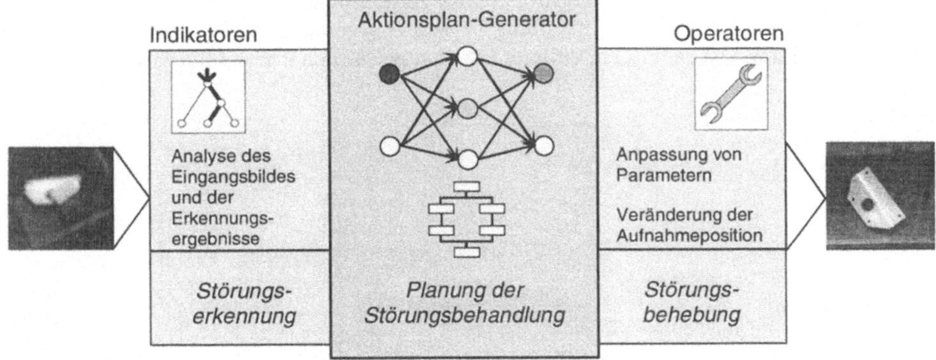

Abb. 2. Aufbau der Störungsbehandlungseinheit

Wird das Erkennungsergebnis als korrekt erachtet, werden die Objektkoordinaten an die Simulation zur Generierung eines kollisionsfreien Greifprogramms weitergereicht. Liegt eine Störung vor, kann wie oben beschrieben situationsgerecht reagiert werden. Basierend auf den Ergebnissen der Störungsindikatoren wird ein Aktionsplan generiert, der die zur Behebung der Störung notwendigen Handlungsanleitungen enthält. Dieser Aktionsplan wird von den jeweiligen Störungsoperatoren ausgeführt. Zunächst wird dabei versucht, die aufgetretene Störung innerhalb der Sensoreinheit z.B. durch Variation von Parametern zu beheben. Wenn dies nicht zum Erfolg führt, wird auf externe Reaktionen zur Störungsbehebung mit dem Führungsrechner des mobilen Roboters zurückgegriffen.

Zusammen mit dem jeweiligen Indikator bildet ein Operator ein auf einen Basisfehler spezialisiertes Störungsbehandlungsmodul. Die Störungsbehandlungseinheit besteht, wie in Abb. 2 zu sehen, aus mehreren Modulen sowie einem gemeinsamen Aktionsplan-Generator.

2.4 Ablauf der Objekterkennung mit Störungsbehandlung

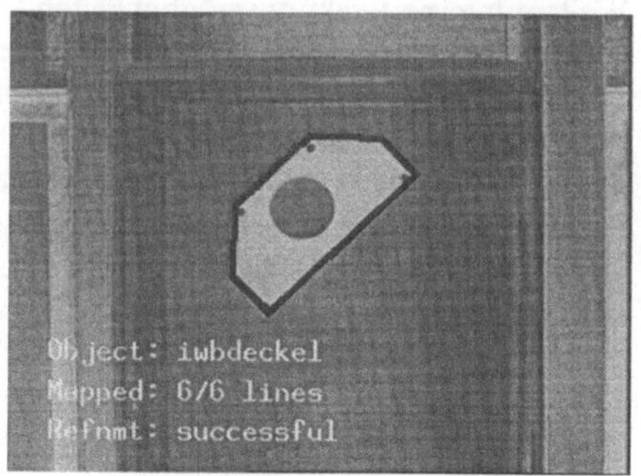

Abb. 3. Objekt nicht vollständig sichtbar

Abb. 4. Objekt nach Störungsbehandlung
vollständig sichtbar

Anhand eines Beispiels soll der Ablauf der Objekterkennung mit Störungsbehandlung verdeutlicht werden. Vom Führungsrechner des mobilen Roboters wird die Sensoreinheit beauftragt, die Position eines Objekts zu bestimmen. Das aufgenommene Videobild wird gleichzeitig an Objekterkennung und Störungsindikatoren weitergeleitet. Wie in Abb. 3 zu sehen, ist das Objekt zuerst nicht vollständig sichtbar. Die Objekterkennung meldet deshalb eine gescheiterte Erkennung, was zur Generierung eines Aktionsplans führt. Während der Bearbeitung dieses Aktionsplans durch die Störungsbehandlung verfährt der Roboter in eine andere Aufnahmeposition, von der aus ein weiterer Erkennungsversuch (siehe Abb. 4) gestartet wird.

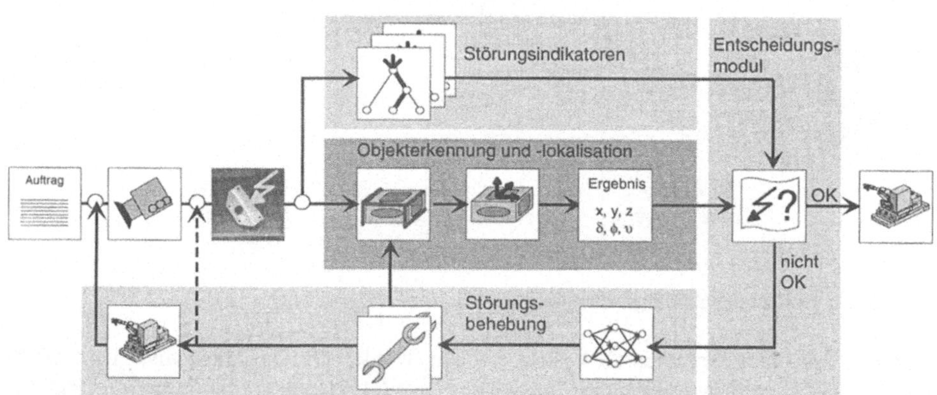

Abb. 5. Regelkreisstruktur der störungstoleranten Objekterkennung

Diesmal meldet die Objekterkennung ein sicheres Ergebnis, was von den Störungsindikatoren, die keine Anzeichen einer Störung finden konnten, bestätigt wird. Ein derartiger Erkennungsvorgang kann iterativ (siehe Abb. 5) durchlaufen werden, bis die Ursache für eine nicht zu behebende Störung bestimmt oder ein zuverlässiges Erkennungsergebnis erzielt werden kann. In jedem Fall wird das Ergebnis, sei es die Position des gesuchten Objekts oder die Störungsursache, an den Führungsrechner des mobilen Roboters zurückgemeldet. Dieser übergibt die ermittelten Objektpositionen sowie Aufträge zur Planung von Handhabungsvorgängen an das 3D-Simulationssystem USIS.

3 Automatische Planung der Handhabung mit der 3D-Simulation

3.1 Aktualisierung des Umgebungsmodells

Das 3D-Bewegungssimulationssystem USIS verfügt über ein Modell der Produktionsumgebung, das auf 3D-CAD-Daten basiert. In dieses Modell werden die von der Objekterkennung ermittelten Positionsdaten des gesuchten Objekts eingetragen. Dazu wird das Fahrzeug des mobilen Roboters im Simulationsmodell zunächst an die gleiche Position wie das reale Fahrzeug gefahren und der simulierte Roboter in die gleiche Achswinkelstellung wie der reale Roboter bewegt. Dies ist für den Abgleich erforderlich, da die Objektpositionen relativ zum Werkzeugkoordinatensystem des Roboters angegeben werden. Aus der Lage des Werkzeugkoordinatensystems des Roboters und der von der Objekterkennung ermittelten Objektposition wird die neue Absolutposition des Objekts im Simulationsmodell ermittelt. Nachdem das Objekt im Simulationsmodell in die neue Position transformiert wurde, zeigt die simulierte CCD-Kamera die gleiche Szene wie die reale CCD-Kamera (s. Abb. 6).

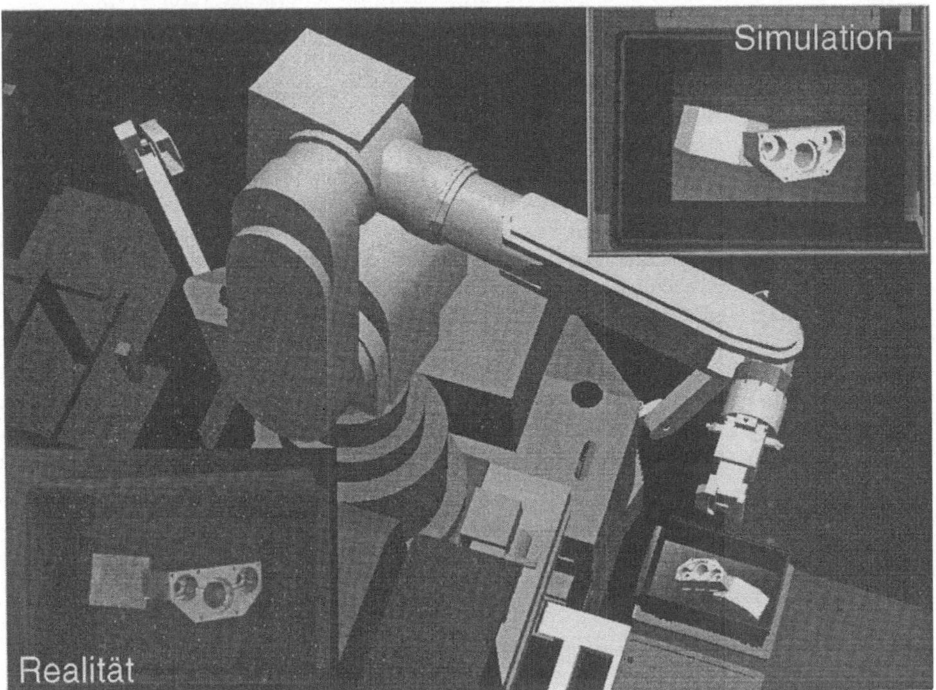

Abb. 6. Simulationsmodell nach dem Positionsabgleich mit realem und simuliertem Kamerabild

Die 3D-Simulation ermöglicht eine einfache Plausibilitätsprüfung der Objektlage. Durchdringt das Objekt andere Elemente wie z. B. Paletten, so ist die von der Objekterkennung errechnete Position zu ungenau und muß noch einmal bestimmt werden. Mit Hilfe der Objekt-

Abb. 7. Bestimmung des erforderlichen Fahrzeugversatzes

erkennung werden so die Positionen von zu greifenden Objekten relativ zum Roboter abgeglichen.

Darüberhinaus können auch Positionsungenauigkeiten des Fahrzeugs des mobilen Roboters im Modell erfaßt werden. Dazu werden die Positionen statischer Objekte bestimmt. In der Simulation wird dann eine neue Position des Fahrzeugs berechnet, so daß die Positionen des Gehäuses relativ zur Kamera in Simulation und Realität übereinstimmen. Im Beispiel von Abb. 7 muß das Fahrzeug dazu näher an die Montagepalette fahren.

Basierend auf dem aktualisierten Umgebungsmodell und der gewünschten Endposition des Objekts kann dann ein Handhabungsprogramm für den Roboter erzeugt werden [4].

3.2 Automatische Planung des Handhabungsablaufs

Der Schwierigkeitsgrad der automatischen Planung des Handhabungsablaufs hängt von der Position und der Geometrie des zu greifenden Objekts ab. Situationen, bei denen sich Objekte nicht in ihrer Sollage befinden, können z. B. durch das Herunterfallen oder Abrutschen eines fehlerhaft gegriffenen Teils entstehen. Das Objekt bleibt dann oft in einer ungünstigen Position liegen oder verkantet sich sogar. Dies bringt vor allem dann Probleme mit sich, wenn das Objekt nur in einer ganz bestimmten Relativposition zum Greifer korrekt an seiner Sollposition abgesetzt werden kann. Eine Position des Objekts relativ zum Greifer wird im folgenden als Greifkonfiguration bezeichnet. Bisher konnte in USIS mit Hilfe der implementierten Greif- und Bahnplanungsalgorithmen nur ein Handhabungsprogramm automatisch erzeugt werden, wenn sich der Handhabungsvorgang aus einem Greifvorgang, einem Transfervorgang und einem Ablegevorgang zusammensetzen ließ [5]. Dies ist z. B. nicht möglich, wenn es keine Greifkonfiguration gibt, die zugleich für das Greifen und das Ablegen geeignet ist. Zur Handhabung in derartigen Situationen wurde bei der Programmgenerierung nun auch die Möglichkeit des Umgreifens vorgesehen. D. h. der Roboter greift das Objekt, transferiert es an eine

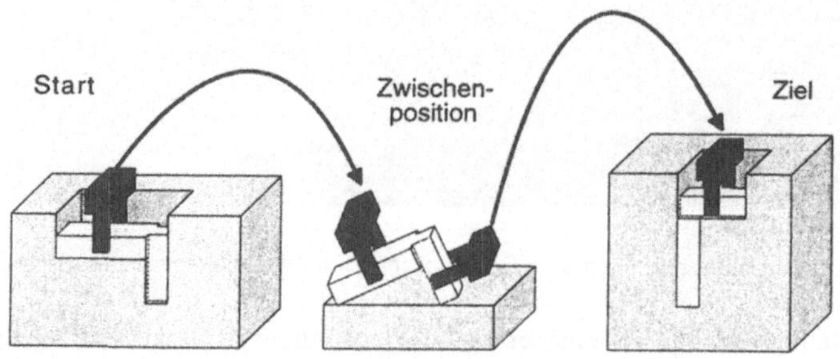

Abb. 8. Handhabungsplanung in zwei Teilschritten

zum Umgreifen geeignete Zwischenposition und legt es dort ab. Von der Zwischenposition nimmt er es dann mit einer anderen zum Ablegen geeigneten Greifkonfiguration erneut auf.

Die Zwischenposition für das zu bewegende Objekt wird in USIS automatisch bestimmt. Das Objekt muß an dieser Zwischenposition stabil liegen und sowohl mit der Greifkonfiguration der Ausgangsposition als auch mit der Greifkonfiguration der Zielposition gegriffen werden können [8]. Zur Beschränkung der möglichen Zwischenpositionen soll das Objekt auf einer ebenen Fläche abgelegt werden. Diese Einschränkung ist insofern sinnvoll, als auch der Mensch beim Umgreifen entweder die zweite Hand zu Hilfe nimmt oder das Objekt meist auf einer ebenen Platte bzw. einem Tisch absetzt.

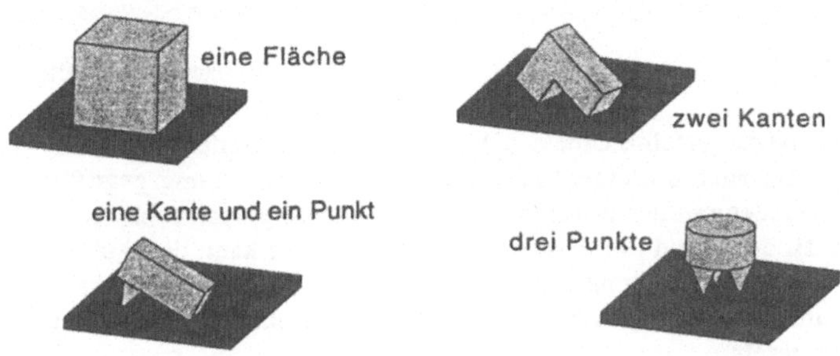

Abb. 9. Vorbedingung für stabile Lagen

Für die Zwischenposition kommen dann zunächst diejenigen Objektlagen in Frage, bei denen bestimmte Geometrieelemente die Auflagefläche berühren. Dabei gibt es vier verschiedene Fälle von der flächigen Auflage bis zur Auflage an drei Punkten, die Abb. 9 zu entnehmen sind. Damit kann die Menge der zulässigen Zwischenpositionen erheblich eingeschränkt werden. Die endgültige Überprüfung der Stabilität einer Zwischenposition wird mit Hilfe der Simulation physikalischer Effekte in USIS durchgeführt [10]. Diese beinhalten u.a. die Simulation von Gravitation, Impulserhaltung und Reibung. Bewegt sich das Objekt in der Zwischenposition nicht, so ist die Lage stabil. Bewegt es sich nur minimal, so wird die nach der Bewegung erreichte Position als Zwischenposition verwendet. Bei größeren Bewegungen muß eine andere Zwischenposition untersucht werden.

Jedoch können viele Störungen durch Umgreifen allein nicht behoben werden, weil keine Zwischenposition für beide Greifkonfigurationen existiert. Hier bietet sich eine Lösung durch optimale Nutzung der zur Verfügung stehenden Betriebsmittel, insbesondere unterschiedlicher Greifer an. Der mobile Roboter des iwb führt in der Regel drei verschiedene Greifer mit sich. Ist die Handhabungsaufgabe mit einem Greifer nicht zu lösen, so kann an einer zum Umgreifen geeigneten Zwischenposition ein Greiferwechsel stattfinden und die Handhabung mit einem anderen Greifer erfolgreich abgeschlossen werden. Die Berücksichtigung der Möglichkeit eines Greiferwechsels ist auch dann von Bedeutung, wenn für das zu handhabende Objekt ein eigener Greifer mit Formschluß existiert. Da dieser das Objekt sehr stabil greifen kann, wird zunächst immer versucht, das Objekt mit dem Formschlußgreifer zu greifen, was aber insbesondere bei verkanteten Objekten oft unmöglich ist. Es muß dann auf einen anderen Greifer ausgewichen werden können.

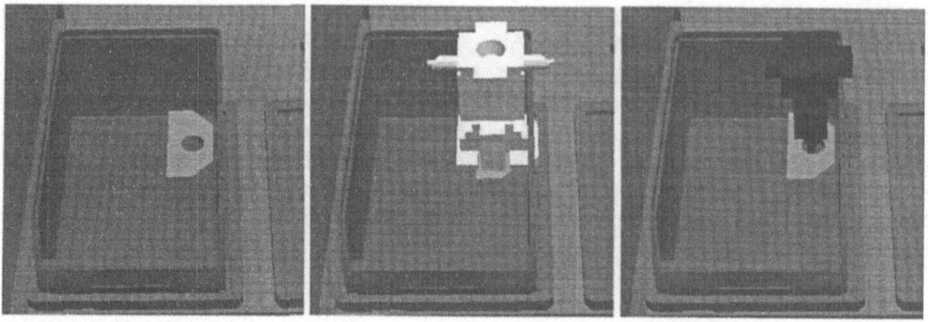

Abb. 10. Automatische Auswahl des zur Handhabungsaufgabe passenden Greifers

Für das in Abb. 10 dargestellte Objekt steht z. B. ein Außengreifer mit Formschluß zur Verfügung. Es kann aber auch mit einem Innengreifer an seiner Bohrung gegriffen werden. In der Regel wird der Außengreifer verwendet. Liegt das Objekt jedoch sehr nah an einem anderen Objekt, wie z. B. der Wand der Schäferbox in Abb. 10, so kann der Außengreifer nicht verwendet werden. Die Handhabungsplanung untersucht dann, ob das Objekt mit einem der anderen verfügbaren Greifer gegriffen werden kann. Die Bohrung ist erreichbar, also wird der Innengreifer eingesetzt.

3.3 Gewährleistung kollisionsfreier Roboterbewegungen

Nach der Bestimmung des Handhabungsablaufs und der zugehörigen Greifkonfigurationen, müssen kollisionsfreie Roboterbewegungen zwischen den durch das Greifen und Ablegen festgelegten Roboterpositionen bestimmt werden.

Da USIS bei der Simulation von Roboterbewegungen RC-Programme der realen Robotersteuerung abarbeitet, wird für einen Greiferwechsel das RC-Programm des realen Roboters bzgl. Kollision überprüft und nur im Kollisionsfall ein neues Programm mit einer kollisionsfreien Roboterbewegung zum Greiferwechsel erzeugt. Für einen Handhabungsvorgang werden zunächst in USIS die entsprechenden Roboterparameter belegt. Die Roboterparameter bestehen im wesentlichen aus den Roboterkoordinaten für das Greifen und das Ablegen des zu handhabenden Objekts. Anschließend wird das parametrisierte Programm mit simultaner Kollisionsüberprüfung ausgeführt. Nur bei Kollision wird mit Hilfe des in USIS integrierten Bahnplanungsverfahrens eine neue Bewegungsbahn bestimmt und in einem Roboterprogramm abgelegt, das dann an die reale Robotersteuerung übertragen wird [5]. Kann das parametrisierte Programm verwendet werden, so werden lediglich die entsprechenden Parameter in der realen Robotersteuerung gesetzt.

4 Zusammenfassung

Die vorgestellte störungstolerante Objekterkennung in Verbindung mit der automatischen Generierung geeigneter Roboterprogramme bietet dem mobilen Roboter auch in schwierigen Situationen die Möglichkeit zur Objekthandhabung. Grundlage dafür ist eine sichere Objekterkennung und die Integration einer Störungsbehandlungseinheit. Die Bestimmung der Störungsursache durch Indikatoren ermöglicht situationsangepaßte Reaktionen des Systems.

USIS gewährleistet entsprechend den Ergebnissen der Objekterkennung eine erfolgreiche und kollisionsfreie Handhabung. Bei der Planung von Handhabungsvorgängen werden alle zur Verfügung stehenden Betriebsmittel sowie ein eventuell erforderliches Umgreifen des zu handhabenden Objekts berücksichtigt.

Danksagung

Die vorliegende Arbeit wurde im Rahmen des Sonderforschungsbereichs „Informationsverarbeitung in autonomen, mobilen Handhabungssystemen" (SFB 331), Teilprojekte M1, M2, M3, von der Deutschen Forschungsgemeinschaft (DFG) gefördert.

Literatur

1. Ansorge, D.; Glüer, D.; Hofner, C.: Flexible Produktionsstrukturen für den Einsatz autonomer Systeme. In: Schmidt, G.; Freyberger, F. (Hrsg.): 12. Fachgespräch Autonome Mobile Systeme AMS '96, München. Springer, Berlin.
2. Blessing, S.; Lanser, S.; Zierl, C.: Vision-based handling with a mobile robot. In: International Symposium on Robotics and Automation. ASME Press, New York, 1996.
3. Blessing, S.; Reinhart, G.: Fault detection and recovery in a mobile robot vision system. In: European Symposium on Lasers, Optics and Productivity in Manufacturing I, 1996.
4. Kugelmann, D.: Autonomous Robotic Handling Applying Sensor Systems and 3D Simulation. In: Proceedings of th 1994 IEE International Conference on Robotics and Automation, San Diego, USA. Los Alamitos: IEEE Computer Society Press 1994, S. 196-201 (Vol. 1).
5. Kugelmann, D.; Reinhart, G.: Automatische Online-Generierung von Handhabungsprogrammen mit der 3D-Simulation. In: Levi, P.; Bräunl, Th. (Hrsg.): Autonome Mobile Systeme 1994. Berlin: Springer 1994, S. 349-360.
6. Lanser, S; Zierl, C.: MORAL: Ein System zur videobasierten Objekterkennung im Kontext autonomer, mobiler Systeme. In: G. Schmidt (Hrsg.): 12. Fachgespräch Autonome Mobile Systeme AMS '96, München. Springer, Berlin.
7. Pischeltsrieder, K.: Steuerung autonomer mobiler Roboter in der Produktion, iwb Forschungsberichte Vorabdruck, Springer Verlag, Berlin, Heidelberg, New York, 1994.
8. Reinhart, G.; Kugelmann, D.: Robot Handling in Case of Disturbances with 3D Simulation. In: Mayorga, R.V. (Hrsg.): Proceedings of the Third IASTED International Conference on Robotics and Manufacturing 1995, Cancún, Mexiko. Anaheim: IASTED/ACTA Press 1995, S. 228-232.
9. Roßgoderer, U.; Kugelmann, D.: Automatical Layout Generation with 3D Simulation. In: Dal Cin, M. u.a. (Hrsg.): 7th European Simulation Symposium ESS '95, Erlangen. Ghent: The Society for Computer Simulation International 1995, S. 647-651.
10. Stetter, R.: Rechnergestützte Simulationswerkzeuge zur Effizienzsteigerung des Industrieroboterreinsatzes, iwb-Forschungsberichte 62, Springer Verlag, 1993.
11. Welling, A.: Effizienter Einsatz bildgebender Sensoren zur Flexibilisierung automatisierter Handhabungsvorgänge, iwb Forschungsberichte 73, Springer Verlag, Berlin, Heidelberg, New York, 1994.

Kooperation, Koordination

Kollisionsvermeidung mobiler autonomer Roboter durch koordinierte sensorgeführte Manöver

Torsten Rupp, Thomas Cord
Forschungszentrum Informatik (FZI)
Abteilung Technische Expertensysteme und Robotik
Haid-und-Neu-Straße 10-14
76131 Karlsruhe

Kurzfassung

Für den Transport in Produktion und Fertigung sowie für die Handhabung von Gütern in Logistikzentren werden heute vielfach fahrerlose Transportsysteme (FTS) eingesetzt. In den Umschlagsystemen für Container einiger See- und Flughäfen werden FTS bereits in größerer Zahl genutzt. Die Sensorsysteme dieser Fahrzeuge haben einen hohen Sicherheitsstandard erreicht. Sie halten zuverlässig an, wenn Menschen, unbekannte Hindernisse oder andere Roboter ihren Weg behindern. Wünschenswert wäre jedoch, daß die Fahrzeuge, statt einfach anzuhalten, selbstständig koordinierte Ausweichbewegungen planen und ausführen, um so eine bessere Kollisionsvermeidung zu ermöglichen. Dieser Beitrag beschreibt ein robustes Steuerungs- und Navigationssystem, das mit Hilfe von Sensordaten und Informationen über die Routen anderer Fahrzeuge sichere und koordinierte Ausweichbewegungen ermöglicht. Durch ein solches intelligentes Verhalten der Fahrzeuge in Störsituationen eröffnen sich neue Einsatzgebiete für mobile Roboter im industriellen wie nichtindustriellen Bereich.

1.   Einführung

Bis Mitte des Jahres 1994 waren weltweit 350.000 Roboter im Einsatz, in Deutschland allein rund 40.000 [1]. Die meisten Roboter sind in industrielle Fertigungsprozesse eingebunden und besitzen nur einen geringen Grad an Anpassungs- und Kooperationsfähigkeit. Die wichtigsten Gründe dafür sind:

1) Aktive oder passive Leitsysteme schränken die Flexibilität und Autonomie der einzelnen Fahrzeuge ein.
2) Verfahren zur Koordination und Kooperation von mobilen Robotern werden bisher nicht eingesetzt.

Selbst in neuen Verladeanlagen, wie dem Containerterminal von Europe Combined Terminals BV (ECT) in Rotterdam, sind kooperatives Verhalten und Autonomie nicht vorhanden. 50 fahrerlose Dieselfahrzeuge transportieren Schiffscontainer von den Kaikränen zum Flächenlager. Die Fahrzeuge sind reine Befehlsempfänger ohne jegliche Autonomie [2].

Die Arbeiten auf dem Forschungsgebiet der Bewegungssteuerung von autonomen mobilen Systemen haben daher die Steigerung der Flexibilität bei Transportaufgaben durch Erhöhung ihrer Autonomie zum Ziel. Dabei wird eine Verbesserung der Fähigkeit, unvorhergesehene Ereignisse und Veränderungen der Umwelt zu beherrschen, angestrebt. Außerdem kann durch den Einsatz leistungsfähiger Sensoren und Navigationssysteme auf aktive und passive Leitspuren verzichtet werden. Hierdurch wird eine flexiblere Nutzung von Fahrtrassen und Rangierflächen bei reduziertem Aufwand für Hallen- und Bodeninstallationen möglich. Den Fahrzeugen wird so eine größtmögliche Unabhängigkeit und Flexibilität gegeben.

Das Navigations- und Hinderniserkennungssystem eines autonomen mobilen Roboters muß u. a. die folgenden Aufgaben bewältigen, um die geplanten Bewegungsbahnen, auf denen Kollisionen mit bekannten Hindernissen vermieden werden, kollisionsfrei zu befahren (siehe auch [3]):

- Erkennung von Gefahrensituationen, die durch
    - stehende und nicht vorhersehbare Hindernisse, wie eine Kiste, die sich auf der geplanten Bewegungsbahn des Fahrzeugs befindet, hervorgerufen werden oder durch
    - bewegliche Hindernisse, wie Fahrzeuge, welche die Bewegungsbahn kreuzen oder durch Menschen, die sich im Arbeitsbereich des Roboters befinden.
- Bewältigung dieser Störsituationen durch die Bestimmung von sicheren Ausweichrouten.

Häufig werden in fahrerlosen Transportsystemen (FTS) mehrere Roboter eingesetzt, die unabhängig voneinander Transportaufträge erhalten und ausführen. Daher kommt es nicht selten vor, daß zwei oder mehrere Roboter bei der Auftragsausführung in einen Interessenkonflikt geraten, wenn sie sich zum Beispiel auf einer Wegkreuzung begegnen. Wenn eine Kollision vermieden werden soll, muß man für solche Fälle Vorsorge treffen. Bisher hat man entweder versucht, Konfliktsituationen dieser Art ganz zu vermeiden, indem man die Auftragsausführung entsprechend gestaltet hat oder man hat sie auf sehr einfache, aber meist ineffiziente Weise gelöst. Oft genug gehen die Konfliktlösungen zu Lasten der Auftragsausführungsgeschwindigkeit oder sie werden mit einem unverhältnismäßigen Ressourcenverbrauch erkauft. Durch eine enge Kopplung von Sensorik zur Erfassung von Objekten im Umfeld des mobilen Roboters und einer Kommunikationseinrichtung zum Austausch der beabsichtigten Trajektorien ist ein koordiniertes autonomes Verhalten der Roboterfahrzeuge erreichbar [4].

2. Stand der Forschung

Zur Kollisionsvermeidung autonomer mobiler Roboter mit statischen oder dynamischen Hindernissen sind verschiedene Ansätze entwickelt worden. Die einfachsten Ansätze arbeiten mit festen Trajektorien, die vom Roboter selbst nicht geändert werden können. Andere erlauben eine Anpassung von Geschwindigkeit oder der räumlichen Bewegungen. In der Literatur findet man folgende Verfahren:

- **Präventive Kollisionsvermeidung:** Kollisionen werden durch eine entsprechende Planung bei der Wegsuche vermieden. Ist die Wegsuche abgeschlossen, können die Trajektorien nicht mehr geändert werden. In [5] wird ein solches Verfahren vorgestellt, das die Fahrstraßen in Zellen einteilt und durch einen Block-Mechanismus, wie bei Zugstrecken, garantieren kann, daß Kollisionen der Roboter nicht auftreten können. An Kreuzungen werden sogenannte „constraint points" und „unlock points" definiert. Will ein Roboter die Kreuzung passieren, teilt er mittels lokaler Kommunikation den anderen Robotern mit, daß er den „constraint point" erreicht hat und die Kreuzung blockiert ist. Sobald der Roboter den „unlock point" erreicht, gibt er die Kreuzung wieder frei. Ist die Kreuzung bei Erreichen des „constraint point" bereits blockiert, muß der Roboter warten. Ein ähnliches Verfahren, das ebenfalls auf dem Blockieren und Freigeben von Zellen beruht, wird in [6] beschrieben.
- **Räumliche Kollisionsvermeidung:** Einer der in Konflikt geratenen Roboter ändert seine Bewegungsrichtung so ab, daß eine Kollision ausgeschlossen wird. Beispielsweise kann ein Roboter, der auf einer Straße einem anderen Roboter begegnet, durch eine Ausweichbewegung in Form einer doppelten S-Kurve seine Bewegungsbahn anpassen und so eine Kollision verhindern [7, 8, 9].

- **Zeitliche Kollisionsvermeidung:** Durch Veränderung der Geschwindigkeit des Roboters wird eine zeitliche Trajektorienanpassung vorgenommen. Dieses Verfahren realisiert die Kollisionsvermeidung dadurch, daß ein Roboter an einer Kreuzung seine Geschwindigkeit reduziert oder stehenbleibt, so daß der andere Roboter die Kreuzung vor ihm passieren kann. In [10] ist ein System skizziert, das durch Änderung von Geschwindigkeitsprofilen eine zeitliche Trajektorienanpassung realisiert. Alle relevanten Objekte werden als Polyeder modelliert und in einem Kachelmodell eingetragen, das eine Zeitachse und eine Achse für die Bogenlänge der Trajektorie besitzt. In den freien Kacheln wird mit einem Wegsuchverfahren ein befahrbarer Weg ermittelt, in dem das Geschwindigkeitsprofil als zu fahrende Wegstrecke je Zeiteinheit enthalten ist. Eine Kollisionsvermeidung mit statischen Hindernissen ist bei diesem Verfahren nur eingeschränkt möglich.
- **Zeitliche und räumliche Kollisionsvermeidung:** In [11] wird ein Verfahren zur raum-zeitlichen Kollisionsvermeidung vorgestellt. Dabei wird zwischen den kollisionsgefährdeten Robotern der raum-zeitliche Kollisionsvektor berechnet, der sich als minimaler raum-zeitlicher Abstand zwischen zwei Raumzeittrajektorien ergibt. Aus dem Kollisionsvektor kann durch Linearisierung der Trajektorien in der Kollisionsregion ein Ausweichvektor berechnet werden, der der Trajektorie des ausweichpflichtigen Roboters überlagert wird. Der beschriebene Ansatz berücksichtigt sowohl statische als auch dynamische Hindernisse und modelliert räumliche und zeitliche Unsicherheiten.

  Ein weiteres Verfahren, bei dem eine Kollision sowohl durch räumliche als auch zeitliche Anpassung der Trajektorie verhindert wird, ist in [12] beschrieben. Bei diesem System wird der Kollisionsort, die Orientierung und der räumliche Kollisionsvektor des Roboters zur Kollisionszeit berechnet. Die räumliche Ausweichbewegung wird bei linearisierten Trajektorien analytisch bzw. allgemein durch ein Iterationsverfahren berechnet. Gegebenenfalls wird durch Reduktion der Geschwindigkeit vor dem Hindernis eine zeitliche Anpassung der Trajektorie durchgeführt.

3. Koordinierte sensorgeführte Roboterbewegungen

Verfahren zur Kollisionsvermeidung, die ausschließlich präventiv arbeiten oder eine zeitliche bzw. räumliche Trajektorienanpassung vornehmen, haben einen entscheidenden Nachteil: in vielen Fällen kann eine Kollision nicht sicher und effizient verhindert werden. Beispielsweise kann ein Verfahren mit zeitlicher Trajektorienanpassung prinzipiell keine statischen Hindernisse berücksichtigen, während ein Verfahren zur räumlichen Trajektorienanpassung beim Überholen eines nahezu gleichschnellen Objekts auf einer Straße mit Gegenverkehr in vielen Fällen nicht ausreichend sein kann. Es bietet sich daher an, Trajektorienanpassungen sowohl zeitlich als auch räumlich vorzunehmen, um die Nachteile der Verfahren zu kompensieren. An ein solches System sind mehrere Anforderungen zu stellen:

- Kollisionen mit statischen Hindernissen sollen erkannt und durch die Berechnung einer räumlichen Ausweichtrajektorie verhindert werden.
- Kollisionen mit anderen Robotern sollen ebenfalls erkannt und durch Berechnung einer raum-zeitlichen Ausweichtrajektorie ausgeschlossen werden.
- Die Bestimmung von Konfliktsituationen und Ausweichbewegungen soll in Echtzeit ablaufen.

Das raum-zeitliche Kollisionsvermeidungsverfahren wird durch das im folgenden SMC (Sensor based Motion Control) genannte Modul realisiert. SMC stellt einen Teil des Navigationssystems dar. Es erhält von einem Bahnplanungsmodul fertige Bewegungsbahnen, die den Roboter vom Startpunkt bis zum Zielpunkt bringen. Vorab bekannte statische Hindernisse, wie Wände, Säulen oder Löcher in der Fahrbahn sollen vom Bahnplanungsmodul bereits berücksichtigt werden. SMC fallen damit folgende Aufgaben zu:

- Entgegennehmen der vom Bahnplaner erzeugten Bewegungsbahnen und Berechnung eines Geschwindigkeitsprofils.
- Einlesen der Abstandsdaten vom Sensorsystem und Kollisionsprüfung mit erkannten, statischen Hindernissen.
- Kollisionsprüfung mit Trajektorien anderer Roboter und Koordination der Ausweichbewegungen bei Kollisionsgefahr.
- Weitergabe der auf Kollisionsfreiheit geprüften Trajektorien an die Bewegungsausführung.

Bis auf die Wegsuche durch einen Bahnplanungsalgorithmus stellt SMC ein vollständiges Navigationsmodul dar. Die von einem Bahnplanungsmodul vorgegebene Trajektorie wird durch ein Sensormodul auf Kollision mit statischen Hindernissen geprüft. Parallel dazu sendet der Roboter über das Inter-Roboter-Kommunikationssystem ständig seine Position an alle anderen Roboter und empfängt gleichzeitig deren Positionen. Kommen sich zwei Roboter zu nahe, fordern sie sich gegenseitig auf, ihre zukünftigen Trajektorien zu senden. Dadurch können die sich nähernden Roboter ihre eigene Trajektorie mit der vom anderen Roboter gesendeten Trajektorie auf Kollision prüfen. Kann eine Kollision mit einem statischen Hindernis oder einem anderen Roboter festgestellt werden, muß die Berechnung einer Ausweichbewegung zur Kollisionsvermeidung durch mindestens einen Roboter eingeleitet werden. Der Roboter, der den unwichtigsten Transportauftrag bearbeitet, ist verpflichtet, eine Ausweichtrajektorie zu bestimmen und auszuführen.

3.1 Erkennung von Kollisionen raum-zeitlicher Bewegungen

Die Trajektorien der Roboter können durch Raumzeitkurven dargestellt werden. Sie setzen sich aus ansteigenden Geraden- und schraubenförmigen Linienstücken zusammen und enthalten neben den Koordinatenwerten für die Position des Roboters im Raum (inkl. der Orientierung Θ) und gegebenenfalls einem Krümmungswert bei Kreissegmenten ein Geschwindigkeitsprofil. Das Geschwindigkeitsprofil legt implizit die Einordnung der Bewegung in der Zeit fest. Geradeausbewegungen können in der Raumzeit durch ansteigende Geraden dargestellt werden, Kreisstücke ergeben schraubenförmige Kurven. Diese Kurven werden Weltlinien genannt [4]. In Abb. 1 ist eine raum-zeitliche Weltlinie eines Roboters dargestellt, der auf einer Kreisbahn fährt.

Wenn ein Roboter mit einem anderen Roboter kollidiert, heißt das, daß sich die Roboter zu einem bestimmten Zeitpunkt an der gleichen räumlichen Position befinden. Daraus kann abgeleitet werden, daß eine Kollision zwischen zwei Robotern immer dann vorliegt, wenn sie sich an der gleichen raum-zeitlichen Position befinden. Durch die räumlichen Ausdehnungen der Roboter liegt eine Kollision jedoch nicht nur dann vor, wenn sich die Roboter exakt an der gleichen raum-zeitlichen Position befinden, sondern auch dann, wenn die Roboter nur „nahe" beinander stehen. Ein Verfahren, das Kollisionen in der Raumzeit berechnet, muß daher die räumliche Ausdehnung der Roboter berücksichtigen. Um jedoch den Rechenaufwand minimal zu halten, wird die räumliche Ausdehnung des Roboters nicht exakt in die Rechnung einbezo-

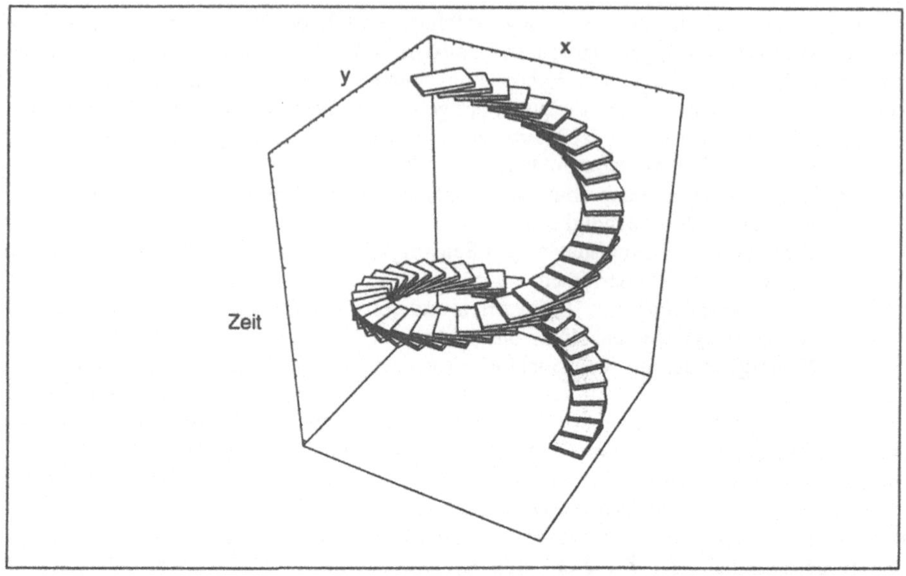

Abb. 1:   Darstellung der Trajektorie als raum-zeitliche Weltlinie

gen, sondern stattdessen der Roboter durch ein einfacheres Objekt, wie seine konvexe Hülle, ersetzt und die Berechnungen mit dieser Hülle durchgeführt. Als einfachste Form einer konvexen Hülle bietet sich eine Kugel mit einem Durchmesser an, der der größten Ausdehnung des Roboters entspricht, oder ein Quader mit entsprechenden Abmessungen.

Eine Kollision liegt dann vor, wenn der minimal raum-zeitliche Abstand zwischen den Weltlinien einen vorgegebenen minimalen Wert unterschreitet. Um die Berechnung des minimalen raum-zeitlichen Abstands zweier Weltlinien einfach und effizient zu halten, werden die Trajektorien in Segmente unterteilt. Die Auflösung sollte dabei ausreichend hoch gewählt werden, um die Positionen zwischen zwei Punkten vernachlässigen zu können. Der minimale raum-zeitliche Abstand kann mit einem Verfahren zur Berechnung des dichtesten Punktepaares bestimmt werden.

3.2 Kollisionsvermeidung

Hat ein Roboter eine Kollisionsgefahr erkannt und ist er ausweichpflichtig, so muß dieser Roboter seine Trajektorie so ändern, daß die Kollision unter sonst gleichen Bedingungen verhindert wird. Die Kollision kann vermieden werden, wenn der ausweichpflichtige Roboter die Weltlinie soweit verschiebt, daß der minimale raum-zeitliche Abstand zwischen der verschobenen Weltlinie und der Weltlinie des anderen in die Kollision verwickelten Roboters eingehalten wird. Dies kann dadurch erreicht werden, daß der ausweichpflichtige Roboter seine Weltlinie entlang eines geeigneten Ausweichvektors verschiebt. Zur Berechnung des Ausweichvektors wird der Kollisionsvektor $\eth$ eingeführt. Der Kollisionsvektor beschreibt Richtung und Betrag des Abstandsvektors zwischen den beiden bei der Kollisionserkennung ermittelten Kollisionspunkten p_1 und p_2. Wird der Kollisionsvektor geeignet zum Ausweichvektor $\eth^*$ verlängert, kann die Weltlinie des ausweichpflichtigen Roboters verschoben und die Kollision verhindert werden. Durch diese Verlängerung wird der Punkt p_1 zum Punkt p'_1 verschoben, durch den die Ausweichtrajektorie verlaufen muß (Abb. 2).

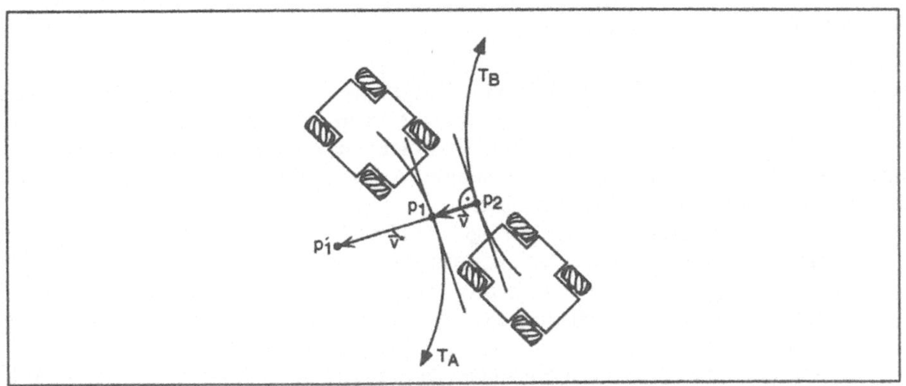

Abb. 2:   Kollisionsvektor und Ausweichvektor

Die Verschiebung des Punkts p_1 entlang des Ausweichvektors $\vec{v}^*$ ist in einigen Fällen jedoch noch nicht hinreichend, um eine Kollision zu vermeiden. Der Ausweichpunkt p_1' liegt zwar bzgl. des Kollisionspunkts p_1 in ausreichender Entfernung zu Punkt p_2, jedoch nicht unbedingt zu allen Punkten der Weltlinie T_B. Aus diesem Grund ist es erforderlich, zu prüfen, ob der Abstand des gewählten Ausweichpunkts zu allen Punkten der Weltlinie T_B hinreichend groß ist. Ist der Abstand an einer Stelle der Weltlinie T_B nicht ausreichend, so ist der Punkt p_1' erneut zu verschieben. Ein weiterer Sonderfall ergibt sich, wenn der Kollisionsvektor der Nullvektor ist. Dieser Fall tritt ein, wenn die Weltlinien sich schneiden. In dieser Situation kann mit dem beschriebenen Verfahren kein Ausweichpunkt bestimmt werden, deshalb wird bei sich schneidenden Weltlinien ein Ausweichpunkt in einer anderen Richtung gesucht.

Ist ein geeigneter Ausweichpunkt p_1' bestimmt, so erfolgt die Berechnung der Ausweichtrajektorie als eine Folge von Bewegungsprimitiven wie Geraden und Kreissegmenten. Die Berechnung der Ausweichtrajektorie mit Hilfe von Bewegungsprimitiven berücksichtigt jedoch ausschließlich die räumlichen Bewegungen des Roboters. Daher muß durch die Wahl eines entsprechenden Geschwindigkeitsprofils für die einzelnen Segmente der Trajektorie dafür gesorgt werden, daß der Ausweichpunkt p_1' zum berechneten Zeitpunkt erreicht wird. Erst wenn auch diese Berechnung erfolgreich abgeschlossen ist, kann die Ausweichtrajektorie ausgeführt werden (Abb. 3).

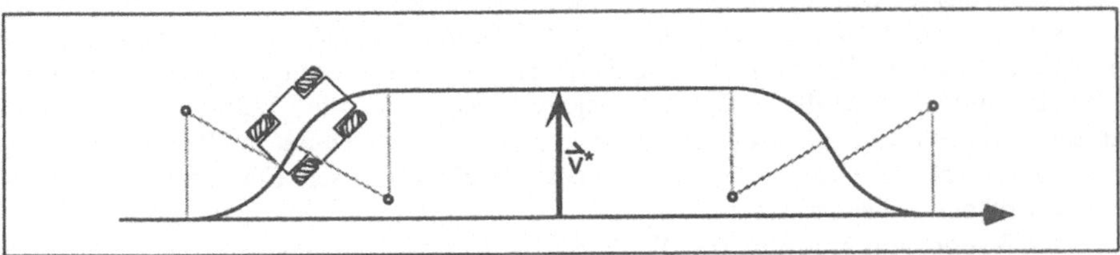

Abb. 3:   Berechnung der Ausweichtrajektorie mit Hilfe von Bewegungsprimitiven

3.3 Inter-Roboter-Kommunikation

Koordiniertes Verhalten der Roboter setzt eine Kommunikationsfähigkeit der Roboter voraus. Da Koordination zur Kollisionsvermeidung nur zwischen nahe beieinanderstehenden Robotern notwendig ist, reicht eine lokale Inter-Roboter-Kommunikationseinrichtung aus, die in der Lage ist, Nachrichten an alle oder an einzelne Roboter zu übermitteln. Die Kollisionsvermeidung wird durch folgendes Verfahren realisiert:

1) Jeder Roboter sendet in regelmäßigen Abständen seine (mit einem Zeitstempel versehene) Position. Parallel dazu empfängt jeder Roboter ständig die Positionsnachrichten anderer Roboter. Für die zeitliche Zuordnung ist eine gemeinsame Zeitbasis aller Roboter erforderlich, die von synchron laufenden Uhren zur Verfügung gestellt wird.

2) Anhand der empfangenen Positionen anderer Roboter überprüft jeder Roboter den räumlichen Abstand. Wird der Abstand zu einem anderen Roboter zu klein, so besteht mit diesem Roboter potentiell eine Kollisionsgefahr.

3) Stellt ein Roboter fest, daß ihm ein anderer Roboter zu nahe kommt, so speichert der Roboter die Position des anderen Roboters und fordert ihn durch Senden einer Nachricht über das Inter-Roboter-Kommunikationssystem auf, seine zukünftige Trajektorie für eine genaue Kollisionsprüfung zu übermitteln.

4) Wird eine angeforderte Trajektorie empfangen, so wird eine Kollisionsprüfung durchgeführt. Kann eine drohende Kollision festgestellt werden, muß geprüft werden, ob Ausweichpflicht besteht und ggfs. eine Kollisionsvermeidung, wie in Abschnitt 3.2 beschrieben, durchgeführt werden.

5) Nachdem eine Ausweichbewegung berechnet worden ist, muß die neue Trajektorie an die anderen Roboter übermittelt werden, um die Beseitigung der Kollisionsgefahr anzuzeigen und ggfs. Folgekollisionen zu erfassen.

4. Evaluierung

Die Funktionsfähigkeit des in den vorangegangenen Abschnitten dargestellten Systems wurde durch Experimente mit den beiden mobilen Robotern *Stan* und *Ollie* des FZI evaluiert. Abb. 4 zeigt die Grundstellung von Testszenario 1. *Stan* (Roboter 1) bewegt sich auf einer Trajektorie in der Form einer „8", *Ollie* (Roboter 2) kreuzt die „8" längs.

Abb. 5 zeigt die Umplanung, die *Stan* auf Grund der erkannten Kollision mit *Ollie* durchführt. Die beiden Kreise markieren die Stellen der nahsten raum-zeitlichen Annäherung. In den Kreismitten liegen die Kollisionspunkte, von denen aus, wie in Abschnitt 3.2 beschrieben, ein Kollisions- und ein Ausweichvektor berechnet werden. Durch den Punkt an der Spitze des Kollisionsvektors wird die Ausweichtrajektorie gelegt. Die schraffierten Bereiche stellen den Grundriß des Gebäudes dar.

Das Testszenario 2 in Abb. 6 stellt die Situation einer Kreuzung nach, auf der sich zwei Roboter begegnen. *Stan* (Roboter 1) ist ausweichpflichtig und berechnet eine Ausweichtrajektorie, die hinter *Ollie* (Roboter 2) vorbeiführt (Abb. 7). Gleichzeitig reduziert Roboter 1 seine Geschwindigkeit auf der Ausweichtrajektorie, um Roboter 2 ausreichend Zeit zu geben, die Kreuzung zu räumen. Anschließend beschleunigt Roboter 1, um wieder auf seine alte Trajektorie zurückzufahren.

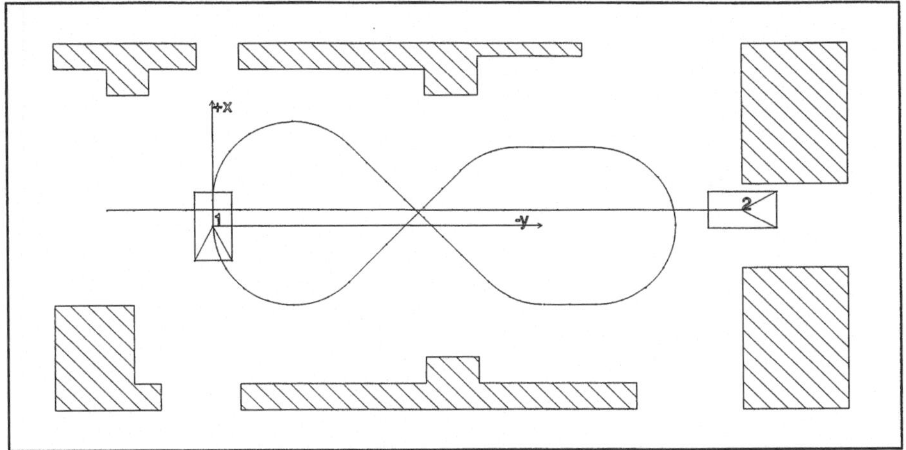

Abb. 4:   Ausgangssituation von Testszenario 1

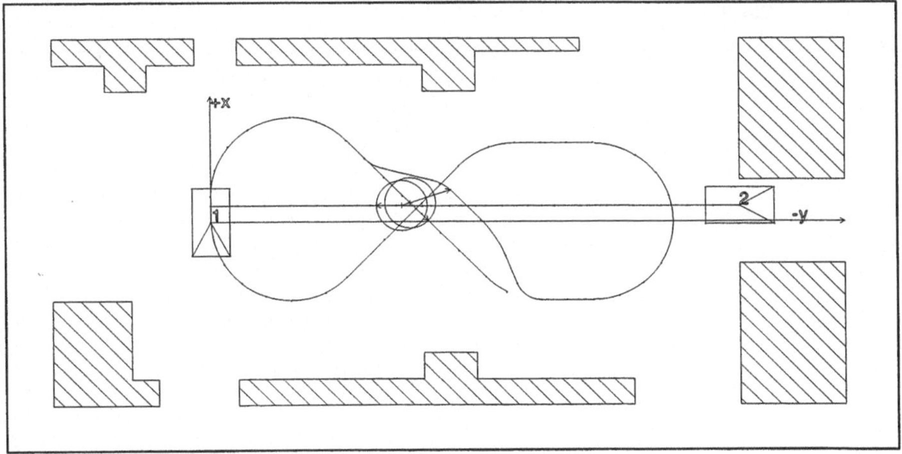

Abb. 5:   Umplanung zur Kollisionsvermeidung durch *Stan*

Das zweite Testszenario zeigt, daß auch bei einer Kreuzungssituation die Berechnung einer sinnvollen raum-zeitlichen Ausweichtrajektorie möglich ist. Die raum-zeitliche Ausweichbewegung bietet die Chance, daß der ausweichpflichtige Roboter nicht anhalten und seine Geschwindigkeit nur geringfügig ändern muß, um die Kollision mit dem anderen Roboter zu vermeiden.

5.   Zusammenfassung und Ausblick

Das in diesem Beitrag beschriebene System ist in der Lage, Kollisionen mit statischen und dynamischen Hindernissen mit Hilfe von Sensorik und Kommunikation sicher zu vermeiden. Dabei gehen die Möglichkeiten zur Kollisionsvermeidung durch die Koordination von Bewegungen über die bisher praktisch eingesetzten Verfahren hinaus. Durch die Betrachtung raum-zeitlicher Bewegungen, der Koordination mit anderen Robotern und ggfs. der Berechnung von

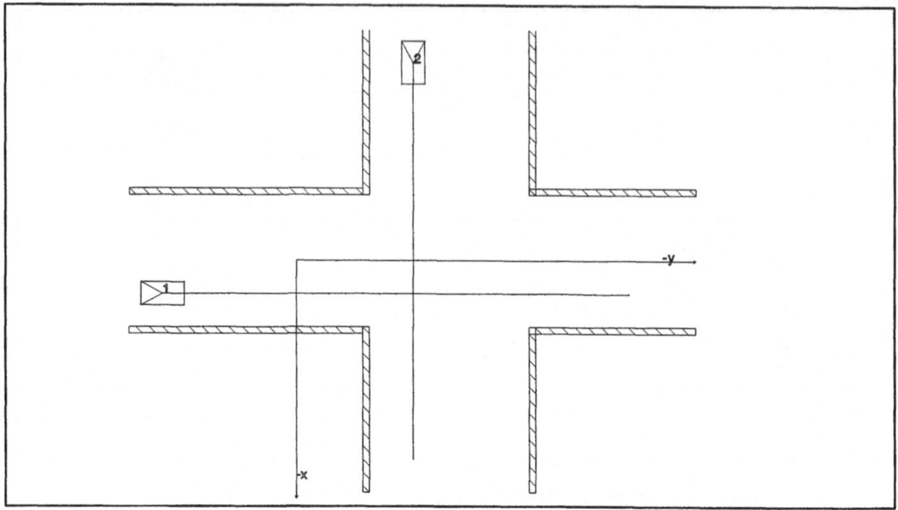

Abb. 6:   Ausgangssituation von Testszenario 2

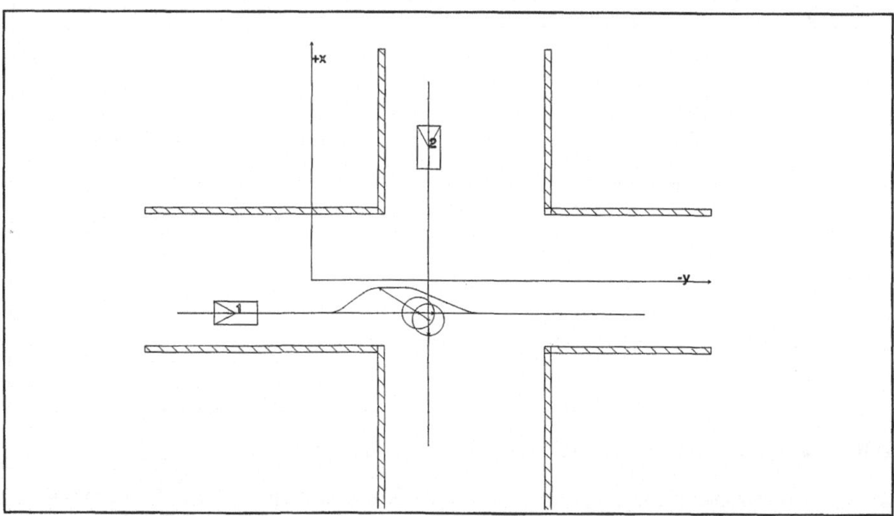

Abb. 7:   Umplanung durch *Stan* bei der Begegnung auf einer Kreuzung

Ausweichtrajektorien in der Raumzeit sind Kollisionen in vielen Fällen frühzeitig erkennbar und Ausweichbewegungen zur Kollisionsvermeidung einfacher und effizienter zu berechnen als dies bei Systemen der Fall ist, die eine Kollisionsgefahr lediglich unmittelbar kurz vor der Kollision erkennen können und dann nur noch in der Lage sind, einen Notstop durchführen. In Mehr-Robotersystemen lassen sich viele Konfliktsituationen wie beispielsweise sich kreuzende Bewegungsbahnen oder direkt aufeinander zufahrende Roboter ohne Eingreifen eines Bahnplaners auflösen und Kollisionen durch geeignet gewählte Ausweichbewegungen sicher vermeiden. Übliche Verkehrsituationen, wie sie an Strassenkreuzungen auftreten, lassen sich bewältigen. Dadurch kann die Effizienz und Autonomie autonomer mobiler Roboter gesteigert werden.

Der Markt für fahrerlose Transportsysteme verspricht steigende Zuwachsraten, da diese neben dem Produktionsbereich zunehmend auch im Service- und Dienstleistungsbereich eingesetzt werden. Diese neuen Einsatzgebiete stellen Anforderungen an mobile Roboter, die durch das vorgestellte Navigationsverfahren erfüllt werden können. Autonome mobile Roboter können in Hotels den Zimmerservice verbessern oder Gepäckstücke der Gäste transportieren. In Krankhäusern könnten autonome mobile Roboter Transportaufträge, wie die Verteilung der Mahlzeiten von der Küche zu den einzelnen Stationen, übernehmen. Die Anforderungen an das Navigationssystem sind wegen der wesentlich geringer strukturierten Einsatzumgebung deutlich höher als in einer Fabrikhalle. Außerdem ist in Konfliktsituationen ein flexibleres Verhalten erforderlich: die Roboter dürfen nicht einfach stehenbleiben und warten, bis sich der entstandene Konflikt von selbst löst oder bis ein Mensch eingreift, sondern sollen selbstständig Lösungen der Konflikte finden und umsetzen.

Schlußbemerkung

Die Autoren danken Prof. Dr.-Ing. U. Rembold von der Universität Karlsruhe für seine Ratschläge und die Unterstützung. Die Arbeiten wurden am Forschungszentrum Informatik (FZI), Abteilung Technische Expertensysteme und Robotik (*Direktor: Prof. Dr.-Ing. U. Rembold*) durchgeführt.

Literaturverzeichnis

[1] C. Reuber, *Vision wird Wirklichkeit - Serviceroboter: Spezialgebiet mit Zukunft*, Elektronik 25, Dezember 1994

[2] G. Scheffels, *FTS für den Containerumschlag*, F+H-Report 1993

[3] P. Hoppen, *Autonome mobile Roboter: Echtzeitnavigation in bekannter und unbekannter Umgebung*, Dissertation an der Universität Kaiserslautern, BI-Wiss.-Verlag, 1992

[4] M. Rude, *Koordinierte Kollisionsvermeidung mobiler Roboter mit Hilfe von Kommunikation und Sensorik*, Dissertation an der Universität Karlsruhe, Fortschr.-Ber. VDI Reihe 8 Nr. 495, 1995

[5] F.R. Noreils, *Coordinated Execution of Trajectories by Multiple Mobile Robot*, International Workshop on Intelligent Robots and Systems IROS 91, Nov. 3-5, Osaka, Japan, 1991

[6] R. Alami, F. Robert, F. Ingrand und S. Suzuki, *Multi-robot Cooperation through Incremental Plan-Merging*, IEEE International Conference on Robotics and Automation, 1995

[7] S. Bouffouix, M. Bogaert und S. Do, *Obstacle Avoidance Algorithm For Teleoperated Vehicles*, Intelligent Autonomous Vehicles, 1st IFAC International Workshop, 1993

[8] E. Modolo und E. Pagello, *Collision Avoidance Detection in Space and Time Planning for Autonomous Robots*, Intelligent Autonomous Systems IAS, 1993

[9] E. Puttkamer, T. Specht und R. Trieb, *Lokale Kollisionsvermeidung durch Ansteuerung der maximalen Hindernisdistanz für einen autonomen mobilen Roboter*, 9. Fachgespräch Autonome Mobile Systeme, Universität München, 1993

[10] Ren. C. Luo, P. Tai-Jee, *On Dynamic Motion Planning Problems*, IEEE International Conference on Robotics and Automation , 1991

[11] M. Rude, J. Loewer und T. Rupp, *Coordination of Mobile Robots by Estimating Relative Spatial and Temporal Uncertainties*, 2nd IFAC Conference on Intelligent Autonomous Vehicles, IAV 95, Espoo Finland, 1995

[12] B. Lammen, *Kollisionsvermeidung in Echtzeit für autonome Fahrzeuge*, 8. Fachgespräch Autonome Mobile Systeme, Universität Karlsruhe, 1992

Verklemmungsfreie Agentenkooperation in verteilten Robotersystemen

Thomas Längle, Tim Lüth und Martin Hesse

Institut für Prozessrechentechnik und Robotik (IPR)
Universität Karlsruhe
email: laengle@ira.uka.de

Abstract. Für die Steuerung komplexer und inhomogener Robotersysteme werden in jüngster Zeit oftmals Multiagentenansätze verwendet, da diese sich im Gegensatz zu zentralen Verfahren durch ihre höhere Flexibilität und Robustheit auszeichnen. Ein Nachteil ist jedoch die potentielle Gefahr des Auftretens von Verklemmungen bei Interaktionen verschiedener Agenten untereinander. Aufbauend auf einer realisierten Kommunikationsplattform für Agenten eines Multiagentensystemes, die eine verklemmungsfreie Verhandlung der Aufgaben nach einem erweiterten Contract-Net-Protokoll garantiert, wird in diesem Artikel das Problem der Kooperation von Agenten bei der Aufgabenausführung untersucht. Es wird hierzu aufgezeigt, unter welchen Bedingungen sich kooperierende Agenten verklemmen können; anschliessend wird ein Ansatz vorgestellt, mit dem dies unter bestmöglicher Ausnutzung von Systemressourcen vermieden werden kann. Die Korrektheit des Verfahrens wird am Beispiel des mobilen Zweiarmroboters KAMRO nachgewiesen.

1 Motivation

Die Thematik der Multi-Agenten-Systeme in der Robotik beschäftigt sich mit der Nutzung von Kooperationsmöglichkeiten zwischen den Teilsystemen eines komplexen Robotersystems und dem Lösen von Interaktionskonflikten. Hierzu wird der Interaktionsraum eines Agenten definiert als der (nicht nur räumliche) Bereich, in dem der Agent auf seine Umwelt und andere Agenten einwirken kann. Es werden vier Fälle für die Relation zwischen den Interaktionsräumen zweier Agenten unterschieden (Abbildung 1).

Viele Betrachtungen zu Multiagentensystemen beschäftigten sich mit Agenten, deren Interaktionsräume sich nicht oder nur unwesentlich überlagern, wie z.B. Transportsysteme einer Fertigungszelle. Setzt man eine geeignete Kommunikationsplattform voraus, können solche Systeme verklemmungsfrei entworfen werden, indem verschiedene Agenten keine gleichen Betriebsmittel beanspruchen. In komplexen Anwendungen sind die Interaktionsräume der Agenten häufig aber nicht überlagerungsfrei. Dies ist z.B. der Fall, wenn Agenten gleiche externe Betriebsmittel bean-spruchen oder mehrere Agenten eine Aufgabe kooperierend gemeinsam lösen. Die Kooperation der Agenten des Systems und die Verwaltung der Betriebsmittel müssen daher so gestaltet sein, dass auch bei Überlagerung

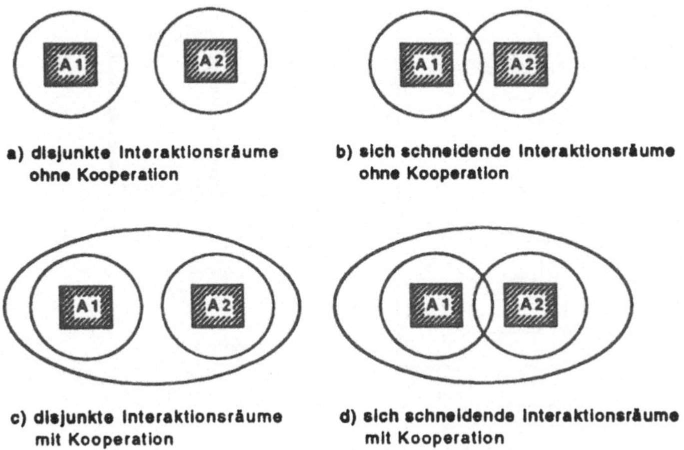

Fig. 1. Agentenbeziehungen

der Interaktionsräume von Agenten ein verklemmungsfreies System garantiert ist. Ziel dieses Artikels ist es, die hierzu notwendigen Methoden bereitzustellen.

2 Die Karlsruher Multi-Agenten-Architektur KAMARA

Die in Karlsruhe entwickelte Multi-Agenten-Architektur KAMARA dient als Infrastruktur zur komfortablen Realisierung von verteilten Steuerungen für komplexe inhomogene Robotersysteme. Die Agenten in KAMARA verhandeln nach einem erweiterten Contract-Net-Protokoll über einen gemeinsamen Kommunikationskanal, das Missionboard, um die Ausführung zu lösender Aufgaben. Die Ausführung der Aufgaben bleibt dann den beauftragten Agenten überlassen. Das hierbei verwendete Agentenmodell geht auf das Esprit-Projekt IMAGINE zurück und ist in Abbildung 2 zu sehen. Ein Agent besteht demgemäss aus den Komponenten Kommunikator, Kopf und Körper.

Der Kommunikator eines Agenten ist nur einmal vorhanden. Über ihn läuft die Kommunikation der anderen Instanzen des Agenten mit der Aussenwelt. Er sequentialisiert die an ihn herangetragenen Kommunikationsanforderungen, um gegenseitige Störungen zu vermeiden.

Der Kopf eines Agenten ist unterteilt in eine Planungsinstanz, den planenden Kopf, und eine Ausführungsinstanz, den ausführenden Kopf. Der planende Kopf ist für die Bewerbung des Agenten um Aufgaben zuständig und ermittelt hierzu die eigene Leistungsfähigkeit. Planende Köpfe eines Agenten gibt es genau so viele, wie Aufgaben auf dem Missionboard ausgeschrieben sind, die der Agent potentiell lösen kann.

Der ausführende Kopf dient der Aufgabenbearbeitung, wobei er den Agentenkörper zur Ansteuerung eventuell vorhandener physikalischer Komponenten benutzt. Der Agentenkörper besteht aus den Körperoperationen und der lokalen

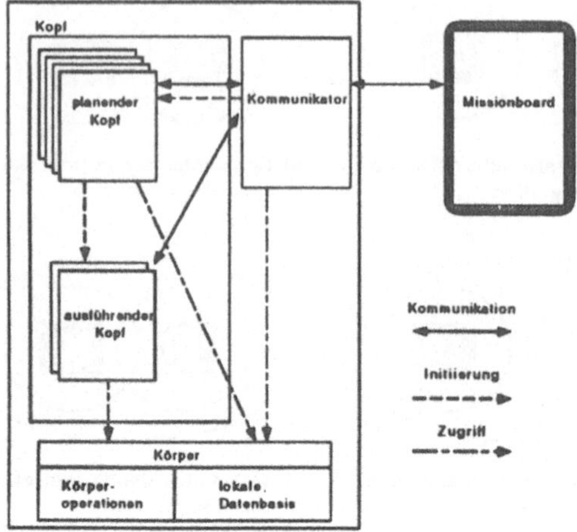

Fig. 2. Prozessstruktur eines Agenten (vergl. [Ruppert 1994])

Datenbasis. Die Körperoperationen dienen der Ansteuerung realer Komponenten. Die lokale Datenbasis enthält Daten, die nur für den Agenten selbst von Bedeutung sind.

3   Kooperation in KAMARA

Die Kooperation zwischen Agenten in einem Multi-Agenten-System ist wie folgt definiert:

Definition 1. Agentenkooperation ist das Zusammenwirken von Agenten im Sinne einer Auftraggeber-/ Auftragnehmerbeziehung zum Lösen einer Aufgabe unter Verwendung einer geeigneten Kommunikationsform. Der Auftragnehmer befindet sich dabei immer in der Phase der Aktionsausführung.

Bei der Kooperation kommt es zu einem Daten- bzw. Aktionsfluss vom Auftragnehmer zum Auftraggeber. Für den Steuerfluss existieren vier Varianten:

Zentraler Steuerfluss: Es gibt eine zentrale Instanz, die während der Kooperation sowohl den Auftraggeber als auch den Auftragnehmer steuert. Die Kommunikation findet dabei implizit durch die steuernde Instanz statt.

Verteilter Steuerfluss, auftraggeberinitiiert: Der Steuerfluss geht vom Auftraggeber aus und wird an den Auftragnehmer weitergegeben. Dies passiert in der Regel über einen gemeinsamen Kommunikationskanal.

Verteilter Steuerfluss, auftragnehmerinitiiert: Der Steuerfluss geht vom Auftragnehmer aus und wird an den Auftraggeber weitergegeben. Dies passiert in der Regel über einen gemeinsamen Kommunikationskanal.

Dezentraler Steuerfluss: Die beiden Agenten steuern sich jeweils selbst und reagieren durch Sensor-Aktor-Kopplung auf aufgenommene Reize.

Die Varianten mit verteiltem und zentralem Steuerfluss müssen durch eigene Interaktionsmuster realisiert werden. In KAMARA sind dies das *Agententeam* respektive der *Spezialagent*.

3.1 Agententeam

Agenten, die miteinander kooperieren, um eine Aufgabe zu lösen, bilden im Regelfall ein Agententeam. Die Kommunikation zur Verwirklichung der Kooperation findet in diesem Fall über das Missionboard statt, die Agenten bearbeiten die Aufgaben jedoch selbständig.

Die Agenten eines Agententeams gehen bei der gemeinsamen Bearbeitung einer Aufgabe eine lose Kopplung ein. Es werden zwar mehrere Agenten zur Aufgabenbewältigung benötigt; die Teilaufgaben bedingen jedoch nur eine asynchrone Kommunikation. Diese ist über den gemeinsamen Kommunikationskanal, das Missionboard, realisierbar.

Hierbei gibt es zwei Arten von Abhängigkeiten. Die schwächere Abhängigkeit erlaubt dem Agenten, während er auf das Ergebnis einer von ihm initiierten Aufgabe wartet, weitere Aufgaben zu bearbeiten, d.h. sie lässt explizite Parallelität im Sinne von [Wettstein 1993] zu. Die stärkere Abhängigkeit entsteht, wenn der Agentenkörper zum Zeitpunkt, an dem die Abhängigkeit auftritt, nicht zur Bearbeitung einer anderen Aufgabe freigegeben werden kann. Teams mit schwächerer Abhängigkeit werden im folgenden Teams *erster Ordnung*, solche mit stärkerer Abhängigkeit Teams *zweiter Ordnung* genannt.

Komplexe Anwendungen in der Robotik verlangen aber unter Umständen ein synchrones Zusammenarbeiten mehrerer Agenten, d.h. die Handlungen der Agenten müssen nicht nur parallel ablaufen, sondern sie müssen auch synchronisiert sein. Genau dieses Konzept wird durch den Spezialagenten bereitgestellt.

3.2 Spezialagent

Der Spezialagent erlaubt die Kontrolle mehrerer Agenten durch eine Instanz, ohne die vorhandenen Strukturen zu stark aufzubrechen. Er stellt den zentralen Ansatz der Agentenkooperation dar, da die Agenten unter seiner Kontrolle ihre Eigenständigkeit verlieren. Intern ist der Spezialagent aufgebaut wie ein normaler Agent. Analog zu diesem besitzt er einen Kommunikator, der mit dem Missionboard kommuniziert, und mehrere Köpfe, die für die Aufgabenbewertung und -ausführung zuständig sind. Für die Ausführung der ihm zugeteilten Aufgaben benötigt der Spezialagent jedoch die Körper anderer Agenten, da er selbst keinen Körper besitzt (vergleiche Abbildung 3). Während der Spezialagent eine Aufgabe löst, sind die Agenten, die von ihm zusammengefasst werden, nicht mehr zur Lösung eigener Aufgaben in der Lage, da die Kontrolle über ihren Körper beim Spezialagenten liegt. Dieser steuert die Körper mittels eines einzigen (Kopf-)Prozesses und kann daher Aufgaben lösen, die synchrone Handlungen der Agenten erfordern. Da der Spezialagent wie ein gewöhnlicher Agent aufgebaut ist und an der Aufgabenverhandlung über das Missionboard teilnimmt, kann auch er an einem Agententeam teilnehmen, da er von aussen als ein Agent betrachtet wird.

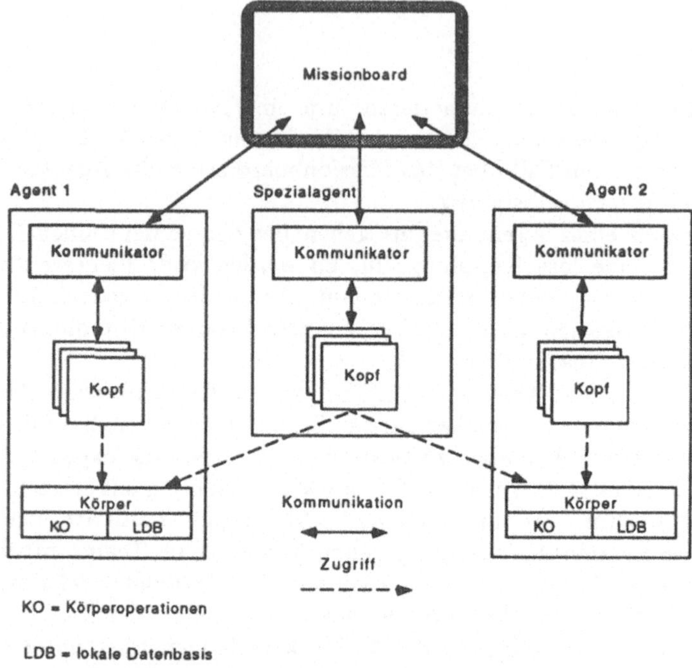

Fig. 3. Aufbau eines Spezialagenten in KAMARA

4 Verklemmungen in KAMARA

Für die Behandlung von Verklemmungen an Betriebsmitteln in einem Multiagentensystem lassen sich die bekannten Theorien zum Thema der Verklemmung an Betriebsmitteln heranziehen. Nach [Wettstein 1993] gibt es für den Umgang mit der Verklemmungsproblematik die Methoden

- Verklemmungsvermeidung,
- Verklemmungsverhinderung und
- Verklemmungserkennung/-behebung .

Da es in einem Multiagentensystem keine zentrale Instanz gibt, die das Prozessgeschehen überwacht, kommt hier nur die Verklemmungsvermeidung in Frage. Diese kann durch Sammelbelegung oder Reihenfolgebelegung der Betriebsmitteln realisiert werden.

4.1 Verklemmungen durch Agentenkörper/externe Betriebsmittel

Verklemmungen, an denen Agentenkörper und externe Betriebsmittel beteiligt sind, sind unangenehm, da sie zwei Betriebsmittelbereiche berühren, die meist getrennt verwaltet werden. Der Agentenkörper wird von den Kopfprozessen der Agenten belegt und freigegeben und ist in der Regel nicht in eine Verwaltung externer Betriebsmittel integriert. Eine Lösung des Problemes ist das Vorgeben einer Reihenfolge bei der Belegung derart, dass der Agentenkörper immer *zuletzt* belegt werden muss. Das hat zur Folge, dass ein Agent alle externen Betriebsmittel, die er benötigt, belegt hat, wenn er den Agentenkörper anfordert. Hier kann er daher nur noch blockiert werden, da der Prozess, der den Körper belegt hält, ebenso alle benötigten externen Betriebsmittel erfolgreich belegen konnte und somit nach endlicher Zeit terminiert.

4.2 Verklemmungen von Spezialagenten

Die Verklemmungen, die für Spezialagenten spezifisch sind, d.h. die Verklemmungen, die durch die parallelen Körperbelegungen mehrerer Spezialagenten entstehen, lassen sich dadurch vermeiden, dass die Belegungen nach dem Prinzip der Sammelbelegung oder Reihenfolgebelegung erfolgen. Bei allen anderen Arten der Verklemmung verhalten sich Spezialagenten wie normale Agenten.

4.3 Verklemmungen von Agententeams

In den folgenden Betrachtungen wird unter einem Team immer ein Team zweiter Ordnung verstanden, da ein Team erster Ordnung sich nicht anders verhält als eine Menge nichtkooperierender Agenten. Bei einem Team zweiter Ordnung sind zwei Fälle zu unterscheiden:

Verklemmungsfreiheit innerhalb eines Teams: Das Team habe die in Abbildung 4 gezeigte Aufrufstruktur. Die Agenten sind mit zwei Indizes versehen. Der obere gibt die Ordnungszahl des Abstiegszweiges an, während der untere Index die Nummer des Agenten innerhalb dieses Zweiges beziffert. Jeder Abstieg, der einem oder mehreren Aufstiegen in der Hierarchie folgt, hat die Erhöhung der Ordnungszahl zur Folge. Für die Abhängigkeiten zwischen den Agenten wird eine Funktion *dep*(dependence) definiert:

Definition 2. Die Agenten eines Teams bilden die Menge T der Teamagenten. Für jeden Agenten ist die Menge der von ihm abhängigen Agenten durch die Funktion

$$dep : T \to 2^{T}$$

$$dep(A_k^i) \mapsto \begin{cases} dep(A_{k-1}^i) \cup A_{k-1}^i, \text{ falls } k > 1 \\[2ex] dep(A_m^n) \cup A_m^n, \text{ falls } k = 1 \text{ und } A_m^n \text{ der Agent ist,} \\ \text{der } A_k^i \text{ beauftragte} \\[2ex] \emptyset, \text{ sonst} \end{cases}$$

definiert.

Die Menge *dep(A)* eines Agenten enthält gerade die Agenten, deren Körper zum Zeitpunkt der Ausführung der Teilaufgabe von *A* noch belegt sind. Für die Verklemmungsfreiheit eines Teams kann damit die folgende hinreichende Bedingung formuliert werden:

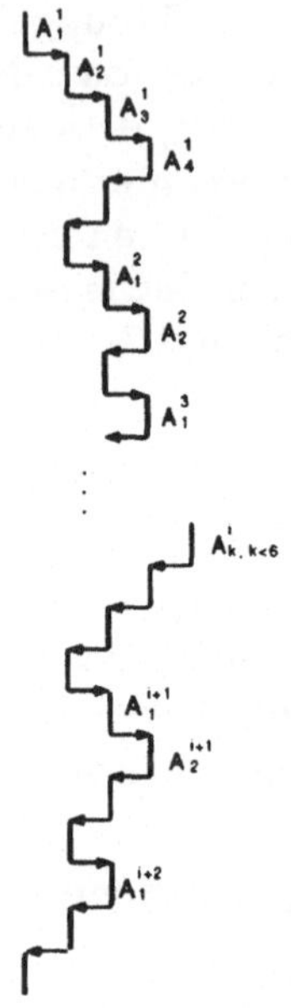

Fig. 4. Aufrufhierarchie eines Teams

Satz 1 *Sei T ein Team von Agenten mit der in Abbildung 4 gezeigten Aufrufstruktur. Dann gilt:*

$$\forall l : A_l \in T \land A_l \notin dep(A_l) \Rightarrow T \text{ ist verklemmungsfrei.}$$

Verklemmungsfreiheit unter mehreren Teams: Bei mehreren Teams kann es, auch wenn die einzelnen Teams nach Satz 1 verklemmungsfrei sind, zu Verklemmungen kommen, wenn die Teams gleiche Agenten enthalten. Seien nun t Teams im System vorhanden und sei $\mathcal{K}$ die Menge der Agententeams. Sei weiterhin $2^{\mathcal{K}}$ die Potenzmenge von $\mathcal{K}$. Die Agenten innerhalb eines Teams seien alle verschieden, d.h. kein Team enthalte einen Agenten mehrfach. Dann gilt folgender Satz:

Satz 2

$$\forall \mathcal{U} \in 2^{\mathcal{K}} (\forall T_i, T_k \in \mathcal{U}, i \neq k : |T_i \cap T_k| < 2) \wedge$$

$$(|\bigcup_{\substack{T_i, T_k \in \mathcal{U} \\ i \neq k}} T_i \cap T_k| < |\mathcal{U}|)$$

$$\Rightarrow \mathcal{K} \text{ ist verklemmungsfrei}$$

5 Protokoll für ein verklemmungsfreies MAS

Die aufgezeigten Bedingungen für Verklemmungsfreiheit eines Multiagentensystems werden nun in entsprechende Mechanismen für das KAMARA-System umgesetzt.

5.1 Kommuniaktionsmechanismen

Basis des Systems ist eine Kommunikationsplattform, die zur Aufgabenverhandlung und zum Informationsaustausch dient. Dieser Plattform ist ein Komunikationsmechanismus aufgesetzt, der die Kommunikation zwischen den Agenten stabil und verklemmungsfrei gestaltet: Alle Zugriffe auf die Kommunikationsplattform, das blackboardartige Missionboard, sind exklusiv, d.h. sowohl Lese- als auch Schreibzugriffe sind jeweils nur durch einen Agenten möglich.

5.2 Kooperationsmechanismen

Um auch die Agentenkooperation verklemmungsfrei zu ermöglichen, muss die Plattform um einen Kooperationsmechanismus erweitert werden. Hierbei müssen zwei Fälle betrachtet werden:

Spezialagent: Die Verklemmungsfreiheit von Spezialagenten wird gewährleistet, indem sie die Körper der Agenten, die sie benötigen, mittels Reihenfolge- oder Sammelbelegung anfordern.

Agententeam: Die Verklemmungsfreiheit eines Teams wird durch das Einhalten der Bedingung von Satz 1 garantiert. Da diese Bedingung für eine praktische Verwendung zu unhandlich ist, wird sie durch die stärkere Bedingung ersetzt, dass kein Agent in einem Agententeam mehr als einmal teilnehmen darf. Dadurch geht zwar etwas Parallelität verloren, die stärkere Bedingung lässt sich aber auf die Sammel- bzw. Reihenfolgebelegung von Betriebsmitteln abbilden, was für die Realisierung günstiger ist.

5.3 Koordinationsmechanismen

Mehrere Teams zweiter Ordnung können sich dann nicht verklemmen, wenn Satz 2 gilt. Diese Bedingung muss durch einen Koordinationsmechanismus garantiert werden, damit keine Verklemmungen auftreten.

5.4 Dynamische Effekte

Zum Abschluss fehlt nun noch ein Mechanismus zur Verhinderung von Verklemmungen durch dynamische Effekte an externen Betriebsmitteln. Hier kann eine geeignete verklemmungsfreie Verwaltung externer Betriebsmittel, die sich der Verfahren der Sammel- oder der Reihenfolgebelegung bedient, Anwendung finden.

6 Evaluierung des Konzeptes

Die aufgeführten Konzepte wurden an Hand des mobilen Robotersystems KAMRO evaluiert. Hierzu wurden die Teilsysteme des KAMRO (2 Manipulatoren, Overheadkamera, 2 Handkameras sowie die mobile Plattform) als Agenten modelliert, die um Aufgaben konkurrieren (Abbildung 5). Neben diesen Hardwareagenten müssen noch Agenten eingeführt werden, die durch die Verteilung des Planungsprozesses notwendig werden (globale Datenbasis, Manager zur Anbindung an gegebenenfalls vorhandene höhere Hierarchieebenen). Die Interaktionsräume der Agenten des KAMRO sind aus Abbildung 6 ersichtlich.

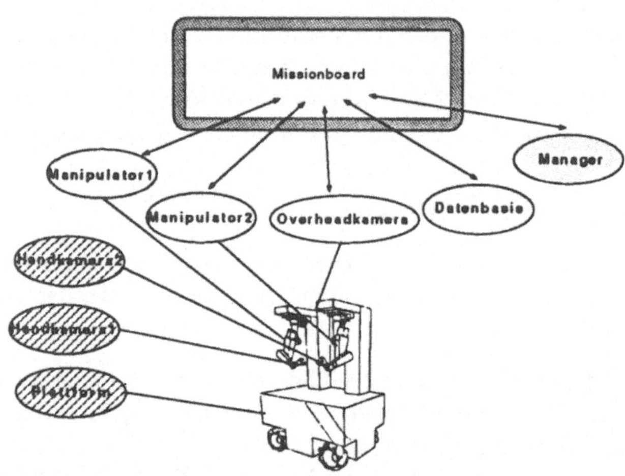

Fig. 5. KAMRO unter KAMARA

Experimentell wurde die Leistungsfähigkeit des Gesasmtsystems durch die Durchführung einer Benchmarkmontage in der Simulation bestätigt. Die zu montierenden Objekte waren dabei so plaziert, dass es zur Bildung mehrerer Teams zweiter Ordnung kam. Die Manipulatoren mussten Werkstücke untereinander austauschen und an Werkstücken umgreifen. Durch die Parallelität der Planung wäre es hierbei zu Verklemmungen gekommen, wenn die Kopfprozesse der Agenten die Betriebsmittel in beliebiger Weise hätten belegen können. Durch die Realisierung der beschriebenen Mechanismen im Datenbasisagenten konnte die Benchmarkmontage jedoch reibungslos durchgeführt werden.

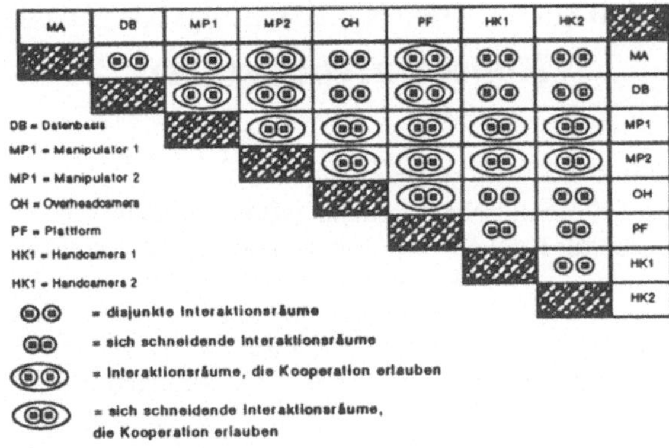

Fig. 6. Interaktionsräume der KAMRO-Agenten

7 Danksagung

Diese Arbeit wurde am Institut für Prozessrechentechnik und Robotik (IPR), Prof. Dr.-Ing. U. Rembold und Prof. Dr.-Ing. R. Dillmann, Fakultät für Informatik, Universität Karlsruhe, durchgeführt. Das Projekt war Teil des Sonderforschungsbereichs Küstliche Intelligenz und wissensbasierte Systeme (SFB 314), gefördert von der Deutschen Forschungsgemeinschaft (DFG).

References

[Hesse 96] M.Hesse:*Konzeption und Realisierung von Kooperationsmustern in einem verteilten Robotersystem*, Diplomarbeit, Institut für Prozessrechentechnik und Robotik, TH Karlsruhe, 1996.

[Längle und Lüth 1994] Th. Längle, T. Lüth: *Decentralized Control of Distributed Intelligent Robots and Subsystems*. Extended abstract accepted at AIRTC '94, Valencia, Spain.

[Längle und Lüth 1994] Lüth, T.C.; Längle, Th. *Task Description, Decomposition and Allocation in a Distributed Autonomous Multi-Agent Robot System*. IROS IEEE/RSJ Int. Conf. on Intelligent Robots and Systems, Munich, Germany, Sept 12-16 1994, pp. 1516-1523.

[Ozaki et al. 1992] Ozaki, K.; Asama, H.; Ishida, Y.; Matsumoto, A.; Kätsu, H.; Endo, I. *The Cooperation among Multiple Mobile Robots using Communication System*. DARS Int. Symp. on Distributed Autonomous Robotic System, Wako, Japan, Sept. 21-22, 1992

[Rembold et al. 1993] Rembold, U.; Lüth, T.C.; Hörmann, A.*Advancement of Intelligent Machines*. ICAM JSME Int Japan, August 2-4, 1993, pp. 1-7.

[Ruppert 1994] M. Ruppert:*Modellierung von Agenten in einem verteilten Robotersystem unter Berücksichtigung von Interaktionsmustern*. Diplomarbeit, Institut für Prozessrechentechnik und Robotik, TH Karlsruhe, 1994.

[Wettstein 1993] H. Wettstein: *Systemarchitektur*. C. Hanser Verlag, 1993.

Entscheidungsnetzwerke für selbstorganisierende Roboterarchitekturen

M. Muscholl, P. Levi
Praktische Informatik – Bildverstehen
Institut für Parallele und Verteilte Höchstleistungsrechner
Universität Stuttgart
Breitwiesenstr. 20-22
D-70565 Stuttgart
{mmuschol, levi}@informatik.uni-stuttgart.de

1   Einleitung

Im COMROS-Projekt (Cooperative Mobile Robots Stuttgart) werden kooperative, autonome Systeme in Form von mobilen Robotern im Verkehr (Konfliktlösung an Kreuzungen und bei der Konvoibildung) sowie in der Produktion (Planung und Steuerung fahrerloser Transportsysteme) untersucht. Es werden Roboteragenten-Systeme modelliert, die exemplarisch an den drei mobilen Fahrzeugen (Athos, Aramis und Portos [LB+94]) validiert werden. Die Roboterarchitektur gliedert sich in drei Ebenen, die reflexive, die taktische und die strategische Ebene. Jede Ebene besteht aus nebenläufigen Einheiten (Autonomiezyklen), die untereinander konkurrieren und kooperieren. Die Autonomiezyklen ([LMB95], [ROL95]) besitzen ein Modell der Umwelt, sowie eine Menge von Plänen, Aktionen und Zustände. Die Ausführung erfolgt zyklisch und wird von einer Entscheidungseinheit gesteuert.

In dieser Arbeit werden Netzwerke aus Entscheidungseinheiten vorgestellt, mit denen Abhängigkeiten zwischen Autonomiezyklen modelliert werden und anhand derer die Entscheidungseinheiten kooperativ Konflikte beheben.

Anhand einer umfangreichen Aufgabe in Abschnitt 4 wird demonstriert, wie Entscheidungsnetze mit Autonomiezyklen zusammenarbeiten, die über Datenflußnetzwerke aufgabenbezogen interagieren. Die Aufgabenstellung ist angelehnt an eine Fertigungsumgebung: Zwei fahrerlose Transportsysteme sollen einen Träger transportieren, der die Tragfähigkeit eines einzelnen überschreiten würde. Diesem Schwertransport wird ein lotsendes Fahrzeug vorausgeschickt, um zu überprüfen, ob die Korridore für den Konvoi passierbar sind.

2   Datenflußnetzwerke

Das Datenflußnetzwerk bildet das Rückgrat einer Anwendung. Es beschreibt, wie Autonomiezyklen zur Lösung von Aufgaben verschaltet werden und wie sie interagieren. Die Autonomiezyklen (Rechtecke) kommunizieren über Datenpuffer (Kreise), die beliebige Datentypen aufnehmen können. Datenpuffer werden auch als Schnittstellen zwischen Ebenen oder zwischen verschiedenen Roboteragenten verwendet. Zur Unterscheidung von gewöhnlichen Puffern werden sie durch andere Symbole (Fünf- oder Dreiecke) dargestellt.

Die Datenflußnetzwerke können als erweiterte Petri-Netze aufgefaßt werden, was detailliert in [LMB95] vorgestellt wurde. Ein Datenflußnetzwerk einer Anwendung ist die Vereinigung von einfacheren Datenflußnetzwerken, die einzelne Teilaufgaben der Anwendung lösen. Verschiedene Teilaufgaben nutzen gemeinsame Autonomiezyklen, welche zwischen den Teilaufgaben datengetrieben wechseln. In Abschnitt 4 wird eine Aufgabe mit mehreren Teilaufgaben vorgestellt.

Abb. 1 zeigt eine Folge von Datenflußnetzwerken mit steigender Komplexität der Aufgabenstellung. Netz I zeigt einen Navigator (N), der Trajektorien an einen Piloten (P) weiterleitet. Dieser wandelt sie in einzelne Fahrbefehle um und schickt sie an einen Roboterantrieb (R). In Netz II überwacht P zusätzlich die Umgebung mit Ultraschall (U), um vor Hindernissen rechtzeitig zu stoppen. Der Ultraschallzyklus ist in diesem Netzwerk so konfiguriert, daß er fortlaufend feuert. Sobald neue Abstandswerte vorliegenm werden sie an P weitergeleitet. In Netz III erhält P von einer Hinderniserkennung nun Informationen über die Position von Objekten innerhalb des Fahrweges, welchen er nun ausweichen kann. In Netz IV greifen sowohl P als auch H auf U zu. Der Ultraschallzyklus ist nun so konfiguriert, daß er nur auf Anforderung (von P und H) feuert. Neu hinzugekommen ist auch, daß H erkannte Objekte den Hinderniserkennungen anderer Roboteragenten mitteilt.

3   Entscheidungsnetzwerke

Wie im letzten Abschnitt beschrieben, werden Aufgaben durch die Vernetzung von spezialisierten Autonomiezyklen gelöst. Jeder Autonomiezyklus besitzt ein auf seine Funktion abgestimmtes, partielles Weltmodell, dessen Konsistenz über interne Mechanismen sicherstellt wird. Die Strukturierung einer Anwendung in einzelne miteinander vernetzte Autonomiezyklen gewährleistet eine funktionale Trennung, jedoch sind die Weltmodelle der Autonomiezyklen untereinander nicht disjunkt. Eine Hinderniserkennung benötigt z.B. ein Verständnis von Geschwindigkeit als einen den Anhalteweg bestimmenden Parameter, dessen Kontrolle einem Piloten unterliegt. Über die Modellierung des Datenflusses hinaus ist es notwendig, die Schnittmenge der Weltmodelle untereinander konsistent zu halten. Um Konsistenz zu erreichen, müssen bei Konflikten Entscheidungen getroffen werden, welches partielle Weltbild bestimmend für andere Weltbilder wird, oder wie verschiedene partielle Weltbilder so kombiniert werden können, daß alle konsistent zueinander sind. Hierfür stellen wir im folgenden Netzwerke aus Entscheidungseinheiten vor.

Ein *Entscheidungsnetzwerk* vernetzt die Entscheidungseinheiten der Autonomiezyklen, deren Weltmodelle sich überlappen und besteht im einzelnen aus

- einem Restriktionsnetz, das Abhängigkeiten zwischen den in der Schnittmenge der Weltmodelle liegenden Parameter modelliert. Die Parameter sind dabei den Entscheidungseinheiten des (einzigen) Autonomiezyklus zugeordnet, dessen Aufgabe es ist, diese Parameter zu steuern;

- einem Verhandlungsmechanismus, über den Konflikte zwischen den Entscheidungseinheiten gelöst werden. Konflikte treten auf, wenn entschieden werden muß, wie Inkonsistenzen des Restriktionsnetzes durch Relaxieren von Restriktionen behoben werden sollen;

- Verhandlungsstrategien, welche eine Entscheidungseinheiten in Abhängigkeit vom Zustand des Autonomiezyklus wählt;

- dynamischen Priorisierungsmechanismus, der die Verhandlungsposition einer Entscheidungseinheit festlegt.

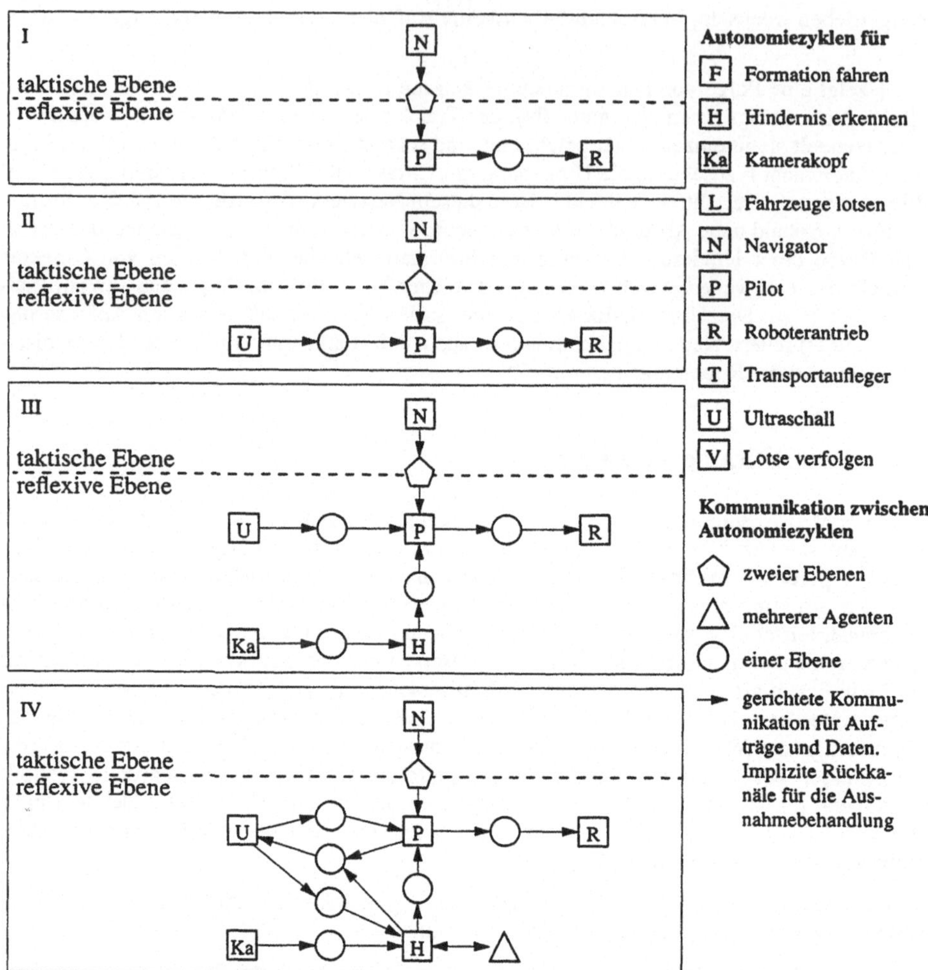

Abbildung 1. Datenflußnetzwerke auf reflexiver Ebene

3.1 Restriktionsnetz

Das Restriktionsnetz, welches den Kern eines Entscheidungsnetzwerks bildet, wird für jede Teilaufgabe entworfen. Es wird eine minimale Menge von Entscheidungseinheiten bestimmt, die sich durch ihre Parameterfestlegungen gegenseitig beeinflussen. Meist besteht im Datenflußnetzwerk dann eine direkte Nachbarschaft zwischen den beteiligten Autonomiezyklen.

Verfolgt ein Fahrzeug gleichzeitig mehrere Teilaufgaben, so können sich einzelne Restriktionsnetze überlappen. In der Schnittmenge zweier Restriktionsnetze befinden sich Untermengen von Parametern, welche die jeweiligen Entscheidungseinheiten in das Netzwerk einbringen. Die Aufgabe der zugehörigen Entscheidungseinheiten ist es sicherzustellen, daß die Werte ihrer Parameter in allen Restriktionsnetzen konsistent sind.

3.2   Verhandlungsmechanismus

Den Verhandlungsmechanismus kann man in drei Phasen unterteilen, einer *Initialisierungs-phase*, einer *Propagierungsphase* und einer *Relaxierungsphase*. Vor Antritt einer Fahrt oder Aufgabe muß sichergestellt werden, daß die Wertemengen der Parameter in den Restriktions-netzen konsistent sind. Ist dies in der *Initialisierungsphase* sichergestellt worden, so kann mit der Ausführung der Aufgabe begonnen werden.

Erfordert die Aufgabe aufgrund von äußeren Einwirkungen Änderungen der Wertebereiche von Parametern einer Entscheidungseinheit, so benachrichtigt sie die betroffenen Einheiten und *propagiert* die Änderungen durch eine ihr lokal vorliegende Kopie des Netzwerkes. Ist das Netz weiterhin konsistent, so wird die ermittelte Lösung den anderen Einheiten mitgeteilt. Diese können nun in einer anschließenden *Verhandlung* die Lösung akzeptieren oder Gegen-vorschläge unterbreiten (ein entsprechendes Verhandlungsprotokoll wurde in [HL92] vorge-stellt).

Kann keine konsistente Wertebelegung gefunden werden, so wird die *Relaxierungsphase* akti-viert. Die im Restriktionsnetzwerk modellierten Abhängigkeiten sind Konsistenzbedingungen zwischen verschiedenen Weltmodellen und können nicht relaxiert werden. Jede Entschei-dungseinheit besitzt jedoch interne Restriktionen, nach denen sie die Wertemenge der Parame-ter aufstellt. Sie haben entweder die Form von absoluten Intervallen, oder stehen in Relation mit anderen Parametern des Weltmodells. Diese internen Restriktionen sind abhängig von der Planmenge, welche die einzelnen Autonomiezyklen hinsichtlich ihrer Funktion bereithalten. Einschränkungen oder Erweiterungen der Planmenge führen zu Änderungen der im Weltmo-dell hinterlegten Zusammenhänge und somit zu veränderten internen Restriktionen. Ziel der Relaxierungsphase ist es, über eine Änderung in den Planmengen der Autonomiezyklen eine Abschwächung der Restriktionen zu erreichen und somit die Konsistenz im Entscheidungs-netzwerk wieder herzustellen.

3.3   Verhandlungsstrategien

Die Entscheidungseinheiten verfügen über Heuristiken, die abhängig von dem Zustand im Autonomiezyklus und der Historie der Wahrnehmung Strategien festlegen, nach denen eine Entscheidungseinheit bereit ist, Einschränkungen in der Wertemenge der Parameter zu akzep-tieren oder interne Restriktionen zu relaxieren.

Praktische Untersuchungen werden zeigen, inwieweit das Bekanntgeben eigener Strategien die Lösungsfindung vereinfacht und wie hoch der Aufwand ist, der durch ein kontinuierliches Bekanntgeben von Änderungen in den Strategien entsteht.

3.4   Verhandlungsposition

Die Verhandlungsposition einer Entscheidungseinheit bestimmt, ob sie von anderen Entschei-dungseinheiten Beschränkungen akzeptiert, oder ihre eigenen Bedingungen durchzusetzen versucht. Gelingt es einer Entscheidungseinheit über mehrere Verhandlungen zu dominieren, so kann man eine Masterrolle identifizieren, hinsichtlich der Bestimmung des Verhaltens des Netzwerkes. Andererseits kann ein Mastering-Mechanismus dazu dienen, die Verhandlungspo-sitionen festzulegen, um zu zielgerichteten Entscheidungen zu gelangen.

In [LMB95] wurde ein Mastering-Verfahren vorgestellt, welches angelehnt an den Informiert-heitsgrad eines Autonomiezyklus die dynamische Priorität des Autonomiezyklus verändert.

4   Aufgabe: lotsenbasiertes, kooperatives Transportieren eines Trägers

Im folgenden wird an einer umfangreicheren Aufgabenstellung demonstriert, wie Entscheidungsnetzwerke mit Autonomiezyklen zusammenarbeiten, die über Datenflußnetzwerke aufgabenbezogen interagieren. Der Verhandlungsmechanismus wird nicht im Datenflußnetzwerk modelliert, da er nur indirekt zur Lösung einer (Teil-)Aufgabe beiträgt. Die Datenflußnetzwerke sind in Abb. 2, eine Übersicht über die Entscheidungsnetzwerke in Abb. 5 dargestellt.

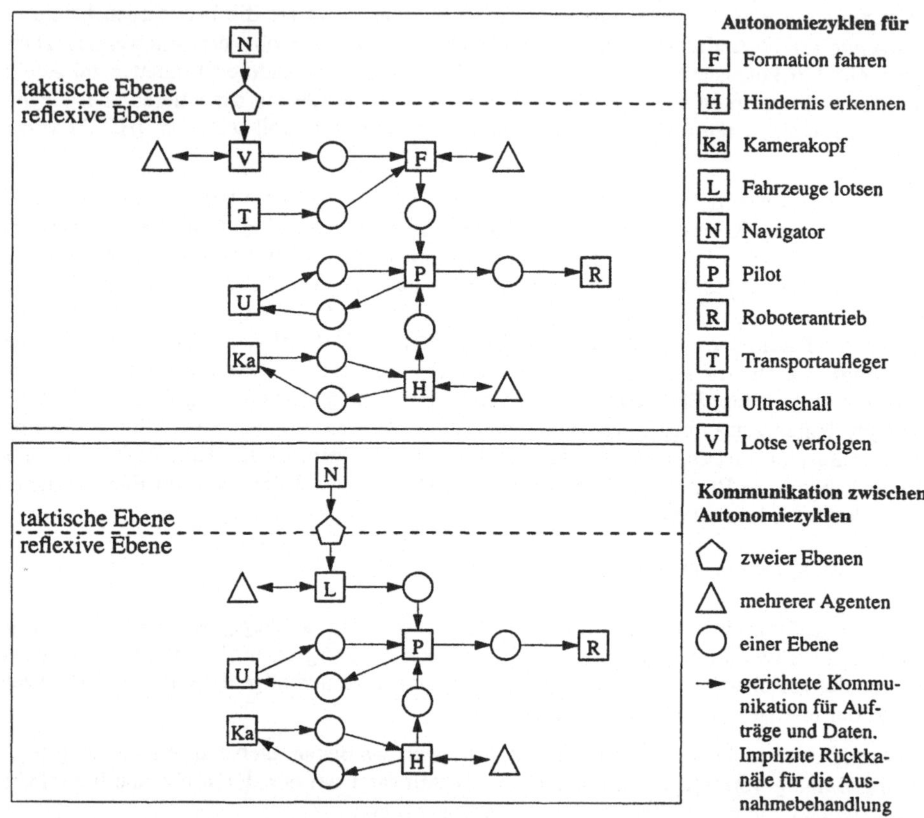

Abbildung 2. Datenflußnetzwerke zur Aufgabe; das obere definiert den Datenfluß der Transportfahrzeuge, das untere den des lotsenden Fahrzeugs.

In einer Fertigungsumgebung soll sperriges Material in Form eines Trägers von fahrerlosen Transportsystemen befördert werden. Hierzu sind zwei mit einem Transportaufleger ausgerüstete Roboterfahrzeuge nötig. Zusätzlich wird ein lotsendes Fahrzeug benötigt. Dieses fährt voraus und überprüft, ob die Korridore für den Konvoi passierbar sind.

Für den Lotsen, Transporter 1 und Transporter 2 lassen sich folgende Teilaufgaben identifizieren, die gleichzeitig verfolgt werden müssen:

- Fahrweg auf statische Hindernisse untersuchen. Diese Teilaufgabe gehört zum Grundrepertoire eines autonomen Fahrzeugs. Darüberhinaus sollen hier klassifizierte Objekte und deren Position anderen Fahrzeugen mitgeteilt werden. Als Sensor wird ein in einer Achse schwenkbarer Kamerakopf eingesetzt.

- Manövrieren in engen Durchfahrten. Die Fahrzeuge sollen in der Lage sein, den Raum in abknickenden Korridoren vollständig auszunutzen. Hierfür wird ein Ultraschallgürtel von 24 Sensoren je Fahrzeug eingesetzt.

- Transporter 1 und Transporter 2 befördern gemeinsam den Träger. Dieser liegt auf je einem Transportaufleger auf, dessen eingebaute Sensoren die Relativbewegung der beiden Fahrzeuge innerhalb gewisser Grenzen messen kann.

- Der Lotse gibt in Zeitabständen eine Route frei, die für die Transportfahrzeuge passierbar ist. Die Route wurde den Fahrzeugen vorab von ihren Navigatoren bekanntgegeben. Die Strecke muß bis zu einem vorgegebenen Termin zurückgelegt werden. Ist dies nicht möglich, wird eine Fehlermeldung an die Navigatoren zurückgegeben, sobald dies festgestellt wird.

4.1 Datenflußnetzwerke

Die Hinderniserkennung H aktualisiert fortlaufend eine Karte, die Hindernisse enthält. Sie überwacht den Fahrbereich, den der Pilot P spezifiziert und meldet erkannte Hindernisse an ihn weiter. Der Fahrbereich wird von P durch zwei Radien (nach links bzw. nach rechts) angegeben, innerhalb deren Grenzen P Fahrbefehle generiert. Will P eine engere Kurve fahren, so garantiert H keine rechtzeitigen Hindernismeldungen. Die Restriktionen zwischen dem Fahrbereich, der gewählten Geschwindigkeit und dem von der Kamera zu überwachenden Bereich werden über ein Ka-H-P-Entscheidungsnetzwerk (Abb. 4) abgestimmt.

Der Pilot P fragt den Ultraschall U für die Kontrolle des Seitenabstandes beim Fahren und während des Rangierens ab.

Die Teilaufgabe des Formationsfahrens wird von den Autonomiezyklen F (Formation fahren) und T (Transportaufleger) erbracht. Hierbei berechnet F ausgehend von der Sensorinformation von T in kurzen Abständen Trajektorien für P. Die für P zugängliche Umweltinformation in Form von zulässigen Fahrbereichen bringt P in ein F-P-Entscheidungsnetzwerk ein.

Das gelotste Fahren wird in den Transportfahrzeugen vom Autonomiezyklus V (Lotse verfolgen) koordiniert. V erhält Trajektorien vom Autonomiezyklus L des lotsenden Fahrzeugs und reicht sie an F weiter. Notwendige Abstimmungen werden über ein F-V-L-Entscheidungsnetz vorgenommen.

4.2 Entscheidungsnetzwerke

Die Abhängigkeiten zwischen Kamerakopf, Hinderniserkennung und Piloten werden durch den Algorithmus festgelegt, mit dem H den zu überwachenden Bereich bestimmt. Dieser Bereich wird durch je einen Blickwinkel (nach links bzw. nach rechts) sowie durch einen Mindestabstand (Anhalteweg) und einem maximalen Abstand eingegrenzt. Unterhalb des Mindestabstandes ist ein rechtzeitiges Erkennen eines Hindernisses unmöglich, so daß durch andere Verfahren (z.B. durch Eintragen vorausgehender Auswertungen in eine Karte), Hindernisfreiheit zugesichert werden kann. Für Objekte jenseits des maximalen Abstands ist es ausreichend, wenn sie später klassifiziert werden.

Abb. 3 zeigt, wie der Blickwinkel definiert wird. Sei t_Σ die Reaktionszeit der Pipeline Ka-H-P-R und T_H definiere die Periode, nach der die Kamera ein Bild unter dem gleichen Blickwinkel aufnimmt. Dann berechnet sich der Anhalteweg l bei einer konstanten Geschwindigkeit v und einer Bremsverzögerung a, der auf einem Kreisbogen mir Radius R zurückgelegt wird, zu $f_l(v, a, t_\Sigma, T_H)$: $l = v^2/(2a) + (t_\Sigma + T_H)v$.

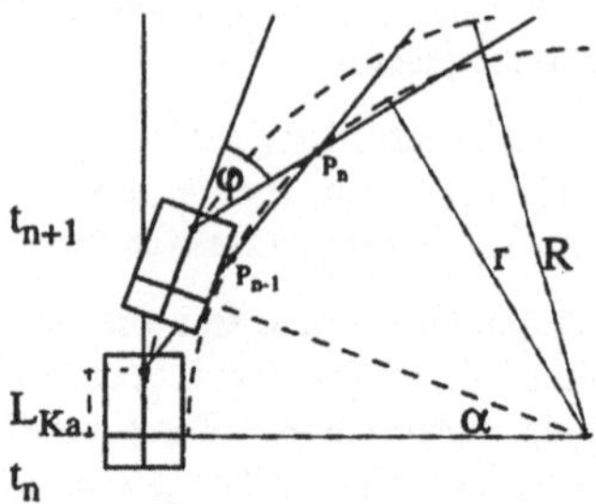

Abbildung 3. Blickwinkel der Kamera für eine überwachte Fahrt entlang eines Kreises

Der Kreis habe den Radius R. Die Bildanalysezeit sei $\Delta t = t_{n+1} - t_n$. Das Fahrzeug fährt währenddessen bei konstanter Geschwindigkeit v einen Bogen der Länge l. Der zurückgelegte Winkel des Kreises beträgt $\alpha = l/R$. Ausgehend von der Position der Kamera zum Zeitpunkt t_n und t_{n+1} ziehen wir zwei Geraden, die sich und den Kreis mit Radius r in einem Punkt schneiden. Sei φ als der Winkel definiert, der die Steigung beider Geraden (bezogen auf das Roboterkoordinatensystem zum Zeitpunkt t_i) festlegt.

Anschaulich bestimmt der Winkel φ eine Grenze des Gesichtsfeldes einer Hinderniserkennung, welches unter der Annahme überwacht wird, daß nur statische Hindernisse existieren. Gegeben der Radius R, muß um Kollisionsfreiheit zusichern zu können, ein um die Breite des Fahrzeugs verringerter Radius r eingesehen werden. Dabei sind alle Objekte die sich in der Kreisfläche um die Kamera zwischen P_{n-1} und P_n befinden, zu klassifizieren.

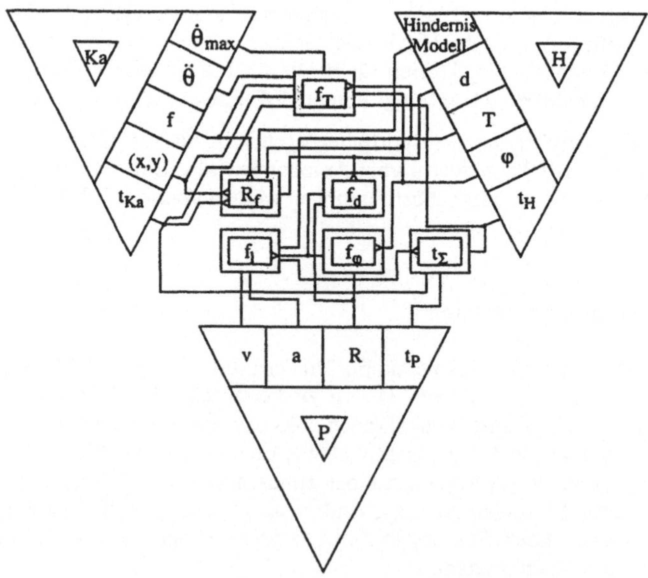

Abbildung 4. Ka-H-P-Entscheidungsnetzwerk.

Der Blickwinkel φ ergibt sich mit $f_\varphi(R, l)$: $\varphi = \mathrm{acot}\dfrac{L_{Ka}RA - r\sqrt{-r^2 + (L_{Ka}^2 + R^2)A}}{r^2 - R^2 A}$. Dabei

sei $A = (2 - 2\cos\alpha)/(\sin\alpha)^2$ und r der um die Breite des Fahrzeuges verringerte Radius R. Die zu klassifizierenden Objekte liegen dann in einer Entfernung zur Kamera von $f_d(l, R)$: $(d_{\min}, d_{\max}) = (d(P_{Ka}, P_{n-1}), d(P_{Ka}, P_n))$.

Ist der Blickwinkel größer als das Gesichtsfeld der Kamera (bestimmt durch R_f), so muß der Kamerakopf geschwenkt werden. Die Periodendauer wird mittels eines Planungsmoduls f_T berechnet.

Die Algorithmen der Bildverarbeitung benötigen für das kleinste in H modellierte Hindernis eine Mindestanzahl von Pixeln. Nun legt die Brennweite der Kamera, zusammen mit der konfigurierten Auflösung des Frame Grabbers, eine maximale Entfernung fest, jenseits der das Objekt nicht mehr als Hindernis erkannt werden kann. Insbesondere muß $d_{\max}$ kleiner als diese Entfernung sein. $d_{\max}$ erhöht sich proportional zu dem Anhalteweg, also z.B. durch höhere Geschwindigkeiten oder durch längere Periodendauern. Die Periodendauer wird maßgeblich durch die Kamerakopfbewegungen bestimmt, um Bilder aus unterschiedlichen Sektoren, links und rechts der Fahrtrichtung aufzunehmen. Wird φ erhöht, so steigt die für die Bewegung des Kamerakopfes benötigte Zeit in diskreten Schritten, abhängig von der Brennweite des Objektivs. Somit steigt die Periodendauer und die Entfernung des zu überwachenden Bereichs, der aber durch die Bildauflösung beschränkt ist. Höhere Auflösungen führen auch zu höheren Grabb-Zeiten.

Das Entscheidungsnetzwerk zwischen P (Piloten) und F (Formation fahren) dient der Abstimmung der Trajektorie, die P abfahren darf. P kann die Trajektorie in vorgegebenen Grenzen autonom anpassen. Muß der Pilot des vorausfahrenden Fahrzeugs (P_1) z.B. vor einem Hindernis ausweichen, und überschreitet er dabei die ihm vorgegebenen Grenzen, so stimmt P_1 die Trajektorie über das F_1-P_1-F_2-P_2-Entscheidungsnetzwerk der Fahrzeuge ab. Somit wird sichergestellt, daß die Fahrzeuge sich nicht zu weit voneinander entfernen und der Träger nicht verlorengeht.

Das Entscheidungsnetzwerk zwischen L (Fahrzeuge losten), $V_{1,2}$ (Lotsen verfolgen) und $F_{1,2}$ (Formation fahren) wird benötigt, um die Trajektorie abzustimmen, nach der die Formation die Korridore abfährt. $F_{1,2}$ bringen ihre Parameter über physische Beschränkungen der Formation ein. $V_{1,2}$ koordinieren die Anordnungen beim Verfolgen des Lotsen (hintereinanderfahren, nebeneinanderfahren, Festlegen des vorderen bzw. linken Fahrzeugs). L stimmt die zulässige Entfernung ab, die der Lotse den folgenden Fahrzeugen voraus sein darf und verwaltet Termine, die während der Fahrt eingehalten werden müssen.

Das Entscheidungsnetzwerk zwischen den $U_{1,2,3}$ (Ultraschall) und $P_{1,2,3}$ (Pilot) der Fahrzeuge wird benötigt, um Störungen zwischen den Ultraschallsensoren der Fahrzeuge zu minimieren. Es wäre bereits ausreichend nur $U_{1,2,3}$ untereinander abzustimmen, jedoch können durch die Hinzunahme von $P_{1,2,3}$ die Sensorabfragen aneinander angepaßt werden. Die Piloten stimmen über das $U_{1,2,3}$-$P_{1,2,3}$-Entscheidungsnetzwerk ihre Abfragen so ab, daß ihnen Antwortzeiten für ihre Abfragen garantiert werden. Dies ist für Formationsfahrten wichtig, da das Ausbleiben eines Sensorergebnisses sich auf den Konvoi auswirkt, indem er z.B. zum Halten gezwungen wird.

Nachdem die Entscheidungsnetze eingeführt wurden, wird nun beschrieben, wie das System sich verhält, wenn es aufgrund eines äußeren Ereignisses aus einem Gleichgewichtszustand gebracht wird. Das Ereignis sei durch ein sich auf der Fahrroute befindendes Objekt gegeben, das von der Hinderniserkennung des vorderen Transportfahrzeugs nicht rechtzeitig klassifiziert werden konnte. Die Hinderniserkennung wird ein weiteres Bild auswerten und feststellen, daß es sich um eine Bodenunreinheit handelt und nicht um ein Hindernis. Die Aufgabe der Entscheidungsnetze ist es, die Geschwindigkeit zu reduzieren, um Zeit für eine zweite Bildauswertung zu schaffen. Hierzu muß der Konvoi abbremsen und der Lotse über die Verzögerung informiert werden. Es wird angenommen, daß keine Termine einer Verzögerung entgegenstehen (andernfalls würde die Bodenunreinheit als Hindernis angesehen werden und vom Konvoi umfahren werden müssen).

Im folgenden werden abstrakt eingeführte Begriffe *kursiv* hervorgehoben. Die Abkürzungen (H, P, F, V, L) stehen für die Entscheidungseinheiten der Autonomiezyklen mit gleichen Namen. In Abb. 5 werden die Entscheidungsnetzwerke der Aufgabe dargestellt.

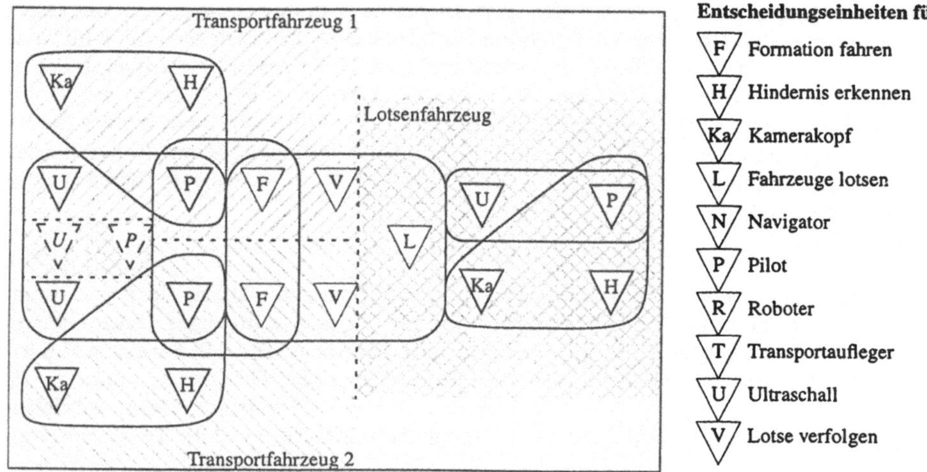

Abbildung 5. Verknüpfung zwischen den Entscheidungsnetzwerken der Aufgabe

Da das genannte Objekt nicht im ersten Bild klassifiziert werden konnte, benötigt H (Hinderniserkennung) ein weiteres Frame unter derselben Blickrichtung. Während dieser Zeit würde sich das vordere Fahrzeug bei gleichbleibender Geschwindigkeit so nah an das Objekt annähern, daß ein sicheres Ausweichen nicht mehr möglich wäre. H erzeugt also eine interne Restriktion für das Intervall (d_{min}, d_{max}) des Beobachtungsbereiches, so daß bei der zweiten Aufnahme das Objekt darin enthalten ist. Daraufhin propagiert H das Intervall durch das Restriktionsnetz und berechnet eine Lösung für die verringerte Geschwindigkeit (*Propagierungsphase*). In der folgenden *Verhandlung* verfolgt H die *Strategie*, wenn nötig φ zu reduzieren, um durch eine sich somit verkürzende Periode T_H Zeit für die Klassifikation zu erhalten.

H unterbreitet nun P den Vorschlag, eine geringere Geschwindigkeit zu fahren. P kann nur in Absprache mit dem nachfolgenden Fahrzeug die Geschwindigkeit ändern, was durch interne Restriktionen für P (Parametereinschränkungen aus dem F-P-Entscheidungsnetz) festgelegt wird. P hat nun die Wahl die Parametereinschränkungen zu relaxieren, oder einen Gegenvorschlag unter Berücksichtigung der Einschränkungen zu machen. In diesem Beispiel versucht P, die Geschwindigkeit im F-P-Entscheidungsnetz zu verringern.

P (P_1) *propagiert* die von H vorgeschlagene Geschwindigkeit und unterbreitet den Verhandlungspartnern im F-P-Netz (F_1, P_2, F_2) die berechnete Lösung: die Trajektorie soll von den beiden Transportfahrzeugen mit geringerer Geschwindigkeit abgefahren werden. P verfolgt die Strategie, die Verhandlung dann abzubrechen, wenn eine Einigung nicht direkt möglich ist.

Die Verhandlungspartnern von P überprüfen daraufhin ihre internen Restriktionen und stimmen zu, wenn sie nicht verletzt sind. Ansonsten berechnen sie einen Gegenvorschlag. F_1 ermittelt nun ob im F-V-L-Netzwerk Restriktionen hinsichtlich Verzögerungen vorliegen. Dies sei in unserem Beispiel nicht der Fall, so daß F_1 dem Vorschlag von P zustimmt. Nachdem auch P_2 und F_2 zugestimmt haben, kann P an H seine Zustimmung melden.

H bestätigt das Verhandlungsergebnis im Ka-H-P-Netz, (P im P-F-Netz) und daraufhin verringern P und P_2 die Geschwindigkeit.

Nun kann H das benötigte zweite Bild analysieren, und das Objekt erfolgreich als kein Hindernis klassifizieren. Die Einwirkung durch das äußere Ereignis ist damit abgeschlossen und H kann die interne Restriktion für (d_{min}, d_{max}) zurücknehmen. Dies führt zu einer erneuten *Propagierung* durch das Ka-H-P-Netz und über den beschriebenen Mechanismus wird die Geschwindigkeit wieder angehoben.

5 Ausblick

Das hier vorgestellte Konzept für die Abstimmung zwischen Entscheidungseinheiten von Autonomiezyklen ist aus der Einsicht entstanden, daß eine Kooperation zwischen den Autonomiezyklen nicht nur durch Austausch von Aufträgen und Weiterreichen von Berechnungsergebnissen erfolgen kann. Vielmehr ist es nötig sicherzustellen, daß die Entscheidungen, die in den parallel agierenden Autonomiezyklen getroffen werden, zueinander konsistent sind, so daß ein stabiles, zielgerichtetes und allen Teilaufträgen gerecht werdendes Verhalten erreicht wird.

Weitere Arbeiten sind hinsichtlich der Bestimmung der Verhandlungsposition einzelner in Konflikt stehender Entscheidungseinheiten notwendig. Studien praktischer Beispiele sollen zeigen, welches dynamische Verhalten sich ergibt, und ob sich hieraus Ordnungsparameter und Stellgrößen für die Vergabe von Verhandlungspositionen finden lassen.

Literatur

[HL92]   S. Handel, P. Levi: Restriktionsbasiertes Verhandlungskonzept für eine dezentrale, kooperative Aktionsplanung. In: Konferenzband der 8. Fachgespräche Autonome Mobile Systeme, Karlsruhe, 1992

[LB+94]   P. Levi, Th. Bräunl, M. Muscholl, A. Rausch: Architektur und Ziele der Kooperative Mobilen Robotersysteme Stuttgart. In: Konferenzband der 10. Fachgespräche Autonome Mobile Systeme, Stuttgart, 1994

[LMB95]   P. Levi, M. Muscholl, Th. Bräunl: Cooperative Mobile Robots Stuttgart: Architecture and Tasks. In: Proceedings of the 4th International Conference on Intelligent Autonomous Systems, Karlsruhe, 1995

[ROL95]   A. Rausch, N. Oswald, P. Levi: Cooperative crossing of traffic intersections in a distributed robot system. In SPIE, Sensor Fusion and Networked Robotics VIII, Vol. 2589, Philadelphia, Oktober 1995

Mensch/Roboter-Schnittstelle

Kommandierung eines Serviceroboters mit natürlicher, gesprochener Sprache

C. Fischer, P. Havel, G. Schmidt

Lehrstuhl für
Steuerungs- und Regelungstechnik
Technische Universität München
D-80290 München

J. Müller, H. Stahl, M. Lang

Lehrstuhl für
Mensch-Maschine-Kommunikation
Technische Universität München
D-80290 München

email: {fischer, havel, gs, mue, sta, lg}@{lsr, mmk}.e-technik.tu-muenchen.de

Kurzfassung. Dieser Beitrag beschreibt die Verwendung natürlicher, gesprochener Sprache zur Kommandierung eines als persönlicher Assistent eingesetzten Serviceroboters. Im ersten Schritt wird dazu aus der gesprochenen Äußerung der Bedeutungsinhalt extrahiert. Bei der anschließenden Generierung der Roboterbefehle werden falsche Anweisungen abgewiesen und fehlende Information durch ein Umgebungsmodell oder über eine Rückfrage an den Bediener ergänzt. Das Verfahren ist Bestandteil der Mensch-Roboter-Schnittstelle des mobilen Serviceroboters ROMAN.

1 Einführung

Mobile Serviceroboter gewinnen zunehmend an Bedeutung. Bereits heute umfaßt ihr Aufgabenbereich die Essensverteilung in Krankenhäusern oder die Reinigung von Flugzeughüllen. Weitere Einsatzgebiete liegen im Dienstleistungsbereich als persönlicher Assistent zur Übernahme einfacher Botenaufgaben und zur Unterstützung älterer oder behinderter Menschen bei manuellen Tätigkeiten, sowie im Bereich des Teleservice und der Tele-

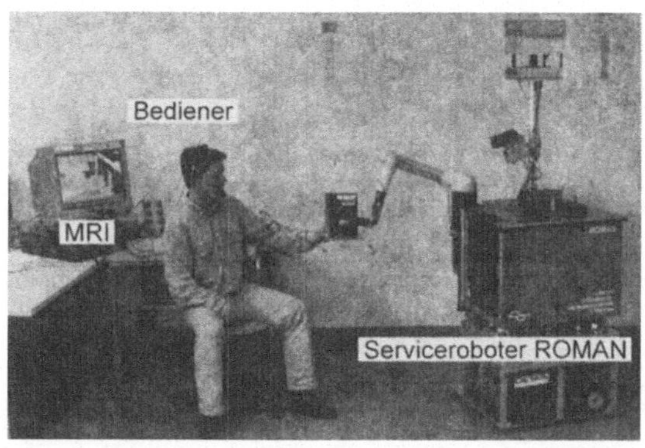

Abb. 1. Serviceroboter ROMAN mit Bediener am MRI

diagnose von industriellen Anlagen. Im Idealfall führt der Roboter seinen Auftrag vollkommen autonom aus. Mit den derzeit zur Verfügung stehenden technischen Mitteln aus dem Bereich der künstlichen Intelligenz ist jedoch noch keine selbstständige Durchführung komplexer Serviceaufgaben in unbekannten Situationen möglich. Einen realistischen Kompromiß auf dem Weg zu erhöhter Autonomie bilden semiautonome Robotersysteme, welche bei Bedarf durch das Wissen und die Entscheidungsfähigkeit des Bedieners unterstützt werden. Dabei kommandiert, überwacht und unterstützt der Bediener den Serviceroboter über eine geeignete Mensch-Roboter-Schnittstelle (huMan-Robot-Interface - MRI), siehe Abbildung 1.

Mit dem Vordringen der Serviceroboter in die unmittelbare Umgebung des Menschen ändern sich im hohen Maße die Anforderungen an die Mensch-Roboter-Kommunikation. Zur Steigerung der Akzeptanz kommt es dabei vor allem darauf an, Menschen auf die gleiche Art und Weise mit dem Roboter kommunizieren zu lassen, wie sie es von einem Mensch-zu-Mensch-Dialog gewohnt sind. Eine unkomplizierte, menschengerechte Kommunikation zeichnet sich durch die folgenden, an die Realisierung gestellten Anforderungen aus: 1. Dialoggeführte natürlichsprachliche und sprecherunabhängige Kommandoeingabe. 2. Visuelle bildschirmgeführte Überwachung und Roboterunterstützung. 3. Haptische Überwachung und Unterstützung bei der mobilen Handhabung. 4. Gesprochener Kommentar bei der Ausführung von Aufgaben.

Der vorliegende Beitrag konzentriert sich auf die sprecherunabhängige Kommandierung eines Serviceroboters mit natürlicher, gesprochener Sprache. In der Literatur sind mehrere Ansätze zur sprachlichen Steuerung eines Roboters bekannt: In [1] wird die Notwendigkeit nach einer einfachen, für den Menschen gewohnten Kommandoeingabe betont. Verwendung findet ein sprecherabhängiger Spracherkenner, mit dem im System vorhandene Makropakete ausgewählt werden können. Die Repräsentation natürlicher Sprache in Bezug auf eine Roboterumgebung bildet den Schwerpunkt der in [2] vorgestellten Arbeit. Dabei wird aus einer textuellen Eingabe direkt ein Roboterbefehl generiert. Eine Unterscheidung der Spracheingabe in Standardeingabe und Telesteuerung nimmt [3] vor. Mit der Interpretation räumlicher Ausdrücke bei der Kommandierung eines Montageroboters beschäftigt sich [4]. Die Übermittlung von Anweisungen bei der Montage wird in [5] durch eine begrenzte Anzahl interner Sensoren gelöst. Dieses Vorgehen bietet die Möglichkeit, fehlende Informationen gezielt nachzuliefern. Trotz vieler Teilergebnisse sind leistungsstarke Gesamtsysteme zur Kommandierung eines Serviceroboters mit sprecherunabhängiger, natürlicher, gesprochener Sprache noch weitgehend unbekannt. Am Beispiel der Einbindung eines bestehenden sprachverstehenden Systems [6] in die Domäne des Serviceroboters RO-MAN [7] wird in dem vorliegenden Beitrag die Umsetzung eines akustischen Sprachsignals in Roboteranweisungen aufgezeigt, siehe Abbildung 2.

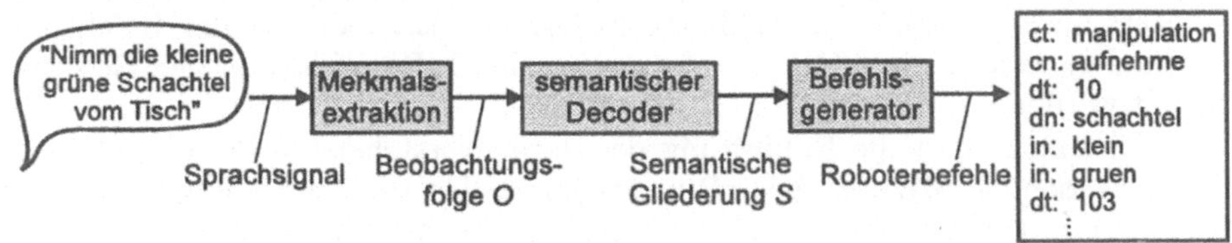

Abb. 2. Natürlichsprachliche Mensch-Roboter-Schnittstelle

Im folgenden Abschnitt wird der Sprachumfang der Roboterdomäne festgelegt und auf die Befehlsschnittstelle zum Serviceroboter eingegangen. Fragen der Decodierung des semantischen Inhalts eines Serviceauftrags behandelt Abschnitt 3 im Zusammenhang mit trainierten, probabilistischen Wissensbasen. Abschnitt 4 beschreibt die nachfolgende Umsetzung der semantischen Gliederung in roboterverständliche Anweisungen. Anhand eines typischen Szenarios aus dem Bereich persönlicher Assistenz wird in Abschnitt 5 die Tragfähigkeit und Robustheit des Gesamtsystems aufgezeigt. Eine Zusammenfassung mit Ausblick schließt den vorliegenden Beitrag.

2 Sprach- und Befehlsumfang der Roboterdomäne

Der Umfang einer Sprache wird durch ihren Wortschatz und die zur Kombination der einzelnen Wörter herangezogene Grammatik definiert. Die Komplexität der deutschen Sprache läßt sich leicht anhand der ca. 300.000 verwendeten Wörter erahnen. Da es neben dem Menschen kein sprachverstehendes System gibt, welches in der Lage ist, einen solch großen Sprachumfang zu verstehen, müssen technische Systeme sich somit auf einen relevanten Teil der Sprache konzentrieren. Dabei ist es sinnvoll, nicht etwa einen repräsentativen Querschnitt durch die menschliche Sprache zu bilden, sondern vielmehr einen Teilbereich (Domäne) möglichst vollständig abzudecken.

2.1 Sprachumfang der Roboterdomäne

Bei der in diesem Beitrag verwendeten Domäne handelt es sich um das Arbeitsfeld eines Serviceroboters zur Ausführung mobiler Handhabungsaufgaben in Innenraumumgebungen. Der Sprachumfang leitet sich dabei von den verschiedenen an den Roboter gestellten und an den anatomischen und planerischen Fähigkeiten orientierten **Serviceaufträgen** ab: 1. Aufnehmen und Abstellen von Objekten, wie z.B. Geschirr, Bücher oder Werkzeug. 2. Bedienen von Einrichtungsgegenständen, wie z.B. Türen, Schränke oder Schalter. 3. Transportaufgaben. 4. Kontinuierliche Bearbeitung auf Boden, Wand oder Mobiliar. Neben der eigentlichen Aktion können vom Bediener eine Fülle von Gegenständen, Räumlichkeiten und symbolischen Positionen in einem Auftrag miteinander kombiniert werden. Dies beinhaltet auch die Verwendung bedeutungstragender Attribute, wie Adjektive, oder sogennanter bedeutungsloser Füllwörter, wie z.B "bitte". Außerdem hat der Bediener die Möglichkeit, den Serviceauftrag durch Verwendung von Synonymen oder unterschiedlicher Detaillierung auf verschiedene Art und Weise zu spezifizieren. So gibt der Bediener mit "Nimm die kleine grüne Schachtel vom Tisch" einen sehr detaillierten Befehl, wohingegen bei "Nimm die grüne Schachtel bitte" von einem Grundwissen über die Position seitens des Roboters ausgegangen wird. Fehlt dieses Grundwissen oder ist der Befehl unvollständig, so muß die fehlende Information durch Rückfrage an den Bediener ergänzt werden.

Abbildung 3 zeigt die Einbettung des Sprachverstehens in die Eingabeseite eines bestehenden MRI. Etwaige Rückfragen an den Bediener erfolgen über die Ausgabeseite genauso wie die für die visuelle Beurteilung durch den Bediener wichtige Darstellung aufbereiteter Sensorinformation. Vom MRI aus lassen sich die vom Planer des Serviceroboters bereitgestellten Fähigkeiten über einen definierten Befehlssatz ansprechen. Durch die Kombination bereits existierender Funktionalitäten zu komplexeren Aufträgen, den sogenannten Makros, können die Funktionalitäten des Gesamtsystems (Serviceroboter und MRI) durch das MRI weiter ausgebaut und somit wachsenden Anforderungen der Domäne angepaßt werden. Es ist auch möglich, die neu definierten Makros in die Wissensbasis der Planungsebene nachzuladen und dadurch den Befehlsumfang des Serviceroboters zu erweitern. In der Planungsebene werden dann durch Kombination von abgelegtem Wissen mit aktueller Sensorinformation Bewegungen generiert. Dabei kann es vorkommen, daß die Fähigkeiten des Planers nicht ausreichen, den

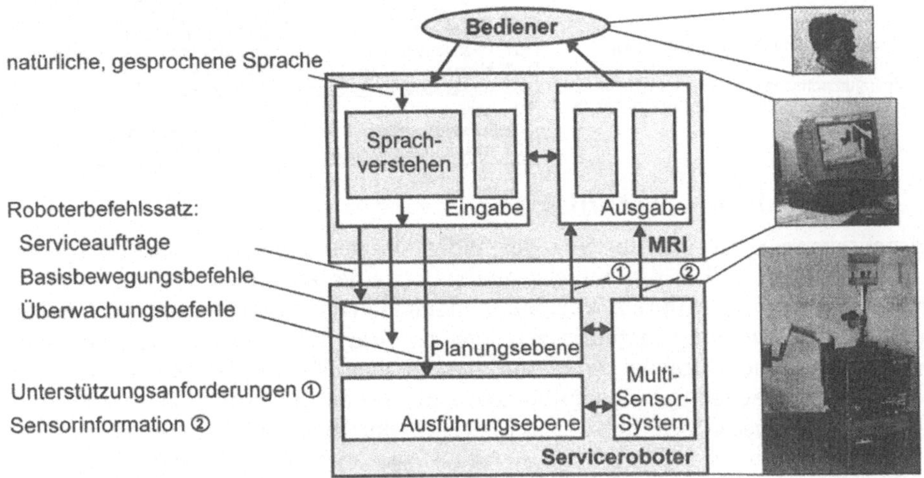

Abb. 3. Ankopplung des Sprachverstehens an einen Serviceroboter

Auftrag erfolgreich auszuführen, und somit eine Unterstützung durch den Bediener erfordern. Ferner sind Situationen denkbar, in denen der Bediener aus Sicherheitsgründen sofort eingreifen muß. Aus diesen Anforderungen heraus lassen sich neben den **Serviceaufträgen** zwei weitere Kategorien von Befehlen, die durch den Sprachumfang beschrieben werden müssen, unterscheiden: Roboterspezifische **Basisbewegungsbefehle** zur Unterstützung, mit denen die Komponenten des Roboters (wendiges Fahrzeug, Effektor, Kamera) direkt angesprochen werden: *"Bewege Dich etwas nach links"*, *"Öffne den Greifer"*, *"Schwenke die Kamera nach unten"*, ... **Überwachungsbefehle** zur sofortigen Beeinflussung des Bewegungsablaufs: *"Stop"*, *"Mach' weiter"*, *"Brich ab"*, ...

Aus den drei Befehlskategorien resultiert der gesamte Sprachumfang, mit dem eine natürliche, d.h. dem Menschen vertraute, Kommunikation zwischen Mensch und Roboter ermöglicht wird. Der derzeitig verwendete Wortschatz beträgt 409 Wörter, mit dem ungefähr 30 verschiedene Einzelaktionen unterstützt werden.

2.2 Erweiterbare Roboterbefehlsstruktur

Zur Repräsentation der verschiedenen Befehle wird eine für den Planer verständliche Struktur gewählt, mit der sich ohne Änderung neue Befehle implementieren lassen. Jeder Befehl besteht aus einem Header mit Befehlstyp ct und Befehlsname cn, gefolgt von einer aktionsspezifischen Anzahl von Datenblöcken. Mit Hilfe der Datenblöcke werden die Befehle näher beschrieben. So läßt sich je nach Aktion ein Objekt, die dazugehörige Objektposition oder eine Zielposition unterscheiden. Andere Befehle benötigen wiederum nur eine Mengenangabe oder Zusatzinformation. Um bei komplexeren Befehlen, den Makros, auch unterschiedliche Zielpositionen unterscheiden zu können, ist die Reihenfolge genauso wie die Anzahl der Datenblöcke durch den Befehl vorgegeben. Jeder dieser Datenblöcke besteht aus einem Datentyp dt, einem Datennamen dn und weiteren Datenelementen. Mögliche Datenelemente sind die Datenmenge da, ein Positionsvektor po und Zusatzinformationen in. Das folgende Beispiel repräsentiert die Äußerung *"Nimm die kleine grüne Schachtel vom Tisch"*. Die nebenstehende Tabelle listet alle zur Verfügung stehenden Datentypen dt auf:

```
[
  [ct:mobile_manipulation][cn:aufnehme]
  [
    [dt:10][dn:schachtel][da:1][in:klein][in:gruen];
    [dt:103][dn:tisch][po:3540,2000,800,0,0,0]
  ]
]
```

dt	name	dt	name
10	object	203	absolute location
101	relative location	204	object referenced location
102	absolute location	30	relative amount
103	object referenced location	31	identifier
20	goal	32	force amount
201	relative location	33	length amount
202	absolute angle value	40	information

3 Semantische Decodierung

Spracherkenner zur Decodierung der Wortkette einer gesprochenen Äußerung sind nicht neu. Selbst die sprecherunabhängige Verarbeitung fließender Sprache ist bei eingeschränktem Vokabular möglich. Weitestgehend ungelöst ist jedoch die Einbeziehung semantischer oder gar pragmatischer Aspekte zum Verstehen natürlicher Sprache. Dabei muß zusätzliches Wissen über die Struktur der domänenspezifischen Sprache miteingebracht werden. Bei den derzeit untersuchten Verfahren lassen sich die zwei kontrovers diskutierten Ansätze der reinen *Statistik* und der ausschließlich *regelbasierten Vorgehensweise* unterscheiden. Üblich sind mehrstufige Systeme, bei denen die signalnahen Verarbeitungsschritte zur Ermittlung der Wortketten mit stochastischen Methoden und die anschließende linguistische Analyse regelbasiert erfolgen. Die dabei auftretenden Defizite beim Abgleich der verwendeten Wissensbasen und der hohe Ressourcenaufwand erfordern jedoch eine noch engere Verzahnung der beiden Verfahren. Im hier vorgestellten Ansatz erfolgt die Decodierung des Bedeutungsinhaltes (dargestellt durch die semantische Gliederung) der Äußerung in einer einzigen Stufe mit Hilfe von zuvor trainierten stochastischen Wissensbasen, wie dies in Abbildung 4 dargestellt ist.

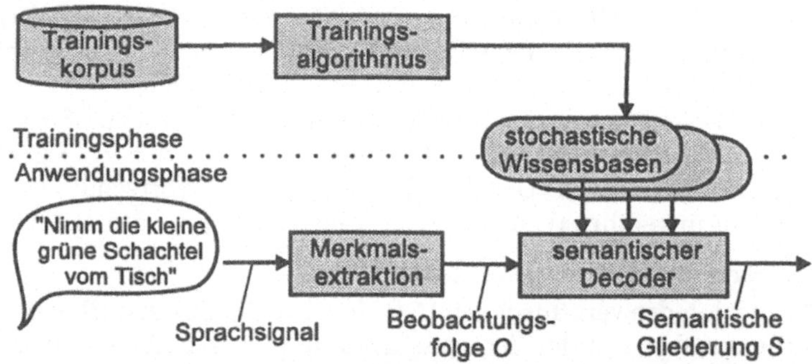

Abb. 4. Ermittlung des Bedeutungsinhalts mit stochastischen Methoden

Die Merkmalsextraktion erzeugt alle 10 ms einen 64-dimensionalen Merkmalsvektor, welcher die spektralen Eigenschaften des Sprachsignals innerhalb eines kurzen Zeitabschnittes beschreibt. Die zeitliche Abfolge solcher Merkmalsvektoren wird als Merkmalsvektorenfolge oder Beobachtungsfolge O bezeichnet. Sie dient als unmittelbare Eingabe-Symbolfolge für den semantischen Decoder.

3.1 Stochastische Maximum-a-posteriori-Klassifikation

Die semantische Decodierung bedient sich stochastischer Methoden, bei denen die menschliche Spracherzeugung als verrauschter Kanal zur Abbildung des Bedeutungsinhaltes S auf die Beobachtungsfolge O der Äußerung aufgefaßt wird.

Im gewählten Maximum-a-posteriori(MAP)-Ansatz wird nun diejenige semantische Gliederung S_E gesucht, welche die höchste Rückschluß(a-posteriori)-Wahrscheinlichkeit $P(S|O)$ zur gegebenen Beobachtungsfolge O aufweist. Diese Wahrscheinlichkeit läßt sich mit dem Satz von Bayes umformen:

$$S_E = \underset{S}{\mathrm{argmax}}\, P(S|O) = \underset{S}{\mathrm{argmax}}\, \frac{P(O|S) \cdot P(S)}{P(O)} = \underset{S}{\mathrm{argmax}}[P(O|S) \cdot P(S)] \quad (1)$$

$P(O)$ wird bei der Maximierung nicht berücksichtigt, da sie bei gegebenem O konstant ist. Die direkte Bestimmung der Abbildungswahrscheinlichkeit $P(O|S)$ ist aufgrund der Vielfalt möglicher Kombinationen aus O und S nicht möglich. Das Modellierungsproblem für $P(O|S)$ wird daher in ebenenspezifische Teilprobleme überführt, indem die zusätzlichen Repräsentationsebenen Wortkette W und Lautfolge Ph eingeführt werden:

$$S_E = \underset{S}{\mathrm{argmax}} \sum_{\text{alle } W} \sum_{\text{alle } Ph} [P(O|Ph) \cdot P(Ph|W) \cdot P(W|S) \cdot P(S)]. \quad (2)$$

Wird angenommen, daß nur die wahrscheinlichste Wortkette W und wahrscheinlichste Lautfolge Ph relevant sind, lassen sich die Summen zu Maximierungen über bedingte Wahrscheinlichkeiten vereinfachen:

$$S_E = \underset{S}{\mathrm{argmax}}\, \underset{W}{\max}\, \underset{Ph}{\max}[P(O|Ph) \cdot P(Ph|W) \cdot P(W|S) \cdot P(S)] \quad (3)$$

Aus dieser wahrscheinlichsten Kombination einer semantischen Gliederung S, einer Wortkette W, einer Phonemkette Ph und der gegebenen Beobachtungsfolge O wird die erkannte semantische Gliederung S_E extrahiert. Dabei liefern vier stochastische Wissensbasen (semantisches, syntaktisches, phonetisches, akustisches Modell) die zur Maximierung benötigten bedingten Wahrscheinlichkeiten. Neu hierbei ist die Trennung von semantischem und syntaktischem Wissen [6], die eine MAP-Decodierung der semantischen Gliederung überhaupt erst ermöglicht.

Die stochastischen Wissensbasen modellieren die zur Decodierung benötigten Wahrscheinlichkeiten nicht als ganzes, sondern als Produkt mehrerer, als stochastisch unabhängig angenommener Wahrscheinlichkeiten. Das hat zum einen den Vorteil, daß die Anzahl der Parameter in den Modellen gering gehalten werden kann, und somit die Fähigkeit zum Generalisieren bereits bei einer kleinen Trainingsstichprobe gegeben ist. Zum anderen ermöglichen die Modelle die Realisierung eines sehr effektiven Algorithmus zur semantischen Decodierung, da sie in der Lage sind, die Wahrscheinlichkeiten zeitlich inkrementell in kleinen "Portionen" zu liefern [8].

3.2 Semantische Gliederung S

Als Schnittstelle zum nachfolgenden Befehlsgenerator dient die semantische Gliederung. Sie ist durch die folgenden Punkte charakterisiert [9]:

- Eine semantische Gliederung S ist ein Baum, bestehend aus N semantischen Untereinheiten (*Semunen*) s_n : $S = \{s_1, s_2, ..., s_n, ..., s_N\}$.
- Jedes Semun s_n besitzt einen Typ $t[s_n]$ und einen Wert $v[s_n]$.

– Jedes Semun s_n verweist auf eine bestimmte Anzahl $X \geq 1$ von sogenannten Nachfolger-Semunen $q_1[s_n], ..., q_X[s_n] \in \{s_2, ..., s_N, \text{leer}\} \setminus \{s_n\}$.
– Das leere Semun 'leer' steht für ein Blatt des Baumes. Es besitzt den Typ $t[\text{leer}] = $ 'leer', keinen Wert und keinen Nachfolger.

Abbildung 5 zeigt beispielhaft eine Wortkette W und die zugehörige semantische Gliederung S als unterschiedliche Repräsentationsformen einer Äußerung.

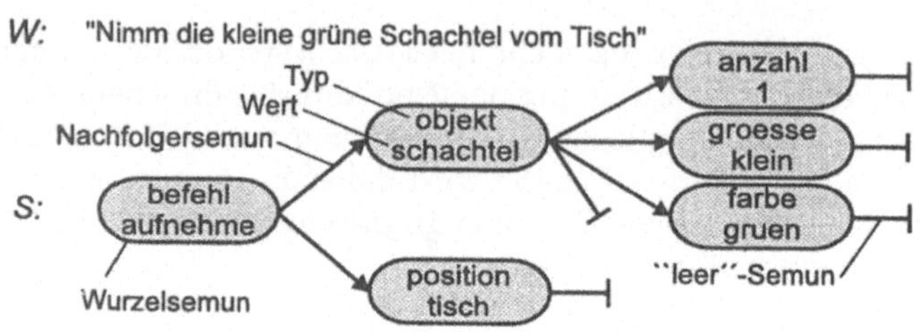

Abb. 5. Wortkette W und semantische Gliederung S

3.3 Bereitstellung der stochastischen Wissensbasen

Die Parameter des **semantischen und syntaktischen Modells** werden mit geeignetem Trainingsmaterial abgeschätzt. Zu jeder Äußerung werden Wortkette und semantische Gliederung mit Hilfe eines geeigneten Typ- und Werteinventars, welches den Bereich der zu erwartenden Bedeutungsinhalte abdeckt, gebildet und zum Training herangezogen. Für Äußerungen außerhalb der Domäne (z.B. *"heute ist schönes Wetter"*) werden keine Typen und Werte definiert. Der derzeitige Trainigskorpus besteht aus 285 Sätzen, die von mehreren Sprechern gesammelt wurden. Bei der Auswahl der Sätze müssen folgende Punkte beachtet werden:

– Ansprechen jeder möglichen Funktion des Roboters
– Benennung aller möglichen und zukünftigen Serviceaufgaben
– Unterbringung aller Objekte, Orte und Positionen
– Abdecken der gewünschten quantitativen Einheiten (Abstände, Winkel, usw.)
– Verwendung verschiedener Worte und syntaktischer Konstrukte

Das **phonetische Modell** wurde als sogenanntes Transkriptionslexikon ausgeführt, das zu jedem Wort, welches beim Training der Grammatik verwendet wurde, jeweils die zugehörige Standardaussprache enthält. Erstellt wurde dieses Lexikon rein manuell unter Zuhilfenahme des Duden. Die **akustische Modellierung** wurde von einem bestehenden Spracherkennungssystem übernommen [10]. Das Training erfolgte mit domänenfremdem Trainingsmaterial, wobei durch Verteilung des Traingsmaterials auf 200 verschiedene Sprecher ein hohes Maß an Sprecherunabhängigkeit der Modellierung erzielt wurde [11].

4 Umsetzung in Roboterbefehle

Nach der Decodierung der semantischen Gliederung S generiert der Befehlsgenerator im nächsten Schritt den korrespondierenden Roboterbefehl, vergleiche Abbildung 2. Dieser planerverständliche Roboterbefehl, der sich an die in Abschnitt 2.3 definierte Befehlsstruktur hält, wird schließlich dem Servicerobter übermittelt.

4.1 Anforderungen an die Umsetzung

Die Umsetzung der semantischen Gliederung in einen Roboterbefehl ist nicht immer ohne weiteres möglich. Es lassen sich verschiedene vom Nominalablauf abweichende Situationen erkennen: 1. Die vom Decoder generierte semantische Gliederung ist *nicht sinnvoll*. 2. Es fehlen für den Befehl wichtige Daten, d.h die semantische Gliederung ist zwar korrekt aber *unvollständig*. 3. Die in der semantischen Gliederung spezifizierten Daten, wie z.B. Objekte oder Räumlichkeiten, sind dem Gesamtsystem *nicht bekannt*. 4. Es handelt sich um einen *hochprioren* Überwachungsbefehl. Faßt man die verschiedenen Situationen zusammen, so lassen sich die folgenden Anforderungen an den Befehlsgenerator ableiten:

— Übersetzung der semantischen Gliederungen in Roboterbefehle
— Validierung der Befehle auf Plausibilität und Vollständigkeit
— Einbindung aktueller Umgebungsinformation und des Roboterzustandes
— Dialoggeführtes Einbeziehen des Bedieners zur Vervollständigung der Befehle unter Ausnutzung der zur Verfügung stehenden MRI-Ressourcen
— Einfache Anpassung an neue Eingabecodes bzw. eine neue Domäne

4.2 Befehlsgenerator

Der in Abbildung 6 gezeigte Befehlsgenerator wandelt die semantische Gliederung schrittweise in die Struktur des Befehlsstrings um. Durch auftretende Redundanz oder Mehrdeutigkeit kann die Ersetzung nicht ohne weiteres erfolgen. Oftmals muß der Nachfolger eines Semuns bekannt sein. Die in einem Umsetzmodell zusammengefaßte Ersetzungsstrategie bietet somit die Möglichkeit, Ersetzungen bedingt durchzuführen oder Datenelemente direkt zu übernehmen. Mit Hilfe des Umsetzmodells wird sowohl die Konsistenzprüfung während der Ersetzung als auch die Vollständigkeitsuntersuchung durchgeführt. Bei unvollständigen oder mehrdeutigen Bedienereingaben wird der Befehl nicht verworfen, sondern durch eine Rückfrage an den Bediener ergänzt. Anschließend erfolgt eine erneute Prüfung. Mit Hilfe der statischen und dynamischen Wissensbasen wird die Existenz der verwendeten Objekte und Räumlichkeiten überprüft. Die mit Namen vorhandenen Objekte und Räumlichkeiten werden dabei zusätzlich durch ihre kartesische Position ergänzt. Bei Nichtvorhandensein oder Mehrdeutigkeiten wird der Bediener nochmals zur genaueren Spezifikation eingeschaltet. Im letzten Schritt erfolgt für einen Makrobefehl die Expansion in von der Planungsebene unterstützte Aufträge. Mit der Möglichkeit, Rückfragen an den Bediener zu stellen, steht ein leistungsstarker Befehlsgenerator zur Verfügung, der einen nicht ganz verstandenen Befehl nicht sofort verwirft, sondern gezielt nachhakt.

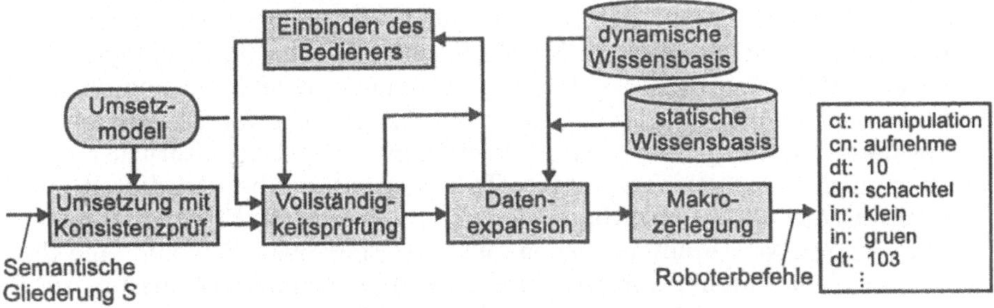

Abb. 6. Befehlsgenerator

4.3 Einsatz weiterer MRI-Ressourcen

Nicht immer ist es ausreichend bzw. zweckmäßig, den Servicerobter ausschließlich über die Spracheingabe zu kommandieren. Weitere, einfach zu bedienende Ressourcen sollten auf Seiten des MRI dem Bediener bereitgestellt werden. Wesentlich einfacher ist es z.B., mit dem Finger auf ein Objekt zu zeigen oder eine kartesische Position zu spezifizieren. Dies kann durch Anklicken des interessierenden Objektes in einer das Arbeitsumfeld darstellenden virtuellen Welt per Computermaus oder Touchscreen erfolgen. Aber auch die präzise Telemanipulation des Roboters durch Vorgabe kleinster Relativbewegungen ist mittels sprachlicher Steuerung umständlich und langwierig. Entsprechende Eingabeelemente für Kraft und Position werden zusätzlich bereitgestellt. Auf der Ausgabeseite kommen ebenfalls unterschiedliche Ressourcen zum Einsatz. Zur bildschirmbasierten Kommandierung, Überwachung und Unterstützung dient das Bild des virtuellen Arbeitsumfelds und das reale Videobild von einer onboard-Kamera. Meldungen erscheinen in einem Textfenster oder werden über eine Sprachausgabe an den Bediener weitergeleitet.

Es ist wichtig, eine leistungsstarke und transparente Verwaltungsstruktur für die unterschiedlichen MRI-Ressourcen bereitzustellen. Sie stellt sicher, daß anforderungsabhängig eine gezielte Einbindung unterschiedlicher Ein- und Ausgabemedien in das MRI möglich wird. Die Ressourcen müssen sich dabei über die Verwaltungsstruktur zu einem Gesamtsysten zusammenfügen, das es dem Bediener erlaubt, einfach und schnell mit dem Roboter zu kommunizieren.

5 Experimentelle Ergebnisse

5.1 Experimentierplattform ROMAN und MRI

Mit der Experimentierplattform ROMAN steht ein semiautonomer Serviceroboter für Innenraumumgebungen zu Verfügung, siehe Abbildung 1 [7]. ROMAN besteht mit seiner kompakten Bauweise aus dem Mehrgelenkmanipulator MANUS, erweitert durch eine Hoch/Tief-Linearachse, und einer sehr wendigen Plattform, welche den Arbeitsraum des Manipulators gezielt erweitert oder reine Transportaufgaben ermöglicht. Die verwendete Sensorik besteht aus einer der absoluten Positionsbestimmung dienenden Lasernavigationseinheit mit kreiselbasierter Koppelnavigation, dem Ultraschallring zur Hindernisvermeidung und einer Videosensorik zur Objekterkennung und -verfolgung. In der Planungsebene des Roboters stehen Grundfunktionalitäten zur Verfügung, welche ein flexibles und situationsabhängiges Verhalten ermöglichen [12].

Mit dem MRI ist ROMAN über ein Funkethernet und eine Hochfrequenz-Videostrecke verbunden. Das MRI basiert auf einer Grafikworkstation mit eingebautem Videoboard zur online-Darstellung der Kamerabilder. Das Virtual-Reality-Tool AnySIM stellt die aktuelle Roboterposition und Konfiguration im virtuellen Arbeitsraum dar. Meldungen erfolgen über eine Sprachausgabe an den Bediener oder an Personen im Arbeitsraum. Zur Eingabe von Kommandos dient das in diesem Beitrag vorgestellte System zum Verstehen natürlicher, gesprochener Sprache. Das dazu aufgestellte Trainingsmaterial besteht derzeit aus 285 Wortketten, das daraus ableitbare Vokabular enthält 409 Wörter. Es werden 42 Typen und 214 Werte unterschieden. Weitere Eingabemedien sind eine Spacemouse zur Unterstützung von Operationen und die Computermaus zur Auswahl von Objekten und Positionen im virtuellen Arbeitsraum [13].

5.2 Experimente

Im ersten Experiment gemäß Abbildung 7 fordert der Bediener den Serviceroboter auf, ihm die Kaffeetasse vom seinem Schreibtisch zu holen. Die generierte semantische Gliederung spezifiziert die Serviceaufgabe vollständig. Als Ziel ist der den Auftrag gebende Bediener eingesetzt. Nach der Umsetzung werden die Datenblöcke 2 und 3 noch um die korrespondierende kartesische Position ergänzt. Dies geschieht durch einen Blick in die statische bzw. dynamische Wissensbasis auf Seiten des MRI. Bevor der Makrobefehl an den Roboter geschickt wird, erfolgt eine Zerlegung in die beiden Teilaufträge *aufnehmen* und *abstellen*. Daraufhin führt der Roboter den Auftrag aus.

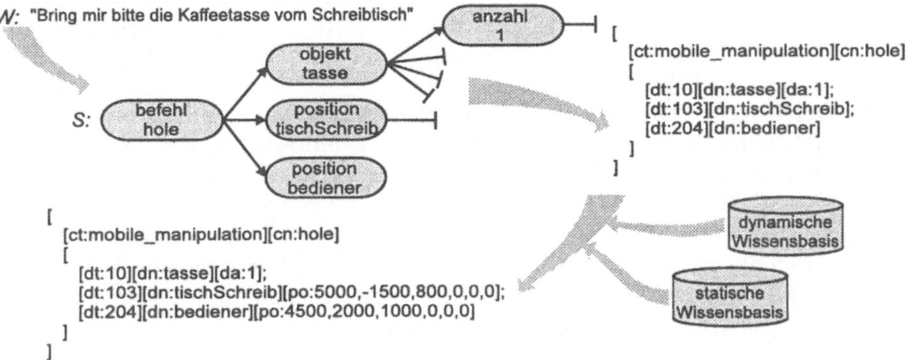

Abb. 7. Experiment ohne Rückfrage an den Bediener

Ausgangspunkt des in Abbildung 8 dargestellten zweiten Experiments ist der unvollständige Befehl, die Kaffeetasse wegzuräumen. Die Vollständigkeitsprüfung ergibt zwei fehlende Datenblöcke, zum einen die Objektlage und zum anderen die Zielposition. Der Bediener wird daraufhin eingebunden und spezifiziert die fehlenden Daten durch Anklicken in der virtuellen Welt. Der ergänzte Makrobefehl wird dann zerlegt und zur Ausführung an den Planer des Roboters weitergeschickt.

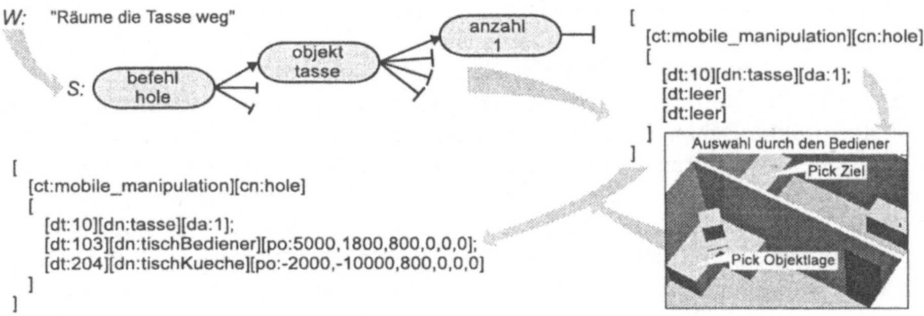

Abb. 8. Experiment mit Rückfrage an den Bediener

5.3 Bewertung

Für die semantische Decodierung von Äußerungen, die vollständig im Trainingskorpus der Grammantik enthalten sind, wurde in [8] eine Trefferrate von 75%

erzielt, allerdings über der Domäne eines Grafikeditors mit ähnlicher Anzahl von Typen und Werten, aber doppelter Vokabulargröße (854 Wörter). Es ist zu erwarten, daß aufgrund des nur halb so großen Vokabulars der Roboterdomäne deutlich weniger Verwechslungen von Wörtern auftreten, was sich positiv auf das Ergebnis auswirkt.

Äußerungen von Benutzern, die nicht mit dem System vertraut sind, werden in der Regel nicht im Trainingskorpus enthalten sein. Probleme bereitet eine solche Äußerung prinzipiell dann, wenn sie neue, unbekannte Wörter aufweist. Dieser sogenannte OOV(Out-of-Vocabulary)-Fall ist unerwünscht, resultiert er doch meist in einem Fehler bei der semantischen Decodierung. Nach [14] läßt sich die OOV-Rate für das verwendete Trainingsmaterial zu 53% abschätzen. Um die OOV-Rate auf unter 10% zu senken, müßte der Trainingskorpus um 8.800 weitere Wortketten erweitert werden. Das resultierende Vokabular umfaßt dann etwa 2.915 Worte.

Der Befehlsgenerator setzt richtig verstandene, womöglich unvollständige semantische Gliederungen immer korrekt in einen Roboterbefehl um. Dazu können bei der Vervollständigung sowohl alle MRI-Ressourcen als auch der Bediener gefordert sein. Falsch decodierte semantische Gliederungen können zum großen Teil durch Konsistenzprüfung erkannt und somit verworfen werden. Um aber auch die Befehle zu erkennen, die zwar falsch sind, aber sich korrekt in einen Roboterbefehl übersetzen lassen, muß zur Gewährleistung 100%-iger Sicherheit immer eine Rückfrage an den Bediener erfolgen.

6 Zusammenfassung und Ausblick

Das hier vorgestellete Konzept bildet einen Beitrag zur einfachen, dem Menschen vertrauten Kommandierung eines semiautonomen Servicerobotors. Grundlage dafür ist die Verwendung sprecherunabhängiger, natürlicher, gesprochener Sprache. Basierend auf der Definition der domäneneigenen Sprache konnten die Sprachmodelle generiert werden. Der domänenunabhängige semantische Decoder stellt mit der semantischen Gliederung eine definierte Schnittstelle zu der sich anschließenden Befehlsgenerierung dar. Bei der Umsetzung in Roboterbefehle werden falsche semantische Gliederungen abgefangen und unvollständige Befehle durch das Einbinden des Bedieners ergänzt. Der resultierende Roboterbefehl genügt einer Befehlsstruktur, in der alle zur Verfügung stehenden Informationen dem Planer des Roboters geordnet bereitstellt werden. Der durchgängige Ansatz von einem akustischen Signal bis hin zum korrespondierenden Roboterbefehl ist durch hohe Flexibilität, Sicherheit und Robustheit gekennzeichnet. Das System zum Verstehen natürlicher, gesprochener Sprache ist in das bestehende MRI integriert und dient der Kommandierung des Serviceroboters ROMAN.

Zukünftige Arbeitsschwerpunkte werden sich mit der Erweiterung des Wortschatzes der Domäne und der Verwendung englischer Sprache beschäftigen. Ferner ist daran gedacht, weitere Umgebungsinformationen mit in die Umsetzung einzubinden.

Danksagung

Der vorliegende Beitrag ist das Ergebnis einer Zusammenarbeit zwischen dem Lehrstuhl für Steuerungs- und Regelungstechnik und dem Lehrstuhl für Mensch-Maschine-Kommunikation, beide TU München. Das Projekt ROMAN wird im

Rahmen des Sonderforschungsbereichs *Informationsverarbeitung in autonomen, mobilen Handhabungssystemen* (SFB 331) von der Deutschen Forschungsgemeinschaft (DFG) gefördert.

Literatur

1. K. Kawamura, M. Iskarous, "Trends in service robots for the disabled and the elderly", in *Proceedings of the International Conference on Intelligent Robots and Systems (IROS)*, München, Deutschland, 1994, S. 1647–1654.
2. V. Dahl et al., "Driving robot through natural language", in *Proceedings of the IEEE International Conference on Systems, Man and Cybernetics*, Vancouver, Canada, 1995, S. 1904–1908.
3. B. Caprile, G. Lazarri, "Commanding a robot by voice: Speech and autonomous navigation for the mobile robot of MAIA", in *Robotics in Alpe-Adria Region*, Springer Verlag, Wien, New York, 1994, S. 153–157.
4. E. Stopp, Th. Laengle, "Natürlichsprachliche Instruktionen an einen autonomen Serviceroboter", in *Tagungsband zum 11. Fachgespräch Autonome Mobile Systeme*, Karlsruhe, Deutschland, R. Dillmann, U. Rembold, T. Lüth (Hrsg.), Springer Verlag, 1995, S. 299–308.
5. S. Förster, K. Peters, "Sprachliche Steuerung behaviourórientierter Systeme", in *Tagungsband zum 11. Fachgespräch Autonome Mobile Systeme*, Karlsruhe, Deutschland, R. Dillmann, U. Rembold, T. Lüth (Hrsg.), Springer Verlag, 1995, S. 309–318.
6. H. Stahl, J. Müller, "A stochastic grammar for isolated representation of syntactic and semantic knowledge", in *Proceedings of the European Conference on Speech Communication and Technology*, Madrid, Spanien, 1995, S. 551–554.
7. W. Daxwanger et al., "ROMAN: Ein mobiler Serviceroboter als persönlicher Assistent in belebten Innenräumen", in *Tagungsband zum 12. Fachgespäch Autonome Mobile Systeme*, München, Deutschland, G. Schmidt, F. Freyberger (Hrsg.), Springer Verlag, 14.–15. Oktober 1996.
8. H. Stahl, J. Müller, M. Lang, "An efficient top-down parsing algorithm for understanding speech by using stochastic syntactic and semantic models", in *Proceedings of the International Conference on Acoustics, Speech, and Signal Processing (ICASSP)*, Atlanta, USA, 1996, S. 397–400.
9. J. Müller, H. Stahl, "Die semantische Gliederung als adäquate semantische Repräsentation für einen sprachverstehenden Grafikeditor", in *Angewandte Computerlinguistik, Reihe "Sprache und Computer"*, Band 15, Georg Olms Verlag, Hildesheim, Deutschland, 1995, S. 211–225.
10. X.D. Huang et al., "Hidden markov models for speech recognition", in *Edinburgh University Press*, Edinburgh, England, 1990.
11. B. Pompino et al., "PhonDat Datenformate", in *Forschungsbericht Nr. 30, Institut für Phonetik und sprachliche Kommunikation, Ludwig-Maximilians-Universität*, München, Deutschland, 1992.
12. C. Fischer, M. Buss, G. Schmidt, "Soft control of an effector path for a mobile manipulator", in *Proceedings of the International Symposium on Robotics and Manufacturing (ISRAM)*, Montpellier, Frankreich, 1996.
13. C. Fischer, M. Buss, G. Schmidt, "Hierarchical supervisory control of service robot using human-robot-interface", in *Proceedings of the International Conference on Intelligent Robots and Systems (IROS)*, Osaka, Japan, 4.–8. November 1996.
14. J. Müller, H. Stahl, M. Lang, "Predicting the out-of-vocabulary rate and the required vocabulary size for speech processing applications", in *Proceedings of the International Conference on Spoken Language Processing (ICSLP)*, Philadelphia, USA, 3.–6. Oktober 1996.

Komponenten, Anwendungen

Autonome Fahrzeugführung in der pflanzlichen Produktion

Gerhard Jahns
Institut für Biosystemtechnik
Bundesforschungsanstalt für Landwirtschaft
Bundesallee 50
38116 Braunschweig-Völkenrode
E-Mail: jahns@bst.fal.de

1 Einleitung

Landwirtschaftliche Fahrzeug-Geräte-Kombinationen sind hochentwickelte Arbeitsmaschinen. Die Überwachung und Regelung ihres Einsatzes mit dem Ziel einer effizienten Prozeßführung ist die Hauptaufgabe des Fahrers. Das Lenken ist eine notwendige zusätzliche Aufgabe, da in der Landwirtschaft, im Gegensatz zu den meisten industriellen Produktionen, Geräte mit den Werkzeugen an die ortsfesten Bearbeitungsobjekte, die Pflanzen und Böden, herangeführt werden müssen. Diese „Nebenaufgabe" beansprucht aber einen großen Teil der Aufmerksamkeit des Fahrers und beeinflußt die Qualität des Prozeßablaufs. Es hat daher in der Vergangenheit nicht an Anstrengungen gefehlt, den Fahrer von dieser Aufgabe zu entlasten. In den 70er Jahren, in denen weltweit an dem Problem der fahrerlosen Fahrzeugführung in der Landwirtschaft gearbeitet wurde, konnten die damit verbundenen regelungstechnischen Probleme im wesentlichen gelöst werden. Praktische Lösungen entstanden aber nur für spezielle Anwendungen z.B. im Weinbau, für Gewächshäuser, für Maishäcksler oder für Gantryfahrzeuge [1,2,3]. Eine befriedigende universelle Lösung scheiterte, da es nicht gelang, ein geeignetes Sensorsystem zu schaffen.

Aufgrund der seither deutlichen Leistungssteigerung der Elektronik bei gleichzeitiger Kostenreduktion wurde Ende der 80er Jahre das Thema der automatischen Lenkung landwirtschaftlicher Fahrzeuge wieder aufgegriffen, da es aussichtsreich erschien, eine universelle, autonome Führung landwirtschaftlicher Fahrzeuge auf der Basis der Bildverarbeitung ergänzt durch Satellitennavigation zu realisieren. Ausgehend von den Anforderungen des Einsatzes in der Landwirtschaft wird ein modulares, offenes System vorgeschlagen, das durch die Verwendung ohnehin verfügbarer Komponenten den erforderlichen Aufwand minimiert.

2 Besonderheiten und Anforderungen

Will man auf Vorbereitungen und Installationen im oder auf dem Feld verzichten, so kommen als Leitlinie die beim jeweiligen Arbeitsprozeß entstehenden Fahr- und Arbeitsspuren in Betracht. Die Ausprägung dieser Leitlinien ist sehr unterschiedlich. So kann es sich einmal um gut zu erkennende Schnittkanten handeln, das andere mal jedoch um den kaum zu erkennenden Unterschied einer mit Pflanzenbehandlungsmitteln behandelten und einer unbehandelten Fläche. Die Leitlinie kann sich dabei wechselnd rechts oder links des Fahrzeugs befinden. Manchmal wird erwartet, daß das System bestehende Unregelmäßigkeiten der Leitlinie ausgleicht, ein anderes Mal, beispielsweise beim Konturpflügen, soll das System einer gekrümmten Kurve folgen. Andererseits müssen Geräte mit Arbeitsbreiten von 30 und mehr Metern so geführt werden, daß sich die bearbeiteten Flächen nicht überlappen, aber auch keine Lücken entstehen. Dies erfordert eine Führungsgenauigkeit von wenigen Zentimetern. Darüber hinaus sind die Vorgewende zu erkennen und auf ihnen unterschiedliche u.U. auch von den Geräten eingeschränkte Wendemannöver vorzunehmen. Diese Forderungen und die, alle Arbeiten auf dem Felde ohne Vorbereitungen durchführen zu können, lassen Verfahren der Bilderkennung in Verbindung mit Satellitennavigationssystemen als am aussichtsreichsten erscheinen. Dies vor allem deshalb, weil zu erwarten ist, daß in Zukunft berührungslos arbeitende Verfahren der Bildverarbeitung ohnehin auf landwirtschaftlichen Fahrzeugen für andere Zwecke eingesetzt werden. Das Gleiche gilt für Satellitennavigationssysteme. Eine nicht zu vernachlässigende Restriktion stellt die schwache finanzielle Situation der landwirtschaftlichen Betriebe dar. Aus diesem Grund ist die Übernahme von Lösungen aus anderen Bereichen und die Nutzung von ohnehin vorhandener Baugruppen geradezu ein Muß. Auch dieser Gesichtspunkt spricht für eine autonome Führung landwirtschaftlicher Fahrzeuge auf der Basis der Bildverarbeitung ergänzt durch Satellitennavigationverfahren, die für alle anfallenden Feldarbeiten geeignet ist.

2.1 Besonderheiten

Eine Besonderheit landwirtschaftlicher Fahrzeuge ist, daß sie sowohl auf öffentlichen Verkehrswegen als auch auf dem Felde eingesetzt werden. Für eine autonome Führung landwirtschaftlicher Fahrzeuge auf öffentlichen Verkehrswegen ist derzeit kein Bedarf zu erkennen. Dies nicht zuletzt deshalb, weil bei diesen Fahrten meist aus betrieblichen Gründen auch in Zukunft eine Person mitfahren wird und außerdem die zurückzulegenden Entfernungen nicht sehr groß sind. Da außerdem an der autonomen Führung von Fahrzeugen auf öffentlichen Verkehrswegen an anderer Stelle intensiv gearbeitet wird, soll diese Einsatzform landwirtschaftlicher Fahrzeuge hier nicht näher behandelt werden. Die nachfolgenden Überlegungen konzentrieren sich daher nur auf die autonome Führung landwirtschaftlicher Fahrzeuge auf dem Felde, während des Arbeitsprozesses.

Hinter dem Sammelbegriff landwirtschaftliches Fahrzeug verbergen sich sehr unterschiedliche Fahrzeug-Geräte-Kombinationen, die wichtigsten Merkmale sind in **Tafel 1** wiedergegeben.

Antrieb	Lenkung	Geräteanbau
Vorderrad	Vorderrad	gezogen
Hinterrad	Hinterrad	Frontanbau
Allrad	Knick	Heckanbau
	Allrad	Seitenanbau
	Panzer	Unterbau
		Mittelanbau

Tafel 1: Antrieb, Lenkung und Anbau landwirtschaftlicher Fahrzeug-Geräte-Kombinationen

Über die sich daraus ergebenden Kombinationen hinaus gibt es aber auch noch weitere Sonderbauarten. Des weiteren ist zwischen selbstfahrenden Arbeitmaschinen und Universalfahrzeugen zu unterscheiden. Selbstfahrende Arbeitsmaschinen wie z.B. Mähdrescher sind Einzweckfahrzeuge, im Gegensatz zu Universalfahrzeugen, wie Schlepper und Tracs. Schlepper und Tracs werden mit sehr unterschiedlichen Geräten eingesetzt werden. Dabei sind Front- und Heckanbau ebenso möglich wie die gleichzeitige Verwendung von angebauten und gezogenen Geräten. Die gezogenen Geräte können starre oder gelenkte Achsen haben. Eine besondere Stellung nehmen auch Gerätemehrfachkombinationen ein. Ein weitere Besonderheit ist die Arbeitsbreite der Geräte. Sie kann 30 m und mehr betragen. Bei diesen Geräten stellt das Anschlußfahren selbst für geübte Fahrer ein besonderes Problem dar. Auch die Fahrmanöver, die Fahrzeug-Geräte-Kombinationen ausführen können, sind unterschiedlich.

Eine weitere Besonderheit besteht darin, daß eine autonome Fahrzeugführung in der pflanzlichen Produktion zumindest in naher Zukunft nicht gleichbedeutend mit einer fahrerlosen Fahrzeugführung sein wird. Es ist vielmehr davon auszugehen, daß der Fahrer auch weiterhin auf dem Fahrzeug bleibt, um den Produktionsablauf zu überwachen. Ein Grund hierfür ist der Aufwand, der für eine Automatisierung aller Funktionen von Fahrzeug und Gerät sowie für die notwendigen Sicherheitseinrichtungen erforderlich wäre. Die Kosten hierfür würden in den meisten Fällen die für eine automatische Lenkung deutlich übersteigen. Ganz abgesehen davon ist es zweifelhaft, wann und ob die juristischen und versicherungstechnichen Hindernisse, die einer fahrerlosen Fahrzeugführung auf landwirtschaftlichen Flächen entgegenstehen, überwunden werden können. In anderen Ländern, z.B. den USA, gibt es andere Vorstellungen hierzu.

Aus der Annahme, daß der Fahrer an Bord des Fahrzeuges bleibt, ergibt sich der Vorteil, daß die Aufgabe einer autonomen Fahrzeuglenkung stufenweise gelöst und auch stufenweise in die Praxis umgesetzt werden kann. Beispielsweise in der Art, daß das Fahrzeug in einer ersten Entwicklungsphase nur einer Leitlinie zu folgen in der Lage ist und erst zu einem späteren Zeitpunkt weitere autonom ablaufende Funktionen hinzukommen, wie das Konturfahren, das autonome Wenden von Fahrzeug und Gerät, die Hinderniserkennung, das Umfahren von Hindernissen und ähnliches.

2.2 Anforderungen

Aufgrund der Erfahrungen mit bisherigen Systemen zur automatischen Führung landwirtschaftlicher Fahrzeuge ist eine Akzeptanz und ein wirtschaftlicher Einsatz nur von Systemen zu erwarten, wenn folgende Bedingungen erfüllt werden:
- Sie müssen universell, d.h. für alle Feldarbeiten und unter allen Produktionsbedingungen einsetzbar sein.
- Vorbereitungen oder Installationen auf oder im Felde oder im Gelände sollen nicht erforderlich sein.
- Auf Vorbereitungen oder Setup-Prozeduren für Fahrzeug und Gerät durch den Fahrer oder andere Personen sollte ebenfalls verzichtet werden.
- Die Bedienung muß einfach und unabhängig von der jeweils verwendeten Fahrzeug-Geräte-Kombination sein.
- Eine autonome Führung landwirtschaftlicher Fahrzeuge auf dem Felde muß kostengünstig sein.

<table>
<tr><td>Schnittkanten - Getreide
Schwad - Getreide, Gras
Düngerspuren - Gülle, Granulat,
           Flüssigkeit
Pflanzenbehandlungsmittelspuren
Fahrspuren
Pflugfurchen
Schaumspuren
Hackfruchtdämme</td></tr>
</table>

Tafel 2: Arten von Leitlinien in der Landwirtschaft

Aus den beiden ersten Anforderungen ergibt sich fast zwangsläufig die Verwendung von berührungslos arbeitenden Verfahren wie z.B. die der Bildverarbeitung zur Gewinnung des

Leitsignals. Die Art der zu erkennenden Leitlinie kann dabei je nach Arbeitsaufgabe sehr unterschiedlich sein. In der **Tafel 2** sind die wichtigsten zusammengestellt. Dabei ist zu berücksichtigen, daß landwirtschaftliche Fahrzeuge nicht nur am Tage, sondern auch nachts eingesetzt werden. Die Fahrgeschwindigkeiten beim Feldeinsatz liegen bei etwa 3 bis 12 km/h (ca. 1 bis 3 m/s).

3. Kursbeschreibung und Sytemstruktur

3.1 Symbolische Kursbeschreibung

Vorbild für ein System zur autonomen Fahrzeugführung ist zweifellos der Mensch. Er verwendet bei der Durchführung von Lenkaufgaben außer numerisch-metrischen Informationen zusätzlich, zum Teil auch ausschließlich, symbolische, d.h. nicht metrische Wegbeschreibungen, die sich an Merkmalen wie dem Vorgewende orientieren. Dadurch ist beispielsweise bei der Führung entlang der Schnittkante die Länge des zurückgelegten Weges von untergeordneter Bedeutung, nicht aber Richtung und Abstand zur Schnittkante.

Mittels einer strukturierten symbolischen Kursbeschreibung läßt sich die Gesamtaufgabe einer autonomen Fahrzeuglenkung in einzelne einfache Abschnitte unterteilen, denen dann bestimmte eindeutige Operationen zugeordnet werden können, wie z.B. das erwähnte Fahren entlang einer Schnittkante oder das Heranfahren an eine Schnittkante oder verschiedene Formen der Wendemanöver u.s.w.. Jede dieser Operationen wird solange ausgeführt, bis eine Entscheidung und ein Umschalten zu einer anderen Operation erforderlich wird. Diese Art der Aufgabenzerlegung wurde von Gilg und Schmidt [4] für eine diesem Szenario vergleichbare Führung von Roboterfahrzeugen in Innenräumen vorgeschlagen. Gilg und Schmidt entwickelten dafür eine Syntax, eine Art Programmiersprache, die dazu geeignet ist, einfache Fahraufträge in Innenräume zu spezifizieren.

Diese Vorgehensweise erscheint auch für das autonome Führen von Fahrzeugen und Geräten auf dem Felde geeignet. Sie hat den Vorteil, daß Operationen von einer lokalen Planungs- und Entscheidungseinheit ohne Kenntnis des Gesamtauftrages schrittweise ausgeführt werden können, und daß auch eine Umplanung während der Ausführung eines Auftrages möglich ist. Zu einer solchen Umplanung gehört auch der Wechsel zwischen einer autonomen Fahrzeugführung und einer manuellen, d.h. Eingriff des Fahrers oder umgekehrt die Übergabe an das Sytem zur autonomen Fahrzeugführung. Jede Operation wird bis zum Eintritt eines terminierenden Ereignisses beibehalten. Derartige Ereignisse sind z.B. Landmarken wie das Vorgewende. Beim Auftreten eines terminierenden Ereignisses erfolgt ein Weiterschalten von einer Operation zur nächsten. Hierbei können auch Alternativen für die Fortsetzung des Fahrtablaufes bestehen. So kann z.B. bei einem schmalen Vorgewende eine andere Art des Vorgewendemanövers gewählt werden, als bei einem breiten Vorgewende. Darüber hinaus wird Art und Form des Wendemanövers durch die Art der Geräte und ihre Kopplung mit dem Fahrzeug eingeschränkt oder vorgeschrieben. Für derartige Umschaltungen ist ein Selektor erforderlich. Ergänzend hierzu werden noch Attribute verwendet, die zusätzliche Informationen über das zu erwartende Ereignis oder die auszuführende Funktion enthalten. Ein derartiges Attribut kann z.B. beim Folgen einer Schnittkante ein Tensor ähnlich wie bei einer Splineapproximation sein, der festlegt in welchem Maß die vorgegebene Schnittkante geglättet wird. Dabei wird das Ergebnis zwischen einer Geraden oder einer mehr oder weniger gekrümmten Kontur lie-

Operation	Ereignis	Selektor	Attribut
Fahren	Spur folgen	Gerade	Richtungsfehler minimieren
Fahren	Spur folgen	Gerade	Abstandsfehler minimieren
Fahren	Spur folgen	Kontur	Richtungsfehler minimieren
Fahren	Spur folgen	Kontur	Abstandsfehler minimieren

Tafel 3: Beispiel für symbolische Kursbeschreibungen

gen, z.B. beim Konturpflügen. Zeilen einer derartigen symbolischen Kursbeschreibung sind in **Tafel 3** wiedergegeben: Die erste und dritte Zeile könnte beispielsweise für das Drillen von Getreide gelten, bei dem Wert darauf gelegt wird Unregelmäßigkeiten der vorhergehenden Spur möglichst auszugleichen. Zeile zwei und vier könnten ein Beispiel für das Drillen von Zuckerrüben sein, bei dem Unregelmäßigkeiten der vorhergehenden Spur zwar geglättet werden sollen, doch wird der Minimierung der Abweichung des Abstandes zur vorangegangenen Spur bzw. Saatreihe ein höherer Stellenwert eingeräumt, damit bei der Ernte problemlos mehrreihige Erntegeräte eingesetzt werden können. Geringfügige Richtungsabweichungen werden also bewußt in Kauf genommen. Im dritten und vierten Fall soll das Fahrzeug an Stelle einer Geraden einer Kontur folgen, kleine Unregelmäßigkeiten der vorhergehenden Spur aber trotzdem ausgleichen.

Für unterschiedliche Fahrzeug-Geräte-Kombinationen in der Landwirtschaft reicht der Sprachumfang jedoch nicht aus. Es ist zusätzlich noch eine Beschreibung der Konstellation erforderlich, z.B. vorderradgelenktes Fahrzeug mit gezogenem Gerät, mit heckangebautem fahrzeugfestem Gerät oder frontangebautem fahrzeugfestem Gerät oder aber hinterradgelenktes Fahrzeug mit festem Frontanbau usw..

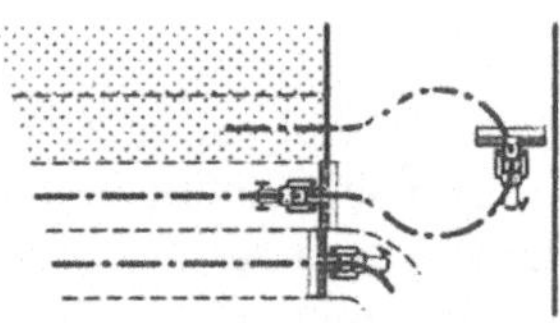

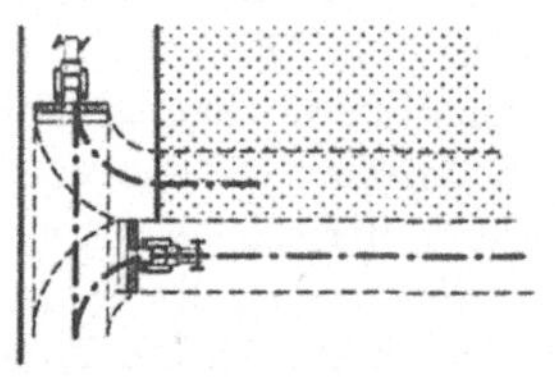

Bild 1: Fahrspuren und Manöver eines Mähdreschers

Je nach Konstellation müssen zur Erfüllung eines optimalen Bewegungsablaufes unterschiedliche Regelstrategien zum Einsatz kommen. Das **Bild 1** zeigt Fahrspuren wie sie z.B. von einem Mähdrescher gefahren werden könnten. Die **Tafel 4** gibt die dazugehörige Kursbeschreibung wieder.

Im Vergleich zu mobilen, autonomen Handhabungssystemen und Fahrten auf öffentlichen Wegen kann die Wegplanung auf dem Felde im Rahmen der Arbeitsvorbereitung vor Fahrtantritt erfolgen. Es kann unterstellt werden, daß die Topographie des Geländes bekannt ist und als digitale Karte im Rahmen des GIS (GIS = Geographical Information System) zur Verfügung steht. Die Routenplanung und Kursbeschreibung kann auf dem Betriebsrechner des Landwirtes durchgeführt und mit einer Chipkarte auf das Fahrzeug übertragen werden.

Bei der Bewältigung von Hindernissen sind zwei Arten zu unterscheiden, permanente und temporäre. Permanente Hindernisse wie Absturzkanten oder übermäßiges Gefälle sind durch das GIS ausreichend dokumentiert und können im Rahmen der Fahrtroutenplanung berücksichtigt werden. Das gleiche gilt für permanente Hindernisse wie Bäume, Wasserläufe u.ä.. Zur Erfassung temporärer Hindernisse wird man vor allem auf Ergebnisse und Verfahren aus anderen Gebieten der autonomen Fahrzeugführung zurückgreifen. Eine Besonderheit, die seit jeher ein Problem darstellt, ist das Erkennen von Tieren, die auch vom Fahrer nur schlecht oder gar nicht erkannt werden, weil sie sich artbedingt (z.B. Rehkitze) bei Gefahr auf den Boden pressen, nicht bewegen und eine Tarnfarbe besitzen.

Operation	Ereignis	Selektor	Attribut
Umschalten	manuell/Automatik	-	-
Fahren	Leitlinie	rechts aufsuchen	-
Fahren	Leitlinie folgen	rechts folgen	Tensor groß
Wenden	T-Manöver	links aufsuchen	-
Fahren	Leitlinie folgen	links folgen	Tensor groß
Wenden	Ω-Manöver	rechts aufsuchen	-
.			
.			
Umschalten	Automatik/manuell.	-	-

Tafel 4: Systemdiagramm der symbolischen Kursbeschreibung

Im Vergleich zu der autonomen Führung von Fahrzeugen im Straßenverkehr entfällt beim Fahren auf dem Felde die Aufgabe, Verkehrszeichen, Ampeln, Kreuzungen und eine von mehreren Fahrspuren zu erkennen. Die Fahrgeschwindigkeit landwirtschaftlicher Fahrzeuge (bis 12 km/h) auf dem Felde liegt deutlich unter der auf öffentlichen Straßen und ermöglicht ein schnelles Anhalten. Darüber hinaus stellt sich das Problem des gemischten Verkehrs auf dem Feld kaum. Das gleiche gilt für unverhofft auftauchende Personen oder Gegenstände.

3.2 Systemstruktur

Für das System wird eine hierarchisch gegliederte, modulare Struktur vorgeschlagen. Das **Bild 2** gibt eine solche Struktur wieder. Dadurch kann auf bereits vorhandene Systeme zurückgegriffen werden und der Aufwand für die autonomen Führung landwirtschaftlicher Fahrzeuge deutlich reduziert werden. Erforderliche Zusatzinformationen wie das Positionssignal und der Fahrauftrag werden über das „Landwirtschaftliche BUS-System" (LBS) [5] abgerufen. Das Ergebnis, das Lenksoll- und Antriebssollsignal, wird auf dem LBS bereitgestellt. Die entsprechenden Datenobjekte sind bereits in der Norm DIN 9684 - eine ISO Norm hierzu ist ebenfalls in Vorbereitung - berücksichtigt.

Die Umsetzung des Lenksignals erfolgt in einem eigenen Modul. Dieser beinhaltet auch den Noteingriff durch den Fahrer und die erforderlichen Sicherheitsvorkehrungen gegen Ausfall des Bordnetzes oder der Hydraulik und ist Stand der Technik [6,7]. Getriebe und Motormanagement zur Umsetzung des Fahrsignal sind zwar in der Landwirtschaft noch nicht Stand der Technik, von ihrer Einführung kann jedoch ausgegangen werden [8].

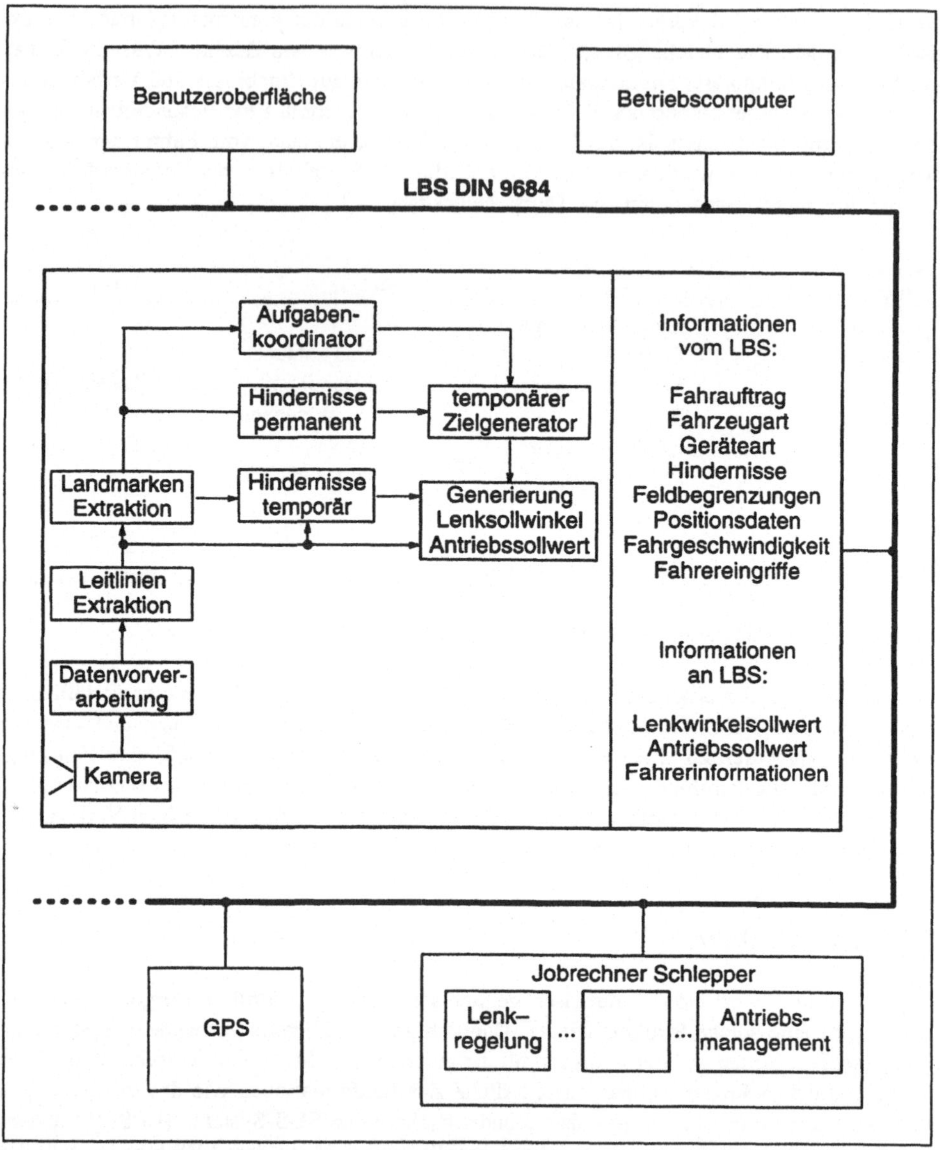

Bild 2: Struktur eines Sytems zur autonomen Führung landwirtschaftlicher Fahrzeuge

Die Routenplanung und Kursbeschreibung kann zweckmäßigerweise im Rahmen der ohnehin erforderlichen Arbeitsvorbereitung auf dem Betriebsrechner des landwirtschaftlichen Betriebes erfolgen. Der Datenaustausch zwischen dem Betriebsrechner und dem jeweiligen Fahrzeug sowie die universelle Ein-/Ausgabeeinheit auf dem Fahrzeug sind ebenfalls Gegenstand des LBS. Alle diese Komponenten, bis auf die Software zur Routenplanung und Kursbeschreibung, sind für landwirtschaftliche Fahrzeuge verfügbar, d.h. sie sind bereits auf dem Markt oder ihre Markteinführung wird erwartet.

Satelliten-Navigationssysteme werden bereits heute im Rahmen einer teilflächenspezifischen Pflanzenproduktion* in der Landwirtschaft eingesetzt. Obwohl sich mittels Differential-GPS (DGPS) Genauigkeiten im Zentimeterbereich erzielen lassen, ist dieses Verfahren als alleiniges Mittel für eine Fahrzeugführung nicht ausreichend, da die Berechnung der Position sehr zeitaufwendig ist. Da Satelliten-Navigationssysteme aber ohnehin auf landwirtschaftlichen Fahrzeugen Verwendung finden, bieten sie sich als Ergänzung einer Fahrzeugführung mittels Bilderkennung geradezu an. Auf die Errichtung und den Betrieb von Referenzstationen auf landwirtschaftlichen Betrieben kann verzichtet werden, da die „Arbeitsgemeinschaft der Vermessungsverwaltungen der Länder der Bundesrepublik Deutschland" (AdV) derzeit ein Netz von Referenzstaionen aufbaut, mit dessen Hilfe Dienste unterschiedlicher Genauigkeit angeboten werden sollen [9]. Erste Stationen haben Ihren Probebetrieb bereits aufgenommen. Für die landwirtschaftliche Anwendung ist die mit dem geplanten „hochpräzisen Echtzeitpositionierungsservice" (HEPS) erzielbare Genauigkeit von wenigen Zentimetern bei einer Updaterate von etwas mehr als einer Sekunde ausreichend. Auch dieses Datenobjekt wurde bei der Normung des LBS bereits berücksichtigt.

4. Schlußbemerkung

Der vorgeschlagene modulare Aufbau eines offenen Systems zur autonomen Führung landwirtschaftlicher Fahrzeuge auf dem Felde erlaubt eine weitgehende Nutzung bereits jetzt oder in Zukunft vorhandener Systeme und dadurch eine weitgehende Kostenreduktion. Grundlage für den erforderlichen Datenaustausch zwischen den Modulen ist das landwirtschaftliche BUS-System (LBS). Die Generierung des Leitsignals mittels Bilderkennung ergänzt durch ein Satellitennavigationssystem verspricht eine erfolgreiche für alle Anwendungsformen in der Pflanzenproduktion geeignete Lösung. Für Verfahren der Bilderkennung sprechen mehrere Gründe. So arbeiten optische Verfahren berührungslos, sind überaus anpassungsfähig und erlauben bei vorhergegangenen Arbeitsgängen entstandene Stukturmerkmale im Felde als Leitlinie zu nutzen, wodurch Vorbereitungen und Installationen im oder am Feld entfallen können. Bei vielen dieser Strukturmerkmale spielen spektrale Merkmale eine wichtigere Rolle, während Formunterschiede u.U. kaum oder gar nicht vorhanden sind. Auch dies spricht für eine Bilderkennung. Erste Versuchsfahrzeuge auf der Basis der Bilderkennung wurden bereits erfolgreich erprobt. Generell ist zu erwarten, daß Verfahren der Bilderkennung auch aus anderen Gründen Eingang in die Pflanzenproduktion finden werden, da sich mit ihnen wertvolle Informationen für die Produktion gewinnen lassen, beispielsweise über den Zustand der Pflanzen, die Verunkrautung, Krankheiten, Bodenzustände usw.. Auf dem Gebiet der Bilderkennung selbst ist zu erwarten, daß aufgrund intensiver Forschungsarbeiten und eines Bedarfs in verschiedenen Bereichen außerhalb der Landwirtschaft in naher Zukunft mit erheblichen Leistungssteigerungen zu rechnen ist. Für die globale Satelliten-Navigations-Systeme gilt ähnliches. Letztere werden bereits heute in der Landwirtschaft für teilflächenspezifische Bearbeitungen verwendet. Sie sind weltweit einsetzbar bei einer ständig steigenden Zahl von Anwendungen und Anwendern, was zu einem ständig steigenden Preis-Leistungs-Verhältnis führt.

---

* Unter teilflächenspezifischer Pflanzenproduktion wird die Bewirtschaftung landwirtschaftlicher Flächen verstanden, die der Variabilität der Böden Rechnung trägt.

Schrifttum

[1] Jahns, G.: Possibilities for Producing Course Signals for the Automatic Steering of Farm Vehicles. In: Automatic Guidance of Farm Vehicles Hrsg.: R.E. Young Agric. Eng. Dep.Series No. 1, Agric. Exp. Station Auburn Alabama Nov. 1976, S. 3-16

[2] Jahns, G.: Automatic Guidance in Agriculture - a Review ASAE-Paper NCR 83-404 (1983)

[3] Tillett, N.D.:Automatic Guidance Sensors for Agricultural Field Machines: A Review. J. Agric. Engng. Res. 50 (1991), p. 167-187

[4] Gilg, A. und Schmidt, G.: Führung eines Roboterfahrzeuges, gestützt auf symbolische Kursbeschreibung und schnelle Landmarkendetektion. at 43 (1995) H. 3, S. 416-423

[5] DIN 9684: Landmaschinen und Traktoren - Schnittstellen zur Signalübertragung.
     Teil I: Punkt-zu-Punkt-Verbindung (Norm)
     Teil II: Serieller Daten-BUS (Gelbdruck)
     Teil III: Systemfunktionen, Identifier (Gelbdruck)
     Teil IV: Benutzerstation (Manuskript der LBS Normengruppe in der Normengruppe
                Landmaschinen und Ackerschlepper (NLA))
     Teil V: Datenübertragung zum Management-Informations-System, Auftragsbearbeitung
                (Manuskript der LBS Normengruppe in der NLA)
Beuth Verlag, Berlin.

[6] Lichtenberg, G.: Entwurf eines Zwischenplattenventils Diplomarbeit Institut für Landmaschinen und Institut für Landtechnische Grundlagenforschung 1975

[7] Busse, W., Coenenberg, H., Feldmann, F. und Crusinberry, T.F.: The first Serial Produced Automatic Steering System for Corn Combines and Forage Harvester Proceedings of the International Grain and Forage Harvesting Conference, Sept. 1977, p 43-47

[8] Jaufmann, A.: Traktormanagementsystem. Zur Veröffentlichung vorgesehen in: Jahrbuch Agrartechnik 1997

[9] Hankemeier, P.: GPS-Augmentation: State of the Art. DGON Seminar SATNAV 95 Satellitennavigationssysteme - Grundlagen und Anwendungen, 09.-12. Oktober 1995 Freising-Weihenstephan, (1995), S.31-40

Ein vielsegmentiger Roboter zur autonomen Inspektion von Abwasserkanälen

W. Ilg, K. Berns, St. Cordes, M. Eberl, R. Suna

Forschungszentrum Informatik, Gruppe Interaktive Planungstechnik
Haid-und-Neu-Str.10-14, 76131 Karlsruhe

Abstract. Schadhafte Abwässerkanäle stellen eine akute Gefährdung des Grundwassers dar. Die derzeit eingesetzten Inspektionsverfahren sind extrem kostenintensiv und können nur einen Teil der Abwässerkanale abdecken. Wesentliche Einschränkungen bei der Inspektion werden dabei von den eingesetzen Kanalinspektionsfahrzeugen bedingt, welche nur in gereinigten und gerade verlaufenden Kanalabschnitten mit sehr geringer Reichweite eingesetzt werden können. In diesen Artikel wird ein Konzept einer vielsegmentigen räderangetriebenen Kanalroboterplattform vorgestellt, die mit wesentlich gesteigerter Mobilität autonom in Abwasserkanalsystemen navigiert und Inspektionsaufgaben verrichtet.

1   Einleitung

Derzeit werden zur Kanalinspektion von nicht begehbaren Abwasserkanälen fast ausschließlich eingliedrige, räderangetriebene Kanalfahrzeuge (Abbildung 1) eingesetzt, welche ein Schleppkabel zur Energieversorgung, Kommunikation und Fernsteuerung durch den Operateur im Leitstand (Abbildung 2) mitführen. Die Reichweite dieser mobilen Plattformen wird einerseits durch das mitgeführte Schleppkabel und andererseits durch auftretende, nicht überwindbare Hindernisse, wie Muffenversätze und sohlenungleiche Kanalanschlüsse stark eingeschränkt.

Die verminderte Mobilität verursacht wesentliche Einschränkungen in der praktischen Handhabbarkeit der Inspektionsvorgänge. Einerseits muß der mobile Leitstand sehr oft seine Position ändern, um das Kanalfahrzeug an einem anderem Kanalschacht einzusetzen. Diese Verfahrensweise beansprucht sehr viel Zeit und macht einen nicht unwesentlichen Teil des Gesamtaufwandes aus. Andererseits ist der Einsatz dieser Kanalfahrzeuge auf nicht in Betrieb befindliche und gereinigte Kanalsysteme begrenzt, da das Überwinden von Ablagerungen und sonstigen Hindernissen damit nicht realisierbar ist. Eine ausführliche Beschreibung der eingesetzten Verfahren und Inspektionsfahrzeuge findet sich in [11] und [13].

Im Rahmen einer Machbarkeitsstudie[1] des BMBF wurden Lösungsansätze zur

---

[1] Projektpartner der der vom BMBF unter Kennzeichen 01 IW 501 A geförderten Machbarkeitsstudie LAOKOON waren das Forschungszentrum Informatik Karlsruhe, die rhenag (Rheinische Energie Aktienge sellschaft) und die Gesellschaft für Mathematik und Datenverarbeitung (GMD) in St. Augustin.

Fig. 1. Das mobile Kanalfahrzeug KRA4 mit dem Schwenkkopfkamerasystem ARGUS der Firma IBAK [6] als Beispiel derzeit eingesetzter Inspektionsplattformen.

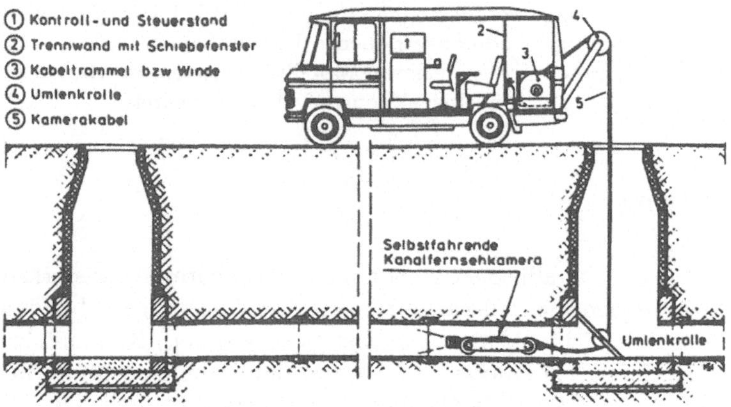

Fig. 2. Prinzipskizze der derzeit üblichen, teleoperativ geführten optischen Inspektion (aus [2]).

Realisierung eines autonomen Kanalroboters entwickelt, der aufgrund wesentlich erhöhter Mobilität und Autonomie eine effizientere und leistungsfähigere Inspektion und Wartung von nicht begehbaren Kanälen verspricht und neue Anwendungsfelder im Bereich des Kanalbetriebs ermöglicht. Eine ausführliche Beschreibung der Studie findet sich in [7].

In folgenden werden zunächst die Anforderungen an eine mobile Kanalroboterplattform seitens der Navigation im Kanal und bezüglich industrieller Anwendungen spezifiziert. Basierend auf diesen Anforderungen erfolgt eine Diskussion verschiedener mobiler Roboter aus Forschung und Technik bezüglich Aufbau und Antriebsysteme für den Einsatz im Anwendungsfeld Kanalinspektion. Als Ergebnis dieser Diskussion wird ein Konzept eines vielsegmentigen räderangetriebenen

Kanalroboterplattform ausführlich vorgestellt. Dabei werden neben der Mobilität besonders auch Aspekte der Autonomie (Energieversorgung, Steuerung, Kommunikation) und die industrielle Anwendbarkeit betrachtet. Der Einsatz des Kanalroboters wird in verschiedenen Entwicklungsstufen und Anwedungsszenarien beschrieben.

2 Einsatz mobiler Roboter in Abwasserkanälen

Um die Einsatzmöglichkeiten mobiler Roboter in Anwendungsfeld Abwassrkanal zu untersuchen, werden zunächst die Anforderungen an ein solches System näher spezifiziert. Dabei werden einerseits die in Abwasserkanälen typischen Kanalverläufe und Hindernisse beschrieben und andererseits die Randbedingungen erläutert, die bei der Realisierung einer kommerziell zur Inspektion eingesetzten Roboterplattform beachtet werden müssen. Diese Betrachtungen werden anschließend zur Diskussion verschiedener mobiler Roboter herangezogen, um das Konzept einer für den industriellen Einsatz in Abwasserkanälen geeignete Roboterplattform zu entwickeln.

2.1 Anforderungen

Die Anforderungen an die Mobilität der Kanalroboterplattform werden von den typischen Verläufen der Abwasserkanäle vorgegeben. Diese bestehen zu einem sehr großen Teil aus gerade und mit leichten Steigungen verlaufenden Haltungen zwischen Kanlschächten (Abbildung 2). Probleme beim Befahren dieser geraden Abschnitte können durch Muffenversätze (Versätze in den Verbindungen zwischen 2 Kanalrohren) oder durch auftretende Hindernisse (Wurzeleinwuchs, abgebröckelter Beton) entstehen. Weitere Probleme beim Befahren von Kanalsystemen bestehen beim Auftreten von Kreuzungen und T-Abbiegungen, sowie beim Abbiegen in nicht sohlengleiche Nebenkanäle (Abbildung 3). Bei der Betrachtung der Mobilitätsanforderungen müssen die Bedingungen im Kanal beachtet werden. Die Kanäle sind im allgemeinen naß und glitschig und führen oft einige Zentimeter hoch Wasser. Weiterhin muß mit Ablagerungen und Verschmutzung verschiedener Art gerechnet werden. Die Mobilitätsanforderingen bestehen im einzelnen aus:

- Befahren von Kanalverläufen mit 30-80 cm Durchmesser
- Fahren von sohlengleichen und nicht sohlengleichen Abzweigungen bis 90o
- Überwinden von Hindernissen wie Sockel oder Muffenvorsprünge

Zusammenfassend kann man sagen, daß die Kanalverläufe verglichen mit Rohrverläufen in Industrieanlagen (Kernkraftwerken) weniger komplex sind, da beispielsweise keine vertikalen Rohrleirungen überwunden werden müssen. Wesentlich erschwert wird die Navigation in den Kanalsystemen durch die wiedrigen und teilweise unvorhersehbaren Kanalbedingungen.

274

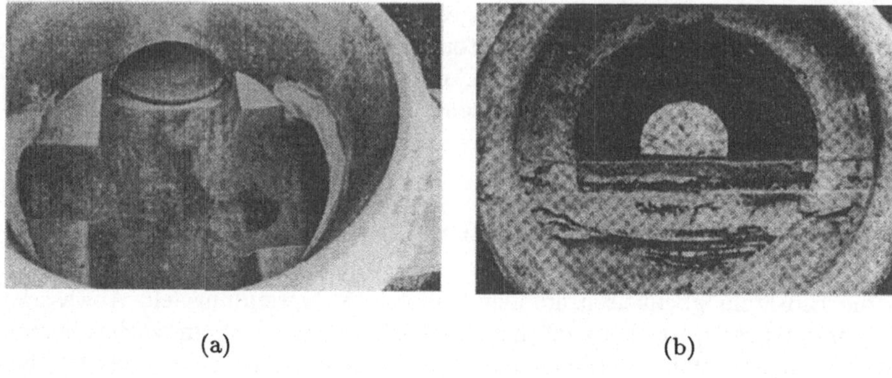

(a)   (b)

Fig. 3. Problembereiche bei der Fortbewegung in Kanalsystemen: Kanalkreuzung mit scheitelgleichen Rohrverläufen (a) und verfestigte Ablagerungen am Kanalboden.

Neben den reinen Mobiltätsanforderungen müssen weiterhin die Randbedingungen zum Einsatz der Roboterplattform zur autonomen Inspektion berücksichtigt werden. Dies sind im einzelnen:

- Energieeffizientes und zügiges Fahren im Normalbetrieb
- hohe Nutzlastkapazität zur Unterbringung von Energieträgern, Sensoren, Informationsverarbeitungseinheiten und Datenträgern
- hohe Ausfallsicherheit sowie einfache Handhabbarkeit im Betrieb

2.2 Mobile Roboter

Um ein geeignetes Konzept für eine Kanalroboterplattform zu entwickeln, wurden verschiedenartige mobile Roboter mit unterschiedlichem Aufbau und Antriebssystemen (Räder, Ketten, Beine, Hybride Systeme) untersucht. Dabei wurden sowohl speziell zur Bewegung in Röhren und Schächten entwickelte als auch auf anderen Anwendungsfeldern eingesetzte Systeme betrachtet.

- *Radangetriebene Systeme* realisieren im Normalbetrieb der geraden Kanalverläufe eine sehr effiziente und energetisch günstige Fortbewegung. Um auch in Abbiegungen und gekrümmten Kanal-und Rohrverläufen verfolgen zu können, werden in den neueren Forschungs- und Entwicklungsarbeiten flexible vielsegmentige Plattformen statt monolytischen Robotern realisiert [4]. Weiterhin werden innerhalb von Rohren die Räder zur stabileren Fortbewegung über den gesamten Querschnitt verteilt wobei der Roboter dann den gesamten Rohrdurchmesser ausfüllt [12]. Dies hat die Nachteile, daß einerseits nur vollständig gesäuberte und im Durchmesser nur gering variierende Rohre durchfahren werden können.

- *Beinangetriebene Systeme* [8], [9] realisieren potentiell die flexibelste Fortbewegung in komplexen Kanal- und Rohrsystemen. Mit Lauf- oder Klettermaschinen ist es aufgrund der im allgemeinen hohen Anzahl von Freiheitsgraden prinzipiell möglich, durch komplexe Bewegungsabläufe Hindernisse zu überwinden und sogar vertikale Rohre hochzuklettern. Die Realisierung eines solchen Kanalroboters beinhaltet Probleme hinsichtlich der industriellen Anwendung in bezug auf die Robust- und Ausfallsicherhheit, Komplexität der Steuerung sowie der sehr hohen Energieaufnahme solcher Systeme. Die beschränkte Komplexität der betrachteten Kanalverläufe erfordern im Gegensatz zu Industrieanlagen keine derart komplexen Bewegungsabläufe, die auschließlich mit beinangetriebenen Systemen realisiert werden können.

- *Kettenangetriebene Systeme* [5] erfüllen prinzipiell die gestellten Mobilitätsanforderungen und sind mit herkömmlichen Steuerungsmethoden sehr robust. Neben der energetisch sehr aufwendigen Fortbewegung sind beim praktischen Einsatz in Kanalsystemen Probleme aufgetreten, wenn Schmutz und Geröll in die Kettensysteme eintritt.

- *Hybride Systeme* [1] weisen durch ihre Redundanz in den Fortbewegungsmechanismen erhöhte Flexibilität und Ausfallsicherheit auf. Beispielsweise kann je nach Anforderung umgeschalten werden zwischen effizienter Bewegungsabäufen (Räder- oder Kettenantrieb) und komplexen Bewegungsabläufen. Diese Systeme erfordern allerdings einen hohen Entwicklungsaufwand und komplexe Steuerungsmechanismen.

Eine Übersicht der betrachteten mobilen Systeme gibt Tabelle 1. Die Studie der verschiedenen Antriebs- und fortbewegungsmechanismen führte zu dem Schluß, daß ein räderangetriebenes vielsegmentiges System mit aktiv ansteuerbaren Gelenken zwischen den einzelnen Segmenten die gestellten Anforderungen seitens Mobilität und industrieller Anwendbarkeit in Kanalsystemen am besten erfüllt.

Roboterplattform	Antriebskonzept	spezielle Mobiltät	Bemerkungen
Mechanische Schlange [10]	Schlangen-bewegung	Umwinden von Hindernissen	Bewegungsform im Rohr schlecht einsetzbar
Inpipe-Robot [12]	Räder mit Spreizantrieb	Abbiegen in T-Stücken	Ausfüllen des Rohrkörpers
ACM IV [4]	ansteuerb. Gelenke, Räder	Abbiegen, Stufen	gleichartige Freiheitsgrade
Rohrkletterer [8], [9]	Beine mit Spreizantrieb	vertikale Kanalverläufe	aufwendige Steuerung, hoher Energieverbrauch
Quadruped Robot [1]	Beine u. Ketten	effiziente o. flexible Bewegung wählbar	hybrides Antriebskonzept

Table 1. Aufstellung der beschriebenen mobilen Systeme zur Fortbewegung in Rohren und Schächten.

3 Konzept der vielsegmentigen Kanalroboterplattform

Basierend auf den oben angestellten Studie wird im folgenden das Konzept einer vielsegmentigen autonomen Kanalroboterplattform sowie die ersten Realisierungen beschrieben. Dabei wird auf den Aufbau der mechanischen Konstruktion, die angestrebte Rechner- und Steuerungsarchitktur sowie weiterer Aspekte der autonomen Navigation in Abwasserkanälen eingegangen.

3.1 Aufbau

Den prinzipiellen Aufbau des vielsegmentigen Kanalroboters zeigt Abbildung 4. Die vielsegmentige Konstruktion mit aktiven, ansteuerbaren Gelenken zwischen den einzelnen Segmenten gewährleistet erhöhte Flexibilität und Mobilität, so daß Abzweigungen in Nebenkanäle und Kurven ebenso durchfahren werden können, wie Hindernisse (Muffenversätze bei Rohrverbindungen)(Abbildung 5), die für die derzeit eingesetzten Kanalfahrzeuge oft unüberwindbare Schranken darstellen und zu einem Abbruch des Inspektionsvorgangs führen.

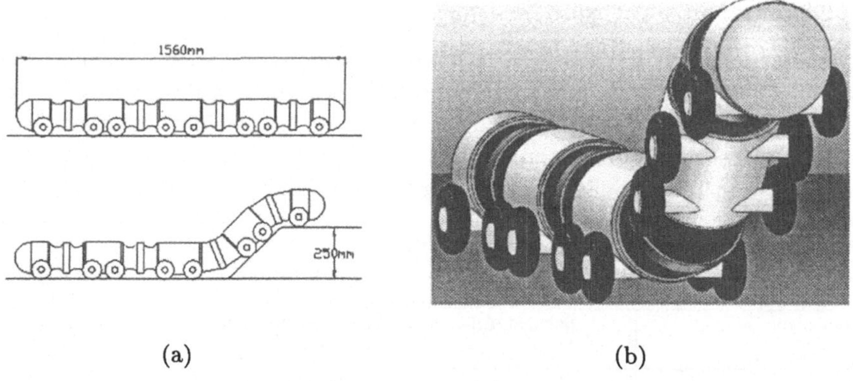

Fig. 4. CAD-Modelle des vielsegmentigen Kanalroboters. In (a) sind die Ausmaße und die Steigfähigkeit des 5 segmentigen Kanalroboters dargestellt. Abbildung(b) zeigt den ersten CAD-Entwurf für die Roboterkonstruktion, die bereits als mechanisches Modell im Maßstab 1:2 realisiert wurde.

Ein weiterer Vorteil des vielsegmentigen Aufbaus liegt in der modularen Umrüst- und Erweiterbarkeit des Roboters. Bei Bedarf kann der Grundaufbau des Roboters bestehend aus Energie-, Antriebs-, Sensor-, und Informationsverarbeitungssegmenten umgerüstet bzw. erweitert werden. So besteht bespielsweise die

Möglichkeit, bei besonderen Inspektions- und Wartungsaufgaben spezielle Sensorelemente und Werkzeuge anzukoppeln. Auch ein Segment zur Wasserprobenentnahme kann hier eingesetzt werden. Diese leicht handhabbare Modularität eröffnet den flexiblen Einsatz in unterschiedlichen Anwendungsfeldern.

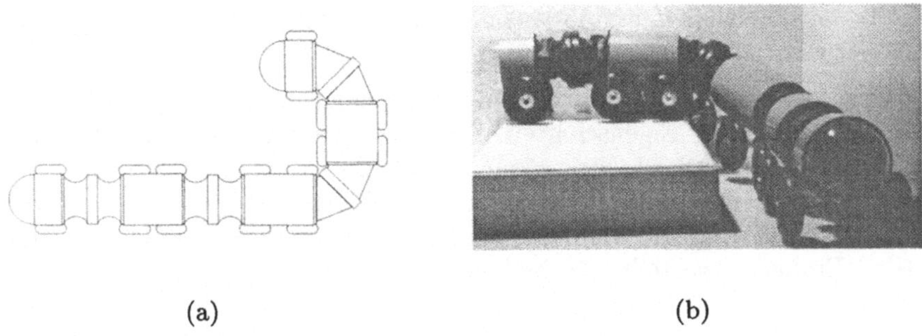

(a)   (b)

Fig. 5. Abbiegevorgänge mit gleichzeitiger Überwindung eines Vorsprunges in in der CAD-Konstruktion (a) und mit dem mechanischen Modell (b).

3.2 Rechner- und Steuerungsarchitektur

Die wesentlichen Anforderungen an die Rechner- und Steuerungsarchitektur sind Echtzeitfähigkeit, Fehlertoleranz beim Verarbeiten verrauschter Sensordaten, Robustheit, Erweiterbarkeit und Ausfallsicherheit. Um diesen Anforderungen gerecht werden zu können und die entstehende Systemkomplexität beherrschbar zu machen, wurde eine modular aufgebaute, hierarchische Steuerungsarchitektur ausgewählt. Einzelkomponenten können dadurch sukzessiv realisiert und in Betrieb genommen werden. Die Fehlersuche vereinfacht sich und führt zu einer kürzeren Entwicklungszeit. Das System wird überschaubarer, es ist einfacher zu entwickeln und zu warten.

Die Modularität kann sowohl auf Software- als auch auf Hardwareebene umgesetzt werden. Mehrere Funktionseinheiten arbeiten zusammen, um das gewünschte Gesamtverhalten zu erreichen. Ein modularer Ansatz bietet auch den Vorzug, das System leicht erweitern zu können.

Eine zusätzliche Methode, die Systemkomplexität in den Griff zu bekommen, liegt in der Einführung von unterschiedlichen Abstraktionsebenen in der Systemsicht. Die Abstraktionsebenen bilden eine hierarchische Struktur zur Beschreibung des Systems. Höhere Verhaltensweisen werden durch das Zusammenwirken einfacherer Verhaltensweisen realisiert, übergeordnete Ebenen nutzen für die Aufgabenerfüllung Dienste aus untergeordneten Schichten.

Die oberste Abstraktionsebene beschreibt den Kanalroboter als mobilen Roboter, der sich in Kanalisationssystemen fortbewegen kann (Abbildung 6b). Die nächsttiefere Schicht stellt den Roboter als ein System mit höherer Sensorik und Bewegungsapparat dar. Die Sicht der Körperebene umfaßt den Bewegungsapparat oder Körper, der sich in Körpersensorik und Antriebsebene aufgliedert. In der Antriebsebene werden Knickgelenke und Antriebseinheiten zusammengefaßt. Die Knickgelenke halten jeweils die Sensorik für die Kardangelenke und die dazugehörigen Aktoren.

Die hierarchische Steuerungsarchitektur besitzt hinsichtlich der geforderten Echtzeitfähigkeit günstige Eigenschaften. Die einzelnen Funktionseinheiten können unabhängig voneinander realisiert und parallel in Hardware ausgeführt werden. Die Verwendung einer einzigen (hoch-)leistungsfähigen, informationsverarbeitenden Komponente entfällt, vielmehr wird die Informationsverarbeitung auf viele kleine Einheiten verteilt, die bedeutend einfacher gestaltet werden können. Durch den Einsatz vieler paralleler Einheiten wird eine hohe Verarbeitungsleistung zur Verfügung gestellt. Zwangsläufig wird dadurch der Kommunikationsaufwand erhöht. Dieser zusätzliche Aufwand wird jedoch durch die Bereitstellung der insgesamt höheren Datenverarbeitungsleistung kompensiert.

Die schematische Einteilung der Steuerungsebenen sowie die Kommunikationsverbindungen, die durch einen CAN-Bus realisiert werden sollen, wird am Beispiel der Bewegungskoordination in Abbildung 6a aufgezeigt.

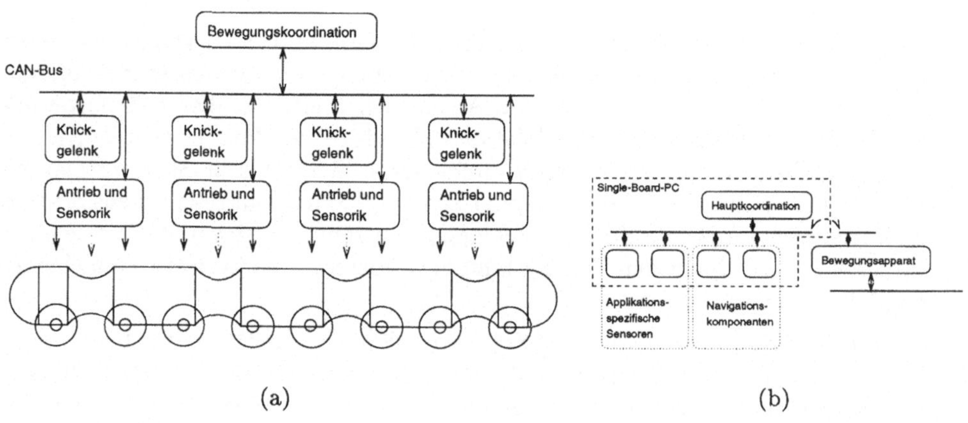

Fig. 6. Aufbau der Steuerungsarchitektur bezüglich Bewegungskoordination (a) und zur Gesamtsteuerung (b).

3.3 Autonomieaspekte

Die Autonomie des Kanalroboters, die auf längere Sicht die Arbeit des Operateurs in der mobilen Leitwarte weitgehend ersetzen und Langzeiteinsätze im Kanal ermöglichen soll, bezieht sich neben der Steuerung im wesentlichen auf die Aspekte der Energieversorgung, Informationsverarbeitung und Kommunikation. Durch das Fehlen des Schleppkabels, was einerseits eine deutlich höhere Mobilität und Reichweite ermöglicht, werden andererseits hohe Anforderungen an Ausfallsicherheit und Bergungsstrategien gestellt.

Funkverbindung Da die Ausbreitung breitbandiger Funksignale in erdverlegten Rohren problematisch ist und eine Funkverbindung durch größere Strecken Erdreich nicht erzielt werden kann, muß die Kanalroboterplattform mindestens kurzzeitig in der Lage sein, völlig autonom, ohne Fernsteuerung durch einen Operateur im Kanalsystem zu navigieren.

Energieversorgung Die Energieversorgung in Form von aufladbaren Batterien ist ebenfalls auf dem Roboter untergebracht. Falls der Roboter ein Absinken der Energie feststellt, sendet er ein Notsignal, und begibt sich an einen der definierten Ausgangsschächte.

Bergungsproblematik Aufgrund des Fehlens des Schleppkabels müssen Störfall- und Bergungsstrategien entwickelt werden, da der Roboter nicht wie herkömmlich einfach am Schleppkabel herausgezogen werden kann (wobei es in der Praxis allerdings immer wieder zu Verklemmungen des Roboters im Kanal kommt). Auch hier muß die automatische Fehlerdiagnose, Absenden eines Notsignals und das Erreichen des nächsten Ausgangsschachtes sichergestellt werden. Durch die Redundanz des vielsegmengtigen Roboters ist dieser auch bei partiellem Ausfall einzelner Gelenke oder Antriebe noch in der Lage, grundlegende Fortbwegungsmechanismen, wie geradeausfahren mit kleineren Hindernissen, auszuführen.

Informationverarbeitung Neben der Informationsgewinnung durch die auf dem Kanalroboter mitgeführten Sensoren stellen die verfügbaren Katasterdaten, Zustandsbeschreibungen und vorhandene Aufzeichnungen von früheren Inspektionsfahrten eine zusätzliche Informationsquelle zur autonomen Navigation und Durchführung der Inspektionsaufgaben dar. Im Forschungszentrum Informatik wurde zur Unterstützung des Kanalbetreibers und des Einsatzes von Kanalrobotern ein Kanalinformationssystem [3] entwickelt.

4 Anwendungsszenarien im teleoperativen Einsatz

Im Rahmen dieses Forschungsprojektes wird ein ganzheitliches Konzept zur teilautonomen Kanalinspektion und Überwachung entwickelt. Die Realisierung des autonomen Kanalroboters wird in mehreren Entwicklungsstufen mit unterschiedlichem Autonomiegrad erfolgen. Der derzeit in der Entwicklung stehende erste

Prototyp wird in bezug auf die Energieversorgung und wesentlicher Bereiche der Steuerung autonom im Kanal navigieren können. Schon in dieser Entwicklungsphase steigt die Leistungsfähigkeit verglichen mit den heute eingesetzten Kanalwagen aufgrund der wesentlich höheren Mobilität beträchtlich. Mit der Realisierung eines autonomen mobilen Kanalroboters können so einerseits die Inspektion und Wartung in Abwasserkanälen wesenlich effizienter durchgeführt und innovative Anwendungen im Bereich des Kanalbetriebs (mobile Einleiterkontrolle, Probeentnahme von Wasser und Schlick, Einsatz von Bio- und Chemosensoren) ermöglicht werden.

References

1. H. Adachi, T. Arai, N. Koyachi, and K. Homma. Six degrees of freedom and posture control for a quadruped robot. In *Intelligent Autonomous Vehicles*, pages 133–138, 1995.
2. Abwassertechnische Vereinigung (ATV). *Inspektion, Instandsetzung, Sanierung und Erneuerung von Abwasserkanälen und -leitungen. Teil 2: Optische Inspektion (Merkblatt M 143, Teil 2)*, 1991.
3. M. Eberl and S. Cordes. Offenes Informationssystem für die Intergration kommunaler Umweltinformationen. In *10. Symposium Informatik für den Umweltschutz*, sept. 1996.
4. Shigeo Hirose. *Biologically inspired Robots - Snake-Like Locomoters and Manipulators*. Oxford Sciens Publications, 1993.
5. Shigeo Hirose. A proposal for cooperative robot gunryu composed of autonomous segments. In *Intelligent Robots ans Systems , IROS*. Oxford Sciens Publications, 1994.
6. IBAK, Wehdenweg 122, 24148 Kiel. *Schwenkkopfkamera ARGUS*, June 1993. Produktinformation.
7. K.Berns, J. Hertzberg, W.Ilg, E. Rome, and H.Stapelfeld (ed.). *BMBF-Machbarkeitsuntersuchung LAOKOON:Abschlußbericht*. Forschungszentrum Informatik Karlsruhe, rhenag Köln , GMD Sankt Augustin, März 1996.
8. W. Neubauer. A spider-like robot that climbs vertically in ducts or pipes. In *Proceedings International Conference on Intelligent Robots and Systems*, volume 2, pages 1178–1185, Munich, Germany, 1994.
9. Th. Roßmann and F. Pfeiffer. Simulation und regelung eines rohrkrabblers. In *Autonome Mobile Systeme*, pages 80 – 89, 1995.
10. Y. Shan and Y. Koren. Design and motion planning of a mechanical snake. *IEEE Transactions on Systems, Man and Cybernetics*, 23(4):1091–1100, 1993.
11. D. Stein and W. Niederehe. *Instandhaltung von Kanalisationen*. Ernst & Sohn, Berlin, 2 edition, 1992.
12. K. Taguchi and N. Kawarazaki. Development of in–pipe locomotion robot. In *Fifth International Conference on Advanced Robotics ICAR*, pages 297–302, 1991.
13. U. Winkler. Abwässerkanäle inspizieren. *Umwelt*, 23(11):626–628, Nov. 1993.

Navigations- und Steuerungssysteme
für die freie Navigation von Radfahrzeugen

Dr.-Ing. Günter Ullrich
Frog Navigation Systems, D-Duisburg

Einleitung

Fahrerlose Transportsysteme (FTS) können als erste Anwendung von automatischen Radfahrzeugen, die nicht schienengebunden sind, angesehen werden. Seit den 70er Jahren sind die in der Vergangenheit zumeist leitdrahtgeführten Systeme im industriellen Einsatz. Der in den Boden verlegte und stromdurchflossene Leitdraht war einfach von der Fahrzeugsensorik (zwei Spulen unterhalb des Fahrzeuges) zu detektieren, hatte aber den prinzipbedingten Nachteil, daß Fahrkursänderungen nur umständlich und darüber hinaus allein vom FTS-Lieferanten vorgenommen werden konnten.

Nicht nur die Navigations- sondern auch die Steuerungstechnik wurde in den Anfängen des FTS einfach gehalten: Entstammten doch alle FTS-Hersteller der ersten Stunde dem klassischen Maschinenbau (Hersteller von Gabelstaplern, Lagertechnik und starrer Fördertechnik), waren projektbezogene Eigenentwicklungen auf durchweg niedrigem Niveau sowohl der FTS-Leit- als auch der Fahrzeugsteuerung die logische Konsequenz. Die in den folgenden Entwicklungsstufen vorgestellte leitdrahtlose Navigation und intelligente Steuerungskonzepte kamen zu spät und waren zu teuer, um das Abflauen der Euphorie für das FTS zu verhindern. Die Automobilindustrie, zuvor größter FTS-Anwender, wendete sich zu Beginn dieses Jahrzehntes gänzlich vom FTS ab und im Zuge der Lean Production einfacheren und billigeren Lösungen zu.

Als Notlösung präsentierten einige Firmen Mitte der neunziger Jahre eine Kombination aus Leitdrahtnavigation und Koppelnavigation ohne Peilung („Freiflug" oder aber Blindflug). Die Fahrzeuge bewältigten kurze Strecken, z.B. Kurven oder Stichstrecken, mit einer reinen Koppelnavigation (Drehwinkelgeber an den Rädern), auf den Hauptwegen war weiterhin der Leitdraht Lotse.

Wir wollen im folgenden betrachten, wie fortschrittliche Steuerungs- und Navigationstechnik heute aussieht und sich im industriellen Einsatz bewährt. Um bewährte Technik wird es gehen, denn egal ob für den zivilen, militärischen oder industriellen Einsatz - der Kunde verlangt preiswerte und leistungsfähige Systeme mit deutlich über 95 % Verfügbarkeit.

Modulare Steuerungsstrukturen

Zunächst muß der Gültigkeitsbereich der folgenden Aussagen definiert werden: Die Radfahrzeuge, um die es hier geht, sind automatisch, d.h. nicht vom Menschen geführt. Es handelt sich also nicht um den klassischen Gabelstapler oder den LKW (vom Menschen direkt gesteuert) und auch nicht um ferngesteuerte Fahrzeuge (Manipulatorfahrzeuge). Der Fahrweg soll jedoch vorgegeben sein; ein Kennenlernen und Zurechtfinden in unbekannter Umgebung sowie eine Umwelterkennung ist nicht erforderlich.

Die verbleibende Gruppe von Fahrzeugen sind die Fahrerlosen Transportfahrzeuge (FTF), ggf. mehrere von ihnen eingebunden in ein FTS. Die Einsatzmöglichkeiten sind für das FTS allerdings definitionsgemäß derart eingeschränkt, daß ihre Hauptfunktion der innerbetriebliche

Materialfluß ist [1]. Auf diese Einschränkung wollen wir hier verzichten, die Begriffe FTS und FTF aber dennoch benutzen.

Der im vorigen Absatz vorgenommene Ausschluß des Kennenlernens und Zurechtfindens in unbekannter Umgebung orientiert sich an den Erfordernissen der Fahrerlosen Transportsysteme: Alle uns bekannten Versuche, die Fahrzeuge selbst, d.h. ohne jegliche Fahrweg-Vorgaben, den kürzesten Weg planen und dazu Hindernisse umfahren zu lassen, endeten in einer Beschneidung dieser Möglichkeiten. Ein Grund dafür ist, daß in einem derart automatisierten Bereich eine gewisse Ordnung und Disziplin notwendig und auch real vorhanden ist. Wesentlich aber ist, daß die in diesen Bereichen arbeitenden Menschen derart frei, aber auch unvorhersehbar agierende Fahrzeuge nicht akzeptieren. Um es ganz deutlich zu sagen: der Anwender will nicht nur Start- und Zielpunkte vorgeben, sondern auch den zu fahrenden Weg bestimmen!

Zeitgleich mit dem Beginn der Rezession und dem Verlust der Automobilindustrie als FTS-Kunden wurde damit begonnen, der FTS-Steuerung größere Bedeutung beizumessen. So lautete 1991 das Thema der Ersten Duisburger FTS-Fachtagung „Die Steuerungsstruktur des FTS bestimmt die Zukunft der Produktionslogistik". Neben dem reinen Transport sollte das FTS nunmehr als Organisationsmittel eingesetzt werden, z.B. zur Realisierung eines durch das FTS zwangsgeführten flexiblen Fließliniensystems oder aber des Taxiprinzips, nach dem die FTF ähnlich Taxen agieren, gesteuert von einer „Taxi"-Zentrale. Die technischen Voraussetzungen waren lange gegeben: Geeignete Rechnersysteme standen ebenso wie die Sensorik zur Verfügung, um die freie Navigation (leitdrahtlos), die Sicherheitsfunktionen (virtuelle Bumper) und einen intelligenten Fahrzeugeinsatz gewährleisten zu können [2].

Von Forschungsinstituten aber auch von einer Vielzahl von Betreibern kam der generelle Wunsch nach mehr Kompatibilität und Modularität auf. Der VDI-Ausschuß „Fahrerlose Transportsysteme" trug dem Rechnung und brachte eine Richtlinie, die die offene Steuerungsstruktur für Fahrerlose Transportsysteme beschreibt [3]. Hier ist definiert:

Eine Steuerungsstruktur ist offen, wenn sie sowohl hardware- als auch softwareseitig modular aufgebaut ist und einheitliche bzw. standardisierte Schnittstellen verwendet. Die Schnittstellen der einzelnen Module sind offengelegt, d.h. allgemein bekannt und vom Anwender nutzbar.

Aus dieser Definition leiten sich allgemeine Anforderungen und die Randbedingungen für eine offene Steuerung ab. In dieser Richtlinie wird die Fahrzeugsteuerung in einzelne, klar voneinander abgegrenzte Funktionsmodule untergliedert (Bild 1). Der inhaltliche Schwerpunkt der Richtlinie liegt dann in der Schnittstellenbeschreibung jedes einzelnen Funktionsmoduls. Abschließend wird das Beispiel einer einfachen Steuerung eines induktiv geführten Fahrzeuges gegeben. Es wird gezeigt, daß mit einer solchen einheitlichen, auf Funktionsmodule basierenden Beschreibung sowohl komplexe als auch einfache Steuerungskonzepte realisierbar sind.

Üblicherweise wird die operative Ebene in dieser Darstellung im Fahrzeugrechner realisiert, deshalb wird sie in diesen Fällen Fahrzeugsteuerung genannt. Hier geht es dann für den Manager darum, die Fahraufträge auszuführen. Dies tut er, indem er für ein reibungsloses Zusammenwirken der Funktionsblöcke Lastaufnahme, Sicherheit, Energieversorgung, Fahren und Kommunikation sorgt.

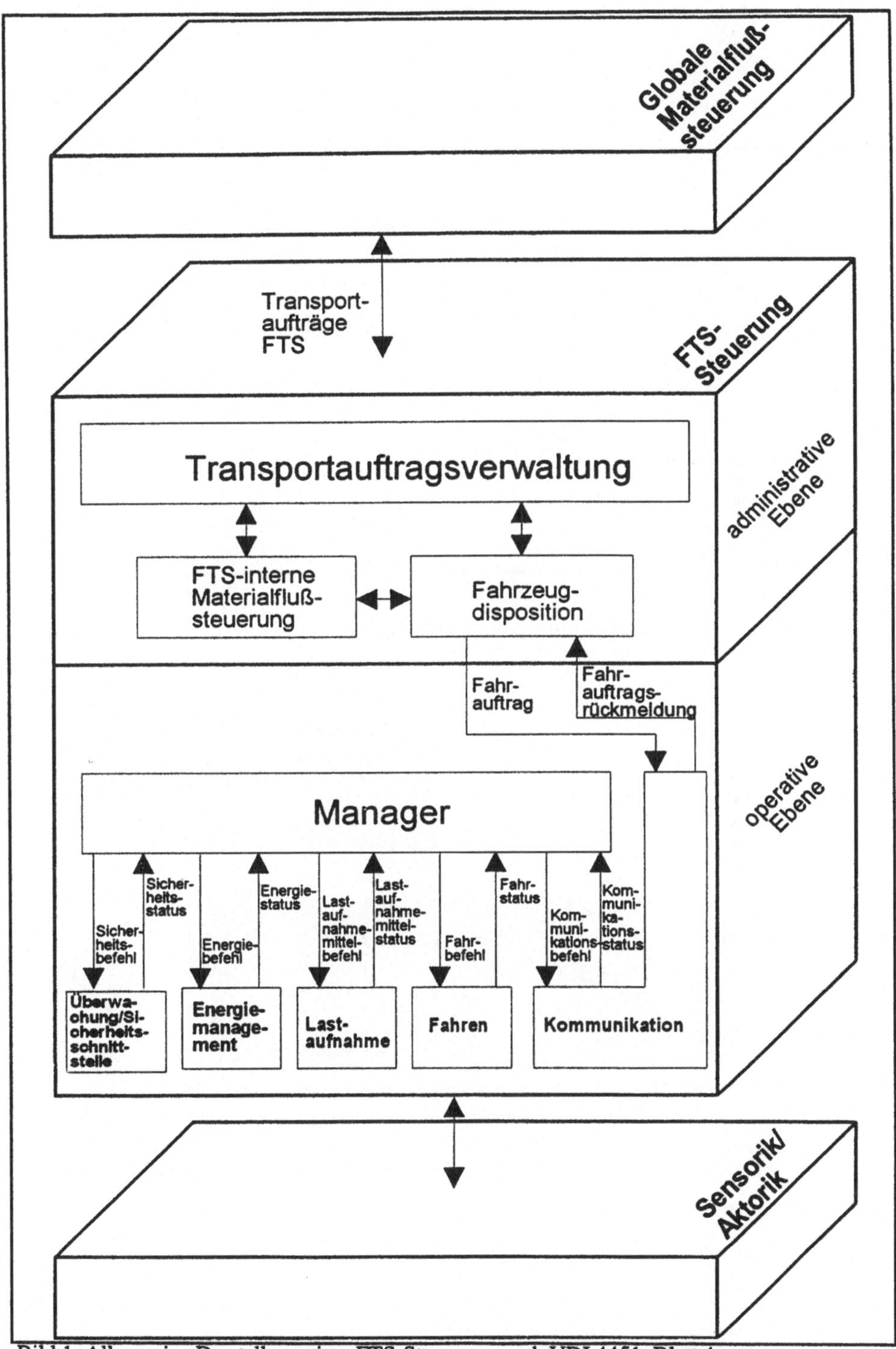

Bild 1: Allgemeine Darstellung einer FTS-Steuerung nach VDI 4451, Blatt 4.

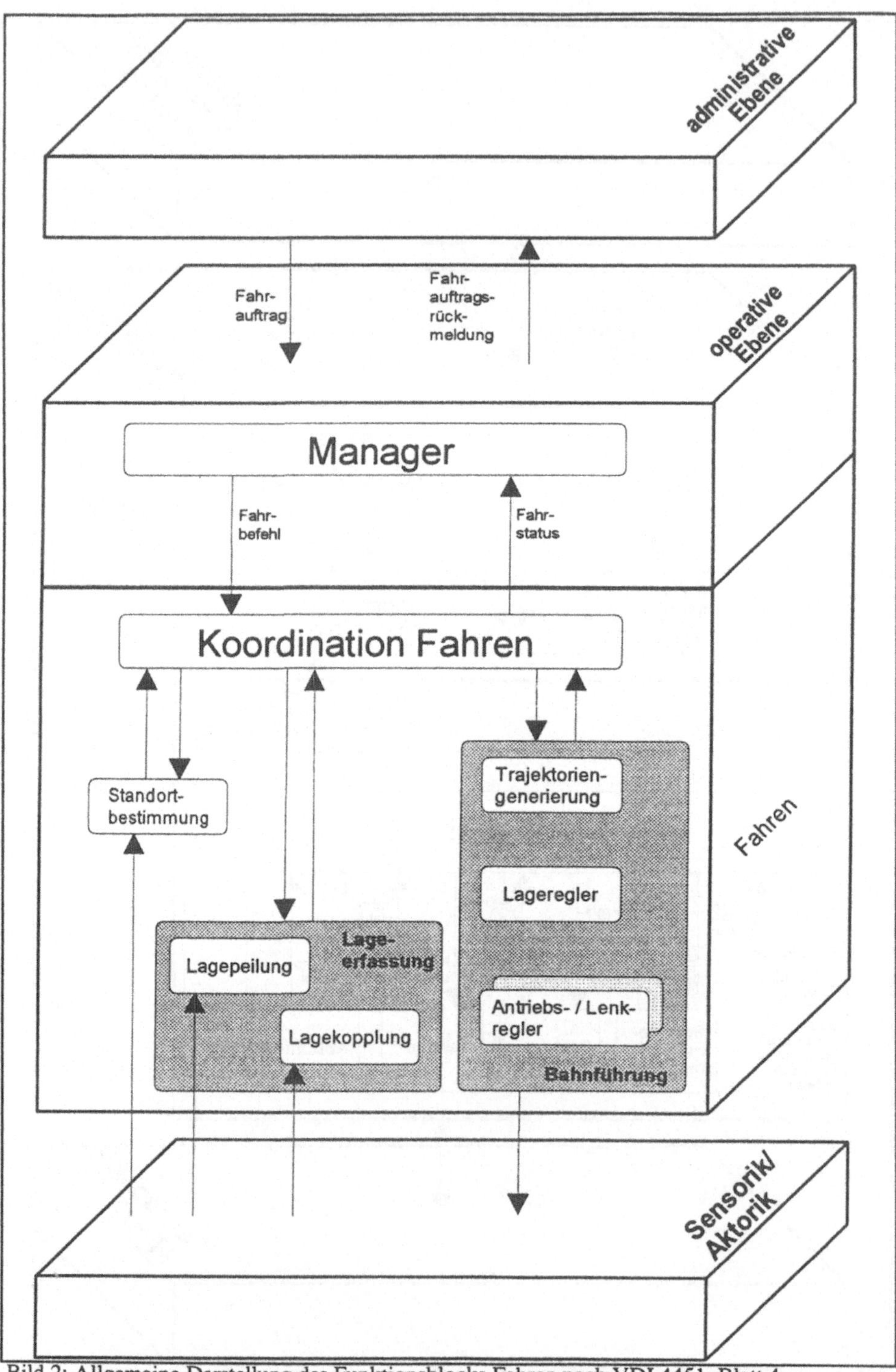

Bild 2: Allgemeine Darstellung des Funktionsblocks Fahren nach VDI 4451, Blatt 4.

Jeder dieser Funktionsblöcke ist über klar definierte Befehle vom Manager kontrollierbar. Die Befehle sind einheitlich aufgebaut und bestehen aus dem Befehlsnamen und den sogenannten Primär- und Sekundärinformationen (Sekundärinformationen sind optional). Alle Funktionsblöcke sollen und können in diesem Beitrag nicht im einzelnen beschrieben werden[1]. Wir wollen uns deshalb auf den Funktionsblock „Fahren" konzentrieren, weil hier dann auch die Navigation steuerungstechnisch abgebildet wird (Bild 2). Im Funktionsblock Fahren werden drei Funktionen erfüllt: 1. Bahnführung.   2. Lageerfassung.   3. Standortbestimmung

Analog zum Manager in der operativen Ebene übernimmt die „Koordination Fahren" die Ablaufsteuerung der drei genannten Funktionen. Die Bahnführung umfaßt die Trajektoriengenerierung, den Lageregler und den Antriebs-/Lenkregler. Sie steuert letztlich die Antriebsaktorik im Fahrzeug an. Dazu gehören Antriebsmotoren, Lenkmotoren und die Bremsen. Die Trajektoriengenerierung bestimmt die Sollage für jeden Zeitpunkt (diskrete Werte, online berechnet). Der Lageregler ermittelt aus der Sollage und der jeweiligen Lageinformation (Ist-Wert), die von der Lageerfassung ermittelt wird, die erforderlichen Stellgrößen für die einzelnen Achsen. Der Antriebs-/Lenkregler steuert entsprechend der vorgegebenen Stellgrößen die Antriebsaktorik an.

Die Lageerfassung dient der exakten Bestimmung der Fahrzeuglage (Lageinformation). Die Lage wird beschrieben durch die x- und y-Koordinaten und den Verdrehwinkel κ in der Ebene. Die Lageerfassung geschieht mittels einer dem jeweiligen Anwendungsfall angepaßten Kombination von Lagekopplung und Lagepeilung. Die Lagekopplung bestimmt die Lage des Fahrzeuges zwischen zwei Peilvorgängen durch Integration interner Bewegungsgrößen, die sie durch fahrzeuginterne Koppelsensorik (z.B. inkrementale Weg- und Winkelaufnehmer an Antriebs- und Lenkmotoren) ermittelt (Koppelnavigation). Die Integration erfolgt - ausgehend von einem Startpunkt - in kleinen, zeitlich diskreten Intervallen.

Koppelnavigation ist prinzipiell fehlerbehaftet (Schlupf zwischen Fahrweg und Rädern sowie Veränderungen der Radumfänge aufgrund von Last- und Temperaturunterschieden und Verschleiß). Sie muß deshalb regelmäßig mittels Lagepeilung kontrolliert und korrigiert werden. Die Lagepeilung ermittelt die Lage des Fahrzeuges relativ zu Merkmalen oder Sensoren im Raum, deren Lage zum Zeitpunkt der Messung bekannt sind. Die fahrzeugexterne Peilsensorik besteht häufig aus optischen Sensoren, das sind sogenannte „Marken", also besondere Merkmale oder Sensoren im Raum. Diese werden entweder speziell für diesen Zweck eingerichtet oder aber in der vorhandenen Umgebung definiert (künstliche oder natürliche) Marken. Die Wahl des Abstandes zweier Peilmarken, d.h. die Häufigkeit der Anwendung der Lagepeilung, unterliegt den Kriterien: Art des Peilverfahrens, Genauigkeitsanforderungen an die Fahrbewegungen des Fahrzeuges und Güte der Koppelnavigation.

Die Standortbestimmung ist erforderlich, um alternativ oder zusätzlich zur (von der Lageerfassung ermittelten) Ist-Lage des Fahrzeugs dessen Standort zu erkennen. Standorte können eine bestimmte Abzweigung, eine Arbeits- oder Lastübergabestation, eine Andockstation, Batterielade- oder Servicestation oder ein Bahnhof (Warteplatz für Fahrzeuge ohne Fahrauftrag) sein. Die erforderliche Sensorik kann einfache, z.B. im Boden eingelassene magnetische Marken erkennen.

---

[1]   Außerdem wird auf die Beschreibung der Leitsteuerung komplett verzichtet, weil sie für die Technik des Fahrens nur mittelbar relevant ist. Zur Zeit ist jedoch eine VDI-Richtlinie zur Modularen Leiststeuerung von FTS in Arbeit [4]. Der Autor leitet den entsprechenden Arbeitskreis.

Freie Fahrzeugnavigation bedeutet also immer eine geeignete Kombination von Koppeln und Peilen in einer Karte des Einsatzbereiches. Die hierzu in der Praxis eingesetzten Technologien werden im nächsten Abschnitt beschrieben.

Navigations- und zugehörige Sensortechniken

Als Basis einer funktionierenden Navigation dient die Karte. In ihr ist das Anlagenlayout, also die Einsatzumgebung des Fahrzeuges abgebildet und im Onboard-Computer gespeichert. Die Karte enthält folgende Elemente (Bild 3):

- Hindernisse, also die Bereiche, die für die Fahrzeuge gesperrt sind (z.B. Maschinen, Gebäudesäulen, reine Fußwege etc.)
- Haltepunkte, wie zum Beispiel Lastübergabepunkte, Batterieladepunkte, Bahnhöfe usw.
- Benutzerzonen, das sind Arbeitsbereiche, in denen bestimmte Aktionen ausgelöst werden sollen, wie das Öffnen von Türen, das Anschalten der Beleuchtung, oder das Abbremsen des Fahrzeuges.
- Verkehrszonen zur Verhütung von Fahrzeugkollisionen. Es ist nur jeweils einem Fahrzeug erlaubt, in eine Verkehrszone einzufahren.
- Bevorzugte Fahrstrecken: Obwohl die Fahrzeuge in der Lage sind, stets den kürzesten Weg zu wählen, ist es wie oben beschrieben sinnvoll, die Fahrzeugbewegungen auf vorhersagbare Strecken zu beschränken.

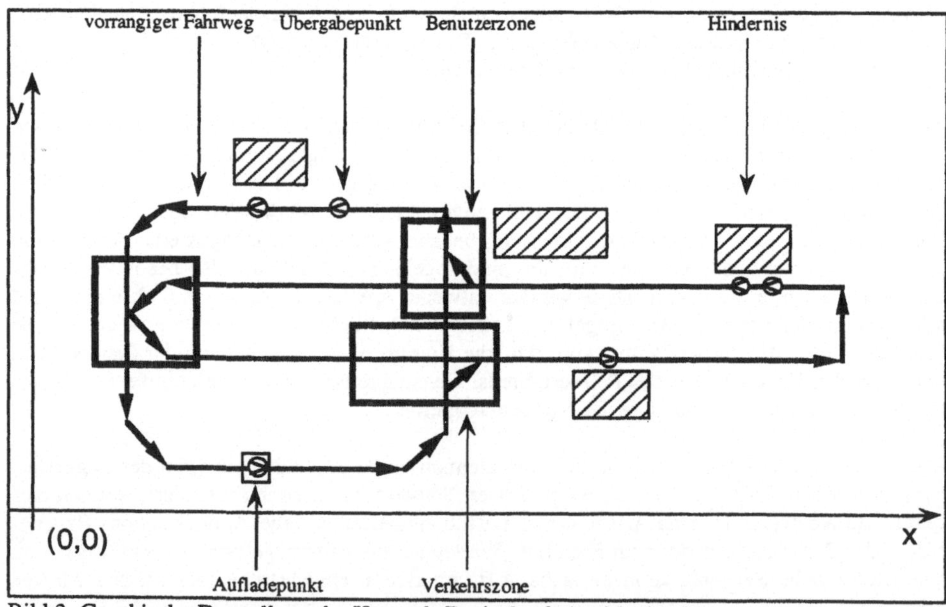

Bild 3: Graphische Darstellung der Karte als Basis der freien Navigation.

Mit solchen wenigen aber effektvollen Symbolen kann ein Layout-Editor aufgebaut werden, der auf dem FTS-Leitrechner verfügbar ist und den Benutzer in die Lage versetzt, Layoutänderungen selbst durchzuführen - sogar während des laufenden Betriebs. Die software-definierten Layoutelemente können leicht hinzugefügt, bewegt oder modifiziert werden, so daß sich das FTS innerhalb kürzester Zeit an neue Situationen anpassen läßt. Standard-CAD-Pakete sind für

FTS-Anwendungen ungeeignet, weil sie zu viel können und zu schwer erlernbar sind. Andererseits ist es natürlich möglich, vorhandene CAD-Layouts direkt zu übernehmen.

Auf Basis der Karte wird dann mit Hilfe von fahrzeuginternen Sensoren gekoppelt. Hier geht es im wesentlichen um die Erfassung und Auswertung von Winkelwerten an den Rädern, dem Lenkmotor sowie ggf. an Meßrädern. Dazu werden Inkrementalgeber (optisch, induktiv oder magnetisch), Absolutwinkelgeber oder aber Potentiometer verwendet.

Optional ist es möglich, das Ergebnis der Koppelnavigation zu verbessern, indem die durch ein Kreiselsystem gewonnene Orientierung des Fahrzeuges mit in die Berechnung der Fahrbewegungen einbezogen wird. Dabei zeichnet sich insbesondere der Faserkreisel durch seinen kompakten und robusten Aufbau aus. Das Licht eines externen Lasers wird durch eine Glasfaser geleitet und dient zur Messung des Drehwinkels und der Drehgeschwindigkeit. Der Effekt beruht darauf, daß die Rotation je nach Rotationsrichtung den Weg der links- oder rechtsumlaufenden Welle verkürzt, was zu einer Phasendifferenzänderung der interferierenden Welle führt. Das Ausgangssignal ist also eine Pulsfolge, deren Frequenz der Drehrate proportional ist. Der aktuelle Drehwinkel entspricht der Anzahl der Pulse, die durch Interferenzen in der Glasfaser entstehen.

Ob Koppelnavigation mit oder ohne Kreiselunterstützung, eine Lagepeilung ist in jedem Falle erforderlich. Sieht man einmal von den verschiedenen Möglichkeiten ab, die Leitlinie physikalisch vorzugeben (z.B. Leitdraht oder Farbspur), so gibt es prinzipiell zwei Möglichkeiten zur Realisierung der Lagepeilung, nämlich stationär angebrachte Peilmarken oder aber stationäre Sender.

Stationär angebrachte Peilmarken

Hier kommen häufig Bodenmarkierungen zum Einsatz. Dies sind optische Marken, Bodenmagnete oder aber Transponder. Alle diese Elemente lassen sich sowohl als Punktfolge (liniengebunden, Reduzierung eines gedachten Leitdrahtes durch einzelne diskrete Punkte) oder als Raster[2] installieren.

Ein optisches Raster kann z.B. realisiert werden durch die Hell-/Dunkelübergänge verschiedenfarbiger Fliesen, durch kontraststarke Fugen zwischen einfarbigen Fliesen oder durch Aufkleber auf dem Boden. Bei den Bodenmagneten handelt es sich um kleine zylindrische Dauermagnetpillen der Größe 5 x 10 $\varnothing$ mm aus verzinktem Neodym-Eisen-Bor (NdFeB). Transponder wirken induktiv und sind bedeutend größer als Bodenmagnete (nämlich ca. 15 cm Durchmesser). Unterhalb des Fahrzeugs angebrachte Spulen induzieren in ihnen einen Strom, der dazu genutzt wird, ihre Kodierung dem Fahrzeug zu übermitteln. Es handelt sich also um eine absolute Kodierung (gegenüber der relativen beim optischen oder magnetischen Raster), die üblicherweise bei sehr großen Fahrzeugen verwendet wird (meist Outdoor-Einsatz).

Bodenfreie Markierungen können künstlich (also extra für diesen Zweck angebracht) oder aber natürlich sein. Als abtastende Sensoren sind Laser, Kamerasysteme und Ultraschallsensoren denkbar. Systeme, die mit natürlichen Marken arbeiten, sind bisher nur als Ultraschall- und Bildverarbeitungssysteme entwickelt worden, kommen aber bis heute in der Praxis nicht vor. Bewährte Technik ist dagegen die Lasernavigation, die mit künstlichen Laserbaken (Reflektoren) arbeitet. Die sogenannte Laser-Triangulation ermittelt die Position des Fahrzeu-

---

[2]   Frog Navigation Systems besitzt die weltweiten Patente auf die Rasternavigation
(FROG = Free Ranging On Grid).

ges, indem mit Hilfe eines rotierenden Laserstrahls die Winkel zu mindestens drei dieser Laserbaken gemessen werden und daraus die aktuelle Lage des Fahrzeuges berechnet wird.

Stationäre Sender

Prinzipiell ist es möglich, Fahrzeuge mittels bestehender Funksysteme zu navigieren. Beispiele sind das Loran C-Verfahren (Laufzeitmessung von Sendeimpulsen, 70 - 130 kHz, 300 - 500 m Genauigkeit, Überdeckung der nördlichen Halbkugel, störanfällig), das Decca-Verfahren (Phasenmeßprinzip, Sendefrequenz ist Vielfaches der Decca-Grundfrequenz von 14 kHz, 200 - 500 m Genauigkeit, bekannt bei Hobbyseglern in Nord- und Ostsee, sowie dem Mittelmeer) und das Omega-Verfahren (Phasenmeßprinzip im Längstwellenbereich: 10 kHz, weltweite Überdeckung, geringe Genauigkeit von 2.000 bis 4.000 m). Die gebotenen Genauigkeiten reichen für die hier betrachteten Fahrzeuge normalerweise nicht aus.

Der Aufbau eines eigens für die Applikation arbeitenden Funksystems ist aufwendig und problematisch. Wenn z.B. große Lager- oder Produktionshallen mit einer solchen Peiltechnik ausgestattet werden sollten, gäbe es hohe Ungenauigkeiten und Störungen durch Reflektionen. Funkpeilanlagen haben deshalb für Fahrerlose Transportsysteme keine Bedeutung.

Vermehrt Bedeutung erlangt die Satellitenpeilung. Hier gibt es im wesentlichen das amerikanische NAVSTAR Global Positioning System GPS und das russische Global Navigation Satellite System GLONASS. Aufgrund der großen Bedeutung wollen wir uns hier auf das amerikanische System beschränken.

Das GPS liegt im Verantwortungsbereich des Verteidigungsministeriums der Vereinigten Staaten. Das Prinzip: Satelliten senden modulierte elektromagnetische Wellen auf die Erdoberfläche. Es gibt insgesamt 24 Satelliten, die in 20.000 km Höhe auf sechs nahezu kreisförmigen Bahnen (vier Satelliten pro Bahn) fliegen. Die Radiosignale enthalten Zeit- und Satellitenbahninformationen und erlauben die Ermittlung der Signallaufzeiten. Die gleichzeitige Beobachtung von vier Satelliten mit einem GPS-Empfänger an einem beliebigen Punkt auf der Erdoberfläche liefert Ort und Zeit.

Prinzipiell senden die Satelliten zwei Arten von Codes: 1. den C/A-Code (Civil Access oder Coarse Aquisition Code) für die zivile Nutzung und 2. den P-Code (Protected oder Precision Code) für die militärische Nutzung. Die Sendefrequenz liegt bei 1.575,42 MHz. Der Systembetreiber behält sich vor, die Genauigkeit im Bedarfsfall künstlich zu verschlechtern. Das sog. Selective Availability (SA) ermöglicht die nahezu stufenlose Steuerung der erreichbaren Genauigkeit. Diese liegt heute offiziell bei 100 m (95 % Wahrscheinlichkeit) und 300 m (99,9 % Wahrscheinlichkeit).

Die erste Stufe der Genauigkeitserhöhung mündet im Differential GPS (dGPS). Der Gesamtfehler, der beim GPS auftritt, ist zeit- und ortsabhängig. Nutzt man nun einen stationären GPS-Referenzempfänger, dessen Position exakt bekannt ist, zur Ermittlung des aktuellen Fehlers und übermittelt diesen geeignet an den mobilen Empfänger im FTF, so wird die Genauigkeit deutlich erhöht: Genauigkeiten von weniger als 0,5 m sind erreichbar. Diese Verbesserungen hängen natürlich wesentlich davon ab, wie weit der stationäre von dem mobilen GPS-Empfänger entfernt ist.

Eine einfach zu nutzende Form des dGPS befindet sich in der Test- und Installationsphase: Die Deutsche Telekom und das Institut für Angewandte Geodäsie bieten das sog. Langwellen-Real-

Time-DGPS (LW-Real-Time-DGPS) an. Über einen Daten-Langwellensender (in Mainflingen, 30 km südöstlich von Frankfurt/Main) werden die Echtzeit-Korrekturdaten jedem Nutzer zur Verfügung gestellt. Die Daten werden auf einer Sendefrequenz von 123,7 kHz im RDS-Format ausgestrahlt.

Frog Navigation Systems verwendet bereits eine weitere Stufe der Genauigkeitserhöhung des GPS: Beim Real-Time-Kinematic-dGPS werden die Daten von insgesamt fünf Satelliten ausgewertet, und zwar mit einer speziellen FROG-Software, die sich immer auf den aktuellen Ergebnissen der Koppelnavigation stützt. So kann eine Genauigkeit von bemerkenswerten 2 bis 10 cm erreicht werden.

Eine zusammenfassende Bewertung der heute eingesetzten fortschrittlichen Peilverfahren zeigt Tabelle 4.

Methode der Lagepeilung				
Methode		*Genauigkeit*	*Indoor*	*Outdoor*	*Eigenschaften*

Methode der Lagepeilung					
Methode		*Genauigkeit*	*Indoor*	*Outdoor*	*Eigenschaften*
Raster-	optisch	2 - 10 mm	ja		Konstante Genauigkeit, zuverlässig und sicher
navi-	magnetisch	5 - 20 mm	ja	ja	
gation	Transponder	10 - 100 mm	ja	ja	
Laser-Triangulation		5 - 50 mm	ja	nein	Freie Sicht zu Laserbaken erforderlich
GPS	dGPS	10 - 50 cm	nein	ja	zuverlässig
	RTK-GPS	20 - 100 mm	nein	ja	abhängig von den äußeren Bedingungen

Tabelle 4: Fortschrittliche Methoden der Lagepeilung.

Abschließend soll ein Beispiel für den praktischen Einsatz der Satelittennavigation bei frei navigierenden Radfahrzeugen vorgestellt werden. Es handelt sich um eine der ersten (wenn nicht die erste) praktischen Anwendungen, weshalb sie es wert ist, hier etwas näher betrachtet zu werden.

Anwendungen mit Satellitenpeilung (GPS): Mooncat

Das holländische Verteidigungsministerium war auf der Suche nach einem automatischen System, mit dem die Panzerausbildung, insbesondere die Schießübungen realitätsnaher durchgeführt werden könnte. Die Überlegungen führten zu Mooncat, einem unbemannten frei navigierenden Bodenfahrzeug zum Ziehen von Zielen, auf die die Panzer im Rahmen ihrer Schießausbildung feuern. Es ist seit Anfang 1995 in Betrieb und hat leicht einsehbare Vorteile gegenüber einem fahrerbedienten Fahrzeug. Auch heutige Simulationswerkzeuge erfüllen nicht annähernd den Zweck einer wirklichkeitsnahen Ausbildung. Die wichtigsten Gründe für ein frei navigierendes Fahrzeug mit FROG-Navigationstechnik waren:

* Das Fahrzeug sollte unbemannt sein.
* Es sollten verschiedene Ziele angehängt und verschiedene, wählbare aber reproduzierbare Trainingsszenarien abgerufen werden können.
* Auf dem vorhandenen Gelände (Nordseestrand) sollte mit einstellbarer Geschwindigkeit frei gefahren werden können.
* Auch unter erschwerten Bedingungen, also absoluter Dunkelheit, Nebel, Rauch, ... sollte die Funktionserfüllung garantiert sein.

Bild 5 zeigt Mooncat: Es handelt sich um ein vierrädriges Fahrzeug mit luftgefüllten Gummireifen und Dieselantrieb (70 KW über vier Hydraulikmotoren mit in die Räder integrierten Planetengetriebe). Es ist 4,9 t schwer, 4,90 m lang, 2,20 m breit und hoch, und ist in der Lage, mit maximal 25 km/h über den Strand einer holländischen Nordseeinsel zu fahren.

Bild 5: Mooncat, Peilung per dGPS.

Das Gelände, in dem das Fahrzeug fährt, ist ein 2.000 x 1.000 m großer Strandabschnitt mit einem zentralen Steuerstand. Hier befindet sich die Leitsteuerung, die per Funk mit dem Fahrzeug kommuniziert. Obwohl das Fahrzeug autonom ist, steht es unter ständiger Kontrolle der Leitsteuerung. Auf der graphischen Oberfläche werden die durchzuführenden Übungen programmiert, gestartet und überwacht.

Mooncat wird unter extremen Bedingungen eingesetzt, z.B. wenn der Strand mit Wasser und Eisschollen bedeckt ist, sowie bei Schnee, Regen, Sturm oder Nebel. Die vom Betreiber zuvor geforderte Genauigkeit von ± 1,8 m wird deutlich unterschritten. Aufgrund des Integrationscharakters einiger Navigations-Algorithmen wird typischerweise eine Genauigkeit von ± 20 cm erreicht.

Zusammen mit dem Mooncat-Betreiber wurde bereits das Lastenheft für die nächste Entwicklungsstufe formuliert: Zukünftige Fahrzeuge sollen auch an Land, und zwar auf unbefestigten Wegen zwischen Bäumen und Sträuchern agieren können. Es sind bereits Tests durchgeführt worden, die zeigen, daß ein GPS-Einsatz im Wald möglich ist. Zwar ist für eine verläßliche GPS-Positionsmessung ein freier Öffnungswinkel über dem Fahrzeug von ca. 15 ° erforderlich. Doch die Kombination aus Koppelnavigation und GPS-Peilung (zur Stützung der Koppelnavigation) ermöglicht eine solche Navigation auch unter erschwerten Bedingungen.

Die neuen Fahrzeuge werden mit einer Geschwindigkeit von bis zu 55 km/h frei fahren können. Die Ziele, auf die gefeuert werden soll, befinden sich nicht mehr auf einem Anhänger, wie bei Mooncat, sondern auf dem Fahrzeug selbst, und zwar mit der Möglichkeit, jederzeit zwischen sichtbar und nicht-sichtbar zu wechseln. Die Navigations-Software wird um eine Funktion erweitert, die unerwartete Bewegungen des Fahrzeuges zuläßt. Verschiedene Wege und Wegstrecken werden alternativ vorgegeben, und das Fahrzeug entscheidet sich erst während der Operation für einen Weg. Dies kann zufällig, oder aber durch Laserimpulse getriggert geschehen.

Zusammenfassend läßt sich sagen, daß heute ausreichend Technologie vorhanden ist, um die freie Navigation von Radfahrzeugen unter den unterschiedlichsten Randbedingungen zu realisieren. Achtet man auf einen modularen Aufbau der Steuerungshard- und -software, hält sich auch der Engineering-Aufwand für die verschiedenen Projekte in Grenzen.

Literatur

[1]   VDI 2510 „Fahrerlose Transportsysteme (FTS)". Ausgabe 11.92, Beuth Verlag, Berlin.

[2]   Ullrich, G.: Von der VDI-Richtlinie 2510 zur realen Steuerung - Wie aus einem mobilen Roboter ein Sonder-FTF wurde. Tagungsband 1. Duisburger FTS-Fachtagung "Die Steuerungsstruktur des FTS bestimmt die Zukunft der Fertigung und der Produktionslogistik", Duisburg: Fertigungstechnisches Labor der Universität -GH-Duisburg 1991, S. 137-160 (ISBN 3-930153-02-5).

[3]   VDI 4451 E, Blatt 4 „Offene Steuerungsstruktur für Fahrerlose Transportfahrzeuge". Ausgabe 01.95, Beuth Verlag, Berlin.

[4]   Ullrich, G.: Unbeirrtes Streben nach mehr Kompatibilität bei Fahrerlosen Transportsystemen. Logistik im Unternehmen 10 (1996) Nr. 4 - April 1996, S. 70-71, VDI-Verlag Düsseldorf.

[5]   De Jong, Tim und Kleijberg, N.: The use of GPS in autonomous, free-ranging ground vehicles. Proceedings of the UV '96 (Unmanned Vehicles), Fourth Annual International Conference & Exhibition, 20/21 June 1996, Le Meridien Paris Etoile Paris, France.

Frog Navigation Systems GmbH
Bismarckstraße 142
D-47057 Duisburg
Tel: +49 (0) 203 / 306 - 1980
Fax: +49 (0) 203 / 306 - 1999
E-Mail: Ullrich@frog.du.eunet.de

Ein integriertes Navigationssystem zur Ortung und Führung von Flächenpeilschiffen auf Binnenwasserstraßen

M. Sandler, M. Faul, E. D. Gilles
Universität Stuttgart
Institut für Systemdynamik und Regelungstechnik
Pfaffenwaldring 9
70550 Stuttgart

1 Einleitung und Aufgabenstellung

Der Verkehrsträger „Binnenschiffahrt" erbringt in Deutschland einen wesentlichen Anteil der Transportleistung. Hierzu stehen in Deutschland ca. 6500 km an Wasserstraßen zur Verfügung, die von der Wasser- und Schiffahrtsverwaltung des Bundes (WSV) unterhalten werden. Eine wichtige Aufgabe bei der Unterhaltung der Wasserstraßen ist es, eine regelmäßige Inspektion des Gewässergrundes durchzuführen, um Fehltiefen in der Fahrrinne oder Hindernisse aufzufinden.

Auf dem Neckar, der von Mannheim bis Plochingen auf einer Länge von ca. 200 km schiffbar ist, wird für diese Zwecke das Peilschiff „Neckar" eingesetzt. Zu beiden Seiten dieses Schiffes sind ausklappbare Ausleger angebracht. An diesen Trägern und im Boden des Schiffes sind im Abstand von 50 cm Ultraschallwandler befestigt, mit denen die Wassertiefe an der betreffenden Stelle gemessen werden kann. Es ist mit diesem Schiff möglich, die Tiefen in einem Streifen von 20 m Breite zu erfassen. Die Erfassung der gesamten Wasserstraße geschieht in mehreren Fahrten mit überlappenden Steifen. Auf dem Neckar wird halbjährlich eine routinemäßige Verkehrssicherungspeilung durchgeführt, daneben sind z.B. nach Hochwassern an kritischen Stellen weitere Messungen durchzuführen.

Am Institut für Systemdynamik und Regelungstechnik (ISR) der Universität Stuttgart wurde seit mehreren Jahren im Rahmen des Sonderforschungsbereichs 228 „Hochgenaue Navigation" an der Entwicklung eines integrierten Navigationssystems für Binnenschiffe gearbeitet. Dieses System ermöglicht es, Schiffe weitgehend automatisch entlang einer vorgegebenen Linie zu führen. Im Rahmen des von der Deutschen Forschungsgemeinschaft (DFG) neu eingerichteten Transferbereichs 3 „Ortung und Führung von Vermessungsschiffen" soll nun das am ISR entwickelte Navigationssystem einer Anwendung bei der vorher skizzierten Erfassung der Gewässertiefen zugeführt werden. Im Rahmen dieses Beitrags soll ein Überblick über die hierzu eingesetzten Techniken und Vorgehensweisen gegeben werden.

Das integrierte Navigationssystem soll im Rahmen des Transferbereichs auf dem Peilschiff „Neckar" installiert und in ein kommerzielles Gewässervermessungssystem eingebunden werden. Die Aufgaben, die das integrierte Navigationssystem dabei zu erfüllen hat, lassen sich in zwei Bereiche untergliedern. Die erste Aufgabe

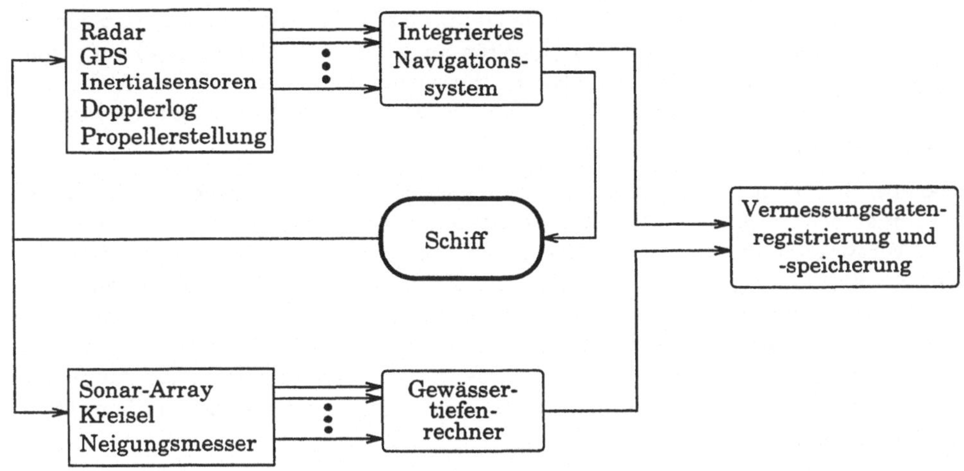

Abbildung 1: Gerätekonfiguration auf dem Flächenpeilschiff

ist die schiffsautarke Ortung des Fahrzeugs in Echtzeit, d. h. die Bestimmung seiner Position in allen drei Koordinaten. Anforderungen an die Ortung sind eine horizontale Positionsgenauigkeit von 50 cm und eine Höhengenauigkeit von 5 cm. Die hohen Anforderungen an die Höhe beruhen darauf, daß über die geodätische Höhe des Fahrzeugs und die gemessene Wassertiefe die geodätische Höhe des Gewässergrundes bestimmt wird. In weiteren Auswertungen wird aus diesen Daten z.B. der Umfang durchzuführender Baggerarbeiten ermittelt. Die zweite Aufgabe besteht darin, das Schiff automatisch und hochgenau entlang von vorgegebenen Bahnen zu führen. Dabei sind die Ergebnisse der Ortung die Grundlage für die Bahnregelung.

Abbildung 1 zeigt schematisch die Gerätekonfiguration, wie sie für das Peilschiff „Neckar" vorgesehen ist. Oben in Abbildung 1 ist das integrierte Navigationssystem dargestellt. Es verarbeitet Meßdaten verschiedener Sensoren, um die Ortungsaufgabe zu lösen. Die Ortungsergebnisse werden an einen Rechner zur Datenregistrierung und Aufzeichnung weitergeleitet, der Teil des kommerziellen Gewässervermessungssystem ist. Daneben hat das integrierte Navigationssystem die Möglichkeit, die Stellung der Antriebspropeller auf der „Neckar" vorzugeben, um so das Schiff auf seiner Bahn zu führen. Ein anderer Teil des kommerziellen Vermessungssytems ist ein spezieller Gewässertiefenrechner, der die Messungen der Ultraschallwandler erfasst, eine Neigungskorrektur durchführt und die Tiefenwerte entsprechend der Vorausrichtung des Schiffes orientiert. Dieser Rechner ist unten in Abbildung 1 dargestellt. Die Speicherung der so aufbereiteten Tiefenwerte erfolgt in dem bereits erwähnten Registrierungsrechner.

Als alternative Möglichkeiten zur Ortung von Peilschiffen stehen gegenwärtig zwei andere Methoden zur Verfügung bzw. sind in der Erprobungsphase. Ein Ortungssystem benutzt ein Laser-Zielverfolgungssystem, das an Land aufgestellt wird. Die Ergebnisse der Zielverfolgung, also die Koordinaten des Peilschiffes, werden zur Registrierung per Funk auf das Peilschiff übertragen. Der Nachteil dieses Systems insbesondere für einen Einsatz auf dem Neckar ist die Forderung nach einer Sichtverbindung zwischen Zielverfolgungssystem und Peilschiff. Zudem muß aufgrund der begrenzten Reichweite des Zielverfolungssystems (ca. 1 km), dieses oft ab- und an anderer Stelle wieder aufgebaut werden. Dies reduziert die mögliche Peilleistung derartiger Schiffe erheblich.

Daneben befinden sich gegenwärtig Ortungssysteme in der Erprobung, die allein mit einer hochgenauen GPS-Trägerphasenauswertung (siehe Abschnitt 3) arbeiten. Voraussetzung für den Einsatz dieser Systeme ist aber sowohl die ständige Sichtbarkeit einer genügenden Anzahl von Satelliten als auch die Funktion einer Funkübertragungsstrecke zwischen Peilschiff und einer an Land einzurichtenden GPS-Referenzstation. Bei einem Einsatz auf dem Neckar stellt nach unseren Erfahrungen insbesondere die Sichtbarkeit der Satelliten ein Problem dar. Aufgrund des teilweise tief eingeschnittenen Tals und hoher Bäume dicht am Ufer kommt es zu Abschattungen von Satelliten.

Innerhalb des integrierten Navigationssystems wird daher der Ansatz verfolgt, die für die Ortung des Peilschiffs notwendigen Informationen aus einer ganzen Reihe verschiedenartiger Sensoren zu gewinnen. Die Integration dieser Sensoren und von a-priori Wissen innerhalb des Navigationssystems führt zu einer hochverfügbaren Ortung des Peilschiffs, wie sie insbesondere für den Einsatz auf dem Neckar notwendig ist.

In den folgenden Abschnitten soll zunächst näher auf die wichtigsten Sensoren und ihre Auswerteverfahren eingegangen werden. In Abschnitt 4 wird dann die Integration der verschiedenen Informationsquellen erläutert. Auf die Bahnregelung soll in diesem Zusammenhang nicht eingegangen werden, nähere Informationen hierzu sind in [8] zu finden.

2 Auswertung von Bordradarbildern

Eine wesentliche Komponente innerhalb des integrierten Navigationssystems stellt die Auswertung der Bilder des Bordradars dar. Hierzu werden die Signale der Radarantenne in einer eigenentwickelten Hardware verarbeitet, das Signal der Echointensität digitalisiert und die Ergebnisse in den Navigationsrechner übertragen. Dort steht dann in einem polaren Koordinatensystem ein binäres Bild der Navigationsumgebung mit derzeit 720 Strahlen pro Antennenumdrehung zur Verfügung. Die radiale Auflösung der Bilddaten beträgt typischerweise 3 Meter.

Ein Verfahren zur Auswertung der Bilddaten besteht darin, sie mit einer elektronischen Karte der Wasserstraße [3] zu vergleichen, um so die Position in der Kartenebene und die Vorausrichtung des Schiffes zu bestimmen. Ausgehend von einer prädizierten Position und Vorausrichtung des Schiffes werden Abstandsvektoren zwischen prädizierter Karte und Radarkonturen bestimmt, aus denen mit Hilfe eines Least-Squares-Ansatzes eine Korrektur der prädizierten Lage des Schiffes bestimmt wird. Die um die Korrektur verbesserte Lage des Schiffes kann somit als eine aus dem Radarbild abgeleitete Messung von Position und Vorausrichtung des

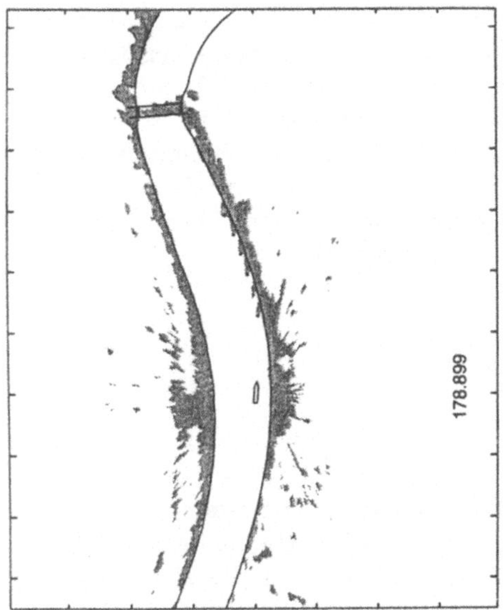

Abbildung 2: Radarbild und elektronische Karte, Neckar bei Stuttgart

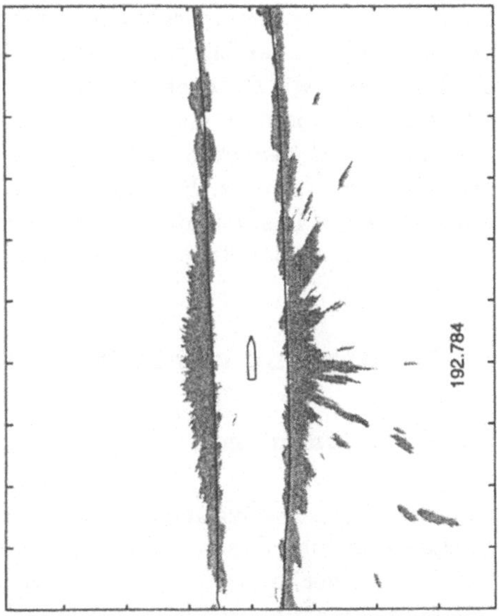

Abbildung 3: Typisches Radarbild bei Uferbewuchs, Neckar bei Esslingen

Schiffes verstanden werden. Einzelheiten zu diesem Bildvergleichsverfahren sind z.B. in [4, 5, 7] zu finden.

Abbildung 2 zeigt das Ergebnis des Bildvergleichs für eine Situation auf dem Neckar bei Stuttgart. Die „Neckar" wird durch die Umrisslinie in der unteren Bildmitte dargestellt, die in den Navigationsrechner eingelesenen Radarechos sind als graue Gebiete wiedergegeben. Den Radarechos ist die elektronische Karte überlagert. Oben im Bild ist eine Brücke zu sehen, in Vorausrichtung des Schiffes einige Dalben im Wasser. Die Entfernungsmarken am Rand haben einen Abstand von 100 Metern.

Maßgeblich für die Genauigkeit der mit Hilfe des Bildvergleichs bestimmten Position ist die Genauigkeit, mit der die elektronische Karte, d.h. das geometrische Modell der Umgebung, die im Radarbild sichtbaren Konturen beschreibt. Die bisher am ISR vorhandenen Karten des Neckars wurden aufgrund von Papierkarten erstellt, die uns von der Wasser- und Schiffahrtsverwaltung zur Verfügung gestellt wurden. Diese Karten enthalten die Bauwerke und Uferlinien der Wasserstraße, wie auch in Abbildung 2 dargestellt. Von wesentlichem Einfluß auf das Aussehen des Radarbilds ist aber darüberhinaus auch die Vegetation entlang der Wasserstraße. Große Büsche oder Bäume, deren Äste über die Wasserfläche hängen, können zu lokalen Abweichungen zwischen Radarkontur und Uferlinie von mehreren Metern führen. Abbildung 3 zeigt diesen Einfluß anhand eines Radarbilds des Neckars bei Esslingen. Die Entfernungsmarken am Rand sind hier 50 m voneinander entfernt. Um die gesetzten Anforderungen an die Positionsgenauigkeit innerhalb des Radarbild - Karten - Vergleichs erfüllen zu können, sind im Rahmen dieses Vorhabens die vorhandenen Karten um die Berücksichtigung der Vegetation zu erweitern.

Beim Einsatz des Bildvergleichsverfahrens kann die Schwierigkeit auftreten, daß die Genauigkeit der Längspositon auf der Wasserstraße beim Fehlen entsprechender Merkmale wie Brücken oder Flußbiegungen deutlich abnimmt. In diesen Fällen ist es notwendig, den oben skizzierten Radarbildvergleich mit anderen Auswerteverfahren und Sensoren zu integrieren, um die gewünschten Genauigkeiten zu erreichen. So ist es z. B. möglich, ein weiteres Bildvergleichsverfahren parallel einzusetzen, das stationäre Objekte im Radarbild mit entsprechenden Radarreflektoren, die in der Karte verzeichnet sind, vergleicht [7].

3 Auswertung von GPS-Messungen

3.1 GPS-Grundlagen

Das Satelliten-Navigationssystem GPS (Global Positioning System) ist ein klassisches dual-use System. Es wurde vom US-Verteidigungsministerium für militärische Zwecke geplant und entwickelt, ist aber auch für die zivile Nutzung mit allerdings eingeschränkter Genauigkeit freigegeben. Das System besteht aus 24 Satelliten, die in 20 200 km Höhe auf sechs Bahnen die Erde umkreisen und stellt ein weltweit, rund um die Uhr verfügbares, wetterunabhängiges Zeit- und Entfernungsmeßsystem dar, das gleichermaßen für Navigation und Vermessung eingesetzt werden kann [1].

Die GPS-Satelliten senden auf zwei Frequenzen Signale aus, der L1-Frequenz mit 1575,42 MHz sowie der L2-Frequenz mit 1227,60 MHz. Diesen Trägerfrequenzen ist ein Code aufmoduliert, aus dem mit Hilfe von Korrelationstechniken im GPS-Empfänger die sogenannten Pseudoranges, fehlerbehaftete Entfernungen zwischen Empfänger und Satellit, bestimmt werden können. Darüberhinaus ist den GPS-Signalen noch eine Navigationsnachricht aufmoduliert, die unter anderem aktuelle Bahndaten der Satelliten, die sogenannten Ephemeriden, enthält. Neben dem Code können in geeigneten Empfängern auch direkt die Trägerwellen für Messungen genutzt werden. Für die in einem Empfänger möglichen Messungen der GPS-Signale wird auch der Begriff „Beobachtung" verwendet.

Für den einfachsten Fall der Positionsbestimmung mit GPS ist es notwendig, Pseudorange-Beobachtungen zu mindestens vier Satelliten zur Verfügung zu haben. Damit kann auf die unbekannte Position in den 3 Koordinaten sowie auf die unbekannte Zeitdifferenz zwischen der Empfängeruhr und den untereinander synchronisierten Satellitenuhren geschlossen werden.

GPS bietet zwei Dienste unterschiedlicher Genauigkeit, den Standard Positioning Service (SPS) und den Precise Positioning Service (PPS). Der Standard Positioning Service, der allen Nutzern unentgeltlich zur Verfügung steht, besteht aus dem C/A-Code auf der GPS L1-Frequenz und der Navigationsnachricht. Die spezifizierte Positionsgenauigkeit beträgt 100 m horizontal und 156 m vertikal bei 95 % Wahrscheinlichkeit . Der Precise Positioning Service auf den beiden GPS-Frequenzen L1 und L2 ist ausschließlich für authorisierte Nutzer verfügbar.

Die im SPS erzielbaren Genauigkeiten sind das Ergebnis der selective availability (SA), einer absichtlichen künstlichen Verschlechterung der C/A-Code Positionsbestimmung, die die nahezu beliebige Steuerung der von nicht authorisierten (zivilen) Nutzern erreichbaren Navigationsgenauigkeit bedeutet. Dies wird durch Verfälschung der Satellitenuhrzeit (SA-dither) und Angabe falscher Ephemeridenwerte (SA-epsilon) in der Navigationsnachricht ereicht.

3.2 Differential GPS (DGPS)

Der Einsatz von Differential GPS ermöglicht eine Genauigkeitssteigerung durch Eliminierung systematischer Fehlerquellen, wie Uhrenfehler der Satelliten und Empfänger, Orbitfehler und Fehler, die durch ionosphärische und troposphärische Einflüße verursacht werden. Dabei werden in einer Referenzstation, deren Koordinaten genau bekannt sind Differenzen zwischen den gemessenen und berechneten Beobachtungsgrößen ermittelt und als Korrekturwerte per Funk zu einem navigierenden Empfänger übertragen. Der Gedanke dabei ist, daß sich einige dieser systematischen Fehler bei der Beobachtung der selben Satelliten auf benachbarten Empfängerstationen ungefähr gleich auswirken, und daß sich diese Effekte bei der Differenzbildung der entsprechenden Beobachtungen aufheben bzw. zum großen Teil reduzieren. Dies betrifft insbesondere die nachteiligen Effekte der SA.

3.3 Differentielles Pseudoranging

Das für Navigationszwecke am häufigsten angewandte Verfahren ist das differentielle C/A-Code-Pseudoranging. Dabei werden in einer Referenzstation Differenzen zwischen wahrer Entfernung Empfänger - Satellit und gemessener Entfernung Empfänger - Satellit berechnet und als Korrekturwerte zu einem navigierenden Empfänger übertragen.

Den Anwendern in Deutschland stehen zur Zeit zwei Systeme zur Verfügung. Für die Navigation auf See und in Küstenregionen ist ein Netz von DGPS-Referenzstationen entlang der europäischen Küste installiert worden [9]. Diese Stationen erfüllen die Systemanforderungen, die der internationale Verband der Seezeichenverwaltungen (IALA) für die Funkübertragung der DGPS-Korrekturdaten festgelegt hat. Die Datenformatierung erfolgt nach der RTCM-Empfehlung SC-104.

Zur Unterstützung der Navigation auch im Binnenbereich, senden inzwischen fast alle Rundfunkanstalten der ARD DGPS-Korrekturdaten über den transparenten Datenkanal (TDC) des Radio Data Systems (RDS) [6]. Das digitale RDS-Datensignal wird mittels eines Hilfsträgers dem stereophonen Multiplex-Signal hinzugefügt. Auf der Empfängerseite können mit einem speziellem RDS-Dekoder die Korrekturdaten dekodiert und dem GPS-Empfänger zugeführt werden. Auch hier wird das RTCM SC-104 Datenformat verwendet. Dieser Service kann auf allen Binnenwasserstraßen in Deutschland genutzt werden und wird RASANT (Radio Aided SAtellite Navigation Technique) genannt. Damit werden Positionsgenauigkeiten im 2 - 3-Meterbereich erzielt.

3.4 Phasenmessung des Trägers

Die Meßgröße bei diesem Verfahren ist die Phase der Schwebungswelle, die sich als Differenz der Phase des von einem Satelliten ausgesandten Trägersignals und der Phase des im Empfänger erzeugten konstanten Referenzsignals ergibt. Damit wird aber nur der gebrochene Anteil der Phase der Trägerwelle gemessen. Der ganzzahlige Anteil der Wellenzüge, die auf der gesuchten Entfernung Satellit - Empfänger liegen, ist zunächst noch unbekannt. Diese Unbekannte wird als cycle ambiguity bezeichnet. Solange beim Empfang des Satellitensignals im Empfänger keine Störungen auftreten, wird die ganze Anzahl von Zyklen ab einer Bezugszeit intern hochgezählt und ist somit bekannt. Erfolgt jedoch eine Unterbrechung im Empfang des Satellitensignals, so wird dieser Wert nicht mehr hochgezählt, und es treten sogenannte cycle slips in den Beobachtungen auf. Im Vergleich zu den Pseudorange-Messungen tritt bei der Phase pro Satellit eine ambiguity-Unbekannte zusätzlich auf, die die Lösung des Positionierungsproblems erschwert.

Der entscheidende Vorteil liegt jedoch in der Genauigkeit, mit der die Phasenbeobachtungen durchgeführt werden können. Die Wellenlängen der Trägerfrequenzen der GPS-Signale liegen bei ca. 20 cm. Unter der Annahme, daß die Genauigkeit der Phasenmessung 1 % der Wellenlänge beträgt, können für die einzelnen Phasenmessungen somit Genauigkeiten von ca. 2 mm erwartet werden.

Mit modernen Zwei-Frequenz-Empfängern und entsprechender Software [10] auf schnellen Rechnern kann eine Phasenlösung in Echtzeit berechnet werden. Hierzu ist es notwendig, neben Korrekturwerten zu den Pseudorange-Beobachtungen auch Phasenkorrekturen zu übertragen. Dies geschieht entweder im Rahmen des in RTCM SC 104 - Version 2.1 definierten Formats oder auch in speziellen, etwas kompakteren Formaten. Die Funkstrecke muss dazu über eine Übertragungskapazität von 2400 bis 9600 Bit/s verfügen. Die Zeiten zur Bestimmung der Mehrdeutigkeiten der Phase liegen in der Größenordnung von 30 - 60 Sekunden [10]. Die Genauigkeit der Positionsbestimmung liegt dann im Bereich weniger Zentimeter. Die GPS-Phasenauswertung ist damit eine wesentliche Voraussetzung für die Höhenbestimmung des Peilschiffes.

Die Arbeitsgemeinschaft der Vermessungsverwaltungen der Länder der Bundesrepublik Deutschland (AdV) ist dabei, unter dem Namen HEPS einen Dienst für GPS-Phasenkorrekturdaten einzurichten [2]. Da hierbei für die nächste Zeit noch keine Abdeckung des Neckars vorgesehen ist, muß man davon ausgehen, daß für die Anwendung auf der „Neckar" eine eigene Referenzstation und Funkübertragungsstrecke benutzt werden muß.

4 Integrierte Ortung

Eine zentrale Funktion des Navigationssystems besteht darin, aus den verschiedenen, zur Verfügung stehenden Informationsquellen eine bestmögliche Schätzung des Bewegungszustands des navigierenden Schiffes zu bestimmen. Unter Informationsquellen sind dabei in erster Linie die verschiedenen Sensoren zu verstehen, daneben wird aber auch a-priori Wissen in Form eines dynamischen Schiffsmodells und der elektronischen Karte in die Verarbeitung eingebracht.

Die Integration der verschiedenen Informationsquellen erfolgt im Rahmen eines erweiterten Kalmanfilters. Aus den von den Sensoren bereitgestellten Meßdaten sind dabei im allgemeinen über verschiedene Auswertungsschritte Größen abzuleiten, die mit dem Bewegungszustand des Schiffes in Verbindung gebracht und somit in einem Meßupdate verarbeitet werden können. Als Beispiel sei hierzu an die Verarbeitung des Radarbilds erinnert. Über den in Abschnitt 2 vorgestellten Bildvergleich wird aus den Bilddaten eine Messung von Position und Vorausrichtung abgeleitet, die dann im Kalmanfilter verarbeitet wird. Dem dynamischen Modell des Schiffes fällt im Rahmen des Kalmanfilters die Aufgabe zu, die zeitliche Verbindung zwischen den verschiedenen, im allgemeinen asynchron vorliegenden Messungen herzustellen.

Es ist vorgesehen, im Rahmen des hier beschriebenen Vorhabens die ebene Bewegung des Schiffes auf dem Wasser und die Höhenbestimmung entkoppelt zu bearbeiten. Daher sind beide Aufgaben im Folgenden auch getrennt dargestellt.

4.1 Horizontale Lagebestimmung

Für die Erfassung der ebenen Bewegung des Schiffes stehen auf dem Peilschiff „Neckar" folgende Sensoren zur Verfügung:

Bordradar: Über einen Vergleich von Karte und Radarbild kann eine Messung von Position und Vorausrichtung des Schiffes abgeleitet werden.

GPS-Empfänger: Aus den GPS-Messungen kann die Position des Schiffes sowie dessen Geschwindigkeit über Grund bestimmt werden.

Ultraschall-Dopplerlog: Dieses Gerät bestimmt die Geschwindigkeit des Schiffes über Grund. Es ist bereits auf der „Neckar" installiert und kann an das Navigationssystem angeschlossen werden.

Kreiselkompass: Dieser Sensor liefert eine Messung der Orientierung des Schiffes gegenüber Nord. Ein Einbau dieses Geräts auf der „Neckar" ist vorgesehen, der Kreiselkompass selbst wurde bisher bei der WSV anderweitig eingesetzt. Er soll vom Navigationssystem und dem Gewässertiefenrechner (siehe Abschnitt 1) gemeinsam genutzt werden.

Wendezeiger: Dieses Gerät erfasst die Drehgeschwindigkeit des Schiffes um die Hochachse. Eine derartige Messung ist insbesondere für die Bahnregelung des Fahrzeugs wünschenswert.

Das Peilschiff „Neckar" wird von zwei Schottel-Propellern angetrieben, die unabhängig voneinander um 360 Grad geschwenkt werden können. Das dynamische Modell des Schiffes verwendet die Richtungen der beiden Propeller als Eingangsgröße für die Modellierung der Drehbewegung um die Hochachse. Die Roll- und

Stampfbewegung des Schiffes wird vernachlässigt. Die Längsgeschwindigkeit gegenüber Wasser wird als unbekannte, aber annähernd konstante Größe modelliert.

Bei dem Einsatz auf Binnenwasserstraßen muß damit gerechnet werden, daß einige Sensoren zeitweise nicht verwendet werden können. Unter Brücken sind typischerweise weder GPS-Messungen noch Radarbildauswertungen möglich. Es erfolgt dann eine Koppelnavigation gestützt auf Dopplerlog, Kreiselkompass und Schiffsmodell. Bei GPS-Störungen aufgrund von Satellitenabschattungen steht trotzdem noch die Radarbildauswertung als Positionsmessung zur Verfügung.

In Voruntersuchungen zu diesem Vorhaben mit der Sensorkonfiguration Radar / GPS / Wendezeiger wurden ohne Differential-GPS-Verfahren Genauigkeiten von ca. 0.5 m in Flußquerrichtung erreicht. Die Genauigkeiten in Flußlängsrichtung lagen bei einem bis mehreren Metern, je nach dem Vorhandensein von Merkmalen zur Bestimmung der Längsposition im Radarbild.

4.2 Höhenbestimmung

Die Bestimmung der geodätischen Höhe des Schiffes mit der gewünschten Genauigkeit von 5 cm stellt sicher den anspruchsvollsten Teil der Ortungsaufgabe dar. Für die Erfassung der senkrechten Bewegung des Schiffes sind zwei Sensoren vorgesehen:

GPS-Empfänger: Um die geforderten Genauigkeiten zu erreichen, ist es notwendig, eine Trägerphasenauswertung (siehe Abschnitt 3) durchzuführen.

Beschleunigungsmesser: Zur Erfassung schneller Höhenänderungen z.B. durch Wellen vorbeifahrender Schiffe ist die GPS-Höhenbestimmung durch eine Messung der senkrechten Schiffsbeschleunigung zu stützen.

Als a-priori Wissen soll in der Wasserstraßenkarte zusätzlich das stationäre Profil der Wasserspiegelhöhe abgelegt werden. Dieses Profil ist vor einer Peilfahrt durch Pegelablesungen an den benachbarten Schleusen an die aktuellen Verhältnisse anzupassen.

5 Zusammenfassung und Ausblick

Ziel der hier vorgestellten Arbeiten ist es, ein leistungsfähiges Ortungssystem für Peilschiffe zu realisieren, das insbesondere für den Einsatz bei für die reine GPS-Auswertung schwierigen Verhältnissen geeignet ist. Gegenüber dem Einsatz eines Zielverfolgungssystems zur Ortung des Peilschiffs ergibt sich eine wesentliche Erhöhung der Peilleistung des Fahrzeugs, da die Wartezeiten beim häufigen Versetzen des Zielverfolgungssystems entfallen. Die hochgenaue automatische Bahnführung des Peilschiffes, auf die in diesem Zusammenhang nicht eingegangen wurde, ermöglicht es darüberhinaus, die Überlappungen zwischen den vom Peilschiff erfassten Steifen zu minimieren. Gleichzeitig bedeutet sie eine wesentliche Entlastung für den Schiffsführer.

Die Arbeiten in diesem Projekt können als ein Beispiel dafür angesehen werden, daß sowohl navigatorische als auch geodätische Aufgaben mit den gleichen Methoden und Werkzeugen gelöst werden können. Ein Motor dieser Entwicklung ist die Verfügbarkeit hochgenauer GPS-Auswertungen in Echtzeit.

Literatur

[1] *Alfred Leick:* GPS satellite surveying. John Wiley & Sons, Inc., New York, 1995.

[2] *Hankemeier, N. und Müller, A.:* GPS-Augmentation: State of the Art. Proc. SATNAV 95, The German Institute of Navigation (DGON), Weihenstephan 1995.

[3] *Kabatek, U., Sandler, M., Neul, R., und Gilles, E. D.:* Eine elektronische Flußkarte als Wissensbasis in einem integrierten Navigationssystem. Zeitschrift für Vermessungswesen 117 (1992), S. 35–45.

[4] *Neul, R.:* Positionsbestimmung eines navigierenden Schiffes durch kartengestützte Radarbildverarbeitung. Diss., Universität Stuttgart, VDI-Verlag, Düsseldorf, 1993.

[5] *Neul, R. und Gilles, E. D.:* Schiffsnavigation durch Vergleich von Radarbildern und elektronischer Karte. Proc. Autonome Mobile Systeme. 6. Fachgespräch (Hrsg.: Rembold, U., Dillmann, R., und Levi, P.), Karlsruhe 1990, S. 197–219.

[6] *Raven, P. und Schoemackers, G.:* DGPS corrections on the air in Nordrhein-Westfalen. Proc. 3rd International Conference on Land Vehicle Navigation, DGON, Dresden 1994.

[7] *Sandler, M., Kabatek, U., Neul, R., und Gilles, E. D.:* Guiding Ships on Waterways. Proc. ISPRS Commission II Symposium, International Society for Photogrammetry and Remote Sensing, Ottawa 1994, S. 63–75.

[8] *Sandler, M., Wahl, A., Zimmermann, R., Faul, M., Kabatek, U., und Gilles, E. D.:* Autonomous guidance of ships on waterways. Proc. Intelligent Autonomous Systems (Hrsg.: Rembold, U. et al.), IOS Press. März 1995, S. 643–650.

[9] *Speckter, H.:* Aufbau und Nutzung zweier deutscher Weitbereichs - DGPS - Referenzstationen und möglicher Einfluß auf VTS-Aufgaben. Proc. VTS Symposium 94, DGON. 1994, S. 143–159.

[10] *Wübbena, G., Bagge, A., und Seeber, G.:* Developments in real-time precise DGPS applications – concepts and status. Proc. IAG Symposium G1, Boulder 1995.

Praxisgerechte Sensorstrategien für die Lokalisierung eines mobilen Mauerroboters auf der Baustelle

G. Pritschow, M. Dalacker, J. Kurz, S. McCormac, J. Zeiher

Universität Stuttgart
Institut für Steuerungstechnik der Werkzeugmaschinen und Fertigungseinrichtungen
Abteilung Roboter- und Maschinensysteme
Seidenstraße 36, 70174 Stuttgart
Telefon: 0711/121-2406
Telefax: 0711/121-2413

Kurzfassung

Der Beitrag beschreibt Sensorkonzepte für die automatisierte Erstellung von Mauerwerk auf der Baustelle mit Hilfe eines mobilen Roboters. Im einzelnen werden die Fehlerquellen beim automatisierten Mauern aufgezeigt, die Genauigkeitsanforderungen an den mobilen Roboter definiert, und zwei baustellengerechte Sensorstrategien zur Bestimmung der Position und Orientierung des Roboters detailliert vorgestellt. Abgeschlossen wird der Beitrag durch eine Bewertung der erreichbaren Positioniergenauigkeit mit den vorgestellten Sensorstrategien.

1. Einleitung und Problemstellung

Beeinflußt durch die Bauautomatisierung in anderen Ländern, insbesondere in Japan /1/, den niedrigen technischen Standard in vielen Gewerken und den verstärkten Wettbewerbsdruck infolge ausländischer Billiganbieter werden die Forderungen nach der Einführung von Robotern in die Bauwirtschaft in jüngster Zeit immer lauter /2, 3/. Gute Chancen in technischer und wirtschaftlicher Hinsicht werden dabei insbesondere Robotern zur Erstellung von Mauerwerk eingeräumt, die dem Menschen als intelligentes Arbeitsmittel dienen und ihn von den körperlich schweren Arbeiten wirksam entlasten. Verstärkt wird diese Entwicklung beim Mauerwerksbau noch durch den Anstieg der Steingewichte infolge der neuen Wärme- schutzverordnung /4/ und dem Zwang zu höherer Produktivität. Grundlegende Konzepte und Basistechnologien für einen mobilen Mauerroboter sowie der am Institut für Steuerungstechnik der Werkzeugmaschinen und Fertigungseinrichtungen (ISW) der Universität Stuttgart zusammen mit einem Industriekonsortium entwickelte Prototyp BRONCO wurden von den Autoren bereits in den vergangenen Jahren vorgestellt. /5 - 8/.

Eine Schlüsselfrage der automatisierten Mauerwerksfertigung mit mobilen Robotern ist die Sicherstellung der erforderlichen Positioniergenauigkeit beim Versetzen der Steine in einer weitgehend unstrukturierten Baustellenumgebung. Hierzu müssen drei Teilaufgaben gelöst werden, nämlich

(1) die Bestimmung der Position und Orientierung des Roboters auf der Geschoßdecke,

(2) die Kalibrierung der Steinlage bezüglich des Greiferbezugspunktes (TCP) nach dem Greifvorgang sowie

(3) das positionsgenaue Versetzen der Steine im Mauerwerksverband.

Gesucht sind daher Sensorstrategien, welche die wesentlichen Forderungen nach Genauigkeit, Baustellentauglichkeit sowie Wirtschaftlichkeit erfüllen. Der vorliegende Beitrag beschränkt sich dabei auf Teilaufgabe (1), da diese für die erzielbare Genauigkeit von entscheidender Bedeutung ist.

2. Zielsetzung und Anforderungen

Das Ziel des Beitrags besteht in der Herleitung und Untersuchung praxisgerechter, baustellentauglicher Sensorstrategien, die eine zuverlässige und möglichst genaue Bestimmung der Position und der Orientierung des Mauerroboters innerhalb der Geschoßdecke unter baustellenüblichen Randbedingungen erlauben. Die Auswahl des am besten geeigneten Verfahrens soll durch eine quantitative Analyse der erzielbaren Genauigkeiten unterstützt werden. An die Sensorstrategien werden die folgenden Anforderungen gestellt:

- möglichst hohe Genauigkeit (Position: $\pm$ 2 cm, Orientierung: $\pm 0.01°$), um den Aufwand für eine eventuelle Zusatzsensorik gering halten zu können,

- Bestimmung der Position und Orientierung in Absolut-/Weltkoordinaten,

- vollautomatische Durchführung des Einmeßvorgangs,

- geringer stationärer Aufwand, z.B. für die Installation künstlicher Landmarken,

- Messung an jedem Arbeitspunkt der Geschoßdecke möglich.

Da der Roboter während des Meßvorgangs mechanisch abgestützt wird, kann die Messung im Stand erfolgen, d.h. es ist keine Navigation erforderlich.

3. Bestimmung der Position und Orientierung des Roboters

Die Untersuchung erfolgt für zwei besonders aussichtsreiche Sensorstrategien, deren Auswahl in /9/ erläutert ist:

(1)   Absolutmessung mit Laser-Scanner und künstlichen Landmarken,

(2)   Relativmessung bezüglich der ersten Steinreihe mittels am Greifer angebrachter Abstandssensoren.

3.1 Definition von Koordinatensystemen

Für die mathematische Beschreibung der Meßstrategien ist es sinnvoll, die in Bild 1 dargestellten und im folgenden erläuterten kartesischen Koordinatensysteme einzuführen:

Das Weltkoordinatensystem ^{W}K wird durch die idealisierte Geschoßdecke und eine Vertikale definiert, die sinnvollerweise durch einen Eckpunkt des Gebäudegrundrisses verläuft. Die gesamte Wandplanung einschließlich der Vorgaben für die Arbeitspositionen des Mauerroboters, die Palettenstandorte sowie eventuell erforderliche Landmarken beziehen sich auf dieses Koordinatensystem ^{W}K, das dem Maschinenführer aus der Anschauung vertraut ist.

Das Roboterkoordinatensystem ^{B}K ist definiert durch die Aufstandsfläche der hydraulischen Vierpunktabstützung und die Grunddrehachse des Mauerroboters. Dadurch werden eventuelle

Neigungsfehler berücksichtigt. Die roboterspezifische Vorwärts- und Rückwärtstransformation und damit auch die Bewegungsbefehle der Anwendungsprogramme beziehen sich auf ^{B}K.

Das Koordinatensystem ^{O}K beschreibt die Drehung des Oberwagens gegenüber dem Roboterkoordinatensystem, und ^{H}K definiert das Bezugssystem eines roboterfest angebrachten Sensors. Dabei kann es sich beispielsweise um einen Laser-Scanner handeln.

Im Greiferkoordinatensystem ^{G}K, das durch den Mittelpunkt der Saugplatte und eine Normale zur Saugfläche definiert wird, werden die Abstandssensoren ausgewertet. Relativmessungen zwischen Greifer und Mauerwerk stellen demnach bei gleichzeitiger Auswertung der Vorwärtstransformation und der Plandaten der Wand eine Beziehung zwischen dem Weltkoordinatensystem ^{W}K und dem Roboterkoordinatensystem ^{B}K her.

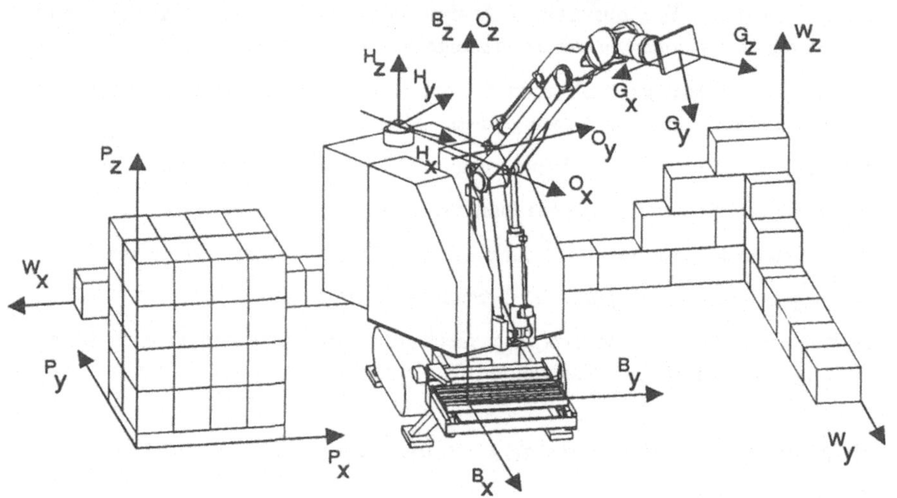

Bild 1: Koordinatensysteme zur mathematischen Beschreibung der Meßstrategien

In den folgenden Abschnitten werden für die beiden genannten Sensorstrategien die Algorithmen zur Bestimmung der Roboterposition und -orientierung aus den Meßdaten hergeleitet. Die mathematische Formulierung wird dabei für den zweidimensionalen Fall vorgenommen, d.h. Neigungsfehler des Roboters werden zunächst vernachlässigt. Die erforderlichen sensortechnischen Maßnahmen und die Erweiterung der Algorithmen bei dreidimensionaler Betrachtung werden dann im Anschluß diskutiert.

3.2 Strategie 1: Absolutmessung mit rotierendem Laser-Scanner und künstlichen Landmarken

Die prinzipielle Funktionsweise eines Laser-Scanners, der aus Winkelmessungen bezüglich ortsfest installierter Reflektoren mittels Triangulation seine eigene Position und Orientierung ermittelt, ist in /10/ beschrieben. Dieses Meßverfahren soll zur Bestimmung von Position und Orientierung des Mauerroboters eingesetzt werden. Hierzu werden der Laser-Scanner am Oberwagen angebracht und die Reflektoren auf der Geschoßdecke aufgestellt (vgl. Bild 2). Als

Meßwerte stehen die Ausgangsgrößen x_H, y_H und γ_H des Laser-Scanners im Weltkoordinatensystem $^W K$ sowie der Drehwinkel φ_1 der Grunddrehachse im Roboterkoordinatensystem $^B K$ zur Verfügung. Bezeichnet man gemäß Bild 2 die Richtung der Scanner-Bezugsachse bezüglich der Mittelachse des Oberwagens mit φ_0, so ergibt sich für die Orientierung des Mauerroboters im Weltkoordinatensystem $^W K$ die folgende Beziehung:

$$\gamma_B = \gamma_H - \varphi_1 - \varphi_0 \tag{1}$$

Der Ansatz zur Berechnung der Position x_B und y_B lautet:

$$^W r_B = {}^W r_H - {}^W r_{BH} = {}^W r_H - {}^{WB}T \cdot {}^{BO}T \cdot {}^O r_{BH} = {}^W r_H - {}^{WO}T \cdot {}^O r_{BH} \tag{2}$$

Mit $^O r_{BH} = \begin{bmatrix} -L_H \\ 0 \end{bmatrix}$, den Sensor-Meßwerten $^W r_H = \begin{bmatrix} x_H \\ y_H \end{bmatrix}$ und γ_H sowie

$$^{WO}T = \begin{bmatrix} \cos(\varphi_1 + \gamma_B) & -\sin(\varphi_1 + \gamma_B) \\ \sin(\varphi_1 + \gamma_B) & \cos(\varphi_1 + \gamma_B) \end{bmatrix} = \begin{bmatrix} \cos(\gamma_H - \varphi_0) & -\sin(\gamma_H - \varphi_0) \\ \sin(\gamma_H - \varphi_0) & \cos(\gamma_H - \varphi_0) \end{bmatrix}$$

ergibt sich für die gesuchten Werte aus Gleichung (2):

$$x_B = x_H + L_H \cdot \cos(\gamma_H - \varphi_0) \tag{3a}$$

$$y_B = y_H + L_H \cdot \sin(\gamma_H - \varphi_0) \tag{3b}$$

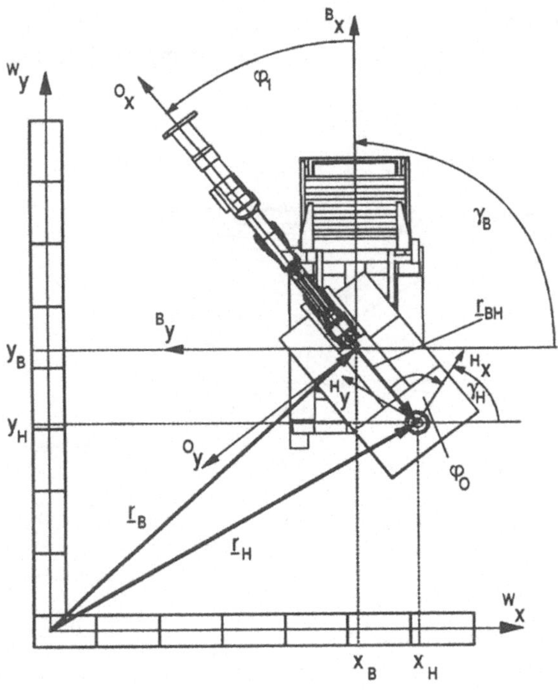

Bild 2: Bestimmung der Position und Orientierung des mobilen Mauerroboters mit Hilfe eines Laser-Scanners

3.3 Strategie 2: Abstandsmessung relativ zur ersten Steinreihe

Wie bereits am Anfang des Abschnitts ausgeführt, kann das Einmessen des Mauerroboters auch mit Hilfe lokaler Abstandssensorik im Greifer gegenüber natürlichen Umgebungsmerkmalen erfolgen. Eine einfache Möglichkeit ergibt sich dann, wenn die erste Steinreihe manuell angelegt wurde und der Roboter über zwei am Greifer angebrachte Abstandssensoren verfügt.

Dem Meßverfahren liegt der folgende Gedanke zugrunde: Zunächst wird der Greifer im Weltkoordinatensystem exakt horizontiert und so vor der ersten Steinreihe positioniert, daß die durch die Steine erzeugte Referenzlinie im Meßbereich der Abstandssensoren liegt. Dann werden die beiden Abstandssensoren aktiviert und der jeweilige Abstand zur ersten Steinreihe gemessen. Aus den Meßwerten a_1 und a_2 können dann mit Hilfe einfacher Beziehungen der Abstand d_M und die Orientierung γ_M des Greifers bezüglich der im Weltkoordinatensystem bekannten Steinreihe berechnet werden (vgl. Bild 3).

$$\gamma_{M,i} = \arctan \frac{a_{1,i} - a_{2,i}}{d_A} \qquad , \qquad i = 1,2 \qquad (4a)$$

$$d_{M,i} = \frac{1}{2} \cdot \left(a_{1,i} + a_{2,i} \right) \qquad , \qquad i = 1,2 \qquad (4b)$$

Dabei bezeichnt d_A den Abstand zwischen den beiden Sensoren. Mit Hilfe des aus der Koordinatentransformation bekannten geometrischen Zusammenhangs zwischen Greifer und mobiler Basis kann dann auf die Position und Orientierung des Roboters zurückgeschlossen werden.

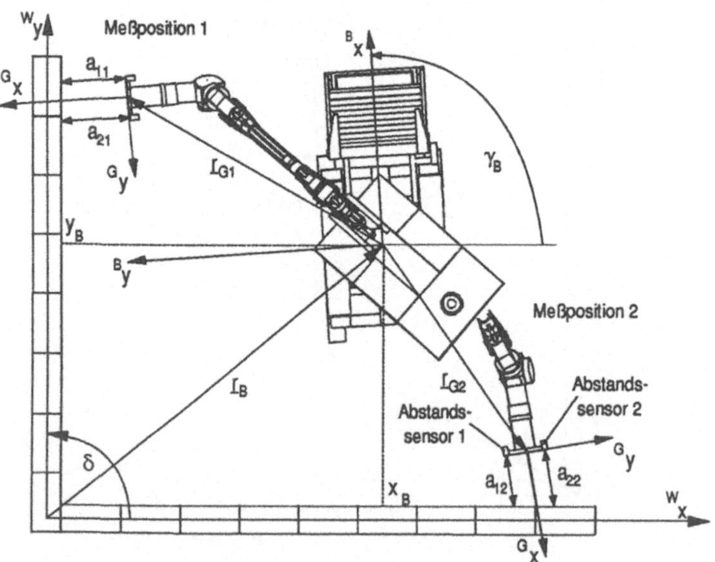

Bild 3: Bestimmung von Position und Orientierung des mobilen Mauerroboters durch zweifache Abstandsmessung zur ersten Steinreihe

Mit einer Messung der beschriebenen Art können jedoch lediglich zwei Freiheitsgrade des Robotersstandorts berechnet werden, da sie keine Information über die Ortskoordinate in Mauerlängsrichtung liefert. Zur eindeutigen Bestimmung von x_B, y_B und γ_B müssen daher mindestens zwei solche Messungen durchgeführt werden. Dabei sind zwei verschiedene Steinreihen als Referenzlinien zu benutzen, die einen Winkel $\delta \neq 0°$ bzw. $180°$ einschließen müssen. Bild 3 zeigt beispielhaft ein derartiges Szenario.

3.4 Kompensation von Neigungsfehlern in der mobilen Basis und im Greifer

Aufgrund unvermeidlicher Bodenunebenheiten steht die Plattform des Roboters im allgemeinen nie exakt horizontal, sondern ist gegenüber der xy-Ebene des Weltkoordinatensystems $^W K$ um die Winkel α_B bzw. β_B geneigt. Dieser Sachverhalt wird durch Bild 4 verdeutlicht.

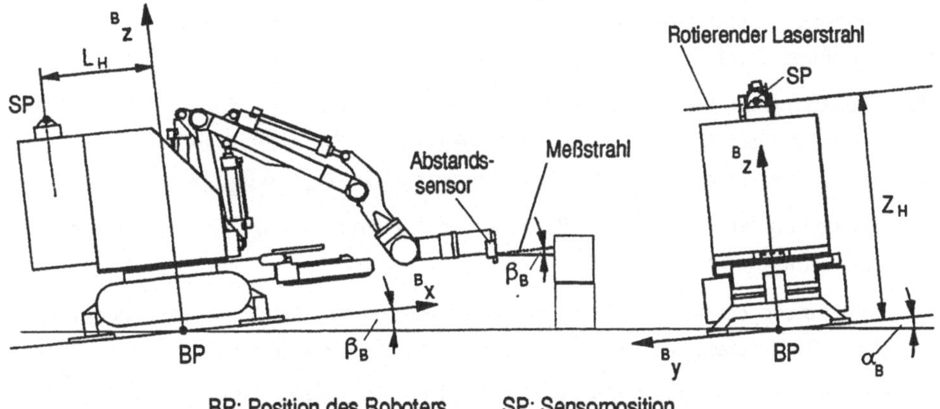

Bild 4:   Neigungsfehler und deren Auswirkung auf die Meßgenauigkeit

Wegen des großen vertikalen Abstands zwischen dem zu bestimmenden Roboterbezugspunkt B und dem Laser-Scanner ($Z_H \approx 1.5$ m) führen solche Neigungsfehler unter Umständen zu erheblichen Positionsabweichungen und dürfen daher nicht vernachlässigt werden. Speziell bei der Sensorstrategie 1 treten zusätzliche Fehler auf, da die Abweichung der Laserebene von der Horizontalen zu einer Verfälschung der Winkelmessungen und damit zu einer fehlerhaften Bestimmung der Scannerposition und -orientierung führt. Aber auch die Abstandsmessungen zur ersten Steinreihe werden durch diese Neigungen beeinflußt.

Die Erfassung der Neigungswinkel α_B und β_B des Roboters ist also unverzichtbar, wenn die genannten Fehler erkannt und wirkungsvoll kompensiert werden sollen. Für die Messung der Neigungswinkel können Inklinometer eingesetzt werden, die entweder an der mobilen Basis oder am Oberwagen des Roboters angebracht werden und bei der Sensorstrategie 2 ist eine direkte Messung der Neigungen am Greifer ebenfalls möglich.

Falls die Basisneigungen α_B und β_B gemessen werden, können die korrespondierenden Neigungen α_H und β_H des Laser-Scanners am Oberwagen bei Kenntnis der beiden Winkel φ_0 und φ_1 (vgl. Bild 2) nach den folgenden Gleichungen berechnet werden:

$$\alpha_H = \arctan\left[\cos(\varphi_0 + \varphi_1)\tan\alpha_B + \sin(\varphi_0 + \varphi_1)\tan\beta_B\right] \tag{5a}$$

$$\beta_H = \arctan\left[\cos(\varphi_0 + \varphi_1)\tan\beta_B - \sin(\varphi_0 + \varphi_1)\tan\alpha_B\right] \tag{5b}$$

Mit Hilfe der beschriebenen Verfahren zur Bestimmung der Neigungsfehler von mobiler Basis und Laser-Scanner sowie zur Horizontierung des Greifers, können nun die gesuchten Größen x_B, y_B und γ_B für den dreidimensionalen Fall auf der Grundlage der in den Abschnitten 3.2 und 3.3 vorgestellten Strategien berechnet werden. Hierzu empfiehlt es sich, neben den definierten ebenen Koordinatensystemen $^W K$, $^H K$ und $^B K$ die jeweiligen geneigten Systeme $^{W'} K$, $^{H'} K$ bzw. $^{B'} K$ einzuführen und zusammen mit den gemessenen bzw. gemäß Geichung (5a,b) berechneten Neigungswinkeln in die Transformationen mit einzubeziehen. Für die Strategie 1 ergibt sich beispielsweise der folgende Lösungsweg:

(1) Umrechnung der Ausgangsgrößen $^{W'} x_H$, $^{W'} y_H$ und $^{W'} \gamma_H$ des (geneigten) Laser-Scanners ins ebene Weltkoordinatensystem $^W K$ mit Hilfe der Neigungswinkel α_H und β_H aus Gleichung (5a,b).

(2) Transformation der Ausgangsgrößen $^{W'} x_H$, $^{W'} y_H$ und $^{W'} \gamma_H$ des (geneigten) Laser-Scanners ins ebene Roboterkoordinatensystem $^B K$ mit Hilfe der bekannten Robotergeometrie und der gemessenen Basisneigungen α_B und β_B.

(3) Berechnung von $^W x_H$, $^W y_H$ und $^W \gamma_H$ durch Transformation der Scannerposition und -orientierung von $^B K$ nach $^W K$.

(4) Bestimmung der resultierenden Roboterposition ($^W x_B$, $^W y_B$) und -orientierung $^W \gamma_B$ durch Gleichsetzen von $^W x_H$, $^W y_H$ und $^W \gamma_H$ gemäß (1) bzw. (3).

Die Vorgehensweise für die Strategie 2 ist ähnlich, dort werden jedoch die Meßdaten der Abstandssensoren ausgewertet und zusammen mit den kinematischen Informationen aus der Vorwärtstransformation zur Berechnung von $^W x_B$, $^W y_B$ und $^W \gamma_B$ herangezogen. Eine quantitative Auswertung der Algorithmen für den dreidimensionalen Fall wird anläßlich einer Fehlerbetrachtung für beide Strategien im nachfolgenden Abschnitt vorgenommen.

3.5 Erreichbare Positioniergenauigkeit

Bei der Auswahl der besten Strategie zur Bestimmung von Position und Orientierung des Mauerroboters spielt die erreichbare Genauigkeit eine entscheidende Rolle. Um hierzu grundlegende Untersuchungen durchführen zu können, wurden die Algorithmen beider Strategien für den dreidimensionalen Fall, d.h. mit Berücksichtigung der Neigungsfehler, auf einem Simulationssystem implementiert. Ziel dieser Simulationen war es, die Auswirkungen unterschiedlicher Fehlerquellen auf die Genauigkeit quantitativ zu ermitteln und daraus detaillierte Aussagen über die Tauglichkeit der jeweiligen Sensorstrategie abzuleiten. Im einzelnen wurden die folgenden Fehlerquellen betrachtet:

- Positionsfehler der Reflektoren durch ungenaues Aufstellen bzw. Einmessen,

- Neigungsfehler des Roboters bzw. des Laser-Scanners,

- Meßfehler der an der Positionsbestimmung beteiligten Meßsysteme und Sensorkomponenten, insbesondere
  - des an der mobilen Basis angebrachten Inklinometers,
  - des Laser-Scanners,
  - des Winkelmeßsystems der Grunddrehachse,
  - der Abstandssensoren am Greifer,

- Fehler beim Anlegen der ersten Steinreihe, d.h.
  - Positionsfehler und
  - Winkelfehler sowie

- Fehler in der Vorwärtstransformation (z.B. Achslage- und Achswinkelfehler).

Die Simulation des Einmeßvorgangs erfolgt anhand eines realitätsnahen Beispiels, nämlich für den Start der Mauerwerksfertigung in einer Ecke des Gebäudes gemäß Bild 5.

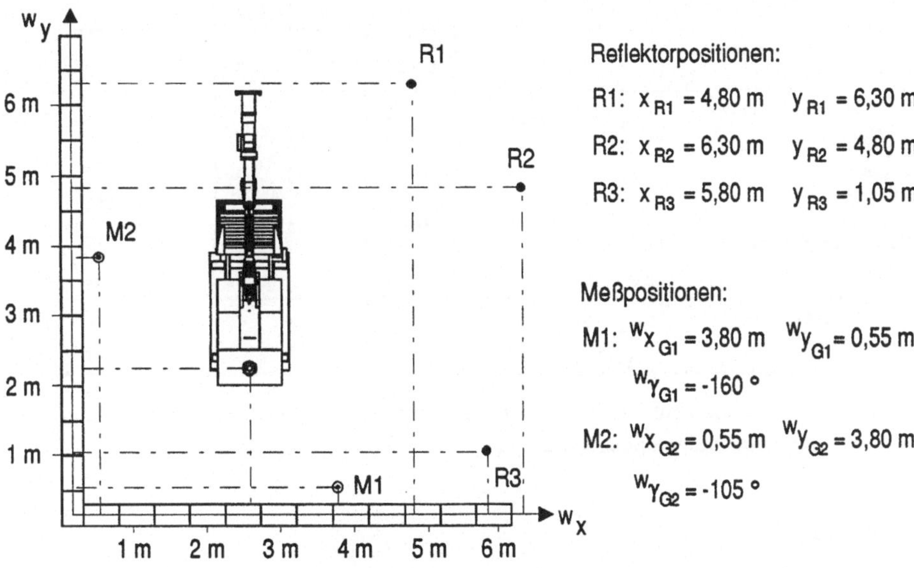

Bild 5: Beispielszenario für die quantitative Untersuchung der Sensorstrategien

Für das entsprechende Szenario wurden die folgenden Voraussetzungen getroffen:

- Die Sollkoordinaten des Roboters im Weltkoordinatensystem, dessen Ursprung mit der Gebäudeecke zusammenfällt, lauten $x_B = 1900\,mm$, $y_B = 2300\,mm$, $\gamma_B = 0°$.

- Die erste Steinreihe wurde bereits vorab manuell angelegt.

- Sonstige Geometrie- und Roboterdaten:

$L_H = 500\,mm$, $\varphi_0 = 0°$
$Z_H = 1500\,mm$, $\varphi_1 = 0°$

Die Simulationsergebnisse, d.h. die jeweiligen Abweichungen Δx_B, Δy_B und $\Delta \gamma_B$ der gesuchten Positions- und Orientierungswerte des Roboters von den tatsächlichen Werten x_B, y_B und γ_B in Abhängigkeit der genannten Fehlerquellen, sind in Tabelle 1 quantitativ dargestellt. In der zweiten Spalte der Tabelle sind die Zahlenwerte der Fehler aufgeführt, welche der jeweiligen Simulation zugrunde liegen.

Auftretende Fehler		Strategie 1			Strategie 2		
Fehlerquelle	Zahlenwert	Δx_B [mm]	Δy_B [mm]	$\Delta \gamma_B$ [Grad]	Δx_B [mm]	Δy_B [mm]	$\Delta \gamma_B$ [Grad]
Positionsfehler der Reflektoren	$\Delta x_{Ri}=\Delta y_{Ri} = 10\,mm$	6	-8	0,15			
	$\Delta x_{Ri}=\Delta y_{Ri} = 20\,mm$	12	-16	0,20			
Neigungsfehler des Roboters	$\alpha_B=\beta_B = 1°$	27	24	0,027	0,07	0,07	0
	$\alpha_B=\beta_B = 5°$	155	82	0,62	1,7	1,7	0
Meßfehler des Inklinometers (Kompensation aktiv)	$\Delta\alpha_B=\Delta\beta_B = 0,01°$	-0,35	-0,055	-0,003	0,03	-0,013	0
Meßfehler des Laser-Scanners	$\Delta\alpha_i = 0,002°$	0,018	$-3 \cdot 10^{-7}$	-0,002			
Meßfehler des Meßsystems der Grunddrehachse	$\Delta\varphi_1 = 0,001°$	$-8 \cdot 10^{-12}$	10^{-11}	0,001			
Meßfehler der Abstands- sensoren	$\Delta\alpha_{1,2} = \pm 1\,mm$				11	-9,5	0,42
Positionsfehler der ersten Steinreihe	$\Delta y_0 = 10\,mm$				0	-10	0
	$\Delta y_0 = 20\,mm$				0	-20	0
Winkelfehler der ersten Steinreihe	$\Delta\psi = 0,1°$				-2	-5	-0,05
	$\Delta\psi = 0,5°$				-8	-25	-0,25
Fehler der Vorwärts- transformation	$\Delta x_{G1}=\Delta y_{G1} = 10\,mm$				0	10	0
	$\Delta x_{G1}=\Delta y_{G1} = 20\,mm$				0	20	0

Tabelle 1: Auftretende Fehler und Auswirkungen auf die erreichbare Positioniergenauigkeit bei den untersuchten Sensorstrategien

4. Ergebnisse

Die Untersuchungen zeigen, daß grundsätzlich beide Strategien für den Einsatz bei einem mobilen Mauerroboter geeignet sind. Insgesamt lassen sich mit Strategie 1 die besseren Ergebnisse erzielen. Falls die Fehler beim Anlegen der ersten Steinreihe gering gehalten werden, ist Strategie 2 ebenfalls anwendbar. Zum Gesamtfehler tragen insbesondere die folgenden Fehleranteile maßgeblich bei:

- Positionsfehler der Reflektoren und Neigungsfehler des Roboters bei Strategie 1 sowie

- Winkelfehler der ersten Steinreihe und Meßfehler der Abstandssensoren bei Strategie 2.

Zur Sicherstellung einer möglichst hohen Positioniergenauigkeit sind demnach die folgenden Maßnahmen zu treffen:

(1)   exaktes Aufstellen und Einmessen der Reflektoren (± 10 mm),

(2)   Messung und steuerungsinterne Kompensation der Neigungsfehler des Roboters,

(3)   exaktes Anlegen der ersten Steinreihe,

(4)   Verwendung hochgenauer Abstandssensoren.

Im Rahmen der weiteren Forschungsarbeiten ist geplant die vorgestellten simulativen Ergebnisse auf einer Versuchsbaustelle anhand von Experimenten zu verifizieren. Ein weiterer Schwerpunkt wird die Erhöhung der Genauigkeit beim Positionieren der Steine im Mauerwerk mittels Sensorik sein.

Literatur

/1/ H.-G. Hilpert. *Die japanische Bauwirtschaft bereitet sich auf das 21. Jahrhundert vor.* IFO Schnelldienst 32/93.

/2/ S. Kämpfer. *Serviceroboter drängen in neue Märkte.* VDI nachrichten 48 (1994).

/3/ N.N. *Positionspapier der IG Bau-Steine-Erden zum Robotereinsatz in der Bauwirtschaft.* Frankfurt/Main, Mai 1995.

/4/ N.N. *Verordnung über einen energiesparenden Wärmeschutz bei Gebäuden (Wärmeschutzverordnung) vom 16.08.1994.* Bundesgesetzblatt 1994, Teil 1, S. 2121 - 2132, Ausgabe vom 24.08.1994.

/5/ G. Pritschow, M. Dalacker, J. Kurz. *Gesamtkonzept und praxisgerechte Realisierung eines mobilen Roboters zur automatischen Erstellung von Mauerwerk auf der Baustelle.* Tagungsband zum 9. Fachgespräch über Autonome Mobile Systeme, München, 28./29. Oktober 1993, S. 357 - 368.

/6/ G. Pritschow, M. Dalacker, J. Kurz. *Automatisierte Mauerwerksfertigung mit mobilen Robotern: Neue Herausforderungen für die Steuerungs- und Sensortechnik.* Tagungsband zum 10. Fachgespräch über Autonome Mobile Systeme, Stuttgart, 13./14. Oktober 1994, S. 326 - 337.

/7/ G. Pritschow, M. Dalacker, J. Kurz, M. Gaenssle. *Technological Aspects in the Development of a Mobile Bricklaying Robot.* Automation and Robotics in Construction XII: Proceedings of the 12th International Symposium on Automation and Robotics in Construction (ISARC), Warsaw, Poland, 30 May - 1 June, 1995, pp. 281 - 290. Edited by IMBiGS.

/8/ G. Pritschow, J. Kurz, M. Dalacker, A. Lußmann. *Mobile Mauerroboter für den Baustelleneinsatz: Programmierung, Wirtschaftlichkeit und erste experimentelle Ergebnisse.* Tagungsband zum 11. Fachgespräch über Autonome Mobile Systeme, Karlsruhe, 30. Oktober - 1. November 1995, S. 10 - 19.

/9/ G. Pritschow, M. Dalacker, J. Kurz, M. Gaenssle, J. Haller. *Application Specific Realisation of a Mobile Robot for On-Site Construction of Masonry.* Automation and Robotics in Construction XI: Proceedings of the 11th International Symposium on Automation and Robotics in Construction (ISARC), Brighton, U.K., 24 - 26 May, 1994, pp. 95 - 102. Elsevier Publishers B.V.

/10/ L.de Vos, H. Schouten. *The Computer Aided Positioning System CAPSY, a Low Cost Positioning System for Construction.* Proc. 6th Int. Symp. on Automation and Robotics in Construction (ISARC), San Francisco, USA, 6 - 8 June, 1989, pp. 387 - 395.

Sonderbeiträge zu den technischen
Demonstrationen aus dem
Sonderforschungsbereich 331
„Informationsverarbeitung in autonomen,
mobilen Handhabungssystemen“

ROMAN: Ein mobiler Serviceroboter als persönlicher Assistent in belebten Innenräumen

W. Daxwanger, E. Ettelt, C. Fischer, F. Freyberger, U. Hanebeck, G. Schmidt

Lehrstuhl für Steuerungs- und Regelungstechnik
Technische Universität München
D-80290 München

email: roman@lsr.e-technik.tu-muenchen.de

Kurzfassung. Dieser Beitrag beschreibt Schlüsselkomponenten für mobile, weitgehend autonom handelnde, Serviceroboter, wie eine wendige Lokomotionsplattform, einen anthropomorphen Manipulatorarm, ein Multisensorsystem und eine multimodale Mensch–Roboter–Schnittstelle. Mit dem Demonstrator ROMAN werden Hard– und Softwarekonzeption dieser Komponenten und deren informationstechnische Integration zu einem Gesamtsystem beispielhaft vorgestellt. ROMANs Einsatz als persönlicher Assistent im Rahmen alltäglicher Serviceaufgaben belegt die Tragfähigkeit des entwickelten integralen Ansatzes und die Leistungsfähigkeit der Schlüsselkomponenten.

1 Einleitung

In den nächsten Jahren werden mobile Manipulatoren als persönliche Dienstroboter wachsende wirtschaftliche Bedeutung gewinnen [1]. Das Projekt ROMAN verfolgt deshalb das Ziel, Schlüsselkomponenten für derartige Serviceroboter zu entwickeln, in ein Gesamtsystem zu integrieren und in repräsentativen Szenarien zu erproben. Der mobile Serviceroboter ROMAN wurde für den Einsatz in Innenraumumgebungen wie Büros, Labors oder Krankenhäusern entwickelt. ROMAN dient einem Menschen als persönlicher Assistent und übernimmt dabei Routinetätigkeiten wie 1. Kleinteiltransport (Post, Bücher, Geschirr, ...), 2. einfache Aufräumarbeiten oder 3. flächendeckende Be-

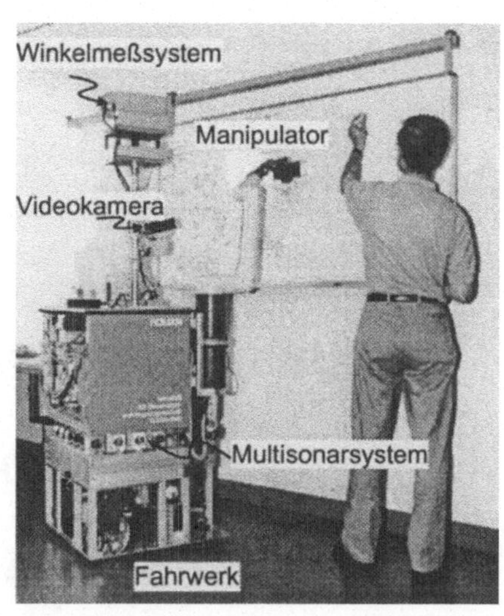

Abb. 1. Der mobile Serviceroboter ROMAN beim Tafelreinigen.

arbeitung. Da der Roboter sich bei diesen Aufgaben in einer für Menschen konzipierten Umgebung bewegt, sind dem Menschen vergleichbare Dimensionen, Arbeitsräume, Beweglichkeit etc. notwendig. Der Roboter muß ferner die Fähigkeit besitzen, sich in einer belebten und nur unvollständig bekannten engräumigen Umgebung automom zu bewegen. Als Lokomotionsplattform wurde ein omnidirektionales Radfahrwerk konzipiert, welches eine hervorragende Beweglichkeit aufweist und eine ausreichende Geschwindigkeit erreicht. Der Roboter ist mit verschiedenen Sensorsystemen ausgestattet, welche bei variierenden Umgebungsbedingungen die absolute Roboterlage mit hoher Genauigkeit bereitstellen und unerwartete Hindernisse zuverlässig detektieren und lokalisieren. Bei der Durchführung einer Serviceaufgabe muß der Roboter Einfluß auf seine Umgebung nehmen, d.h. Türen oder Schubladen öffnen, Gegenstände aufnehmen und ablegen, Schalter bedienen und einfache Reinigungsoperationen ausführen, Abb. 1. Zu diesem Zweck ist er mit einem Manipulator ausgerüstet, dessen Abmessungen und Bewegungsfreiheitsgrade dem menschlichen Arm entsprechen. Um den beschränkten Arbeitsbereich des Manipulators zu erweitern, wird dieser beim Ausführen einer gewünschten Bewegung ggf. durch eine Hoch/Tief–Linearachse und die Lokomotionsplattform unterstützt. Eine videobasierte Objekterkennung bestimmt während der Manipulation die relative Lage des Effektors zum zu manipulierenden Objekt. Die Qualität eines persönlichen Assistenten wird durch eine einfache und natürliche Interaktion zwischen Mensch und Roboter erreicht. Diesem Zweck dient zum einen eine natürlichsprachliche Schnittstelle zwischen Mensch und Roboter, zum anderen kann der Mensch den Roboter in einem virtuellen Arbeitsraum verfolgen. Der Roboter kommentiert mit einem Sprachausgabesystem den aktuellen Stand der Abarbeitung einer kommandierten Serviceaufgabe.

2 Informationsverarbeitende Struktur

Die Informationsverarbeitungsstruktur von ROMAN besteht aus Expertenmodulen für Lokomotion, Manipulation, Sensorik, interne Kommunikation und Mensch–Roboter–Interaktion, Abb. 2. Diese Experten tauschen über einen Blackboard–Server und eine dynamische Kommunikationsweiche untereinander Daten aus. Der Blackboard–Server bietet jedem Experten die Möglichkeit, wichtige Daten öffentlich zur Verfügung zu stellen, so z.B. die absolute Roboterlage durch den Experten für absolute Lokalisierung. Die Kommunikationsweiche stellt abhängig von Situation und Aufgabe Kommunikationskanäle zwischen den Experten bereit. Beim Öffnen einer Tür werden z.B. die Experten für Objekterkennung und Hindernisdetektion mit dem Experten für die Mobile Manipulation verknüpft, während bei weiträumigen Fahrten der Experte für Hindernisdetektion mit dem Experten für Weiträumige Lokomotion verbunden ist.

Im folgenden werden wesentliche Schlüsselkomponenten eines mobilen Serviceroboters beschrieben. Abschnitt 3 gibt eine Übersicht über Verfahren zur Mobilen Manipulation und Weiträumigen Lokomotion. Die zur sicheren Bewegung im Arbeitsraum notwendige absolute Lokalisierung von ROMAN und die schnelle Detektion und Lokalisierung von unerwarteten Hindernissen werden in

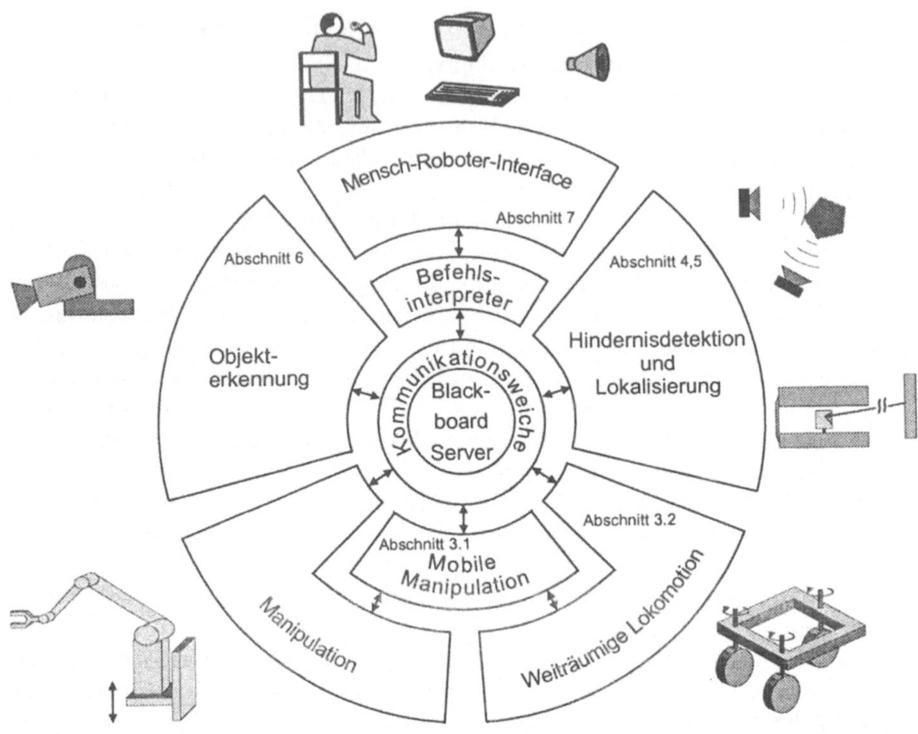

Abb. 2. Die Informationsverarbeitungsstruktur des Serviceroboters ROMAN.

den Abschnitten 4 und 5 beschrieben. Die videobasierte Objekterkennung und
–lokalisierung zur kontinuierlichen Unterstützung von Greifvorgängen wird in
Abschnitt 6 vorgestellt, die Kommunikation zwischen Roboter und Mensch in
Abschnitt 7. Implementierungdetails sind in Abschnitt 8 zusammengefaßt. Abschnitt 9 demonstriert schließlich die Fähigkeiten von ROMAN in einem typischen Innenraumszenario.

3 Bewegungssteuerung

Die Durchführung unterschiedlichster Handhabungsaufgaben mit einem mobilen Manipulator läßt sich durch Kombination zweier Expertenfunktionen unterstützen: 1. Die *Weiträumige Lokomotion* zur Annäherung an das Ziel, ohne dabei Handhabungsaufgaben durchzuführen. 2. Die *Mobile Manipulation*, die sich in eine *Armvorbereitungsphase*, die eigentliche *Effektorbahnfolgephase* und die *Armnachbereitungsphase* zum Einnehmen einer Transportkonfiguration unterteilt, Abb. 3. In den nachfolgenden Abschnitten werden die Expertenfunktionen im Detail beschrieben.

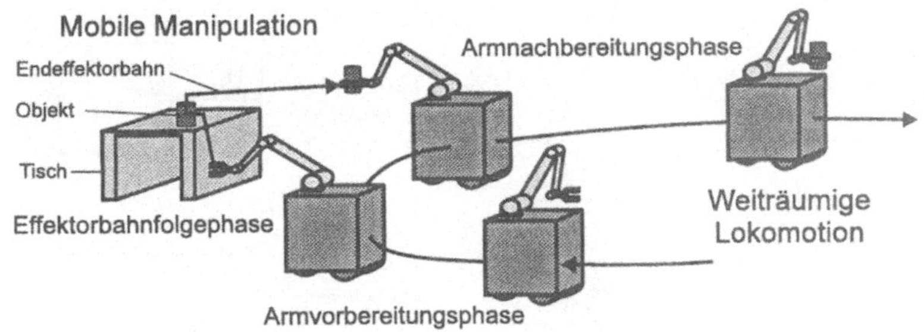

Abb. 3. Unterteilung einer mobilen Handhabungsaufgabe.

3.1 Mobile Manipulation

Der Experte für Mobile Manipulation ist für die flexible Handhabung von Objekten zuständig. Betrachtet man einen stationären Manipulator, so ist er zwar in der Lage, einer Endeffektorbahn innerhalb des gesamten lokalen Arbeitsraumes zu folgen; verläuft die Bahn jedoch außerhalb, kann er nur durch einen Standortwechsel der Vorgabe des Bahnplaners oder Bedieners nachkommen. So unterstützt z.B. der Mensch seine Hand- und Armbewegungen durch gezielte Variation seiner Position und Ausrichtung und geht gegebenenfalls noch zusätzlich in die Knie. Die Unterstützung des Roboterarms orientiert sich an diesem menschlichen Vorgehen und verwendet neben den durch die omnidirektionale Lokomotionsplattform bereitgestellten Freiheitsgraden auch eine Hoch/Tief–Linearachse zur Erweiterung des Arbeitsraums.

Ansatz Der hier verwendete Ansatz zum Bahnfolgen beruht auf der natürlichen Trennung der beiden Bewegungssysteme für Lokomotion und Manipulation, Abb. 4. Die Hoch/Tief–Linearachse wird dabei als zusätzlicher Freiheitsgrad der Lokomotion betrachtet. Die Regelung des Endeffektors auf die bezüglich eines beliebigen Koordinatensystems vorgegebene Trajektorie übernimmt der Manipulator. Gemäß der Nullraumtheorie ist der Manipulator somit für die Einhaltung der externen Bewegung alleine verantwortlich [2]. Optimiert wird das gesamte Bewegungsverhalten durch gezielte Änderungen des Lokomotionszustandes, welche damit die internen Bewegungen des Gesamtsystems initiieren. Der Manipulator regelt weiterhin auf die vorgegebene Endeffektortrajektorie und reagiert zusätzlich durch interne Bewegungen auf die Konfigurationsänderungen der Lokomotion [3], [4].

Vergleicht man den Ansatz mit einer global optimierten Roboterbewegung, bei der alle n Freiheitsgrade des Gesamtsystems aus Lokomotion und Manipulation dazu verwendet werden, eine interne Bewegung zu verursachen, wird durch die hier vorgenommene Trennung die Komplexität von n auf $n-6$ ($6 \cong 6$ Raumfreiheitsgrade) reduziert. Der Verzicht auf eine global optimierte Ausführung, welche aufgrund ihrer Komplexität auf eine kleine Anzahl von Freiheitsgraden n oder auf rein simulative Untersuchungen beschränkt ist, ermöglicht den Einsatz zeiteffizienter Strategien zur Stellgrößengenerierung. Etwaige durch Plattformbewegungen bedingte Störungen der Endeffektorbahn werden durch eine schnelle Endeffektor–Regelung kompensiert.

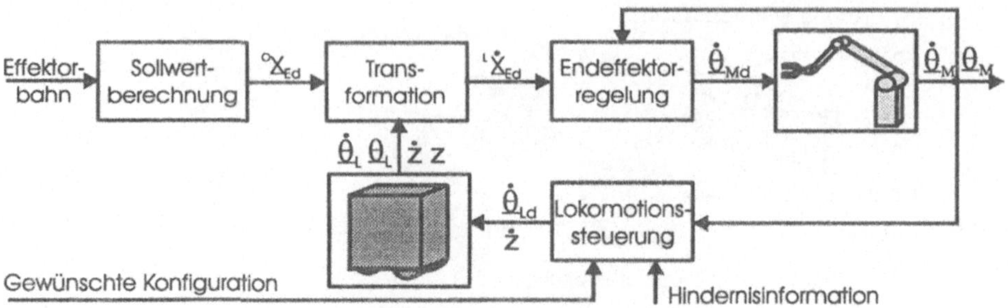

Abb. 4. Regelungsstruktur der Bahnfolgephase.

Verhaltensvorgaben Im Hinblick auf eine gezielte Unterstützung des Manipulators durch die Lokomotionssteuerungsstrategie in der *Bahnfolgephase* werden folgende Verhaltensvorgaben formuliert:

- Erweiterung des lokalen Arbeitsraums

- Erhaltung guter Manipulierbarkeit des Roboterarms

- on–line Variation der Roboterkonfigurationsvorgaben

- Vermeidung von Kollisionen mit statischen und dynamischen Hindernissen

- Einhaltung von Gelenkwinkelbegrenzungen und ausreichendem Hindernisabstand

- natürliches, d.h. anthropomorphes Bewegungsverhalten

Mit der im Gesamtsystem zur Verfügung stehenden Redundanz $r = n - 6$ wird die Konfiguration des Roboters dahingehend variiert, daß die oben genannten Verhaltensvorgaben erfüllt werden. Die für den Roboterarm „unbequemen" Armstellungen werden ebenso vermieden wie singuläre Konfigurationen und Bewegungen in der Nähe von Gelenkwinkelbegrenzungen. Zur Beschreibung dieses Verhaltens wird ein Satz von speziellen, von der aktuellen Armkonfiguration abhängigen Kriterien $\underline{k}$ definiert, welche die durch die Lokomotionsplattform zur Verfügung gestellten Freiheitsgrade binden. Das heißt, es werden genauso viele unabhängige Kriterien wie redundante Freiheitsgrade r benötigt. Im vorliegenden Fall handelt es sich um $r = 4$ redundante Freiheitsgrade und somit um $r = 4$ unabhängige Kriterien. Neben den 3 unabhängig einstellbaren Freiheitsgraden der Lokomotionsplattform wird zusätzlich die am Fußpunkt des Manipulators angebrachte Hoch/Tief–Linearachse zur Unterstützung herangezogen. Zur Vermeidung von Verrenkungen oder Gelenkverdrehungen werden folgende 4 Kriterien für den verwendeten Standardmanipulator definiert, Abb. 5:

k_1: horizontaler Abstand zwischen Handwurzel und Schulter

k_2: Schulterwinkel, d.h. Armstellung bezüglich Plattform

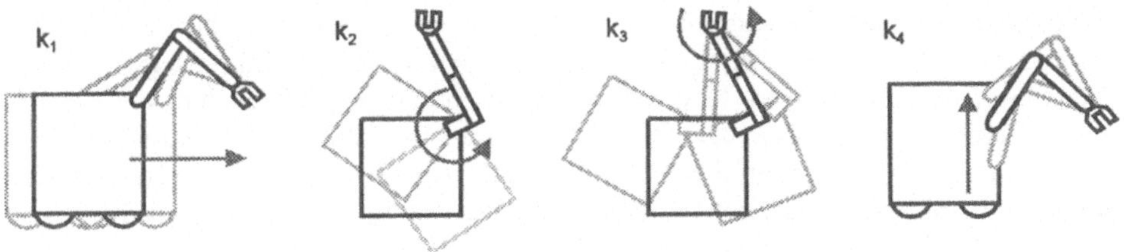

Abb. 5. Veranschaulichung der Kriterien k_{1-4} zur Redundanzbindung.

k_3: Handwurzelgelenkwinkel, d.h. Handverdrehung gegenüber Unterarm

k_4: vertikaler Abstand zwischen Handwurzel und Schulter

Lokomotionssteuerungsstrategie Die Lokomotionssteuerungsstrategie generiert mit Hilfe der eingeführten Kriterien $\underline{k}$ und der gewünschten optimalen Konfiguration $\underline{k}_{OPT}$, z.B. $[50\text{cm}, 20^\circ, 20^\circ, 0\text{cm}]^T$, eine korrespondierende Zustandsänderung der Lokomotion $\underline{\dot{\theta}}_L = [\dot{x}_L, \dot{y}_L, \dot{\Psi}_L]^T$ und der Linearachse $\dot{z}$. Dabei werden zusätzlich die momentane Hinderniskonfiguration und andere feste Beschränkungen, z.B. der Gelenkwinkel, berücksichtigt. Zur Umsetzung aller Forderungen wird eine aus mehreren Stufen bestehende fuzzybasierte Lokomotionssteuerungsstrategie verwendet [3], [4].

3.2 Weiträumige Lokomotion

Der Experte für die Weiträumige Lokomotion verbindet Arbeitsbereiche der Mobilen Manipulation durch weiträumige Bewegungen der Lokomotionsplattform. Hierzu wird ein Weg definiert, der aus einer Abfolge von Pfadknoten besteht. Zur Verbindung dieser Pfadknoten stehen sowohl trajektorienbasierte als auch modellbasierte Bewegungsprimitive zur Verfügung, die auf der Annahme einer virtuellen Lokomotionsplattform beruhen, Abb. 6. Eine abstrakte Schnittstelle beschreibt die inkrementelle Bewegung der virtuellen Lokomotionsplattform durch die aktuelle Lage des Drehzentrums (Center of Rotation) κ_1, ϕ_1 und die Geschwindigkeit v_1 des virtuellen Rades. Diese Vorgaben werden durch einen unterlagerten Regler in physikalische Stellgrößen ϕ_i, v_1 zur koordinierten Bewegung der drei unabhängigen Radsätze umgesetzt. Dadurch nutzen die Bewegungsexperten die volle Omnidirektionalität der Lokomotionsplattform aus, ohne deren realen Aufbau berücksichtigen zu müssen.

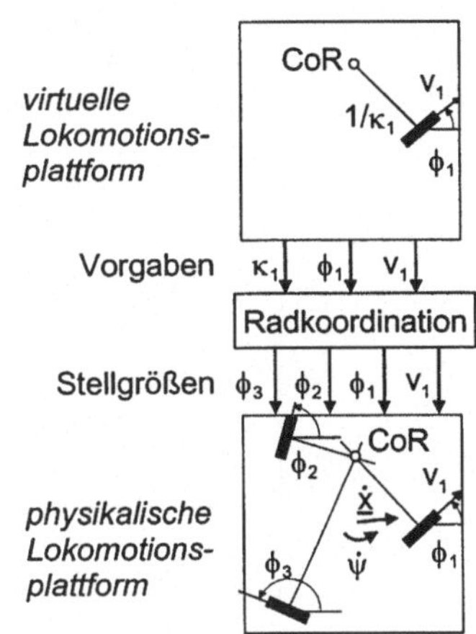

Abb. 6. Abstrakte Schnittstelle zur omnidirektionalen Lokomotionsplattform.

Pfadsuche Zur Generierung eines Weges wird ein graphentheoretischer Ansatz verwendet. Dabei wird ausgehend von einer geometrischen Liniensegmentkarte ein Graph erstellt, dessen Knoten und Kanten die Topologie der frei befahrbaren Fläche wiedergeben. Die Knotenattribute bestimmen die kartesische Position $[x_K, y_K]^T$ der anzufahrenden Knoten, während die gerichteten Kanten neben der Robotergeschwindigkeit die Orientierung des Roboters und die davon unabhängige Durchfahrtrichtung definieren. Die Topologieknoten werden so plaziert, daß ihre direkten Verbindungen auf der Grundlage der Liniensegmentkarte kollisionsfrei sind. Die für eine Wegsuche notwendige Gewichtung der gerichteten Kanten ergibt sich zunächst aus den euklidischen Abständen der Topologieknoten in der Karte. Zusätzlich werden in die Gewichtungen Informationen eingebracht, die den Aufwand beim Durchfahren der Verbindung wiedergeben, wie z.B. beim Passieren von eventuell zu öffnenden Türen. Dynamische Topologieveränderungen wie Trassenblockaden können ebenso eingebracht werden. In diesem Topologiegraphen wird der kürzeste Weg nach dem Dijkstra–Algorithmus ermittelt.

Da der ermittelte Pfad nur auf Basis der statischen Liniensegmentkarte kollisionsfrei ist, obliegt es den unterlagerten Komponenten, welche die Pfadknoten durch Bewegungsprimitive verbinden, die Kollisionsfreiheit während der Ausführung sicherzustellen.

Bewegungsprimitive Reaktive Manöver unter Nutzung aller drei Freiheitsgrade werden durch einen Fuzzy–Referenzmodell–Regler erreicht. Üblicherweise geben Fuzzy–Navigationssysteme in Abhängigkeit von der aktuellen Situation Vorgaben an die Lokomotionsplattform. In diesen Anweisungen muß der Anwender formulieren, *wie* ein gewisses Manöver ausgeführt werden soll. Dies ist im vorliegenden Fall eines omnidirektionalen Roboters sehr schwierig, bedeutet es doch die jeweils sinnvolle Plazierung des CoR. Darum wird hier eine linguistische Beschreibung der *gewünschten* kartesischen Roboterbewegung in der Form

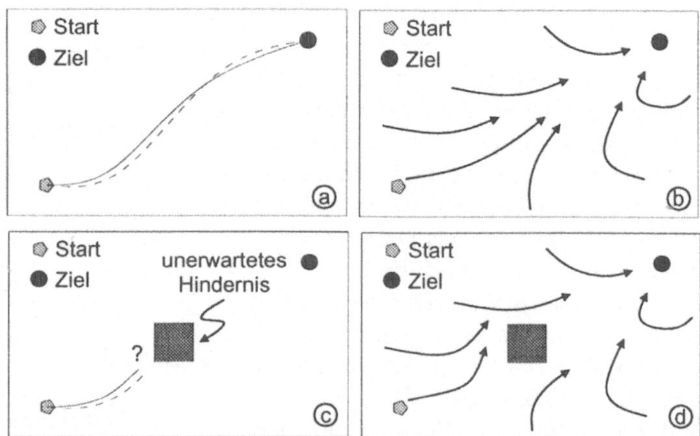

Abb. 7. Gegenüberstellung der *trajektorienbasierten* und *modellbasierten* Bewegungsprimitve a), c) ohne und b), d) mit unerwartetem Hindernis.

eines Fuzzy–Robotermodells [5] vorgenommen. Der Anwender formuliert also nur Anweisungen, *was* für ein Manöver in einer vorliegenden Situation angemessen ist, Abb. 7 b). Ein mit Hilfe der Lyapunov–Stabilitätstheorie entworfener nichtlinearer Regler generiert daraus Vorgaben an die Lokomotionsplattform, so daß der reale Roboter dem Referenzmodell stabil folgt [6].

Ein eigenständiges Fuzzy–System analysiert die sensorisch erfaßte Hinderniskonfiguration und generiert Bedingungen für den Bewegungsvektor des Roboters. Auf dieser Grundlage wird dann der Bewegungsvektor bestimmt, welcher möglichst nah am Referenzmodell liegt und alle Nebenbedingungen erfüllt, Abb. 7 d).

Bei den modellbasierten Bewegungsprimitiven ergibt sich die Bewegung des Roboterfahrzeugs implizit. Die daraus resultierenden Trajektorien sind also *nicht* a priori geschlossen geometrisch bestimmbar, was für einige Anwendungen (z.B. [7]) aus technologischer Sicht ungünstig ist. Abhilfe schaffen *trajektorienbasierte* Bewegungsprimitive, wobei hier kartesische und polare Splines 5. Ordnung verwendet werden. Ausgehend von der momentanen Lage des Roboters und der gewünschten Ziellage wird eine Referenztrajektorie geplant, der während der Ausführung mit einem beschränkten Regelfehler stabil gefolgt wird, Abb. 7 a). Offensichtlich ist dabei ein Nachteil, daß beim Auftreten von unerwarteten Hindernissen eine u.U. aufwendige Umplanung der Referenztrajektorie zum Ausweichen notwendig ist, Abb. 7 c).

Durch Nutzung der gleichen abstrakten Schnittstelle zur Lokomotionsplattform können die modell- und trajektorienbasierten Bewegungsprimitive kombiniert eingesetzt werden. Dies vereinigt eine einfache geometrisch geschlossene Beschreibungsform der Bewegung des Roboterfahrzeugs im hindernisfreien Fall mit der Eigenschaft, unerwarteten Hindernissen geschmeidig auszuweichen.

4 Absolute Lokalisierung

Eine wichtige Voraussetzung für den Einsatz eines in der Ebene beweglichen mobilen Roboters ist die ausreichend genaue Kenntnis seiner Lage $[x_I, y_I, \Psi_I]^T$ bezüglich eines Inertialkoordinatensystems. Hierzu schätzt das Verfahren zur absoluten Lokalisierung zunächst die initiale Roboterlage und frischt diese dann während der Fahrt rekursiv auf.

Der mobile Roboter befindet sich in einer Innenraumumgebung, welche neben beweglichen Objekten auch ortsfeste Strukturen wie Wände, Türen und Schränke enthält. Diese ortsfesten Strukturen dienen als natürliche Landmarken zur Bestimmung der Roboterlage und werden durch künstliche Landmarken ergänzt. Die Lagen der Landmarken werden entweder 1. einem Gebäudeplan entnommen, 2. manuell vermessen, oder 3. mit den Meßsystemen des Roboters während einer Erkundungsfahrt unter menschlicher Aufsicht einmal bestimmt. Neben den Lagen der Landmarken werden auch ihre Lageunsicherheiten als Attribute in eine Umweltkarte eingetragen.

Zur Lokalisierung anhand dieser Landmarken sind zwei Geometriesensortypen im Einsatz, welche sich durch einfachen Aufbau, niedrigen Preis und weite Verbreitung auszeichnen: 1. Ein rotierendes *Laser–Winkelmeßsystem*, welches

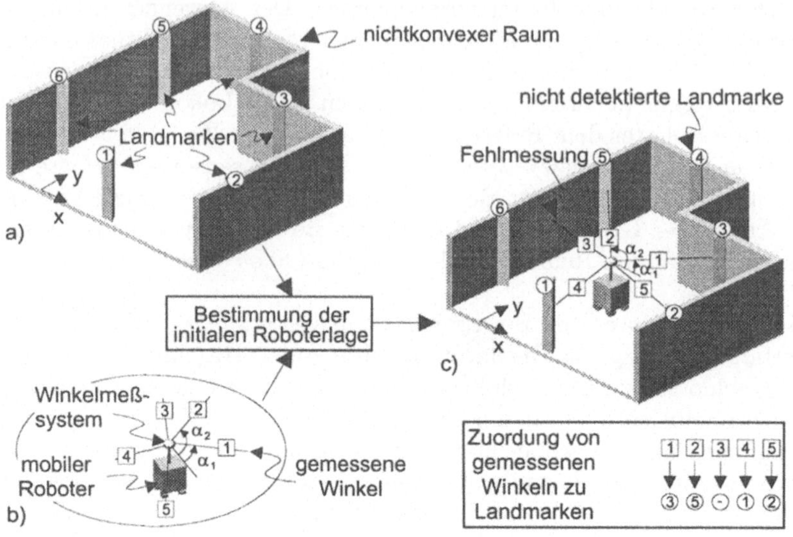

Abb. 8. Bestimmung der initialen Roboterlage mit Hilfe von Winkelmessungen zu bekannten Landmarken, wobei zunächst die Zuordnung von Winkelmessungen zu Landmarken unbekannt ist. a) Die Karte der bekannten vertikalen Landmarken. b) Der Satz der bezüglich des Roboterkoordinatensystems gemessenen Winkel. c) Erfolgte Zuordnung von Winkelmessungen zu Landmarken, wobei der Datensatz Fehlmessungen enthielt und einige Landmarken nicht detektiert wurden.

Winkel zu künstlichen Landmarken mißt, und 2. ein *Multisonarsystem*, welches Distanzen zu natürlichen Landmarken bestimmt. Die Daten beider Geometriesensoren sind durch korrelierte und systematische Fehler gestört, was im Rahmen der Sensordatenfusion berücksichtigt wird.

4.1 Bestimmung der initialen Roboterlage

Zur Initialisierung der Roboterlage wird ein einfaches, aber effizientes Verfahren verwendet, welches sich auf einem gemessenen Satz von $N \geq 3$ Winkeln zu bekannten, aber ununterscheidbaren Landmarken abstützt, Abb. 8. Das Initialisierungsverfahren toleriert 1. Verdeckungen durch unbekannte Objekte, 2. Fehlmessungen und kann 3. auch in nichtkonvexen Räumlichkeiten eingesetzt werden. Weiterhin wird Vorwissen über die Roboterlage genutzt, um den Initialisierungsprozeß zu beschleunigen. Den Kern des Verfahrens bildet eine geschlossene Lösung für die Bestimmung von Roboterlagewerten aus Winkelmessungen, Abschnitt 4.3. Hierbei wird auch überprüft, ob die berechneten Roboterlagewerte kompatibel mit den a priori angegebenen Fehlergrenzen für die Messungen und Landmarkenpositionen sind.

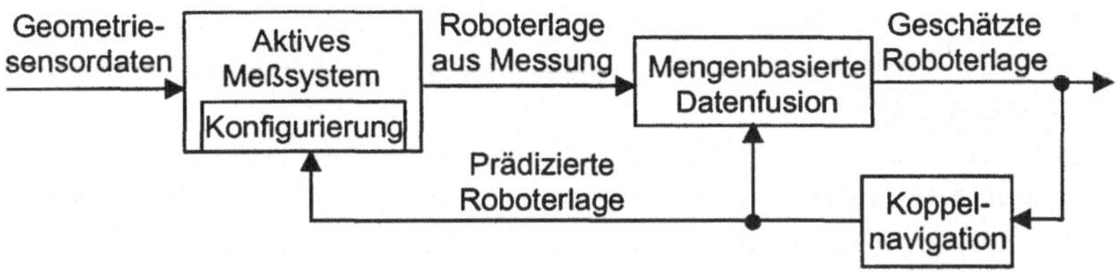

Abb. 9. Schema zur rekursiven Lokalisierung von ROMAN.

4.2 Rekursive Lokalisierung in schneller Fahrt

Während der Fahrt wird die Roboterlage durch ein odometriebasiertes Koppel-navigationsverfahren fortgeschrieben, welches die bei omnidirektionalen Robo-tern auftretenden systematischen Fehler bei der inkrementellen Lageschätzung berücksichtigt. Ein Koppelnavigationsystem leidet wegen des fehlenden Umwelt-bezuges unter der Akkumulation der Fehler, so daß die geschätzte Roboterlage laufend durch die Daten von Geometriesensoren aufgefrischt werden muß. Hierzu wird ein rekursives Verfahren zur Lageschätzung in schneller Fahrt verwendet, Abb. 9, welches jeweils die aktuelle Lageprädiktion zur optimalen Konfigurie-rung und Fokussierung des Sensorsystems in Abhängigkeit von der aktuellen Umgebung und den erwarteten Umweltmerkmalen nutzt. Dieses Vorgehen ver-mindert den Einfluß von Störungen und führt zu einer drastischen Erhöhung der Datenrate. Insbesondere für das in der Implementierung verwendete Ultraschall-sensorarray werden Abtastfrequenzen von 450 Hz pro Landmarke erreicht.

Alle auftretenden Unsicherheiten werden mit Verfahren der mengenbasierten Zustandsschätzung behandelt. Diese Vorgehensweise ermöglicht auch für den Fall systematischer oder stark korrelierter Fehlerquellen den Entwurf von nicht-linearen Schätzern geringer Komplexität und hoher Effizienz.

Ein dezentrales Schema wird zur Fusion der konkurrierenden Lageschätzun-gen der Sensoren im Multisensorsystem verwendet, welche Daten an verschiede-nen Orten mit unterschiedlichen Abtastraten asynchron zur Verfügung stellen. Dieses Fusionsschema unterstützt unmittelbar die verteilte Implementierung und ist beliebig skalierbar. Durch Verwendung identischer Fusionsprozesse für die ein-zelnen Sensoren wird die Komplexität des Multisensorsystems beherrschbar und das System wird tolerant gegenüber partiellen Ausfällen.

4.3 Effiziente Bestimmung von Geometriedaten

Geschlossene Lösungen wurden 1. für die Bestimmung der Lage eines Roboters aus *reinen* Winkelmessungen und 2. für die Bestimmung von Landmarkenposi-tionen aus *reinen* Distanzmessungen entwickelt. Beiden Lösungen ist gemeinsam, daß die Berücksichtigung der Unsicherheiten in den Landmarkenpositionen und in den Messungen *integraler Bestandteil* der Lösung ist und nicht wie üblich im nachhinein durchgeführt wird.

Winkelmeßsystem Das inhärent nichtlineare Problem der *Lagebestimmung* aus N Winkelmessungen zu bekannten Landmarken wird exakt in ein lineares Problem transformiert [8]. Dabei ergibt sich ein System von $N-1$ linearen Gleichungen für die *Position* und ein System von N linearen Gleichungen für die *Orientierung* des Roboters.

Distanzsensorarray Ein einfaches und effizientes Verfahren zur aktiven Lokalisierung von Umweltmerkmalen wird in [9] vorgestellt. Das Verfahren ermittelt kartesische Landmarkenpositionen aus Distanzmessungen, welche mit einem Distanzsensor–Array beliebiger Topologie gewonnen werden, dessen Elemente auf der Außenhaut des Roboters befestigt sind. Die Positionsschätzung führt zum einen auf genauere Ergebnisse als rasterbasierte oder angenäherte Verfahren und ist zum anderen weniger rechenintensiv als iterative Methoden.

5 Detektion von Hindernissen

Zur Detektion unerwarteter Hindernisse werden M Ultraschall–Sender und N Ultraschall–Empfänger verwendet. Wegen der Omnidirektionalität des verwendeten Roboters und seiner hohen Arbeitsgeschwindigkeit ist eine *schnelle* Detektion der den Roboter *umgebenden* nächsten Hindernisse und deren *präzise* Lokalisierung notwendig.

5.1 Methode des virtuellen Punktwandlers

In bisher veröffentlichten Arbeiten werden zur Hindernisdetektion üblicherweise mehrere Sensoren unabhängig voneinander betrieben. Die gegenseitige Beeinflussung wird entweder durch abwechselnden Betrieb oder durch nachträgliche Fehlerkorrektur beseitigt. Hier [10] wird nun ein Array von vielen Einzelsendern in einer Weise betrieben, daß das Schalldruckfeld eines einzigen virtuellen Punktwandlers *approximiert* wird, Abb. 10. Für ein Echo, welches an einem bestimmten Empfänger detektiert wurde, muß nicht entschieden werden, von welchem physikalischen Sendeelement der Sendeimpuls stammt. Damit wird ein paralleler Betrieb aller Sensoren in einem Array möglich.

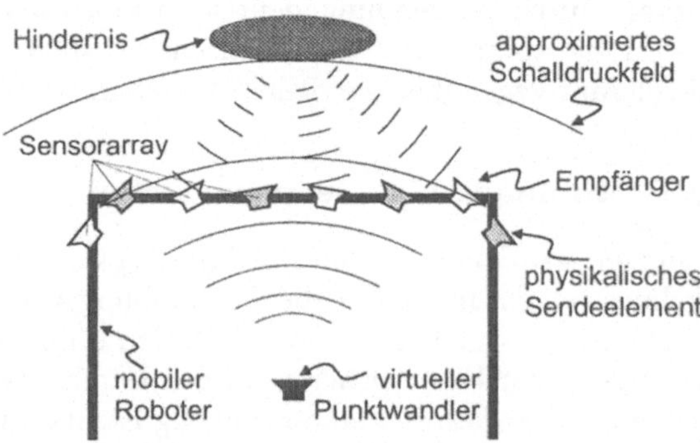

Abb. 10. Hindernisdetektion mit Hilfe eines virtuellen Punktwandlers.

5.2 Hindernisextraktion und Aufbau einer Hinderniskarte

Mit Hilfe der Methode des virtuellen Punktwandlers erhält man zu jedem Abtastschritt N Distanzmessungen, die Zuordnung der gemessenen Distanzen zu Hindernissen ist aber unbekannt. Weiterhin ist sowohl die Anzahl der Hindernisse als auch deren Typ unbekannt. Ein Verfahren zur schnellen Zuordnung unter diesen Bedingungen ist in [11] beschrieben. Nach der Zuordnung wird das in Abschnitt 4.3 angegebene Verfahren zur effizienten Berechnung der kartesischen Hindernispositionen verwendet. Die detektierten Hindernisse werden in eine lokale Hinderniskarte eingetragen und durch eine Liste repräsentiert.

6 Videobasierte Objekterkennung

Bei der Abarbeitung von Serviceaufgaben müssen bekannte und durch den Auftrag spezifizierte Objekte manipuliert werden. Um diese Objekte präzise zu greifen, muß ihre Position relativ zum Roboter mit der entsprechenden Genauigkeit bekannt sein. Die Bestimmung der Position mittels Ultraschallsensorik scheidet aus, da neben größeren Objekten wie Möbeln oder Türen auch Kleinteile erfaßt werden sollen, die nicht im Sichtbereich des Ultraschallringes liegen, sondern auf dem Boden, auf einem Tisch oder in einem Regal. Hierfür eignet sich eine Video–Kamera, wobei die Modellvorstellung für die Objekterkennung und –lokalisierung neben der Geometrie des Objektes und optischer Eigenschaften auch bekannte Einschränkungen der Objektlage einschließt. Beispielsweise ist bei einem Türblatt neben der Form auch die ungefähre Lage des Türrahmens in der Welt, die Griffhöhe und der Türanschlag bekannt, während der Öffnungswinkel des Flügels gegenüber dem Rahmen möglicherweise unbekannt ist bzw. von einem dynamischem Umgebungsmodell [12] nur grob vorgegeben wird. Die Vorinformationen werden verwendet, um ausgehend von einem Erkennungsauftrag z.B. des Manipulationsexperten die Kamera auf das gewünschte Objekt auszurichten, damit das Objekt sicher im Bildfeld der Kamera erscheint. Anschließend wird das Objekt quasikontinuierlich erkannt und lokalisiert, bis das Objekt gegriffen ist. Bei der Objekterkennung in Bildfolgen wird das Objekt zunächst in jedem Bild isoliert extrahiert; anschließend werden die Einzelergebnisse verknüpft.

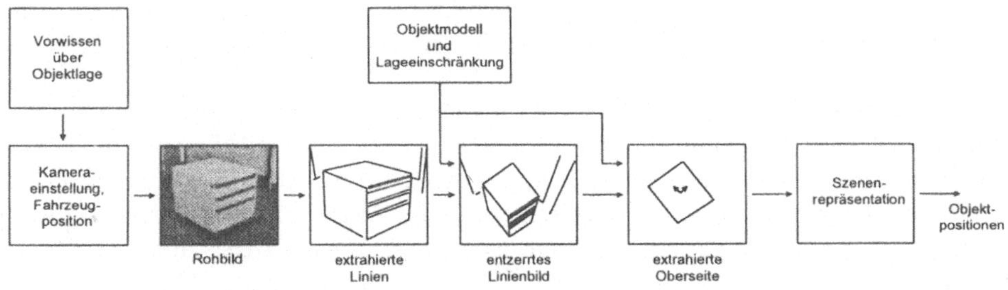

Abb. 11. Schritte der videobasierten Objekterkennung und –lokalisierung.

6.1 Objekterkennung in Einzelbildern

Für eine robuste und schnelle Objekterkennung werden zunächst Linien extrahiert, da alle betrachteten Objekte gerade Kanten aufweisen. Durch die perspektivische Abbildung ist im Allgemeinen ein 3D–Vergleich der Bildlinien mit den Modellinien notwendig [13], was aber zu einer hohen kombinatorischen Komplexität führt und deshalb bei üblicher Rechenleistung nicht mit der erforderlichen Geschwindigkeit durchgeführt werden kann. Daher wird in einem zweiten Schritt eine perspektivische Entzerrung der Linien durchgeführt, die z.B. im Falle des Rollcontainers, Abb. 13 e), zu einer flächen– und winkeltreuen Abbildung der Oberseite des Objekts führt. Diese kann nun im weiteren mittels einfacher 2D–Erkennung extrahiert werden und liefert direkt die Koordinaten des gesuchten Objektes relativ zum Serviceroboter. Das Verfahren ist also dann vorteilhaft anwendbar, wenn bestimmte Freiheitsgrade der gesuchten Objekte bekannt sind und eine entsprechende Bezugsebene zur Verfügung steht, die durch die perspektivische Transformation der 2D–Erkennung zugänglich gemacht werden kann. Diese Einschränkung ist in vielen praktisch relevanten Fällen gegeben und führt damit zu einer Objekterkennung für wichtige Basisfunktionen des Serviceroboters. Das entwickelte Verfahren ist robust durch die Verwendung von Vorwissen über die Lage der Objekte und schnell, da dieses Vorwissen bereits bei der Erkennung des Objekts eingesetzt wird und so die Komplexität dieser Aufgabe reduziert [14].

6.2 Hypothesenfortschreibung

Bei der quasikontinuierlichen Objekterkennung in Bildfolgen muß neben der Auswertung der Einzelbilder eine geeignete Verknüpfung aller Einzelergebnisse stattfinden. Hierzu werden in einem Hypothesenspeicher alle Erkennungsergebnisse gespeichert und neue Ergebnisse mit den bisherigen verglichen. Dadurch können Fehldetektionen erkannt werden und die Lageposition richtiger Ergebnisse durch Mittelung verbessert werden. Diese Hypothesenfortschreibung kann für verschiedene Objekttypen durchgeführt werden und stellt damit eine im Vergleich zum Rohbild abstrakte und mit Objektnamen versehene Beschreibung der Szene zur Verfügung, auf deren Basis der Bediener beispielsweise in Kommunikation mit dem Roboter ein bestimmtes Objekt auswählen kann.

7 Kommunikation zwischen Roboter und Mensch

Das Mensch–Roboter–Interface (MRI) bildet die Schnittstelle zwischen dem Roboter und dem Bediener sowie zu weiteren Personen im Arbeitsraum. Durch verschiedene Informationskanäle kommandiert, unterstützt und überwacht der Bediener den Serviceroboter. Zur Steigerung der Akzeptanz von Servicerobotern kommt es vor allem darauf an, Menschen auf ähnliche Weise mit dem Roboter kommunizieren zu lassen, wie sie es von einem Mensch–zu–Mensch–Dialog gewohnt sind. Dies hat zur Folge, daß hohe Anforderungen an die Mensch–Roboter–Kommunikation zu stellen sind [15].

Das zur Interaktion mit dem Serviceroboter ROMAN konzipierte multimodale MRI ermöglicht eine visuelle bildschirmgeführte Überwachung und Roboterunterstützung. Neben dem durch das Videobild der onboard–Kamera vermittelten Eindruck der realen Roboterumgebung dient ein animiertes dreidimensionales Modell, wie im vorliegenden Falle eines ganzen Stockwerkes, einer weitreichenden Verfolgung des Serviceroboters, Abb. 13 d). Informationen, welche zur gezielten Unterstützung während der Aufgabenausführung benötigt werden, resultieren aus dem Vergleich der in die Sichtweise der onboard–Kamera transformierten virtuellen Umgebung mit dem Videobild. Zur Eingabe der Bedienerkommandos wird das in diesem Berichtsband näher beschriebene Verfahren zum Verstehen natürlicher, gesprochener Sprache verwendet [16]. Für eine direkte Vorgabe der Roboterbewegungen durch den Bediener dient die SPACE MOUSE mit ihren 6 Freiheitsgraden und ein Kraftpedal für die Steuerung des eigentlichen Greifvorganges. Die Kommentierung der Auftragsausführung erfolgt über eine Sprachausgabe an den Bediener oder an Personen im Arbeitsraum.

8   Implementierungsdetails

Die beschriebenen Schlüsselkomponenten wurden in dem Demonstrator RO-MAN prototypisch implementiert und zu einem Gesamtsystem integriert. Im folgenden sind einige Details zur Implementierung des mobilen Roboters RO-MAN zusammengefaßt. ROMAN ist 0.63 m breit, 0.64 m tief und 1.8 m hoch und erreicht bei einem Gesamtgewicht von 250 kg eine maximale Geschwindigkeit von 2 m/s.

8.1   Systemarchitektur

Die Systemarchitektur von ROMAN spiegelt den Gedanken eines aufgabenorientierten leicht erweiterbaren Verbundes aus Standard–Industrierechnern wieder. Dieser Verbund untergliedert sich in eine stationäre und mobile Rechnergruppe. Die stationäre Gruppe (Abb. 12 links), welche der videobasierten Objekterkennung (Abschnitt 6) und der Mensch–Roboter–Kommunikation zwischen dem Bediener und ROMAN (Abschnitt 7) dient, ist mit der mobilen Gruppe (Abb. 12 rechts) mittels eines drahtlosen Funkethernets und einer Videofunkübertragungsstrecke gekoppelt. Durch die Trennung der Rechnergruppen wird die Autonomie der sicherheitskritischen Basisfunktionalitäten von RO-MAN bei Experimenten gewährleistet. Die mobile Rechnergruppe besteht aus einem enggekoppelten heterogenen Mehrrechnernetz. Für die in Abschnitt 3 aufgeführte Algorithmik der Bewegungssteuerung stehen für die Aufgaben der Bewegungsausführung je ein MC 68040 basierter Rechner zur Verfügung. Der Manipulationsrechner kommuniziert dabei mit dem Steuerungsrechner des Manipulators über eine CAN–Buskopplung, während der Lokomotionsrechner eine Signalprozessor–basierte Mehrachsreglerkarte über die in Abschnitt 3.2 beschriebene abstrakte Schnittstelle ansteuert. Für die überlagerte Algorithmik der Bewegungsplanung steht ein Sparc 2 Rechner zur Verfügung. Zur lokalen echtzeitfähigen Auswertung der Basissensorik (vgl. Abschnitt 4 und 5) wird ein aus INMOS T805 bestehendes verteiltes Transputernetzwerk verwendet. Die Kommunikation mit den Rechnern der Bewegungssteuerung erfolgt über eine als Blackboard–Server dienende Transputer–VMEbus–Brücke, die als systemweite geteilte Speicherresource für die mobile Rechnergruppe dient. Während das Transputernetzwerk als Verbund betriebssystemloser Prozessoren arbeitet, werden die Rechner der Bewegungssteuerung unter dem echtzeitfähigen Unix–Derivat LynxOS betrieben. Das Programmier–Paradigma des Multithreadings gewährleistet dabei eine hohe Reaktivität der echtzeitkritischen Algorithmen. Die gute Wartbarkeit und ein geringer Einarbeitungsaufwand trägt dem Gedanken Rechnung, ROMAN als universellen Demonstrator in verschiedensten Bereichen und Aufgaben der Servicerobotik einzusetzen.

8.2 Lokomotionsplattform

Die Mechanik der Lokomotionsplattform besteht aus drei voneinander unabhängig um $360°$ lenkbaren Radsätzen. Einer dieser Radsätze ist mit einem Motor zum Vortrieb des Roboters ausgestattet. Die aus dieser speziellen Kinematik resultierende Beweglichkeit von ROMAN erinnert an ein Luftkissenfahrzeug und ist mit Fahrzeugen vergleichbar, welche MECANUM–Räder verwenden. Der Einsatz von hartgummibeschichteten Standard–Rädern mit 20 cm Durchmesser erlaubt ROMAN allerdings eine vibrationsarme Fortbewegung auf unterschiedlichen Bodenbelägen bis hin zu Teppichböden.

Um einen sinnvollen Fahrbetrieb ohne seitlichen Schlupf der Räder zu ermöglichen, muß die Existenz eines momentanen Fahrzeugdrehpunkts (Center of Rotation) gewährleistet sein. Hierzu müssen die Lenkwinkel der Radsätze so koordiniert werden, daß sich ihre Normalachsen im CoR schneiden. Die Koordination der Lenkwinkel ϕ_i wird durch eine geometrisch–prädiktive Kaskadenregelung erreicht. Während in der inneren Kaskade Standard–Regler für die Lenkmotore

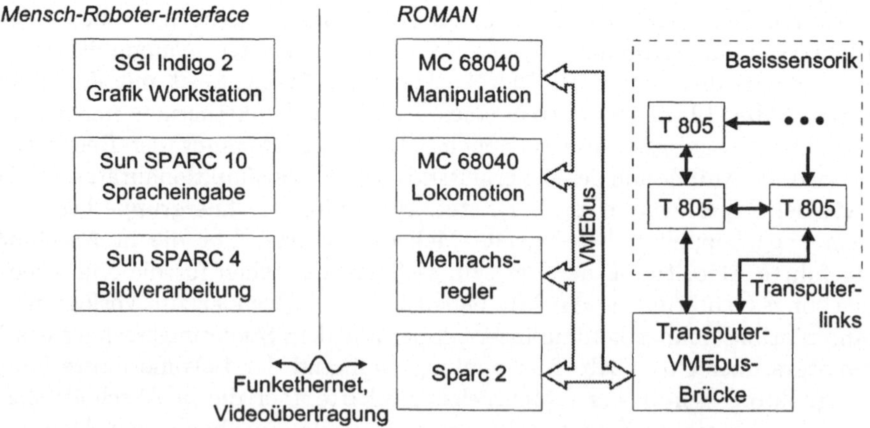

Abb. 12. Systemarchitektur des mobilen Serviceroboters ROMAN.

eingesetzt werden, gewährleistet eine Verhältnisregelung in der äußeren Kaskade die Existenz des momentanen Drehpunkts. Durch eine Prädikton der Lage des CoR wird die äußere Kaskade an die Dynamik der inneren Kaskade angepaßt.

8.3 Manipulationseinheit

Die Manipulationseinheit von ROMAN besteht aus dem Mehrgelenkmanipulator MANUS, dessen Zwei–Finger–Greifer sowie einer Hoch/Tief–Linearachse. Die gesamte Einheit ist an einer Ecke von ROMAN angebracht.

MANUS–Manipulator Der 17 kg leichte MANUS–Manipulator der Firma EXACT Dynamics erreicht mit seinen 6 Achsen eine Reichweite von 800 mm und eine Wiederholgenauigkeit von ca. $1-5$ mm. Im gestreckten Zustand kann der Arm mit einer Nutzlast von max. 1.5 kg belastet werden. Der durch eine Zahnriemenübertragung realisierte Antrieb der einzelnen Gelenke ermöglicht ein freies Rotieren und garantiert somit eine maximale Beweglichkeit im gesamten Arbeitsraum. Angesteuert wird der Manipulator über einen CAN–Bus. Die Regelungsstruktur besteht aus einem Jacobi–Regler mit Vorsteuerung und unterlagerten Geschwindigkeitsservos. Als Bezugskoordinatensysteme dienen für die kartesische Regelung das Fußpunktkoordinatensystem des Manipulators, das Weltkoordinatensystem oder ein durch Videosensorik bereitgestelltes relatives Objektkoordinatensystem. Ein Kollisionsschutz verhindert interne genauso wie externe Kollisionen des Manipulators.

Zwei–Finger–Greifer Der verwendete Zwei–Finger–Greifer ist eine modifizierte Version des Standard–MANUS–Greifers mit einer Öffnungsweite von 90 mm. Neben einer Regelung für die Öffnungsweite ist zusätzlich eine Kraftsteuerung realisiert. Mit Hilfe einfacher taktiler Sensoren an den beiden Fingern und der zum Kraftaufbau vorhandenen Feder läßt sich eine bis zu 15 N große definierte Greifkraft aufbauen.

Hoch/Tief–Linearachse Die Hoch/Tief–Linearachse dient der vertikalen Erweiterung des Manipulatorarbeitsraums. Mit dem Verfahrweg von 475 mm wird für die Arbeitsraumhöhe ein Bereich von $0-1850$ mm erreicht.

8.4 Multisensorsystem

Koppelnavigation Zur Bestimmung der Lageänderung des Roboters stehen ein Odometriesystem und ein Kreisel zur Verfügung, welche zur Koppelnavigation verwendet werden. Die Omnidirektionalität des Roboters erschwert den Einsatz von separaten Meßrädern, weshalb das Odometriesystem ausschließlich auf den Tragrädern beruht. Dabei werden die zurückgelegten Wege und Lenkwinkel aller drei Räder gemessen und verarbeitet.

Winkelmeßsystem Zur hochgenauen absoluten Lokalisierung ist ROMAN mit einem laserbasierten Winkelmeßsystem ausgestattet, welches die Winkel zu künstlichen vertikalen Landmarken bestimmt. Ein kontinuierlich ausgesendeter, augensicherer Laserstrahl wird von einem schnell rotierenden Umlenkspiegel abgelenkt und tastet die Umgebung in einer horizontalen Ebene ab. Der von einer Landmarke reflektierte Strahl wird von einer Empfangsdiode detektiert.

Als Landmarken werden vom Winkelmeßsystem nicht unterscheidbare retro–reflektierende Streifen von 4 cm Breite verwendet. Der Umlenkspiegel rotiert mit 20 Umdrehungen pro Sekunde. Die absolute Meßgenauigkeit des Systems beträgt etwa 0.02^o bei einer Reichweite von 20 m. Ein lokaler Transputer sorgt für die vor Ort benötigte Rechenleistung. Zur Verringerung von Verdeckungen ist das System auf einer Höhe von 1.8 m montiert.

Distanzsensorarray ROMAN ist mit einem Array von akustischen Signalquellen und Empfängern versehen, welche auf einer Höhe von 50 cm auf der Außenhaut des Roboters befestigt sind [17]. Dieses Multisonarsystem beruht auf dem Puls–Echo–Verfahren und besteht aus jeweils 24 identischen Quellen und Empfängern mit einer Trägerfrequnz von 40 kHz. Die minimale Reichweite, die sogenannte Totzone, beträgt 25 cm; die maximale Reichweite beträgt je nach Objekttyp etwa 3 – 4 m. Jede Signalquelle ist mit einer Ansteuerschaltung zur Pulserzeugung versehen; jeder Empfänger ist mit einem analogen Echodetektor verbunden. Nachgeschaltete digitale Zähler, welche in den Adressraum von vier T805–Transputern eingeblendet sind, bestimmen die einzelnen Pulslaufzeiten. Die zu einem lokalen Netzwerk verschalteten Transputer übernehmen die Konfigurierung des Systems, die Bestimmung der Sendezeitpunkte und die Verarbeitung der rohen Pulslaufzeiten.

Videosensor Als Videosensor wird eine Standard–NTSC–CCD–Kamera mit einer Auflösung von 512 x 768 Pixeln bei einer Bildrate von 30 Hz eingesetzt. Die Kamera ist auf einem Neigekopf befestigt, um sowohl Objekte auf dem Boden als auch in Regalen erfassen zu können. Die Auswertung des Videosignals erfolgt auf einer stationären Workstation, vgl. Abschnitt 8.1, im 100 ms Takt, was zu einer quasi–kontinuierlichen Regelung der Endeffektorbahn ausreicht. Ein robustes Ergebnis entsteht durch Fusion mehrerer Bilder etwa 1 sec nach Beginn der Bildauswertung.

9 Ein typisches Szenario

Abbildung 13 zeigt in einer Szenenfolge den Ablauf einer typischen Serviceoperation. Der Auftrag wird in natürlicher Sprache formuliert und lautet: „Hole den Behälter aus dem Rollcontainer im Großlabor", Abb. 13 a). Dieser Auftrag ist eindeutig und vollständig, d.h. er spezifiziert die Aktion, hier also das Holen, das Objekt selbst, den Raum, in dem sich das Objekt befindet und als weitere Einengung des Suchbereichs die Angabe des Rollcontainers. Gemäß diesen Informationen fährt ROMAN auf einem automatisch generierten Pfad, gestützt auf seine kontinuierliche Selbstlokalisierung, in den angegebenen Raum. Bei dieser Operation wird der Freiraum durch die Ultraschallsensorik ständig überwacht, um unerwartete Hindernisse wie Personen zu detektieren und ihnen gegebenenfalls auszuweichen, Abb. 13 b), oder mittels Sprachausgabe die Person anzusprechen und um Freigabe des blockierten Weges zu bitten. Vor der Durchfahrt durch Türen wird der aktuelle Öffnungszustand der Tür mittels Videosenorik bestimmt [12] und, abhängig vom Ergebnis, die Türe geöffnet, Abb. 13 c), und der Weg fortgesetzt. Der Anwender kann die Bewegung von ROMAN ständig am MRI verfolgen und durch verbale Kommandos in den Ablauf eingreifen, z.B.

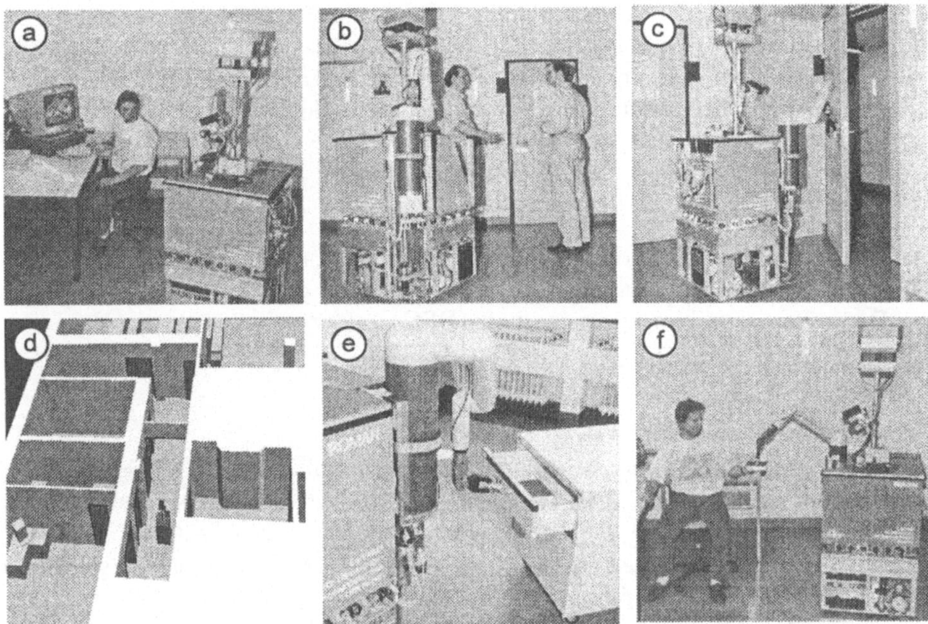

Abb. 13. a) MRI mit Bediener. b) Ausweichmanöver. c) Öffnen einer Türe.
d) ROMAN im virtuellen Arbeitsraum. e) Öffnen der Schublade und
Entnehmen des Behälters. f) Übergabe an Bediener.

ROMAN schnell anhalten, Abb. 13 d). Im Zielraum fährt ROMAN zum angegebenen Rollcontainer, dessen Position mittels Videosensorik bestimmt wird, um
die Schublade zu öffnen. Bei dieser Operation wird ROMAN gleichzeitig in allen 10 Freiheitsgraden der Lokomotion und Manipulation gesteuert, wobei der
Erhalt einer größtmöglichen Bewegungsfreiheit angestrebt wird und Hindernisse
im Arbeitsraum berücksichtigt werden. Der Behälter wird videobasiert lokalisiert und daraufhin entnommen, Abb. 13 e). Anschließend fährt ROMAN mit
dem Behälter zurück und übergibt ihn dem Bediener, Abb. 13 f).

10 Schlußfolgerungen

Dieser Beitrag beschreibt Schlüsselkomponenten für mobile Serviceroboter unter besonderer Berücksichtigung der koordinierten Lokomotion und Manipulation, der sensorischen Unterstützung von Bewegungs- und Greifvorgängen, der
Mensch–Roboter–Interaktion und der Integration in ein funktionsfähiges Gesamtsystem. Hierzu mußten richtungsweisende, über den aktuellen Stand der
Technik hinausgehende Konzepte und Verfahren entwickelt werden, die mit dem
Demonstrator ROMAN im Rahmen typischer Serviceszenarien und –aufgaben
experimentell validiert wurden. Diese Schlüsselkomponenten sind erprobte Bausteine, aus denen spezialisierte und kostenoptimierte Serviceroboter für verschie-
denste zukünftige Anwendungen konfigurierbar sind.

Die Autoren sind der Überzeugung, daß mit der Entwicklung von ROMAN die Zukunft der Servicerobotertechnik einen Schritt nähergerückt ist und die mit diesem System gewonnenen theoretischen und praktischen Erfahrungen bei kommenden Serienprodukten ihren Niederschlag finden werden.

Danksagung

Das Projekt ROMAN wird im Rahmen des Sonderforschungsbereichs *Informationsverarbeitung in autonomen, mobilen Handhabungssystemen* (SFB 331) von der Deutschen Forschungsgemeinschaft (DFG) gefördert.

Literatur

1. R. D. Schraft, "Vom Industrieroboter zum Serviceroboter — Stand der Technik, Chancen und Grenzen," *VDI Berichte 1094: Intelligente Steuerung und Regelung von Robotern*, pp. 1–19, 1993.

2. O. Khatib, "Sensor-based control of robots," in *Proceedings of the International Conference on Recent Advances in Mechatronics*, (Istanbul, Turkey), pp. 1120–1125, 1995.

3. M. Seidl und C. Fischer, "Feed-forward locomotion control strategy for a manipulator mounted on a mobile platform," in *Proceedings of the Teleman-HCM European Union Undergraduate Students Telerobotics Congress*, (Noordwijkerhout, The Netherlands), pp. 101–106, 1995.

4. C. Fischer, M. Buss, und G. Schmidt, "Soft control of an effector path for a mobile manipulator," in *Proceedings of the International Symposium on Robotics and Manufacturing (ISRAM)*, (Montpellier, France), 1996.

5. U. D. Hanebeck und G. Schmidt, "Genetic optimization of fuzzy networks," *Journal of Fuzzy Sets and Systems, Special Issue on Neuro–Fuzzy Techniques and Applications*, vol. 79, pp. 59–68, 1996.

6. S. Maier und U. D. Hanebeck, "Fuzzy Guidance of Omnidirectional Mobile Robots Including Sensor–Based Obstacle Avoidance," in *Proceedings of the TELEMAN Student Research Projects Congress, July, Noordwijkerhout, The Netherlands*, pp. 95–100, 1995.

7. C. Hofner und G. Schmidt, "Path Planning and Guidance Techniques for an Autonomous Mobile Cleaning Robot," in *Intelligent Robots and Systems 1994 (IROS'94)* (V. Graefe, ed.), pp. 241–257, Amsterdam: Elsevier Science, 1995.

8. U. D. Hanebeck und G. Schmidt, "Set–theoretic Localization of Fast Mobile Robots Using an Angle Measurement Technique," in *Proceedings of the 1996 IEEE International Conference on Robotics and Automation, Minneapolis, Minnesota*, vol. 2, pp. 1387–1394, 1996.

9. U. D. Hanebeck und G. Schmidt, "Closed–Form Elliptic Location with an arbitrary Array Topology," in *Proceedings of the 1996 IEEE International Conference on Acoustics, Speech, and Signal Processing, Atlanta, Georgia, 7.-10. Mai*, vol. 6, pp. 3070–3073, 1996.

10. U. D. Hanebeck und G. Schmidt, "A New High Performance Multisonar System for Fast Mobile Robots," in *Proc. of the 1994 IEEE/RSJ/GI Int. Conf. on Intelligent Robots and Systems, Munich, Germany*, pp. 1853–1860, 1994.

11. U. D. Hanebeck und G. Schmidt, "Schnelle Objektdetektion mit Ultraschallsensor-Arrays," in *Autonome Mobile Systeme 1995, (11. Fachgespräch, 30. Nov. – 1. Dez. 1995, Karlsruhe)* (R. Dillmann, U. Rembold, und T. Lüth, Hrsg.), pp. 162–171, Springer, 1995.

12. N. O. Stöffler, A. Hauck, und G. Färber, "Ein geometrisch-symbolisches Umgebungsmodell zur Unterstützung verschiedener Perzeptionsaufgaben autonomer, mobiler Systeme," in *Tagungsband zum 12. Fachgespäch Autonome Mobile Systeme 14. – 15. Oktober* (G. Schmidt und F. Freyberger, Hrsg.), München, Germany: Springer, 1996.

13. S. Lanser und C. Zierl, "MORAL: Ein System zur videobasierten Objekterkennung im Kontext autonomer, mobiler Systeme," in *Tagungsband zum 12. Fachgespäch Autonome Mobile Systeme 14. – 15. Oktober* (G. Schmidt und F. Freyberger, Hrsg.), München, Germany: Springer, 1996.

14. E. Ettelt und G. Schmidt, "Vision Based Guidance and Control of a Mobile Forklift Robot," in *Proceedings of International Conference on Recent Advances in Mechatronics, ICRAM'95, August 14-16, Istanbul, Turkey*, pp. 180–186, 1995.

15. C. Fischer *et al.*, "Kommandierung eines Serviceroboters auf der Basis natürlicher, gesprochener Sprache," in *Tagungsband zum 12. Fachgespäch Autonome Mobile Systeme, 14. – 15. Oktober* (G. Schmidt und F. Freyberger, Hrsg.), München, Germany: Springer, 1996.

16. C. Fischer, M. Buss, und G. Schmidt, "Hierarchical supervisory control of service robot using human-robot-interface," in *Proceedings of the International Conference on Intelligent Robots and Systems (IROS), 4.-8. November*, (Osaka, Japan), 1996.

17. U. D. Hanebeck und G. Schmidt, "A New High Performance Multisonar System for Fast Mobile Robot Applications," in *Intelligent Robots and Systems 1994 (IROS'94)* (V. Graefe, ed.), pp. 1–14, Amsterdam: Elsevier Science, 1995.

Flexible Produktionsstrukturen für den Einsatz autonomer Systeme

D. Ansorge *, D. Glüer **, C. Hofner **

Technische Universität München
* Institut für Werkzeugmaschinen und Betriebswissenschaften
Karl-Hammerschmidt-Straße 39, D-85609 Aschheim
e-mail: as@iwb.mw.tu-muenchen.de

** Lehrstuhl für Steuerungs- und Regelungstechnik
Arcisstraße 21, D-80290 München
e-mail: {glueer,hofner}@lsr.e-technik.tu-muenchen.de

Kurzfassung. Ständig wandelnde Märkte fordern neue flexible Produktionsstrukturen. Der Einsatz von autonomen Systemen mit lokaler Planungs- und Ausführungsintelligenz ermöglicht in automatisierten flexiblen Produktionsumgebungen eine Optimierung der Aufgabenbearbeitung. Für eine zielorientierte Gesamtplanung ist eine Integration der lokalen Intelligenz in eine übergeordnete Aufgabenplanung notwendig. Die dazu eingesetzte Koordinierungsinstanz verteilt mittels eines neu entwickelten Verhandlungsmechanismus die Aufgaben an die einzelnen Systeme. Durch eine geeignete Grobplanung der Koordinierungsinstanz und die Verhandlungsfähigkeit wird den autonomen Systemen größtmöglicher Planungs- und Entscheidungsfreiraum gewährt. Die Leistungsfähigkeit dieses Konzeptes wurde durch die Entwicklung autonomer Systeme und ihrer Integration in eine Produktionsumgebung in einem Beispielszenario evaluiert und demonstriert.

1 Einleitung

Produktionsbetriebe sehen sich aufgrund der Sättigungserscheinungen der Märkte und der steigenden Innovationsdynamik einer stark wandelnden Marktsituation ausgesetzt. Diese Änderungen des Umfeldes erschweren es Unternehmen, mit den Methoden Kostenführerschaft, Produktdifferenzierung und Marktnischenkonzentration Marktvorteile zu erringen. Deshalb sind neue organisatorische und technische Lösungen zu entwickeln, die eine flexible und schnelle, am Gesamtoptimum orientierte Reaktion des Unternehmens ermöglichen [11].

Es entstehen Lösungsansätze, die starre hierachische und zentralistische Strukturen aufgeben und die Potentiale von dezentralen, verteilten Strukturen nutzen. Gerade in der Produktion erweisen sich unflexible Anlagen und zentralistische Produktionsplanungssysteme als Hemmnis, die konkurrierenden Vorgaben aus hohem Kosten-, Termin-, Qualitäts- und Innovationsdruck zu vereinen. In diesem Beitrag wird die Integration der im Rahmen des Sonderforschungsbereiches *Informationsverarbeitung in autonomen, mobilen Handhabungssystemen* (SFB 331) entwickelten Systeme in eine neu strukturierte Produktion vorgestellt und beispielhaft ihr Zusammenwirken demonstriert.

2 Zukunftsweisende Produktionsstrukturen

2.1 Situation der flexiblen Produktion

Schon heute wird durch den Einsatz flexibler Fertigungs- und Montagesysteme eine hohe Produktivität in dynamischen Produktionsumgebungen erreicht. Als autonom werden diese Systeme bezeichnet, wenn sie durch geeignete Situationserfassungs-, Planungs- und Steuerungskomponenten in der Lage sind, eigenständig Abläufe zu optimieren und auf aufgetretene Störungen mit geeigneten Maßnahmen zu reagieren [9].

In vielen Fällen werden diese Fähigkeiten nicht in vollem Umfang genutzt. Dies liegt größtenteils an den Defiziten der Integration der Systeme in die gesamte Produktion. Insbesondere durch die Einbindung in zentrale, übergeordnete Planungsstrukturen wird die Leistungsfähigkeit autonomer Systeme wenig genutzt. Bei diesen konventionellen Ansätzen wird im allgemeinen vom Einsatz nichtautonomer Produktionssysteme ausgegangen. Diese erhalten ihre Anweisungen von einem zentralen Leitsystem, das seine Planungsdaten in imperative Anordnungen umsetzt. Störungsbedingte, aber auch gewollte Veränderungen im Fertigungsablauf, wie z.B. Änderungen der Auftragsreihenfolge, müssen durch eine Um- bzw. Neuplanung des zentralen Planes abgeglichen werden. Infolge der Komplexität des zentralen Planes ist es oft nicht möglich, einen geänderten oder neuen Plan in beschränkter Zeit zu erstellen und nach logistischen Kenngrößen zu optimieren.

Dagegen ermöglichen verschiedene dezentrale Ansätze ein Maximum an verteilter Aufgabenplanung und somit auch die Kooperation von autonomen Systemen. Bei diesen Ansätzen wird auf eine zentrale Instanz verzichtet und die Planung der Aufgaben auf die Produktionssysteme verteilt [1], [2], [5], [8] und [13]. Dadurch können lokale Informationen schnell und unmittelbar bei der Planung berücksichtigt werden. Durch die informationstechnische Vernetzung der lokalen Einheiten wird eine hohe Flexibilität bei der Aufgabenplanung und -ausführung erreicht. Ein wesentlicher Nachteil ist jedoch, daß das Planungsergebnis mangels der Durchsetzung übergeordneter Zielvorgaben oftmals nicht die gewünschte Qualität hinsichtlich logistischer Zielgrößen, wie z.B. Termintreue und Durchlaufzeit, erreicht.

2.2 Autonomie und Kooperation als Lösungsansatz für flexible Produktionsstrukturen

In einer dynamischen Umgebung ist es erforderlich, flexible Systeme einzusetzen. Die Fähigkeit, Aufgaben zu planen und auf Störungen angemessen zu reagieren, ist dabei eine wesentliche Voraussetzung für deren Aufbau, damit sie im Sinne der Autonomie selbständig und aufgabenorientiert arbeiten können.

Oftmals können Störungen in der Produktion nicht durch einzelne Systeme behoben werden. In solchen Fällen muß auf die Unterstützung von außen, d.h. auf andere Systeme, zugegriffen werden. Dafür ist zum einen die gemeinsame Planung von Aufgaben, zum anderen die Interaktion zwischen verschiedenen Systemen erforderlich. Ein solch temporärer Zusammenschluß von mehreren autonomen Systemen zur Lösung spezieller Aufgaben wird als Kooperation bezeichnet.

Die Entwicklungen im Bereich autonomer, *mobiler* Systeme zeigen bereits die Vorteile der Autonomie- und Kooperationsfähigkeit bei der Aufgabenbearbeitung. Autonome, mobile

Systeme lassen sich vielerorts einsetzen, um wirkungsvoll und schnell zur Behebung von Störungen beizutragen. Geeignete Sensoren und Aktoren sowie eine lokale intelligente Planung und Ausführungssteuerung ermöglichen unter Berücksichtigung lokaler Umgebungsinformationen eine selbständige Aufgabenbearbeitung und Interaktionsfähigkeit.

Somit gewinnen autonome, mobile Systeme für materialflußtechnische Aufgaben in der Produktion an Bedeutung. Sie nehmen damit nicht nur eine Schlüsselfunktion für diese Aufgaben in einer dynamisch veränderlichen Umgebung ein, sondern unterstützen auch die Kooperation zwischen Fertigungs- und Montagesystemen.

2.3 Integration autonomer Systeme in eine Gesamtstruktur

In einer automatisierten flexiblen Produktionsumgebung sollen sowohl autonome Fertigungs- und Montagesysteme als auch autonome mobile Systeme eingesetzt werden. Sie sind durch ihre intelligente selbständige Aufgabenplanung und -Ausführung charakterisiert. Diese Systeme werden im weiteren als autonome Einheiten bezeichnet.

Ihr Einsatz erfordert insbesondere die Integration ihrer lokalen Planungsfähigkeiten in eine übergeordnete Aufgabenplanung. Nur dadurch kann über die lokale Bearbeitung von Aufgaben hinaus zusätzlich ein Optimum in der Auftragsbearbeitung hinsichtlich übergreifender logistischer Ziele erreicht werden. Diese Ziele müssen unterschiedlich gewichtbar sein, was zum einen eine hohe Termintreue gegenüber Kunden, zum anderen eine niedrige Durchlaufzeit bei hoher Auslastung der Produktionsmittel bedeuten kann. Um eine einheitliche Zielorientierung zu ermöglichen, muß deshalb eine Koordinierungsinstanz eingesetzt werden. In Abb. 1 ist die beschriebene Struktur mit verschiedenen autonomen Systemen, der Koordinierungsinstanz und einer verteilten Wissensbasis dargestellt.

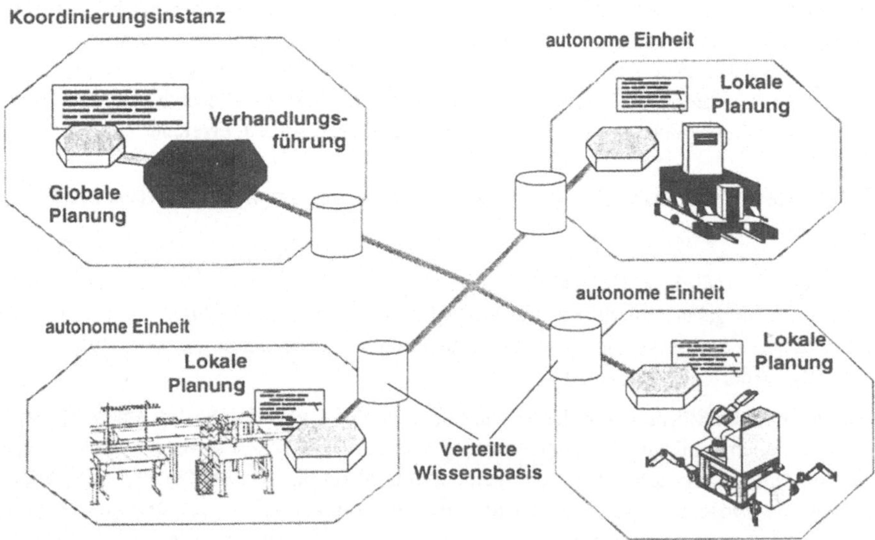

Abb. 1 Gesamtstruktur

Durch die Vereinheitlichung der Kommunikationsschnittstellen zwischen den autonomen Einheiten und der Koordinierungsinstanz, wird die Voraussetzung für die Verteilung und gemeinsame Planung von Aufgaben geschaffen. Die verteilte Wissensbasis organisiert dabei den Informationsaustausch und stellt systemübergreifende Dienste zur Verfügung [10].

2.4 Konzept der verhandlungsbasierten Koordinierung der Produktion

Aufbauend auf den beschriebenen zentralen und dezentralen Ansätzen zur Produktionsplanung und den Anforderungen an eine zukünftige Produktionsstruktur, wurde im SFB 331 ein Konzept einer verhandlungsbasierten Produktionskoordinierung entwickelt. Dieses verbindet die Vorteile einer verteilten dezentralen Planung und der zielorientierten Aufgabenerfüllung der zentralen Ansätze, bei maximaler Nutzung der lokalen Fähigkeiten autonomer Einheiten.

Die Verteilung der Aufgaben erfolgt mittels Verhandlungen, da dieses Prinzip gerade für die verteilte Lösung von Problemstellungen geeignet ist [9]. So können die autonomen Einheiten je nach ihrer lokalen Situation Aufträge von der Koordinierungsinstanz annehmen oder ablehnen. Die Koordinierungsinstanz übernimmt bei den Verhandlungen die Verhandlungsführung und berücksichtigt dabei die übergeordneten Zielvorgaben.

Bei der Verhandlung einer Aufgabe durch die Koordinierungsinstanz werden zur Reduzierung des Kommunikationsaufwandes nur die notwendigsten Angaben an die autonomen Einheiten übermittelt. Alle weiteren zu einer Aufgabe gehörenden Informationen stehen den autonomen Einheiten direkt zur Verfügung. Im Rahmen der Verhandlungen kann eine autonome Einheit prüfen, ob eine Aufgabe eingeplant werden kann und gegebenenfalls veränderte Planungsbedingungen vorschlagen. In bestimmten Situationen, wie z.B. Störungen oder lokalen Engpässen, können die autonomen Einheiten durch lokale Verhandlungen mit anderen Einheiten dezentral Probleme beheben, indem sie z.B. betroffene Aufträge selbst umverteilen.

Da die Einplanbarkeit einer Aufgabe dezentral geprüft wird, benötigt die Koordinierungsinstanz zur groben Planung aller Aufgaben wesentlich weniger Daten als zentralistisch organisierte Leitsysteme. Folglich ist eine schnelle Aktualisierung der globalen Planung an veränderte Umgebungsbedingungen möglich. Erfüllt die Gesamtheit der lokalen Pläne nicht mehr die vorgegebenen Zielvorgaben, so ist eine erneute Verhandlung der einzelnen noch nicht ausgeführten Aufgaben notwendig.

3 Planung und Verhandlungsführung der Koordinierungsinstanz

3.1 Globale Aufgabenplanung

Für die globale Planung der Aufträge werden im wesentlichen folgende Ziele verfolgt. Es soll ein einfacher, robuster Plan mit minimalem Datenbestand und Rechenaufwand erzeugt werden. Dadurch ist eine schnelle, oft wiederholte Planung möglich, die eine ständige Aktualisierung des Planes erlaubt. Zudem muß in diesem Plan ausreichend Planungsfreiraum für autonome Einheiten berücksichtigt werden können, um lokale Optimierung zu ermöglichen. Nicht zuletzt müssen, wie bereits erläutert, übergeordnete logistische Ziele erreichbar sein. Optimale Planungsergebnisse werden deshalb durch ein geeignetes Zusammenspiel der übergeordneten globalen Planung der Koordinierungsinstanz und der lokalen Planung der einzelnen autonomen Einheiten erzielt.

Damit den autonomen Einheiten der notwendige lokale Planungsfreiraum zur Verfügung steht, werden die Arbeitsvorgänge (AVOs) der Aufträge nicht auf einzelne Ressourcen bezogen, sondern bezogen auf Gruppen von Einheiten (Kapazitätsgruppen) geplant. In einer Kapazitätsgruppe befinden sich all diejenigen Einheiten, die für die Ausführung einer bestimmten Aufgabe in Frage kommen. Zudem werden durch die Koordinierungsinstanz nicht die Start- und Endtermine der Aufgaben errechnet, sondern lediglich Zeitintervalle (sog. Planungsräume) bestimmt, innerhalb denen eine Aufgabe ausgeführt werden soll. Nimmt eine autonome Einheit mehrere Aufgaben an, so hat sie i. d. R. durch die Planungsräume die Möglichkeit, die Abarbeitungsfolge von Aufgaben zur lokalen Optimierung zu variieren. Durch Wahl der Größe der Kapazitätsgruppen und der Planungsräume kann der lokale Planungsfreiraum in einem großen Bereich skaliert werden.

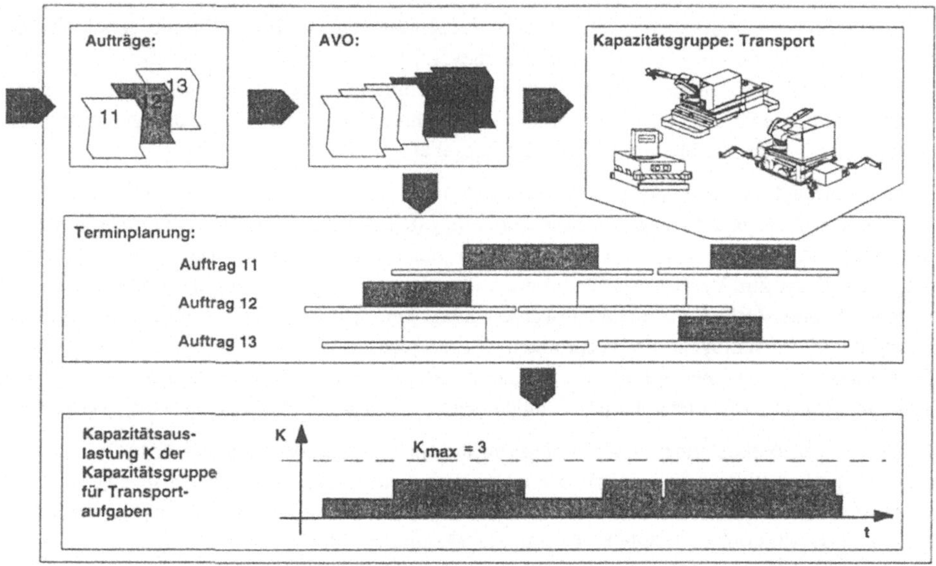

Abb. 2 Schematischer Planungsablauf

Abb. 2 zeigt schematisch einen Planungsablauf. Die in Arbeitsvorgänge (AVOs) gegliederten Aufträge werden zunächst den entsprechenden Kapazitätsgruppen zugeordnet. Dies ist am Beispiel einer Kapazitätsgruppe für Transportvorgänge dargestellt. Im folgenden Planungsschritt werden die Arbeitsvorgänge, ausgehend von den Endterminen der Aufträge, in der globalen Planung mittels Rückwärtsterminierung eingeplant. Dabei wird unter Berücksichtigung verschiedener Kriterien, wie dem geplanten Start- und Endtermin des Auftrags und der mittleren Durchlaufzeit der Arbeitsvorgänge sowie unter Bewertung der momentanen kapazitiven Situation in der Produktion ein auftragsspezifischer Streckungsfaktor ermittelt. Dieser wird mit der Dauer der einzelnen Arbeitsvorgänge der Aufträge multipliziert. Die sich daraus ergebenden Zeitspannen bilden die Planungsräume, innerhalb denen die Arbeitsvorgänge beliebig verschoben werden können (Abb. 3).

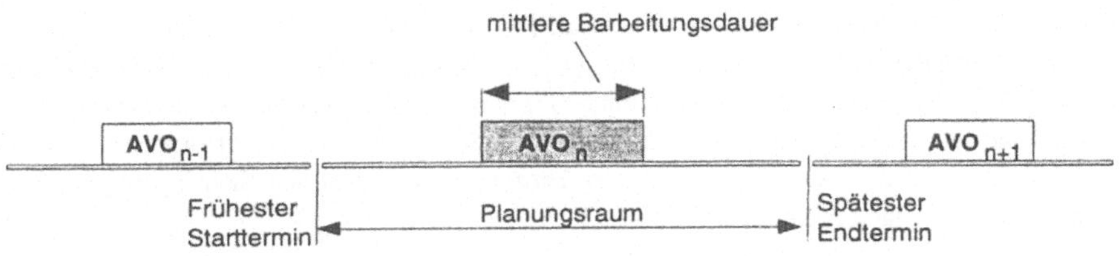

Abb. 3 Darstellung von Planungsraum

Die terminliche Konsistenz bleibt gewahrt, wenn eine Überlappung der Planungsräume technologisch aufeinanderfolgender Arbeitsvorgänge vorerst ausgeschlossen wird. Da es trotz der Planungsräume zu zeitlichen Kapazitätsengpässen kommen kann, werden diese explizit lokalisiert und aufgelöst.

Die Berechnung der Auslastung erfolgt kapazitätsgruppenweise durch Summieren der eingeplanten Aufgabeninhalte. Bei Kapazitätsüberschreitungen ist eine weitere Streckung der Planungsräume betroffener Arbeitsvorgänge und damit ein Herabsetzen der Gesamtkapazität notwendig. Zur Kapazitätsberechnung wird eine gleichmäßige Verteilung des Arbeitsinhaltes über den gesamten Planungsraum angenommen. Wird jedem Arbeitsvorgang für seine mittlere Bearbeitungsdauer die Kapazität 1 zugewiesen, so berechnet sich der Kapazitätsbedarf aus dem Produkt der mittleren Bearbeitungsdauer und der Kapazität mit dem Wert 1. Auf den Planungsraum bezogen, ergibt sich dann eine benötigte Kapazität k aus dem Quotienten des Kapazitätsbedarfes und des Planungsraumes (Abb. 4).

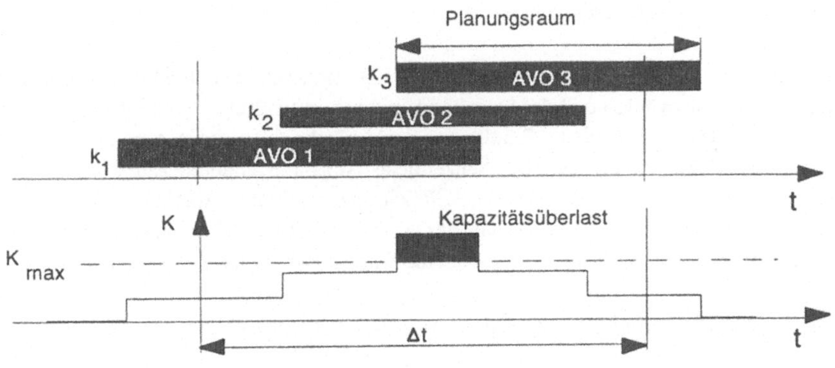

Abb. 4 Beispielhafte Kapazitätsberechnung

Nach der Planung kann mit den autonomen Einheiten über die Arbeitsvorgänge verhandelt werden.

3.2 Der Verhandlungsmechanismus

Die Verwendung eines Verhandlungsmechanismus nach dem Prinzip von Angebot und Nachfrage zur Verteilung von Aufgaben, erlaubt eine bestmögliche Nutzung der lokalen Planungsfähigkeit und Entscheidungskompetenz der autonomen Einheiten und ist Voraussetzung für Kooperationen zwischen autonomen Einheiten. Das dazu verwendete Verhandlungsprotokoll baut auf dem Contract-Netz-Protokoll [16] auf, das um Elemente zur Planung von Produktionsaufgaben erweitert worden ist [15]. Ein Auftraggeber bietet in Form einer Ausschreibung (1) eine Aufgabe mit terminlichen und fertigungsspezifischen Angaben an (Abb. 5). Kann eine autonome Einheit diese Aufgabe annehmen, erhält der Auftraggeber in einem Angebot Informationen, zu welchen genauen Terminen und unter welchen Bedingungen die Ausführung der Aufgabe möglich ist.

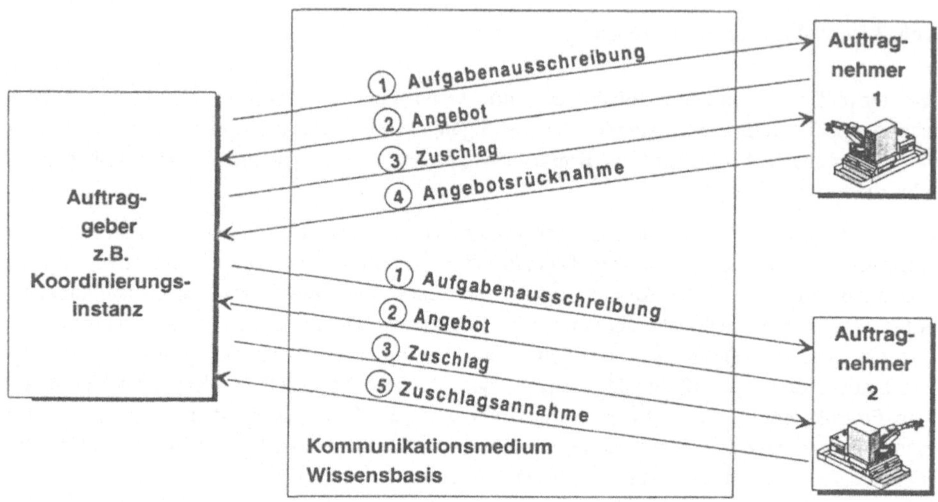

Abb. 5 Verhandlungsmechanismus

Der Auftraggeber wird bei mehreren Angeboten (2) nach seinen individuellen Kriterien das optimale Angebot auswählen und der betreffenden autonomen Einheit einen Angebotszuschlag erteilen (3). Falls eine verbindliche Einplanung der Aufgabe, z.B. durch veränderte Planungsrandbedingungen oder durch die zwischenzeitliche Annahme anderer Aufgaben nicht mehr möglich ist, kann die betreffende autonome Einheit jetzt noch eine Ablehnung (4) erteilen. Im Falle einer verbindlichen Einplanung erhält der Auftraggeber eine Zuschlagsannahme (5). Alle anderen Einheiten erhalten für ihre Angebote eine Angebotsablehnung.

3.3 Die Verhandlungsführung der Koordinierungsinstanz

Die Verhandlungsführung der Koordinierungsinstanz koordiniert den Verhandlungsablauf bei der Vergabe der global geplanten Aufgaben (Abb. 6). Dazu werden bereits in der Planungsphase der Aufträge der Verhandlungszeitpunkt, die Verhandlungsabfolge und die aufgabenspezifischen Bedingungen festgelegt. Verhandelt wird nach terminlicher Abfolge der Arbeitsvorgänge, wobei zur Einhaltung der technischen Konsistenz innerhalb eines Auftrages ein Vorgang erst nach erfolgter Verhandlung seines Vorgängers ausgeschrieben wird. Durch die Bedingungen kann die Wichtigkeit der einzelnen Aufgaben wiedergegeben werden. Ihre Festlegung erfolgt in Ausschreibungsparametern nach globalen Zielgrößen, Kennlinien und Erfahrungswerten aus vergangenen Verhandlungen. Dadurch kann z.B. auf die Einhaltung des Endtermines Einfluß genommen werden.

Die Kriterien zur Auswahl des besten Angebots sind auf Koordinierungsebene globale Zielgrößen, durch die eine Gesamtoptimierung der Auftragsabwicklung erreicht werden soll. Treffen keine Angebote ein oder erfüllen diese nicht die globalen Zielvorgaben, so muß die Koordinierungsinstanz durch Modifikation der Ausschreibung einen neuen Verhandlungszyklus mit veränderten Ausschreibungsparametern starten, wobei u.U. eine Verschlechterung der Zielerfüllung in Kauf zu nehmen ist. Führt auch diese Maßnahme zu keinem Erfolg, so ist eine Umplanung und eine erneute Verhandlung notwendig.

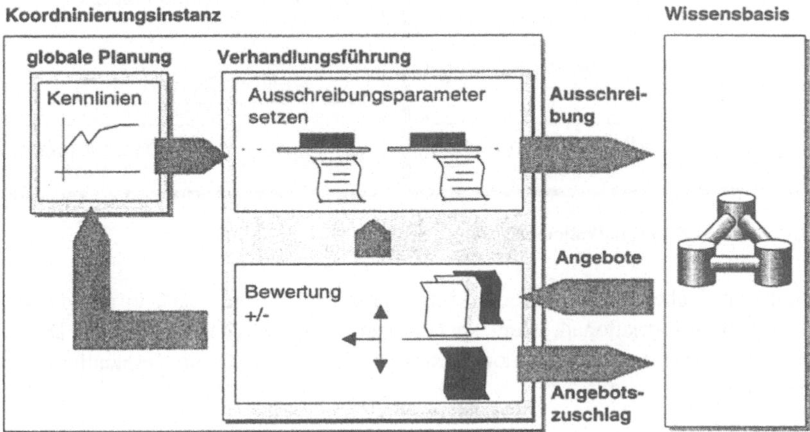

Abb. 6 Einordnung der Verhandlungsführung

Um den Verhandlungspartnern den Vergleich der Sichtweisen mehrerer autonomer Einheiten zu ermöglichen, müssen die Bewertungen der Angebote quantifizierbar sein. Dazu wird für eine erste Realisierung ein Punktesystem mit Bonus- und Maluspunkten eingesetzt. Bonuspunkte erhält der Auftragnehmer, der eine Aufgabe bearbeitet. Maluspunkte müssen gezahlt werden, wenn eine Aufgabe nicht oder nicht rechtzeitig bearbeitet wurde. Der Auftraggeber muß Maluspunkte zahlen, wenn er die in einer Ausschreibung zugesagten Voraussetzungen, wie z.B. die Bereitstellung von Rohteilen, nicht zum vorgegeben Zeitpunkt zur Verfügung stellen kann. Bei diesem System wird vorausgesetzt, daß die Einheiten kein spekulatives Verhalten zeigen.

4 Das Kommunikationsmodell

Das Konzept der verteilten Planung führt automatisch zu höheren Anforderungen an die Kommunikationsfähigkeit der Systeme. Die Möglichkeit der lokalen Planoptimierung unter Berücksichtigung globaler Ziele hat zur Folge, daß sowohl zwischen der Koordinierungsinstanz und den autonomen Einheiten, als auch zwischen den Einheiten selbst ein ständiger Informationsaustausch stattfindet. Das im Rahmen des SFB 331 entwickelte Kommunikationsmodell hat zur Bewältigung dieser Anforderungen die in Abb. 7 dargestellte Struktur.

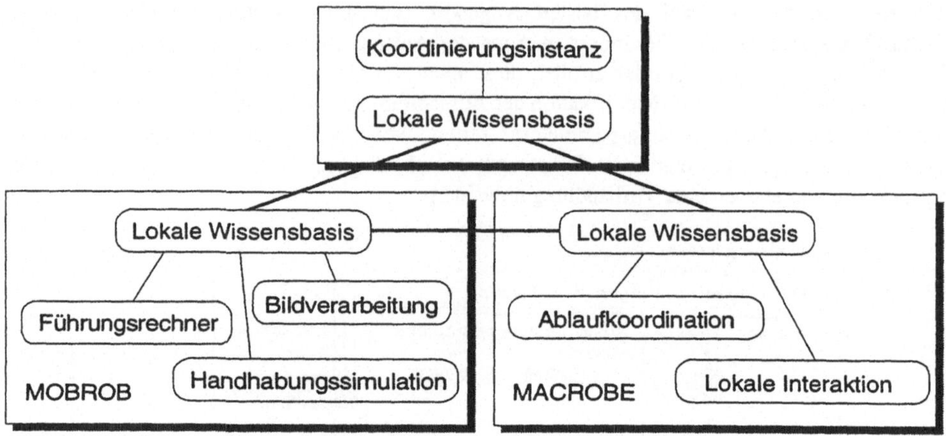

Abb. 7 Struktur des Kommunikationsmodells

Jede autonome Einheit verfügt über eine eigene lokale Wissensbasis, in der die Einheiten, neben anderen Informationen, ihre spezifischen Umgebungsdaten halten. Die verteilte Wissensbasis repräsentiert die Kommunikationseinheit, in der auch die Verhandlungsprotokolle integriert sind.

5 Beispielhafte autonome Einheiten

Die vorgestellte Produktionsumgebung ermöglicht die system- und informationstechnische Integration autonomer, mobiler Systeme wie sie im Rahmen des SFB 331 entwickelt wurden:

FLEXL-II ist eine flächenbewegliche, spur*un*gebundene Transporteinheit, die als Last wahlweise Paletten oder den mobilen Roboter MOBROB [4] aufnehmen kann. In Verbindung mit MOBROB bildet FLEXL-II eine freibewegliche mobile Handhabungseinheit.

Dagegen zeichnet sich MACROBE als universelle frei navigierende Einheit dadurch aus, daß sie unterschiedliche Serviceaufgaben, z.B. Transporte oder flächendeckende Inspektionen in veränderlicher Umgebung ausführen kann [3]. Basis der Fähigkeiten von MACROBE ist eine Systemstruktur, wie sie in Abb. 8 dargestellt ist.

Die Aufträge, die MACROBE angenommen hat, werden in der *Koordinationsschicht* expandiert und der unterlagerten sogenannten *Expertenschicht* sequentiell und stoßfrei überlappend zur Ausführung übergeben. Kennzeichen der Module in der Expertenschicht ist ein spezifischer Perzeptions-, Planungs- und Ausführungszyklus, der in Echtzeit durchlaufen wird. Zur Perzeption bedienen sich die Experten des *Multisensorsystems* [17] und wählen für die Teilaufgabe geeignete (virtuelle) Sensoren aus. Die Expertenschicht erlaubt darüberhinaus ein einfaches Austauschen und Erweitern von Modulen und damit der autonomen Eigenschaften und Funktionen des Serviceroboters.

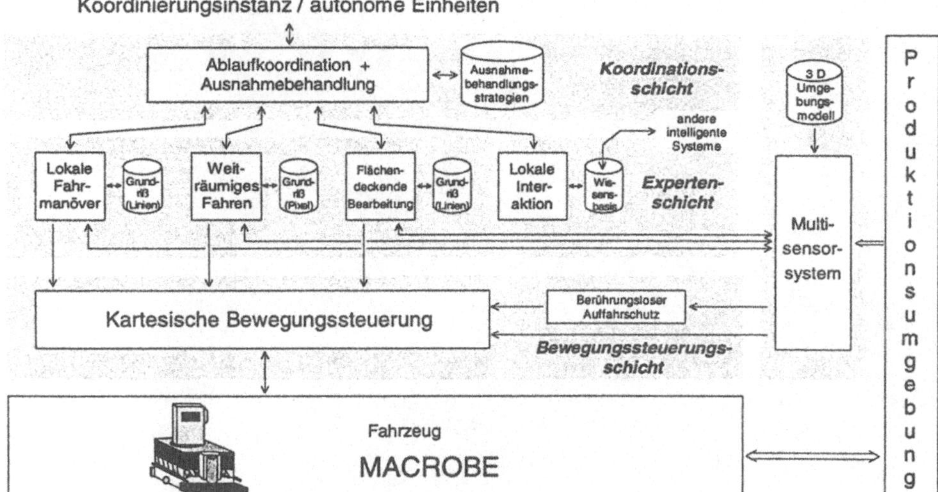

Abb. 8 Systemstruktur von MACROBE

Eine weitere Aufgabe der Koordinationsschicht ist die kontextabhängige Behandlung von aufgabenbezogenen Ausnahmen, wie z.B. Einschieben dringender Aufträge, zur Neigung gehende Hilfsmittel, Trassenblockaden etc. Dazu verfügt MACROBE über eine Ausnahmebehandlung, die sich auf in Relationen abgelegtes Wissen stützt. Es zeigte sich, daß diese Repräsentationsform für autonome mobile Serviceroboter geeigneter ist, als in umfangreichen Regelsätzen abgelegtes Wissen [6].

Mit Hilfe dieser lokalen Mechanismen erlangt MACROBE ein hohes Maß an Autonomie und kann so - im Rahmen der vorgebenen Freiräume - eine Vielzahl von lokalen Planänderungen vornehmen, ohne andere (zentrale) Systeme konsultieren zu müssen.

6 Evaluierung in einem Demonstrationsszenario

Am Institut für Werkzeugmaschinen und Betriebswissenschaften (iwb) der TU München werden die vorgestellten Konzepte beispielhaft umgesetzt. Das Szenario umfaßt dabei mehrere autonome Einheiten; hierzu gehören Bearbeitungszellen, verschiedene Materiallager sowie die mobilen Systeme MACROBE, MOBROB und FLEXL-II.

Es werden verschiedene Produktions- und Serviceaufgaben demonstriert, unter anderem die Fertigung hydraulischer Papierlocher, Materialflußverkettung durch mobile Systeme und typische automatisierbare Dienstleistungen wie die Inspektion oder die Reinigung großer Flächen [18]. Wesentliche Arbeitsschritte für die Durchführung der Produktionsaufgaben werden dabei von der Koordinierungsinstanz grob geplant und durch Verhandlungen an geeignete autonome Einheiten vergeben. Treten während des Produktionsprozesses Störungen auf, versuchen die autonomen Einheiten zunächst, aufgrund ihrer lokalen Planungs- und Entscheidungsfähigkeit, selbständig geeignete Maßnahmen zur Störungsbehebung durchzuführen. Kann die Störung aber allein nicht behoben werden, fordern sie über Verhandlungen einen Kooperationspartner an.

Abb. 9 Produktionsumgebung am iwb mit autonomen Einheiten

Im ungestörten Produktionsablauf werden die erforderlichen Bauteile auf Paletten von den Bearbeitungsstationen zur Montageeinheit transportiert, während zeitgleich eine flächendeckende Inspektion des Hallenbodens von dem Serviceroboter MACROBE durchgeführt wird. Welche der Fahrzeuge für die Transportaufgaben einzusetzen sind, wurde zuvor über den beschriebenen Verhandlungsmechanismus mit der Koordinierungsinstanz abgestimmt.

Tritt während der Lochermontage der Störungsfall ein, daß sich zu wenig Bauteile auf den Paletten befinden, verhandelt die Montageeinheit zunächst mit den verfügbaren Lagern über eine Nachlieferung. Sind mehrere Lager vorhanden, die das fehlende Locherteil zur Verfügung stellen können, erhält das nächstgelegene Lager den Zuschlag.

In einem weiteren Verhandlungsschritt wird aus dem Pool der mobilen, autonomen Einheiten bevorzugt diejenige ausgewählt, die über die notwendigen sensorischen und aktorischen Fähigkeiten zur Beschaffung der fehlenden Teile verfügt.

Den Auftrag erhält im Beispielszenario MOBROB, da er mit Hilfe seiner Bildverarbeitung die Lage eines Locherteils am Lager detektieren und anhand der sensorisch gewonnenen Informationen einen geeigneten Handhabungsvorgang planen und ausführen kann. Zur Ausführung des Auftrages muß MOBROB zum Lager und zur Montage transportiert werden und verhandelt deshalb direkt mit den vorhandenen Transporteinheiten.

Sobald MOBROB das Lager erreicht, überprüft er, ob die benötigten Locherteile vorrätig sind. Er detektiert, daß aufgrund einer unvollständigen Lieferung Teile fehlen. Durch eine erneute Verhandlung zwischen den Lagern und MOBROB ergibt sich, daß sich weitere Teile nur noch in einem weiter entfernten Lager befinden, welches jedoch für MOBROB nicht zugänglich ist. Um dennoch der Montage alle benötigten Locherteile zur Verfügung zu stellen, schreibt MOBROB im Rahmen dieser neuen Störung einen Auftrag für die Beschaffung der im externen Lager befindlichen Teile aus.

Für diese Aufgabe eignet sich im Beispielszenario MACROBE, die aufgrund ihrer Planungs- und Navigationsfähigkeiten eine zielorientierte Fahrt auch über längere Fahrstrecken in nur teilweise bekannter Umgebung durchführen kann. Insbesondere wird bei nicht vorhergesehenen Hindernissituationen durch lokale Ausweichbewegungen sichergestellt, daß MACROBE ihr Ziel, in diesem Fall das externe Lager, erreicht.

Da MACROBE aber zur Zeit einen Inspektionsauftrag bearbeitet, muß dieser für den dringenden Transportauftrag unterbrochen werden. Hierbei generiert die Ausnahmebehandlung von MACROBE eine Sequenz von Maßnahmen, die gewährleistet, daß nach der Lieferung der Teile an MOBROB der unterbrochene Auftrag fortgesetzt werden kann.

Nachdem MACROBE am externen Lager die Teile mit Hilfe ihrer Hubgabel aufgenommen hat, fährt sie an einen durch die verteilte Wissenbasis vermittelten Übergabeort. Nach einem sensorgestützten Andockmanöver wird über die Wissensbasis eine lokale Kooperation zu MOBROB aufgebaut (Abb. 10).

Abb. 10 Kooperation von MACROBE und MOBROB

Die Kooperationsphase gliedert sich typischerweise in folgende Abschnitte:

1. Lagevermessung der Teile mit der Bildverarbeitung von MOBROB

2. Bedarfsabhängiges Korrekturmanöver von MACROBE bei nicht möglicher Handhabung durch MOBROB.

3. Greifen der Teile durch MOBROB nach erfolgreicher Lagevermessung.

4. Quittierung durch MOBROB und Verlassen des Interaktionsbereiches.

Darüberhinaus könnten während dieser Kooperationsphase auch kontextabhängig komplexere Aktivitäten von MACROBE durch die Ausnahmebehandlung ausgelöst werden, wie z.B. die Beschaffung weiterer Teile.

Nach Beendigung der Kooperation wird MOBROB zur Montage transportiert und legt die nachgelieferten Teile auf der Montagepalette ab. Anschließend kann die Montageeinheit den unterbrochenen Auftrag wieder aufnehmen.

So kann trotz der geschilderten Störungen die Montage der Locher in der von der Koordinierungsinstanz vorgesehenen Zeit ausgeführt werden. Eine weitere Umplanung des Produktionsplanes ist somit nicht notwendig. Hätte andernfalls die verzögerte Beendigung des Auftrags eine Auswirkung auf die Termine anderer Aufträge, müßte durch die globale Planung der Koordinierungsinstanz eine Terminanpassung aller betroffenen Aufträge durchgeführt werden, gegebenenfalls einschließlich neuer Verhandlungen.

Während die Lochermontage zu Ende geführt wird, setzt MACROBE den zurückgestellten flächendeckenden Inspektionsauftrag an der Stelle fort, an dem er unterbrochen wurde. Der hierfür eingesetzte Experte zeichnet sich durch einen spezifischen Perzeptions-, Planungs- und Ausführungszyklus aus, der auflaufende Lagefehler überwacht und selbständig korrigiert. Darüberhinaus erfolgt bei Hindernissen eine automatische Anpassung des Kurses [7], wobei die dadurch entstehenden Restflächen in ein „Gedächtnis" übernommen werden. Diese werden automatisch nachbearbeitet, nachdem unter Berücksichtigung von Hindernissen eine aus technologischer Sicht größtmögliche Flächenabdeckung erreicht wurde [18].

Abb. 11 veranschaulicht den gesamten, im Rahmen der Inspektion und des Transports von MACROBE zurückgelegten Weg.

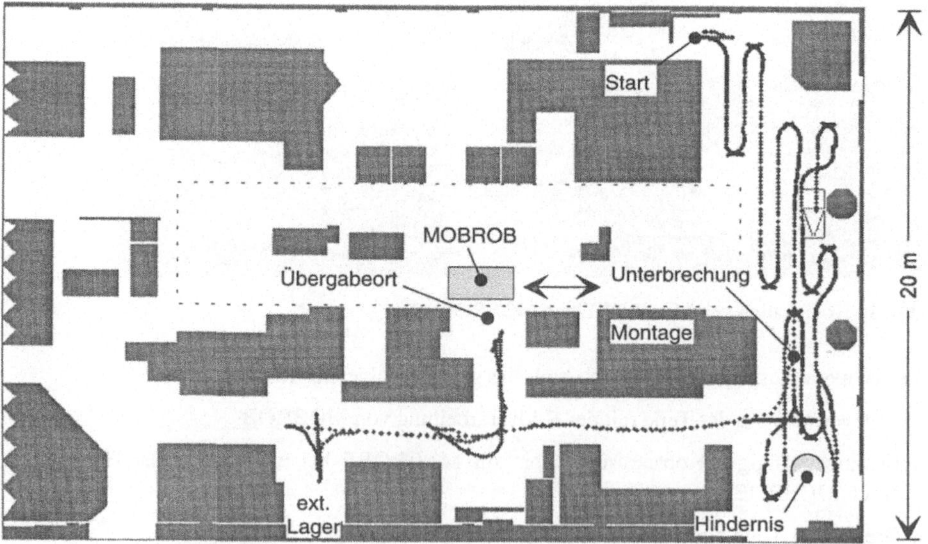

Abb. 11 Zurückgelegter Weg von MACROBE

7 Zusammenfassung und Ausblick

Es wurde eine Produktionsumgebung beschrieben, in der autonome Einheiten verhandlungs-basiert unter Einsatz einer Koordinierungsinstanz zur globalen Aufgabenplanung und einer Wissenbasis für das Kommunikationsmanagement, in einer flexiblen Produktion effizient genutzt werden können. Besonders eignen sich hierfür die im Rahmen des SFB 331 entwickelten autonomen Einheiten MACROBE, MOBROB und FLEXL-II.

Die Planung und Verhandlungsführung der Koordinierungsinstanz ermöglichen dabei eine zielorientierte globale Ausrichtung der Produktion während die autonomen Einheiten die zur Verfügung gestellten Freiräume lokal nutzen.

Weiterführend werden nun intelligente Verhandlungsführungsstrategien erprobt und evaluiert. Darüberhinaus sollen aufbauend auf der Speech-Act-Theorie Verhandlungsmechanismen entwickelt werden, die im Verhandlungsablauf variabler sind und sich dynamisch an unterschiedliche Situationen anpassen.

Danksagung

Die vorliegende Arbeit wurde im Rahmen des Sonderforschungsbereichs „Informationsverarbeitung in autonomen, mobilen Handhabungssystemen" (SFB 331) von der Deutschen Forschungsgemeinschaft (DFG) gefördert.

Literaturverzeichnis

1. Ahluwalia, R. S.; Ji, P.: A distributed approach to job schedulding in a flexible manufacturing system. In: Computers Industrial Engeneering Vol. 20 (1991) 1, Great Britain: Pergamon Press, S. 95-103.
2. Ayel, J.: Decision coordination in production management. In: Proceeding of the 4th MAAMAW: Pre-Proceeding of the 4th European Workshop Modeling Autonomous Agents in a Multi-Agent World, (1992).
3. Azarm, K.; Bott, W, Freyberger, F; Glüer, D.; Horn, J.; Schmidt, G.: Autonomiebausteine eines mobilen Roboterfahrzeugs für Innenraumumgebungen. Informationstechnik und Technische Informatik 36 (1994) 1, S. 5-11.
4. Blessing, S.; Kugelmann, D.; Reinhart, G.: Sichere Handhabung mit 3D-Simulation und videobasierte Sensorik. In: Schmidt, G.; Freyberger, F. (Hrsg.): 12. Fachgespräch Autonome Mobile Systeme (AMS '96), München. Springer-Verlag 1996.
5. Duffie, N. A.; Chitturi, R.; Mou, J.: Fault-Tolerant Heterachical Control of Heterogeneous Manufacturing System Entities. Journal of Manufacturing Systems 7 (1988) 4, S. 315-328.
6. Glüer, D.; Schmidt, G.: A New Flexible Exception Handling Approach for Autonomous Mobile Service Robots. 2nd World Automation Congress / 6th International Symposium on Robotics and Manufacturing (WAC/ISRAM'96), Montpeiller, France, 1996.
7. Hofner, C.; Schmidt, G.: Path Planning and Guidance Techniques for an autonomous mobile Cleaning Robot. Intelligent Robots and Systems (IROS '94), (Hrsg.) Volker Graefe, Elsevier Science Verlag 1995, S. 241 - 257.
8. Iwata, K. u.a.: Random Manufacturing System: a New Concept of Manufacturing Systems for Production to Order. Annals of the CIRP 43 (1994) 1, S. 379-383.

9. Koch, M.R.: Autonome Fertigungszellen - Gestaltung, Steuerung und integrierte Störungsbehandlung. Berlin: Springer, 1996 (iwb Forschungsberichte 98).

10. Koller, A.; Stöffler, N.O.: Basisfunktionen zur Steigerung der Autonomie mobiler Systeme. In: Schmidt, G.; Freyberger, F. (Hrsg.): 12. Fachgespräch Autonome Mobile Systeme (AMS '96), München. Springer-Verlag 1996.

11. Milberg, J.: Unsere Stärken stärken - Der neue Weg zu Wettbewerbsfähigkeit und Standortsicherung. In: Milberg, J.; Reinhart, G. (Hrsg.): Unsere Stärken stärken - Der Weg zu Wettbewerbsfähigkeit und Standortsicherung, Referate des Münchner Kolloquiums 94. Landsberg/Lech: MI Verlag 1994. S. 11-31.

12. Milberg, J.; Koch, M. R.: Autonomous Manufacturing Systems (Past, Present and Future of FMS). In: Peklenik, J. (Hrsg.): Flexible Manufacturing Systems: Past - Present - Future. Ljubljana: Faculty of Mechanical Engineering 1993, S. 143-162.

13. Raulefs, P.: Cooperating agent architecture to manage manufacturing processes. 4. Internationaler GI-Kongres (1991), S. 6-17.

14. Reinhart, G.; Koch, M.: Autonome, kooperative Produktionssysteme. In: Wildemann, H. (Hrsg.): Schnell lernende Unternehmen - Quantensprünge in der Wettbewerbsfähigkeit. Münchner Management Kolloquium, München. München: TCW Transfer-Centrum, 1995.

15. Reinhart, G.; Pischeltsrieder, K.: Flexible Electrically-Powered Transport Vehicles in Future Production Structures. In: Rembold, U. (Hrsg.); Dillmann, R. (Hrsg.); Hertzberger, L.O. (Hrsg.); Kanade, T. (Hrsg): Proc. of the Int. Conf. on Intelligent Autonomous Systems (IAS4), Karlsruhe. Amsterdam: IOS Press 1995. S. 15-25.

16. Smith, R.G.: The Contract Net Protocol: High Level Communication and Control in a Distributed Problem Solver. In: IEEE Transaction on computers. 1980, Vol. C-29.

17. Stöffler, N.O.; Hauck, A.; Färber, G.: Ein geometrisch-symbolisches Umgebungsmodell zur Unterstützung verschiedener Perzeptionsaufgaben autonomer, mobiler Systeme. In: Schmidt, G.; Freyberger, F. (Hrsg.): 12. Fachgespräch Autonome Mobile Systeme AMS '96, München. Springer-Verlag 1996.

18. Videofilm: Der SFB 331: Informationsverarbeitung in autonomen, mobilen Handhabungssytemen, TU München, 1996.

Basisfunktionen zur Steigerung der Autonomie mobiler Systeme

Andreas Koller, Norbert O. Stöffler

Sonderforschungsbereich 331
Technische Universität München
email: {koller@informatik,stoffler@lpr.e-technik}.tu-muenchen.de

Kurzfassung. Wirkliche Autonomie können mobile Systeme nur dann erreichen, wenn sie in der Lage sind, unabhängig von einer zentralen Steuerung zu planen und zu agieren. Wesentlich hierfür ist die Fähigkeit, die Umgebung selbständig zu erfassen, um eine stets aktuelle Grundlage für Entscheidungen zur Verfügung zu haben. Darüber hinaus sind Mechanismen zur dezentralen Koordination und Kooperation mit parallel operierenden Systemen erforderlich. Dieser Beitrag gibt einen Überblick über die an der TU München im Rahmen des Sonderforschungsbereichs 331 entwickelten Konzepte und exemplarischen Realisierungen der geforderten sensorischen und kommunikativen Fähigkeiten.

1 Einleitung

Die aktuelle Entwicklung der Marktsituation bedingt neue Anforderungen an moderne Produktionsanlagen. Steigende Innovationsdynamik führt zu immer kürzeren Produktlebenszyklen, die Individualisierung der Kundenwünsche zu einem Ansteigen der Variantenvielfalt. Dieser Wandel hat die Unternehmen dazu gezwungen, die Produktion immer stärker zu flexibilisieren. Auch in anderen Domänen der Automatisierungstechnik ist dieser Trend zur Flexibilisierung und Individualisierung zu beobachten. Die damit einhergehende Steigerung der Komplexität, zusammen mit der Forderung nach Störungstoleranz, führte zur Entwicklung neuer Konzepte für zukünftige Systeme.

Reduktion der Komplexität, Erhöhung der Verfügbarkeit und Flexibilität der Konfiguration einer automatisierungstechnischen Anlage können durch Verlagerung der Kompetenz von zentralistischen Steuerungen an Subsysteme erreicht werden [12]. Es entstehen *autonome* Einheiten, die in der Lage sind, Störungen lokal zu behandeln und auf veränderte Umgebungen und Anforderungen selbständig zu reagieren. Besonders bei *mobilen* Systemen ist die Flexibilität gegenüber der Umgebung essentiell.

Erst durch diese Steigerung der individuellen Reaktivität erschließen sich für autonome, mobile Systeme auch Einsatzbereiche, die über die klassischen Automatisierungsanwendungen hinausgehen. So gewinnen beispielsweise mobile Service-Roboter zunehmend an Bedeutung.

Der Sonderforschungsbereich 331 an der TU München beschäftigt sich seit mehr als 10 Jahren mit der Informationsverarbeitung in autonomen, mobilen Systemen. Als Grundlage dedizierter Lösungen für die einleitend angesprochenen Probleme wurden auch eine Reihe von Basisfunktionalitäten realisiert, die die Autonomie mobiler Systeme unterstützen. Diese Basisfunktionalitäten sollen im Folgenden vorgestellt werden.

Grundlage für alle Konzepte zur flexiblen Umgebungsbehandlung ist eine robuste Sensorik, die Interaktion mit variierenden Umgebungsbedingungen erst ermöglicht. Ihr ist das Kapitel 2 gewidmet. Um Koordination mehrerer Systeme unter Vermeidung einer zentralen Instanz untersuchen zu können, wurden Kommunikationskonzepte mit aufgabenorientierter Struktur, der Möglichkeit gemeinsamen, aber verteilten Wissens, Mechanismen zur dynamischen Teambildung und lokale Verhandlungskonzepte entwickelt. Hierzu sei auf Kapitel 3 verwiesen.

Zur Durchführung von Experimenten entstand eine Reihe von Demonstratoren. Nur kurz erwähnt seien hier das mobile Handhabungssystem MOBROB, das wahlweise von den Fahrzeugen FLEXL-II und Demag-FTS aufgenommen werden kann, das multifunktionale Roboterfahrzeug MACROBE, die Sensorikplattform MAC 1 und der mobile Servicemanipulator ROMAN. Details finden sich in [15], [2], [19] und [5].

2 Sensorik

Voraussetzung für Mobilität in einer dynamischen Umgebung ist die sensorgestützte Navigation. Die Auswertung der Sensordaten muß Fähigkeiten zur globalen Lokalisation und zur Kollisionsvermeidung bereitstellen. Sind darüberhinaus auch Manipulationsaufgaben durchzuführen, muß auch Lokalisation relativ zu relevanten Objekten möglich sein.

Prinzipiell lassen sich diese sensorischen (oder *Perzeptions-*) Aufgaben mit unterschiedlichen physikalischen Sensoren und entsprechender Sensordatenverarbeitung bewältigen. Ein grundlegender Ansatz der entwickelten Algorithmen ist der Vergleich mit einem Umgebungsmodell. Hypothesen über Positionen und Hindernisse werden solange algorithmisch variiert, bis sich entsprechende Prädiktionen anhand des Modells mit den Sensordaten zur Deckung bringen lassen.

Je nach den Anforderungen der jeweiligen Perzeptionsaufgabe im Hinblick auf Distanzen, Orts- und Zeitauflösung, Genauigkeit etc., wurden unterschiedliche Sensorsysteme entwickelt und auf den Demonstratoren des SFB erprobt und evaluiert. Sowohl Standardsensoren der Robotik wie Laser-Baken-Navigationssysteme und Ultraschallringe [9] als auch neuartige Laser-, CCD- und Radarsensoren (vgl. Kapitel 2.1, 2.2 und 2.3) finden Verwendung. Zur flexiblen, videobasierten 3D-Objekterkennung und Lokalisation entstand das System MORAL [13]. Ein weiteres, auf die mobile Manipulation optimiertes, videobasiertes Erkennungssystem wird in [5] beschrieben.

Ein einheitliches Umgebungsmodell für alle Sensoren und Perzeptionsaufgaben wird in [16] und [18] vorgestellt.

2.1 3D-Laserentfernungskamera

Einer der beiden neu entwickelten Sensoren des Roboterfahrzeugs MACROBE ist
eine 3D-Laserentfernungskamera [7]. Zur Abstandsmessung wird ein modulier-
ter Laserstrahl verwendet, wobei die Phasendifferenz des ausgesandten und des
am Umweltobjekt rückgestreuten Laserlichts ausgewertet wird. Mittels zweier
synchronisierter Spiegel (siehe Abb. 1) wird der Laserstrahl über die zu erfas-
sende Szene geführt. Bei einem Elevationswinkelbereich von $[-52^{\circ}, 0^{\circ}]$, einem
Azimutwinkelbereich von $[-28.4^{\circ}, 28.4^{\circ}]$ und einem Entfernungsmeßbereich bis
15 m werden Entfernungsbilder mit einer Bildtaktrate von 2.5 Hz erzeugt. Jedes
Bild besteht aus 41 Zeilen mit je 321 Pixeln. Die Kamera wird zur Hindernisdetektion und Landmarkenvermessung eingesetzt. Eine weitere, für die autonome
Lokomotion grundlegende Applikation dieses Sensorsystems ist die absolute Lokalisation.

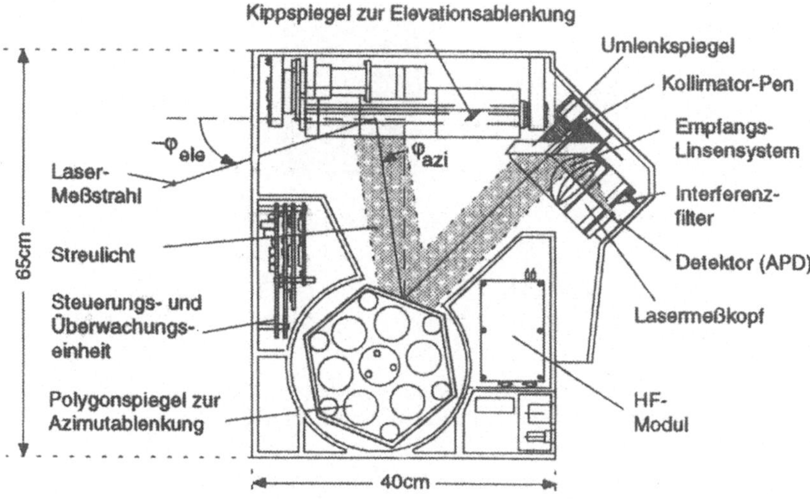

Abb. 1. Mechanischer Aufbau der 3D-Laserentfernungskamera

Hierzu werden aus dem Entfernungsbild der Kamera natürliche Landmarken,
vertikale ebene Flächen, z.B. Wände, extrahiert und mit den von einem Umgebungsmodell [16] prädizierten Landmarken verglichen. Dabei wird unter Verwendung der Methode der kleinsten Quadrate die absolute Fahrzeuglage bestimmt.
Zur kontinuierlichen Lokalisation werden diese absoluten Lagedaten fortlaufend
mit den inkrementellen, von der odometriebasierten Koppelnavigation gewonnenen Lagedaten statistisch fusioniert [11].

Abbildung 2 zeigt ein repräsentatives closed-loop Experiment mit dem Roboterfahrzeug MACROBE. Innerhalb einer Laborumgebung wurde ein Rundkurs
von 46 m Länge wiederholt im Dauertest abgefahren. Die Testdauer wurde durch

die Kapazität der onboard-Stromversorgung des Fahrzeugs auf 96 min begrenzt. Hierbei wurde eine Strecke von 1664 m zurückgelegt. Dargestellt ist die Bahn von MACROBE gemäß Koppelnavigation und kontinuierlicher Lokalisation sowie die zur Lokalisation verwendeten Wände. Bei diesem Experiment betrug der maximale Fehler der Koppelnavigation in der x-Position ca. 2 m, in der y-Position ca. 7 m und in der Orientierung ca. 37°. Wie das Bild zeigt, bleiben dagegen Positions- und Orientierungsfehler der kontinuierlichen Lokalisation stets innerhalb hinreichend enger Toleranzbereiche, so daß die sichere Fahrzeugführung gewährleistet wird.

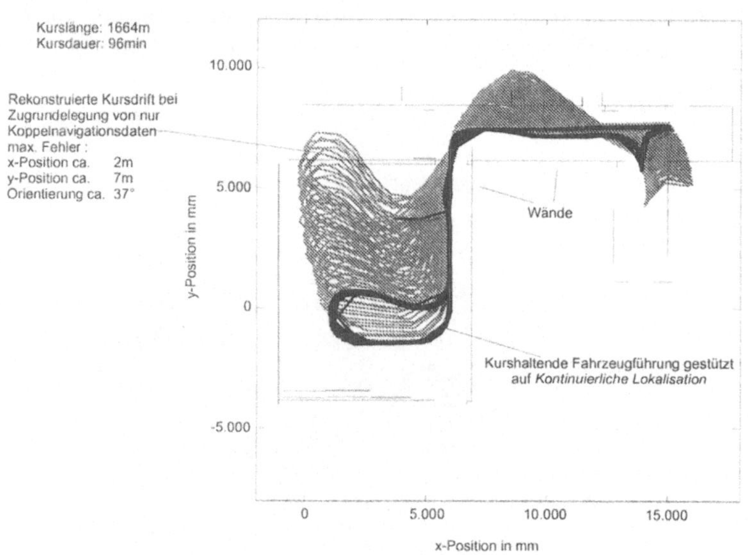

Abb. 2. Testfahrt zur kontinuierlichen Lokalisation

2.2 Verzerrungsfreier Weitwinkel-Videosensor mit aktivem Lichtschnitt

Speziell für die schnelle Vermessung und Überwachung des Fahrzeugnahbereichs wurde ein neuartiger Videosensor mit extremer Weitwinkelsicht entwickelt und in das Multisensorsystem von MACROBE integriert [8]. Ein asphärischer Umlenkspiegel und ein spezielles Weitwinkelobjektiv legen den den Fahraufgaben angepaßten Sichtbereich von 4 m x 4 m fest. Durch die Spiegelgeometrie wird unter Berücksichtigung der nichtlinearen Abbildungseigenschaften des Weitwinkelobjektivs eine nahezu verzerrungsfreie Aufsichtperspektive erreicht. Sämtliche zur Bodenebene parallelen Objektkonturen werden dabei im gesamten Sensorsichtbereich längen– und winkeltreu abgebildet (s. Abb. 3). Im Gegensatz zu konventionellen Kameraanordnungen ergibt sich eine nahezu konstante Ortsauflösung.

Abb. 3. Kamerarohbild einer Beispielszene mit zugehörigem binarisierten Gradientenbild

Abb. 4 zeigt die prinzipielle Anordnung des Videosensors. Kombiniert mit aktivem Lichtschnitt wird eine 3D-Umgebungserfassung ermöglicht. Dabei werden nicht nur Erhebungen (z. B. Objekte auf der Fahrtrasse), sondern auch Absenkungen (z. B. Bahnsteigkanten) im Sichtbereich vermessen.

Synchronisiert mit der Aufnahme zweier Halbbilder erfolgt eine Hell– bzw. Dunkeltastung der Lichtebenen, so daß nach Differenzbildauswertung nur noch die von den Lichtebenen erfaßten Objektkonturen weiterverarbeitet werden.

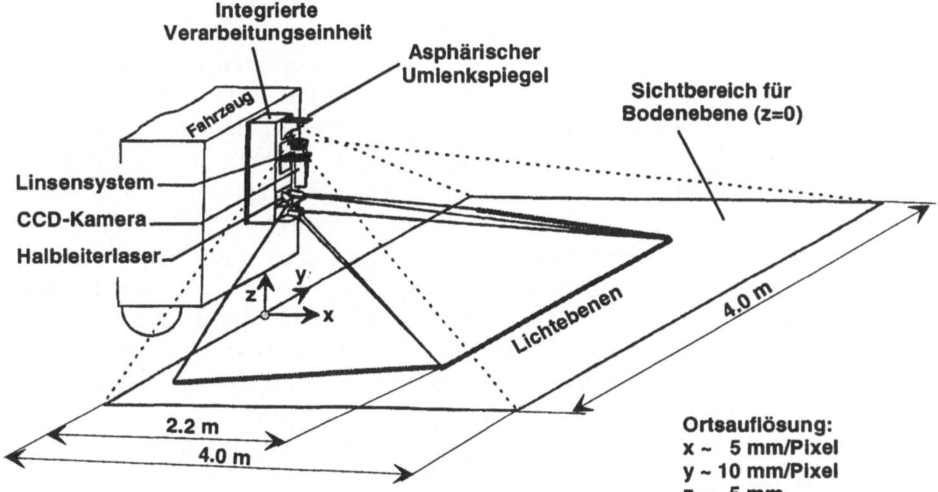

Abb. 4. Aufbau des Videosensors mit aktivem Lichtschnitt

Über eine Kalibriertabelle erfolgt die schnelle Zuordnung zwischen einem Bildpunkt auf dem CCD–Chip und dem korrespondierenden Konturpunkt im Sensorsichtbereich. Programmierbare Hardwarefilter erlauben eine Vorverarbeitung der Videobilder im Pixeltakt. Segmentierung, Verdünnung und Verkettung von Konturen zu Liniensegmenten werden direkt im Arbeitsspeicher eines RISC-Prozessors durchgeführt. Der Aufbau einer robusten Sensorkarte erfolgt durch Fortschreibung der Liniensegmente anhand der Fahrzeugkoppelnavigation. Typische Zykluszeiten zum Kartenaufbau betragen weniger als 200 ms und erfüllen somit die Anforderungen des Kollisionsschutzes und der Online–Wegeplanung für Fahrgeschwindigkeiten von MACROBE bis 1 $\frac{m}{s}$.

Das Videosensorsystem wird erfolgreich in verschiedenen Experimenten eingesetzt, z. B. zur Hindernis Detektion, zur Erkennung und Aufnahme von Paletten [4], zur Freiflächenvermessung für flächendeckende Bearbeitungsaufgaben [10], zur Landmarkenerkennung für symbolische Fahrzeugführung [8], sowie zum bildgeführten neuro-fuzzy-basierten Einparken [6].

2.3 Radarsensor

Speziell für den Einsatz auf autonomen, mobilen Systemen ist ein Sensor entwickelt worden, der die Vorteile der Radartechnik aus der klassischen Freiraumanwendung auf Innenräume überträgt. Da die Wellenausbreitung im Frequenzbereich der Millimeterwellen nahezu unabhängig von den atmosphärischen Bedingungen ist, können in Kombination mit einer kohärenten Signalauswertung Reichweiten bis zu 100 m bei extrem geringer Sendeleistung erreicht werden. Zusammen mit einer Geschwindigkeitsmessung von Objekten über den Dopplereffekt lassen sich damit die sensorischen Fähigkeiten autonomer Systeme deutlich erweitern, denn der Erfassungshorizont vergleichbarer aktiver Sensoren wie Laser-Scanner oder Ultraschallsensoren reicht kaum über 15 m hinaus.

Der Sensor ist so ausgelegt, daß sowohl Entfernung als auch Geschwindigkeit der im Radarstrahl erfaßten Objekte direkt gemessen werden können. Die Entfernung wird über eine Puls-Laufzeitmessung bestimmt. Dabei kommen extrem kurze Pulse mit einer Dauer von 2 ns zum Einsatz, was zu einer Radialauflösung von 25 cm führt. Die Entfernung bereits aufgelöster Objekte läßt sich dann bis auf 5 mm genau bestimmen. Die Objektgeschwindigkeit spiegelt sich direkt im Doppleranteil des Empfangssignals wider. Die Nutzung des Dopplereffekts erfordert eine feste Phasenbeziehung zwischen Empfangs- und Sendesignal und damit eine kohärente Signalquelle. Zu diesem Zweck wird ein leistungsstarker IMPATT-Oszillator mit einem phasenstabilen Gunn-Oszillator synchronisiert. Die hohe Trägerfrequenz von 94 GHz führt zu Dopplerfrequenzen von 625 Hz pro 1 m/s Objektgeschwindigkeit und erlaubt damit eine genaue Geschwindigkeitsanalyse in sehr kurzer Zeit.

Wie in Abb. 5 zu sehen ist, fokussiert eine Fresnellinse den Radarstrahl, um eine hohe Winkelauflösung des Sensors zu erreichen. Der gebündelte Strahl mit einem Öffnungswinkel von 2° wird von einem Spiegel mit zwei Freiheitsgraden abgelenkt und ermöglicht eine dreidimensionale Abbildung der Umgebung.

Auf der Basis dieser Abbildungen sind in den vergangenen Jahren verschiedene Basisfunktionen für autonome, mobile Systeme demonstriert worden, wie z.B. Standortbestimmung [23], Schutzraumüberwachung [19] und Bewegungserfassung [21]. Die wichtigsten Systemparameter des Sensors sind in Tabelle I aufgeführt.

Tabelle I
Systemparameter des Radarsensors

Frequenz	94 GHz
Wellenlänge	3,2 mm
Pulsspitzenleistung	10 mW
mittlere Sendeleistung	20 μW
Reichweite	0 ... 80 m
Entfernungsauflösung	25 cm
Entfernungsmeßgen.	2 cm
Winkelauflösung	2°
Winkelmeßgenauigkeit	0.15°
Geschwindigk.-Meßber.	±8 m/s
Geschwindigk.-Meßgen.	10 mm/s
Datenrate	10.000 Voxels/s

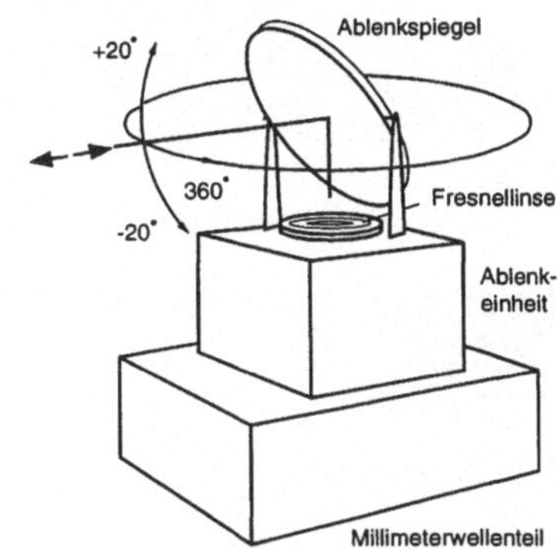

Abb. 5: Erfassungsbereich des Sensors

2.4 Sensorkoordination

Für Fusionsexperimente diversitärer Sensoren wurde die mobile Plattform MAC 1 (siehe Abb. 6) mit einer Videokamera und dem Millimeterwellen-Radar (siehe Kapitel 2.3) bestückt. Beide Sensoren entfalten ihre Stärken bei unterschiedlichen Perzeptionsaufgaben. Während sich der Videosensor für Objekterkennung und Feinlokalisierung anbietet (vergleiche [13]), ist der Radarsensor bei weiträumigen Erkundungen, der Detektion von Veränderung und Bewegung in der Umgebung und der globalen Lagebestimmung des mobilen Systems im Vorteil.

Durch Aufbrechen von komplexen Perzeptionen (Beispielsweise die Erkennung eines neu hinzugekommenen Objekts) in einen Ablauf von Perzeptionsphasen (im Beispiel Detektion und Erkennung) lassen sich die Vorteile beider Sensoren kombinieren. Die Ergebnisse der einzelnen Phasen werden geometrisch fusioniert. So können neue Objekte vom Radar detektiert, und über eine ebenfalls vom Radar bestimmte grobe Positionshypothese der Aufmerksamkeitsbereich der Bildverarbeitung fokussiert (siehe Abb. 7) werden. Verarbeitungszeit als auch Erkennungssicherheit verbessern sich dadurch signifikant [19]. Auch die Trennung von Bildvordergrund und Bildhintergrund läßt sich auf Basis der Entfernungsinformation des Radarsensors erleichtern [14].

Nach der videogestützten Feinlokalisierung des neuen Objektes relativ zum Fahrzeug wird über die vom Radarsensor schritthaltend bestimmte Weltposition

Abb. 6. Sensorikplattform MAC 1 und Sicht des Videosensors

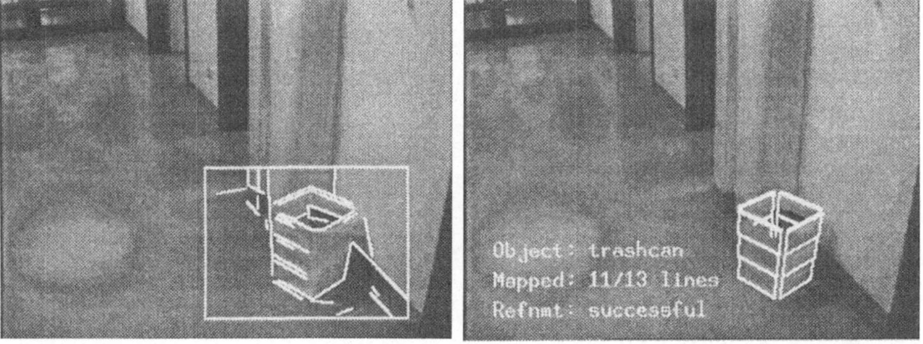

Abb. 7. Radargestützte Definition eines Aufmerksamkeitsbereiches und Resultat der Bildverarbeitung

des Fahrzeugs die Lage des Objekts in der Welt ermittelt, so daß dieses im Umgebungsmodell instantiiert werden kann [18]. Über die in Kapitel 3.1 vorgestellten Kommunikationsmechanismen wird die Information auch anderen autonomen Einheiten zur Verfügung gestellt.

3 Kooperation

Die bereits in der Einleitung beschriebene Entwicklung von autonomen Systemen für Fertigungsumgebungen führt zu neuen Anforderungen an die Informationsverarbeitung. Im Bereich der Sensorik wurde dies bereits im vorhergehenden Kapitel vorgestellt. Dieses Kapitel untersucht die Kommunikation auf der abstrakteren Ebene der autonomen Einheiten. Im Zuge der Spezialisierung der Systeme entstehen heterogene Sichtweisen auf die Umwelt. Daneben erwächst für die autonomen Systeme die Notwendigkeit, zur Lösung komplexer Probleme zusammenzuarbeiten. Beispiel hierfür sind die Koordinierung der Fahrwege verschiedener mobiler Systeme, sowie die Lösung von gemeinsamen Transport- oder

Handhabungsaufgaben. Um beiden Aspekten Rechnung zu tragen werden Konzepte vorgestellt, die einerseits durch die Verteilung der Daten mit Hilfe einer verteilten Wissensbasis die Modellierung lokaler und heterogener Daten ermöglichen, aber andererseits durch Einführung eines dynamischen Teamkonzepts den Austausch des lokalen Wissens zum Zweck der Kooperation unterstützen. Reale Umgebungen erfordern Realzeitfähigkeit der beteiligten Systeme. Auch hierzu dienen die Verteilungskonzepte der Wissensbasis. Im Anschluß an die Konzepte werden ausgewählte Anwendungsaspekte u.a. anhand koordinierten Fahrverhaltens dargestellt.

3.1 Die verteilte Wissensbasis

Allgemeines. Als Antwort auf die eingangs erwähnten Anforderungen wurde eine objektorientierte, verteilte Wissensbasis entwickelt. Wesentliche Bestandteile sind aktive Mechanismen zur Verteilung von Wissen (Dämonenkonzept). Die speziellen Anforderungen einer realen Umgebung führen darüberhinaus zu den in diesem Kapitel vorgestellten Verteilungskonzepten.

Verteilung. Die Wissensbasis stellt Mechanismen für die Repräsentation lokalen und globalen Wissens bereit. Unter lokalem Wissen versteht man Wissen, das nur für ein bestimmtes autonomes System oder Anwendungsprogramm von Bedeutung ist. Globales Wissen andererseits wird von mehreren autonomen Systemen benutzt. Betrachtet man z.B. eine wirkungsvolle dezentrale Wegeplanung, so müssen alle autonomen Fahrzeuge den Aufenthaltsort der anderen Fahrzeuge der Fabrikumgebung kennen. Das Wissen um den Aufenthaltsort der einzelnen Systeme gehört also zum globalen Wissen.

Lokale Wissensbasen. Um diese Fähigkeiten anbieten zu können, besteht die verteilte Wissensbasis aus einer Menge von lokalen Wissensbasen. Jede lokale Wissensbasis ist einem oder mehreren Anwendungsprogrammen zugeordnet. Ein Beispiel für eine derartige Organisation findet sich in Abb. 8. Dort sind fünf lokale Wissensbasen abgebildet, die drei verschiedenen autonomen Systemen bzw. deren Anwendungsprogrammen zugeordnet sind.

Da das globale Wissen eines Agenten aus dessen Sicht auch lokales Wissen ist, wird das globale Wissen in der Wissensbasis mit den gleichen Repräsentationsformen wie das lokale Wissen modelliert. Für die Verwaltung des globalen Wissens sind zwei Fälle zu unterscheiden. Erstens kann globales Wissen in mehreren lokalen Wissensbasen repräsentiert sein. Die Gründe für diese redundante Modellierung können etwa die Zugriffseffizienz, heterogene Wissensstrukturierung, unterschiedliche Sichten auf das Wissen oder Detailabstraktion sein. Folglich benötigt man in der realzeitfähigen, verteilten Wissensbasis erstens einen Mechanismus, mit dem repliziertes Wissen gezielt aktualisiert werden kann. Zweitens kann globales Wissen nur in einer lokalen Wissensbasis physikalisch gespeichert sein, aber Anwendungsprogramme, die anderen lokalen Wissensbasen zugeordnet sind, müssen auf das Wissen zugreifen können. Mögliche Gründe für diese Form

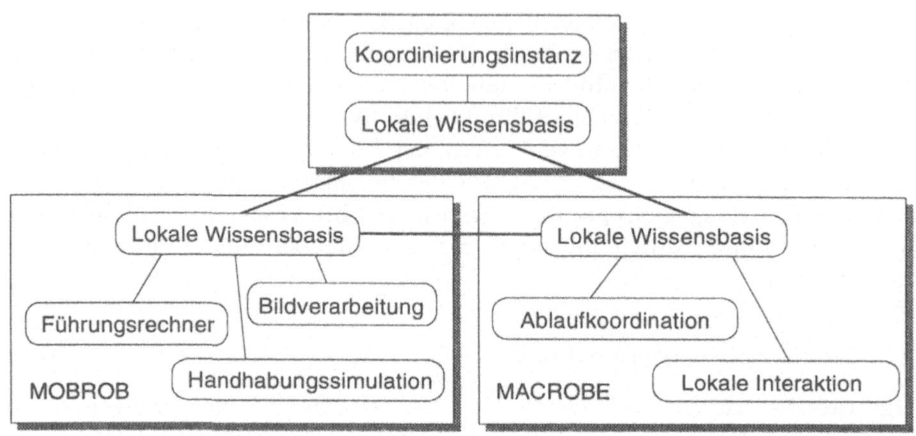

Abb. 8. Beispiel einer verteilten Wissensbasis mit zugeordneten autonomen Systemen und Anwendungsprogrammen

der Modellierung sind die Vermeidung von Redundanz, unnötigem Netzverkehr und Konsistenzproblemen. Der Zugriffsmechanismus soll also hinsichtlich des Ortes des gespeicherten Wissens transparent sein.

Gezielte Datenaktualisierung. Mit dem Mechanismus der gezielten Datenaktualisierung können Beziehungen zwischen kompatiblen Wissensteilen zweier lokaler Wissensbasen eingerichtet und ausgewertet werden. Kompatible Wissensteile sind Wissensteile, die bezüglich der Granularität der Wissensrepräsentation aufeinander abgebildet werden können. Jede Aktualisierungsbeziehung besteht u.a. aus der Angabe eines Quellobjekts, eines Zielobjekts, eines Triggerobjekts und einer Aktualisierungsbedingung. Nach jeder Veränderung des Triggerobjekts wird überprüft, ob die Aktualisierungsbedingung erfüllt ist. Falls diese erfüllt ist, wird das Objekt in der Zielwissensbasis mit dem Original aus der Quellwissensbasis überschrieben. In Abb. 9 wird, sobald der Auftragstatus den Wert „Übernahme-bereit" annimmt, die Andockposition in der Zielwissensbasis aktualisiert. Daneben besteht bei der gezielten Datenaktualisierung die Möglichkeit, eine Initialisierungsroutine bzw. eine im Moment der Aktualisierung durchzuführende Aktion anzugeben.

Ortstransparenter Wissenszugriff. Mit dem Mechanismus des ortstransparenten Wissenszugriffs können Verweise zwischen kompatiblen Wissensteilen zweier lokaler Wissensbasen eingerichtet und ausgewertet werden. Im Gegensatz zur gezielten Datenaktualisierung wird hierbei nicht auf einem Replikat, sondern auf dem Original gearbeitet, auf das der Verweis der Ortstransparenzbeziehung zeigt. Dadurch erreicht man, wie oben gefordert, beim Zugriff auf das globale Wissen eine Transparenz hinsichtlich des Ortes, an dem die Daten physikalisch gespeichert sind.

In Abb. 9 wird der "bearbeitete Teilauftrag" nur einmal physikalisch gespeichert und von anderen Wissensbasen ortstransparent referenziert. Weitere Informationen zu den beschriebenen Mechanismen finden sich in [17].

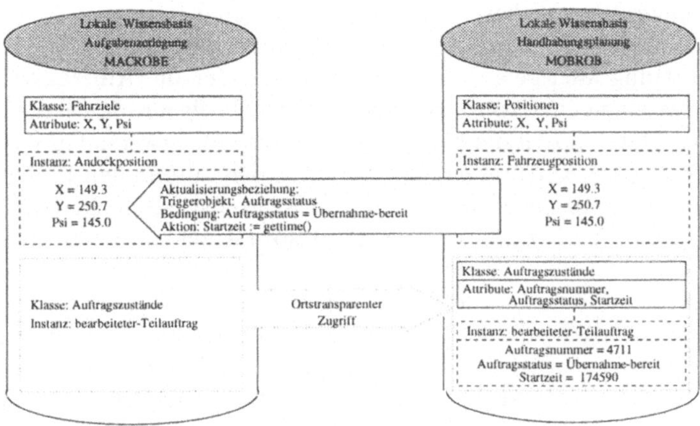

Abb. 9. Beispiel für Ortstransparenz und Aktualisierungsmanagement

Teamkonzept. Die bei den Verteilungskonzepten dargestellten Kooperationsbeziehungen sind abhängig von der Aufgabe, die die autonomen Agenten aktuell zu bearbeiten haben. Daraus folgt, daß die Anwendungsprogramme eine Möglichkeit benötigen, die Kommunikationskonzepte, entsprechend der Aufgabe, die sie gerade bearbeiten, dynamisch zu aktivieren bzw. zu deaktivieren.

Der Mechanismus, den die Wissensbasis dafür anbietet, ist das sogenannte "Teamkonzept". Das Teamkonzept ordnet jeder Aufgabenstellung ein Team von lokalen Wissensbasen zu. Innerhalb eines Teams von lokalen Wissensbasen gelten die für die Bearbeitung der Aufgabe notwendigen und sinnvollen Aktualisierungs- und Ortstransparenzbeziehungen. Jedes Anwendungsprogramm stellt seine Anfragen an seine lokale Wissensbasis als Mitglied eines bestimmten Teams von lokalen Wissensbasen. Die lokalen Wissensbasen des Teams kooperieren durch gezielte Datenaktualisierung und ortstransparente Wissenszugriffe, um das für die Bearbeitung der Aufgabe benötigte Wissen bereitzustellen. Dabei kann eine lokale Wissensbasis auch gleichzeitig in mehreren Teams mitarbeiten. Da die gezielte Datenaktualisierung und die ortstransparenten Wissenszugriffe implizit und innerhalb der Bearbeitung der Anfragen erfolgen, bleibt dem Anwender die Teamarbeit zwischen den lokalen Wissensbasen verborgen. Es wird dem Anwendungsprogramm, das eine Anfrage an ein Team von lokalen Wissensbasen stellt, auch nicht mitgeteilt, welche lokalen Wissensbasen an der Bearbeitung seiner Anfrage beteiligt waren.

Das Teamkonzept wird ausführlich vorgestellt in [17].

3.2 Kommunikation in den Demonstrationsszenarien

Mit den vorgestellten Eigenschaften kann die verteilte Wissensbasis als zentrales Kommunikations- und Koordinationsmedium zwischen den realisierten Demonstratoren eingesetzt werden.

In verschiedenen lokalen Wissensbasen werden heterogene Umgebungsmodelle der autonomen Systeme gespeichert. Darüberhinaus wird die Wissensbasis zur Übermittlung aller relevanten Informationen für die Auftragsvergabe zwischen den Systemen eingesetzt. Hierunter fällt z.B. die automatische Ergänzung symbolischer Daten durch die vom jeweiligen System verwendeten Geometriedaten. Für die flexible Auftragsvergabe zwischen den autonomen Einheiten wurde ein Verhandlungskonzept entwickelt. Die Wissensbasis stellt die entsprechenden Schnittstellen zur Verfügung. Ergänzende Information zu diesem Bereich findet sich in [1].

Durch Einsatz der aktiven Komponente leitet die Wissensbasis auch Umgebungsveränderungen, die von autonomen, mobilen Systemen mit Hilfe ihrer Sensorik detektiert wurden (vgl. Kapitel 2.4), an andere Systeme weiter. Aktualisierte Objektbeschreibungen stehen jedem System in der systemspezifischen Sichtweise zur Verfügung. Ein Beispiel für unterschiedliche Sichtweisen sind unterschiedliche Koordinatensysteme, absolute oder relative Positionsangaben. Die verteilte Wissensbasis wird zudem für Suchanfragen und für die Wegeplanung der autonomen mobilen Systeme verwendet. Dies wird in [20] beschrieben.

3.3 Kooperatives Fahrverhalten

Wird eine Gruppe autonomer Roboterfahrzeuge in einer Umgebung eingesetzt, so können sie bei der Nutzung gemeinsamer Fahrflächen, wie z.B. beim Passieren einer Türdurchfahrt oder einer Kreuzung, einer Begegnung im engen Gang, der Nutzung der Ausweichstellen etc., miteinander in Konflikt geraten. Im Sinne der Autonomie erfolgt die Auflösung derartiger Konflikte durch eine lokale Interaktion der am Konflikt beteiligten Roboter und *ohne* Einsatz eines zentralen Systems. Dieses kooperative Fahrverhalten ist damit eine notwendige Ergänzung zum individuellen Fahrverhalten und ermöglicht das sichere und effiziente Verkehrsgeschehen in einem dezentralisierten Multirobotersystem.

Ist eine Konfliktsituation erkannt, so kooperieren die beteiligten Roboter, um durch Verhandlung eine gemeinsame Lösung auszuarbeiten. Ziel ist die *dynamische Priorisierung*, d.h. die Bestimmung der Reihenfolge, nach der die Roboter einander ausweichen. Zu diesem Zweck tauschen die Roboter Informationen über ihre beabsichtigten Fahrwege aus. Basierend auf dieser Information kann jeder Roboter mittels seines Multiroboterplaners [3]. modifizierte Wege berechnen. Die Roboter bewerten diese geplanten Fahrwege und können durch den Vergleich der Bewertungen den kostenoptimalen Satz der Fahrwege bzw. die zugrundeliegende Prioritätsordnung als Lösung des vorliegenden Konfliktfalls auswählen. Diese Wege werden anschließend koordiniert ausgeführt, so daß die Roboter nach erfolgreicher Beendigung der Konfliktsituation erneut ihre individuellen Bewegungen fortsetzen können.

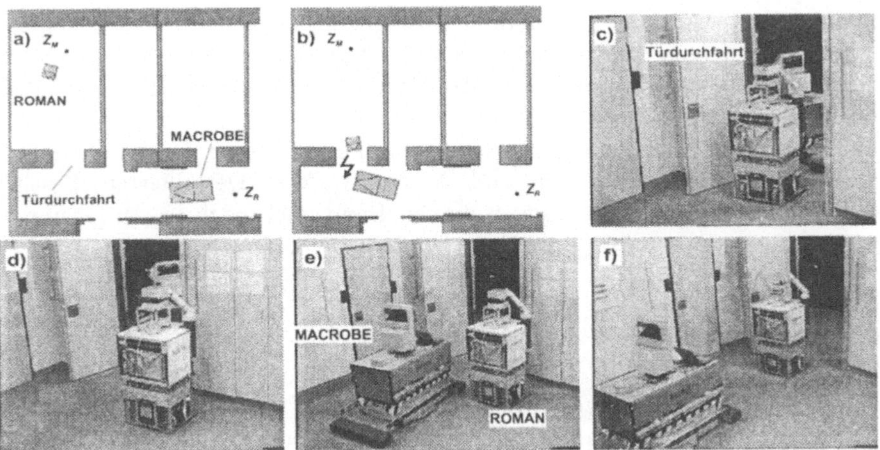

Abb. 10. Die Roboterfahrzeuge MACROBE und ROMAN kooperieren, um eine Konflikt-situation zu lösen

Experimentell wurde das Verfahren mit den Roboterfahrzeugen MACROBE und ROMAN erprobt. Die Roboter wurden für weiträumige Fahroperationen eingesetzt und konnten unter Verwendung des o.g. Verfahrens kooperativ unterschiedliche Konfliktsituationen lösen. Abb. 10 zeigt Schnappschüsse aus einem Experiment, bei dem sich die Roboter während ihrer weiträumigen Fahroperationen (Zielpunkte der Roboter: Z_M und Z_R) in einer Türdurchfahrt begegnen. Die Roboter verhandeln miteinander, um dynamisch die Prioritätsordnung festzulegen. Als Folge davon erhält ROMAN eine niedrigere Priorität und modifiziert seinen Weg, um MACROBE vorbeizulassen (Abb. 10c-e). Nach erfolgreicher Beendigung des Konflikts fährt jeder Roboter auf seinen individuellen Zielpunkt zu (Abb. 10f).

4 Zusammenfassung und Ausblick

Die in diesem Beitrag dargestellten Konzepte stellen wesentliche Basisfunktionen zur Verwirklichung realer autonomer Systeme dar. Im ersten Teil wurde die im SFB 331 erreichte Einbindung und Entwicklung verschiedenartiger Sensorik angeschnitten. Fernziel wäre hier eine Vereinheitlichung der Konzepte und die Realisierung immer komplexerer Perzeptionsaufgaben mit Standardsensoren wie Videokameras. Aufgrund der vielen ungelösten Probleme bei der Interpretation von Videobildern und der starken Überschneidung mit Konzepten der künstlichen Intelligenz erschließt sich hier noch ein breiter Forschungsspielraum.

Der zweite Teil beschäftigte sich mit der Kommunikation und Kooperation autonomer Systeme. Wesentliches hier entwickeltes Konzept ist eine verteilte Wissensbasis. Sie ermöglicht die Modellierung heterogenen Wissens bei gleichzeitigem Erhalt der Fähigkeit zum Austausch der Daten. Zur Garantie von Realzeitbedingungen wurde ein dynamisches Teamkonzept eingeführt. Weitergehende Arbeiten befassen sich auch hier mit der Standardisierung von Konzepten und Schnittstellen wie beispielsweise der Integration der *Object Query Language* (OQL) (siehe auch [20]).

Anwendungen aller Konzepte werden im SFB 331 in konkreten Fertigungs- und Serviceszenarien untersucht und weiterentwickelt. Detailliertere Beschreibungen der Szenarien finden sich in diesem Band auch noch in [1], [5] und auf dem Videofilm [22].

Danksagung

Die in diesem Beitrag vorgestellten Arbeiten wurden von der *Deutschen Forschungsgemeinschaft* im Rahmen des *Sonderforschungsbereichs 331, "Informationsverarbeitung in autonomen, mobilen Handhabungssystemen"* unterstützt.

Literatur

1. D. Ansorge, D. Glüer und C. Hofner. Flexible Produktionsstrukturen für den Einsatz autonomer Systeme. In G. Schmidt und F. Freyberger (Hrsg.), *Autonome Mobile Systeme*, Informatik aktuell. Springer-Verlag, 1996.
2. K. Azarm, W. Bott, F. Freyberger, D. Glüer, J. Horn und G. Schmidt. Autonomiebausteine eines mobilen Roboterfahrzeugs für Innenraumumgebungen. *Informationstechnik und Technische Informatik*, 36(1):7–15, 1994.
3. K. Azarm and G. Schmidt. A Decentralized Approach for the Conflict-Free Motion of Multiple Mobile Robots. In *Proc. of IEEE/RSJ Int. Conf. on Intelligent Robots and Systems (IROS'96)*, Osaka, Japan, November 1996.
4. W. Bott. *Automatische Planung und Ausführung lokaler Fahrmanöver für Roboterfahrzeuge*. Dissertationsschrift, Fakultät für Elektrotechnik der TU München (in Vorbereitung), 1996.
5. W. Daxwanger, E. Ettelt, C. Fischer, F. Freyberger, U. Hanebeck und G. Schmidt. ROMAN: Ein mobiler Serviceroboter als persönlicher Assistent in belebten Innenräumen. In G. Schmidt und F. Freyberger (Hrsg.), *Autonome Mobile Systeme*, Informatik aktuell. Springer-Verlag, 1996.
6. W. Daxwanger and G. Schmidt. Skill based visual parking control using neural and fuzzy networks. In *Proc. of the IEEE Conf. on Systems Man and Cybernetics*, volume 2, Seiten 1659–1664, Vancouver, Canada, 1995.
7. C. Fröhlich und G. Schmidt. Laser-Entfernungskamera zur schnellen Abbildung von 3-D Höhen- und Tiefenprofilen. In *ITG-Fachbericht 126: Sensoren – Technologie und Anwendungen*, Seiten 543–548, 1994.
8. A. Gilg. *CCD-Lichtschnitt-Sensorsystem zur Führung eines mobilen Roboters durch symbolische Wegespezifikation*. Dissertationsschrift, Fakultät für Elektrotechnik der TU München (in Vorbereitung), 1996.
9. U. D. Hanebeck und G. Schmidt. Schnelle Objektdetektion mit Ultraschallsensor-Arrays. In Tim Lüth R. Dillmann und U. Rembold (Hrsg.), *Autonome Mobile Systeme 1995, (11. Fachgespräch, 30. Nov. – 1. Dez. 1995, Karlsruhe)*, Seiten 162–171. Springer-Verlag, 1995.

10. C. Hofner and G. Schmidt. Path Planning and Guidance Techniques for an Autonomous Mobile Cleaning Robot. In Volker Gräfe (Hrsg.), *Intelligent Robots And Systems (IROS 94)*, Seiten 241–257. Elsevier Science Verlag, 1995.

11. J. Horn and G. Schmidt. Continuous Localization for Long-Range Indoor Navigation of Mobile Robots. In *Proceedings of the 1995 IEEE International Conference on Robotics and Automation*, Seiten 387–394, Nagoya, Japan, May 1995.

12. M. Koch und G. Reinhart. Autonome, kooperative Produktionssysteme. In H. Wildemann (Hrsg.), *Schnell lernende Unternehmen - Quantensprünge in der Wettbewerbsfähigkeit, Münchner Management Kolloquium*, München, 1995. TCW Transfer-Centrum-Verlag.

13. S. Lanser und C. Zierl. MORAL: Ein System zur videobasierten Objekterkennung im Kontext autonomer, mobiler Systeme. In *Autonome Mobile Systeme*, Informatik aktuell. Springer-Verlag, 1996.

14. O. Munkelt, P. Levi, B. Radig, M. Rožmann und J. Detlefsen. Integration eines hochauflösenden Radarsensors in ein videobasiertes Objekterkennungssystem. In *9. Fachgespräch "Autonome Mobile Systeme", München*, Seiten 299–312, 1993.

15. H. Naber. *Aufbau und Einsatz eines mobilen Roboters mit unabhängiger Lokomotions- und Manipulationseinheit.* Dissertationsschrift, Fakultät für Maschinenwesen der TU München, 1990.

16. H. J. Russ. Sensornahe Umgebungsmodellierung mit echtzeitfähigen Zugriffsfunktionen. In *Fortschritt-Berichte VDI*, number 364 in 10, Düsseldorf, 1995. VDI-Verlag.

17. J. Schweiger, K. Ghandri, and A. Koller. Concepts for a Distributed Real-Time Knowledge Base for Teams of Autonomous Systems. In *Proceedings of IEEE/RSJ/GI International Conference on Intelligent Robots and Systems*, Seiten 1508–1515, Federal Armed Forces University Munich, Germany, September 1994.

18. N. O. Stöffler, A. Hauck und G. Färber. Ein geometrisch-symbolisches Umgebungsmodell zur Unterstützung verschiedener Perzeptionsaufgaben autonomer, mobiler Systeme. In G. Schmidt und F. Freyberger (Hrsg.), *Autonome Mobile Systeme*, Informatik aktuell. Springer-Verlag, 1996.

19. N. O. Stöffler and T. Troll. Model Update by Radar- and Video-based Perceptions of Environmental Variations. In *International Symposium on Robotics and Manufacturing*. ASME Press, New York, 1996. To appear.

20. S. Stöhr. Using a Distributed Knowledge Base to Coordinate Autonomous Mobile Systems. In *To appear at: the Seventh International Dexa Conference and Workshop on Database and Expert Systems Applications*, Zürich Switzerland, September 1996.

21. T. Troll und J. Detlefsen. Bewegungserfassung mit einem Millimeterwellen-Sensor. In G. Schmidt und F. Freyberger (Hrsg.), *Autonome Mobile Systeme*, Informatik aktuell. Springer-Verlag, 1996.

22. Videofilm. Der SFB 331: Informationsverarbeitung in autonomen, mobilen Handhabungssystemen. TU München, 1996.

23. M. Rožmann and J. Detlefsen. Environmental exploration based on a three-dimensional imaging radar sensor. In *Proc. IROS*, Seiten 422–429, Rayleigh, NC, 1992.

Autorenverzeichnis